THE BLUNTS' ARABIAN TRAVELS

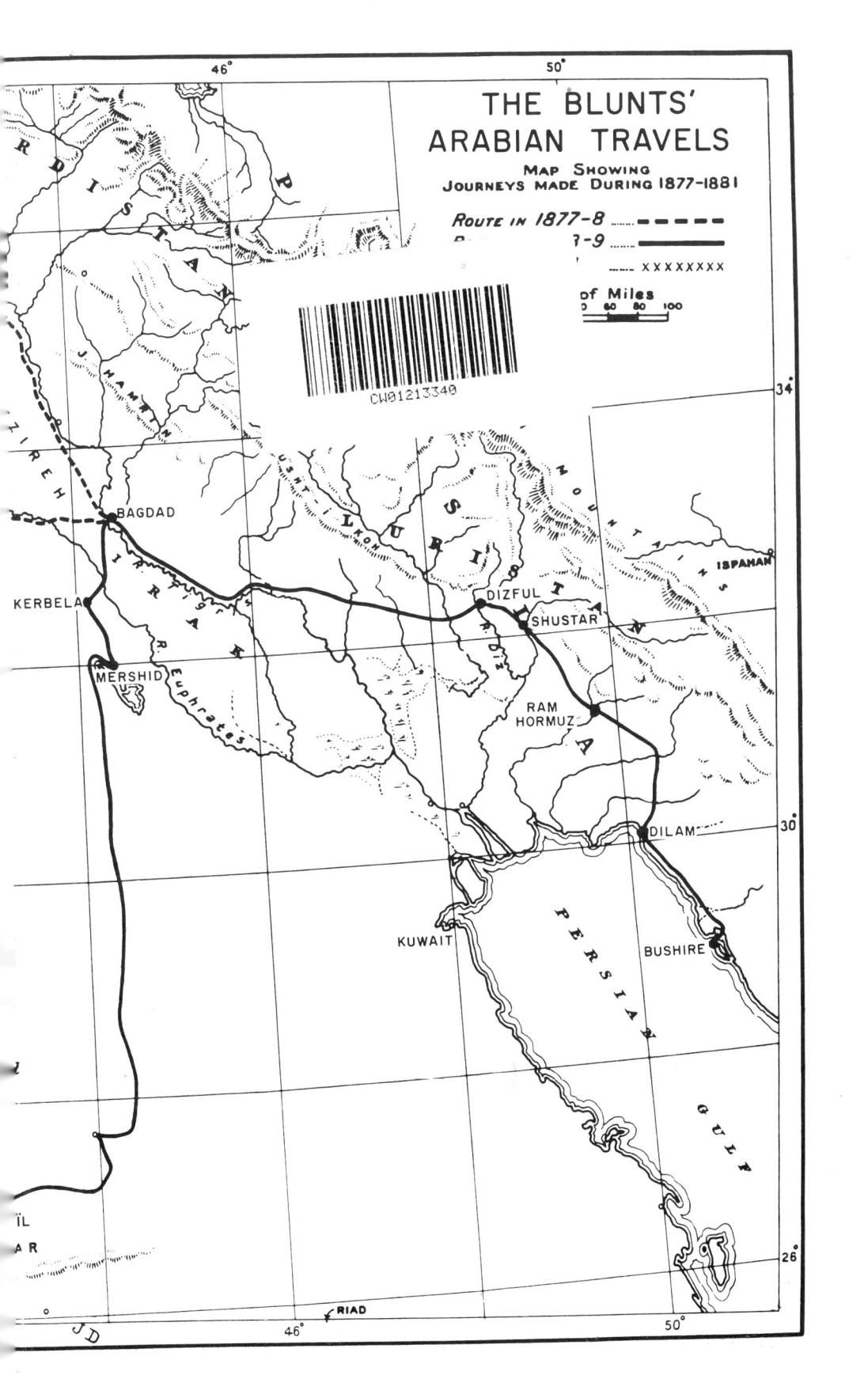

Map Showing Journeys made during 1877-1881

Route in 1877-8 — — — —
Route in 1878-9 ————
xxxxxxxx

Scale of Miles

THE
CRABBET
ARABIAN STUD

Its History & Influence

Crabbet from the East in 1876

THE
CRABBET
ARABIAN STUD

Its History & Influence

ROSEMARY ARCHER
COLIN PEARSON · CECIL COVEY

WITH BETTY FINKE

Foreword by
H.R.H. PRINCESS ALICE
OF ATHLONE

Alexander Heriot

Alexander Heriot & Co. Ltd
P.O. Box 1 Northleach
Gloucestershire

Text copyright © 1978 and 1994 Rosemary Archer and Alexander Heriot
Tables copyright © 1978 and 1994 Alexander Heriot

All rights reserved. No part of this publication may be
reproduced, stored in a retrieval system, or transmitted, in
any form or by any means, electronic, mechanical, photocopying,
recording or otherwise, without the prior permission of
Alexander Heriot & Co. Ltd

ISBN 0 906382 13 0

First published 1978
New edition 1994

Design and production
Colin Reed and Peter Loveday

Printed in Great Britain by
Woolnough Bookbinding, Irthingborough.

FOREWORD

It is a great honour to have been invited to introduce this fascinating book about the Crabbet Arabian Stud and its phenomenal influence upon the Arab Horse world.

I venture to do so for two reasons. Firstly because I am one of the few people still alive from the era when Lady Anne and Wilfrid Blunt were building the foundations of the Stud; and secondly because, some sixty years after the Blunts' own travels in Arabia, I and my husband had the good fortune to make, albeit in a less arduous manner, a rather similar journey to that country.

We went as guests of that great man, King Ibn Saoud. How times had changed since the Blunts were there! For instead of horses, we used motor cars to cross the desert from Jeddah, on the Red Sea, to Bahrein – a distinct contrast to the perilous and uncomfortable journey of the Blunts. But as the days went on, we were able to visualize something of their wanderings. The Bedouin camps had not changed, nor the circular, low-walled stables, like those the Blunts visited at Haïl, around which the mares and colts were fed. The enchanting foals were running loose around their mothers' legs and came readily to sniff us and be patted.

At the end of our visit we were presented with five Arabians, two of which unfortunately died after being walked all the way from Hofuf to Jeddah. Another, a beautiful young colt, was drowned when he leapt off the boat. But a rather elderly mare and a charming bay filly reached England safely and though the mare did not survive many weeks, the filly, called Nuhra, became the foundation mare at my daughter's stud at Barton Lodge. Nuhra was mated to Irex to produce the filly Nuhajjela. She, in her turn, had a chestnut daughter named Rajjela, by Lady Wentworth's Champion stallion, Grand Royal. Rajjela had only two foals, both colts, called Rajmek and Darjeel but they went on to establish two British records by being made Senior and Junior Champions at the Arab Horse Society Show in the same year.

And so, even in our relatively small way, I think I can claim that we are continuing the work of the Blunts and Lady Wentworth. For me, Aleppo in 1878 is not such an age away as it will be to most people.

The results of the Blunts' stay there with Mr Skene have reverberated not only around the world of Arab Horse breeding but also of the many other breeds to which the Arabian has made, and continues to make, so essential a contribution. This truly absorbing book should be compulsory reading for anyone who is even remotely interested in this unique animal.

Alice Mary

H.R.H. Princess Alice, Countess of Athlone
V.A., G.C.V.O., G.B.E.

Kensington Palace,
July 1978

Lady Anne Blunt
Photo courtesy of the Earl of Lytton

PUBLISHER'S NOTE

Fifteen years having elapsed since the first publication of this book, certain alterations have become necessary before offering it again to the public. These comprise corrections of fact together with some refurbishment of parts of the text in order to reflect current opinion concerning horses that were too young in 1978 to be properly evaluated. To spare readers who possess both editions the labour of sifting through them to identify the corrections, these have been listed separately on the opposite page.

The additional task of bringing the text up to date has been undertaken by Rosemary Archer in Chapter 13 (The Families Summarised) and the Overseas Section dealing with Australia, South Africa and the United States of America; and by Betty Finke who has divided Russia and Poland into two chapters and usefully increased the scope of the book to cover all the principal Arab horse-breeding countries of Europe.

It is finally the Publisher's sad duty to report the death since first publication of two of this book's co-authors, Cecil Covey (1985) and Colin Pearson (1987), and of the author of the Foreword, H.R.H. Princess Alice, Countess of Athlone (1981). Others mentioned as being alive in 1978 are also no longer so and in such cases, both equine and human, readers are requested to adjust for themselves the present tense to the past.

CORRIGENDA
TO THE FIRST EDITION

The factual corrections that have been incorporated in the text of the new edition of The Crabbet Arabian Stud are as follows:

Page
- 51   Miss Dillon's first name was Etheldred and not Ethelred.
- 66   The 'disappointing' book was a quite different work, by Abd el Kadr's son.
- 78   El Hami Pasha died in 1860 and not 1861.
- 95   and 257 For BINT NURA (ES SHAKRA) read BINT BINT NURA (ES SHAKRA).
- 96   Bint Nura, the dam of Bint Bint Nura, was bay and not grey.
- 98   For JELLAIBEH read JELLABIEH.
- 100   The dam of MAHRUSS (1893) was Bint Bint Nura and not Bint Nura.
- 111   IBN NURA: for Khalil el Hajrej read Khalil el Hajry.
- 113   YEMAMA: for [Fate unknown] read: Given away in 1906 to El Shafei el Tihawi.
- 115   Miss Dillon's horses were not sold at the Langston Arms but on the cricket ground in Chipping Norton.
- 118   For Barakhat read Barakat.
- 154   The 'Saadun filly' was Durra.
- 188   Oran had five and not four crosses to the Queen of Sheba line.
- 229   Ben Azrek's dam was Shemse and not Riad.
- 251   For Zemzem read Zem Zem.
- 257   and 258 For H.C. Stevens read H.C. Stephens.
- 260   For Ibn Aafuz read Ibn Aafas.
- 283   Sindh was not by Oran but by Oran's son, Silver Vanity.
- 292   For Nejmet et Subh read Nejmet es Subh.
- 340   Chez Nous Shah Rukh was the sire of Vidiko Yram Shah and the horses listed beneath him.
- 341   Quantock II was the sire of Rynet Sirex Shah and the horses listed beneath him.
- 358   Greatheart was the sire of Bayard and the horses listed beneath him.

Back endpaper: the reference F in the panel should read Windfall and not Woodfall.

Other alterations either correct literals or introduce new material.

ACKNOWLEDGEMENTS

The authors wish to acknowledge their gratitude to the Trustees of the British Library for access to the Wentworth Bequest and to the Syndics of the Fitzwilliam Museum for access to the papers of Wilfrid Scawen Blunt. Quotations from these archives are included by kind permission of Mr C.G. Covey and the Syndics of the Fitzwilliam Museum.

The task of sifting these collections has been greatly lightened by the unfailing courtesy and assistance of Miss J.M. Backhouse, Assistant Keeper of the Department of Manuscripts at the British Library, and Mr Paul Woudhuysen, Keeper of Printed books and Manuscripts at the Fitzwilliam Museum.

Lady Anne Lytton has provided invaluable help with her recollections of the Stud, as has Mrs Barbara Hucker. Lady Longford has given generously of her advice upon matters in common with her biography of Wilfrid Scawen Blunt.

Without the professional skill of Walter Rawlings, many of the photographs in this book could never have been reproduced. The authors also wish to thank the following for the use of photographs: Lady Anne Lytton, John Scouller, Rachael Kydd, Popard Photos, Michael Pitt-Rivers, Mrs A.D.D. Maclean, Mrs Valerie Males, Mr Michael Bowling, Carol Mulder, Mrs J. Grobbelaar, Mrs E.B. Arnold, Mrs T.W.I. Hedley and Mr G. North.

Information about Major R.D. Upton and his connections with Australia has been kindly supplied by Mrs M. D. Ireland and Mrs Sheila Stump.

Mrs C.P. Willes drafted the tables and Kees Mol read them in typescript.

The authors finally wish to thank their editor, James Fleming, for his efforts in making this book what it is.

Revised Edition
Charmaine Grobbelaar and Michael Bowling have again been of very great assistance and I thank them accordingly. I am also grateful to Lord Lytton, Bazy Tankersley, Coralie Gordon, Mrs V. Breakwell, Joan Flynn and Jacquie Webby both for the loan of photographs and for information so readily supplied.

R.A.

CONTENTS

FOREWORD	v
PUBLISHER'S NOTE	viii
CORRIGENDA TO THE FIRST EDITION	1
ACKNOWLEDGEMENTS	2
ILLUSTRATIONS	5
BIBLIOGRAPHY	9
INTRODUCTION	13

PART ONE
by Rosemary Archer

1	Early Days	23
2	The First Arrivals	34
3	Later Horses and The Newmarket Race	43
4	The Stud is Established	59
5	Sheykh Obeyd and Ali Pasha Sherif	73
6	The Foundation Stock	93
7	Partition – 1906	114
8	Troubled Times	137
9	The Lawsuit	156
10	Crabbet Prospers	165
11	The End of an Era	186
12	Some Memories of Crabbet *by Cecil Covey*	203
13	A Century's Work – The Families Summarised	225
	Appendix I	257
	Appendix II	260

PART TWO
by Colin Pearson
with Betty Finke

THE INFLUENCE OF CRABBET OVERSEAS

Argentina	265
Australia	268
New Zealand	276
Egypt	294

Europe:
 Russia   307
 Poland   319
 Spain   322
 The Netherlands   325
 Germany   330
 Denmark   332
 Sweden   333
 France   334
South Africa   336
United States of America   343
Canada   352

TABLE OF DESCENT FROM RODANIA   359
GENERAL INDEX – INDEX OF HORSES   373

ILLUSTRATIONS

Unless otherwise acknowledged, all illustrations are the property of Rosemary Archer and may not be reproduced without written permission. The relevant British Library Addn. MS numbers are 54085, 53970 and 53979.

Foundation Stock between pages 104 and 105
AZREK · BASILISK · DAJANIA · FEYSUL
HADBAN · MAHRUSS · MESAOUD · QUEEN OF SHEBA

Front endpaper Map of the Blunts' Arabian travels
Back endpaper Crabbet house and grounds about 1923: an aerial view
Frontispiece Crabbet from the East in 1876

Page
- vii Lady Anne Blunt (*The Earl of Lytton*)
- 7 Wilfrid Blunt in youth and old age (*The Earl of Lytton*)
- 27 Wilfrid Blunt in Buenos Aires, 1868 (*The British Library*). Lord Wentworth (*The British Library*). Lady Anne Blunt painting Kars (*The British Library*).
- 31 Wilfrid Blunt with Turkeycock. (*The British Library*). Lady Anne Blunt with Judith and Sherifa (*The British Library*).
- 33 Wadi Roseh
- 36 Wilfrid and Lady Anne Blunt in the desert
- 45 Ibn Rashid's stables at Haïl
- 46 Kars, the Stud's first stallion
- 51 Mares in the Cricket Park at Crabbet
- 52 Pharaoh. Sale day for the Blunts, *ca* 1886
- 60 Nefisa at Newbuildings. Rose of Sharon (*p.61*)
- 62 Fred Holman at Crabbet (*The British Library*). The 'Desert' at Crabbet, with Sherifa and foal (*The British Library*).
- 67 Meshura. Rose of Jericho
- 74 Wilfrid Blunt and Sherifa (*The British Library*). The tomb of Sheykh Obeyd (*The British Library*).
- 81 Lady Anne Blunt's notes on the Ali Pasha Sherif horses (*The British Library*)
- 82 The Pink House at Sheykh Obeyd
- 85 The staff at Crabbet *ca* 1885 (*The British Library*). Shahwan, purchased 1892 (*p.86*)
- 90 Judith Blunt with Ibn Nura. Mutlak with the dog Berk (*The British Library*).
- 115 Bint Helwa with her filly by Mesaoud
- 119 Sobha (*The Earl of Lytton*). Mares and foals at Crabbet
- 123 Sale Day in 1902
- 125 Ahmar, Bukra and Berk
- 128 Wilfrid Blunt on Yemama
- 130 Daoud and Nasra
- 135 THREE GREAT MARES: Narghileh, Rosemary and Ridaa
- 139 Rim, and Riyala
- 142 Geoffrey Covey
- 155 The final resting place of a great lady (*John Scouller*).
- 169 Nejiba, Ajjam, Anne Lytton with Kaftan (*The Earl of Lytton*).
- 172 Lady Wentworth with Risala, Ajjam, Kibla, Riyala and Rim
- 173 Lady Wentworth and Skowronek

ILLUSTRATIONS

Page

174 Rafeef and Nezma
175 Rasim and Raseem
178 Astrella, Razina and Riffal (*Mrs A.D.D. Maclean*).
180 King Fuad of Egypt; Prince Faisal ibn Saoud at Crabbet
183 Reyna, Jalila and Mirage
189 Silver Fire, Silver Gilt and Silver Vanity
190 Faris, Rissalix and Blue Domino (*Photonews*).
193 Dargee, Darjeel, (*Photonews*), Royal Crystal, Dancing Sunlight (*Mrs R.M. Kydd*), and Rissalma II
198 Mikeno (*Photonews*), and Indian King (*Popard Photos*). (*p.199*)
201 Sirella, Hanif, Haroun (*Mr M. A. Pitt-Rivers*), and Dancing Diamond
203 Cecil and Grace Covey
208 The Richmond Show, 1928
216 A post-war parade at Crabbet: Indian Magic. Bright Shadow (*Photonews*), and Silver Shadow
221 Naziri and Blaze (*p.220*)
222 Oran, Royal Diamond and Grand Royal
223 Raktha, General Grant (*Mrs T.W.I. Hedley*), and Indian Magic
231 Rijm, Nureddin II, and Shareer
233 Sotamm, Naufal, Sindh (*Mrs A.D.D. Maclean*), and Shafreyn (*Mrs A.D.D. Maclean*).
234 Ferhan and Indian Gold
237 Naseem, Irex and Rissam
240 Nasifa, Neraida, Niseyra, Nisreen and Indian Crown
241 Sharima, Grey Royal, Sharfina and Serafilla
246 Risala, Rissla and Risslina (p.247)
249 Selma, Somra, Silver Grey (*Photonews*) and Selima
253 Silent Wings, Indian Sylphette (*B. Finke*) and Hanif (*G. Plaister*)
254 Nerinora, Rikitea and Ludo
255 Golden Treasure (*Mrs P.A.M Murray*), King Cotton Gold (*Mrs P.A.M Murray*) and Somerled (*Joan Flynn*)
256 Aliha (*Mrs J. Maxwell*), Carmargue (*Gari Dill-Marlow*) and Seheran
269 Rossfennick (*Mrs A.D.D. Maclean*), Silver Moonlight (*Mrs A.D.D. Maclean*) and Rakib (*Mrs A.D.D. Maclean*)
271 Nuralina (*Mrs A.D.D. Maclean*), Rafina (*Mrs A.D.D. Maclean*) and Nasirieh (*Mrs A.D.D. Maclean*)
273 Indian Light, Ralvon Pilgrim (*Mrs Valerie Males*), Greylight (*Mrs A.D.D. Maclean*) and Electric Silver (*Mrs A.D.D. Maclean*)
311 Rixalina and Rissalma
313 Star of the Hills and Ruellia
327 Amal (*B. Finke*), Bint Sylvan Lass (*B. Finke*), Mangani (*B. Finke*) and Warandes Plakat (*B. Finke*)
337 Grantchester (*Mrs C. Grobbelaar*), Shalwan (*Mr G. North*) and Raktha (*Mrs E.B. Arnold*)
338 Dancing Wings (*Mrs E.B. Arnold*), Zena (*Mrs C. Grobbelaar*) and Jamani Rashani (*Mrs C. Grobbelaar*) p.335
346 Rissletta, Ferda (*Mr M. Bowling*), Incoronata and Crabbet Sura
347 Nasik, Anne Lytton with Rifala and Raffles, and Raffles in America in 1934
353 Xanthium (*Mrs Bazy Tankersley*), Khemosabi (*Mrs R. Husband*) and AM Canadian Beau (*Mrs Bazy Tankersley*)
355 Abu Zeyd, Serafix, Silver Drift and Nizzam

Wilfrid Blunt in youth and old age
Photo courtesy of the Earl of Lytton

BIBLIOGRAPHY

The following works have been referred to for the Introduction:

Doughty, C.M. *Travels in Arabia Deserta.* Repr. London, 1926.
Finati, G. *Narrative of the Life and Adventures of* . . . Translated from the Italian, London, 1830.
Forbis, J. *The Classic Arabian Horse.* New York, 1976.
Guarmani, C. *El Kamsa.* 2nd edn. Jerusalem, 1866.
Guarmani, C. *Northern Najd: A Journey from Jerusalem to Anaiza.* Translated by Lady Capel-Cure. Introduction and Notes by Douglas Carruthers. London, 1938.
Hammer-Purgstall, J. von. *Mines de l'Orient.* Volume 5. Vienna, 1816.
Hogarth, D.G. *The Penetration of Arabia.* London, 1905.
Hunt, Vere D. *The Horse and his Master.* London, 1859.
Journal des Haras, des Chasses et des Courses de Chevaux. Paris, 1828–63.
Lance, Général Mennessier de la. *Essai de Bibliographie Hippique.* Repr. Nieuwkoop, 1971.
Napier, Col. E. *Wild Sports in Europe, Asia and Africa.* London, 1844.
Nolan, Capt. L-E. *Cavalry, Its History and Tactics.* London, 1860.
Palgrave, W.G. *Narrative of a Year's Journey through Central and Eastern Arabia.* London, 1865.
Philby, H.St.J.B. *Northern Najd,* by C. Guarmani. *Royal Central Asian Journal* for January, 1939.
Poland, the Pure-Bred Arab Horse in. Warsaw. n.d.
Public Record Office. Foreign Office documents for Aleppo.
Sadlier, G.F. *Diary of a Journey across Arabia.* Repr. Cambridge, 1977.
Schiele, E. *The Arab Horse in Europe.* London, 1970.
Upton, Major R.D. *Gleanings from the Desert of Arabia.* London, 1881.
Upton, Captain. *The Thoroughbred Horse.* London, 1867.
Upton, Captain Roger. *Arabian Horses Studied in their Native Country in 1874/5.* Published in *Frasers Magazine,* September, 1876.
Vyse, Col. H. *Operations carried on at the Pyramids of Gizeh in 1837.* London, 1840–42.
Wrangel, Graf C.G. *Ungarns Pferdezucht in Word und Bilt.* Stuttgart, 1893–5.

Other printed works consulted:
Assad, T.J. *3 Victorian Travellers.* London, 1964.
Black, R. *Horse-Racing in England.* London, 1893.

Blunt, Lady Anne. *Bedouin Tribes of the Euphrates.* London, 1879.
Blunt, Lady Anne. *A Pilgrimage to Nejd.* London, 1881.
Blunt, Wilfrid Scawen. *Secret History of the English Occupation of Egypt.* London, 1907.
Blunt, Wilfrid Scawen. *India under Rippon.* London, 1909.
Blunt, Wilfrid Scawen. *The Poetical Works of Wilfrid Scawen Blunt.* London, 1914.
Blunt, Wilfrid Scawen. *My Diaries.* London, 1919 & 1920.
Blunt, W. *Cockerell.* London, 1964.
Blunt Spurs. *The Griffin's Aide-de-Camp.* New edn, Madras, 1858.
Borden, S. *The Arab Horse.* Repr. California, 1961.
Bowden, B.V. (Ed.) *Faster than Thought.* London, 1953.
Brown, W.R. *The Horse of the Desert.* Repr. Hildesheim, 1977.
Conn, Dr G.H. *The Arabian Horse in America.* Revised edn. New York, 1974.
Egremont, Max. *The Cousins.* London, 1977.
Finch, Edith. *Wilfrid Scawen Blunt.* London, 1938.
Forbis, J. *The Royal Arabians of Egypt and the Stud of Henry B. Babson.* Texas, 1976.
Gazder, P.J. *Arab Horse Families.* 1875–1973. New edn. Heriot 1993.
General Stud Book, The.
Greely, Margaret. *Arabian Exodus.* New edn. London, 1976.
Lutyens, Lady Emily. *A Blessed Girl.* London, 1953.
Lytton, Neville. *The English Country Gentleman.* London, n.d.
Lytton, the Earl of. *The Desert and the Green.* London, 1957.
Lytton, the Earl of. *Wilfrid Scawen Blunt.* London, 1961.
Meysey-Thompson, Col. R.F. *The Horse.* London, 1911.
Moore, Doris Langley. *Ada, Countess of Lovelace.* London, 1977.
Parkinson, M.J. *The Kellogg Arabian Ranch, the First Fifty Years.* California, 1975.
Prior, C.M. *The History of the Racing Calendar and Stud-Book.* London, 1926.
Raswan, C. *The Raswan Index.* Repr. Colorado, 1969.
Reese, H. *The Kellogg Arabians, their Background and Influence.* California, 1958.
Ridgeway, W. *The Origin and Influence of the Thoroughbred Horse.* London, 1905.
Rolland, S. **Raffles, his Sons and Daughters.* Iowa, 1974.
Schmidt, Margaret Fox. *Passion's Child, the Extraordinary Life of Jane Digby.* London, 1977.
Travelers Rest Arabian Horses. Repr. n.p., n.d.
Wentworth, Lady. *Thoroughbred Racing Stock and Its Ancestors.* London, 1938.
Wentworth, Lady. *The Authentic Arabian Horse and His Descendants.* London, 1945.
Wentworth, Lady. *The Swift Runner.* London, 1957.
Wentworth, Lady. *The World's Best Horse.* London, 1958.

BIBLIOGRAPHY

MANUSCRIPT MATERIAL
The Stud Books of Lady Anne Blunt and Lady Wentworth.
Papers of Wilfrid Scawen Blunt in the Fitzwilliam Museum, Cambridge.
Private papers of Lady Wentworth.
The Wentworth Bequest held by the British Library. The Additional MS numbers of material quoted from the Wentworth Bequest are as follows:

Chapter 1 53844/889; 54029/095/108
2 53889/894/895/896; 54095
3 53908/911/917/933/945
4 53978/984/985/996: 54008/011/147/623
5 53957/969/970/982/988/991/992/994/955: 54004/005/013/093/102
7 54006/007/008/010/011/015/016/017/097/104
8 54020/022/023/108/114/116/143/148
10 54099
13 54138

Since first publication of this book, a number of works have appeared which add substantially to our knowledge of Crabbet, the Blunts and the influence of Crabbet blood overseas.

Archer, R (Ed.) *Lady Anne Blunt: Journals and Correspondence 1878–1917.* Heriot, Northleach 1986.
Australia, The Arabian Horse in, volumes I, II and III. Australia 1980–89.
Courthouse Arabian Stud of Bill Musgrave Clark. Heriot, Northleach 1992.
Covey, Cecil. *Crabbet Arabians.* Sussex 1981.
Crabbet Convention, The. Sussex 1985.
Crabbet Influence Today: Collectors I and II. USA 1992/3.
Crabbet: World Symposium on Crabbet Breeding. USA 1983.
Dano, E. *The Sheykh Obeyd Arabian in the U.S.A.* USA 1991.
Fahlgren, B. *The Arabian Horse Families of Poland, 1790–1987.* Heriot, Northleach 1991.
Gordon, C. *The Crabbet Silver Family in Australia.* Queensland 1987.
Gordon, C & Flynn, J. *The Crabbet Arabian Imports to Australia.* Queensland 1988.
Hyde, D. *40 Years of British Arab Horse Champions 1953–1992.* Heriot, 1992.
Maxwell, Joanna. *Spanish Arabian Horse Families, 1898–1978.* Heriot, Northleach 1983.
Pearson, Colin with Mol, Kees. *The Arabian Horse Families of Egypt, 1870–1980.* Heriot, Northleach 1988.
Upton, Peter. *Desert Heritage: The Blunts Original Arab Horses.* London 1980
Upton, Peter. *The Arab Horse.* Marlborough 1989.

INTRODUCTION

A century ago the pure-bred Arabian was to be found, outside its native land, in only a handful of studs scattered through a small number of countries. Today its numbers are legion. That this transformation has been possible is largely due to the efforts and genius of Wilfrid and Lady Anne Blunt, and their daughter Judith, later Lady Wentworth.

The purpose of this book is to explain how the Blunts built up their stud at Crabbet Park in Sussex and to describe how the horses that they and Lady Wentworth bred have come to exert so profound an influence in the world of Arabian horse breeding. But in order to appreciate fully the immensity of the Blunts' achievements, it is first necessary to place the Crabbet Arabian Stud in its historical perspective.

The most remarkable feature of the Stud in this context is that it should have been founded in a country which for over a hundred years had displayed a marked antipathy towards the Arabian. This attitude was in complete contrast to that in Europe where the breed had always been held in the highest esteem. The reasons for this difference are fairly clear.

On the Continent, the frequency of land-based military campaigns made essential a ready supply of utility riding horses with the hardiness and stamina that could be achieved only by infusions of Arabian blood. Through stallion depots, breeding centres and government studs, successive European powers strove to encourage the production of a prime all-round horse. Since the qualities of the Arabian could be spread more quickly and more widely by the use of top crosses of Arab stallions, it was naturally upon the acquisition of these and not mares that breeders concentrated. It is true that as a consequence, the idea of breeding the Arab pure was alien to most European studs. But on the other hand, the mere recognition of the fact that the qualities of the Arabian were vital to light horse breeding as a whole, ensured for it the highest possible respect. It is only necessary to look at the dedication of such famous breeders as von Fechtig, Brudermann, the Sanguszkos and the Potockis, Branicki and Dzieduszycki, to realise the importance of the Arabian in European breeding.

In England, however, matters were very different since there was no military pressure to produce the European type of light horse. For economic and constitutional reasons, standing armies were not maintained in peacetime while in war England preferred, where possible, to persuade her allies to provide the men while she supplied the gold. Moreover, as her naval power grew and became central to her strategic policy, so the incentive to consider the needs of her cavalry was even further reduced. An exception may be made for the army in India, where horses of more or less Arabian character were widely used, but in England itself breeding revolved principally around civilian requirements; the carriage horse, the hunter and above all, the Thoroughbred. It is in relation to the latter that may be found the main reason for the decline in the Arabian's popularity in England.

The evolution of the Thoroughbred in the early eighteenth century, from crossing imported Arabian stallions with indigenous mares, is well known. Whether the enormous increase in speed that resulted was in fact due to the Arabian influence is a matter of conjecture. What is important is that breeders thought that it might have been, and when they failed to produce a horse even faster than the Thoroughbred by repeating the experiment, they laid the blame squarely upon the Arabian. In the absence of any military criteria, the only yardstick by which horses were judged was their performance on the Turf. If, so the argument ran, the Arabian could no longer increase the speed of the Thoroughbred, it must, *ex hypothesi*, be an inferior animal. The falseness of a proposition that looked for the one quality in the Arabian that it has never possessed was not apparent to people who had never had the opportunity to observe at first hand its real attributes.

The disfavour in which the Arabian was held by the racing (and breeding) fraternity was paradoxically reinforced in the 1850s by a surge in the public's interest in the breed and its homeland. As the Middle East became familiar to people in the nineteenth century, so a ready market arose in England for popular accounts of the Orient and its mysteries. And the Victorian appetite for romance was seldom more easily appeased than when fed with fabulous tales of the Arab and his horse. Caroline Norton's *The Arab's Farewell to His Steed*, and Whyte Melville's *The Arab's Ride to Cairo, a Legend of the Desert* are typical of the literary fare served to an avid and impressionable public. To the less credulous men of the Turf, however, these sentimental outpourings merely confirmed their long-held belief that the Arabian horse was an iridescent gewgaw that flattered to deceive, doubtless very suitable for ladies to sigh over in picture-books but completely devoid of substance when pitted against the size of the Thoroughbred.

Not all Englishmen shared this view, however, in the same way that not all Europeans preferred the Arab to the Thoroughbred. In 1825 an Italian traveller recorded hearing of a British cavalry officer trying to buy Arabians in Egypt but was unable to discover any details. Some twenty years afterwards when Colonel Vyse and later Colonel Napier visited Mohammed Ali's stud at Shoubra, they both showed a keen knowledge and appreciation of the breed. Opposition to the primacy of the Thoroughbred became explicit when in 1854 the Crimean War demonstrated that British horse-breeding was not the unqualified success that its admirers claimed for it. 'Our cavalry horses are feeble . . . the blood they require is not that of the weedy race horse (an animal more akin to the greyhound and bred for speed alone) but it is the blood of the Arab and Persian, to give them that compact form and wiry limb in which they are wanting,' wrote Captain Nolan. In the same vein, Vere D. Hunt pleaded for more Arabian blood to supply those 'essential excellencies *once* derived from him, and wantonly sacrificed to a debasing thirst for gold'. But these were only a few voices crying from the wilderness. The England of 1878 was by and large as staunchly pro-Thoroughbred and anti-Arabian as it had been a hundred years earlier.

Such then was the unlikely soil in which Crabbet was planted. But in the long term the importance of the Blunts has not been as innovators. It has been that they preserved the Arabian horse if not from extinction at least from decimation; that they bred it pure, and that in their selection of stock they adopted a standard of authenticity that was arguably more uncompromising than any previously known. The ways in which the Blunts acquired their horses are related in later chapters. At this point it is appropriate only to look at the methods used by the horse-buyers that preceded them in the Arabian peninsula.

With the exception of the trade with India, of which at present little is known, the export of horses from Arabia before 1878 lay principally in the hands of European and Egyptian breeders.

So far as Egypt is concerned, the history of the Arabians collected by the Viceroy Mohammed Ali and his successors has been very ably told elsewhere. It is unfortunate that the records relating to these horses and their origins have not survived in their entirety, especially as for many years no breeding register was kept by Mohammed Ali. We know as yet little more than that the horses were drawn from the finest stock available in northern Arabia, at allegedly very high prices. Some caution, however, needs to be exercised here, as those two eminent authorities, Douglas Carruthers and D.G. Hogarth, have observed. Both Mohammed Ali and Abbas Pasha I were at various times concerned to break away from the rule of Constantinople and looked to the Arab tribes as natural allies in their ambition. In a country such as Arabia where discreet methods of subversion were few, the suggestion that the horse trade was the least suspicious way of putting money into the right hands is by no means implausible. It is certainly curious that twenty-five years after Abbas Pasha had paid £1,000 for a fifteen-year-old mare, the Blunts, who were finding good horses 'exceedingly rare' and 'a luxury reserved only for princes', should have paid little more than £100 for the 'celebrated' mare Rodania. And for Mohammed Ali to have employed as horse-coper the Swedish Arabist Wallin, a man of great learning who later became professor at Helsingfors University, when he had at his disposal hundreds of real horse-copers, may perhaps indicate that the Egyptian horse trade in those days was not all that it appeared to be. But whatever the methods and motives of these great Egyptian breeders, it is indisputable that they did assemble a stock of horses containing the most reputable blood in all Arabia, from which the Blunts themselves were to profit enormously.

Mohammed Ali and Abbas Pasha held a distinct advantage over the European horse-buyers in that for many years they had first refusal, as it were, on the horses of Nejd. The area occupied by the main horse-breeding tribes of north Arabia may be divided very roughly between Nejd in the south and the Syrian desert in the north. There may or may not have been a difference between the horses of Syria and Nejd (according to Doughty one were as well to distinguish between London and Middlesex pheasants) but the fact is that Nejd was at all times accessible to Egypt whereas, with the exception of G.F. Sadlier in 1819, it was unexplored by Europeans until the middle of the nineteenth century.

The first Europeans to visit Nejd after Sadlier were probably W.G. Palgrave in 1862 and Carlo Guarmani in 1864. Since he neither bred nor bought Arabians, Palgrave does not really fall within the scope of this introduction. He is commonly referred to as a primary authority on the horses of Nejd but it is questionable whether he in fact deserves this credit. His character, his accuracy and his truthfulness, the political motives for his journey and the commercial aspects behind the publication of his account of it, have all tended to discredit him as a dependable source of information. In Wilfrid Blunt's opinion, 'Palgrave's chapter on horses is just such as might have been written as an afterthought to supply an important omission in his account of the country.' Whether or not this was the case, Palgrave's description of the horses of Nejd had an important result. For it was a principal factor behind the decision of his employer, Napoleon III, to commission Guarmani to go to Nejd and buy some of the horses that Palgrave had seen.

Guarmani set out only two years after Palgrave. The combination of the timing and the common patron, together with certain geographical inconsistencies in his account, has tended, unjustifiably, to put Guarmani's motives and veracity under the same shadow of suspicion as those of Palgrave. However, the three men best qualified to judge the issue – Carruthers, Hogarth and H.St.J. Philby – are unanimous in acquitting Guarmani of deception. Hogarth even compares his knowledge of the tribes with that of Doughty, which is praise in no uncertain fashion.

Carlo Guarmani was born in Italy in 1828. In 1850 he left for the East where over the following years he travelled extensively among the tribes, combining a post in the Imperial French Postal Service with sundry trading activities. In 1864 he had published a slender and outspoken book on the Arabian horse entitled *El Kamsa*. Two years later his account of the expedition to Nejd for Napoleon appeared. It was intended to be only an itinerary to *El Kamsa* for, as he said, 'I could not write on the Arab horse and its noble race without describing, in some manner, the land which from the beginning of the world has been the cradle of the most perfect type of equine species.'

Guarmani's particular importance is that, like the Blunts, he lived in the East and knew the tribes intimately. Since he was especially scornful of previous European horse-buyers, it is of great interest that he should have listed the qualifications necessary in anyone wishing to purchase good horses from the Arabs. That person must, he said, have lived in the Levant for some time, be able to speak Arabic perfectly, know the customs and traditions of the people themselves and be willing to understand and sympathise with their way of life. Without these, 'one can only have an imperfect and often completely false knowledge of these matters; nor, which is worse, will one send to Europe anything other than stallions of doubtful parentage which are not accepted by the Arabs themselves although often purchased at the highest prices of which the greater part remains in the hands of disloyal servants.' Guarmani did have considerable advantages over other European horse-buyers. For not only had he the opportunity to acquire the qualifications that he mentioned, but he also knew both Syria and Nejd, whereas other Europeans bought horses only in Syria.

In contrast to central Arabia, Aleppo and the fringes of the Syrian desert had been familiar to the West for centuries and because of the relative accessibility of its tribes, had become the natural destination of all early horse-buying missions from Europe. The allegiances of these expeditions were varied. Rzewuski was commissioned privately by the rulers of Württemburg; Damoiseau was a member of the de Portes party, sent by the French Government to repair the loss of horses during the Napoleonic Wars; Puckler-Muscau and the several emissaries of the Sanguszkos were buying on their own account while Dambly, von Herbert and Brudermann were directly employed by state studs. In most instances we know little either of their itineraries or of the great majority of the horses they brought back. Occasionally a note of scepticism was sounded in the journals of the day about the origins of some of these importations, as in remarks such as 'arabes prétendus' and 'généalogie obscure'; and Guarmani was so openly contemptuous of many of these purchases that it would be of great value to know more precisely where, how and from whom the horses were acquired.

The situation is not made clearer by the way in which these (and even more recent) exploits have been subject to a certain amount of colourful exaggeration. Count Rzewuski, for example, sent from Syria between 1817 and 1819 a total of 137 Arabians to the royal stud at Weil. In the process, we are told, 'he wrote a separate page in the history of the expeditions in search of original Arab horses'. For during these two years he is supposed, when not arranging his finances in Constantinople, to have travelled as far as Muscat in the east and Jebel Shammar in the south, and to have been adopted as emir of seventeen different tribes in addition to being made Prince of Aleppo and Baghdad. As he himself wrote, 'tout enfin me fit comparer au héros favori des arabes, au célèbre Antar'. That Rzewuski purchased these horses is undoubted. But this sort of romantic embroidery upon his tale cannot but influence belief in him as a serious horse-buyer. As Hogarth wrote to Wilfrid Blunt about Palgrave, 'he is so inaccurate in matters historical and geographical, indeed one might say so devoid of "scientific conscience" that one never feels safe with him'. The ability to feel 'safe' is paramount when the source material is so sparse.

We are on much firmer ground with the stud buyers, Dambly, von Herbert and Brudermann, who have left fairly detailed accounts of their travels. From these it is possible to reconstruct the general pattern of such missions. They would land either at Alexandretta (now Iskenderun) and work south *via* Aleppo and Damascus to re-embark at Beirut, or they would land at Beirut and make the same circuit northwards. On both cases they were well placed to visit the Ruala and Weld Ali from Damascus, and the Fedaan and S'baa Anazeh from Aleppo. It seems to have been customary to use agents to provide guides, interpreters and provisions as well as to make preliminary enquiries among the tribes. But it is doubtful whether these expeditions penetrated very deeply. This was partly because travelling in the desert could still be very dangerous; partly because, as we know happened in the case of Dambly, agents had already collected the horses before he arrived, leaving only the final choice to be made, and partly because in general the standard of horse required was of relative rather than absolute excellence, for reasons that have already been discussed. It is probably also the case, as Guarmani implies, that the tribes most frequently visited had come to regard such missions as a very profitable outlet for horses they did not want to keep themselves.

To say this is not, however, to deny that in 1857 Brudermann could have found round Homs and Hama 'sehr schöne und edle Pferde'. Seven years before Wallin had put Abdullah's stud at Haïl at about two hundred head and said that most of the wealthier families in Jebel Shammar owned horses. At that time good horses were not rare. But the danger of buying in settled or semi-settled land and not from the desert itself were well illustrated by Captain Roger Upton in 1874. He had been riding into Aleppo one day when he witnessed the purchase by Egyptian agents of horses of 'more or less breeding'. 'These horses', he wrote, 'would figure in Egypt as valuable Arabians. I mention this occurrence to show how seldom Arab horses, or horses of Arab blood, are obtained. Not that I consider these I have mentioned as specimens of the pure breed of the desert . . . but they were what are usually seen by travellers and considered as high-class Arabs.'

Upton is the last horse-buyer of importance before the Blunts. He was born in 1827 and at the age of twenty-four was commissioned into the 1st West Indies Regiment of Foot. In 1855 he exchanged into the 9th (Queen's Royal) Lancers, then stationed in India, and served with them until 1861 when he resigned his commission and left the regular army. From then until his death from typhoid fever in January, 1881, his only occupation of which a record exists was as adjutant to two volunteer cavalry regiments, first in Essex and then in Northumberland. He appears to have done some writing under a pseudonym and in 1866, after a correspondence in *The Field* that arose from Palgrave's account of the Nejd horses, he tried to raise a subscription to import into England some of these 'exquisitely well-shaped' animals, declaring that it would benefit the nation 'from the sovereign downwards'.

Upton seems to have made only one journey to Arabia; that of 1874/5 on behalf of Henry Chaplin M.P. and the Australians W.J. and A.A. Dangar. Its purpose was to upgrade native stock and though lines from one of the mares, Kesia, exist to this day, the horses purchased did not prove particularly successful at stud. Lady Wentworth considered Upton's opinions on the Arabian to be often incorrect – 'myth: quite absurd', 'hopelessly muddled', 'quite untrue'. Nevertheless he was a dedicated believer in the merits of the Arabian and his unbiased and factual observations upon the horse situation in Syria have considerable value. His main handicap was probably a lack of personal funds and had he been as affluent as the Blunts there can be little doubt that he would have himself attempted to fill 'the grand opening for private enterprise' that he saw in exporting horses from Arabia.

In November, 1877, Wilfrid and Lady Anne Blunt set out from England for the East. They took the train to Marseille and from there a steamer to Constantinople and Alexandretta, where they landed on December 5th. Within three weeks they had purchased a yearling filly that was to be called Dajania and with her they founded the Crabbet Arabian Stud.

J.R.F.

PART ONE

by Rosemary Archer

CHAPTER I

Early Days

Wilfrid Scawen Blunt and Lady Anne Isabella Noel King were married in London on June 8th, 1869, at St George's, Hanover Square. The wedding was a great social occasion and of interest to many, for Lady Anne was the only granddaughter of the poet Lord Byron, and the charm and devastating good looks of Wilfrid Blunt had been conspicuous for some years past among social and diplomatic circles in Europe.

The Blunts had been landowners in Sussex since the middle of the seventeenth century. The original seat of the family had been Springfield House, bought in 1660, but this had changed when in 1762 Wilfrid Blunt's great-great-grandfather had acquired by marriage the estates of Crabbet and Newbuildings (some sixteen miles apart), together with the Manor and forest lands at Worth.

Francis Blunt, Wilfrid's father, joined the army as a young man but during the Peninsular War was permanently lamed and obliged to give up soldiering. He thereafter led a life of adventurous respectability, dividing his time between his estates and various sporting activities. In 1838 he married Mary Chandler. They had three children; Francis Scawen, born in 1839, Wilfrid Scawen in 1840 and Alice, in 1842. Within a few months of the birth of his last child, Francis Blunt died. The children were made wards in Chancery and the Blunt property was entailed upon Francis, the elder son.

For the next few years Mary Blunt moved restlessly round England and the Continent with her young family. In 1848 she became a Roman Catholic and four years later her three children were also received into that faith. Wilfrid Blunt was never as devout as his brother or sister, and was later to dally with both Mohammedanism and atheism. His mind was too unresting and exploratory to abide for long by one creed, unlike his wife whose belief in her religion was steadfast.

At an early age Wilfrid Blunt showed signs of artistic ability and after one unhappy period at school it was suggested that he learn to be a painter. Arrangements were made for him to be apprenticed to the portrait painter G.F. Watts but these were abandoned when his mother fell ill and died in June, 1853. Wilfrid and his brother and sister now came under the care of their aunt, Mrs Wyndham, who left the boys at Oscott, the school at which they had begun shortly before their mother's death. Here Wilfrid fell under the influence of Dr Charles Meynell, a remarkable Yorkshireman, who not only introduced him to the spirit and romance of poetry but also awakened in him an instinct for enquiry and critical reasoning that freed him from the intellectual confines of his religion. When Wilfrid Blunt left Oscott at the age of seventeen, it was not as a shy and unhappy orphan but as a self-assured young man who was ready to discover what the world had to offer. In 1858 he joined the Diplomatic Service, a normal career for a second son with slender expectations of inheriting the family property. Over the next eleven years he occupied posts in Athens, Frankfurt, Madrid, Paris and finally Buenos Aires. His duties were few and undemanding, and left him ample time to savour the many distractions that contemporary Europe offered. By the time he married Lady Anne, Wilfrid Blunt was certain that there was a great deal of pleasure to be had from life. The fortune that his wife had inherited from Lady Byron was considerable and shortly after their marriage Blunt resigned from the Diplomatic Service.

Blunt had true artistic feeling and could have excelled in any of the arts. Almost unknown is the sculpture he made of his brother Francis which is in the Franciscan Friary in Crawley. It has been described as a masterpiece and was carved by Blunt in alabaster as a memorial to the brother he loved so dearly. Blunt's daughter Judith wrote that he had 'an inherent sense of beauty and good taste in all the arts which made him collect round him everything that was best of its kind in architecture, books, rare birds, beautiful flowers, pictures and the like'. It was, she said, his 'love of symmetry and beauty which drew him specially to Arabian horses'.

Wilfrid Blunt did not have a robust constitution and was plagued by illness throughout his life. In 1873, when he was with Lady Anne in Constantinople, he caught pneumonia and either that, or the galloping consumption that the doctors also diagnosed, left one lung permanently damaged. He nevertheless continued to live with unbounded energy. He enjoyed all country pursuits and had a deep love of nature, particularly for wild flowers and woodlands. He was especially fond of Sussex, the county of his birth, and of the family estates, which ran into no less than sixteen different parishes.

> Nor has the world a better thing,
> Though one should search it round,
> Than thus to live one's own sole king,
> Upon one's own sole ground.

Blunt's published poetry occupies ten separate works and was produced in a collected edition of two volumes in 1914. He was frequently compared with Byron and Shelley, less perhaps for their poetic similarities than for the position they shared as aristocratic rebels against the system. With his total disregard for convention and a mercurial, and at times explosive, temper, Blunt was to incur time and again the wrath of the Establishment. Throughout his life he rarely wavered in his condemnation of what he saw as the essential evil of imperialism. But unpalatable though they were to most people at the time, it was less his opinions and more the unrelenting persistence with which he expounded them, that constituted his major weakness. For whether in his political battles or in the family quarrels that so beset his later life, Blunt never knew when to leave well alone. When he fought, he did so to the bitter end. Compromise was not a word he understood.

It has been said of Blunt that he was too gifted in many ways to be supreme in any one. It would be quite false to pretend that his part in the Crabbet Arabian Stud does anything like justice to his achievements and character. In the pages that follow it is his blemishes and not his virtues that are mainly apparent. His importance as a traveller, poet and political visionary are only marginally relevant to the story, while his separation from Lady Anne and the bitter confrontations with his daughter are central. Yet in her later life Judith, after all that had passed between them, still remembered with pride her father's originality and independence of mind, and his indefinable magnetism and arresting charm 'which made him unique'. As for Lady Anne, she had loved him with a deep sincerity, although she was caused much trouble and sorrow by his tempestuous way of life. In her old age she wrote sadly of her 'undying affection to think of what he *might* be – and is not'.

Lady Anne Blunt was born three years before Wilfrid, in 1837. Her father was William, the 8th Baron King until he was created first Earl of Lovelace in 1838. Her mother was Ada, the only child of Byron and his wife, Anne Milbanke.

Ada, Countess of Lovelace, was a remarkable woman. Apart from being an accomplished musician, she had an extraordinary skill in mathematics. She was introduced at an early age to Charles Babbage, then engaged upon the construction of his Difference Engine, the prototype almost of the modern computer, with which he intended to work to twenty decimal places. While her contemporaries regarded it with the same sort of expression that 'some savages are said to have shown on first seeing into a looking glass', Miss Byron (as she then was) comprehended its principles instantly. She later published a learned paper on it and for the rest of her life continued to correspond closely with Babbage and the most distinguished mathematicians of her day*.

She had always been fond of horses and had an unfortunate weakness for horse-racing. She is said to have invented an 'infallible' system of betting but when it proved otherwise she found herself in grave financial trouble and had to pawn the family jewels. After a long and painful illness, she died in 1852 at the age of thirty-seven.

She left behind her three children who inherited many of their mother's talents; Byron Noel, who died at the age of twenty-six, Lady Anne, and the youngest, Ralph, who succeeded his brother as the 13th Lord Wentworth. Their father, Lord Lovelace, became remote and unapproachable after his wife's death and as a result the children received an unorthodox upbringing.

As a young child, Lady Anne had spent two years with her grandmother, Lady Byron, who was largely responsible for the children's education since their mother Ada was too absorbed in her scientific studies to be able to devote much attention to them. Lady Anne had little formal schooling and relied heavily upon her brother Ralph, to whom she was deeply attached, to procure books for her and to help her learn. The lack of a proper education did not restrict the development of a naturally fine mind and during her life Lady Anne became fluent in several languages, particularly Arabic. She began to take Arabic lessons after she and Wilfrid returned from their first major journey in Arabia. She had various teachers, among them Sheikh Abdur Rahman Aleysh in Cairo, a friend of Blunt's called Sabunji in London, and a gentleman in Paris with an incurable fondness for highly-scented hair lotion. She learned a written Arabic stated to be used only in the highest scholastic circles and to be taught only rarely to women. Lady Anne became so imbued with the East that according to her family she would think in Arabic and was even known to make her responses at Mass in Arabic. But unlike Wilfrid, who was apt to pretend to a greater knowledge of Arabic than he had, Lady Anne

* In 1980 a software language was named 'Ada' in her honour which four years later became a trademark of the U.S. Department of Defense.

right Wilfrid Blunt in Buenos Aires, 1868
above Lord Wentworth, Lady Anne Blunt's brother
below Lady Anne Blunt painting Kars with Molony looking on. Judith Blunt is seated on the grass

was never one to parade her learning. For as she once told her daughter, her object was 'to pass through life unobserved'.

After her mother had died and when she inherited her share of the Milbanke fortune from her grandmother, Lady Anne left the family home and spent much time living on the Continent with musical friends. On one occasion she visited Clara Schumann. Brahms was there also and Lady Anne described how he would wander off into the woods to find inspiration. She was a persevering musician who enjoyed practising the scales on her violin and playing duets with her brother Ralph. According to her daughter, Lady Anne at one time owned two of the world's famous Stradivarius violins and Mozart's viola.

Lady Anne was more fluent as an artist than as a musician. She studied under Ruskin and the watercolours with which she filled her notebooks on her desert journeys are vivid. She also painted in oils; one picture is the life-size portrait of Wilfrid Blunt on the stallion Pharaoh, for which the horse was held for hours on the lawn at Crabbet. Blunt proved a more difficult subject and could rarely be persuaded to stay on Pharaoh for longer than five minutes.

On her travels with Blunt, Lady Anne faced situations and suffered injuries that would have daunted all but the strongest character and without doubt she possessed extraordinary inner reserves of courage. She also had behind her the strength of her faith. When they were in Persia in 1879, Wilfrid Blunt fell seriously ill. They were encamped in mountainous country among unfriendly tribesmen and having only their Arab servants with them, there was nobody to whom Lady Anne could go for help. One night, as Wilfrid's condition grew critical, she went outside the tent and saw 'for some few moments that Glory which may not be described . . . *I knew*'. The intensity of the vision remained in her memory until her death. That night proved to be the turning point in Blunt's illness and he made what they both came to regard as a miraculous recovery. The following year Lady Anne was received into the Roman Catholic Church.

Her son-in-law, Neville Lytton, said of Lady Anne that there were only three things she could not abide; the world, the flesh and the devil. There was certainly a streak of puritanism in her. She strongly disapproved of smoking and over-indulgence in the worldly pleasures of eating and drinking. At first acquaintance she could appear a little remote but beneath the reserve she was capable of great wit and vitality. One of her finest qualities was her unfailing sincerity and honesty.

She was incapable of telling an untruth, as her family constantly testified. Generous in her gifts to charity, she was invariably kind and thoughtful and in the words of her daughter, commanded 'something like adoration from family retainers and all those around her'.

One member of Lady Anne's staff was to play a particularly important part in the Blunts' life – Isabella Mary Cowie, known always as Cowie. Officially Lady Anne's maid, there was nothing that Cowie could not and did not do. When she went with them on their travels she was cook and nurse, when they were at Crabbet she was housekeeper and general manager. She was often entrusted by Lady Anne with her business appointments. When rooms were needed in London or in some coastal resort for Judith, it was Cowie who inspected them. She even campaigned with Lady Anne when Blunt was standing for Parliament. Above all, she provided an element of stability, cheerfulness and peace in the house until her death in 1903. Many years later Judith described the sort of duties that came Cowie's way.

> She was of Huguenot ancestry, [she wrote] and had a refined and delicate humour which assisted her to deal with refractory lizards, live scorpions (in bottles), hawks, owls and other compulsory-voluntary undertakings on their [the Blunts'] return from Spain. These included Felipe Pedro da Croz, a black negro slave bought in Africa for 10/- and known familiarly as Pompey, a pair of Spanish horses, two barbs, an eagle, a pair of owls, and an old penniless Irish painter, one Molony (picked up in the art galleries of Madrid) all of which were imported to Crabbet.

The Blunts' first child was born in late 1870 at Newbuildings Place. A boy, named Wilfrid Scawen after his father, he died after only a few days. Lady Anne later had twin daughters who also died soon after they were born. On February 6th, 1873, she gave birth one month prematurely to their only surviving child. Judith Anne Dorothea was born in London, at 45 Brook Street, where the Blunts had taken a house. Her first two names were from Lady Anne's family and the last the name of the saint of the day. 'I had asked a blessing of the Pope,' wrote Wilfrid,' 'he might have made it a boy'. Eleven days later he heard that the Pope had blessed a medal for the infant Judith but the letter arrived with its edges frayed – and no medal. 'It's gone, it must have fallen out – it's gone,' exclaimed Blunt. He was bitterly disappointed at not having had a son and expected Judith to be able to do all the things with him that a boy would have done. At an early age he taught her how to use a gun and together they would make long expeditions rabbiting and trout fishing but throughout his life he never ceased to regret that he had no male heir.

In 1872 Blunt's brother and sister both died from consumption, Francis in April and Alice in August. Alice had married, eight days after the Blunt's own marriage, Nep Wheatley who for a short time was to be their agent at Crabbet. With the death of his brother, Blunt now found himself the owner of the estates at Crabbet and Newbuildings. He and Lady Anne had been living at Newbuildings Place when they were in England and in 1870 he had been given by Francis a lease on it with the option to purchase. But his brother's last words to Wilfrid had been that he should keep Newbuildings as a plaything and actually live at Crabbet. So a month after Francis's death, the Blunts moved into the few habitable rooms at Crabbet.

A survey taken of the house in 1802 had stated that 'the buildings at Crabbet consist of an old mansion a part of which has been taken down and the remainder ought to be so'. By 1811 only a wing of the old house remained. Blunt's father had added a few rooms and the house had then been let to a tenant farmer until Francis moved there.

The Blunts now decided to rebuild entirely the main portion of the house and together they drew up their own designs. Apart from the Portland stone facings, local materials were used. The bricks were made in their own brickyard and the roof of Horsham stone slates. The timber came from the estate and only local labour was used. Today Crabbet, a listed building, stands as a monument to their combined abilities.

Once the house was finished in the spring of 1873, the Blunts set off for Belgrade and Constantinople. Regardless of the consumption diagnosed by Wilfrid's doctors, they went to the horse-market and there bought six country ponies and one 'claiming to be more or less an Arab'. Thus equipped they crossed over into the hills of Asiatic Turkey.

The six weeks that they now spent in the magnificent but poor countryside of the northern provinces provided, as Wilfrid Blunt said, 'a foretaste only but enough to raise in us a thirst for more'. He had made the occasional foray into the country when he had been in Athens, but this was the first time that either he or Lady Anne had ever left the beaten track. They allowed themselves to be absorbed into the timeless routine of daily life in the East and found the experience

above Wilfrid Blunt with Turkeycock, 'the far forerunner of the Crabbet Arabian Stud'

left Lady Anne Blunt with Judith and Sherifa outside Crabbet

richly rewarding. 'It was here,' wrote Blunt, 'that I was first impressed with the solemn dignity of eastern things in contrast with the hurry of the west, the strings of camels in the streets, the slow ox-drawn *arabas*, the sole wheeled vehicles on the few roads broad enough for wheels to run.' The Blunts enjoyed themselves hugely and in fact they were never happier during their marriage than in their eastern travels, when they experienced together a peace and solitude that they could never find in Europe.

When they came home, they brought with them the Arab, 'more or less', that they had purchased in Constantinople. Named Turkeycock, he was the first horse of eastern blood that they had at Crabbet. He was described by Blunt as 'the far fore-runner of the Crabbet Arabian Stud – a valiant beast who had carried me the journey through, in colour grey, and with the characteristics of Arabian blood, if not a pure Kehailan'. It is not known what became of Turkeycock for he is not mentioned as being at Crabbet in 1878 when the Blunts sold most of their horses to make room in the stables for their imported Arabians.

There were to be two further expeditions before 1877. In the winter of 1873 they travelled into the Algerian desert where Lady Anne fell seriously ill. A potentially awkward situation was saved only by the arrival of Ralph Wentworth who was following behind and came to the rescue 'swathed, as his custom was, in a multitude of coats and cloaks, but bare-headed and without other luggage than his violin, a filter and a huge Bologna sausage purchased in Italy'. Two years later they made their first visit to Egypt. From Cairo they travelled north across the Sinai peninsula to Jerusalem and thence to Damascus. It was not an especially memorable journey (though Blunt shot a shark in the Gulf of Aqaba) but it gave them a feeling for Arabia and the Bedouins, and on their return they began to make plans for a far more ambitious excursion into the deserts of Syria and Mesopotamia.

They had thought at first of travelling overland along the caravan routes from Syria to India but could find little information about the terrain or the dangers involved. The only accurate maps that Blunt could discover in the library of the Royal Geographical Society were those that Colonel Chesney had made between 1835 and 1837. So they decided to leave their plans open until they had reached Syria. All the practical arrangements, including organising the letters of credit, were undertaken by Lady Anne and on November 20th, 1877, they left England for the East.

They did have one definite purpose in going to Syria, and that was

Wadi Roseh

to see if they could find any representatives of the strain from which the Darley Arabian had come over a hundred and fifty years before. The Darley Arabian has been, in the male line, the most influential of the Thoroughbred Foundation Sires and whether for this reason, or whether from a desire to solve the mystery of his physical appearance (over which there was then some doubt), the history of the Darley Arabian had been over the years something of an obsession with the Milbanke side of Lady Anne's family. The Milbankes had been famous breeders of the Thoroughbred in its early days. At any rate Lady Anne and her brother Ralph, and to some extent Wilfrid too, were all keenly interested to obtain 'some of the true breed of Arab mares from which the Darley Arabian came'. Lord Wentworth gave Blunt £150 before he left England to be spent on buying a horse of the Darley strain.

The way in which the quest for the blood of the Darley Arabian developed into the Crabbet Arabian Stud was decided for the Blunts by a chance encounter with an engineer on board their ship to Alexandretta. He was in the service of the Ottoman Government and well acquainted with conditions in Syria. When he heard of their indecision about their route when they landed, he advised them to do nothing without first going to Aleppo and consulting Mr Skene, the British Consul. Skene had been in the country for years and was by far the best person to give them the information they wanted. It was a sensible idea and they followed it through.

The consequences of their visit and of the snowstorms that enforced a long stay with Skene, may be found today throughout the Arabian stud-books of the world.

On December 14th, 1877, Lady Anne Blunt wrote in her journal: 'We have made a plan . . . of importing some of the best Anazeh blood to England and breeding it pure there . . . it would be an interesting and useful thing to do and I should like much to try it.'

CHAPTER 2

The First Arrivals

The month that the Blunts spent with the Skenes in that winter of 1877 effectively marks the birth of the Crabbet Arabian Stud. As Blunt later wrote, it was to Skene that 'we owed the idea and . . . our initial knowledge of the Bedouin tradition of horse-breeding, without which it would have been impossible to make our purchases'.

James Henry Skene was then aged sixty-five. After serving for five years in an infantry regiment, he had been appointed in 1845 to be Local Director of Police at Cephalonia and later Zante. In 1852 he had been promoted to the Vice-Consulship at Constantinople and in 1855 to the Consulate at Aleppo. The same year he had been seconded to General Vivian's staff as Private Secretary, Vivian being the commander of a force of irregular cavalry that had been raised to fight in the Crimean War. When peace was declared in 1856, Skene returned to his position at Aleppo where he had remained ever since.

During his many years in Syria, Skene had travelled extensively in the surrounding country. He had become acquainted with the neighbouring sheikhs and had acquired considerable knowledge of the Bedouin tribes and their history. Of greater importance to the Blunts was the fact that he had also become extremely interested in the local traditions and practices of breeding Arabian horses. According to Wilfrid Blunt, Skene had been the first Englishman to have tabulated the various strains of Kehailan blood. Over the years he had had much experience of purchasing horses from the Arabs, having in particular accompanied Upton on his buying mission in 1874.

It so happened that while the Blunts were staying with him, Skene had in his stables a yearling colt which he had bought as a foal from the sheikh of a branch of the Hannadi tribe and which he believed to be of the same strain as the Darley Arabian. The Blunts' interest was immediately aroused for they saw in the colt the link with the original Darley for which they had been looking. They were much impressed by Darley, as he was to be named, and were excited by Skene's enthusiasm for breeding Arabians. When he suggested that they go into partnership together to start a stud of pure-bred Arabs in England, both Wilfrid and Lady Anne were more than receptive to the idea.*

'The plan,' as Lady Anne called it, was that the Blunts and Skene should have equal shares in the enterprise. Skene already had permission to export six horses from Syria and would contribute the Darley colt and two fillies. The Blunts were to buy another colt and two fillies. Lady Anne estimated that the total cost of purchasing and transporting the horses to England would be a little over £600. 'As to making it pay, the sum is not too large that it would matter very much if lost, but if there is any luck it ought not to be a losing business.' The Blunts later agreed with Skene that it would be best to buy young mares in foal instead of fillies so that they could then have four foals by the following spring.

With the purchase of these horses as one of their basic objectives, the Blunts began to make preparations for the desert. They took lessons in Arabic and with Wilfrid doing his best to obtain the geographical information they needed, Lady Anne took charge of the commissariat. It was on these expeditions that Wilfrid and Lady Anne Blunt forged a partnership which, as Hogarth has said, 'remains unique among exploring parties in Arabia'. They travelled for no express scientific, commercial or political purpose but rather from a broad sympathy with the customs of the East that was to be cemented by their interest in the Arabian horse. With Blunt as leader and Lady Anne as storekeeper, saddle-mender, doctor and diarist, they were to cross country seldom seen by Europeans before and at the same time experience some of the happiest months in their lives.

The Blunts had already started to buy horses before they left Aleppo. Their first purchase, made on Christmas Day, 1877, was coincidentally one of the most important they ever made. This was a yearling filly of the Kehileh Dajanieh strain, called variously Lady Hester, Jessamine, Jasmine and finally registered as Dajania. On January 4th they acquired Palmyra, whom they renamed Hagar. Bought as a journey mare, she was to carry Blunt from Aleppo to Baghdad and then back through northern Mesopotamia to Damascus. She proved extremely

* The Blunts later discovered that Skene's information about the original Darley Arabian had been incorrect and that he had been a Managhi and not a Kehilan Ajuz of the Ras el Fedawi like their Darley colt. Darley was sold at the first Crabbet sale, in 1882. Though beautiful as a yearling, he developed faulty hocks and at the age of three, curbs appeared. The Blunts made enquiries about his sire and dam but did not hear of any defect or unsoundness.

Wilfrid and Lady Anne Blunt in the desert

fast when they chased the desert wolves and gazelles. According to Blunt she had the long low stride of an English racehorse and was the fastest of all their early imports. With her gentle temper, Hagar made an ideal journey mare. The Blunts also bought at this time an impressive four-year-old Seglawi Jedran whom they called Kars. He was to be the first stallion used at Crabbet.

Their departure from Aleppo was delayed by Blunt falling ill. Lady Anne described it as an attack of violent neuralgia mixed with toothache, 'caused by the blind stupidity of his tiresome old dentist who mistook and blundered about his teeth'. Since no one reliable could be found at short notice, Lady Anne herself had to do what she called 'some experimental stopping' on Wilfrid's teeth.

On January 9th, 1878, the Blunts finally left Aleppo with Skene, who was to accompany them for the first few days. Word soon spread that they were looking for horses. Numerous animals were brought for their inspection but none came up to the standard they had set and it was soon apparent, as it had been to Upton three years before, that outstanding specimens of the breed were all too rare in the desert. So when on April 7th they saw Beteyen ibn Mirshid, Sheikh of the Gomussa, riding a bay mare 'incomparably superior to anything we have seen here or elsewhere', they immediately determined to buy her.

They were at the time on their way back to Damascus and had camped near the pools of Khabra el Mashluk, some sixty miles to the south east of Palmyra. Beteyen was also on his way home, from an outlying Gomussa camp where he had been to fetch the mare in which he had recently bought a half share from her breeder. Lady Anne described the mare as 'a dark bay (brown) everything perfect for racing, head good', with a 'neatness and finish about every movement' that reminded her of a fawn.

The next day they began negotiations with Beteyen. He had given fourteen camels and £20 for his share and the Blunts did not have enough money with them to be able to offer the 'really overpowering price' that was needed to secure her there and then. They therefore left the matter with Skene who assured them that he would be able to come to an arrangement with Beteyen without difficulty. The full story of how this was accomplished is told in Lady Anne's own words in Chapter 6. Beteyen's mare, as the Blunts referred to her, eventually arrived at Crabbet in 1879 and was there named Queen of Sheba.

On April 17th the Blunts reached Damascus and after leaving money with Skene for the purchase of Beteyen's mare and having arranged with him that he should buy more horses for the Stud, they set off for England.

On their way home they stopped to see Lord Wentworth in Paris. Lady Anne had already told her brother of their plan to start a stud when she had written to him about Skene's Darley colt. His interest had clearly been stimulated; he now expressed a keen desire to be involved in the project and at Lady Anne's request joined the partnership. It was agreed that the Stud should be divided into three equal shares between the Blunts, Skene and Lord Wentworth. The £150 that Lord Wentworth had given Blunt earlier was to be counted as part of his share and he was to send a further sum to Skene to help pay for the latter's purchases.

When the Blunts returned to Crabbet after an absence of six months they found much to be organised before the arrival of the first batch of horses. Permits had to be obtained for their importation and the stables made ready. In the middle of these preparations, an unforeseen problem suddenly arose over the haymaking, a crop that was vital to Crabbet that year in view of the expected increase in horses. The men on the estate were at that time employed on a seasonal basis. Blunt's brother-in-law, Nep Wheatley, who had been appointed agent at Crabbet during the Blunts' absence, had been spending his time in London and had neglected to tell the men that they were wanted for haymaking. So when work started in the fields, the Blunts found to their alarm and annoyance that all their own men had been employed by neighbouring landowners. In the end they themselves had to turn out to help, including even Cowie.

Meanwhile much correspondence had passed between the Blunts and Skene. By early June the number of horses coming to England had risen from six to eleven. Most had been seen by the Blunts but some had been bought by Skene on his own judgement. The Blunts were now finding Skene a rather difficult man to deal with. He had been glad when he heard that Lord Wentworth had joined the 'Association' as he was bargaining for more horses and needed extra money. But now he was always wanting either to exchange horses that had already been bought or to add completely new ones to the list. Of the animal that the Blunts particularly wished to hear, Beteyen's mare, no further news came although they understood that negotiations had been reopened. But everything else was in order by the middle of June, when the Blunts heard that the first shipment of horses was ready to leave for England.

As with all consignments from the East, the horses went by sea to Marseille and then by train to Calais. When they reached Paris, Lord Wentworth took the opportunity to go and see them. He liked Kars but two of the fillies disappointed him and he told the Blunts that Skene should be instructed to buy only the best.

On July 2nd, 1878, history was made. Lady Anne described the event in her journal:

> This evening as we sat at dinner the telegram was brought to me. It was from S. Francis at Folkestone. The horses landed and he would be at Three Bridges tonight by the mail train from Redhill. So I have sent word to Eyles to go down to the station to meet him and the six, Kars, Lady Hester, Palmyra, Jerboa, Darley filly and Zenobia, and I am writing in the hall hoping every minute to hear of their coming. The night has cleared . . .
>
> They have come and Wilfrid and I have been out to see them. Kars is beautiful. Palmyra rather thin, so hungry she would hardly notice us which made the meeting unromantic. Dajanieh very pretty as ever. The Darley filly disappointed us, she is leggy and slight without any particular air. Zenobia after Ralph's disapproval which prepared us for disappointment was less of a delusion than the Darley filly. She is however not good looking, has an enormous head but is probably fast. She is in most wretched condition with a tremendous bruise over the right eye so that I am afraid the sight of that eye may be injured. We saw them in their boxes and then came in.

The names of most of the horses were soon changed by the Blunts and they were actually entered in the Crabbet Stud Book as follows; Kars, Dajania (Lady Hester), Hagar (Palmyra), Jerboa, Wild Thyme (Darley filly) and Burning Bush (Zenobia).

The Blunts were disappointed with two of Skene's purchases, Wild Thyme and Burning Bush, but they were delighted with Kars and the way in which he proved to be a very good ride. It must be emphasised that although the Blunts had bought the horses for breeding, they also expected them to be useful in daily life. The stallions were always ridden and in the early days most were also broken to harness. The mares too were driven and ridden, sometimes, it seems, to excess – Shieha died of a heart attack when out hunting at the age of twenty and Meroe slipped her foal and died after being driven as a wheeler on long journeys when in foal. Younger animals were also used for light work on the farm, such as dragging the bush-harrows.

On August 13th the second batch of horses arrived from Skene and were met at Three Bridges station by the Blunts and Lord Wentworth. The group consisted of Tamarisk, Darley, Damask Rose, Purple Stock, Sherifa and her foal, and an 'insignificant' small bay filly. Sherifa had had a colt when stabled with Skene at Aleppo and thus Saoud, as he was called, became the first foal to be bred by the partnership. The insignificant bay was another of Skene's bad purchases. She would be 'a blot on the stud', wrote Lady Anne and henceforth she was known as Blot. The poor animal's weedy appearance was soon accounted for, as after only a few weeks at Crabbet Blot died and was discovered to have had a diseased liver.

Francis, who had previously been Lord Wentworth's groom, had been put in charge of the horses after the arrival of the first batch, when the Blunts decided to put Kars, Hagar, Jerboa and Burning Bush into training for a small race meeting at Crawley later in the year. They thought it would be interesting to see how their Arabians fared against English horses but in the event they scratched from the race. It was, they decided, too paltry an affair and anyway the horses were not yet completely fit. But at the end of September they had their first runner in public when Kars started in the two mile Streatham Hurdle Plate at Clapham. Although there were other good horses entered, for some reason Kars was given a high weight. He ran well and although he finished some seven lengths behind the winner, satisfied all concerned.

Considerable interest was shown by local people in the new arrivals at Crabbet – an interest, it must be said, that was tempered by scepticism. One day Darley was found to be lame and the Blunts blamed a defective hock. They decided to telegraph Skene in Aleppo to point out that he must be careful in future to purchase horses which were not only sound but also without any faults that could lead to unsoundness. But to ensure that no one locally should hear of Darley's condition through gossip at the post office, Lord Wentworth sent the cable from London.

Correspondence continued between the Blunts and Skene. Lady Anne wrote to Skene's wife to explain that the emphasis should be on quality and not quantity and that they were both counting on her sober and critical mind to influence her husband's decisions. Blunt had meanwhile been in touch with Skene on a very different matter. Throughout the summer of 1878 he had been working enthusiastically on a book about Arabia and its people. He had discussed the project with Skene and was relying on him to supply a certain amount of background information about the tribes. Blunt soon realised that collaboration was impossible at such a distance and urged Skene to come to England. It was now that the truth about Skene emerged. Writing to tell Blunt that he was sending him a synopsis for his part of the book, he mentioned that he was no longer able to put up the money for his share in the Stud. The reason, he explained, was that the proceeds from the sale of his wife's jewellery, which had been intended for the Stud, would now have to be used to pay the legal costs of a suit against him in the Supreme Consular Court in Constantinople.

Skene had retired from the Consulship at Aleppo in March, 1878, on the grounds of ill health. The Blunts had offered to help him find another position and it was not until midsummer that they discovered he was in financial trouble.

In 1855, shortly after Skene had left his post at Constantinople, the government audit department had found a discrepancy in the books of account there. They alleged that certain cash items, such as consular fees and shipping charges, for which Skene was responsible, had been incorrectly declared and sought to recover the deficiency from Skene personally. It is unclear whether this, the case in Constantinople, was the final chapter in a protracted attempt by the audit department to recover the money from Skene or whether it was unconnected with the previous incident. But the net result was that Skene was obliged to sell his house in Aleppo in order to satisfy his creditors. Even this was apparently insufficient, for the Blunts were warned by Henderson, Skene's successor as Consul, that the £500 of Lord Wentworth's money still held by Skene might be claimed by his creditors.

The Blunts were also concerned about Beteyen's mare, whose purchase they had left in Skene's hands. But Skene was still able to act for them despite all his worries, and to the Blunts' great relief they received a cable from him late in the autumn announcing the purchase of Queen of Sheba. Skene was unable to do more and left to Henderson the task of arranging the stabling and despatch of Queen of Sheba and the other horses that he had bought.

The accounts were settled satisfactorily in the end. But Skene was now penniless and even Henderson, who had heard some unpleasant stories about him when he became Consul, found it impossible not to feel sorry for him. Later he took Skene and his wife and young son into his house for a year. The Blunts also pitied Skene. 'It is quite certain,' wrote Lady Anne, 'that had he chosen he could have made us pay a large sum instead of a very small one for Sherifa, and this Darley mare is worth more than the sum she cost. But I fancy that he always intended to act honestly by us in the purchases, but that, at a certain crisis, when driven into a corner and in danger of imprisonment, he could not resist the temptation of helping himself to our money to get out of the immediate difficulty.'

What Lady Anne could not forgive, though, was Skene sending inferior mares to England. It seems that he had a preference for powerfully built horses with potential speed, whereas the Blunts had been looking primarily for quality and sound conformation. Some of Skene's horses were so disappointing that they were put up for sale soon after they had arrived in England and it is noticeable that when the breeding stock for Crabbet was finally selected, neither Skene's purchases nor any of their descendants were retained. But it was only with Skene's help that the Blunts had been able to buy some very important horses such as Queen of Sheba and Pharaoh, 'the stars of the stud', as Lady Anne wrote at the time. They had even heard from Mrs Digby in Damascus that their purchase of these two horses had caused a sensation in the desert. It was being talked about in all the tribes, the mare being described as the best anywhere and the colt as the finest horse among the Anazeh.

With the purchase of Queen of Sheba, Skene disappears from the history of the Crabbet Stud. His place is an important one, for as the Blunts were ready to admit, his was the inspiration that set off the chain of events from which Crabbet grew and prospered.

There now remained only two partners, the Blunts and Lord Wentworth. Lady Anne's accounts show that the total cost of the first two consignments amounted to £1,999 3s. 10d., including transport. Lord Wentworth had contributed £1,000 and continued for some years to share the running costs. Many years later this was to prove a bone of contention between him and Wilfrid Blunt, but for the present harmony reigned. When an agreement was drawn up, the founders of the Crabbet Arabian Stud were stated to be Lord Wentworth and Wilfrid and Lady Anne Blunt.

CHAPTER 3

Later Horses and the Newmarket Race

By the autumn of 1878 the horses had settled in at Crabbet. The stables had been repaired and altered, new drains laid in the yard and six more loose boxes erected. The Blunts appointed Captain Laprimaudaye as agent in place of Nep Wheatley and in November they were ready to set out again for Arabia. Their destination this time was the great desert of Nejd. Blunt saw it as the natural complement to their previous travels through Syria and Mesopotamia. 'Nejd,' he wrote, 'in the imagination of the Bedouins of the North, is a region of romance, the cradle of their race, and of those ideas of chivalry by which they still live.'

By December the Blunts were in Damascus and like most European visitors to the city at that time, took the opportunity to call upon one of its most famous residents, Jane Digby. Sometime Lady Ellenborough, Baroness von Venningen and Countess Theotoky, Mrs Digby, as she then preferred to be known, was aged seventy-one. To the list of her former husbands, she was able, according to well-founded reports, to add a very much longer and even more distinguished list of former lovers. In her forties she had parted from her current *beau*, a Greek brigand chief, and had set out for Syria. There, in 1854, she married a Bedouin, Mijuel el Mizrab, a younger brother of the Sheikh of the Mizrab tribe, and with him had lived happily since. Mijuel had received an excellent education and besides being able to speak several languages, was an authority on desert history. The Blunts were most anxious to see him for they hoped that he would be able to inform them about the tribes and the country that lay ahead. They had met one of his sons in the spring of that year when they had been negotiating for Queen of Sheba with Beteyen ibn Mirshid, and it was through him that they obtained an introduction to Mijuel.

They found him to be a charming and highly knowledgeable man who was able to give them a great deal of valuable advice about their journey. They were also much taken by Mijuel's house which stood in its own garden 'with narrow streams of running water and paths with borders full of old-fashioned English flowers – wallflowers especially'. It was probably on account of this captivating combination of people and place that the Blunts decided to buy their own house in Damascus. They found one nearby with an acre of garden and bought the freehold for £260. Leaving an agent to finalise the purchase for them, on December 13th they set out for Nejd.

Their remarkable crossing of the great Nefud and the many adventures that befell them are recounted in detail in Lady Anne's book, *A Pilgrimage to Nejd*, which together with her account of their first journey, *Bedouin Tribes of the Euphrates*, are classics of their kind. Although the books were published under Lady Anne's name and consist largely of extracts from her journals, they were in reality a joint work in which Wilfrid was responsible for the editing and for the chapters on the history and customs of Arabia. The books also include lengthy notes on Arabian horses. It must be remembered, however, that these passages were written before Lady Anne had begun the enormous amount of research that she was to carry out on Arabian horse-breeding. She later discovered that some of the information in these books was inaccurate and intended to correct it in her definitive work on the Arabian. But this, as we shall see, never got beyond the draft stage during her lifetime.

So far as horses were concerned, the Blunts' journey to Nejd was a disappointment. The horses they had been most looking forward to seeing were those of the Emir Mohammed ibn Rashid, at Haïl. Sixteen years before, at the time of Palgrave's travels, the centre of power in that part of Arabia had been with Feysul ibn Saoud at Riad. According to Blunt, Feysul's stud at Riad had probably been the finest in the country and he doubted whether any collection could now be found of equal merit. Feysul had assembled his stud from all the tribes in Arabia, especially from the Muteyr, Beni Khaled, Shammar and Anazeh. His emissaries had been on the constant lookout for mares and had even, so the Blunts were told, mounted raids with no other object than to obtain a particular animal of a particular strain. But since then the leadership of central Arabia had passed from Riad to Haïl and now only a twentieth part of Feysul's stud remained. Of the rest, most had passed into the hands of Mohammed ibn Rashid's predecessors and it was these horses that the Blunts were eager to inspect.

They reached Haïl on January 24th. Ibn Rashid's horses were then

Ibn Rashid's stables at Haïl

in their winter quarters in open yards in the town itself. In the spring they would be taken out to the desert where a plentiful supply of pasture existed round the wells. When the Blunts first saw them they were looking their worst. Chained to the ground, ungroomed and in the roughest possible condition, they had 'very little of that air of high breeding one would expect', wrote Lady Anne, and it required considerable imagination to picture them as the *ne plus ultra* of breeding in Arabia. But, she added, 'we made the mistake, too common, of judging horses by condition, for mounted and in motion, these at once became transfigured.' It was only after they had witnessed a sham fight outside the city walls that they realised the true qualities of Ibn Rashid's horses. It was a brilliant spectacle, vividly described in their book and in a sketch by Lady Anne.

From Haïl the Blunts travelled north to Baghdad and thus completed the Arabian part of their journey. They then decided to turn south east through Luristan to the Persian Gulf, a detour that turned out to be the most hazardous of all their ventures. Illness, fatigue and great personal danger made it a nightmare for them both. The journey ended at Bushire, on the Gulf, in a 'feverish dream of heat and flies'.

The only purchase the Blunts made during these months was the mare Canora, which they bought in Baghdad and were to sell three years later. In July 1879, they returned to England.

They found their horses thriving. Queen of Sheba was a 'splendid' ride and that winter Kars was to prove outstanding in the hunting field. After one memorable two-hour run, Blunt wrote: 'I never wish to be better carried than I was today – I would back Kars against any horse of his size, 15 hands, in Europe.' A local newspaper reported that only those with a change of horse could possibly have had anything to do with the finish. But Blunt had ridden Kars throughout and was still there at the end. It had been St Valentine's Day:

> Today, all day, I rode upon the Down,
> With hounds and horsemen, a brave company,
> On this side in its glory lay the sea,
> On that the Sussex weald, a sea of brown.
> The wind was light, and brightly the sun shone,
> And still we galloped on from gorse to gorse.
> And once, when checked, a thrush sang, and my horse
> Pricked his quick ears as to a sound unknown.

When they went to stay with friends or relations, the Blunts often took their horses with them, sending them by train with a groom while they travelled separately. If they were going to be in London for any length of time they would take horses to ride in Hyde Park. On more than one occasion they even took a couple to Paris when they went to stay with Lord Wentworth.

Only four foals were born at Crabbet in 1880, the first year of breeding at the Stud. One, a colt by Kars out of Dajania, died when a few weeks old from an injury to the spine and the other three were eventually sold.

The Blunts' Arabians now began to attract attention elsewhere. On May 20th Pharaoh took first prize in the Arabian class at the Islington Horse Show and Kars was placed. Kars was also ridden by Francis in the jumping class and despite knocking down a gate, still won an award. In September Blunt published a long article on the Arabian in the *Nineteenth Century*. The Prince of Wales was reported to have taken up the idea of racing Arabs in England and to have promised to head a subscription list for prize money with £100. Even the Prime Minister, Mr Gladstone, was sufficiently intrigued to apply to Blunt for a treatise on the origin of the Arabian horse.

In the winter the Blunts returned to Egypt for Wilfrid to continue his studies of the Mohammedan religion, with which he had become engrossed during their travels. But their visit is memorable for another reason. On November 23rd, 1880, the Blunts were engaged to dine with a Mr Fitzgerald. 'At Shepherds Hotel,' wrote Lady Anne, 'Mr Fitzgerald came to speak to us on the terrace and said he had spoken to Ali Sherif Pasha about our seeing his stud.' After they had dined, the party went to the theatre and there the Blunts first met Ali Pasha Sherif. 'Ali Pasha came into the box and staid some time talking to Wilfrid and me about his horses and at the first word or two one could perceive he understood all about Bedouin ideas of race and was imbued with them – he invited us to visit his stud.'

Two days later the Blunts made the first of what were to be many visits there. Since several of the horses that she then saw will reappear often in this book and also feature in the pedigrees of some of the Blunts' foundation stock, Lady Anne's account of this occasion is given in full.

> On Thursday very tired – my legs aching from being put into work. But we had a great pleasure the greatest we could have – that of seeing some pure bred Arabians. By appointment we were at Ali

Kars, the stud's first stallion. Purchased at Aleppo on January 5th, 1878

Pasha's house at two. He received us and shewed us his horses first, then a few mares and half a dozen foals – afterwards directed us to go to see the remaining mares at Abassieh. Of the horses most were white or grey. The first 'Shueyman Seba' and of that breed – handsome with fine head, not *very* good shoulder – the second called 'Vizir' [Wazir] a Seglawi Jedran of Ibn Soudan fine all round – 18 years old but with no appearance of age. His head in shape reminded me of both Kars and Basilisk (sire S[eglawi]. J[edran]. of Ibn Sbeyni). The third a young horse and still darkish grey Wadnan Hursan? There were about five more, one a white Seg. Jed. of either Ibn Sbeyni or Ibn Soudan (I have a confused recollection of the name) very good, and fine shoulder – all the horses have splendid legs except a handsome chestnut (Dahman Shahwan) (N.B. Mesaoud's sire, Aziz) with 4 white stockings who has badly curbed hocks – 4 years old only and used for breeding in spite of the defect. Ali Pasha made no allusion to the hocks but said that this horse had been used for the stud at 3 years old, for he had been curious to see whether the 4 white legs would be inherited. He does not like 4 white legs. The marks have not been transmitted and we afterwards saw a foal (filly) 5 days old from a splendid Seglawieh Jedran, Hora, own sister to Vizir, mare – white – which has but one small patch of white just above one hind foot. The chestnut horse was good *except* the hocks – fine long neck, well-arched and head a little like Canora's. In the desert, at Abassieh we saw 2 bay Doheymeh Nejib mares difficult to choose between. The more interesting at first is a 5 year old, bright full bay (like Kars) with 2 white hind feet and small star. Her crest, wither and shoulder exaggerated like the portraits of the Godolphin Arabian. She is a picture and at a little distance very like Kars. The other mare was darker bay and altogether I think the best – legs stouter and more muscle – she is 6 or 7 – a daughter of a celebrated D[oheymeh]. N[ejib]. mare called Norah – who died of the disease when this mare was 2 years old. The first bay is a grand-daughter of Norah. Both of these are daughters of Vizir. The younger one has a head like Jasmine [Dajania] and Kars.

The Blunts were delighted by their visit. Afterwards Ali Pasha promised to let them have a list of his different strains, including those he had lost during the horse plague. Lady Anne thought it likely that several of these were by now extinct since Abbas Pasha had swept the whole of Arabia for specimens of the particular breeds he fancied. At this stage, though, there was no question of the Blunts buying any of the Pasha's horses. A little over eight years were to pass before that happened.

From Cairo the Blunts went by boat to Jeddah, on the Red Sea. There they saw a pretty little mare from Ibn Rashid's stables but they could not discover her exact breeding and so did not buy her. A few days later they met an agent of Ibn Rashid, a man called Yusuf Effendi, who had known Sherifa when she belonged to the Governor of Mecca. The Blunts had hoped to travel inland for a few weeks but while still in Jeddah Blunt went down with a high fever and when his condition did not improve they decided reluctantly to return to Egypt. 'A sad ending for the year,' wrote Lady Anne.

When Blunt had recovered they set off for Damascus. Their mission now was to purchase mares from the horse-breeding tribes south of Palmyra. They also hoped to obtain further information on the horses Skene had bought for them and were successful in establishing the *bona fides* of some, including Basilisk.

At the Gomussa camp they saw the dam of Queen of Sheba who like her daughter had a 'magnificent style of going'. But 'on the whole', wrote Lady Anne, 'we have seen fewer, much fewer, good mares than formerly with the Gomussa. Wilfrid thinks the Managhys are ruining the breed but I think there are perhaps other causes, chiefly the general carelessness about choice in breeding.' They found better horses at the camp of Meshur Agid of the Sebaa, where they bought Dahma, but it was not until they reached the wells of Abu Fayal that they found an animal with the true stamp of quality. This was the 'celebrated' mare Rodania from whom, as Blunt later noted, 'nearly everything of the best at Crabbet is now descended'.

At the same time they bought another mare, the Kebeysheh Zefifieh, a flea-bitten grey which Blunt adopted as his riding mare. 'The mare, which Wilfrid now wishes to call Zenobia, in the tent as usual,' wrote Lady Anne with unusual brevity. Zenobia (who was in fact named Zefifia by the Blunts) was also well known in the desert and as they passed through the tribes they heard remarks like, 'look, there is Mohammed er Robaa's mare.' When they started for Aleppo, they were warned that an attempt might be made to steal her. Every night they kept all the mares under the awning of their tent and as an added precaution tied the head ropes to their arms when they went to sleep. Even so they were nearly taken unawares. One night Wilfrid heard a clank of fetters from the horses. When he went to investigate the blunt end of a lance was thrust into his ribs. He shouted out and the intruder ran off.

When they reached Aleppo they found the situation much changed since Skene's time. Henderson had left the previous day and there was no one to help them get export licences for the horses. The governor of the city telegraphed to Constantinople for the permit and Blunt followed this up with a telegram to the British Embassy there, begging for support for the governor's request.

While they waited for the licence, they went to see the stud of Ali Pasha. He was 'a little wizened man full of information which he likes to air, about horses and I liked hearing him talk and quote poets; as to being "a good fellow" that is quite out of the question'. They bought Meshura, whom they had been offered several months before but had not yet had a chance to see. Meshura's history is a colourful one and is told in full in Chapter Six. While in Aleppo they also bought Jedrania from a Kurd called Ali Agha.

The Blunts were certain that they had been right to buy these further horses. Even though they had had to pay more than for most of their earlier purchases, they foresaw an increasing scarcity of high-class animals and felt that unless they bought the best available now, they might never have another chance to do so. They did not in fact keep all the horses they had acquired on this trip and sold some in Aleppo. They selected five to take back to England: Rodania, Zefifia, Dahma, Meshura and Jedrania.

Eventually the export licence was granted and on April 26th the Blunts left with their horses for Alexandretta. Jedrania had a foal at foot which Lady Anne found asleep beside her one morning. On the 29th they boarded the steamer *Erymanthe* and after a rough voyage arrived home safely a fortnight later. With them they brought Blunt's hawk Rasham, who had accompanied them on their journey through Nejd. Rasham was to live for several years at Crabbet until one day he wandered too far and was shot by a neighbouring gamekeeper.

The Blunts had by now achieved a measure of celebrity as travellers and their homecomings were always worth a paragraph in the local press.

LATER HORSES AND THE NEWMARKET RACE 51

Wilfrid Scawen Blunt Esquire and Lady Anne Blunt of Crabbet Park returned home from their tour in Arabia on Saturday last. It was remarked that both the Squire and his Lady looked well, although somewhat changed by the climate in which they have been sojourning. The beautiful Arabian Stud at Crabbet Park has been increased by five splendid creatures, including a mare and foal. These were accompanied by two Arab attendants – fine looking fellows, their grotesque Oriental costume forming a very interesting picture. It is said these Arabian servants will remain permanently at the Park.

The servants, Khalil and Ibrahim, were in fact far from becoming permanent members of the staff at Crabbet. Within ten days of their arrival they had so annoyed Lady Anne by their misbehaviour that they were sent back to Aleppo forthwith.

More Arabians were now trained to harness and on Derby Day that year Blunt drove their guests to Epsom in a phaeton drawn by Wild Thyme and Meshura. Despite the occasional accident the Arabians proved very good being driven, though some were inclined to make a show of independence. Wild Thyme once objected so vigorously to being harnessed with Sherifa's son Saoud that Cowie preferred to get out and walk.

Among the many visitors to Crabbet that year was the Hon. Miss Etheldred Dillon with her imported Arab stallion El Emir. A match run in the Park proved Pharaoh a much faster horse but Miss Dillon's stallion had tremendous courage and was driven all over England by his owner.

Mares in the Cricket Park at Crabbet in 1882
From left: Zefifia, Sherifa, Hagar, Dahma and Rodania

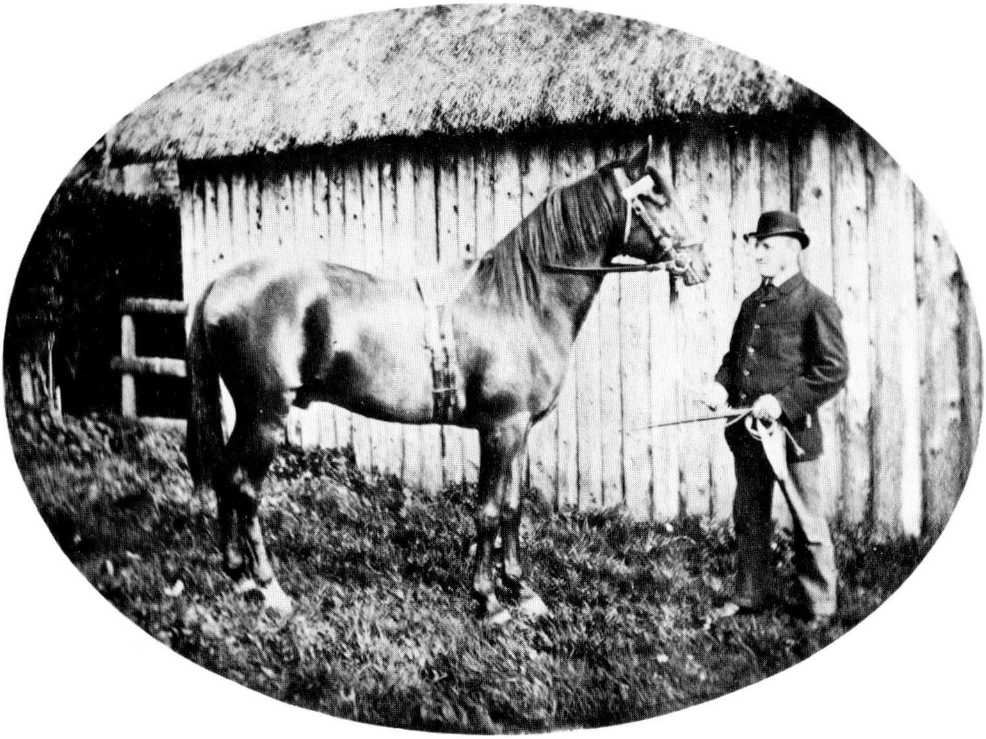

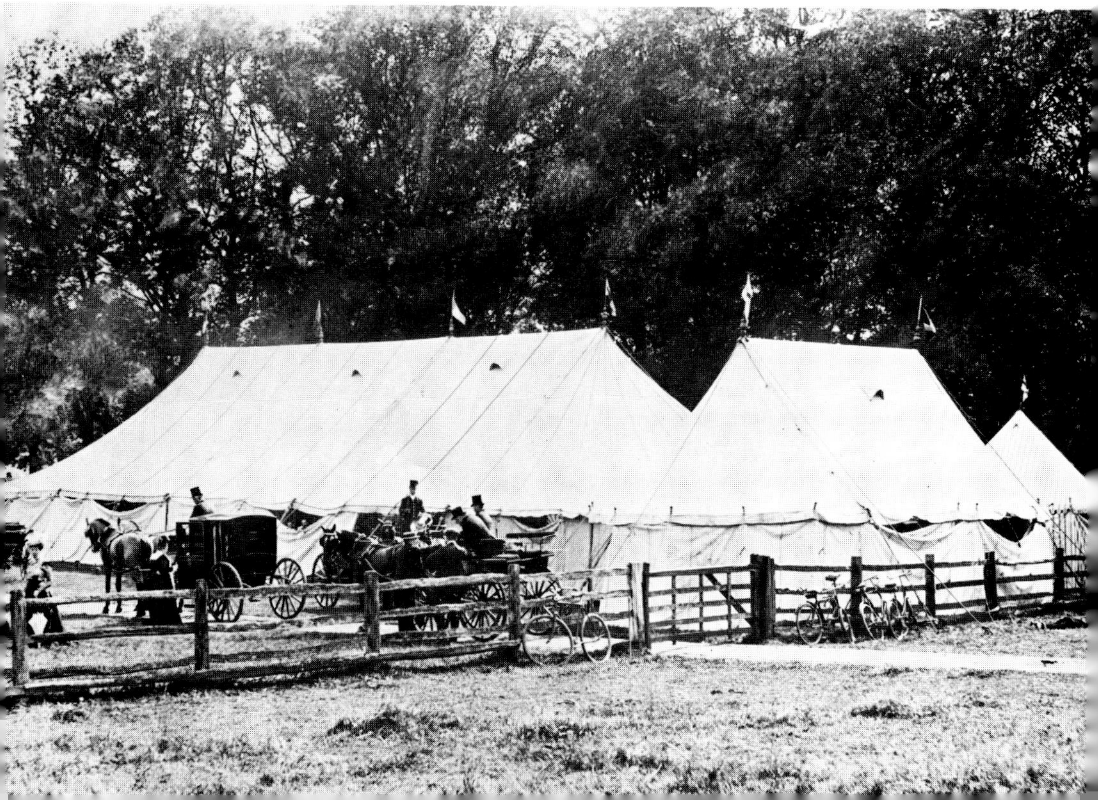

For many years Miss Dillon's Arabian stud was to be the only other of any consequence in England. She built it up with some mares from Crabbet, notably Hagar, Jerud (by Pharaoh out of Jerboa),* Jedrania and Wild Honey (by Kars out of Wild Thyme and renamed Raschida by Miss Dillon), which she put to her stallions El Emir and the famous Maidan. She was an irrepressible enthusiast of the breed and wrote copious letters to the press upon its merits. Her ideas on size and type often differed from those of the Blunts and led to a violent argument between her and Wilfrid. But for all their disagreements, the Blunts admired her as a person and allowed her to sell her horses at the Crabbet auctions.

The Stud expenses were now beginning to alarm Lady Anne. Hitherto any profit on the farm and woodlands at Crabbet had gone to Blunt and the deficiency on the Stud had been made good by Lady Anne. Since she also paid the costs of the household and gardens, most of their expenses abroad and not a few of Wilfrid's personal debts, she felt that her financial obligations were a little too open-ended. In the summer of 1882 she therefore arranged with Blunt that she would pay regular fixed amounts to support Crabbet and the Stud and that he would meet the balance. Neither of them knew whether the auction of horses they were planning for July would make any difference to the Stud's finances. As they had invited some two hundred people for luncheon beforehand, they cannot have been too hopeful for a profit at the end of the day.

The Stud had by now been established for four years and the Blunts wished to dispose of more of the original imports which they considered unsuitable as foundation stock and some of the surplus animals that they had themselves bred. The previous year they had advertised some for sale in *The Field*. As was to be the practice in future, the sales list was drawn up by Blunt. Although Lady Anne was usually consulted, at that time it was invariably Wilfrid who took the final decisions on stud policy.

Fourteen horses were listed in the sale catalogue, including the foundation mares Jerboa, Dajania and Queen of Sheba. But these were only intended to improve the quality of the sale and had extremely high reserves put on them to prevent any chance of being sold. Invitations were sent to friends in society and politics as well as to potential buyers.

* Breeding details, where material, are given the first time the horse is mentioned and not repeated thereafter unless relevant to Chapter 13 or overseas sections.

above Pharaoh. Brown stallion purchased in the desert in October, 1878
below Sale day for the Blunts, *ca* 1886

Mr Tattersall was engaged as auctioneer and elaborate preparations were made for the occasion. In view of the fact that the Stud had been breeding for so short a time, the interest aroused in the sale was surprisingly large. Several visitors went down to look at the horses beforehand, among them a party of three Australians and Count Potocki, who had come over from his stud at Antoniny in Poland.

The auction was held in pouring rain on July 2nd, 1882. A marquee had been erected and after luncheon Mr Tattersall proposed the Blunts' health, praising the objectives of the Stud and the benefits that it would confer upon England. Blunt could not reply as he was showing guests around but since, Lady Anne noted, 'the great Tattersall said it did not matter, I supposed it did not.' As soon as Wilfrid returned, the auction began. The Blunts preferred not to see the bidding and withdrew to the house. David (Blunt's valet) was sent to watch how the first two horses were sold. 'He soon came back and said "110 and 120" which was a good beginning.'

Eleven out of the fourteen horses were sold. Top price was made by Pharaoh who was bought by Count Potocki for 525 guineas, while Purple Stock and Francolin were knocked down to the Australian, Mr Dangar.* The other horses sold were Damask Rose, Wild Thyme, Canora, Purple Iris, Purple Emperor, Faris, Saoud and the gelding Darley. As Blunt had intended, the reserves on Jerboa, Dajania and Queen of Sheba were sufficient to deter buyers.

Mr Tattersall's speech was reported at length in *The Sussex and Surrey Courier* and is worth quoting in some detail.

> 'The country,' Mr Tattersall had said, 'was greatly indebted to Mr Blunt for his endeavour to confer a national good by the introduction of originally pure stock, from which all our Thoroughbreds had been obtained, and he had no doubt that with the assistance of the soil and climate of England the Arab steed would develop and become a larger animal . . . All the animals were entered in the Stud Book and could be traced to ensure their purity . . . Mr Blunt's idea in establishing a stud of Arab thoroughbreds had been to procure the best blood he could find in Arabia, and by selection and

---

*The Dangars were among the earlier importers of Arabs into Australia. In 1872 R.H.E. Upton, then aged sixteen, went to New South Wales and was there employed by A.A. Dangar. Two years later he returned to accompany his father, Major R.D. Upton, on the latter's expedition to Syria for the Dangars and Henry Chaplin. A stallion and a mare, Alif and Jemima, were bought for Mr Dangar. Upton remained with the Dangars until 1886. From 1892 until his death in 1907 he was the manager at Turanville, near Muswellbrook, N.S.W.

careful breeding to improve his stock in the same way Alderney cattle and short horns had been improved out of originally good material, believing the climate of England and proper feeding will greatly develop his stock in size, strength and speed. He did not propose himself to attempt any experiment in cross-breeding, but he believed such experiment would be successful, and he was anxious that it should be made . . . It must be remembered that this is the original material out of which our own racehorses were produced a hundred years ago, and that the blood is the blood of our Thoroughbreds. If the imported animals were small their produce would certainly be larger, and in strength and constitution they must not be judged merely by their appearance. It would be a great mistake to estimate the value of these Arabs merely by the amount of horseflesh they appeared to represent. Blood is nearly everything in breeding, and blood was there.'

The possibility of regenerating the Thoroughbred by a fresh infusion of Arabian blood was at first a dominant factor in Wilfrid Blunt's mind. He found the Thoroughbred far from beautiful: 'There is a meanness about their quarters and style of action, which strikes one continually. They look as if they had been made in sections and clumsily put together.' But like many Englishmen he found it hard to forget that the Arabian had been the progenitor of the Thoroughbred and many years later would still hark back to the blood horse of a century and a half before. He soon abandoned the idea of mixing Arabian and Thoroughbred blood after the poor showing of Arabians on the racecourse, but for the moment he pressed on.

As early as 1880 he had discussed with the Jockey Club the possibility of a race under their rules for Arabians only. The prejudices of that conservative body were well represented by the opinion of Lord Fairhurst that the present Arab horse was descended from 'a degenerated English horse crossed with the ponies of Asia.' But Blunt persevered and in the spring of 1882 he went again to Newmarket to meet the Jockey Club. This time he found them more receptive to the project. Two of the three stewards were in favour of the race and since the third was then rather unpopular for having won too many races, Blunt felt sure of success. After more discussions about its conditions, the Jockey Club agreed to hold the race at Newmarket in 1884, two years later. In order to demonstrate to the racing world at large that the qualities of the Arabian were still vital to the Thoroughbred, it was essential that a good showing was made at Newmarket. The best Arabs in training were then in India so when, in the autumn of 1883, the Blunts set out for that country, they were anxious to persuade the owners of Arabian racehorses there to send their animals to England for the Newmarket race.

Racing and polo were popular pastimes with the British community in India and the demand for Arabians was high. Pre-eminent among the several dealers who were importing horses direct from Arabia was Abdur Rahman Minni in Bombay. His stables, known colloquially as the Bomb Proof, were famed throughout India and always held a number of Arabians in training. Of particular interest to the Blunts was a consignment of young horses recently acquired from the Oteybeh. There was a grey Hamdani Simri described by the Blunts as 'very good', but the best was a Hadban Enzahi which they bought and named Hadban. Later they added Proximo and Rataplan to their purchases, the latter as their representative in the Newmarket race.

Hadban had come from the Oteybeh only a few weeks before the Blunts saw him. He had a lump on his near fore fetlock, the result of a slight accident, and for this reason was offered to them at what they considered the very reasonable price of just over £100. When they were not buying direct from the breeder, the Blunts always took especial care to verify with the owner the authenticity of every horse and this they did as thoroughly for those they bought in India as for those in the desert. It is quite certain that no one selecting original Arabians for breeding has been more careful in checking the ancestry of their horses than the Blunts. Wilfrid stated that the Crabbet Arabian Stud differed from all other studs in Europe (except for Sanguszko's and perhaps Württemburg) in that all its foundation stock was *mazbut* (pure).

Blunt's attempts to get owners of Arab racehorses in India to enter at Newmarket did not meet with much success. Although Weatherbys agreed to put forward the closing date for entries to give him more time, only two runners were secured, Abdur Rahman Minni's Dictator and the famous Kismet, unbeaten for two years in India and the winner of over £30,000 in prize money.

They returned to England in the late spring of 1884. The race was to be held on July 2nd and two days beforehand the Blunts travelled to Newmarket. The horses they had decided to enter were Rataplan and Halfa, a three-year-old filly by Kars out of Hagar. They had been put into training with Yousiffe Mannington and the Blunts went out at dawn to watch them on the gallops.

The race was a sweepstakes, run over two miles, of 25 sovereigns each with £200 added by the Jockey Club and £100 by Wilfrid Blunt. Three-year-olds were set to carry 7st. 10lbs.; 4-year-olds 9 stone, and 5 and upwards 9st. 3lbs.

For some reason there was a long delay at the start. The Blunts, who were riding Proximo and Shehrezad, had positioned themselves at the turn into the home stretch and began to grow worried when the horses did not appear. But at last they saw them approaching 'at what seemed to be a tremendous pace. Then we cantered up to see the finish but steering through a crowd on foot and riding prevented watching the horses as they came up and I only saw as they passed close to the winning post, that Asil and Dictator were in front and Rataplan third, Kismet fourth and Halfa last but one.' They then went to the paddock where they found Halfa very blown. Her jockey, Loates, reported that she had had the speed of them all but had 'pulled and fighted' for the first mile and had then tired through not being completely fit. They tried to see Asil, the winner, 'but he was taken away at once and he not having been paraded before the race I only saw him passing for an instant. A long strong horse with a plain head, not a bit like the Abeyan sire at Aleppo.'

The result was: 1st, Admiral G. Tryon's b.c. Asil, 3 years; 2nd, Mr Abdur Rahman Minni's Dictator, aged; 3rd, W.S. Blunt's Rataplan, aged. The owner of Hadramaut (a full brother to Halfa), who came fifth, complained to Blunt that the winner was not a pure Arabian and wanted him to lodge an objection. This Blunt refused to do. He and Lady Anne knew something of Asil's background and as his dam had come to England when carrying him, they did not believe that Asil was impure.

There were conflicting reports about the race. One of the jockeys described it as fast run but according to the newspapers the pace had been funereal. To doubts about the pedigree of the winner were added suspicions about the genuineness of the race. Lady Anne wrote of

> rumours of the matter being pre-arranged. Francis hears that Halfa was pulled at the turn and taken round outside the horses. An old fellow who has been thirty years in Nat Dawson's stable came and tapped Francis on the shoulder and said he was sorry our mare had not had fair play and said that the jockeys tried them in the first mile to see which was best and then put them according to what had been arranged.

Whether or not the race had been honestly run, it was a great disappointment to the Blunts and for the purposes of demonstrating the ability of the Arabian was little short of a fiasco. The simple fact was that only Asil had been properly trained, as was proved the following year when he was beaten by Hadramaut and then twice by Kismet.

The detractors from the Arab were not slow to comment. One writer said that the performance of Mr Blunt's horses epitomised the 'final and utter collapse' of the Arabian and another that the absurdity of the Newmarket race 'scarcely required ocular demonstration'. Further salt was rubbed into the wound when in 1885 Asil was given 4 stone 7 lbs and a twenty length beating by a very moderate Thoroughbred of the Duke of Portland's.

The Jockey Club was also unimpressed and allowed no more races for Arabians at Newmarket. But in another race for Arabians in 1884, at Sandown Park on July 22nd, Blunt's colours of green, yellow and blue, and red cap were carried into third place by Halfa. The winner was Hadramaut, who had come fifth at Newmarket. Proximo, entered under Lady Anne's name, was unplaced. Interestingly, this race was timed and the Arabs were only one second slower than the Thoroughbreds had been over the same distance in the preceding race.

Despite these setbacks, Blunt apparently still clung to his belief in the racing value of the Arabian. In his speech at the Crabbet sale that year, he pointed out that though breeders could do no better than to rely on sires such as Hermit and St Simon, the cost of their stud fees was far beyond the reach of most people. It was, he said, vastly preferable for anyone unable to afford the best stallions to use pure Arab stock rather than to resort to third rate Thoroughbreds. He reiterated his opinion that one day he might be able to produce an Arab which could hold its own against the Thoroughbred on the racecourse, particularly if given the traditional Goodwood Cup allowance of 28lbs. But as the performance of Asil was to show, his optimism was ill-founded.

The Newmarket race marks the end of the first phase at Crabbet. Thereafter the Blunts gradually relinquished their hopes of rejuvenating the Thoroughbred through the blood of their Arabians. And if 1884 was one turning point, the following year was another, of infinitely greater importance to the Arabian of today.

CHAPTER 4

The Stud is Established

The year 1885 is a landmark in the history of the Crabbet Arabian Stud for it saw the birth of two remarkable mares; Rose of Sharon, through whom the 'R' line is principally carried, and Nefisa, the first of the 'N' line.

Both Nefisa and Rose of Sharon were sired by Hadban,* the horse the Blunts had bought in India. They were his only daughters.

Rose of Sharon (out of Rodania) was very small as a foal and was considered insignificant until over two years old, but she developed into a fine mare. She was the dam of Rafyk (by Azrek), who was bought by Sir James Penn Boucaut for his stud in Australia where a newspaper reported him to be 'perfect'. Her most famous son was Rijm (which is the Arabic for a cairn of stones). Rose of Sharon had five fillies of which the Blunts kept only one, Ridaa (by Merzuk), and it is through her and her three almost legendary daughters, Rim, Riyala and Risala, that the Rodania female line has spread throughout the world.

Nefisa was the only filly that Dajania produced at Crabbet. A bay with three white feet and blaze, she was described by Lady Anne as a perfect brood mare. She was to have twenty-one foals in all, the last at the age of twenty-seven. Two of these died very young and another two before reaching maturity (one from over-eating acorns in Crabbet Park). Many of her offspring were above average height, some being fifteen hands and more by the age of three. Most of her colts were exported; Nemrud went to South Africa, Naaman to Russia and Narenk and Narkise to the Government in India. Several of her daughters also went abroad but the most important, Narghileh (by Mesaoud) and Nasra (by Daoud), remained at Crabbet.

It may be realised from the above how important the export market was to the Blunts. With the exception of a very few enthusiasts such as Miss Dillon, there was then little demand for Arabians in England. The

---

*The General Stud Book gives the sire of Nefisa as Proximo or Hadban and of Rosemary as Proximo or Jeroboam. But Proximo was, in Lady Anne Blunt's words, 'a failure at the stud'. See under Proximo in Appendix 1.

significance, therefore, of the biennial sales at Crabbet was considerable, both as an outlet for surplus stock and as a social occasion and hence a means of trying to popularize the Arabian in England. The sales played an immaterial part in the finances of the Stud since the costs (some £500 a time, all borne by Lady Anne) were usually as great as, and often more than, the proceeds.

From an early date the sales were reported extensively in the daily newspapers. In the opinion of the representative of *The Pall Mall Gazette*, few excursions were more pleasant 'than to run down on a hot July afternoon and idle under the oak trees of the park, passing from group to group of the beautiful mares and foals for which it is famous ... a most agreeable change from the burning pavements of Charing-cross'. The sales were usually held in the week before Goodwood so that society would not be inconvenienced and special arrangements were made for the express trains to stop at Three Bridges. It was all a great occasion, especially for Wilfrid who was much sought after by the reporters.

The Pall Mall Gazette of 1889 has left a good picture of Crabbet at that time.

Nefisa (Hadban–Dajania) with her colt Nadim (by Ahmar), at Newbuildings

The principal portion stands four square, bold in character but not lacking in refinement. To one side the servants' buildings are attached while two sides are fronted by clean-cut lawns and the fourth by a little piece of ground about half an acre in extent, which has been allowed to grow wild. Here is pitched Mr Blunt's travelling tent, with an Arab spear at the entrance and generally a mare tethered close by. 'This,' said Mr Blunt, 'is what we call the "Desert". Some people laugh at me for keeping it so, but it would astonish you what a reputation it has got. I have had the Bedouins in Asia ask me about it. They think I live in England in the midst of a Desert.'

There is much animal life at Crabbet Park. In the fields there were many cattle and mares with their foals, standing under the shade of the trees when I drove through. The stables were full. A couple of cats were chevying round the courtyard an old greyhound named 'Fly', a much-travelled animal. There were Sussex spaniels in kennels, turtle doves in cages, fowls everywhere, and what struck me most, a large flock of pigeons. 'These,' said Mr Blunt,

Rose of Sharon (Hadban–Rodania)

left Fred Holman with spaniels and the greyhound 'Fly' at Crabbet
below The 'Desert' at Crabbet, with Sherifa and foal

'are all descended from two pairs of carrier pigeons, which were used to carry messages during the Franco–German war. They were given to me by the Postmaster-General of Paris after the war. Their descendants have been allowed to revert back more or less to the wood pigeon form, through want of breeding.'

Four years later another journalist visited Crabbet and found Blunt mounted on 'an exquisite old white mare of the type one is familiar with in equestrian protraits of Napoleon'. He remarked upon the ease with which she carried Blunt's weight.

'Yes,' he said, 'they can all carry several stone more weight than you would give them credit for according to English standards, and the carriage of head and tail and the walking action are essential points in judging of this capacity. You were right to notice these. I make it a rule now, after much experience, never to buy unless, at the first glimpse of the animal walking by, I have felt a certain almost electric thrill, the sense of sudden admiration. The thrill of course may deceive you on a nearer inspection, for you may discover defects, but without it and the power of thus "striking the eye" an Arab horse can hardly be of the first quality. He may be speedy, he may be sound, he may be useful, but he can hardly be the horse to breed from.'

Blunt went on to explain that it was the Arabian's strength across the loins which enabled them to carry weight. Breeders of Thoroughbreds always noticed this and he liked to show his horses to men of this class.

The most hopeless class of visitors are hunting men, whose eye is generally vitiated by a long contemplation of ugliness . . . 'Peacocky', they generally say, meaning to disparage, and not recognising the truth that beauty is an essential feature in the Arab, or indeed in any other sire.

Blunt then asked the writer to inspect the horses' feet and to tell him whether he ever saw any better-shaped.

It is the point on which our English horses are probably the most defective. It stands to reason it should be so. Our racehorses are bred for galloping on turf only, and an indifferent foot is no bar to the winning of races . . . I do not like to boast, for it may bring ill luck, but it is really astonishing how little unsoundness of any kind there is here.

The main market for their young stock was overseas. But the weak point in the undertaking was the marked tendency to barrenness in pure Arab stock. With twenty-five brood mares, the Blunts considered themselves fortunate in getting fifteen foals 'and in some years the proportion is less than half'. This failure was not due to the change in climate but to the antiquity of the breed, which had been unmixed for centuries.

> I only state it as a difficulty we have to contend with, one common to most highly selected breeds. It doubtless accounts, too, for the growing rarity of the quite pure blood everywhere. It is now all but impossible to purchase stallions of the first quality even in Arabia ... but I think I may say that as a pure Arab stud this at Crabbet is the best you will find. We have taken infinite pains to make it so. I am therefore, even from a commercial point of view, satisfied with our prospects.

Finally the writer described how the Blunts showed their colts. They moved to a large open yard laid down in peat moss litter where, one after another, the two-year-olds which were for sale were released. 'With head and tail high held ... they galloped to and fro with amazing agility and an accurate change of the leg at each turn, which made their sharpest doublings graceful, and then settled down to a no less wonderful trot, in which the whole mechanism of the animal seemed to partake.'

Seventy years later colts at Crabbet were still being shown loose in small paddocks. As Blunt wrote: 'There is no better test of quality than to turn a colt loose in a paddock and take note of how he moves his shoulders and forearms.'

In contrast to Blunt's guarded optimism for the commercial future of the Stud, his own finances were a constant worry. A degree of extravagance in his way of life combined with only a relatively modest income from the land at Crabbet and his investments, forced him periodically to consider various economies. In the summer of 1890 he decided to try to sell Newbuildings. An unsuccessful auction sale of the house and the estate was held on July 3rd. At the end of the summer Newbuildings Place was let, which pleased Lady Anne who had been against the sale from the start.

Blunt was in Europe for most of the summer, staying with his old friend Lord Lytton, then Ambassador in Paris, and thus missed Charles Doughty and his wife when they visited Crabbet. Doughty was now famous as a result of his book, *Travels in Arabia Deserta*, published two years before. Lady Anne found him 'tall and thin with a red beard and dull coloured hair, a very aquiline nose and eyes muddy brownish – not a colouring very favourable to Arabian travel I should think. He looks in very delicate health, and Mrs Doughty says he will never recover [from] the hardships he underwent on his wonderful wanderings in Arabia followed by exhausting work at writing his book.' Doughty was interested to see their Arabians but admitted he knew little about horses.

More knowledgeable visitors came the next year, 1891. Lord Napier of Magdala proved especially agreeable to Lady Anne. He was one of the 'most enthusiastic people we have had for a long while and even wrote about the horses since they left'. He said 'that after our horses others looked "so woodeny" which is a very good expression'. In 1892 Mr (later Sir) J.P. Boucaut came to Crabbet. The previous year he had bought Rose of Jericho (by Kars out of Rodania), Dahna (by Kars out of Dahma) and Rafyk for his stud in South Australia. He was a 'cheerful fresh looking white haired, and white bearded man full of go and conversation . . . and looked at all we shewed with evident delight'. When visitors came to see the horses Blunt would demonstrate the tractability of the mares by riding Meshura with neither saddle nor bridle, her foal careering round wildly in pursuit.

The foals of 1891 had greatly pleased the Blunts. According to Lady Anne, Queen of Sheba was their best brood mare at the time. Judith Blunt later described her as a 'gorgeous mover' whose offspring were 'all perfect' and considered it a great loss to the Stud that so many of her foals died, largely, she said, through mismanagement. Among the stallions, Azrek, imported in 1888, was outstanding. Blunt thought him 'the best stallion I have ever possessed, and perhaps the best I have ever seen for united quality, constitution and strength. He is in full vigour as a stallion, and I should say has a good eight years before him of undiminished value as such. My experience is that Arab stallions do not come to their full value as sires till they are past eight years old, and that they improve even to twelve and fourteen years.' In 1890 Azrek had sired a bay colt out of Queen of Sheba that was described as the finest colt of his age and with splendid action. This was Ahmar and a full sister called Asfura was foaled the following year. The policy of the Blunts was to sell the older horses, who were naturally in greater demand and fetched higher prices than the youngsters, once they had produced some good stock. In August a Mr Thompson came to Crabbet with a commission to buy two colts for Cecil Rhodes in South Africa. He offered 400 guineas for Azrek which Blunt accepted since the price was a good one. But he refused to sell Ahmar. In Lady Anne's opinion, Thompson had 'a rare "eye" for a horse' and she had 'never seen a visitor take in all the points at a glance so completely as he does'. She was sorry to lose Azrek but expected his sons Ahmar and Shah to represent him well.

The year 1891 was particularly significant for Crabbet since it also saw the arrival from Egypt of Mesaoud, who had been bought by the Blunts from Ali Pasha Sherif two years before. He was to become probably the most influential stallion in the world in Arabian pedigrees and the number of lines that trace to him is enormous. Shortly after his arrival he was pegged out to graze in the Arab fashion as usual but somehow got loose and started to fight Azrek. Webb, one of the grooms, had to run back to the stable with Merzuk, who was 'all agog' to join the fray, in order to obtain help. Judith then 'rushed forward in her anxiety about her beloved Mesaoud and seized and tugged at Azrek's chain at the risk of getting kicked'. Fortunately Holman, another groom, then arrived having heard the noise of the battle and no serious damage was done. In 1892 Mesaoud's first batch of foals were proving 'very promising' and the Blunts thereafter used him extensively.

There were then 61 horses at Crabbet but a cause of great sadness was the death in 1892 of Sherifa. Bred over thirty years before by Feysul ibn Saoud, 'the last of the great Wahhabi princes of that family in Nejd', and famous for her particularly beautiful head, Sherifa had become a firm favourite of the Blunts. Apart from being one of the first mares they imported, she was also something of a character, as may be seen from her description in Chapter Six.

Blunt was now embarked upon a project he had for a book on the Arabian horse. When he had written two chapters he asked Lady Anne to do some research into Abd el Kadr's joint work with General Daumas entitled *Les Chevaux du Sahara*. They had in fact met Abd el Kadr in 1876 when he was exiled in Damascus and had found him most agreeable. But the book* was disappointing. Lady Anne found it 'tiresome' and 'very muddled and rambling'; she would go straight through it 'as the facts worth noting are scattered amid rubbish'. But she persevered and when Blunt suggested that she and Judith might

*In fact the 'book' was a separate work by Abd el Kadr's son.

above Meshura, purchased at Aleppo in April, 1881
below Rose of Jericho (Kars–Rodania)

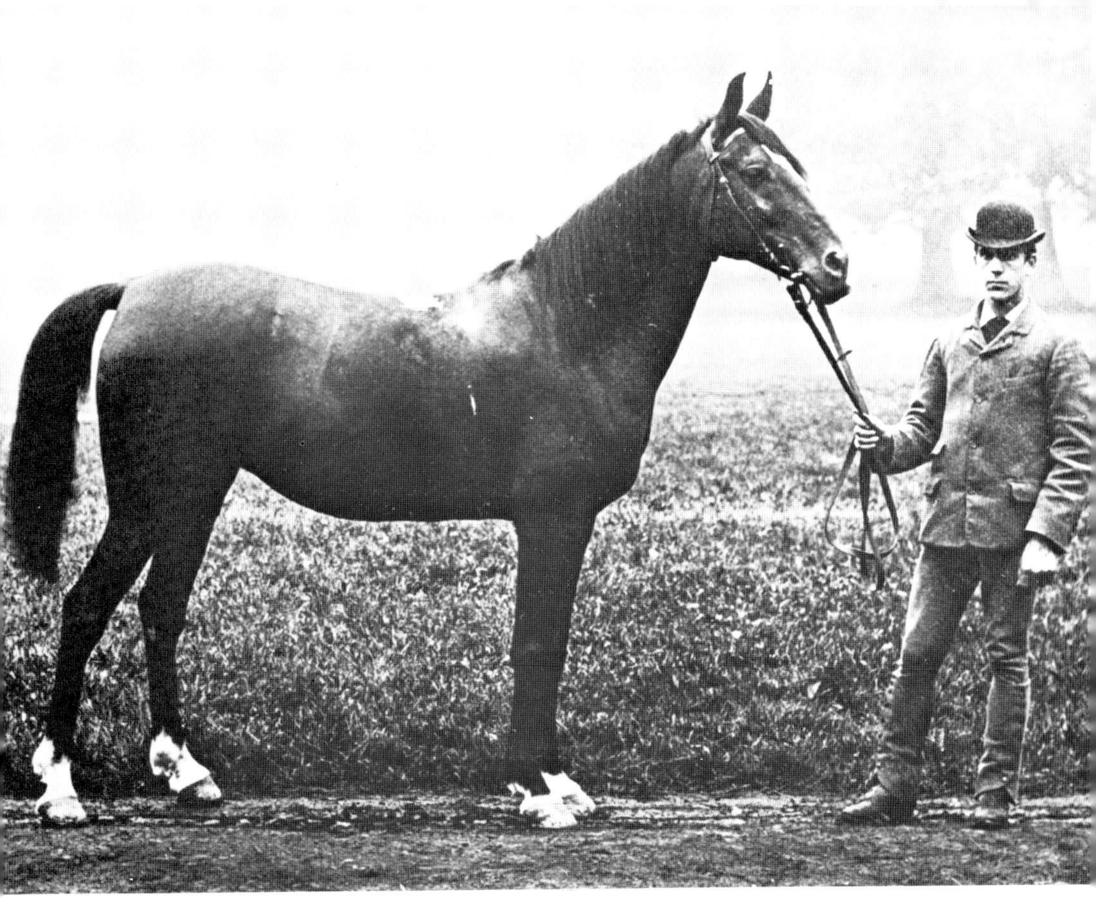

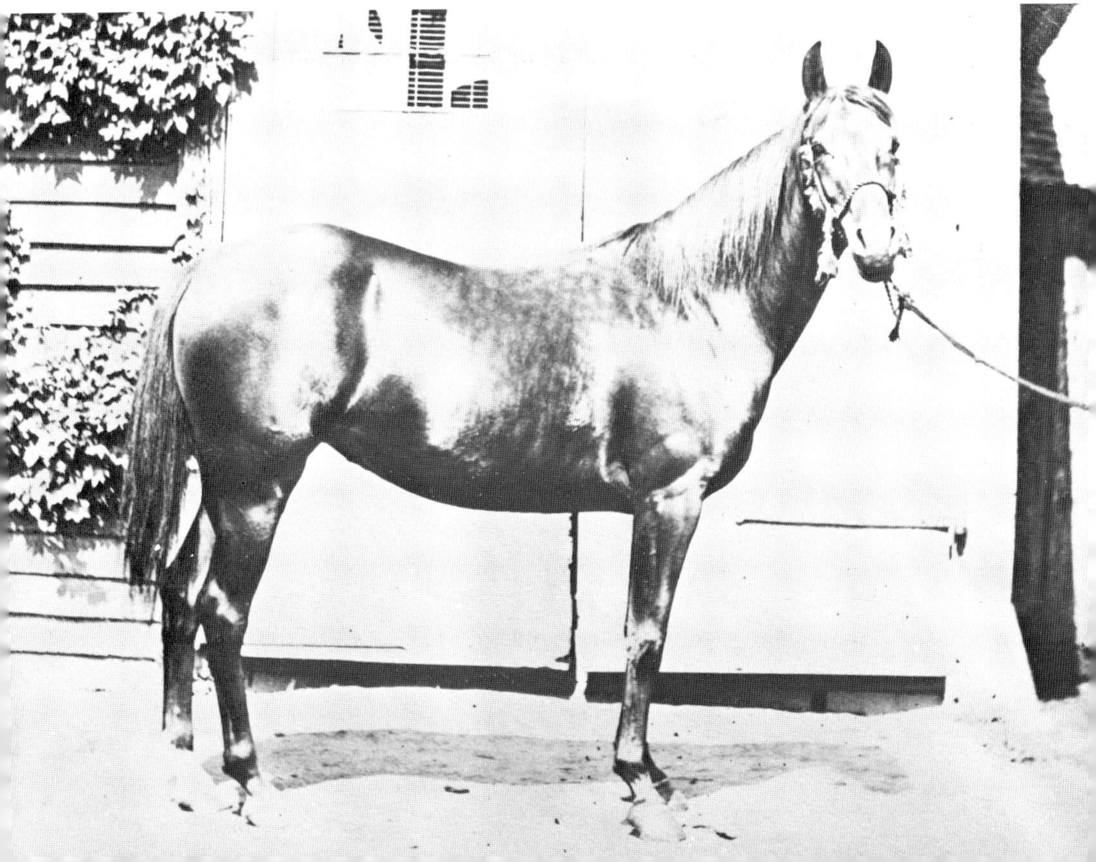

like to finish the book she agreed, on the basis that she would supply the material and Judith would do the writing. For the next twenty-five years they were all three to work intermittently on the project. 'Too busy for the last fortnight with my horse book,' wrote Blunt in 1901. In 1910 he handed over the manuscript for Judith to continue. By this stage it consisted of two books, for in September, 1913, Lady Anne gave Blunt the manuscript of her own work on the Arabian. He was unhappy with it in places and wanted to re-write it but Lady Anne refused to do it as a joint work with him. Two years later at Sheykh Obeyd she completed *The Three Voices*, as she called a section of her work, and on her death *The Times* noted in its obituary that she had recently completed a book on the Arabian which "was likely to become a classic". A classic it was indeed but not until Lady Wentworth published in 1945 extracts from it under her own name in *The Authentic Arabian Horse*.

The family's literary bent was well pronounced. Apart from numerous political and poetical works of his own, Blunt collaborated with Lady Anne to produce two books of Arabian interest. For both *The Celebrated Romance of the Stealing of the Mare* (1892) and *The Seven Golden Odes of Pagan Arabia* (1903), Lady Anne made the translations from the Arabic for Blunt to put into verse. In 1892 Judith wrote her first poem (*On a Jerboa*) and in 1913 *Love in a Mist*, her first book of sonnets, was published. This was followed over the years by a further four volumes of poetry. In addition to her many horse books she also published in 1911 *Toy Dogs and Their Ancestors* which in Blunt's opinion was a work 'quite exhaustive of its subject'.

With this background it is not surprising that the family was drawn into the arena of speculation about the origins of the Arabian. In 1894 Blunt took Judith to see Professor Huxley in Eastbourne. Huxley, he said, agreed that Arabia had doubtless been in former times well watered and 'it was possible a wild horse might have been isolated there in the South (this was my suggestion) long after the drying up of the northern plateaux, but the historical evidence, such as there was, was against it.' Some years later Blunt and Judith entertained the naturalist Lydekker and the head of the Natural History Museum, Andrews, and all agreed that the origin of the wild horse was multiple and that it was quite possible that the Arabian was a separate wild breed. Blunt was interested in the importance that Andrews attached, when discussing the origin of the Arabian, to the depression for the tear gland in their skulls and the set-on of the tail. But 'all these authorities differ so much from each other in what they tell you, that one cannot have much confidence in their knowledge'. In the end Blunt agreed with Huxley that it was all guess work but that, needless to say, did not prevent him attacking others' guess work.

In 1893 he denounced General Tweedie as an 'imposter' and refused to review his book, *The Arabian Horse, Its Country and People*, when it appeared the following year. And when in 1905 Professor Ridgeway's *The Origin and Influence of the Thoroughbred Horse* was published, it was greeted with an awesome barrage of criticism from both Blunt and Lady Anne.

Their chief bone of contention was Ridgeway's argument, expressed at inordinate length, for a Libyan origin for the Thoroughbred as opposed to an Arabian. In reviewing the book in *The Speaker*, Lady Anne accused Ridgeway of 'staggeringly sweeping generalisations' and of jumping to conclusions with acrobatic agility. It was doubtful, she said, whether the author had 'ever contemplated horses from any but a scientific point of view, whether he has ever examined a real live horse'. Blunt was more outspoken in the *Nineteenth Century* and accused Ridgeway of 'plagiarism, ignorance and inaccuracy.' This enraged Ridgeway who challenged Blunt to either stand by his statements or withdraw them publicly. Ridgeway's wrath was increased when the editor of the *Nineteenth Century* refused to allow him space to reply to Blunt and he was obliged to defend himself in the relative obscurity of *The Cambridge Review*. 'These dons have no sense of the ridiculous,' wrote Blunt and attacked Ridgeway as 'a conceited fellow and pilferer from other men's gatherings'.

Life for the Blunts was never leisurely. Blunt was constantly on the move; most summers he went off on a driving tour, taking two of the Arabs and staying with friends or camping in his Arabian tent. Lady Anne would be left to deal with the problems of running the large estate. When 100 head of cattle were turned out with the mares, it was she who had to see to their removal. When the pigeons grew too numerous for the aviary it was she who arranged the drastic culling which resulted in pigeon pie being the staple diet for many days. Then there were letters to Blunt from Egypt to be translated and his replies put back into Arabic, his books and pamphlets to be researched and checked. Her lot, as she said, was 'behind the scenes as organ-blower'.

In 1893 the Blunts were in Constantinople where Lady Anne

suffered a mild re-occurrence of a recent severe illness. Blunt and Judith went without her to see the Sultan's mares in the company of an unexpected admirer of Arabians, the actress Sarah Bernhardt. Of the 150 there, Blunt described most as of no account but of the twelve really good ones, two or three were first-class. The best had come from Ibn Rashid, who two years before had sent the Sultan thirty horses. The Egyptian manager of the stud told Blunt that the Sultan insisted upon having tall horses and that he believed the Bedouins sent their big ones to Constantinople on purpose and kept the smaller and better ones for themselves. But the Blunts did particularly admire one stallion called Saha, a Seglawi from Ali Pasha Sherif, and an immensely showy chestnut from Ferhan Jerba. They also saw some black mares, 'sent as rarities but I doubt if black is ever a good Arab colour'.

The following day they were shown the rest of the Sultan's horses in the stables at Yildiz. It was, wrote Lady Anne, a mark of especial favour since it was normally a privilege reserved for crowned heads and other potentates. They found there a splendid collection of stallions arranged in stalls according to their colours – grey, black or bay but very few chestnuts. In Blunt's opinion the most remarkable were half a dozen sent by the Sheikh of the Montefyk and there were also several fine ones from Ibn Rashid. Unfortunately there was no one to explain the breeding to them but they were 'altogether the grandest Arab collection I have seen, and far superior in quality to the mares we saw yesterday'. It was surpassed, however, by Prince Sanguszko's stud at Chrestowka which Blunt visited two years later. There was, he admitted, a lack of promising young stallions but the mares were magnificent and some of the flea-bitten greys 'quite wonderful'.

Blunt never had the same prejudice against greys that Lady Anne had. In 1894 the French Government, who were trying to establish an Arabian stud in Algeria, sent a party to buy horses from Crabbet. They were very keen on Shahwan, the grey the Blunts had bought from Mohammed Sadyk Pasha two years before, and offered £300 for him. This Blunt refused and Lady Anne wrote, 'we won't go below £400 as we can't get his like again and would not part at all with him were he not grey'. Her dislike of the colour was apparently due to its unpopularity in England and other countries; she maintained that bays and chestnuts were easier to sell. When the question arose later as to whether they should keep the stallion Seyal (by Mesaoud out of Sobha), Lady Anne's opinion was that 'we could not do better except for colour and must risk some greys I suppose'. But she was by no means consistent on this point. Not only did she consider some of their best horses to be greys but she also tried very hard to purchase greys from Ali Pasha Sherif. Judith strongly disagreed with her mother. She thought colour was of secondary consideration; quality was the most important thing and it was incidental that of the earlier horses she liked best some had been grey.

The following year Shahwan was sold to Mr J.A.P. Ramsdell of New York for 250 guineas and another 50 if he won a first prize showing. Though he did enjoy some success in America, a feeling against greys existed there also and for that reason people apparently refused to send their mares to him, although an American newspaper described him as "the most beautiful and typical Arabian horse in this country".

In 1894 four horses from Crabbet were exhibited in the Polo Pony Show at Hurlingham. Shahwan and Ahmar came second and third in the stallion class while Rosemary (by Jeroboam out of Rodania) and Rose of Dawn (by Rataplan out of Rose of Jericho) were first and second in the class for mares. A week later the Blunts showed at Ranelagh. Rose of Dawn came second to an English mare and Mesaoud was second to the Thoroughbred Rosewater and would have won had not one of the judges been 'very anti-Arab'.

The previous year Lady Anne's father, Lord Lovelace, had died and her brother Ralph had succeeded to the title and estate at Ockham. He now wrote to his sister that it was possible they might have as much as £4,000 a year additional income between them. But Blunt again decided that measures would have to be taken to cut down costs. Although Lady Anne paid most of the Stud and estate expenses, and even transferred money direct to his bank account, Blunt's financial position was such that economies had to be made. He proposed to let Crabbet and their Mount Street rooms in London and move to Newbuildings, which would be cheaper to run. In addition he intended to reduce the size of the Stud and to make a further saving by replacing the agent, Laprimaudaye, with a local man called Caffin on a lower salary. At the same time he made a will leaving everything to his cousin George Wyndham. But like many of his plans, much of it remained on the drawing-board. The Stud was not reduced, and five years later he was still in Mount Street. The decision to let Crabbet was, however, put into effect and the move to Newbuildings was made on June 29th, 1895. Blunt was away at the time and Lady Anne wrote with sadness of her last evening at Crabbet. When he returned Blunt took possession of the cottage at Caxtons with the intention of making it his *pied à terre*. Caxtons lies on the southern side of Crabbet Park, about half a mile from the house.

Despite the move, the Blunts continued to keep a number of horses at Crabbet because of the lack of space at Newbuildings. But it was at Newbuildings that on May 31st, 1897 a significant event took place. 'Great excitement of the day,' wrote Blunt, was 'the arrival of Webb from Cairo with five Ali Sherif mares and Mahruss.'* He and Lady Anne went to meet them at Southwater Station. They were 'certainly very beautiful though slight and unsubstantial compared with those we have bred here'. It was the first consignment of their purchases from Ali Pasha Sherif during the previous winter. Although Mesaoud was establishing himself as a first-class sire, the arrival of more Abbas Pasha blood was to make a crucial contribution to breeding at Crabbet. For it was from this blending of the Blunts' original imported desert stock with the best of the Ali Pasha Sherif horses that there have emerged the characteristics of the 'Crabbet type' which have so marked generations of magnificent Arabians.

* In order to avoid confusion between this Ibn Mahruss (registered as Mahruss) and his sire Mahruss and his son called Ibn Mahruss (exported to America *in utero*), this animal is referred to throughout as Mahruss (1893).

CHAPTER 5

Sheykh Obeyd
and Ali Pasha Sherif

Following their visits to Arabia, Blunt wrote a small book in the summer of 1881 entitled *The Future of Islam*. In it he expounded his belief in Islam as 'the Cause of Good' and urged the British Government to support Mohammedans everywhere against territorial encroachment in the East by European powers. 'The sacred land, the cradle of Eastern liberty and true religion' was a constant and irresistible lure and in November 1881 he and Lady Anne set out again for Arabia. They had intended to stay only very briefly in Egypt. But when they reached Cairo they found themselves almost immediately involved in a political movement of the type that appealed powerfully to Blunt throughout his life. The Arabian journey was forgotten and thirty-six years of happy association with Egypt had started.

Blunt's political career – his attempts to enter Parliament, his imprisonment in Ireland and his numerous brushes with the Establishment – is recorded in detail in his various volumes of memoirs. His beliefs, then extremely unfashionable, have a ring that is nowadays familiar. Through pamphlets and newspapers, he continually attacked the expansion of the Colonial powers, their oppression of subject races and customs and the general arrogance and incompetence of Imperialist administration. The Egyptian Nationalist movement of Arabi Pasha, in the middle of which he now found himself, epitomised a struggle for liberation with which Blunt instinctively sympathised and he threw himself into the affair with characteristic passion.

His support for the Nationalists did not endear Blunt to the European community in Cairo. They naturally wished to preserve the Khedivial administration, with all its advantages to them, and regarded Blunt's activities on behalf of Arabi with the greatest suspicion. Very soon, Blunt and Lady Anne found themselves more or less ostracised. They were at the time looking for a house outside Cairo where they could be free from the constraints of city life and still remain in touch with

left Wilfrid Blunt and Sherifa
below The tomb of Sheykh Obeyd

events. They also intended their decision to buy property to be seen as a gesture of confidence in the Nationalist policies, which after Arabi's *coup* earlier in the year had caused a heavy fall in the financial markets.

They had been looking at some land in the Zeitoun district and had even begun negotiations for its purchase when they heard that the garden of Sheykh Obeyd was for sale. It had been named after a saint who, according to local tradition, had been one of the Prophet's companions and whose tomb stood in the garden. The property had originally belonged to Ibrahim Pasha, one of Mohammed Ali's sons, who had laid it out in the 1830s and planted it with fruit trees imported from the Hejaz and Syria. It was said that its pomegranates were of such size that thirty were load enough for a camel and of such excellence that an annual consignment was sent as a gift to the Sultan of Turkey. The garden lay on the edge of the desert at Heliopolis, some nine miles to the north east of Cairo and on February 3rd, 1882, the Blunts went to inspect their future home.

It consisted of a walled garden of thirty-seven acres of rich soil lying in a slight depression, on the one hand secure from the flooding of the Nile and on the other hand low enough to draw upon the underlying water-table. The house itself was in poor condition, but this did not deter the Blunts. Two weeks later and at the cost of £1,500 they found themselves the owners of Sheykh Obeyd garden together with another thirteen acres outside the walls and the steam engine which operated the irrigation system.

In Sheykh Obeyd lay what Blunt later called 'the unique privilege of our life in Egypt'. A bare ten miles

> and one will be out of sight of the Nile valley. It will have faded to a blue line far below . . . and then it will be forgotten, lost, and one will feel oneself projected into another world of being . . . All the nations of Europe, Asia and Africa might be at each other's throats now and it would make no difference here. Humanity might be blotted out – it would not harm us. We should not know.

But the delights of Sheykh Obeyd were not to be theirs for a few years yet. In March of 1882 the Blunts returned to England. Wilfrid continued to involve himself in the Nationalist cause, which had by now assumed international significance. On May 20th the British and French fleets anchored off Alexandria and three weeks later riots broke out there in which a number of Europeans were killed. At this point

Blunt, whose outspoken support for Arabi had already earned him a reputation in England as a dangerous political agitator, wrote a long letter to *The Times* denouncing the Foreign Office's actions in Egypt over the last six months as the most deplorable on record. This provoked a great outcry. The Prince of Wales accused him of having raised over £20,000 for Arabi by selling jewels and furniture and asked if nothing could be done to stop 'this disloyal and eccentric Jesuit'. And when a Reuter's telegram announced that seventeen cases of firearms had been found at Sheykh Obeyd the very worst was believed. Though in fact it was only a box of seventeen rifles and revolvers and one small brass cannon that Blunt had intended to take to Arabia in 1881, the incident seemed to confirm the general suspicion that Blunt's allegiances in this matter were very doubtful.

The events of the following year, 1883, do not therefore come as a surprise. In September the Blunts left England for India to obtain entries for the Newmarket race. On the way they broke their journey in Cairo, and Blunt was unable to restrain himself from taking up the cause of five Egyptians who, he maintained, were being improperly detained in prison. This proved too much for Baring (later Lord Cromer), the Consul-General in Cairo, who without difficulty arranged for Blunt to be banned indefinitely from entering Egypt. For the next four years Sheykh Obeyd was left in the care of a manager.

It was not until 1887 that the Blunts were again able to visit Egypt. They had gone to Italy for the winter, intending that Lady Anne carry on to Cairo with Cowie to look after Sheykh Obeyd. Blunt had meanwhile written to the Foreign Secretary, Lord Salisbury, to ask if he might now be allowed into Egypt. On January 19th he received the reply by cable: 'Your letter. Baring says no objection.'

A dismal sight greeted them at Sheykh Obeyd. Many of the trees were dead or dying through lack of water, the ground had not been tilled and the house was even more dilapidated than before. The Blunts decided to build on a new wing and establishing themselves in their usual travelling tent, set to work. By March they felt they had earned a rest and together with one of their Bedouins, Zeyd Saad el Muteyri, they set out into the desert. They heard of a grey stallion belonging to Ibn ed Derri which was described by Zeyd in glowing terms. This was the famous Azrek whom they eventually purchased some months later thanks to Zeyd's ingenuity and persistence. With him they also bought Ashgar and Jilfa. Azrek was one of Crabbet's best stallions and the account of his extraordinary acquisition is given in detail in Blunt's *My Diaries*.

In the winter of 1888–89 they took Judith to Sheykh Obeyd for the first time. Blunt had felt that the garden might be too inaccessible for a winter home but when he heard that the railway was to be extended in its direction he abandoned all thoughts of leaving it. Already they were able to take the train to Matinah, only two miles away.

On arriving in Cairo, Wilfrid and Lady Anne left Judith and Cowie to rest in their hotel and set out for Sheykh Obeyd.

> A lovely day – found garden however pinched and trees shrivelled – there have been some cut, too – two big trees and most of the *mishmush* (apricots) – also fresh cattle tracks within shewed that the wild grass (*hashish*) was pasture for cattle. Donkeys were in the stables beneath the house. The house itself has been built up as ordered by Wilfrid. This is the work of Mohammed Ner Din so that he has given *some* value for the moneys received while old Seyd Ahmed has done nothing but *take*, and rob, and on a large scale.

They soon discovered that Seyd Ahmed, who had been left in charge, had been selling all the fruit from the garden and keeping most of the proceeds himself. There was much to do to put matters right. On December 18th Judith paid her first visit to Sheykh Obeyd. On their way they met at Matinah an Arab who remembered seeing the Blunts at Haïl in 1879 and was even able to describe correctly the horses they had been riding at the time.

Judith was delighted by Sheykh Obeyd and did not want to return to Cairo. Blunt also thought they should move in at once as all that was needed was a little sand on the mud floors. But Lady Anne insisted that since they had Judith and Cowie with them, they must have proper sleeping arrangements and cooking facilities. They decided to go back to Cairo until the work was nearer completion.

The next day they visited Ali Pasha Sherif's stud. Since his horses have played so important a part in Crabbet's history, it is appropriate to say something of their background.*

In 1805 Mohammed Ali was appointed Viceroy of Egypt by the then sovereign power in Constantinople. In the course of various campaigns in Arabia he built up over the years a stud of the finest Arabian horses.

---

* A chronological table of the principal studs involved in Egyptian breeding will be found in the overseas section under Egypt.

Mohammed Ali was succeeded as Viceroy by his grandson, Abbas Pasha I, in 1848 and died the following year. To the horses Abbas Pasha had already acquired from his grandfather's stud and through his friendship with Feysul ibn Saoud, he now added many more, buying through his agents the best blood in north Arabia. In 1854 he was assassinated and his stud was inherited by his son, El Hami Pasha. El Hami was not, however, in a position to enjoy his new property. Many horses were sold during his lifetime and the remainder by auction after his death in 1860. One of the principal buyers at the auction was Ali Pasha Sherif, the son of a Governor of Syria, who thus founded a stud which at its height was said to contain 400 Arabians. Although many strains were wiped out by horse plague, there were still in 1880 over 100 head of horses. Thereafter it had gone steadily downhill, partly from what Lady Anne Blunt called 'the want of the eye of the owner' and partly from the deterioration in Ali Pasha's personal circumstances.

The Blunts had heard rumours that Ali Pasha was in financial difficulties and might be selling part of his stud but they saw no sign of a break-up or an impending sale. The Palace was rather run down but the horses appeared well looked after. Altogether they saw thirty or more and though not all were good some, Lady Anne remarked, were really beautiful. They were particularly interested to see Aziz again. When they had seen him as a four-year-old in 1880 Lady Anne had been critical of using him as a sire because of one of his hocks. But she now found no sign of trouble, nor in any of his produce, though in several the hocks were small. Aziz was then twelve years old. He had 'rather too long a head but altogether has enormously improved, filled out and strengthened and has very marked type'.

Another impressive horse was the seventeen-year-old Ibn Nadir, whom Blunt described as the 'old one-eyed Seglawi . . . which I consider the finest horse, taken all round, I ever saw'. Judith singled out a grey Seglawi Jedran, a seven-year-old son of Ibn Nadir and consequently with Seglawi blood on both sides of his pedigree. Lady Anne thought him probably the pick of the lot and described him as 'very perfect and strong. Head also fine, very short cannon bones, and quarters and tail remarkably good.'

Among the mares was the bay Doheymeh Nejib, which they had seen on their first visit in 1880. But she was now 'a wreck of her former self. The crest like the Godolphin Arabian has gone but the immense high wither remains. Light of bone, nevertheless, I should not mind having her.' She was then about twelve. They also saw Horra again, the old Seglawieh Jedranieh who had been a beautiful mare in her prime, and two very good daughters of hers.

Finally they came to the great Wazir, who was in the biggest box of all. He seemed well, 'in spite of his great age – twenty-six years. His head very like Sherifa, less good however. He came and snuffed at the railing of the box – very friendly.'

They were now beginning to visit Sheykh Obeyd every day. Blunt had a lesson in pruning and was afterwards much occupied with the trees. At Christmas he decided to live in the newly-built house, finished or not. Cairo was unhealthy, he said, and he was tired of hotel life. After some hectic days buying the household essentials, Lady Anne joined him with Judith and Cowie. 'So ends 1888,' she wrote, 'a year of great moment in my life – I had quite given up hope of such happy arrangements as have come to pass.' Rather less happy was an accident that befell her a few days later. When riding through Cairo her donkey tripped and fell on top of her. 'No hurt, only a bruise or two, of course a crowd collected offering donkeys all of which were described as perfection while the owner of my unlucky one assured me it never stumbled, only it fell from fright at the carriages.'

On December 30th, the Blunts received a message from a Mr Paul Flemotomo that Ali Pasha Sherif wished to sell some horses. Their interest was aroused and they immediately arranged to revisit the stud. They had already decided to start what they then called the 'Sheykh Obeyd Garden Stud' and if Ali Pasha really was willing to sell, the opportunity was far too good to be missed.

Some of the animals that were for sale did not interest them but there were others they were keen to buy. They both agreed that overall the Seglawis of Ali Pasha had 'certain points about them superior to all others perhaps' and they would have liked a grey of this strain. However, after some negotiation and a further visit to the Palace on January 27th, they bought three chestnuts, a filly and two colts, of which the pick was the Seglawi son of Aziz. This was Mesaoud. They could scarcely have chosen better. With the other two (Merzuk and Khatila), the total cost to Lady Anne was £220. They would have liked Ibn Nadir as well but considered him too old unless he had been offered at a very low price. As Lady Anne remarked, 'if we could have *one* horse of this peculiar old fashioned stamp, it would be a great advantage to the stud'.

Judith, who was then nearly sixteen, made a careful note of this episode in her diary.

> Jan 28th, 1889. Yesterday we went to Ali Pasha. The first horse was Ibn Zarifa . . . He was a grey with good head and legs but tail put on too low and quarter not as good as it might be . . . The first colt was a bright chestnut with four white legs and blaze. (Mesaoud.) He is a beauty, holds his tail high in the air. Very showy but rather light of bone . . . [He] will be as fine a horse as ever was seen. The lightness of bone is partly because Ali Pasha's horses never leave the stable.
>
> Jan 29th. The three purchases arrived looking lovely. Zeyd has gone quite crazy over them. He is installed in a tent at the further end of the garden and has been given a pistol to defend himself and the horses with. They have never been out of doors before and never had *bersim*. A lamb was killed and the blood rubbed on their foreheads for luck. When they arrived they were taken a long way round in case El Khreshi should see them and wish them evil. (This was a man reputed to have the evil eye.)

Much importance was attached by Zeyd and the other Bedouins to protecting the new arrivals from the evil eye. Referring to the 'blessing' of the colts by smearing their foreheads with blood, Lady Anne wrote: 'It is curious and interesting to see how firm a belief has remained through all the ages of the need of the offering of a sacrifice . . . whenever any important matter is undertaken.'

Judith later recorded how, when Mesaoud was being broken in, a Bedouin struck him. 'The man Amash was reproached for twenty-four hours by Zeyd and in the middle of the night Zeyd woke him up to say "O Amash, the little lady (me) will dream of that stick that you hit Mesaoud with." That is just what I did do.'

In fact Judith's sixteenth birthday fell shortly after Mesaoud's arrival and her parents decided she should have a very special gift – Mesaoud.

No further purchases were made for the Stud that winter. Several horses were offered to them but all were wanting in what Lady Anne called 'that indefinable thing, "style" '. In 1890 they received a letter from Flemotomo when they were in England enquiring if they wished to purchase more Ali Pasha horses. But Blunt advised against it as they did not know for certainty the breeding of the mares Flemotomo mentioned and besides 'if we are ever to purchase Ali Pasha's *best* mares we must not be too eager about his second best.' It was not until 1891 that they again started to buy horses, when they acquired the mare Sobha from Mahmud Bey.

By then the two Ali Pasha colts, Mesaoud and Merzuk, were being ridden regularly and it was decided to train Mesaoud for a race at Cairo. On February 20th he ran in the Cairo Eclipse Stakes at Ghezireh, over a mile and a half. He started badly and finished seventh out of nine runners although Sitwell, his jockey, said that he was making ground at the end and would have done better over three miles. In fact Mesaoud was sent to Crabbet that spring and never raced again. The Blunts' overall plan for Sheykh Obeyd was to use it as a base for collecting the horses bought and then from time to time to send the best to England. Judith did not favour keeping a stud in Egypt as well as in England as she foresaw (correctly) the difficulties that would arise in managing two separate establishments when they spent only half of every year in each country.

One day in February of the same year the Blunts met Flemotomo in Cairo. He said that Ali Pasha had recently lost several mares and would sell none of his remaining mares or fillies. But he was willing to part with two or three colts and another visit to his stud was therefore arranged.

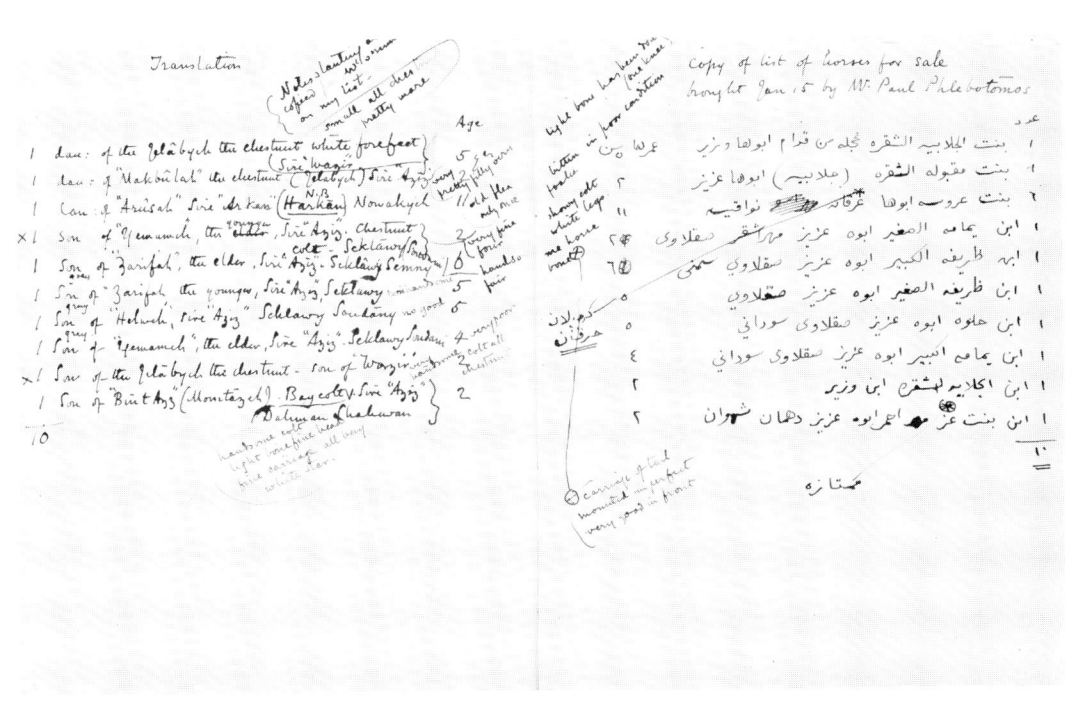

Lady Anne Blunt's notes on the Ali Pasha Sherif horses seen in January 1889 (Mesaoud is fourth on the list.)

Lady Anne was much taken by Amir, the white Seglawi Jedran of Ibn Sudan, by Aziz out of Horra.

> His head is perfection . . . his pedigree is the very best of the best and he is really lovely. The light bone need not be inherited, I *think*, anyhow any foals born out here would be likely to have more bone than those in Ali Pasha's stables: witness the improvement in the three we originally bought, Merzuk, Mesaoud and Khatila.

The second horse they were shown, by Aziz out of a bay Doheymeh Nejiba mare, Lady Anne liked less than any other she had seen in the stud. He had 'a short thick neck with the throat to chest line bulging *out*, and a plain head and small eyes', and his only redeeming feature was good tail carriage. The third and last horse they saw was a two-year-old chestnut with 'very fine carriage of tail – long neck and beautiful shoulder, short cannon bones, well shaped hocks, though the bone of cannon bones light – this colt I like much, he has great length. Wilfrid and Judith both despised him because he is so low, and will be *small*, they say.' Lady Anne gave him as a Dahman Shahwan, by Nazrat out of Montaza.

Further visits were made to Ali Pasha's stud that winter but no purchases were made. Lady Anne and Judith saw Amir again, this time being ridden in a pelham. They were still keen to buy him but Ali

Pasha increased the price to £500. They then discovered that Flemotomo had quarrelled with the Pasha and negotiations thereafter became more difficult. In the spring of the following year they managed to secure from Mohammed Sadyk Pasha a white Dahman Shahwan, which they named Shahwan, for £60. In Lady Anne's opinion this was 'the event of the day and indeed of the winter'. It needed only a glance to see his breeding, 'the unmistakable Ali Pasha Sherif stamp, so fine in all ways, beautiful shoulders with *excellent* action, tail erect in the air'.

During these years the Blunts added to their property at Sheykh Obeyd. Lady Anne bought 'El Kheyshi's land' and some further acres adjoining the garden. In 1895 another ninety-three acres were purchased gaining them 'a strategic frontier against all possible villa builders'.

In 1891 they were building another house. Known as the Pink House, it was initially used for guests. (Lady Anne was to make it her home after 1906.) When it was nearing completion and the builder was finishing off the roof, Lady Anne described the scene. 'Wilfrid sits in a wicker chair on one part of the roof watching his [the builder's] proceedings on the other part. This good old man is named Ali Yusef, *very* old and *very* good and I need hardly add very cunning.' Afterwards they had the whole of the first floor cemented against fleas which, together with the mosquitoes, were among the few drawbacks to Sheykh Obeyd.

They now had more visitors than ever before. Hasher the Oteybeh, who had been Abbas Pasha I's head groom, came out one day and told them how Ali Pasha used to visit him after Abbas Pasha's death to extract details of the horses so that whenever the chance arose he could buy the best. Flemotomo was also still in touch and reported that the new Khedive, Abbas Pasha II, had been buying broken down Thoroughbreds to breed half-breds with his Arabs. To this Blunt characteristically remarked that the invasion of the East by the English horse was almost as pernicious as its invasion by its men. 'In some ways, it is worse, for it mixes the blood as well as usurps the place of the native race.'

On February 11th, 1892, Mesaoud's first colt was born, out of Saada. It was a chestnut with three white feet and was named Ibn Mesaoud. Four days later the customary Bedouin ceremony was performed.

> Then came the operation of the foal's ears. I was present in the shed while the boy Montasser held the mare and Wilfrid and the

The Pink House at Sheykh Obeyd

Spider held the foal down – it lay on its near side – while Khuddr with a very big packing needle, and a coarse worsted threaded in the eye of that needle, pierced the skin of the ears and tied them together . . . Directly it was done up jumped the foal and shook itself and seemed perfectly happy. Not a drop of blood was visible so it was well done. Then Khuddr said, 'What have you named him? Is he not Mesaoud's son?' 'He is,' we said, 'but we have not yet given him a name.' 'Oh but you ought,' Khuddr replied, 'he ought to learn his name at once so that he should know it and he must be called Mesaoud', and before anyone could protest the huge fat figure of Khuddr had rushed at the foal, thrown two sausage like arms round its neck and was bellowing into its ears 'Mesaoud, Mesaoud . . .' in deafening tones which drowned the feeble voices of those who tried to expostulate. 'Now,' drawing himself up in triumph, said Khuddr, 'he will *never* forget *that*.' No indeed, I should think he never would.

The custom of sewing the foals' ears at Sheykh Obeyd was soon stopped by Lady Anne.

The Blunts often visited other studs. They had been before to see the horses of Prince Ahmed Kemal Pasha and had admired them. But when Lady Anne went again in March, 1892, she was greatly disappointed. 'It is painful to see the type going downwards, as he has spoilt his breed of horses through having bad sires. I can't think how he can be so blind as not to perceive this. Among the thirty to forty mares and horses *very* few really good and those are old.' She liked one very much, though, a grey Managhieh called Nura, the daughter of the original Managhieh Sobeylieh from Tellal ibn Shaalan by Ali Pasha's grey Seglawi Jedran.

In April, 1892, the Blunts left for England taking with them Shahwan and two other horses, El Tafuk and Rabdan.* The journey to Marseille proved a nightmare. A day out from Alexandria a gale blew up and except for Lady Anne the entire party was prostrated with seasickness. On deck the horses had the greatest difficulty to keep their footing in the boxes and were terrified by the waves crashing against the ship. When Lady Anne battled her way to them she found only Webb there. She sent a seaman to get some sand to give the horses a foothold

---

*No details can be found for either El Tafuk or Rabdan. They were entered in neither the Blunts' stud books nor the General Stud Book and were probably gelded for riding.

The staff at Crabbet *ca* 1885. Seated, from the left, are: Webb, Pompey, Francis and David (Blunt's valet). The giant is probably Budgen

and with the help of Blunt and a fellow passenger called Dr Kirkwood, the situation was brought under control. But it had been a gruelling and frightening experience, as Lady Anne wrote: 'It is anything but a pleasure to travel with horses, one feels all the risks for them so vividly, and the great hardships for whoever is in charge if he does his duty as Webb did . . . he hardly ever left them, and with that sea voyage and the land journey which lasted till Monday, the tenth day from the time he left Sheykh Obeyd with them, he had a severe experience.'

As on previous occasions, the horses were loaded into a horse-box at Marseille and travelled by train *via* Paris to Calais and thence across the Channel and by rail to Three Bridges. It was a long and tiring journey but though Webb came home with a bad cold, Shahwan arrived with his 'tail over his back'.

Sam Webb had been in their employment for some years. He had previously been a jockey in the Khedive Ismail's stables and had then been with Sir Rivers Wilson in Alexandria. He proved an enormous asset to the Blunts as he had picked up a little Arabic in Egypt and used it to garnish outrageous romances about the horses to impress potential buyers. Apparently this rarely failed and visitors usually ended by taking his advice rather than the Blunts'. His only disadvantage was a tendency to drink and fight and in 1902 he left Crabbet to set up a betting shop in Brighton. Thereafter Blunt found the Stud 'respectable but dull'.

January, 1893, found the Blunts again at Sheykh Obeyd. The garden was by now more beautiful than ever. Ali Pasha Sherif had given them some vines and rose bushes which together with the orange trees, apricots and olives, were a constant delight to the eye. In the wilderness of the garden's edge foxes barked by night while during the day a pair of white turkeys from Prince Ahmed's flock strutted importantly round the courtyard. Wilfrid had once considered importing a herd of roe deer from England but had been put off by the cost. Lady Anne has left a vivid picture of the rural life at Sheykh Obeyd.

> You cannot think how delightful I find the hot weather life – *mine* at least. Breakfast on roof at 4-30 nightingales singing below. Ride far away into desert starting at 5 – seeing the sun rise on the left – often meeting curious birds – a stork all by itself – for example. And the desert lark with its pathetic whistling song. Then coming home any time between 7-30 and 9 and I sit down to read Arabic – generally some tough things to prepare for my professor's weekly

visit. Then a sleep before luncheon. Afterwards perhaps I ride about 2 as I don't mind the heat and it suits me better than the evening air – besides I am in bed soon after (if not at) 7. Riding however often has to be either on business to see after things or to make calls. Building the *sakieh* is a great occupation – looking after livestock too from horses, cows, donkeys down to Wilfrid's cat and kittens.

At this time of the year the horses were tethered out to graze on *bersim*. Acres of it could be purchased or rented and the animals were moved from one area to another, often some distance from Sheykh Obeyd. This was the only green fodder the horses received; for the rest of the year they lived on dry food.

It was now that Blunt began to contemplate shipping part of the Stud at Crabbet to Egypt. The following year when at Sheykh Obeyd he went to see Gorst, the Minister of the Interior, with a view to arranging terms for the move. The difficulty lay in obtaining permission to export the produce that would be foaled in Egypt and in fact the proposal was turned down by the Khedive who understandably wished to keep for himself the export monopoly in horses.

The history of the Sheykh Obeyd Stud is divided into what Lady Anne later called the 'First Attempt' and the 'New Venture'. The First Attempt lasted until 1898 when the greater part of the horses then at Sheykh Obeyd were sold or given away through being either inferior or of doubtful pedigree. The trouble, as they discovered, was that forging pedigrees was all too common among Egyptians wishing to dispose of their horses to wealthy Europeans. On one occasion Lady Anne spotted a flaw in a pedigree and found that Ali Pasha Sherif had been fraudulently named as the horse's breeder. In fact the practice of forging pedigrees was not confined to Egypt but was common among townspeople throughout the Middle East. But the Blunts were at all times meticulous and quite indefatigable in tracing back the ancestry of their breeding stock and were ruthless in discarding any horse that was not unquestionably *mazbut*.

In 1895 the Blunts bought Sherif, an eight-year-old stallion by Ibn Nadir out of Sobha, from Mahmud Bey Akif. Sherif and his half brother Antar (by Aziz), who had come with his dam when she was bought in 1891, were the first two stallions to be entered in Lady Anne's Stud Book for the New Venture. In January 1896 the Blunts bought a three-year-old colt from Ali Pasha Sherif called Ibn Mahruss (Mahruss 1893).

Shahwan, purchased in Egypt in January, 1892
'The unmistakable Ali Pasha Sherif stamp'

When the Blunts returned to Egypt in October, 1896, it was to find their horses suffering from a bad attack of mange, caused by dirt and neglect. The sick animals were cured by being washed and then dosed with small amounts of arsenic but the sight of them so distressed Blunt that he considered abandoning the Stud altogether. This notion, however, was swept from his mind when one morning one of Ali Pasha's grooms, Mutlak, arrived to tell them that the Pasha's property was being inventoried for a sale and that the horses were to be auctioned. The Pasha himself was now restricted to an allowance of £70 a month and Mutlak and the other servants were being paid by the guardian, a man called Sabit Pasha.

A month later the Blunts went to see the horses. They were a pitiful sight. 'Of all that famous stud,' wrote Blunt, 'nothing now remains but three ancient stallions, five old brood mares and a dozen of young stock – a mere ruin.' According to one of the Pasha's sons, the whole stud did not number more than thirty of which several were probably half-bred. In the event twenty-one horses were shown to them and Lady Anne made the following notes:

Horses:
Ibn Nura. Flea-bitten, fine but very old. Magnificent head.
Ibn Sherara. White also fine and very old (hind toes turned in). Like Upton's frontispiece horse. Both the above saddle-backed with age.

Mares:
Bint Azz. Flea-bitten. Fine but very old. Saddle-backed. Beautiful head.
Makbula. White. Dam of the beautiful chestnut filly by Aziz.
Bint Mumtaza (Badiaha). A fine mare but wretchedly poor. Lovely head.
Bint Fereyha. Flea-bitten. Old but a fine mare.
Bint bint Fereyha. [Fulana.] Brown filly, great depth, head moderately good.
Bint Helwa. White with miserable foal [Ghazala] that has been ill and just recovered – rather old but a beautiful mare in spite of rather weak back – fine head and style.

They also saw some young stock of which one, Ibn Bint Nura (named Abu Khasheb by the Blunts) was 'very fine'.

A note was immediately sent to Ali Pasha asking for particulars of the breeding, age and price of nine of the horses seen and thus began hectic negotiations to complete the purchase before the public auction. Mutlak acted as the intermediary. He would ride out every morning to Sheykh Obeyd to deliver Ali Pasha's notes and take back Blunt's replies. A hitch occurred over Blunt's first messages. He wrote them in French but the Pasha, who was unable to read that language,* had to have them translated by a mere *katib*, or secretary, a procedure which greatly offended his dignity and looked likely to prejudice the Blunts' chances. In due course the price list arrived. The Blunts decided to buy five of the horses they had seen: Makbula, Bint Fereyha, Bint Helwa and her foal, Abu Khasheb and Fulana. To insure against further language problems, Lady Anne wrote out the list of those they wanted in Arabic and sent it back with her cheque for £350, the price for the five. She then had to hurry into Cairo to draw on a letter of credit to place enough money in her account at the Ottoman Bank to cover Ali Pasha's cheque. On her way out of the Bank she was met by Mutlak with the news that the horses would be coming the next day at eight o'clock. The following morning Mutlak and three other grooms arrived at Sheykh Obeyd with the animals, having set off from Ali Pasha at four a.m. so that the Pasha's Trustees could not prevent their departure.

But by mistake Bint Mumtaza (Badia) had been sent instead of Bint Helwa. This would be certain to annoy Ali Pasha and if the Blunts made a fuss about it, might endanger the possibility of making more purchases before the sale. To make matters worse, when Mutlak reported back to Ali Pasha, he found with him Sabit Pasha, who was disputing whether Ali Pasha had had the right to sell the horses to the Blunts. According to Sabit Pasha the property was entirely in trust and Ali Pasha had no title to the horses, which could be sold only at the Trustees' direction. Ali Pasha denied this vehemently. Two days later the Blunts heard from Mutlak that he 'had loaded a revolver and said he would shoot any who disobeyed and he would sell his horses as he chose'.

The dilemma over Badia was partially solved by Lady Anne writing to Ali Pasha asking if she could buy her as well as Bint Helwa. (This proposal came to nothing, it seems, for Badia was one of the horses the Blunts bought at the first auction.) The question of whether the

---

* Curiously, for he was educated in Paris.

above Judith Blunt with Ibn Nura in his old age
left Mutlak with the dog 'Berk'

Blunts had a good title to the horses was more serious. There existed in the Palace a powerful faction strongly in favour of Sabit Pasha bringing a lawsuit against the Blunts to recover the horses. At this stage the Blunts called upon Carton de Wiart, a highly esteemed Cairo lawyer whose legal advice they had often sought before. In his opinion there was a substantial doubt whether Sabit Pasha could make good his claim to the property within the *serai* since originally, when Ali Pasha had been *interdit*, his rights over the horses and other personal possessions had been specifically reserved to him. Moreover it appeared that he had since made full use of this concession to arrange other sales privately to which no objection had been raised. The Blunts were relieved to hear this and since de Wiart's opinion was finally, if reluctantly, accepted by Sabit Pasha, they were able to restore amicable relations all round.

The date of the auction had been set for January 15th and a fortnight before Lady Anne went again to inspect what was left of the stud. About a dozen animals were tethered in the garden of one of the Pasha's palaces with the four old white horses, Mes'ad, Ibn Nura, Ibn Sherara and Ibn Nadir in loose boxes. The others were outside under an arcade, among them Bint Azz, a brown mare Mahrussa, and the '*marwardi* spotted' Bint Makbula (named Manokta by the Blunts). It was a depressing experience. 'Mutlak was there and a sort of casual groom boy looking as dilapidated as the Palace and its grounds. *Sic transit.* It was three p.m. and the horses had not been fed or watered since daybreak . . . a pitiful sight.'

The auction started at ten in the morning. There were sixteen horses. Lady Anne bought Ibn Nura for £30 and Badia for £70. Others she missed after being erroneously informed by a friend that the bids were not genuine. But two days later she bought Bint Bint Jamila el Kebira from Sabit Pasha for £27, and for another £50 she acquired Fasiha, a daughter of Bint Fereyha, from Abd el Hamid, one of Ali Pasha's sons. Altogether the Blunts had purchased thirteen animals from Ali Pasha's stud and as Lady Anne noted, 'we have now therefore secured the larger part of what remained of this famous stud'.

On February 26th that year, Ali Pasha died and a final sale from his stud was arranged for March 26th. The Blunts viewed the horses the previous day and decided to bid for Bint Horra. In the event Lady Anne bought Bint Nura as well and would have had others if Blunt had not been strongly opposed to spending more money on buying horses. Despite this, Lady Anne later acquired Johara from Ibrahim

Bey and Manokta, the latter for her blood lines rather than her looks.

With the animals of 1889, the Blunts could now justly feel that they had bought the best of Ali Pasha's horses. In Blunt's opinion, 'the mere name of having purchased them will be worth much to our stud for they are celebrated the whole East over'. In April they left Egypt and on May 1st Webb was sent out to bring back Mahruss (1893) and five of the best mares, Bint Helwa, Bint Nura, Johara, Badia and Fulana.

Sheykh Obeyd itself ceases at this point to play a material part in the history of the Crabbet Stud. In January 1898 Lady Anne culled from the Stud any animal that was not completely *mazbut*. Of the remaining Ali Pasha Sherif mares, three (Kasida, Jellabieh and Makbula) were sent to England and the rest were kept for Ibn Nura who was too old to make the journey. All the other mares at Sheykh Obeyd were given away or sold, with the exception of Yemama and her descendants. The Blunts continued to breed horses there but on a limited scale and none were to be of any significance to the Crabbet Stud itself, though Ghazala and her daughter Ghadia (Radia) have founded strong lines in America and Egypt.

Early in 1897 the Blunts had engaged Mutlak as a groom. Mutlak el Batal, of the Muteyr tribe, was eventually made stud manager at Sheykh Obeyd and remained there until his death. Under his management the horses were far better kept than before and he became a devoted and trusted servant of Lady Anne.

In 1905 Blunt left Sheykh Obeyd stricken with illness and never to return. But for Lady Anne the garden was to be a paradisial retreat in her later years. As she once wrote poignantly, 'leaving Sheykh Obeyd garden is always to me as a sort of death'.

Many years later Lady Wentworth looked back at Sheykh Obeyd —

> I still can hear the kites as they circled in the sun and had sham quarrels with the crows which nested in the same trees each year. Often small foxes could be seen mouse-hunting, springing up into the air and pouncing on a hidden prey in the clover fields, where the lovely little Egyptian cows were tethered – cows like miniature Jersey cattle.
>
> By night the stars were a heaven of glory and we rode for hours through the palm groves and far into the desert hills. The desert has the same charm as the sea, the same wildness of cloud and wind, the same immensity of horizon and stars.

CHAPTER 6

The Foundation Stock

With the exception of three horses introduced by Lady Wentworth, all the animals that constitute the Crabbet foundation stock were imported by the Blunts themselves. The exceptions are Dafina, Mirage and Skowronek. In the first section of this chapter (Crabbet) will be found these three, the Ali Pasha Sherif horses that produced stock in England, and all horses from which the Blunts had preserved descendants in 1897.

Appendix I contains all other importations recorded in the Crabbet Arabian Stud books, including journey mares and those whose line had died out by 1897. Some of the horses listed here, such as Hagar, Jilfa and Rataplan, have left lines outside Crabbet that date from before 1897 and these are discussed in Chapter 13.

Only those horses that went to England from Sheykh Obeyd are given in the Crabbet section. Those that remained in Egypt and which are true foundation animals, are listed in the Sheykh Obeyd section. When Lady Anne Blunt abandoned the First Attempt in 1898, all the horses that remained from it (with the exception of Yemama) were given away or sold very cheaply. These are listed in Appendix 2.

All the information in this chapter, excluding the details of Lady Wentworth's three horses, has been taken from the stud books which were Lady Anne's personal copies and maintained exclusively by her. This applies for both Crabbet and Sheykh Obeyd. In the cases of Kars and Pharaoh, Lady Anne also included some notes by Wilfrid. These are in inverted commas and are initialled W.S.B. All author's explanations are given either in square brackets or as footnotes. Lady Anne's spelling of some proper names is inconsistent. These differences have been corrected only where demanded by the sense.

It is perhaps worth recalling the importance that Lady Anne attached to authenticating the origins of their purchases:

> Generally speaking the process was to escape from all Ottoman company or surveillance, contrary to the usual custom of Europeans

in search of horses, one is much more welcome to the Nomads in that case. In some rare instances a mare which had been got hold of by officials was purchased after the origin had been investigated. In one instance, that of Basilisk whose dam had been stolen from Ibn ed Derri by one of the Abadat tribe, authentication was not obtained for three years not until we visited Ibn ed Derri in the desert – if we had not succeeded her descendants would not have counted as pure-bred, and no stallion of her or of her posterity could have been used as a sire.

It should also be mentioned that a small number of horses such as Ibn Mesaoud, Babylonia and Ibn Yemama were entered by the Blunts in the General Stud Book but not in the Crabbet stud books since they had no intention of breeding from them.

The decision to take 1897 as the cut-off date is not arbitrary but follows Blunt's own realization, which he spelled out in his memorandum of that year, that by then a watershed had been reached and that future breeding at Crabbet could take place only from lines already established at the Stud.

CRABBET

AZREK
Foaled in 1881, a Seglawi Jedran of Ibn ed Derri of the Resallin tribe of Sebaa Anazeh.

14 hands 2 inches, below the knee 8 inches. A flea-bitten grey stallion, originally and up to 7 years grey with black points and black mane and tail. Afterwards quite white and flea-bitten. A magnificent horse in every way, grand head and arched neck, powerful shoulder with unrivalled trotting action (seen approaching at a trot the soles of the hoofs visible) enormous strength of back and quarter, up to any weight, tail set very high and splendidly carried, legs absolutely perfection the sinews literally 'like steel' to the touch. Great speed, impossible to tire. His stock 1891 superior to any yet bred in this stud.

Purchased in the desert for Mr Blunt by Zeyd Saad el Muteyri sent there for the purpose. Zeyd was despatched from Alexandria to Beyrout in March 1887 and thence via Damascus to the desert to look for the Anazeh. Azrek was purchased from his breeder Mashlab, son of Neddi ibn ed Derri, and brought by land to Egypt (with Ashgar and Jilfa) arriving towards the end of the summer. He was brought to England early in the year 1888.

Azrek was sold in the autumn of 1891 to the Hon. Cecil Rhodes (through his agent Mr Thompson) for exportation to the Cape. Impossible not to regret his departure.

BADIA [BADIAA in Sheykh Obeyd Stud Book]
A Dahmeh Nejiba. A chestnut mare foaled 1884. Bred by Ali Pasha Sherif in Cairo. Purchased from Daïra of Ali Pasha Sherif January 1897. Sire: Aziz. Dam: Mumtaza, a white Dahmeh Nejiba bred by Ali Pasha Sherif. Imported from Sheykh Obeyd in 1897. Given away in 1903 to R. Gregory.

BASILISK
Foaled 1876, a Seglawieh Jedranieh of Ibn ed Derri of the Resallin tribe of Sebaa Anazeh.

14 hands 1 inch. A white mare with black hoofs, a few flea-bitten marks also some patches of pink which shew when the coat is changing, the rest of the skin being black. Great power, up to any weight, wiry legs though not large below the knee, very fine shoulder, drooping quarters but tail carried like a feather in the air, good head and small muzzle. Basilisk has something of the compact wiriness of a wild animal.

Purchased for Mr Blunt by Mr Skene in February 1878 of Abd el Jadir of Deyr. Imported in 1878.

Basilisk's dam was a white Seglawieh Obeyran* stolen by Faris Assaat from the desert. Neddi ibn ed Derri had sold the mare on shares to an Abadat (Sebaa Anazeh) and it was from him that she was stolen. Sire said to be a bay Seglawi of same strain. Faris Assaat sold the dam to Abd el Jadir of Deyr on the Euphrates in whose possession Basilisk was foaled. Basilisk is fast and a good fencer.

Basilisk was sold in August 1884 to the Duke of Westminster and left Crabbet Park, after the foal (Bustard) had been weaned, on the 1st of September.

BINT HELWA
A Seglawieh Jedranieh of Ibn Sudan's strain. A white mare foaled in 1887. White, reddish tint on near side from wither to girth, small pink patch between lower ends of nostrils towards eyes. Black hoofs. Bred by Ali Pasha Sherif.

Sire Aziz, a chestnut Dahman Shahwan bred by Ali Pasha Sherif. Dam Helwa, a white Seglawieh Jedranieh bred by Ali Pasha Sherif. Purchased from Ali Pasha Sherif, Dec. 14, 1896. Imported from Sheykh Obeyd 1897. Destroyed 1907.

BINT BINT NURA (ES SHAKRA)
A Dahmeh Nejiba. A chestnut mare foaled 1885. Chestnut, 3 white feet, the hind ones to about third up cannon bone, the off front to below fetlock

*When purchased, Basilisk was thought to be a Seglawieh Obeyran and was entered as such in the G.S.B. But Lady Anne Blunt was unable completely to satisfy herself about Basilisk's pedigree until 1881, when she found her to be a Seglawieh Jedranieh. Other references to being an Obeyran have been corrected in her stud book and the omission to do so here is clearly an oversight.

in front extending behind, star above eyes and snip. Bred by Ali Pasha Sherif. Sire: Aziz. Dam: Bint Nura, a bay Dahmeh Nejiba bred by Ali Pasha Sherif, her dam Nura (original mare) a grey Dahmeh Nejiba, her sire Zobeyni (original horse) a white Seglawi Jedran of Ibn Sbeyni's strain. Imported from Sheykh Obeyd in 1897. Destroyed 1912.

DAJANIA

Foaled in 1876, a Kehileh Dajanieh, 14 hands 3 inches, just over 7 inches below the knee, girth 70 inches.

A bright full bay mare with black points 3 white feet (both hind and off fore, *mutlak es shemal*) star and snip. Good head, rather short neck, fine ears, short back wonderfully strong, fair shoulder perfect legs, fine action and carriage of tail.

Purchased at Aleppo, Dec. 25th 1877, through Seyd Ahmed, Sheykh of the Hannadi now settled at Haggla, of the person who stole her (we not knowing her to be stolen till some time afterwards). Dajania's (at first named Jasmine and exhibited under that name in the 1880s) dam was a Kehileh Dajanieh stolen from the Sebaa Anazeh by Mohammed Pasha, a Turkoman chief who bred Dajania, her sire a Kehilan Nowag. Dajania was in her turn stolen from her owner and brought to Aleppo where she was sold to Mr Blunt. We were not aware that she had been stolen for our conversation with Seyd Ahmed who had brought the filly to the Consulate, for sale, on the morning of Christmas Day, was carried on through Mr Skene. I believe that Mr Skene was informed of the fact by Seyd Ahmed, but we only learned it in 1881. No doubt it was owing to this that we got her cheap. Extract from journal of Dec. 25, 1877, 'the filly is lovely. Seyd Ahmed asked T£50, Mr Skene said "You will get her for £40." We all went into the drawing room and sat round the *mangal* (brazier) for it was very cold. Mr S. began by offering 30 and ended by 35. Seyd Ahmed offered her for 40. Mr S. stuck to 35. He said when the Sheykh got up and left the room, "You will have her for 35", and so we did.' Imported in 1878. Dajania was sold at the 3rd biennial sale in 1886 to the Turkish ambassador, H.E. Rustem Pasha.

FERIDA

A Managhieh of the strain of Ibn Sbeyel. An imported bay mare foaled in 1886. About three white hairs on forehead. 14 h. 1½ ins. Bred by the Shammar tribe in Mesopotamia from whom she was purchased at Deyr on the Euphrates for Mohammed Khuddr Jemal ed Din by his nephew. Purchased in Egypt of Mohammed Khuddr Jemal ed Din and imported 1891. Given to J.A.D. 1907 by whom a home was found.

THE FOUNDATION STOCK

FEYSUL

A Kehilan Ajuz of the Jellabi strain, or Kehilan Jellabi. A chestnut stallion bred by Ali Pasha Sherif in Cairo 1894. Sire: Ibn Nura, a white flea-bitten Dahman Nejib. Dam: Bint Bint-Jellabiet-Feysul (ie Feysul Ibn Turki, Amir of Riad) a Kehileh Jellabieh bred by Ali Pasha Sherif. Her dam Bint-Jellabiet-Feysul out of Jellabiet-Feysul (original mare) brought to Egypt by Abbas Pasha I, Viceroy of Egypt (for it is said £7,000!) from Feysul Ibn Turki but by him obtained from Ibn Khalifeh, Sheykh of Bahrein who possessed both Dahman Shahwan and Kehilan Jellabi strains having got them from the Ajman tribe in eastern Arabia.

A chestnut, very strong colour, off hind foot white and *seyal* (narrow blaze); fine shoulder, arched neck, head set on like Ibn Nura's and same way of turning it, short legged, good mover. Purchased from Seyyid Mohammed Fathi December 7 1898. Mohammed Fathi had bought him from Saleh Bey Sherif, his purchaser at the 2nd Auction held in March 1897. Imported to England 1904. Destroyed 1917.

FULANA (BINT BINT-FEREYHA EL SAGHIRA)

Seglawieh Jedranieh of Ibn Sbeyni's strain. A brown mare foaled in 1893. Bred by Ali Pasha Sherif. Sire: Ibn Nura. Dam: Bint Fereyha. Purchased from Ali Pasha Sherif Dec. 14 1896. Imported from Sheykh Obeyd 1897. Destroyed 1908.

HADBAN

Foaled in 1878, a Hadban Enzeyhi of the Oteybeh tribe. 14 hands $2\frac{1}{2}$ inches, girth 68 inches, below the knee $7\frac{3}{4}$ inches. A light bay stallion with three white feet (*mutlak al yemin*) the two hind feet white up to half cannon bone, the near fore has white up to over fetlocks, and star. Rope scar on near hock.

Remarkably fine head with prominent forehead full eye and small muzzle, ears well shaped but rather broad, neck somewhat too short, good shoulder and depth and length, stands back at the knee and pasterns, which are long, too much sloped (though no weakness apparent). Lump on near fetlock joint outside from accident on the voyage from Arabia to India. Great style, tail carried, and action free, moves well galloping and appears to have speed, could not be tried owing to accident from which it must take months to recover. On being galloped once after arrival at Crabbet, the horse pulled up lame.

Purchased at Bombay in December 1883 from Ali ibn Amr of Bussora who bought him from Jakin ibn Aghil Sheykh of the Daajini tribe of Oteybeh, and brought him to India. Imported in 1884. Sold to Mr Mackay of New South Wales and sent out with Kars, left Crabbet June 22, 1885 and was shipped on board the *Kent* accompanied by Webb. Boxes had been built in the middle of the ship on purpose for the two horses. In view of the excellence of the only two mares (Nefisa and Rose of Sharon) by Hadban in the Crabbet Arabian Stud it is to be regretted that he should have been parted with.

IBN YASHMAK

A Kehilan Ajuz of the Jellabi strain. An imported chestnut stallion foaled in 1902. Bred at the Sheykh Obeyd stud. Dam: Yashmak, a white Kehileh Jellabieh bred at Sheykh Obeyd stud. [For Yashmak's dam Yemama see Sheykh Obeyd section and for her sire, Shahwan, see below.] Sire: Feysul [see above].

Chestnut, near feet white and blaze. Imported from Sheykh Obeyd to England in September 1904. [Sold to the Royal Agricultural Society of Egypt in 1920.]

JELLABIEH (or BINT BINT JELLABIEH FEYSUL)*

A Kehilet Ajuz of the Jellabi strain belonging to Ibn Khalifeh, Sheykh of Bahreyn. White mare foaled in 1892. Sire: Ibn Nura. Dam: Bint Jellabiet Feysul. Bred by Ali Pasha Sherif. Purchased Dec. 10 1897 from Ayub Bey (who had purchased her from Ali Pasha Sherif). Imported from Sheykh Obeyd in 1898. Sold in Mar. 1912 to Mr [H.] V. [M.] Clark. Destroyed 1914.

JERBOA

A Managhyeh Hedrujieh, foaled in 1874. 14 hands $2\frac{1}{2}$ inches, a light bay mare with three white feet (two fore and near hind) and star. Head shewing breeding though not handsome, eye large and flashing and shewing some temper, ears remarkably good, mane very fine, shoulder well sloped though hardly any wither up to the age of 7, very strong back good sound wiry legs but not large bone, tail well carried, splendid action trotting and fast, and good mover galloping, the stride being smooth and even as a machine, good leader in a team though inclined to kick if annoyed.

Jerboa's dam a bay Managhyeh Hedrujieh long and low and very worn, old and thin when seen at Deyr in 1878. Her sire a Managhy Ibn Sbeyel of the Gomussa. Extract from journal Deyr Jan. 21, 1878 'a bay filly was brought, Managhyeh yet strange to say good looking, and for her we are to treat'. Purchased at Deyr Jan. 24, 1878 from her breeder Othman el Abd of the Obeyd tribe. Imported 1878. Jerboa died in 1893.

JOHARA (or BINT HELWA ES SHAKRA)

A Seglawieh Jedranieh of Ibn Sudan's strain. A chestnut mare foaled about 1880. Near hind foot white to $\frac{1}{3}$ up cannon bone, small splotch of white outside off hind foot, above hoof, and blaze from just below ears to lower level of nostrils.

Sire: Aziz. Dam: Helwa. Bred by Ali Pasha Sherif. Purchased from

* Not to be confused with her half sister Bint Bint Jellabiet-Feysul, the dam of Feysul (q.v.).

Ibrahim Bey Sherif (son of the late Ali Pasha Sherif) April: 19 1897. Imported from Sheykh Obeyd in 1897. Given away to Mrs Pearce 1903.

KARS

Foaled in 1874, a Seglawi Jedran of Ibn Sbeyni of the Fedaan Anazeh. Sire stated to be of the same strain. 14 hands $2\frac{1}{2}$ inches, girth $63\frac{1}{2}$ inches, below the knee $7\frac{1}{4}$ inches.

A bright bay stallion with black points, both hind feet white up to fetlocks, small star on forehead; splendid head with fine jowl, small muzzle, lips like a camel's, nostril large; magnificent shoulder, high wither, rather flat sided, quarter very powerful and somewhat drooping but tail well set and carried well galloping, legs hock and knees perfect, pasterns long and strong, feet good. Mark like a dent in the neck on the near side, called 'the prophet's seal'. His temper perfect.

Purchased at Aleppo January 5th 1878 from Mahmud Aga, a Kurdish Chief of an irregular cavalry force raised in the northern desert during the Russian war, who obtained him as a two year old from his breeder of the Fedaan. Mahmud Aga rode Kars in 1877 to the war in Armenia where nearly every other horse perished, Kars being, as his former owner's brother told me at Aleppo in the spring of 1881, miraculously preserved although twice hit by a bullet and afterwards abandoned on the road. On one occasion a bullet struck him on the cannon bone inside and just below the off knee, knocking over the horse and his rider and rolling them several yards. The second time a shot described as an inch in diameter grazed his shoulder. On the retreat from Armenia to Aleppo the horse appeared so much exhausted that his bridle and saddle were taken off and he was left behind, but he got up again and followed his master. Both reached Aleppo but in so wretched a state that recovery seemed doubtful for either. The one took to his bed and the other, suffering from a frightful back, was fired on the belly as a counter-irritant and was considered hardly out of danger when we saw and offered to buy him in January 1878. His owner, at the point of death, beset by heirs and relations, was persuaded to sell him for £69, a very small sum for a horse of his breed.

Imported in 1878. 'Kars is in shape like the best sort of English thoroughbred and reminds me of the picture of Dungannon and also of Borack. He is a good horse all round, a fast walker trotter and galloper, with fine shoulder action, a brilliant fencer and up to my weight 13 stone to hounds. He has carried me often with the South Down and has (1881) never been beaten or stopped by any fence or given me a fall. In the autumn of 1880 he unfortunately met with an accident, pricking his knee with a thorn, in jumping a made fence in the park at Crabbet, and has remained with an enlarged knee but the blemish has not affected his soundness. His stock are all satisfactory not one of them showing any weakness of limb or constitution.'

W.S.B.

Kars was sold in June 1885 to D. Mackay Esq of New South Wales, for exportation to Australia.

KASIDA (formerly BINT MAKBULA ES SHAKRA)
A Kehilet Ajuz of the Jellabi strain. A chestnut mare foaled 1891. Sire: Nasr. Dam: Makbula [see below]. Bred by Ali Pasha Sherif. Sold Mar: 1897 by the Daïra of Ali Pasha Sherif after his death to Maître Léon Clery. Taken to France April 1897, brought back to Egypt in the winter of 1897–8. Purchased Mar: 2 1898 from Maître Clery (in Cairo). Imported from Sheykh Obeyd in 1898. Destroyed 1913.

KHATILA
A Kehilet Ajuz of the Jellabi strain or Kehileh Jellabieh. An imported chestnut mare foaled in 1887. 14 h. 2 ins.

Bred by Ali Pasha Sherif in Cairo and purchased from him in the winter of 1888–9. Imported in 1891. Sire: Aziz. Dam: Makbula, a chestnut Kehilet Ajuz of the Jellabi strain or Kehileh Jellabieh bred by Ali Pasha Sherif in Cairo, her dam of the strain from Ibn Khalifeh, Sheykh of Bahreyn. Given away to Mr Ruxton in 1909.

MAHRUSS [1893]
A Dahman Nejib. A chestnut stallion bred by Ali Pasha Sherif in Cairo 1893. Sire: Mahruss, a grey Wadnan Hursan bred by Ali Pasha Sherif, his dam a grey Wadneh of the Hursan strain (original mare) of Bender Ibn Saadun, Sheykh of the Montefyk tribe. Dam: Bint Bint Nura.

A bright strong chestnut with 4 white feet, three of them stockings, the off front only to above the pasterns; star rather high and to offside of forehead and joined by a very narrow white line to a snip ending pink between nostrils.

Purchased from his breeder Ali Pasha Sherif Jan. 1896. 'Ibn Mahruss' afterwards called 'Mahruss' and as such entered at Weatherbys was sent to England in May 1897. He was the sire of two colts, one in 1899 out of Badia which broke a front leg and was destroyed as a foal, the other out of Rose of Sharon 1901 (Rijm). Sold 1900 to J. Hamilton Leigh of Stockport. (Note: It would be well to have more of Mahruss's stock.) *

MAKBULA
A Kehilet Ajuz of the Jellabi strain (belonging to Ibn Khalifeh, Sheykh of Bahreyn) or Kehileh Jellabieh. A white mare foaled in 1886. White, a few reddish spots, black hoofs except part of near hind hoof white. Bred by Ali Pasha Sherif. Sire: Wazir. Dam: Makbula.

---

*Mahruss (1893) was used sparingly at stud and his full brother Abu Khasheb (see Appendix 1), scarcely at all. Abu Khasheb was sold the same year that Rijm was foaled, a decision that Lady Anne Blunt may have regretted when Rijm grew older.

Purchased from Ali Pasha Sherif Dec: 14 1896. Imported from Sheykh Obeyd in 1898. Sold at the International Horse Show at Paris (Sept 1–10, 1900) to Count Stroganoff for Russia.

MERZUK

A Kehilan Ajuz of the Jellabi strain or Kehilan Jellabi. A chestnut stallion foaled in 1887. Sire: Wazir. Dam: a chestnut Kehileh Jellabieh of the strain procured by Abbas Pasha from Ibn Khalifeh, the Sheykh of Bahreyn. Bred by Ali Pasha Sherif. A strong chestnut with two white feet, off hind and near fore feet, and a speck of white on near hind foot, and narrow crooked blaze. Very broad forehead and prominent eyes, short ears very pricked, strong back, well ribbed up, remarkably good legs, especially fine hocks. Purchased from his breeder in the winter of 1888–9. Imported in 1891.

Merzuk was sold during the summer of 1891 to Sir Henry Lock, Governor of the Cape for exportation to Basutoland. A horse that would have been valuable for the Crabbet Arabian Stud, but a promise to find a horse for the Cape had to be kept, so he had to be sent out. 1893: Merzuk, after being the sire of about 40 foals, fell a victim to the African horse sickness.

MESAOUD

A Seglawi Jedran of Ibn Sudan's strain. An imported chestnut stallion foaled in 1887, a Seglawi Jedran of the strain formerly belonging to Ibn Sudan of the Roala tribe, a strain no longer existing in the desert, for Abbas Pasha I, Viceroy of Egypt, bought up all he could hear of till none were left, and all that Abbas Pasha's stud possessed, passed into the hands of Ali Pasha Sherif.

Dam: Yemameh, a grey Seglawieh Jedranieh of Ibn Sudan's strain. Sire: Aziz, a chestnut Dahman Shahwan whose dam was granddaughter to the mare of Ibn Nakadan of the Ajman tribe, a Dahmeh Shahwanieh from the stud of Feysul Ibn Turki, then Amir of Riad, but originally from Ibn Khalifeh of Bahreyn (who had obtained her from Ibn Nakadan of the Ajman tribe and who possessed the Dahman Shahwan and the Kehilan Jellabi strains). The Seglawi Jedran strain of Ibn Sudan originally came to that family from Ibn Sbeyni of the Fedaan Anazeh. Bred by Ali Pasha Sherif in Cairo.

Mesaoud was purchased of his breeder in the winter of 1888–9. Imported in 1891.

A bright chestnut with 4 white legs and blaze, a mark of white under the chin, also group of white specks under jowl. Beautiful head and ears, deep jowl, very fine shoulder, great depth in front of girth, powerful quarter, large hocks and knees and remarkably deep cut sinews. Very fine mover, fast walker and trotter. Tail set on very high and carried magnificently. Dark line along the back. Height $14.2\frac{1}{2}$ inches, girth 69, below the knee $7\frac{3}{4}$ inches.

Mesaoud was sold in June 1903 to Wladislas Kliniewski 'à Niezdow près Opole, Royaume de Pologne, Empire de Russie', for stud and taken away in July, a few days after the 15th sale of July 4, 1903.

MESHURA

Foaled 1875, a Seglawieh Jedranieh of Ibn ed Derri of the Resallin tribe of Sebaa Anazeh. Sire a Managhy Hedruj of Ibn Sbeyel. 14 hands 1 inch, girth 67 inches, below the knee $7\frac{1}{8}$ inches.

A bright red bay mare with black points, four white feet, star on forehead with point downwards, snip or rather splotch on the nose not exactly in the middle the off nostril being dark, the other pinkish, the near eye like a human eye oval and shewing the white, a large white patch on each side of the back from saddle galls. Great length and strength, splendid legs, feet large but rather shallow, remarkably fine carriage of tail, well shaped head with good jowl and beautiful ears. A celebrated mare.

Purchased at Aleppo April 24th 1881 from Ali Pasha Governor of Deyr. Imported in 1881.

Meshura's dam was a Seglawieh Jedranieh of Ibn ed Derri of the Resallin tribe of Sebaa Anazeh, her sire a Managhy Hedruz of Ibn Sbeyel, a celebrated horse. By the dam's side she is half sister to Pharaoh. She was bred by Berghi ibn ed Derri brother to Neddi the head of the Ibn ed Derri family and was sold by him in 1879 to Ali Pasha at the price of 44 camels, £100 in cash a total amount of at least £600. Even at this price she was not obtained without some pressure. Ibn ed Derri had refused to sell her, but the Pasha had set his heart upon possessing a mare already famous among the tribes. He seized an opportunity to negotiate with her owner when the latter suspecting nothing had encamped with a section of his tribe near the river bank at a spot where they could be hemmed in by soldiers. This having been effected the Governor sent word that unless the mare was delivered up he should order the troops to open fire. Berghi had no choice but to yield; the Pasha however was an honest man and did not propose to take the mare for nothing. He only wanted to purchase and was prepared to give a handsome price, more especially as it did not come altogether out of his own pocket. The 44 camels conveniently at hand were Government property seized from the Shammar Bedouins in payment of taxes claimed by the Government and these formed two thirds of the value paid to Berghi. Ali Pasha showed his delight at his new acquisition by pampering her with all sorts of dainties and decorating her with a chain and halter of solid silver. Once, too, he lost his temper with her because she was fidgeting when he rode out, and he put her for three days under arrest in irons. But his bargain, according to the gossip of Deyr and Aleppo, brought him no luck. Meshura while in his stables did not produce a foal, and before two years were out the

Pasha's affairs were so involved that he was forced to part with the whole of the stud he had collected. In the winter of 1880–1, knowing that Pharaoh had been sold to us, he sent us a message offering the mare but asking a long price and for all that she was Pharaoh's sister we could not afford such a sum for a mare we had not seen. In the spring of 1881 when on our visit to the various Anazeh tribes east and north east of Damascus we seriously thought of trying to see her with a view to purchase. We had found a sad change in the three years since our former visit, good mares had become rarer among the tribes, first rate seemed hardly to exist and whatever Meshura might be as to looks there was no doubt of her great reputation among the Bedouins. Ali Pasha on his side was still more eager we should see the mare and had sent instructions to his subordinates at Tudmor and Karieteyn to invite us to Deyr without delay. We should have gone but the hot weather set in, the tribes still to be visited had pushed on north and Deyr would have taken us too far out of our way. We gave up all thought of buying 'the Pasha's mare' and made the best of our way to Aleppo. Once there we were too fully occupied with the difficulty of shipping our other purchases to think of regretting her and were taken by surprise when Ali Pasha with all his stud suddenly arrived from Deyr the day before we were to leave Aleppo. He finding we did not come, set off post haste from Deyr and had not been an hour in Aleppo before he sent his son Hassan Bey to call upon us. After seeing Meshura we were not long in coming to terms. We might have secured her for a less sum than we gave had we known Ali Pasha's straitened circumstances for not every day can a European foolish enough to part with his cash be found in Aleppo. The sum fixed upon was paid to a creditor in disguise as the Pasha's 'Secretary' who pocketed the bag of gold and carried off the solid silver chain halter to which we as purchasers had a right according to custom. Meshura died in 1899.

PHARAOH
Foaled in 1876, a Seglawi Jedran of Ibn ed Derri of the Resallin tribe of Sebaa Anazeh, sire a Kehilan Ajuz of the Gomussa tribe of Sebaa. 14 hands 3 inches, girth 67 inches, below the knee $7\frac{3}{4}$ inches.

A dark bay stallion with black points, both hind feet white up to just below the fetlock, narrow strip of white beginning like a large star on the forehead, rather to the off side, above the level of the eyes and tapering down to the upper lip, ending slightly pink; handsome head, good jowl, very beautiful ears, eyes like the human eye oval and shewing the white, slope of shoulder good and length sufficient but forelegs placed about an inch too far back, he stands back too a little at the knee especially with the near foreleg; good depth, splendid barrel well ribbed up, magnificent carriage of the tail walking trotting or galloping; there is never a moment of forgetfulness.

Pharaoh is ever ready to be seen. He is celebrated among the Anazeh tribes as the handsomest colt bred by the Sebaa for twenty years.

Purchased through Mr Skene in October 1878 from Neddi Ibn Ed Derri head of the Ibn Ed Derri family of the Resallin tribe of Sebaa Anazeh, at Beteyen Ibn Mirshid (Sheykh of the Gomussa)'s camp near Palmyra. Imported in 1879.

Pharaoh's dam was a bay Seglawieh Jedranieh of Ibn ed Derri, his sire a bay Kehilan Ajuz belonging to one of the Beteyen Ibn Mirshid's people (Min Jemaat Beteyen) of the Gomussa tribe of Sebaa Anazeh (the Resallin and Gomussa are mixed up altogether). Sire of dam a Seglawi Jedran from Obeyd El Belasi of the people of Ibn Majil of the Roala Anazeh. The Seglawi Jedran of Ibn Ed Derri is considered to be the best strain of blood now remaining to the Sebaa Anazeh. At this moment (1881) the Ibn Ed Derri family possess two mares and two colts, the former a chestnut and a bay and both the latter grey. The chestnut (dam of Azrek) is a half sister to Pharaoh, her sire a Hadban, is very small with one foreleg (the near) crooked when seen in front, and the off knee scarred, the bay is tall 14.3, four years old 1881, a very fine head (resembling Kars) no white except a few hairs on the forehead. Sire Managhy which accounts for a certain coarseness difficult to define but always apparent in the present fashionable strain of that breed. (NB. This was as far as we had seen up to 1881, and refers to a particular Managhy horse in most cases. Other strains of Managhy such as Jerboa's (which was Hedruj) and Ferida (Ibn Sbeyel's) shew great quality.)

'Pharaoh is a fine mover galloping but is unable to stay over a distance, neither is he a free jumper. He has an excellent constitution and is perfectly sound, but two or three of his produce have had defective hocks (his own are excellent). The calf knee however has not reproduced itself in his stock. He is figured in Lady Anne Blunt's portrait of me in Bedouin dress.' W.S.B.

Pharaoh was sold at the 1st Sale July 1882 to Count Joseph Potocki for exportation to Russian Poland. Count Potocki sold him three years later and the horse became the principal stallion in the Emperor of Russia's private stud. In 1899 heard from Colonel Alexandre de Sdanovitch that Pharaoh was at the Derkoul (Russian Government) Stud.

QUEEN OF SHEBA

Foaled in 1875 an Abeyeh Sherrakieh, of the Gomussa tribe of Sebaa Anazeh; 15 hands, girth 69½ inches, below the knee 7¼ inches. A brown mare with four white feet, very small star and snip, a good head remarkably fine nostril and fine ears, muzzle not particularly small, splendid shoulder, strong back and quarter, very free action trotting, great stride galloping and tail carried high. This mare is perhaps, taken altogether, the finest in

AZREK

Grey stallion purchased in the desert in the spring of 1887.

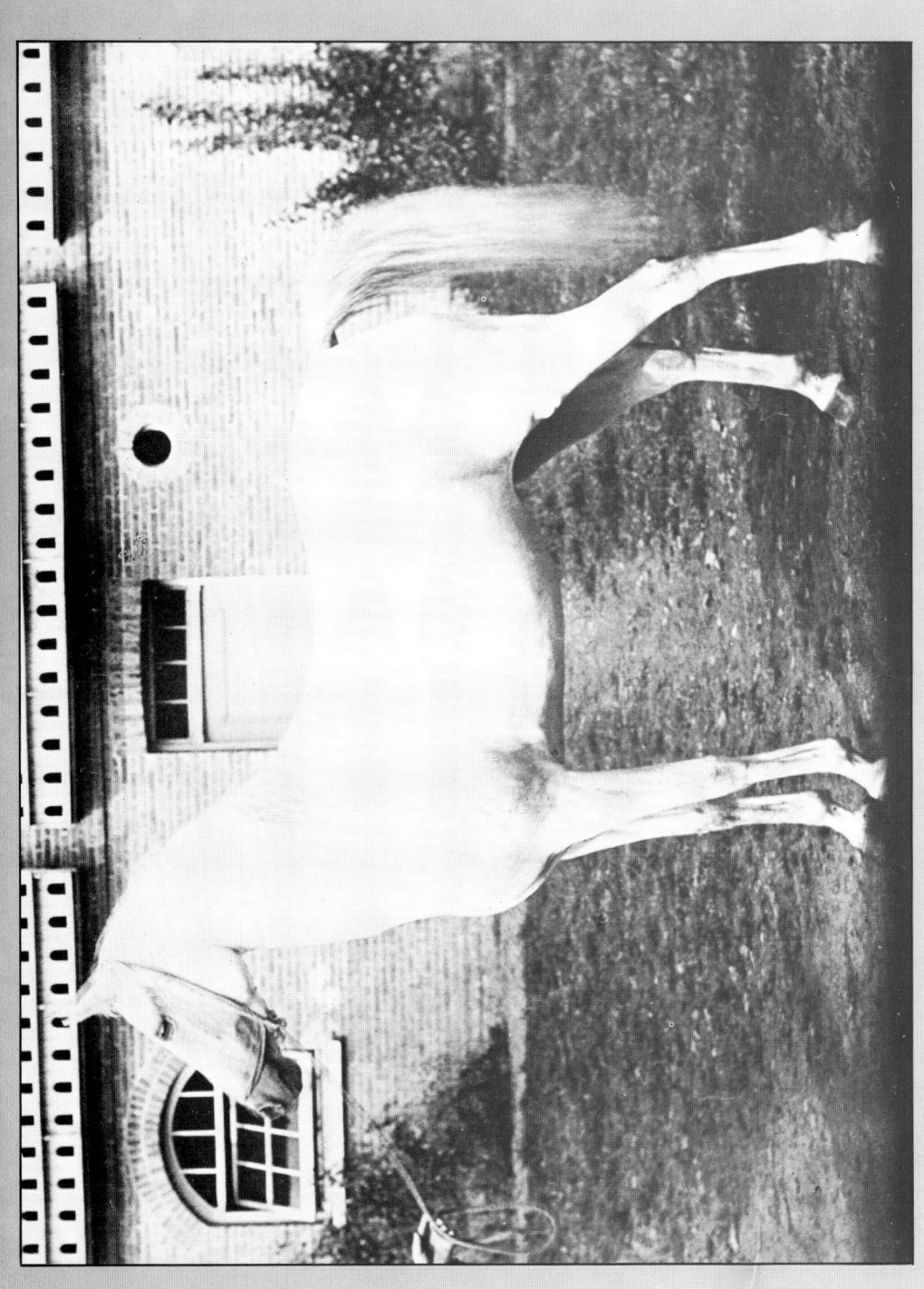

BASILISK

DAJANIA

Purchased at Aleppo on December 25th, 1877. Her foal is Nebuchadnezzar.

FEYSUL

Chestnut stallion purchased in Egypt in December 1908

HADBAN

Bay stallion purchased in Bombay in December, 1883.

MAHRUSS

MESAOUD

Chestnut stallion purchased in Egypt in January, 1889.

QUEEN OF SHEBA

the stud. She is celebrated in the Syrian desert. Sire a Managhi Hedruj of Ibn Gufeyfi of the Gomussa. Purchased in the autumn of 1878 of Beteyen Ibn Mirshid, who owned her on half shares with her breeder. Queen of Sheba's dam was a bay Abeyeh Sherrakieh of the Gomussa belonging to Erheyen Ibn Alian who bred Queen of Sheba and sold her on shares to Beteyen Ibn Mirshid. This mare took us longer to buy than any of the others. We first saw her in 1878 when we were on a visit to Beteyen. He had just brought her to his tent, he holding the bridle share, and at first sight we saw that she was superior to all the mares we had been looking at. Beteyen did not at once refuse to part with her, on the contrary much conversation took place about her between him and Mr Skene who was also at the camp and who undertook to negotiate for us. Mr Skene however unfortunately quarrelled with the Sheykh in a manner which put an end to all hopes of dealing – at least for the time. Our imperfect knowledge of Arabic at that time prevented our being able to counteract the unpleasant impression made on Beteyen by Mr Skene's remarks, and although we knew just enough to make out who was in fault we were helpless to make ourselves understood or to continue bargaining unassisted, and were obliged not only to renounce our hopes but to leave the tribe with this disagreeable incident unexplained. Mr Skene assured us that he could easily send a trustworthy person to buy the mare as soon as the Sheykh's anger should have cooled; we then believed that, though in fault for the quarrel, he would do his best to make the purchase for us, and we placed in his charge the sum of money supposed to be sufficient to complete the transaction. But after our return to England the year passed and still the purchase had not been made. Beteyen, it was said, had been seriously offended and continued to object to whatever was proposed. At last, however, late in the autumn a telegram announced that the mare was to be ours, and soon afterwards, finding that she could not be safely left at Aleppo we had her sent (with Pharaoh, Francolin and Basilisk) to Egypt for the winter. Thus more than two* years passed from our first seeing Queen of Sheba to her arrival at Crabbet. We in fact did not see her until August 1879 on our return from Nejd and India. Destroyed 1901.

RODANIA

Foaled about 1869, a Kehileh of Ibn Rodan (sometimes called 'Rodanyeh' without the prefix Kehileh as Managhy Ibn Sbeyel mares are often called 'Sbeyelyehis'), 14 hands 2 inches.

A chestnut mare near hind foot white to above fetlock and blaze to the mouth with pink on upper lip, fired on quarter, belly and chest, deep jowl, eyes shewing white like the human eye, extraordinary strength and style of going, up to any weight, but uncertain temper. A celebrated mare.

*One year is correct.

Purchased April 12, 1881 in the desert near the Wells of Abu Fayal, of her owner Taïs Ibn Sharban, of the Gomussa tribe of Sebaa Anazeh, who had taken her the previous summer from the Roala. Imported in 1881.

The strain of Kehilan Ajuz of the Rodan is much prized. We had heard of this mare two years before we saw her when on our journey through the Nefud we halted at the well of Shakih. We met there some Roala with a son of Beneyeh Ibn Shaalan, and were told that Beneyeh had quarrelled with his cousin Sotamn Ibn Shaalan, on account of his chestnut mare which Sotamn insisted on having and had taken away from him by force when fair means of persuasion to sell or give had failed. Beneyeh had then left Sotamn to shift for himself in the war with the Sebaa and this withdrawal had contributed to it, it had not caused the reverses experienced by Sotamn who in one of the engagements lost this very mare for whose possession he had sacrificed the interest of his tribe. She was taken by Taïs Ibn Sharban, a Gomussa. We saw him riding her on the 10th of April while we were talking to Afet el Mizrab and Abtan Ibn ed Derri about the latter's Managhyeh (half sister to Meshura). We asked what this chestnut mare was. 'Oh that is Beneyeh Ibn Shaalan's mare,' was the reply. Two days afterwards we bought her, deciding as one must in the desert in a few minutes and having had no opportunity of observing her only defect – a serious one – that of temper. She is the only mare or horse in the stud that can be described as ill tempered and unsafe. She strikes with the forefeet, and kicks too. Her strange temper may possibly be the result of having been knocked about and especially the severe firing she had undergone before we bought her.

Rodania died in 1889.

SAFRA

A Hamdanieh Simrieh. An imported grey mare foaled in 1885. Bred by Mahmud Bay (see under Sobha). Purchased from her breeder and imported in 1891. Sire: Shueyman, a white Shueyman Sbah bred by Ali Pasha Sherif. Dam: Sobha. Safra died 1893.

SHAHWAN

A Dahman Shahwan. A grey stallion foaled in 1887. Sire: Wazir. Dam: a grey Dahmeh Shahwanieh. Dam's grandam, 'the mare of Ibn Khalifeh'. Bred by Ali Pasha Sherif, but foaled in the possession of Mohammed Sadyk Pasha to whom Ali Pasha gave the dam in foal. Purchased from Mohammed Sadyk Pasha in January 1892.

White with black hoofs; about the ears and tail are traces still (in 1892) of the horse having been foaled chestnut. Fine style and surprising carriage of tail, great strength of back and quarters, and free shoulder action. The off knee blemished, said to have been done when a foal.

Shahwan was sold September 1895 to Mr J.A.P. Ramsdell. Exported to U.S.A. (New York). Winner of prizes in America.

SHERIFA

Foaled probably about 1862, a Hamdanieh Simri, 14 hands 2½ inches, girth 65¾ inches below the knee 7⅛ inches.

A white mare with two black hoofs and two white (the two near), a few flea-bitten marks and a dark patch on the off side of the neck, very black skin showing dark when coat is wet; an extraordinary head, very broad forehead very small muzzle, very deep jowl, broad hollow between the jaws, beautiful ears like a gazelle's, large eyes shewing some white, long nostril lying very flat when in repose, with crinkles round the upper end, muzzle very black, except small pink snip on lip, and quite bare of hair in summer (nearly up to the eyes), eyes surrounded by bare black skin (in summer). Good shoulder, great length stands back a little and rather cow hocked, mane and tail of wonderfully fine hair. Scar of spear wound on near quarter just below hip bone. Purchased at Aleppo March 8 1878 for Mr Blunt, by Mr Skene, of the executors of Sheykh Takha Chief of the ibn Ulema of Aleppo. Imported in 1878.

Sherifa was bred in Nejd, her dam a Hamdanieh Simri no certain information of breed of sire but said to be a bay Hamdani Simri at Riad. She was presented by Saoud Ibn Saoud, Emir of Riad, to Takha ed Din Pasha Governor of Mecca, and by him, who brought her to Aleppo, to Sheykh Takha the Chief of the ibn Ulema of that town. On his death, in 1878, she was purchased by his executors for Mr Blunt. Sherifa is 'a unique mare' in more ways than one. Not only as to appearance – though her head surpasses any that we saw in Arabia, but in the stoutness she seems to be equal to the best notwithstanding her age, 19 years. She is of the Nejd type in shape, which we had considered as distinct from the best racing type of Anazeh strains; the strains in fact which have been bred in the northern desert ever since the Anazeh migrated from Nejd and which have in consequence improved in speed; yet she possessed considerably speed as well as staying power. It seemed incredible that an old brood mare, her foal only lately weaned, should after years of idleness, be able suddenly to go into work, as Sherifa did in the summer of 1881. She was then put into harness, perhaps injudiciously for her companion made her do more than her share of the work, and when she found this likely to continue she took to kicking with such pertinacity that she gained her point and harness work was given up. On the last occasion of her being driven she went as a wheeler from Crabbet to Newbuildings and back, 32 miles, and pulled and kicked the whole way going and returning. This was in August, from which time until October 31st she was kept in walking exercise and then given a canter with Pharaoh. The course 2¼ miles which she did in 6m. 30 sec. and then did not want to stop though carrying 12 stone or more. The ground was very rough. Sherifa died in 1892.

SOBHA

A Hamdanieh Simrieh. A white mare foaled in 1879. Bred by Mahmud Bey in Cairo. Sire: Wazir, a white Seglawi Jedran of Ibn Sudan's strain, bred by Ali Pasha Sherif, his dam Ghazieh, a white Seglawieh Jedranieh (original mare) from Ibn Sudan of the Roala tribe bought by Abbas Pasha I Viceroy of Egypt; his sire Zobeyni, a white Seglawi Jedran of Ibn Sbeyni's strain of the Mehed tribe of Fedaan Anazeh (original horse) bought by Abbas Pasha I from Ibn Sbeyni. Wazir a celebrated horse in Egypt and a winner of many races. Wazir died in 1890.

Dam: the Hamdanieh Simrieh (Selma) in Abbas Pasha's stud, purchased by Mahmud Bey with his brother Suleyman Bey at Ismail Pasha's sale of the mares collected by Abbas Pasha. This sale took place about 1868. Mahmud and Suleyman Beys being 'Mamluks' of Ali Pasha Sherif, their horses were kept with his. Mahmud survived Suleyman being still (in 1891) with Ali Pasha Sherif.

Sobha purchased from Mahmud Bey in 1891. Imported in 1891. Sobha sold 1899 to Col. Alexandre de Sdanovich for the Russian Government stud at Derkoul.

IMPORTED HORSES INTRODUCED AFTER LADY ANNE BLUNT'S DEATH

DAFINA

A Kehilet el Krush. White mare bred in Nejd 1921.* Imported through King Ibn Saoud in June 1927. Dam: a Kehilet el Krush. Sire: horse of King Ibn Saoud. Sold to Mrs Elms 1936.

MIRAGE

A Seglawi Jedran Dalia. White stallion bred by the Anazeh tribe. [Exact date of birth unknown.†] Brought by King Faisal of Irak to France and presented to the Italian ambassador Signor de Martino and brought by him to England. [Bought at Tattersalls in 1923.] Sire: a Seglawi Jedran. Dam: a Seglawieh Dalia.

Sold to the USA 1930.

SKOWRONEK

A white Kehilan Ajuz stallion. Bred at Antoniny, Poland 1909‡ by Count J. Potocki. Imported by Mr Walter Winans.

Sire: Ibrahim (imported to Poland from the east by Count Potocki). Dam: Yaskoulka, by Rymnik out of Epopeja, by Dervish out of Lyra.

* The Arab Horse Society Stud Book gives 1926. Dafina's first foal at Crabbet was born in 1928.

† The Stud Book of the Arabian Horse Club of America gives 1909. The Crabbet records indicate it was about 1916.

‡ The English and Polish Arabian Stud Books give 1909. The General Stud Book and the original Potocki pedigree have 1908.

Snow white. Splendid arch of neck and crest. Exquisite head, small sharp cut ears. Enormous strength and breadth of back and loins. Tail set high and arched very high. Dancing prancing action. Purchased in 1920. Died February 1930.

SHEYKH OBEYD STUD

The New Venture (all genuine)

MARES
1. Descendants of Abbas Pasha I collection. (i.e. Mares from stud of Ali Pasha Sherif where they had been preserved, and which came to an end in 1897).
2. Some few direct from Arabia in 1911.
3. And one the dam of which direct from Bahreyn.

STALLIONS
Descendants from collection of Abbas Pasha I.
Two direct from Arabia.

AIDA
A Kehilet el Krush (stated to be the first mare of that strain ever to be brought out of Arabia). Bay mare foaled in 1910. 4 white feet, near hind almost over fetlock, off hind half up cannon bone, near front narrow rim round coronet, off front to beneath fetlock: blaze like star with narrow strip to between nostrils, fine prominent eyes.

Sire: chestnut Hamdani Simri. Dam: grey Kehilet el Krush. Purchased through Ali el Abdallah el Bassam, arrived at Sheykh Obeyd Dec: 11 1911 after a four months' journey. [Fate unknown.]

ANTAR
A Hamdani Simri. A grey stallion bred by Mahmud Bey in Cairo in 1890. Sire: Aziz. Dam: Sobha. Dark grey, very beautiful head, broad forehead, small muzzle. Purchased with his dam from his breeder in January 1891. Antar was sold in 1899 to H. Brook Greville esq., Manager of the Bank of Egypt, Cairo branch.*

AZIZA
A Seglawieh Jedranieh of Ibn Sbeyni's strain. A chestnut mare foaled April 2 1900 at Zeytun near Cairo.

Sire: Aziz. Dam: Bint Jamila. Purchased with her dam and her half sister from Mons. J. Valensin, April 19 1901. Sold January 1912 to Mahmud Mutlak.

* Antar was nevertheless used at stud by Lady Anne Blunt on a number of later occasions.

AZZ (BINT BINT-AZZ)
A Dahmeh Shahwanieh, a white mare foaled in 1895–6. Bred by Ali Pasha Sherif in Cairo. Sire: Ibn Nura. Dam: Bint Azz. Purchased May 11 1906 from Othman Bey Sherif. [Sent to Crabbet 1910. Destroyed in 1916 s.p.]

BINT BINT-JAMILA EL KEBIRA
A Seglawieh Jedranieh of Ibn Sbeyni's strain. A grey mare foaled in 1894. Sire: Aziz. Dam: Bint Jamila. Bred by Ali Pasha Sherif and purchased from the Daïra of Ali Pasha Sherif, Jan: 1897. Destroyed after an accident, 1898.

BINT EL BAHREYN
A Dahmeh Shahwanieh. A bay mare foaled in 1898. Bright bay with four white feet. Bred by Aissa Ibn Khalifeh, Sheykh of Bahreyn in 1898 and brought by him as a gift to Abbas Pasha II, Khedive of Egypt in 1903. Purchased from H. H. the Khedive on Dec: 26 1907. Sold 1912.

BINT FEREYHA
A Seglawieh Jedranieh of Ibn Sbeyni's strain entered in the register of Ali Pasha Sherif as 'Bint Fereyha el Saghira'. A white mare foaled in 1884. Sire: Aziz. Dam: Fereyha. Bred by Ali Pasha Sherif and purchased from him Dec: 14 1896. Died Jan. 24 1905.

BINT HORRA
A Seglawieh Jedranieh of Ibn Sudan's strain. A white mare foaled 1889. White with black hoofs. Bred by Ali Pasha Sherif. Sire: Aziz. Dam: Horra. Purchased from the Daïra of the late Ali Pasha Sherif, with her filly foal by Ibn Nura, Mar: 26 1897. Died Sept. 1897.

BINT JAMILA
A Seglawieh Jedranieh of Ibn Sbeyni's strain. A white mare foaled Jan 21 1881. Sire: Shueyman. Dam: Jamila. Purchased April 19 1901 from M. Jacques Valensin. Bint Jamila was bought by Mons. J. Valensin in Mar: 1897 from the Daïra of Ali Pasha Sherif. Died 1901.

(BINT) NOMA
A Kehilet Ajuz of the Nowak strain. A bay mare foaled in 1901. Bred by Prince Ahmed Kemal Pasha at Mataria in 1901. Sire: Dahman el Azrak, a white fleabitten Dahman Shahwan. Dam: Noma. Purchased from Prince Yusef, only son and heir of Ahmed Pasha Jan: 9 1908. Sold with Yashmak to Abd el Wahab 1912.

BINT RODA
A Seglawieh Jedranieh of a strain from the collection of Abbas Pasha I. A white fleabitten mare foaled in 1896. Black hoofs. Bred by Prince Ahmed Kemal Pasha. Sire: Jamil. Dam: Roda. Purchased from Prince Yusef Bey in April 1909. Given away 1912.

DOHAYYA
A Hamdanieh Simrieh. Grey mare foaled in 1909. Sire: Seglawi Jedran of Ibn Zobeyni's strain. Dam: Hamdanieh Simrieh descended from the mare of Abdallah et Feysul Ibn Saoud. Purchased through Ali el Abdallah el Bassam. Arrived at Sheykh Obeyd Dec 11: 1911. Sold April 7 1916 to Ahmed Shafee.

FASIHA (BINT BINT-FEREYHA EL KEBIRA)
A Seglawieh Jedranieh of Ibn Sbeyni's strain. A grey mare foaled in 1892. Nearly white 1897, black patches on knees and hocks. Sire: Ibn Sherara, a white Kehilan Ajuz of the Jellabi strain. Dam: Bint Fereyha. Bred by Ali Pasha Sherif in Cairo. Purchased from Abd el Hamid Bey Sherif, son of Ali Pasha Sherif Jan: 20 1897. Died winter of 1914.

GHAZALA (BINT BINT-HELWA)
A Seglawieh Jedranieh of Ibn Sudan's strain. A grey mare foaled about May or June 1896. Grey *mawardi*, off hind leg white and blaze narrow above and spreading on muzzle ending pink. Bred by Ali Pasha Sherif. Sire: Ibn Sherara. Dam: Bint Helwa. Purchased from Ali Pasha Sherif Dec: 14 1896. Sold Sept. 1909 to Spencer Borden, U.S.A.

GHAZIEH (BINT BINT-HORRA)
A Seglawieh Jedranieh of Ibn Sudan's strain. A bay mare foaled 1897. Bay, small patch of white above off front hoof (the inside half) and white rim above off hind hoof all round; rather large star above eyes, black hoofs. Sire: Ibn Nura. Dam: Bint Horra. Purchased with her dam from the Daïra of the late Ali Pasha Sherif Mar: 26 1897. Destroyed March 19, 1916.

IBN NURA
A Dahman Nejib. A white stallion bred by Ali Pasha Sherif about 1876. Sire: Sottam, a grey fleabitten Dahman Nejib bred by Ali Pasha Sherif; his dam the white Dahmeh Nejiba (original mare) of Khalil el Hajry; his sire Sueyd a fleabitten Seglawi Jedran (original horse) from Ibn Sudan of the Roala tribe. Dam: Bint Nura.

A fleabitten white. Magnificent horse, head splendid and splendidly set on; neck shoulder and style perfection. Purchased January 15 1897 at the first auction of the remnant of Ali Pasha Sherif's stud by order of the 'curator' Sabit Pasha, at the stables of the Daïra in the Ismailia quarter of Cairo. Ibn Nura died in the spring of 1903.

JAMIL
A Seglawi Jedran of Ibn Sbeyni's strain of the Mehed tribe of Fedaan Anazeh. A chestnut stallion bred by Ali Pasha Sherif in Cairo 1896. Sire: Aziz. Dam: Bint-Jamila. Dark chestnut with some white hairs on flanks, 4 white feet, blaze. Purchased 1901 from Mons. J. Valensin acting for Mon-

sieur Suarès (who had bought Jamil in March 1897 from the Daïra of Ali Pasha Sherif). Presented to the Government breeding Stud at Behtim in March 1917.

JAMILA

A Seglawieh Jedranieh of Ibn Sbeyni's strain. A grey mare foaled on Mar: 18 1901. Grey near front foot white to over fetlock and star. Sire: Sabbah a grey Manaki Hedruj. Dam: Bint Jamila. Purchased with her dam Bint Jamila and her half sister Aziza from Mons. J. Valensin April: 19, 1901. Sold March 3 1906 to F. Eugene Mason.

JAUZA

A Kehilet el Krush. Chestnut mare foaled in 1909. Purchased through Ali el Abdallah el Bassam and arrived Sheykh Obeyd August 1913. Sire: Dahman Shahwan of Sheykh Mubarak ibn Sabah, Amir of Koweyt. Dam: Kehilet el Krush, favourite mare of the late Sheykh Sultan el Duish. [Fate unknown.]

KRUSH

A Kehilan el Krush. Grey stallion bred in 1909. Sire: Kehilan el Sueti of the Harb stock. Dam: grey Kehilet el Krush whose dam was the mare of Ammash el Reja el Duish, known as the 'white Krush' famed for her speed. Purchased in the desert in 1911. [Fate unknown.]

MANOKTA (BINT MAKBULA EL SAGHIRA)

A Kehilet Ajuz of the Jellabi strain belonging to Ibn Khalifeh, Sheykh of Bahreyn. A grey mare foaled 1894. Grey *marwardi* with light spots and blaze. Bred by Ali Pasha Sherif. Sire: Nasr, a bay Dahman Shahwan bred by Ali Pasha Sherif. Dam: Makbula. Purchased Mar: 31 1897 from Mohammed Bey Khuddr Ibn Khuddr Agha. Given to B. V. Noel and exported to Greece Feb 1906.

MEZNA

A Dahmeh Shahwanieh, foaled in 1903. Dark chestnut mare, no white except *seyal*. Bred by H. H. Khedive Abbas Pasha II at Kubba. Sire: Antar (ibn Muniet el Nefus) chestnut Hamdani Simri. Dam: Meshura. Purchased Nov: 26 1909 from Bedr Mohammed. [Fate unknown.]

RODA

A Seglawieh Jedranieh of a strain from the collection of Abbas Pasha I Viceroy of Egypt. Bay mare foaled in 1906. Bay, near hind foot white to below fetlock, no other white. Bred by Prince Ahmed Kemal Pasha at Mataria in 1906. Sire: Sabbah. Dam: Bint Roda. Purchased from Prince Yusef Bey Jan 9 1908. Sold Nov 6 1912 to Mohammed Ahmed el Minshawi.

SAADE
A Kehilet Ajuz of Ibn Aafas. Bay mare foaled in 1909. Sire: Kehilan el Dhobyeh of the Saadun Sheykhs. Dam: a Kehilet Ajuz of Ibn Aafas descended from mare of Mohammed el Abdallah Ibn Rashid. Purchased through Ali el Abdallah of Oneyzeh in Kasim. Arrived in Sheykh Obeyd Dec. 11 1911. Died Jan 16, 1917.

SAADUN (previously called ABEYAN)
An Abeyan Sherrak. Bay stallion bred by Sheykh Meshara Ibn Saadun, of the Montefyk ruling Sheykhs, in 1906. Sire: Abeyan Sherrak. Dam: Abeyeh Sherrakieh. Purchased from his breeder in the desert in 1911. Won three races. Died September, 1917 (evidently from dourine disease).

SABAH
A Kehilet Ajuz of the Mimreh strain. A bay mare foaled in 1906. Bay, blaze shaped like hour-glass, no other white. Bred by Prince Ahmed Kemal Pasha at Mataria in 1906. Sire: Rabdan, a grey Kehilan Ajuz. Dam: Om Shebaka. Purchased from Prince Yusef Bey Jan: 9 1908. Exchanged Nov 26 1909 with Bedr Mohammed for a dark chestnut Dahmah Shahwanieh. [See Mezna.]

SAHAB
A Dahman Shahwan. A white stallion bred by Othman Bey Sherif (son of Ali Pasha Sherif) in Cairo, 1903. Sire: Kaukab, white Dahman Nejib, his dam Bint Nura, his sire Ibn Sherara; Kaukab the property of Yusef Bey Sherif, given to him by his father before the 'interdict'. Dam: Azz. Purchased November, 1909 from Timur Bey. Timur Bey bought the horse from Othman Bey in 1905, and named him 'Ramses' but was unable to manage him; in fact Sahab was perfectly wild when brought to Sheykh Obeyd Stud. [Fate unknown.]

SHERIF
A Hamdani Simri. A white stallion bred in Cairo 1887 by Mahmud Bey. Sire: Ibn Nadir, a white Seglawi Jedran of Ibn Sbeyni's strain bred by Ali Pasha Sherif. His dam Samha, a Seglawieh Jedranieh (original mare) from Ibn Sbeyni, his sire Nadir. Dam: Sobha. Purchased December 1895 from Mahmud Bey Akif. Sherif was sold in April 1898 to the Egyptian Horse Breeding Commission.

YEMAMA
A Kehilet Ajuz of the Jellabi strain, formerly belonging to Ibn Khalifeh, Sheykh of Bahreyn. A bay mare foaled in 1885. Purchased from Ali Pasha Sherif by Moharrem Pasha. Purchased from Moharrem Pasha, through Ali Bey, March 1892. Given away in 1906 to El Shafei el Tihawi.

CHAPTER 7

Partition
1906

The Ali Pasha Sherif mares did not remain for long in the background. Bint Nura was the first to be shown when in 1898 she was placed second to Rosemary in the Arab brood mares class at the Crystal Palace Show. In Lady Anne's opinion the only reason Rosemary was preferred was because the judges admired her foal, the filly Rakima by Mesaoud.

Before that, however, had occurred what Blunt called an 'abominable' incident. One morning at the beginning of June, Bint Helwa had been turned out with Fulana and Johara in the field opposite the entrance to Newbuildings. As Lady Anne described it, 'the three mares appeared perfectly quiet, and did not attempt to gallop about. But it seems no sooner were they left to themselves than they wanted to come home'. They rushed through the fencing at the far end of the meadow, near the corner where the road to Trawlers Farm turns off, over the bank and the ditch and onto the road, where 'Bint Helwa was found with her leg broken, standing waiting, by Webb, who when the other two came home, went to see what had happened'. She had managed to hobble almost to Newbuildings gate.

Both Webb and the vet, a man called Grace, were in favour of putting the mare down but Blunt would not consent. 'I sent for you to vet the mare's leg, not to shoot her,' he told Grace. Thereupon with great difficulty, Bint Helwa was 'got up the hill, into the yard and under the roof of the hovel, where an admirable sling was arranged by Webb. There were splints made of elm bark, which seemed as good a plan as could have been hit on. Plaster of Paris could not have been used in this case.'

By the middle of September she was still gradually improving and 'if when the time comes for trying to use the muscles of the leg, no mistake is made by too much hurry, and that care is taken in cautiously bending the joints gently for the mare, not letting her do it for herself at first, there seems a fair chance of her being able to hobble about

Bint Helwa with her filly by Mesaoud

without much suffering'. And this is in fact what the Blunts did, depriving her of the sling by stages as she grew stronger. In time Bint Helwa was able even to trot though her leg was 'frightfully misshapen'. The incident is made all the more remarkable by the fact that ten days before breaking her leg, Bint Helwa had been covered by Mesaoud. On April 18th she foaled, 'no one being present and she and the foal were found together, all well, in the morning'. Lady Anne observed a curious feature of the foal: 'Foal's front legs sometimes held exactly in the position of the dam's broken limb, bent inwards and as if weak, but it seems able to do this at will. Sometimes the off leg is thus held, at other times the near one, at other times again both. As if the mare... had transmitted it to the mind of the foal.' This characteristic disappeared after a few months but unfortunately the filly died in 1899 in an epidemic of strangles that attacked all the yearling fillies at Crabbet. The Bint Helwa yearling was the third fatality and 'by far the greatest loss', more so as it happened, since the Bint Helwa line died out completely at the Stud itself.

In 1898 the Blunts' main rival as a breeder of Arabians decided to sell many of her horses. Illness, mounting financial problems and disease among her horses had become too great a burden for Miss Dillon and she put most of her stud up for auction, without reserve, in the small Oxfordshire town of Chipping Norton. She kept a few, but in 1905 sold the nucleus of these to Spencer Borden in America, including Imamzada, the grandson of her beloved El Emir.

The Stud deficit at Crabbet for 1898 was the worst they had yet suffered, approximately £1,500, and Blunt proposed to Lady Anne that she increase her subsidy by a further £1,000 per annum instead of paying for the various expenses as they occurred. There was the option of reducing their stock but Blunt thought it would not be easy to replace them. 'Twenty-five brood mares is not too many for a stud which has the position of ours,' he wrote. 'If we are overstocked (which I do not think we are) the practical way is to breed no more for several years, but I think this would in many ways be a pity, nor do I think we are unable to afford £1,500 a year on a hobby which gives us all so much pleasure – you had better consult Judith about this.'

Judith was then in Egypt with Lady Anne and though much involved in the affairs of the Stud, had her mind on a very different matter. She was now twenty-five years old. She had 'come out' and done a season in London like all other girls in her position. She had had many suitors but had never cared for the life that society seemed to offer and was always happier in the country than in London. She and her mother had often been to stay with the Lyttons at Knebworth, where she had met the Lyttons' youngest son Neville, then aged only nineteen. Neville's father Robert, 1st Earl of Lytton, had become a friend of Wilfrid Blunt in 1863 when they had both been attachés in the Embassy at Lisbon. Drawn together by a common love for poetry, they had remained close to each other despite their differing political beliefs. Lord Lytton had gone on to become Viceroy of India and British Ambassador in Paris, where he died in 1891. Four years later his widow, Edith, had been appointed Lady of the Bedchamber to Queen Victoria.

Both the Blunts were fond of Neville and were delighted when he proposed. But they had their doubts about the match on account of his age and when Neville visited Newbuildings in August 1898 to ask for permission to marry Judith, Blunt advised him to think about it and come back in a year's time. This was not to be. On October 1st that year, when out shooting at Crookhorn, Judith told her father that she had become engaged. The official announcement was made on October 14th. Queen Victoria was reported by Neville's mother to be 'deeply interested' though she was also said to have her reservations because of the possible effect on Neville of Blunt's political views. On a less exalted level, Cowie amused Lady Anne by remarking, 'Oh, how dreadful, I did hope for a little peace and quiet.'

It was decided that the marriage should be held in Cairo and in

November that year Judith and Lady Anne set off, travelling *via* Paris where Neville was studying art. Blunt had not recovered sufficiently from an illness the previous winter to enable him to accompany them and felt his duties were done when he persuaded his old protagonist, Lord Cromer, the Consul-General, to give Judith away at the ceremony.

The wedding took place on February 2nd, 1899, in the Roman Catholic church at Zeytun. 'I could not describe the scene, am too tired, but it was brilliant,' wrote Lady Anne. Lord Cromer had put at their disposal his carriage and the Residency's *syces*, resplendent in their dress uniform, and all had gone according to plan. After the marriage ceremony a Mass had been held. Luncheon was then taken by the guests and at three o'clock the bride and bridegroom left for their honeymoon at Sheykh Obeyd. From the station at Ezbet en Nakhle they were escorted to the Pink House by Abu Tawil's horsemen and Mutlak, mounted on Shieha, while Lady Anne 'galloped round by the *serai* to fetch the keys which had been left there. Then left Judith and Neville in possession. They looked the picture of happiness.'

In the evening Lady Anne gave a celebration feast to the *fellaheen* of the five neighbouring villages, for which *The Times* noted that "a whole flock" of sheep were killed. Queen Victoria was moved to cable Lord Cromer to ask if all had gone well, to which Cromer drily replied: 'Marriage duly performed.' In Sussex, *The Horsham Times* (which for some reason contrived to be ten days earlier with its notice than Fleet Street) announced the presentation to the couple of an illuminated address from the tenants on the Crabbet estate. After spending some weeks at Sheykh Obeyd, the Lyttons returned to Paris where Neville continued his art studies.

In England meanwhile Blunt had been entertaining Prince Scherbatoff and his brother-in-law, Count Stroganoff, and was optimistic that they would recommend the Russian Government to buy horses from Crabbet. His hopes were fulfilled, for that summer a Colonel de Sdanovitch came to the Crabbet sale and bought altogether six animals, including the ageing mare Sobha. He also wanted to buy Mesaoud but was told by Lady Anne that 'that could not be at any price this year'.

While Lady Anne had been in Egypt, Blunt had purchased Fernycroft, thirty-one acres of woodland in the New Forest. His anxiety over his day to day finances did not apparently extend to his capital account. In 1898 Trawlers Farm, some 375 acres of pasture and woodland adjoining Newbuildings, had been put up for sale. Unbeknown to Lady Anne at the time, Blunt raised a mortgage of £15,000 on Crabbet and used it to buy Trawlers for £7,600 excluding the timber. Fernycroft cost him £1,000 and in 1901 he rounded off the Newbuildings estate, making it he said, 'complete . . . and as pretty as any in England,' by buying Marlpost Wood and its timber for £3,200.

Blunt spent much of the next few years at Fernycroft, sometimes with Lady Anne but usually on his own. He had had at the outset a typically grandiose scheme for making it 'a branch headquarters' of the Stud but the idea never materialised, although at one time a few mares and some young stock were sent there for the grazing. He had also had a plan to cross one of the Crabbet stallions with pony breeds and bought some Exmoor ponies to run with Nejran, but this too did not last long. The only prolonged experiment the Blunts made with cross-breeding was with Arab stallions and Suffolk mares in the early days of the Stud, which did indeed produce some very fine heavyweight horses for driving. To encourage the improvement of local stock they also allowed their horses to be used on a few outside mares of different breeds.

In 1900 Lady Anne arrived home from Egypt to find that Blunt had put Azrek's son Ahmar on the sale list for that year. This did not please her, for apart from being one of their few representatives of the Azrek line, Ahmar was getting stock of great quality. In particular Lady Anne remarked upon one of his daughters, the four-year-old Siwa, out of Sobha, who had 'not had a saddle on since last year yet she behaved as if she had been ridden daily'. In fact Sobha's family itself was notable for 'its admirable cleverness as well as good temper'. In spite of his colour, Lady Anne had a distinct preference for the grey Seyal, Sobha's son by Mesaoud, over Rosemary's son Rejeb.

Ahmar was not included in the sale, which was not a success in any case. Attendance was poor as many of those invited stayed in London for news of the Peking legations, then besieged by the Boxers. The horses did not show themselves well in the ring and in the end only three were sold. The main item of interest was the purchase afterwards by the Rev. D.B. Montefiore of the mare Barakat for thirty guineas. Montefiore then promptly resold Barakat to the American Mr Eustis for eighty guineas. This so annoyed Lady Anne that when Montefiore wished to buy Sefina, she refused to sell her to him. Montefiore later became the principal co-founder and first Secretary of the Arab Horse Society.

above Sobha, purchased in Egypt in 1891.
'Delightful as a companion and to ride'
below Mares and foals at Crabbet. From left: Risala, Ridaa, the grey Bozra and Rose of Sharon

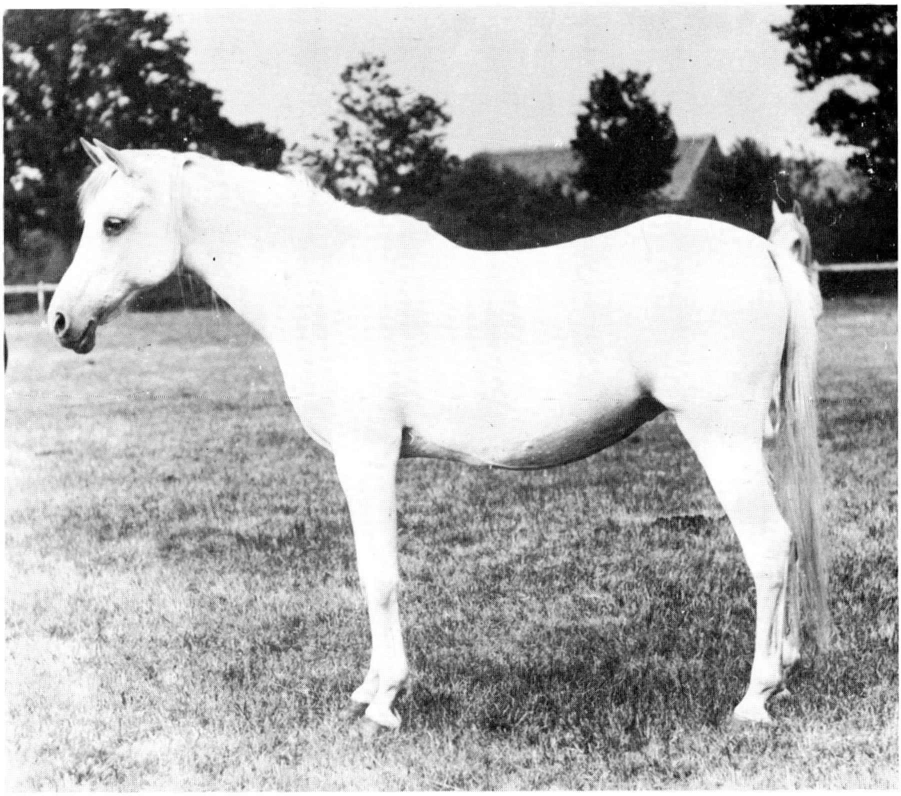

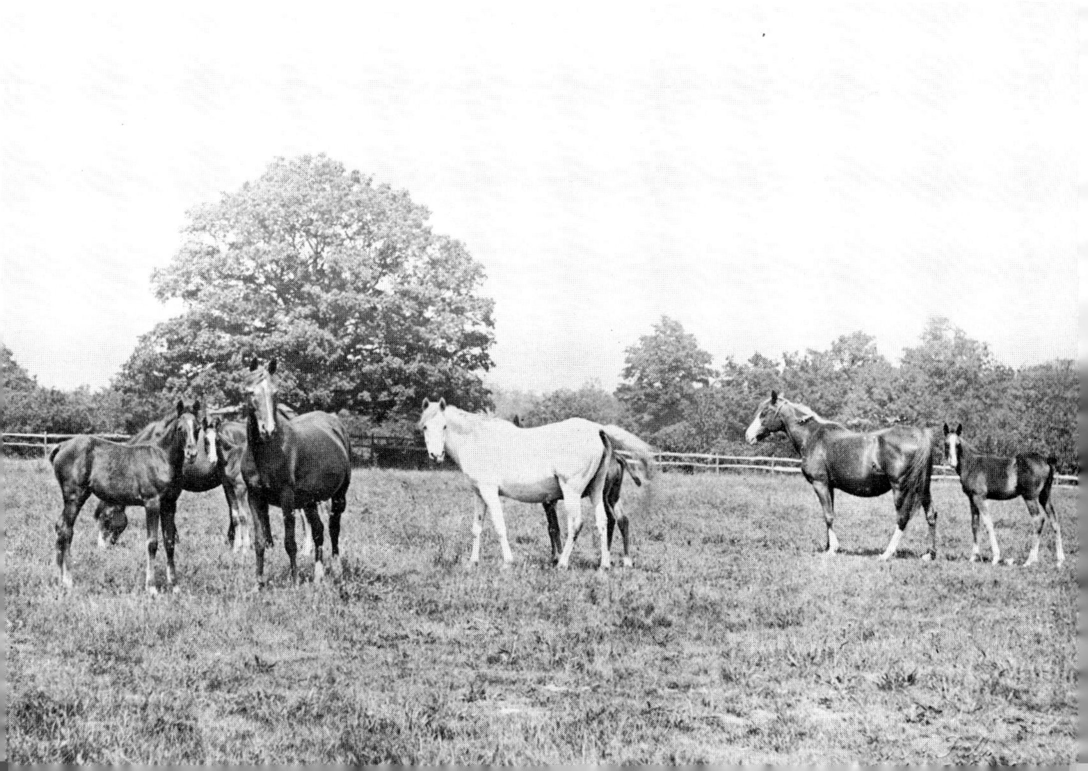

The most important event of the year was the International Exhibition in Paris. It was to include a Horse Show with classes for Arabians in which the best in Europe had been entered. The Blunts had been making plans for it for a long time and had decided to send over nine horses – Mesaoud, Seyal and Abu Khasheb as the stallions and Bint Nura, Rosemary, Bozra (by Pharaoh out of Basilisk), Nejiba (by Azrek out of Nefisa), Mabruka (by Azrek out of Meshura) and Makbula as their mares. Seyal was not in fact exhibited as he hit his head on the way out and suffered a haemorrhage from the nostril. Webb went with the horses and Blunt followed a week later. He found on his arrival on September 4th that the prospects were far from promising. The ripples from the Fashoda incident two years earlier, when France and Britain had nearly come to blows over a 'sandbank', had not abated and there was a strong anti-British feeling. The judges, Blunt noted scornfully, were mostly 'French military men of the same class that sat in court martial on Dreyfus'. To cap it all, the Sultan of Turkey had not only bent the rule that prohibited him from competing by entering his horses under the false name of Muzaffer Pasha, but had also contrived to have his own Inspector of Studs and the manager of the Ottoman Horse Show appointed as judges.

As Blunt had expected, the Sultan's horses swept the board. First prize went to a 'small black stallion, whose colour is his chief recommendation', while the Sultan's best horse (in Blunt's opinion) was not even placed. The Crabbet horses took four prizes; Mesaoud was placed fourth in the stallion class and Bozra, Makbula and Rosemary came fourth, fifth and sixth respectively in the mares' class. According to Blunt the only honest part of the Show was the list of results, which described their awards not as prizes but as recompenses, 'it being not even pretended that the judging is according to merit, the medals being awarded to the exhibitors rather than to the beasts'. But it was not a total disaster; the Crabbet contingent had had many admirers, people 'of a serious kind', and Count Stroganoff bought Makbula for a good price.

The sale of Makbula was not, however, all the good fortune it seemed to be. For on his return to England, Blunt proceeded to claim the sale money for himself. It was not the first time he had appropriated such receipts. On this occasion his action deeply upset Lady Anne. 'Now I will here record that Makbula was actually bought and paid for by me (like many others, in fact most original mares and *all* the Ali Pasha

Sherif ones, several of them against Wilfrid's wishes, as he was always trying to stop my getting them).' With the Stud usually showing a loss, Lady Anne very reasonably maintained that all sale proceeds should be paid into the Stud account. Moreover Lady Anne (self-styled the universal provider) was then paying the expenses of three separate households; Newbuildings and Fernycroft for herself and Wilfrid, and a house at Cheyne Gardens, in London, that she had rented for Judith and Neville Lytton. She had recently suffered losses through poor investment advice and the incident of Makbula struck her as a serious matter. If she was to be able to act as universal provider to her family, she must, she decided, make herself more independent. She accordingly engaged a new solicitor, Francis Smith, to look after her affairs in place of her previous lawyer, Chandler, who had acted for both her and Blunt.

In the summer of 1901 an accident occurred at Sheykh Obeyd that made headlines in the press.

Whenever the Blunts were away, Mutlak had strict orders to allow no one into the garden. This was partly for the sake of the horses and partly because the grounds were kept as a sanctuary for wild life. They were also a natural haven for foxes. One Sunday morning at about five o'clock, a group of officers from the 11th Hussars entered and started to draw the garden with their pack of hounds. Mutlak and the others, 'to whom the arbitrary ways of English foxhunters were altogether a novelty', tried to expel the intruders in accordance with the Blunts' instructions and as *The Field* reported, "something very like a free fight took place". The upshot of the matter was that after proceedings of a murky legality, Mutlak and two other servants were sentenced to terms of imprisonment of between three and six months.

The Blunts were enraged. To Wilfrid it typified 'the unscrupulous methods' used by the administration to 'hide its tampering with the Law Courts and whitewash the misdeeds of the Army of Occupation', while Lady Anne thought that the officer chiefly concerned had behaved 'in the most outrageous manner'. Upon appeal, the sentences were reduced to two months for two of the men and one month for the third. This did not mollify Blunt and he took up the matter with Lord Lansdowne, the Minister of Foreign Affairs, besides bombarding the newspapers with letters of indignation. Questions were asked in Parliament, the Government issued a Blue Paper on the incident and the affair generally simmered away for a year or more until Blunt decided to attack Lord Cromer personally, declaring with colourful licence that 'in big game shooting it is safest to leave the antelopes alone and go straight for the rhinoceros'. With the ensuing publicity Blunt felt that he had run that particular hare far enough and allowed the matter to drop.

An indirect result of this and other of Blunt's tirades against the British administration in Egypt, was the cancellation of a visit which the Khedive, Abbas Pasha II, was scheduled to make to Crabbet in 1903. A special train had been laid on for him to Three Bridges and elaborate arrangements made for his entertainment. At the last minute the Blunts received a cable that owing to 'unexpected circumstances' the Khedive could no longer come to Crabbet. 'H.M. the King must have stepped in', wrote Lady Anne. Five months later they heard in Egypt that the Khedive had been told that the King would be angry if he went to Crabbet. So far as politics were concerned, Wilfrid Blunt was beyond the pale.

The Stud was now in good shape overall and the young horses were very promising. Lady Anne was particularly pleased with Astraled (by Mesaoud out of Queen of Sheba) who 'should not be parted with lightly with his action and quality and colour, in spite of the imperfect profile'. Blunt too thought him beautiful, 'a little race-horse if ever there was one'. Mesaoud's son Daoud (out of Bint Nura) also pleased Lady Anne, who rode him often. She especially admired his action and was strongly opposed when Blunt mentioned the possibility of selling him.

The sale of 1901 was among the most successful ever held. For the first time, Blunt put the horses in Arab *reshmehs*,* 'much to the disgust of the stable people but I knew it would add at least 20 guineas a head to the prices given'. Twelve out of the twenty horses were sold for an average price of about £150. Four horses were bought by the Indian Government, three by Boucaut for Australia, two went to Java and one to Germany. Six weeks later the stallions Regib and Riaz were sold to Japan.

By contrast the sale of 1902 was the least profitable, although socially the most exalted. It was the year of Edward VII's coronation for which many Colonial Prime Ministers had gathered in London. To the officials looking after them, a visit to the Crabbet auction must have appeared an ideal diversion. In conjunction with the British

*Bit-less bridles.

SALE DAY IN 1902

above Wilfrid Blunt greeting the Maharajah of Kashmir
right H. H. The Sultan of Perak arriving
below Lady Anne Blunt receiving guests

Empire League and the fledgeling Automobile Club, a cavalcade of fourteen cars was organised to carry the guests from London to Crabbet. The weather was perfect and the affair 'a brilliant function'. The principal guest was Princess Louise of Schleswig-Holstein who annoyed Blunt by insisting on being shown around after the sale when he only wanted to relax.

The following year Lady Anne had an accident when riding with Blunt to Three Bridges station. At a narrow part of the lane they met a traction engine at which Lady Anne's horse baulked. The driver tried to help and tugged at its bridle whereupon the horse pulled back, lost its balance and fell with Lady Anne underneath. Though in great pain she was able to continue to the station in a fly and thence to Newbuildings where she was kept in bed for several days. The anecdote about her calling in the vet instead of the doctor probably arose on this occasion, when she sent for Grace 'as I did not want to have a regular doctor if it can be avoided'. No damage had been done and the most hurtful aspect was a report in *The Evening Globe* which not only cast aspersions on her ability to sit tight but also asserted that the Crabbet horses were 'badly broken in and dangerous creatures'. Lady Anne was actually an excellent horsewoman. She had light hands and was an extremely sensitive and sympathetic rider. She always took charge of the young or difficult horses, for as Blunt wrote of her after her death, she had 'inexhaustible patience and loved the beasts she rode too entirely ever to lose her temper with them'.

By 1903 Judith and Neville Lytton had a young family. Anthony had been born in 1900, Anne in 1901 and Winifrid was to be born shortly. They now decided to move to Forest Cottage, a house on the Crabbet estate near Worth. For some time Blunt had been considering making over Crabbet to Judith so as to reduce death duties. He had not yet fully recovered from his illness in 1898 and now 62, felt he could hardly live long. After much consultation with his lawyers, on September 17th, 1904 he signed a trust deed giving Crabbet estate to his daughter. Judith had wanted Neville to have a life interest in the estate as well but Blunt refused as Neville was not a blood relation. Blunt made his cousin George Wyndham remainderman after Judith and her issue as 'he was my nearest male relation . . . I had looked upon him as the inheritor after me of our family traditions, and in some measure of my family possessions as trustee and knowing all'. The Lordship of the Manor of Worth and Oram was kept by Blunt, with Worth Forest,

above Bukra (Ahmar–Bozra)
centre Ahmar
(Azrek–Queen of Sheba)
below Berk (Seyal–Bukra)

Springfield, the estate at Newbuildings and the ground at Beeding. On Michaelmas Day that year, Blunt ceased to own Crabbet. 'I went down there and spent a long afternoon wandering in the woods and bidding them farewell, a day of great beauty with a sun as hot as summer.' The Lyttons were unable to move into Crabbet house immediately since the lease of the present tenant had not expired.

Two other aspects of the settlement should be mentioned. One, the condition imposed by Blunt that Judith change her name to Blunt-Lytton;* and the other, that in addition to now owning Crabbet, Judith also found herself responsible for paying the interest on Blunt's mortgage of £15,000.

The same month Feysul and his two sons, Ibn Yemama and Ibn Yashmak, arrived from Sheykh Obeyd Stud. 'The old horse is indeed a little lion', wrote Blunt admiringly. It is interesting that he should have referred to Feysul as 'old' for the horse was only ten. Blunt's comment may have been prompted by an air about him of premature old age that seems to have been common among their Egyptian horses. At any rate Feysul was to live until the age of 23 and was a valuable addition to the Crabbet Stud. After his first crop of foals had arrived, Lady Anne noted that they had 'quality to a high degree'.

Another horse that was showing much promise at the time was Berk, by Seyal out of Bukra. Though only a yearling he was already demonstrating the qualities for which he was to become famous. After a visit to Crabbet, Lady Anne wrote 'but *the* sight of all was Berk lunged, as his action is magnificent – he was a perfect picture in motion and recalled Queen of Sheba, Azrek and Ahmar (this last his grandsire)'.

These were happy enough days but trouble was on its way. The Blunts were now spending much of their time apart. To understand the background to the unhappiness and discord that were periodically to envelop the whole family and eventually to threaten the very existence of the Stud, it is necessary to know a little of their mutual relationships.

Neville Lytton once wrote that Blunt's greatest mistake was not dying at a romantic age. He also said that Blunt lived in an 'electric atmosphere of storm' and that he had a great sense of the reverence due to himself as a husband and father. As a young man, Blunt had been handsome, captivating and brilliant, almost another Byron. But by 1904, age and illness had diminished those qualities and to his family at

*Judith Lytton assumed the name Blunt-Lytton by deed poll on August 24th, 1904.

least he could appear more often than not as a vain and insensitive tyrant.

For years Lady Anne had endured and forgiven his ways and probably would have continued so to do had her home life been unaffected by the other women in Blunt's life. Not only was she grateful for much that he had given her, but she had also loved him with a sincerity and depth that he may have never comprehended. She had always sought for unity in her family, but her tolerance was not infinite. Beneath that gentle exterior lay a good measure of the inner strength that had carried her through their desert journeys. Devoted though she was to her husband, there was a limit to the indignities and wounds that she could stand.

One of the chief causes of the final breach was Blunt's nurse, Miss Elizabeth Lawrence. She had been engaged in 1898, at the age of thirty-six, to help during one of Blunt's illnesses. For the rest of his life she rarely left his side. A powerful and probably rather awkward person, she came to regard herself as much Blunt's protector as his nurse.

With Judith too, it was Blunt's attraction to women that led to the initial rift. Until about the age of twenty, Judith adored her father. He seemed to represent all that was finest in life. For Blunt's part, his 'dearest Bibi', with her precocious wit and tomboyish love of outdoor life, was a continual source of delight. But then she discovered that Blunt was the father of an illegitimate child and that he had asked her closest friend, Emily Lytton, to go with him to Paris. When she succeeded in persuading Emily to refuse the invitation, Blunt was bitterly angry, as much with himself as with Judith for he knew that their friendship could never be the same in future. The affair completely destroyed Judith's faith in her father. Many years later she wrote: 'To me he had once seemed a glorious ideal, which crashed to dust to my eternal grief'. By 1897 Blunt was writing sadly that Judith had 'drifted out of my hearing, we are hardly now within the distance of a shout of each other'. From then on, despite long periods of outward amiability, their relationship contained the seeds of sudden and violent rupture.

For Wilfrid and Lady Anne the turning point was to come in 1905. The previous year Blunt had gone to Damascus to look at a horse. While there he picked up £12 that he had left at Glyn's Bank twenty-three years before. He also tried to find the house that they still owned but was unable to do so without a guide and when he reached it he could not recognise it. (In 1909 Blunt agreed to let it to a young diplomat called Ronald Storrs. Thereafter its fate is unknown.) After spending the summer in England he set out for Egypt. It was to be his last visit.

During the winter the Lyttons joined Blunt and Lady Anne at Sheykh Obeyd and for the last time they were together as a family. One day 'H.F. rode up on Yemama in scarlet and gold and white and black, a splendid apparition – what with Neville taking photographs I got but three minutes or less to dab on my sketch some colours and try to perpetuate the vision.' (After Judith's marriage Blunt was known as H.F. – Head of the Family.) But then Blunt caught malaria and not long after a fever that attacked his lungs and kidneys. Miss Lawrence now took complete charge. She installed herself in the sick room and allowed no one, even Lady Anne, to visit 'her' patient without her

Wilfrid Blunt on Yemama, 'a splendid apparition'

permission. On March 20th Blunt left for England regardless of the consequences for his health. In Venice his condition became critical and Sydney Cockerell, who had been his personal secretary since 1898, felt his life sufficiently at risk to cable Lady Anne to come home. In great alarm the family hastened to London where they arrived on April 15th.

They found Blunt in his rooms in Chapel Street, unaware that Cockerell had summoned them. The doctors had diagnosed Malta fever and when Lady Anne was allowed by Miss Lawrence to see her husband, she found him strangely unwelcoming, probably as a result of the morphia and hashish he took which caused him such severe bouts of depression that he scarcely knew what he was doing. Lady Anne now found Miss Lawrence's attitude more objectionable than ever. She did not seem to realise that Lady Anne had nursed Wilfrid through many dangerous illnesses and, in the words of Neville Lytton, had been of service to him 'such as *no* other woman could have been'. 'Few people,' he wrote, 'realise the amount of bitterness that it must be to Lady Anne to have been supplanted in this her last domestic happiness, namely of being a domestic essential.'

Blunt soon grew restless in London and wanted to move to Newbuildings. He also wished to know what Astraled's first crop of foals was like. Lady Anne went down and reported that they were most promising and 'sure to have fine action'. Daoud's foals on the other hand were disappointing and did not come up to the mark, 'especially considering his splendour'. When Blunt was well enough, he was moved to Newbuildings but he was still very weak and had to have the horses brought up to the house for him to see. He was very impressed by Rijm, then a four-year-old, but complained that the greys they were breeding were too small and attributed this to the stallion Seyal.

The Blunts spent much of the summer together in Sussex. Lady Anne helped Wilfrid with the proofs of a new book and translated the letters he received from Egypt. But the presence of Miss Lawrence was always felt. By now she had made herself indispensable to Blunt, who refused to hear a thing against her although she was causing much unrest among the staff. When Miss Lawrence tried to control Blunt's domestic affairs in a way that appeared completely to usurp her own status in the household, Lady Anne decided that her position had become untenable. Deeply saddened, she left Newbuildings to stay with Judith at Forest Cottage.

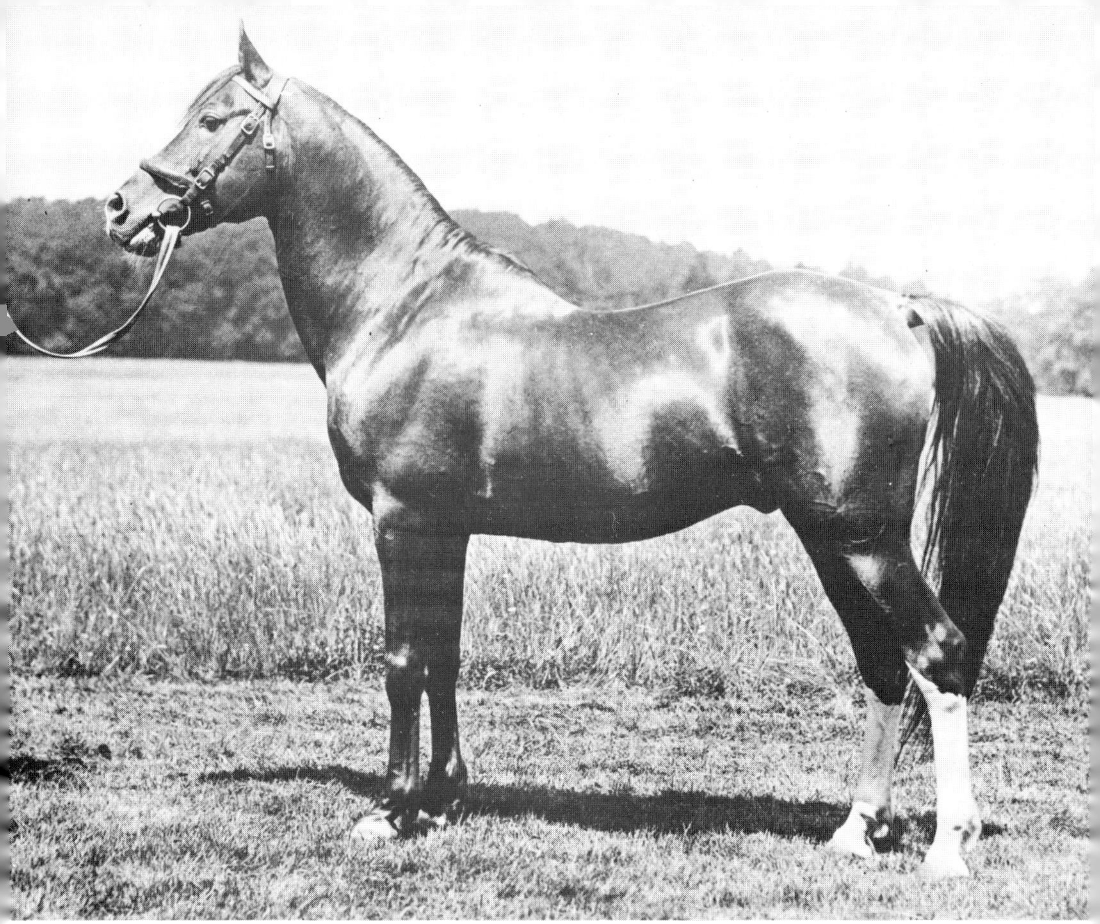

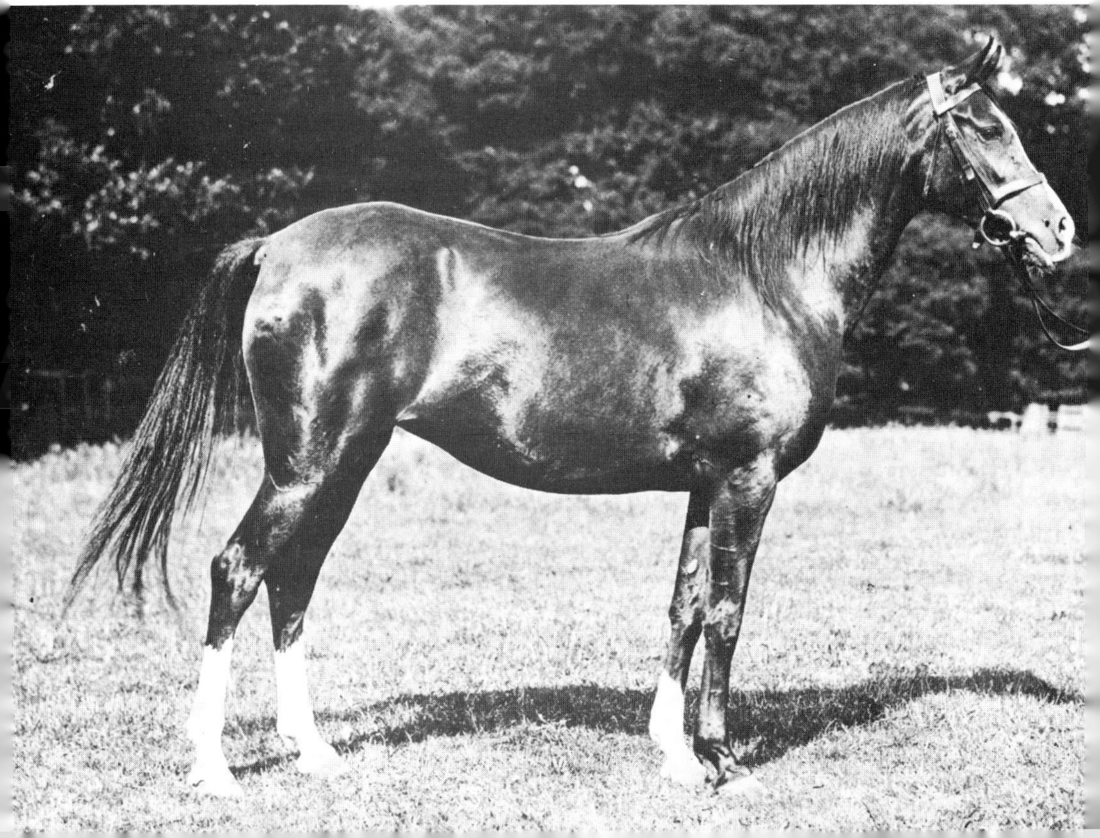

Blunt was now far from inclined to be involved in the worry and expense of running the Stud. After discussing it with Lady Anne, he agreed that she should take over all the horses, the farm and the shooting at Newbuildings and in return be responsible for all the costs. Believing the Stud now to be entirely in her hands, Lady Anne set out in November for Sheykh Obeyd, leaving in control Guy Carleton, a relation of Blunt's who had been made stud manager in June that year.

With the building of the railway and a greater degree of prosperity in the country, a considerable demand had built up for residential land near Cairo and the Blunts had received several enquiries about Sheykh Obeyd. In January Lady Anne wrote to Blunt that she was selling three acres near the station for £300 an acre. In April she sold for £800 an acre land which Blunt had bought in 1893 for £20 an acre and 'thought myself fleeced'. Neither the garden itself nor the land at El Kheyshi's was offered for sale. The news of these events was a tonic for Blunt. In all, he calculated he should receive from the sales about £38,000 which, he noted, 'puts me at my financial ease'. Lady Anne wanted to make Sheykh Obeyd self-supporting as an inheritance for the Lyttons and with some of the proceeds she opened a bank account in Cairo purely for the maintenance of the Stud.

Lady Anne left Egypt in May. Early the following month a General Browne and a Colonel Dean visited Blunt at Newbuildings to buy horses for the Indian Government. They chose Harb (by Mesaoud out of Bint Helwa) and two others and offered £530 for Rijm. At that point Lady Anne arrived home and went first to see the horses at Crabbet. There she met Browne, who made her an offer for Rifaat (by Mesaoud out of Ridaa). This, Blunt wrote after Lady Anne had gone on to Newbuildings on June 19th, was unfortunate as 'I had reserved [Rifaat] for the stud and for some reason Anne had decided to sell . . . and even before she got inside the house a heated argument began.' It was clear that Blunt, having now recovered his health, was choosing to forget that he had made over management and horses to Lady Anne the previous year. The next day he handed Lady Anne a memorandum. In it he acknowledged a joint equal share in the livestock and agreed to give the management to Lady Anne, reserving only the right to veto either the sale of any animal he might think necessary for breeding stock or the employment of any new stallion. Lady Anne was to be responsible for the finances of the Stud, farm and the shooting, while he was to provide the land at Newbuildings and Caxtons.

above Daoud (Mesaoud–Bint Nura)
below Nasra (Daoud–Nefisa). Foaled in 1908, the same year as Daoud's other famous daughter, Somra

When she read the memorandum, Lady Anne wrote 'H.F. handed [me] an elaborate document purporting to be a historical sketch of the origin and progress of the stud winding up with his ideas of an agreement. Not what I could accept and also the historical part is a romance with no attempt at accuracy.' She went on, 'Amongst other things shewing an incapacity to be accurate it was stated in his memorandum that when a new arrangement was made (I think in 1898) it was agreed that "Mr Blunt should *continue* to bear the expenses of the stud but that Lady Anne Blunt should contribute £2,000 a year to them". Whereas in reality I took over the whole expense then and there, started the Crabbet Arabian Stud Account at Drummonds and there was never any question since of his paying *anything* to the stud.'

Lady Anne now decided that she could have no more partnerships with Blunt. She saw no solution but to divide the Stud; as she had not insisted upon a legal document she could not prove that Wilfrid had given her his share, 'though he did so and that most emphatically'. Her sole wish was for the success of the Stud 'and its *permanence* and I do not especially covet the management if that success could be better secured otherwise. With H.F.'s ideas and practice about breeding – the system he has adopted I mean – I am convinced that it must perish.' Lady Anne wondered if in fact the best answer to the problem was not to give the Stud to Judith. 'But I fear H.F. has got into his head a fancy to manage details and to have it all his undertaking. In that case division must happen, and something must be decided soon – after the sale – otherwise the stud may be left stranded without each as I shall pay no more while it is in abeyance, and now there is only the sum of £90 balance whereas since last June I have paid in £2,500 . . . of course there has been the shooting and rates and taxes all of which I undertook to pay in consideration of the stud being made over to me absolutely but if H.F. backs out of the agreement I shall cease to pay the shooting or for his half of the stud.'

The sale to which she referred was an experimental one to be held at Tattersalls instead of the auction at Crabbet. It was not a success. Six horses were sent from Crabbet; those that they most wished to dispose of were sold but the top price was only 61 guineas.

Lady Anne's brother Ralph had by now been drawn into the affair. As one of the Stud's founders nearly thirty years before he felt that he had an interest in its fate. 'You must not weaken in the fight,' he wrote to Lady Anne. 'I am sorry you did not get everything arranged by a lawyer in black and white last year. You have not only yourself to think of but your descendants.' Lady Anne now went to her lawyer, Francis Smith. After a long meeting with him and Neville Lytton, she came away with approval for a letter she had written to Guy Carleton for him to show to Blunt. Smith also advised her not to pay the latest bill for Wilfrid's nurses.

The essence of the letter to be shown to Blunt was that with a 'so-called joint management' Lady Anne would have no chance of carrying out the breeding on the lines she considered necessary. She did not propose to continue to maintain the Stud with policies of which she could not approve and if Blunt now wished to manage her half as well as to take back his own, it was only proper that he should pay for the upkeep. On being shown the letter Blunt declared, 'This is war,' and instructed Carleton to withhold from Lady Anne any sums received for the sale of horses.

In fact Blunt and Lady Anne had by now drifted so far apart that any form of partnership had become impossible, whether in the Stud or in their marriage. Another figure had recently appeared at New-buildings — Carleton's sister Dorothy,* who was beginning to spend much time with Blunt. Lady Anne was feeling more unwanted than ever at Newbuildings and asked Blunt for a meeting to discuss the future. With Guy Carleton acting as intermediary, Blunt proposed to Lady Anne that they divide the Stud between them. When this was agreed, Blunt suggested that Lady Anne might prefer to be 'domiciled' with her half of the Stud. 'We shall have our own separate establishments,' he wrote, 'and manage our own finances in our own way.' Lady Anne's only reservation was that she needed time to find somewhere permanent to live. For the present she could always stay with Judith and Neville Lytton at Forest Cottage and anyway, 'the important thing will be done if we can settle the stud in a right way'.

There was much discussion over the wording of the Partition Agreement. Lady Anne wanted a clause stating that Judith should inherit the whole Stud but Wilfrid preferred that each half should be left to the survivor free of all obligations. Were he to survive his wife, he would of course leave the Stud to Judith; but as Lady Anne commented, wills could be changed but the Partition could not.

The main points of the Partition Agreement were as follows: each half of the Stud was to keep not less than 12 brood mares under sixteen

* Christened Margaret Theodora but always known as Dorothy.

as well as 12 young mares and fillies, with not less than 4 stallions between the ages of four and fifteen; the stallions at present, Astraled and Rijm (Blunt's), and Daoud and Feysul (Lady Anne's), not to be disposed of without mutual consent; other stallions to be entered on 1st January each year and all stallions to be accessible to the other party without fee; no new blood to be incorporated without approval by both parties; a sale list to be exchanged on 1st June each year with either party having the right to buy from it; no animal to be destroyed without notice, each party having the right to acquire absolutely any such animal.

The actual division of the horses was settled 'quite easily', Blunt said. 'We had each of us drawn up a list of what we thought would be a fair division, keeping our own special favourites, and on comparing the two lists, we found them almost identical.'

Besides Astraled and Rijm, the Newbuildings half included Harb and Ibn Yashmak among the stallions; and Ajramieh (by Mesaoud out of Asfura), Ridaa, Bint Helwa, Ferida and Narghileh among the mares. In Lady Anne's half were Feysul and Daoud as the main stallions, together with Berk, and the mares Balis (by Seyal out of Bukra), Nefisa, Belkis (by Seyal out of Bereyda), Bukra (by Ahmar out of Bozra), Rosemary, Siwa, Bint Nura and Rabla (by Mesaoud out of Rosemary).

Ralph Lovelace was strongly opposed to the terms of the Partition and protested vehemently against Blunt ever inheriting or disposing of what he called 'his portion' of the Stud. On the grounds of having been a co-founder of the Stud and of having paid part of the running cost in its early days, he insisted that 'the amount of stock which represents the animals that were provided by me should on no account be directed from the possession of my representative [Lady Anne]'. Although he had actually given his part of the Stud to Lady Anne many years before, he argued that he had done so only on the condition that Blunt never obtained it. Blunt maintained that Lovelace's capital in the Stud of £1,000 had been repaid to him a long time before, in the Eighties. Lovelace admitted this but asserted that he had later re-lent the money to Lady Anne and so still had a legitimate interest in the Stud. Blunt suspected that Lady Anne had put her brother up to raising these objections but it seems more likely that Lovelace, who disliked Blunt intensely, was so incensed by the way his sister was being treated that he acted on his own account. Unfortunately for him, the Partnership Deed recording the foundation of the Stud could not be found, nor

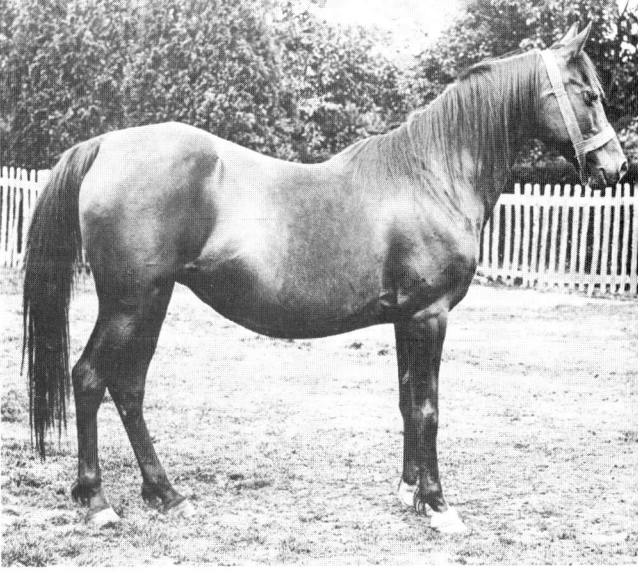

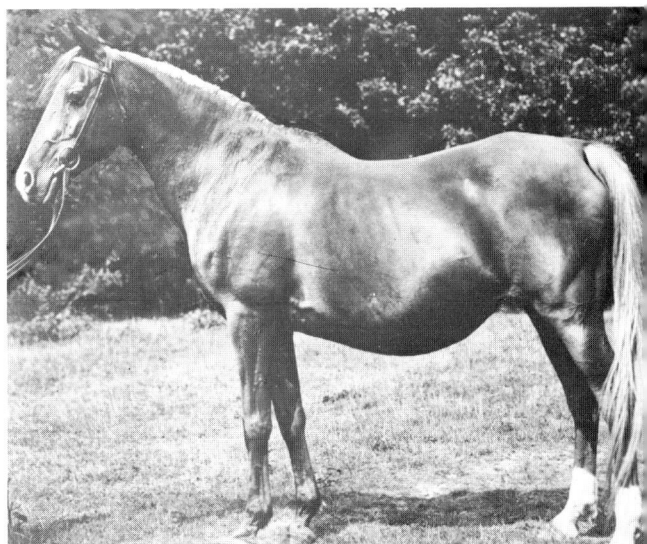

THREE GREAT MARES
above Narghileh
(Mesaoud–Nefisa)
centre Rosemary
(Jeroboam–Rodania)
below Ridaa
(Merzuk–Rose of Sharon)

any other legal documents that might have supported his contention, and he was advised by his lawyers that he had no case.

The Partition Agreement was signed on August 3rd, 1906. There was now no longer any reason for Lady Anne to remain at Newbuildings. The horses went to Caxtons and soon afterwards, after thirty-seven years of married life, Lady Anne left her husband's home for ever. At last, wrote Blunt cheerfully, he would be free to live 'after my own fancy with my own friends'. As for Lady Anne, it was with considerable relief, after the mounting strain of the last few years, that she moved out of Newbuildings to the cottage she had rented in Three Bridges.

CHAPTER 8

Troubled Times

Following her separation from Blunt, Lady Anne's first thought was to put her affairs onto a footing suitable for an independent lady. But when she consulted Francis Smith, she found the wish easier than the practice.

The Blunts had been married before the Married Women's Property Act of 1882. Consequently their financial arrangements were not subject to its provisions but were governed by the law prior to the Act, whereby a woman ceased to be legally entitled to any property of her own once she was married. Lady Anne had already found that through a fault in her marriage settlement Blunt would receive a very considerable income from her personal trusts if she predeceased him. She now discovered that in order to ensure for herself complete security at Sheykh Obeyd she would be obliged to buy from Blunt land for which she had herself paid, since her husband was its owner at law. She was happy to leave the Old House and about three acres in Blunt's possession so long as she could have the Pink House and the land at El Kheyshi's. The unfairness involved in paying her husband for property that she had herself bought did not upset her so much as the fact that she had to settle for his market valuation of £15,000 when its original cost, before the land boom, had been a mere fraction of that sum.

Lady Anne's problems were increased when her brother Ralph died suddenly at Ockham at the end of August, 1906. She had been extremely fond of him, besides having depended on him for forty years and more as a source of independent advice, especially over business matters. In his will Lord Lovelace left his estates to his wife Mary for her life and thereafter to Lady Anne and then to Judith and her children. 'This makes them inheritors of great wealth,' wrote Blunt, and 'makes me more than ever decided to adhere to my own plan for my own remaining property.'

Dorothy Carleton was now living permanently at Newbuildings. In November, 1906, Blunt adopted her formally as his niece. 'All the world requires about such things is a "formula" by which to explain the unexplainable,' he wrote hopefully. But it was not a formula that pleased his family. Lady Anne was both indignant and acutely embarrassed and refused ever to visit Newbuildings so long as Dorothy Carleton was there. Judith too was put in an awkward situation. She wished to remain friendly with her father but at the same time wanted to avoid hurting her mother. As a compromise she stayed away from Newbuildings but allowed her children to go. In the following years the young Lyttons were often at Newbuildings and spent many days of great happiness with their grandfather.

After adopting Dorothy Carleton, Blunt had altered his will 'in accordance with the new conditions here'. These 'new conditions' now gave rise to another problem. Dorothy Carleton's association with Blunt was not approved of by some of her relations and in the summer of 1907 her brother Guy informed Blunt that because of the strength of feeling in the family, he would have to resign as stud manager at Newbuildings. Blunt now decided to reduce the number of horses he would keep. Twelve mares and six stallions would be 'quite stud enough to amuse me and save me much expense and anxiety'. He kept Astraled, Rijm, Ibn Yashmak, Rifaat and two colts; and the mares Hamasa (by Mesaoud out of Bint Helwa), Abla, Narghileh, Shieha, Feluka (by Mesaoud out of Ferida), Narda (by Rejeb out of Narghileh), Ridaa, Ajramieh, Rakima, Rose of Hind (by Rejeb out of Rose Diamond), Kibla (by Mesaoud out of Mabruka) and Kantara. The remainder he offered to Lady Anne and agreed to rent her the farm at Crookhorn, near Newbuildings, for their accommodation. Carleton then became Lady Anne's stud manager and moved to a house near Crabbet.

Lady Anne had meanwhile returned to Sheykh Obeyd, with its calm and seclusion and almost magical powers of healing. There she completed the arrangements which gave her legal possession of the Pink House and the surrounding land. In December 1906 she was visited by Sir Hugh Bell and his daughter Gertrude and was delighted when a month later Gertrude gave her the prints of the photographs she had taken at Sheykh Obeyd.

The next year she was corresponding with Spencer Borden in America. Borden had been in touch with the Blunts since 1896 and in 1905 had come over from America to visit them. He had already bought Arabs from Miss Dillon but this had been the first time he had shown interest in pure Crabbet stock. He had fallen immediately under the spell of Rose of Sharon and despite Lady Anne's reluctance to part

above Rim, full sister to Riyala
below Riyala (Astraled–Ridaa). 'She is truly magnificent'

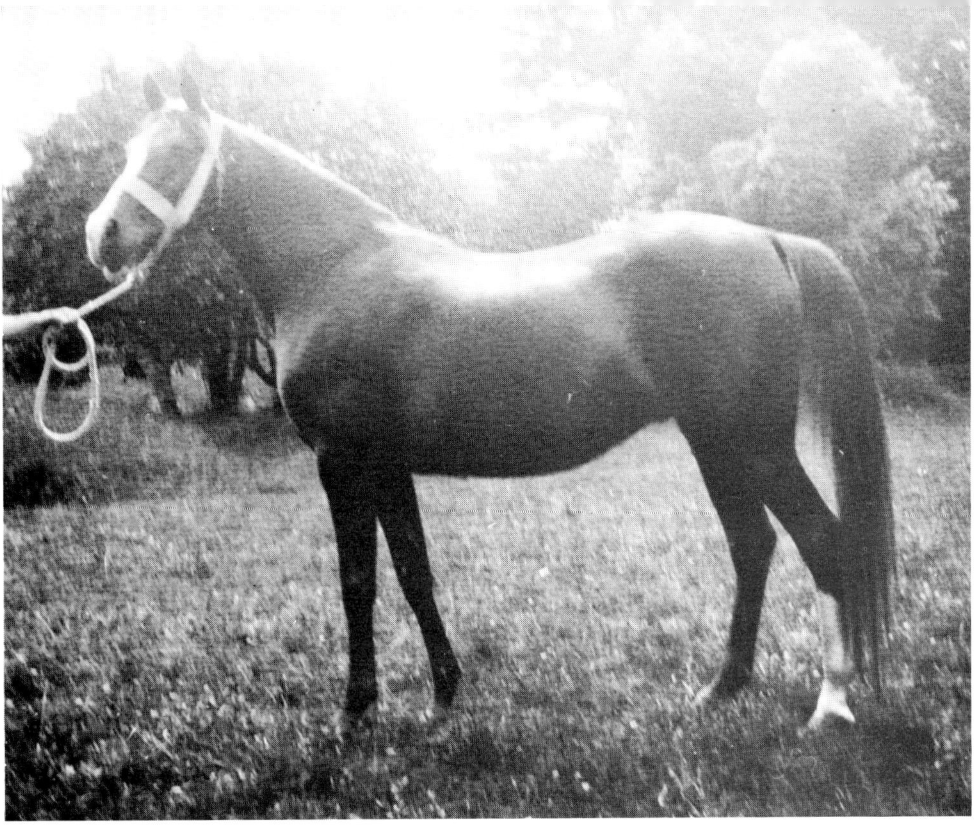

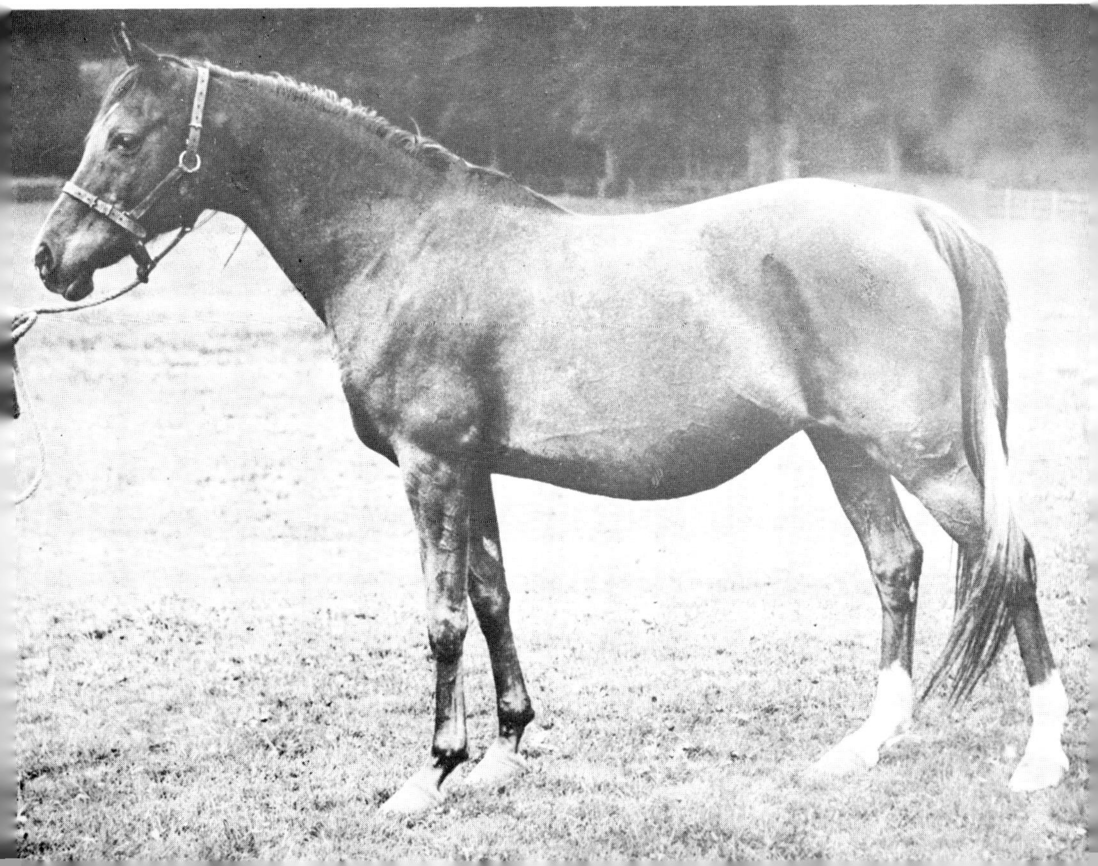

with such a fine mare, succeeded in buying her together with Rumeliya, Rosetta and Antika.

Rose of Sharon had then been in foal to Harb and in 1906 had produced the colt Rodan. Borden was now writing to Lady Anne to tell her that he was thinking of having Rodan gelded on account of his bad temper. Lady Anne counselled him to have patience and to give the horse plenty of exercise and discipline. She told him that neither she nor Mutlak believed that a permanently bad-tempered Arabian could exist. She described how Mutlak had broken in one particularly difficult colt by hours and hours of lungeing while it was tied to a peg driven firmly into the ground. After several days of this Mutlak, who was 'a featherweight as well as a fine horseman,' then backed the animal and had no further trouble. Fortunately for American breeders, Borden took the advice and the grandsire of Gulastra was reprieved from being gelded. Two months later under a new handler, Rodan had become a changed horse.

In the summer of 1908 Borden was again in touch with Lady Anne. He had been unlucky and had lost two fillies and wanted to know if Riyala (by Astraled out of Ridaa) and certain other horses were for sale. Lady Anne was not enthusiastic about selling Riyala. 'She is truly magnificent, however as she is the only available one of those you ask about I will sell her for 300 guineas.' Borden replied that this was a 'fancy' price and received in return a mild rebuke for such ungallant language. The strain, explained Lady Anne, was 'of an all round value besides its extreme beauty and rarity,' and no others of it existed save 'the few at this stud and the few there may be in Nejd now quite inaccessible'.

Under the Partition Agreement the Blunts had to obtain each other's permission before selling a horse not entered on their annual sale lists. As it happened, Blunt had recently received a good offer for Rijm and was therefore very interested in Borden's negotiations with Lady Anne over Riyala. In writing to Lady Anne for her agreement to the offer for Rijm, he said that his stock 'though very good, have too much white about them to be quite satisfactory'. Lady Anne did not think this a good enough reason. In the first place Rijm was the only representative, with the exception of Daoud, of the rare strain of Bint Nura. Secondly he had the advantage over Daoud of combining the Hadban descent through Rose of Sharon. Finally, 'in the case of so remarkable a sire as he is shewing himself to be, it would be too great a risk to let him go until a sufficient number of his stock have reached maturity'. Moreover, as Lady Anne remarked, the bitter experience of having parted too quickly with Pharaoh, Hadban, Merzuk and Azrek should serve as a warning.

Rebuffed over Rijm, Blunt asked to have Riyala sent to Newbuildings for him to inspect before deciding whether she should be sold to Borden. He thought her a first-class mare and one to be kept. But since it was a good price he was prepared to agree to the sale provided that Lady Anne bought Rijm from him for 400 guineas. By this time Judith had joined the discussion and objected so strongly to the sale of Riyala that she eventually bought a half share in her to ensure that the mare remained at Crabbet.

This incident is typical of the way in which horses changed hands after the Partition. In the bigger sales, the buyer could never be certain that the horse was his until he heard whether the other Blunt had vetoed it. In dealings between Crabbet and Newbuildings, horses were bought, sold, exchanged and given with such frequency that it is often hard to draw an exact line between the two studs.

Spencer Borden continued to correspond regularly with Lady Anne. In September 1909 he bought Bint Helwa's daughter Ghazala (by Ibn Sherara). Ghazala had been covered in Egypt by Jamil that February and offered to Borden in place of Riyala. The intention had been for Ghazala to be shipped direct from Egypt to America but this proved impossible and Ghazala had to be sent first to England. The purchase was a good one for America.

Borden and Lady Anne also kept each other informed about the progress of the 'Arab cause' in their countries. The number of breeders, though still small, was gradually increasing, and Lady Anne now told Borden, almost with surprise, that recently there had even been some English buyers for their horses.

One of these was Mr G.H. Ruxton. He had seen Maisuna (by Mesaoud out of Meshura) advertised by the Blunts and in 1907 had bought her for his stud at Craven Lodge near Basingstoke. Three years later he bought the stallion Nadir (by Mesaoud out of Nefisa) by whom Maisuna was to have four foals, the last of which was Joseph. Maisuna was hunted for three seasons and regularly driven. Ruxton later added other horses of Crabbet breeding, notably Rythma, by Berk out of Risala. In due course he bought the stallion Algol, who had been bred by the Prince of Wales (later Edward VIII). Three of Algol's grand-

Geoffrey Covey

parents were of Crabbet breeding but the fourth, Dwarka, was an imported horse owned by the Prince.

Two other breeders in the early part of the century deserve mention, Captain the Hon. George Savile and Colonel J. Hamilton Leigh. In 1903 Savile bought Rose Diamond (by Azrek out of Rose of Jericho) from the Blunts when in foal to Mesaoud. The issue, a colt, was named Lal-i-Abdar and renamed Abu Zeyd after being sold to America where he became a notable sire. Savile also bred Sher-i-Khurshid, by Lal-i-Abdar out of the Crabbet mare Mazna (by Astraled out of Mabruka). According to Lady Wentworth, Sher-i-Khurshid had 'supreme nobility of type' and was unlucky not to have done better in the show ring.

Colonel Hamilton Leigh owned several Crabbet-bred horses at various times. Among them were Fejr (by Rijm out of Feluka), Rokhama (by Astraled out of Rabla), Ranya (by Nasik out of Riyala) and Rayya (by Rustem out of Riada), the latter the dam of Raseyn. He also bought from the Blunts in 1900 their foundation stallion Mahruss (1893).

By March, 1907, the real tennis court that the Lyttons were having built at Crabbet had been finished. It is this that forms the background for many of the photographs taken of the horses. The architect, Joseph Bickley, was well known as a designer of real tennis courts and that at Crabbet was reputed to be a fine example of his work. Both Judith and Neville Lytton played the game well – Neville was world amateur champion in 1911. Since there were only about fifty such courts in existence (and many fewer now, of course) the addition of one more to this select list was the cause of much publicity and the opening match on March 23rd between P. Latham and G.F. Covey was played before a packed gallery. Geoffrey Covey had recently come from Princes Club in London to act as marker for Neville Lytton and thus began an association with Crabbet that was to last for the rest of his life. From being marker and tennis coach (during which time he held the world professional championship for 16 years) he was to become, under Lady Wentworth, manager of the Stud and estate.

The next month Prince Mohammed Ali visited Blunt at Newbuildings. He came down by car and arrived late after losing his way. He and Blunt made a grand tour of the Stud, in the course of which Astraled was particularly admired.

It is interesting to compare Blunt's attitude to the Stud with that of Lady Anne. Blunt was now largely concerned to minimize the cost and worry of the enterprise. Lady Anne regarded it far more seriously, as a permanent institution of which she was the guardian. She wanted to perpetuate it 'as a beautiful thing, or "a thing of beauty" in itself, not as a speculation, although I must keep it on strict business lines, but this *without* the expectation of it *paying*. Horse-breeding will *not* pay now with the human race intent on machine made locomotion not to mention flying'. Some years later she repeated to Holman how she saw the Stud 'as a thing of value to the country', of which she was the trustee for the benefit of posterity. There was no question of it being a mere pastime. 'The word "hobby" used about the stud is as you know quite inapplicable. There was a time when the Squire regarded it in that light but I never did.'

On March 28th, 1908, the Lyttons left Forest Cottage and moved into the house at Crabbet. Blunt was pleased as it meant he could now have a room at Crabbet and stay with Judith, something which had been impossible in the cottage. But when he went to visit her he found an insuperable obstacle. Judith refused to receive Dorothy Carleton into her house. She said that to do so would not only be a sign of acquiescence in a liaison of which she disapproved but that it would also be intolerably painful to her mother. Blunt was incensed. 'Either she is polite to Dorothy or I do not go to her house or she to mine.' Later he wrote Judith a 'declaration of war as extreme as I could make it'. All thoughts of his latest proposal, that she should have a share in the management of his part of the Stud, were dismissed from his mind. But Blunt's wars never lasted long at this time and by the late summer friendly relations had been restored.

With the Partition, the auctions at Crabbet had ceased. In 1909 Blunt revived the practice, though without the participation of Lady Anne. He held it at Caxtons and compared with its predecessors it was a quiet affair. There was no garden party and only forty people sat down to luncheon. But including Lady Anne's purchases from his sales list, Blunt cleared 500 guineas and was well satisfied.

Shortly afterwards Professor Osborn, head of the Natural History Museum in New York, came down to Crabbet and Newbuildings with his daughter. He thought Berk and Ibn Yashmak were 'the most typical' of the horses. It is interesting that he should have singled out Berk. For of all the Blunts' horses that have left important lines, Berk was the only one that no outsider apart from Osborn appears to have remarked upon. Lady Anne had noted his brilliance when moving but Blunt never liked the horse and was glad he had never sent any mares to him as his stock were all 'weedy and second rate'. In view of Berk's record as a sire of such influential mares as Rissla, Rangha, Rythma and Safarjal, the opinion of Blunt and others can only be described as an astonishing blind spot.

Berk won the Eastern Sires class at the Polo Pony Show on two occasions but in 1911 was beaten by Nadir. Blunt did not agree with the placings. With six entries in the class of Crabbet breeding, the first prize had gone to 'the horse I thought least of, Nadir, apparently because he had most bone, for this is the way Arabs are judged in England. But every judge has his own fancy and very few know anything of the Arab points'.

Blunt disliked shows and considered them 'a mistake except perhaps as an advertisement'. Lady Anne agreed with him. Both felt that show results could be misleading and that it was more important that a horse should breed good stock than win prizes in the show ring.

Two days after Osborn's visit, another American, Mr Lothrop Ames, came down with his agent, an Irishman called Dorgan who had previously been a groom in service near Crabbet. Ames had already cabled an offer of 500 guineas for Rijm but Lady Anne had once more vetoed his sale. Ames now bought Shibine (by Mesaoud out of Shobha), Narda with her son Crabbet (by Rijm) and Astraled, whose sale Lady Anne regretted but did not veto.

> It was a lovely day, [wrote Blunt] and Astraled was looking his very best. He certainly is the most perfect horse we ever bred, and I hope he will make his mark as a sire in America, for I am certain that if put to thorough-bred mares he would get racing stock, for he is the picture of the old fashioned blood horse of 150 years ago. In colour he is the darkest possible brown without a speck of white except a very small snip – the carriage of head and tail perfect, large beautiful eyes, splendid shoulders, loins and quarters – everything about him perfect.

Not long after his arrival in America, Astraled was shown at Brackton and won what was described as 'the largest class ever known'. As the sire of Gulastra, Astraled did indeed make his mark in America.

At Ames's request, Shibine stayed at Crabbet to be covered again by Rijm. In 1910 she was shipped to America with Crabbet, and there produced a daughter called Noam. In 1919 Noam, Crabbet and W.R. Brown's Ramla (by Astraled out of Ridaa) competed in one of the earliest endurance tests to be held in America. Ramla was declared winner because of her excellent condition on the morning after the test, during which she gained points for the lowest feed consumption of any of the entrants. But it was the gelding Crabbet whose consistent successes demonstrated the remarkable qualities of the Arabian and thereby did much to popularize the breed in America. Crabbet finished fifth in 1919 and fifth again in 1920, when carrying 245 lbs on the last day he recorded the shortest time ever made by any horse in one day. In 1921 he won the 310 mile test, covering the distance in 49 hours and 4 minutes and finishing twenty minutes in front of the next horse. The following morning he was able to gallop freely and without stiffness.

The sequel to Lady Anne's continued veto to the sale of Rijm came in 1910 when she agreed to give Blunt 400 guineas for him. Rijm arrived at Crabbet on June 23rd. '*Rijm has come!*' wrote Lady Anne. 'Fred [Holman] went over last night and led him from Newbuildings this morning. Went first to see him and then fetched Judith. The horse is splendid and I am only too happy to have got him . . . He really is magnificent.' Ames must somehow have heard of this for within a month he was writing to Lady Anne asking if she would sell Rijm. After consulting Judith, Lady Anne cabled back to say that she had no intention of selling him and that nothing less than 5,000 guineas would be accepted.

Lady Anne was now spending her summers at Hillside, a house near Caxtons, and her winters as usual at Sheykh Obeyd. She had tried to persuade Weatherbys to accept the Sheykh Obeyd horses in the General Stud Book but had failed on account of their refusal to register horses resident in studs outside England.

At Sheykh Obeyd Lady Anne decided to start riding astride. She was then seventy and had been riding side-saddle all her life. Her first expedition astride was a three hour ride into the hills with Mutlak which 'seemed to me nothing'.

In the winter of 1909/10, Lady Anne began her search for the grey stallion which Judith was keen to get for the Stud. Although she still preferred chestnuts and bays, Lady Anne agreed with Judith that the sale of the greys, Azrek and Shahwan, had been a great loss. At one time she had considered sending over a grey colt from Sheykh Obeyd but had changed her mind when it did not come up to expectations. As it happened, she now heard of a chance to buy some horses of the famous Krush strain from Arabia and began to negotiate for them. Nearly two years were to pass before they arrived at Sheykh Obeyd and then only after a journey lasting four months. Unfortunately the stallion in the group, a grey called Krush, did not prove himself at stud and Lady Anne was never able to find the equal of those Blunt had sold.

Lady Anne also took the opportunity to visit the library of Prince Mohammed Ali and copy the Ali Pasha Sherif records. The originals, which were in the possession of the Khedive, had been 'very illegible' and Mohammed Ali had had them written out again. Lady Anne found a record of every single mare and stallion bought for Abbas Pasha I. She enjoyed reading the Abbas Pasha accounts, with their 'interminable' lists of varieties of Kehailan but it gave her 'a heart ache to think how all this was lost – wasted, as nothing remained of it pure-bred except the comparatively few afterwards in Ali Pasha Sherif's stud'.

In the summer of 1910 another American had been to visit the Blunts' Studs. Homer Davenport had come to England with Theodore Roosevelt as the correspondent of *The New York World*. He had been in touch with the Blunts for a number of years, ever since he had visited the Anazeh tribes and 'picked up some knowledge of the subject', as Wilfrid Blunt noted rather patronisingly. Davenport was a cartoonist and his sense of humour (together with his low opinion of Roosevelt) appealed to his host. Blunt particularly liked his comment that the Newbuildings meadows were 'the cunningest little paddocks for breeding that ever I saw'. But Blunt also thought Davenport did not look much like a buyer. In this he was proved right; Davenport bought only three horses in England, the famous Lal-i-Abdar (Abu Zeyd) from Savile, and Berid and Jahil from Lady Anne, whom he visited the next day.

Blunt had always had a deep love for Worth Forest and to enjoy its beauty more closely had a house built in it. Known as Worth Manor, it lay in a commanding position on high ground about two miles from Frogshole Farm. He was fond of holding parties there and entertained many distinguished politicians, including Winston Churchill, whose father Randolph had been a close friend. In October, 1909, Winston Churchill was at Newbuildings. After lunch one Sunday Blunt mounted him on Rijm and took him to Worleys to look at the mares, 'which gave us a fine exhibition of galloping and circling around us. Rijm showed himself nobly, and I promised Churchill he should ride him in the procession there would be one day when he went to open Parliament as the first President of the British Republic'.

In 1911 Blunt had several horses on his sales list. Judith bought Rodan (by Rijm out of Rakima) and Lady Anne two young mares and a colt. Once again Lady Anne did not join the sale at Caxtons. It was not a success and only six horses were sold out of a total of twenty-three.

But Blunt was well pleased with his part of the Stud. 'They are a splendid show, all perfect. There is no doubt that our mares are now vastly finer than the stock we originally imported 33 years ago . . . more powerful and of finer quality. It has been done by selection and a careful avoidance of breeding for mere size.' But as usual he was worried about the cost of keeping them and in 1912 he and Lady Anne agreed to limit the number of mares they would breed from. The demand for Arabians in England was never high and when, as now, the overseas market failed them, the problem of surplus stock became acute.

Blunt's sale in 1913 was a financial disaster. There were only two genuine bidders and he prophesied gloomily that with the advent of motor cars the demand for carriage horses and indeed for any horses other than hunters, would disappear completely. Three weeks after the sale, he proposed to Lady Anne that he make over the whole Stud to her, keeping only some twelve horses for his own use. If she would not take it, 'I shall look for some other person to be its owner'. Judith, with whom he had talked, 'does not seem greatly interested in its fate'. Lady Anne, however, was also worried about the financial outlook, partly because of troubles in the coal-mining industry, on which her income from Ouston (her estate in Durham) was dependent, and partly because the political situation in Europe was depressing bond and share prices. But she took four of Blunt's older mares and when he managed to sell another three horses to Señor Ayerza in South America, the immediate crisis was past.

Blunt had been wrong to suppose that Judith was indifferent about the Stud. She had been involved in its running for many years and after the Partition was consulted continually by her mother. 'It is a joy we are absolutely at one over stud matters,' wrote Lady Anne in 1909. But Judith had the estate and a young family to look after and enough financial problems of her own without taking on any more. Besides, she had another worry to contend with.

Neville Lytton had always had a much greater liking than Judith for London social life and for the last two years had been at Crabbet only at weekends. Despite the growing estrangement between them, they nevertheless decided to proceed with a visit planned to America, where they would combine playing tennis with selling Neville's pictures. They left England in March, 1914, with Geoffrey Covey. The trip was a calamity. They had an appalling passage out, Neville's paintings were lost and they arrived in New York to find a blizzard and nine foot of snow. When Judith tried to enter the tennis court to watch Neville playing, she found herself firmly excluded as the players were apt to walk around in a state of undress. Covey was beaten twice by the American champion, Gould, in Philadelphia. 'It has been a disaster in every way,' Judith wrote to her father.

The outbreak of war in 1914 posed immediate problems. Neville Lytton tried to join the British Expeditionary Force as an interpreter. When this failed, he enlisted in the infantry and was put in charge of raising men locally for a newly formed Sussex regiment. In due course he received his commission as an officer, whereupon Lady Anne offered him Rasim (by Feysul out of Risala) as a charger, but stallions were not permitted in the regiment. As the war progressed, Neville Lytton's appearances at Crabbet became increasingly rare and in 1923 he and Judith were divorced by mutual consent.

The Blunts' greatest worry was for the horses. Arabians were not being requisitioned like other breeds as they were disliked as cavalry horses and were unsuitable in artillery teams or supply units. But with War Office controls over the supply of hay and corn, the fodder situation was to be a constant source of anxiety, particularly to Lady Anne. Later in the war, blackouts were imposed in the Three Bridges area for fear of Zeppelin attacks on the railway junction and many of the staff were called up. Most disturbing of all, the war made it virtually impossible to sell any stock.

For Blunt, however, the winter of 1914 was a happy one. Lady Anne had not been able to go to Egypt and was staying with Judith at Crabbet. At Judith's suggestion, he invited them both to spend Christmas with him at Newbuildings and although Lady Anne declined since Dorothy Carleton would be there, her reply encouraged him to think that a reconciliation between them was possible. The negotiations were slow and not without misgivings on both sides. But with Judith's help, a meeting was finally arranged at Worth Manor and on May 12, 1915, they saw each other for the first time since 1906. They spent an hour together, with Judith present. They took care to avoid controversial subjects and when they parted both Wilfrid and Lady Anne were happy to find that they were able to renew their relationship after so many years apart.

Two days later Blunt drove over to Crabbet and with Lady Anne and Holman made a tour of the Stud. He considered most of the foals first-rate, especially those by Rustem (by Astraled out of Ridaa) and Sotamm (by Astraled out of Selma), the latter now asserting himself 'as our best sire in descent from Mesaoud'. But with the future uncertain and further edicts from the War Office regulating the fodder supply, neither he nor Lady Anne felt particularly optimistic. They were both well into their seventies and were naturally concerned for the future of the Stud. Lady Anne had recently remade her will giving her granddaughter, Anne Lytton, the Sheykh Obeyd Stud. She intended to leave to Judith the thirty or so horses at Crabbet that she had either bought from Blunt or had bred herself and which were therefore her absolute property.

Judith Lytton was now running into serious financial difficulties. Like many others, the war had forced her to make economies. But the mortgage interest was still £750 per annum, none of the principal having been repaid, and Crabbet estate itself was operating at a considerable loss. One day Miss Lawrence reported to Blunt that she had heard from Holman that there was talk of Judith having to sell the estate. Blunt did not see how she could be pressed for money with the income from her marriage settlement and her allowance of £2,000 a year from Lady Anne. In August Caffin, who was agent for both Crabbet and Newbuildings, told Blunt that he was thinking of resigning at Crabbet as he had been accused by Judith of muddling the estate accounts. This infuriated Blunt, who felt that Caffin was being made the scapegoat for Judith's financial problems which, in his opinion, had been caused by the Lyttons' improvident style of living. He cited the tennis court and swimming pool as examples of their extravagance.

Blunt and Lady Anne spent much of September discussing what was to be done with the Stud. Both were keen to reunite the two halves under Lady Anne's control. 'I have no wish in this matter except to retire from all ownership and responsibility in the stud,' wrote Blunt on September 11th. Ten days later they held a conference at Caxtons with Caffin and Chandler. According to Blunt, it was agreed that the Partition Agreement should be revoked and that a new deed be made whereby Blunt would give the entire ownership and management of the Stud to Lady Anne for life, with reversion to him on her death together with a settlement of £3,000 a year for its upkeep. When both of them were dead, it was to pass to Judith, provided that she undertook to spend at least £2,000 a year on its maintenance. Failing this, it was to go to Anne Lytton.

But a week later Blunt had changed his mind after hearing reports from Crabbet that convinced him that Judith intended to sell the estate. 'Nothing shall now induce me to include Judith in any plan we may come to for the future of the stud,' he wrote. On October 13th, Lady Anne signed the 'new stud agreement which makes me sole owner' of the Crabbet Arabian Stud. Blunt, however, refused to sign it, alleging that it contained a 'dangerous' clause, presumably one that made it possible for Judith to inherit. He nevertheless appears to have acquiesced in the new arrangement; five months later, in March, 1916, he and Caffin were planning the removal to Crookhorn of what remained of the Newbuildings section of the Stud, on the following Saturday 'which is Lady Day when my separate ownership of it comes to a final end'.

Lady Anne returned to Egypt that winter for the last time, greatly distressed at Judith's continuing troubles. In February Judith delayed paying the interest on the Crabbet mortgage and was reminded by the

Trustees of their power to call it in. The same month Blunt took his lawyer's advice and asked the Public Trustee* to become an additional Trustee for the Crabbet estate. He hoped thereby to strengthen the Trustees' hand against Judith, who would be unable to sell the estate without their permission. When the March instalment of the interest fell due, Judith was again in default since Lady Anne had not paid her allowance owing to her own financial worries. The Trustees now stepped in and warned Judith that unless the interest was paid immediately, they would call in the mortgage even if this meant selling Crabbet. Either Judith was genuinely unable to find the money, or she had all along intended to part with what she perhaps saw as a financial millstone, for on April 12th she announced she was selling the entire estate, except for 'the mansion house, pleasure grounds and Park'.

'This,' wrote Blunt, 'is mere devilry and an entire absence of all honourable feeling or scruple of honesty.' The mere idea of Blackwater and Frogshole being sold was an 'abomination'. The last time they had been on the market was in 1698. It seemed to him 'monstrous that a woman should have it in her power in a freak of temper, for it is really this, to destroy an estate it has taken a dozen generations of honest men during three hundred years to get together'. Blunt appeared to have forgotten that many years before he had tried to sell Newbuildings estate. In any case Judith was fully the equal of her father when it came to accusations of this sort. 'You prefer fiction, romance and prejudice at all costs,' she replied. Crabbet was insolvent by £1,237 a year, including the interest. The mortgage was Blunt's and not hers. She had no personal debts but had spent her money paying the interest on his. Her dress bill for the last year had been less than £10 and for her father to accuse her of extravagance for which Lady Anne had to pay, was untrue and hypocritical. 'Did not her money purchase and import horses and keep up the stud? Did not her money defend Arabi, fight your elections, pay your law expenses when you were in prison, pay for all your foreign travels, build Crabbet and pay countless debts and extravagances?'

Various attempts at mediation were now made. Lady Anne wrote from Egypt to Chandler to say that she would guarantee the mortgage. Later she offered to buy Woolborough Farm from Judith for £15,000 and thereby pay off the mortgage but was advised against it by her

* A Government Agency established in 1908 to act as executor or trustee for members of the public.

lawyers. Father Lawrence, the priest who took Mass at Crabbet, tried to intercede with Judith but according to Blunt bungled it hopelessly. Judith's lawyers then offered to stop the sale if Blunt paid off the mortgage and gave Judith a clear income of £3,000 a year. This was later reduced to £1,500 a year if Caxtons and Forest Cottage were included in lieu of the balance. But these moves came to nothing, foundering on the prejudices, suspicions or obstinacy of one or other of the parties. On September 20th, 1916, there were sold by auction 1,635 acres of the Crabbet estate together with sundry outlying properties. Lady Anne's representative bought Woolborough Farm and Blunt the farms at Frogshole and Blackwater since they had been particular favourites of his brother Francis.

Lady Anne was deeply saddened. Having striven for years to preserve the unity of her family, she feared that her efforts would now prove worthless and that there would be a complete and irreversible break between Wilfrid Blunt and Judith. They were 'so alike in their *absolutism*', she wrote. She had received widely differing statements from each and all she knew for certain was that instinct told her the sale had been wrong. 'The calamity is beyond words,' she wrote to Blunt and later, when she heard that he had bought Frogshole, 'I am so glad . . . the alder meadows always remind me of the days before the world, our world, became full of troubles, when you and Alice went trout fishing in the brook.'

Marooned in Egypt by the activities of German submarines, and with the mails from England delayed or lost, she felt increasingly sad and helpless. She did have Philip Napier and his family, old friends of Wilfrid, staying in the Old House. But earlier in 1916 she had lost Mutlak, her companion as well as manager, who had died after a long illness, having been 'much more soul than body for years past'. The news from England, when it came, rarely brought her peace of mind. When Holman tactlessly wrote 'if only we could get a little oats', she became very alarmed and believed the horses to be on the brink of starvation. Then Father Lawrence told her that the presence of so many apparently useless horses during wartime was causing bad feeling in Three Bridges and that windows had been broken at Crabbet by malcontents. Lady Anne took this particularly hard since at that very moment she was drawing up a trust 'for the benefit of the nation in future breeding', and had received every encouragement from the Remount Department.

By 1917, with all these troubles and then the sale, Lady Anne was near to despair over the future of the Stud. In April she abandoned the idea of making it into a trust and a month later even contemplated dispersing the English end altogether. Her income had fallen considerably; much of her capital had been spent or given away, and she felt she could no longer afford to make a settlement for the upkeep of the Stud after her death. She believed strongly that once she was no longer there to act as the universal provider, it would be the Stud that would suffer first.

Providentially, as it seemed at first, an offer was now made by Mr H.K. Bush-Brown, Secretary of the Arabian Horse Club of America, for a 'large portion' of the Stud. This news was distorted in transit to England. What Blunt heard was that Lady Anne had offered the whole stud to Bush-Brown. Twenty-five horses perhaps could be spared, 'but the whole stock NO!' Greatly alarmed, he hastened to assure Lady Anne that the fodder shortage had been greatly exaggerated and that it would be a grievous mistake to part with all the horses. Lady Anne was relieved to get his letter. 'Nothing but the fear of starvation extinguishing the results of 40 years' labour, induced me to use so sweeping a phrase, but I cannot regret having done so as it brought me that letter of yours with assurance that you, actually on the spot, are certain that restrictions of feed will be reduced to talks, and also that you yourself will be able to help with grazing ground, last but not least that you care so much for the preservation of results.' In fact no definite offer had been received from Bush-Brown and the negotiations with him came to a standstill.

Lady Anne still found happiness in Egypt with her old friends. She continued to lead an active life and went frequently to Cairo. After a visit to Prince Mohammed Ali's stud in February 1917 she described it as an 'interesting show but of the whole lot *few* were perfect'. At the Kubba Palace she discussed the horses she had offered to the Breeding Section of the Royal Agricultural Society and agreed to give them Jamil, Ghadia and Jemla. Prince Kemal el Dine visited Sheykh Obeyd to thank her for the gift. Frequently parties of convalescent soldiers came to take tea and afterwards to see the horses or walk to the tomb of Sheykh Obeyd. One day a Colonel Fulton dropped in and delighted Lady Anne by remarking of Nasik (whom he had seen at Crabbet), 'I shall *never* forget those glorious eyes.'

On June 18th 1917, Lady Anne's niece Mary died. She had been the only child of Lady Anne's brother Ralph, and on his death had inherited the baronetcy of Wentworth, one of the few titles that can be passed down through the female line. As Mary's closest relation, Lady Anne now inherited the title, the fifth female holder since its creation in the sixteenth century.

That summer her health started to decline, but she still spent much time with her beloved horses. 'In the afternoon sat for some time by Jauza – on her manger in fact. She it is that one can't help loving *personally* more than any. Dalal is interesting and her Saadun filly* is a jewel Only Jauza has some indefinable charm.'

Blunt and Lady Anne were in frequent correspondence over the Stud, or as frequent as the mails allowed. Both were unhappy that they had not settled its future beyond all doubt before Lady Anne had left England in 1915 and they exchanged a number of proposals for the formation of a new trust. Blunt was now full of praise for Nureddin II (by Rijm out of Narghileh) but was dubious about using him at stud because of his size. 'I do not object,' replied Lady Anne, 'Nejd have no objection to height in anything they bred among themselves so that they know about it but in anything from outside it is a cause of additional suspicion – additional to the suspicion *always* lurking for outsiders. Of course increased stature is rare in that country.'

On Sunday, November 4th, Lady Anne had an internal chill and remained in bed. The following Wednesday she managed to get up in the afternoon to receive a party of New Zealand soldiers, 'but since then I have been quite flattened out – this is Saturday 10 and I am a shade better but no Mass for me on Sunday'. This is the last entry in her journal.

Lady Anne's health deteriorated steadily. At the end of the month she was taken to hospital. She asked for letters to be written to Wilfrid and Judith but told Napier that he was not to cable as she did not want her family to come out in wartime conditions. By December 6th she had grown very weak and Napier cabled Blunt to tell him that the family should be warned. On December 15th, Lady Anne Blunt died, aged eighty. She was buried in the nuns' cemetery at Jebel Ahman, in sight of Sheykh Obeyd. On January 3rd, 1918, a Requiem Mass was held for her at St Marks, Shoubra, by an appropriate coincidence the site, so many years before, of the Arabian stud of the Viceroy Mohammed Ali.

* Durra 1917

Among the many tributes to Lady Anne, none was more true than that in *The Egyptian Gazette*.

A gracious personality of scholarly tastes, a writer, an artist and a traveller – possessed of great nobility of character and a kindly dignity, which charmed all who knew her, Lady Anne was, in the fullest sense of the word, a great lady.

The final resting place of a great lady

CHAPTER 9

The Lawsuit

On the death of Lady Anne, Wilfrid Blunt presumed that the Stud would revert to him since nothing had been definitely settled before she died. But unless Lady Anne had made a settlement upon it in her will, he doubted that he would be able to afford it and so began to make contingency plans to reduce it to an economical size.

There were 84 horses in all and at the end of 1917 Blunt singled out seven stallions and colts and twenty mares and fillies to keep for breeding. The remaining animals were to be given away, gelded or destroyed, if old. The younger horses would be auctioned at Tattersalls during the coming summer and the mares and fillies would be sold without pedigree so that no rival stud could use them. For the future Blunt hoped that he would be able to sell enough stallions abroad each year at prices high enough to give him sufficient income to run the Stud. It was then costing about £2,000 per annum, which he estimated could be reduced to £1,200 with only thirty horses.

These notions were dashed when early in the New Year he heard the details of Lady Anne's will. It was dated June 14th, 1917. Nothing had been left to Judith (now Lady Wentworth) for three reasons: by her marriage settlement she had been left the remainder to Lady Anne's estate at Ouston; she had been receiving an ample income from the other interests in her marriage settlement (including £20,000 as a gift from Lady Anne); and because she had already received from her mother personal possessions such as jewellery, plate, gold, silver, musical instruments and books to a very considerable value. All that Lady Wentworth inherited, and from the point of view of the Arabian horse it was a priceless legacy, was Lady Anne's manuscript on the Arabian.

Almost the entire residuary estate had been left by Lady Anne in trust for her granddaughters, Anne and Winifrid Lytton, then aged sixteen and thirteen. The Trustees were named as Philip Napier and the Public Trustee. The only mention of the horses was in connection with the powers of the Trustees who 'in particular may continue and carry on my stud or studs of Arabian horses mares and foals in such manner and on such scale as they deem advisable'. The words 'stud or studs' were to be quite important in Crabbet's history.

In his disappointment Blunt wrote: 'It ends any possibility there may have been of my carrying on the stud except on the very smallest scale – a dozen mares and fillies and three stallions.' A few days later, after studying some discouraging accounts for Newbuildings estate for 1917, he decided he could not afford to continue the Stud 'even on the smallest scale'. He now sold Beeding Farm for £4,000 and instructed Philip Napier to accept an offer of £7,000 which had been made for the last of his own land at Sheykh Obeyd.

Despite these sales, Blunt continued to worry about the cost of the horses. To his mind there was no question but that he owned them; regardless of Lady Anne's will, the Partition Agreement of 1906 had stated clearly that the Stud was to pass to the survivor of Blunt and Lady Anne. He ignored the fact that many of the animals were 'free horses', as Lady Anne had called them in her letters to him; that is, they had been either bought from him, or were the offspring of horses that had been bought, by Lady Anne after the Partition.

In January the Public Trustee received an offer of £1,200 for the horses at Sheykh Obeyd. To this Blunt advised acceptance though he had no idea of the number of animals involved: 'if only a dozen, the price is a good one'. The buyer was probably a Greek called Casdugli who in 1924 sold one of the mares, Durra, to the Royal Agricultural Society of Egypt. But Prince Kemal el Dine was also involved, acquiring in particular the mares Dalal 1910, Zareefa 1911 and Serra 1915. This decision to sell the horses angered Lady Wentworth who later complained that the Trustees had made a grievous mistake in parting with the only horses of the Krush strain that had ever left Arabia.

Blunt now began to eye his daughter with some wariness, especially as he had heard from Holman that she looked upon Rasim as her son Anthony's property and not his. He therefore decided to have Rasim and Sotamm removed from Caxtons to Newbuildings as a precaution against a possible *coup de main* by Lady Wentworth. This was on January 24th. On February 16th Caffin reported that Lady Wentworth's lawyers were preparing a claim to part of the Stud on behalf of the Trustees of Lady Anne's will. In Blunt's eyes this was an act of 'mischief and blackmail' and he started to gather at Newbuildings as many horses as he could. On the 18th Nasik and Razaz arrived from Woolborough. Four days later Risala, Ramla and the filly Battla were taken from Crabbet, to be followed at the beginning of March by another six mares. But Blunt was advised not to take the mare Riyala, 'as having been given her (although I do not believe it) by her mother'. In fact Lady Wentworth had bought a half share in Riyala to prevent her sale to Spencer Borden in 1908. Following the removal of these horses to Newbuildings, Lady Wentworth retaliated by taking three mares from Caxtons to Crabbet where she kept them in padlocked stables.

Meanwhile an American, Charles Hayden, representing the President of the Arabian Horse Club of America, Mr W.R. Brown, had arrived at Newbuildings. Brown himself had been to Newbuildings in May, 1913, but had not bought anything. Blunt now saw in Hayden an ideal opportunity to reduce the stock and told him that he could have any of the stallions except Ibn Yashmak, Rustem, Nureddin II and Rasim at moderate prices, together with twenty to thirty mares and fillies. When he told Holman that he was selling Berk, Holman burst into tears. Lady Wentworth, however, had not been inactive, and on March 17th Blunt received a letter from the Public Trustee asking for an assurance that he would not sell or geld any of the horses that Lady Wentworth claimed without the consent of the Trustees. But Blunt had already agreed to sell several of them to Brown and anyway he did not see how the Trustees could require such an assurance from him. On March 19th, he agreed with Hayden the sale of fourteen mares and three stallions for a total of 1,800 guineas. Two days later, however, Hayden told him that Lady Wentworth maintained that Blunt had no title in the horses that were being sold and that they belonged to her. Blunt advised Hayden to pay no attention to this but did tell the Trustees that he would wait until the end of the month before selling any more of the mares on his daughter's list. But when the end of the month came, it did not bring Blunt good news. For on March 31st he heard that Lady Wentworth was now claiming every brood mare in the Stud, including those in the Newbuildings half, together with all the breeding stallions.

It is as well at this point to outline the legal issues upon which the lawsuit was finally fought, nearly two years later.

Blunt claimed all the horses. His reason was that since the Stud was not specifically covered in Lady Anne's will, her horses only fell into the residuary clause if they had not been subject to prior disposition. He asserted that they had been so disposed of by virtue of the survivor clause of the Partition Agreement and that nothing had happened subsequently to alter that position. In addition, the Newbuildings half was his by right of ownership.

Lady Wentworth claimed some fourteen or fifteen horses for herself on the grounds of having been either given them her by her mother or of having purchased them from her. In the former category lay all the greys in the Stud which Lady Wentworth alleged her mother had intended her to have.

The Trustees of Lady Anne Blunt's will claimed all the horses at Crabbet and Newbuildings that Lady Wentworth had not herself claimed, on behalf of Anne and Winifrid Lytton. They contended that there were in any case the 'free' horses, belonging solely to Lady Anne and not covered by the Partition Agreement; and that between 1906 and 1917, Blunt had made over to Lady Anne the management and *de facto* the ownership of all the horses in the Stud. Consequently there had been no prior disposition, as Blunt claimed, and all the Arabians fell into Lady Anne's residuary estate.

Blunt was very apt to give the management of the Stud to Lady Anne whenever he was particularly ill or had financial worries. It had happened, as we have seen, in 1905, in 1907 and in 1913. But the occasion that counsel for the Trustees brought out with especial care was the proposed trust agreement of 1916. Although it had never been signed by Blunt, it was significant, counsel said, of the true state of affairs in the Stud, since at no stage did Blunt propose to take any part in the management and his name as co-owner was omitted in Lady Anne's draft of the trust. Together with other evidence, such as Blunt leaving all the breeding arrangements to his wife, Lady Anne's apparent ability to negotiate without reference to Blunt in the abortive sale to Bush-Brown in 1917, and the clause of her will that mentioned 'stud or studs', counsel for the Trustees was able to construct a case to show that Blunt had effectively ceased to own any part of the Stud.

From the moment in March when Lady Wentworth and the Trustees put forward their claims, the exchanges between Blunt and his daughter quickly assumed a tone similar to those that had preceded her sale of the land at Crabbet. But Blunt was now an old man and had lost much of his earlier fire and fighting spirit. Statements such as 'the fate of the Arab horse depends on my success in resisting Judith's claims', and that the lawsuit was a 'more important issue perhaps than that of the British Empire for which Haig is fighting', would surely have been phrased a great deal more acidly before Lady Anne's death. Though he played his hand to the last card, his heart was never completely in the struggle and against an opponent who was not only as unscrupulous as he was but very much younger and more determined, half measures were certain to fail.

For the moment, though, Blunt continued to sell horses. On April 3rd, 1918, he sold Rief (by Sotamm out of Ridaa) to an Australian, Captain Browne, for 120 guineas. Two days later he secured Rijm after an altercation in the stable yard at Caxtons and had him brought to Newbuildings. Later that month Hayden informed him that the bankers involved in the Brown sale were refusing to go through with their side of it without a written declaration from the Public Trustee that there would be no opposition to the sale. This consent was given in June, though the stallions Nasik, Karun and Mabruk were excluded, and on July 19th, 1918, the largest single consignment to leave Crabbet so far departed for the docks at London. Seventeen horses were included for a total price of only 1,600 guineas. 'Nothing but what we can well spare,' wrote Blunt. After they had left he had 'the most perfect lot of mares now ever seen together, I am convinced, since the days of Solomon.' A little later the Stud 'never was so splendidly perfect as it is now – every doubtful weeded out. I keep repeating to myself as the mares gallop and wheel in the meadows,

> Whence are ye noble ladies, whence are ye?
> So many and so many and such glee.'

Shortly after this Blunt was visited by Mr S.G. Hough, who had for some time been trying to buy Nureddin II. Blunt did not want to sell him and by way of a polite refusal, asked 1,000 guineas. To his surprise, Hough agreed the price immediately, the biggest ever given for a Crabbet horse. But then Nureddin was exceptional and according to Blunt, one of the best horses bred at the Stud. Holman too was pleased at the price. 'Her ladyship would have been delighted if she had known of it. Perhaps she does,' he remarked. Fortunately for Blunt, Nureddin was not one of the horses that Lady Wentworth could claim as he had never spent so much as a night at Crabbet.

Various proposals for a compromise had by now been made by Lady Wentworth and the Public Trustee. The first was that Blunt and Lady Wentworth should divide the Stud between them. Blunt denounced this as impudence and replied that he would not be party to any arrangement that left a single horse in his daughter's hands. He did, however, offer to treat out of court with the Public Trustee and the Lytton girls on what he described as a money basis. This came to nothing and the Public Trustee put forward another offer; neither Lady Wentworth nor the girls would pursue their claim so long as Blunt undertook to leave the Stud to them on his death. After some consideration, Blunt rejected this as well, since he declined to bind himself when the girls were unmarried and under their mother's influence.

Negotiations continued in a desultory way into the spring of 1919. The intermediary was Philip Napier. Lady Wentworth viewed his interference with alarm and P.N., as she referred to him, soon came to be known as 'the Perfect Nuisance'. Napier seemed to forget at times that 'he is (or ought to be) acting for the children *against* H.F.'. She thought that Blunt 'would twist him round his little finger ... and even his father says he is an ass!!'. Blunt too became impatient with Napier; and with the dispute now in its second year and with the prospect of losing the summer market again, he decided in February that nothing was to be gained from further bargaining and that the issue should be determined in the courts.

By now he had collected a large number of horses at Newbuildings and had, he thought, every point of law on his side 'including the point of possession'. But the Stud had cost him £4,000 in 1918 and although this had been offset by sales of £3,000, this was an exceptional figure and Blunt was seriously worried about the cost of maintaining the Stud without having a free hand to sell as he chose. 'I shall therefore have to make my settlement of the stud, whether to the King or another, now without waiting for my death, and the sooner the better.' For some time Blunt had been attempting to persuade a friend, Lord Ribblesdale, to approach George V over the Stud's future, a move that added further fuel to Lady Wentworth's argument that unless something was done soon there would be no horses left. But in the summer of 1919, Blunt was informed to his chagrin that the King 'already had such a number of studs to keep up that he did not see his way to undertaking any more'. Blunt thereupon offered it to Ribblesdale himself. He declined and suggested that Blunt ask Smuts if the South African government would take it, or failing that, the Duke of Portland. These developments were cut short by the news that the case was to commence at the end of October.

On October 9th, Blunt was visited by Dr A.E. Branch and his wife, acting for the Princes Mohammed Ali and Kemal el Dine. The latter was said to be managing 'what remains of the Ali Sherif stud in Egypt which they have placed under the *Waqf* as a trust and who wants to get together all the blood they can of that stud and especially ours'. Branch was interested in Rustem, Ibn Yashmak and Naufal (by Sotamm out of Narghileh), for whom Blunt asked 1,000 guineas for the three. A few weeks later he received a telegram from Prince Kemal el Dine enquiring the price of four stallions and a mare – Ibn Yashmak, Rustem, Nasik (by Rijm out of Narghileh), Rasim and Risala (by Mesaoud out of Ridaa). Blunt replied that Rasim and Risala were not for sale and that for the others he wanted 1,200 guineas.

These negotiations also had to be abandoned when it was announced that the lawsuit, which had already been postponed from October, was definitely to start on December 23rd.

Since Blunt was not well enough to give evidence in London, arrangements were made for the Official Referee and counsel for both parties to come down that day and cross-examine him at Newbuildings.

Blunt's sense of theatre never left him. On December 20th his hair dresser, a man named Middleton, travelled from London to trim his beard and generally to 'furbish me up', as Blunt described it. When on the 23rd, the Referee, eight lawyers and Sydney Cockerell were led up to his bedroom to begin the proceedings, they found Blunt ensconced in bed amid a pile of cushions and attired in a resplendent Bedouin robe. As they and the shorthand reporter (who in a characteristic aside Blunt recognised as a conscientious objector who had been 'abominably martyred' during the war) arranged themselves around the foot of the bed, they can have been in no doubt who was going to hold the stage. 'It was certainly a great advantage to me to have in this way the central position and by far the most comfortable,' wrote Blunt, 'and fortified with an extra dose of cough mixture, I felt more than usually fit.'

The hearing continued throughout the day and for a few hours on Christmas Eve. Blunt felt that he was still on top, even though Lady Wentworth had yet to give evidence. Another attempt to compromise was now made. Grant, counsel for the Public Trustee, approached Cockerell to see what terms Blunt would agree to. Blunt said that if he could choose forty mares and horses for himself, he would allow his grandchildren to take the remainder. He considered that this 'would leave me all that was necessary to keep the stud going'. Lady Wentworth did not find the proposal acceptable.

The case reopened in London on February 9th and lasted until the 23rd. 'So long for so little,' wrote Blunt, and it does indeed seem that a disproportionate amount of time was taken up by issues that did not strictly relate to the Stud. The accusations and insinuations made by both parties delighted the newspaper reporters but were seldom more than incidental to the point in question.

Shortly after the hearing began, counsel again offered to compromise with Blunt and again he adamantly refused to allow any of the horses to fall into Lady Wentworth's hands. For her part, she 'had no wish to stand 4 days in any witness box, but I always said that I should fight the matter out if he persisted in refusing to let us have any horses at all'. Blunt's counsel had been 'offensive and vindictive' when cross-examining her but had failed to make her lose her temper.

Opinion generally was that Blunt would win. His lawyers were confident and did not anticipate the award of 'more than a few horses' to the Public Trustee. The worst they feared was Rasim going to Lady Wentworth, for he and the mare Riyala had been the most disputed of the horses. The decision was announced on March 5th, 1920. Blunt was asleep at three in the afternoon when his lawyer's telegram arrived: 'Decision against you with all costs but you allowed cost of keeping all horses that you had from January 1918.'

Blunt was not unduly disappointed. In fact he may have even been relieved at the result and he refused to appeal against the verdict. 'Apart from a sense of a sharp blow which any unexpected news of defeat gives for the moment, it has not troubled me much.' He was now free not only of the worry of the whole affair, but also, which was probably more to the point, of the expense of maintaining 'a costly possession which I can no longer enjoy or attend to properly'.

It has not been possible to ascertain Lady Anne's final wishes for the Crabbet Arabian Stud after her death. Her thoughts appear to have been governed by two principal considerations; one, the very grave doubts that she – and Blunt – had for the future of horse-breeding in England, and the other, her conviction that no member of her family would have sufficient funds to maintain the Stud at the size she felt necessary. The most likely explanation is that she was in such despair about the Stud and the relationship between her husband and daughter that she simply left it for her executors to decide. Whether or not the Referee's decision was a good one at law (Blunt's counsel were confident that it would have been overturned on appeal), it was undoubtedly the best from the point of view of the Arabian horse. Had Blunt won the case, it is more than likely not only that he would have been obliged to continue to run down the Stud by selling stock but also that he would have been incapable, through age and infirmity, of ensuring that the horses were properly cared for.

The final terms were somewhat different from the court ruling. They were as follows: 1. Blunt was to pay his costs only; 2. He was to be repaid the £1,000 put on deposit after the sale to W.R. Brown; 3. He was to retain all other sales proceeds received; 4. Lady Wentworth was to pay nothing for maintenance since 1918; 5. All the horses were to be removed from Newbuildings by June 30th of that year.

Lady Wentworth was triumphant. On April 16th she was driven to Crookhorn where Caffin handed over the first batch of horses, the stallions Razaz, Hazzam and Rasim and the mares Nasra and Rim with their foals. Lady Wentworth rode Rasim back to Crabbet herself. 'Not even torrential thunder rain could drench the joy out of that 17 mile ride,' she wrote. The penultimate and probably the most brilliant phase in the history of the Crabbet Arabian Stud had commenced.

CHAPTER 10

Crabbet Prospers

When the horses arrived at Crabbet, Lady Wentworth was faced with many difficulties, the main one being their sheer number. But the most immediate problem was to deal with the poor condition in which many returned.

Lady Wentworth sometimes said that one of the reasons that certain lines died out at Crabbet and that the mares lost many of their foals, was the mismanagement in the early days of the Stud. There is some truth in this. Both Wilfrid and Lady Anne Blunt spent long periods abroad and while they were either at Crabbet or Sheykh Obeyd were unable to ensure that the horses in the other stud were receiving proper attention. However good were the men who had been left in charge during the Blunts' absences, they were no substitute for the personal supervision of the Blunts themselves. The risks involved in running two large breeding studs in different countries without the benefit of modern veterinary skills, had for a long time been apparent to Lady Wentworth. When the Blunts had started breeding in Egypt she had criticised the idea for the very reason that they would be unable adequately to oversee both studs.

Wilfrid Blunt's attitude to the horses' well-being was similar in many ways to his views on their breeding; the more closely conditions reproduced those in the desert, the more likely it would be that the stock were true representatives of their forebears. In breeding terms this was a perfectly valid philosophy since it led to the automatic weeding out of unsuitable animals, but for the purposes of horse management it was a failure.

Since Arabians had to be hardy to survive in their own environment, Blunt expected them to be likewise in England. He said that the only reason for feeding up horses was to make them sell better. Except for the stallions and foals, he reckoned that they should be able to live out all the year round on grass alone, supplemented occasionally with acorns in winter. He did not see this as a cause of unnecessary suffering but rather as a test of their natural characteristics. In 1904 it had been suggested in the local press that he treated his horses better than his labourers. 'The implication,' he replied, 'is the reverse of true. My horses, valuable as they are, are housed, not in handsome modern stables, but in rough farm buildings, old wooden sheds and disused barns. In these they are lodged the winter through without clothing, nevertheless in perfect health . . . This is a matter of notoriety in the county and, I may add, the world over.' Later, in March 1918, when he had been trying to dispose of the Stud, he made a point of taking Lord Ribblesdale to see the mares 'in their starvation camp at Worleys', as it would show him 'what hardy stock they are, for they have been out of doors all winter'.

Had the horses received correct attention in other respects, the lack of corn and the winters outside might have mattered less. But Blunt disliked vets, whom he thought should never be called except for an accident since they carried diseases in their pockets. He was also strongly opposed to money being spent on what he called mere smartness, a remark that prompted Lady Wentworth to comment, 'But a good deal should be spent on cleanliness and disinfection.' In addition he had been immobilised by illness throughout the lawsuit and had been physically unable to inspect the horses regularly. Thus in October 1918, he had three colts gelded but it was not until May the next year that he saw for himself their 'extremely bad state' (from which one, in fact, died soon afterwards).

Although the stallions at Newbuildings had been well cared for, several of the mares returned to Crabbet in such poor condition that they either died or failed to breed again. Some of the fillies had to be rigorously treated for lice, worms and skin diseases. From the first Lady Wentworth kept an eagle eye on all aspects of the Stud. In her early days she would personally supervise everything, even drenching the mares when they were ill. Geoffrey Covey was appointed manager and under him excellent men as heads of department. Some of the staff taken on in the 1920s were to remain at the Stud until its disbandment.

Her other great worry was the number of the horses and where to accommodate them. While the lawsuit had been in progress, many of the foals born at Newbuildings had not been entered in the General Stud Book. When applications were now made to register them, they were turned down as they had been sent in too late. Apart from these youngsters, who clearly could not remain in the Stud without being registered, there were also many other horses that Lady Wentworth felt were superfluous. Luckily Dr Branch was still in England and keen to resume the negotiations that he had begun with Blunt the previous year.

Branch and Lady Wentworth disliked each other from the start. His dour Scottish manner did not appeal to her and even less when he began by telling her that it was useless to try to carry on. Despite being told sharply to mind his own business, Branch continued to take the same line and offered £75 a head for forty-one horses. This was turned down flat and the arguments now became so heated that it is surprising that an agreement was reached at all. Branch was annoyed at not being allowed to buy the best mares and sent his wife over to Newbuildings to stir up Blunt's wrath against his daughter. Lady Wentworth was angry at being taken for a fool and kept hidden the horses that she did not want to sell. Agreement was finally reached whereby for 3,000 guineas Branch bought on behalf of the Royal Agricultural Society of Egypt a total of nineteen horses, including a filly and two geldings. No sooner was this settled than Lady Wentworth had paraded in front of Branch's disbelieving eyes the stallions Skowronek and Nasik, 'for a penance', she said. Branch was so struck by them that he immediately asked why he had not been shown them before since he would certainly have bought them. He was told by Lady Wentworth that if she had allowed him to see them earlier he would never have bought Sotamm – which she wanted to sell.

The sale to Egypt was important, for it reduced the Stud to a manageable size and put Lady Wentworth's finances in a better position. It will be remembered that the horses had belonged, under trust, to Anne and Winifrid Lytton. In the summer of 1920 the Public Trustee had obtained a valuation on them of £2,328 from Montefiore, the Secretary of the Arab Horse Society. Meanwhile Lady Wentworth had been given a guarantee of £3,300 by her aunt Lady Lovelace and on the strength of this was able to buy all the horses from the Trustees.

Anne and Winifrid Lytton were allowed to keep two horses each for their own pleasure. Winifrid was married the following year and soon gave up her horses, but for Anne Lytton* it was the start of an illustrious career as a breeder. She had always been deeply interested in horses, much more so than her brother and sister. Her grandmother had given her every encouragement as a child. She had allowed Anne

---

*The Hon. Anne Lytton assumed the name Lytton-Milbanke in February, 1925. The Milbanke was dropped in 1947 when she became Lady Anne Lytton upon her father's accession to the Earldom.

to accompany her on her daily tours of the stables and had taught her to ride correctly one winter at Sheykh Obeyd. Anne Lytton now chose the mare Ferda (by Rustem out of Feluka) and Nasik (by Rijm out of Narghileh). But she was persuaded by her mother to take the gelding Kaftan instead of Nasik as she would enjoy riding him more than the stallion.

Anne Lytton bred five foals from Ferda, three fillies and two colts, all of which she gave to her mother. The first was Farasin (by Rasim) which Ferda was carrying when she arrived from Newbuildings. Farasin was born in 1920 and was sold to the United States in 1926. In 1922 Ferda had Fantana (by Nasik) who produced three good daughters in Firefly, Josepha and Dil Fireb, and she was followed by Farrash (by Nadir), Fejran (by Rasim) and Ferdisia (by Rafeef). By the time the last was born, negotiations with Mr W.K. Kellogg were under way and at her mother's request, Anne Lytton returned Ferda so that she might be included in the sale with Farasin and Ferdisia. In America Ferda and Farasin were to become famous as brood mares. In exchange for Ferda, Anne Lytton was given Rossana, a Skowronek filly out of Rose of Hind, but this proved an even more temporary gift than Ferda as Rossana also went to Kellogg in 1926.

The way in which Lady Wentworth reclaimed the horses she had given her daughter may appear a little summary but it was actually something of a tradition in the family of which she herself had more than once been a victim. First there had been Mesaoud, her birthday present, and then the greys Bozra and Nejiba. She had been promised Bozra when Bozra's dam Basilisk, who was also a grey and much admired by Lady Wentworth, was sold to the Duke of Westminster. The promise was never kept. Nejiba had been given her as a wedding present only to be taken back a few years later. She had been offered money instead but had considered this no compensation for the loss of the mare.

Lady Wentworth once described how, as a child, she saw the white Seglawi Jedran of Ibn Sudan being led through the vaulted archways of Ali Pasha Sherif's palace and how the memory of 'the silver manes and tails floating in the wind' and the 'crested arch of neck and tail' had been imprinted in her mind. Her father had noted that white horses were 'commonly connected with extreme beauty'. There was no grey stallion at Crabbet in 1920 and only a few grey mares. Lady Wentworth was now to acquire the most famous of all the greys that Crabbet ever had.

above Nejiba (Azrek–Nefisa) at Crabbet before the stables were altered in 1936.
centre Ajjam (Ibn Yashmak–Ajramieh)
below Anne Lytton with Kaftan at the Richmond Show *ca* 1922

Lady Wentworth saw Skowronek at the Pony Show at Islington in March, 1920. Though he was placed second in the stallion class and had not been particularly successful at previous shows, she immediately made up her mind to buy him. Skowronek had been bred by Count Joseph Potocki in Poland and in 1913 had been imported into England by Walter Winans, a sculptor of American birth who was also an enthusiastic breeder of trotters. The horse had then passed into the hands of a Mr Webb-Ware who had ridden him as a hack during the war and had later sold him to Mr H.V.M. Clark, who registered him in the Arab Horse Society's Stud Book and used him on a few mares at his Courthouse Stud.

A month after the Islington Show Skowronek was at Crabbet. Whenever Lady Wentworth herself showed interest in a horse either the owner suddenly decided not to sell or the price of the animal immediately rose. She was not the only person who occasionally had to use the services of an intermediary. The go-between for Skowronek's purchase was the American, Hayden, who had negotiated with Blunt over the sale to W.R. Brown. He was able to persuade Mr Clark to part with Skowronek, probably on the pretext that he was acting for an American buyer. The next that Mr Clark knew was that instead of being at the docks, Skowronek was at Crabbet.

Lady Wentworth had learned something of Skowronek's Polish background from her parents who had visited Antoniny early in the 1880s and had greatly admired many of the mares there. In the summer of 1920 Count Roman Potocki (whose father had bred Skowronek) went to Crabbet and was able to supply the information needed to register Skowronek in the General Stud Book. Skowronek was actually the last imported Arabian to be accepted into the G.S.B. as shortly afterwards it was closed to new imports and only Arabians whose parents were already registered were henceforth eligible for inclusion.

The Arabian section of the G.S.B. had started in 1877 with the importations of Sandeman and Upton. In the following volume in 1880 it was enlarged to include the Blunts' horses. Since then Crabbet horses had always been registered in it and were so until Weatherbys changed to a computer system in 1965 and closed the Arab section. When the Arab Horse Society published its first stud book in 1919, some of the Crabbet horses were included in it. Lady Wentworth continued to register most of her horses with the Society until 1923 when she resigned after a violent disagreement over its policy for new registrations.

The Arab Horse Society had been formed in the spring of 1918 under the aegis of the Rev. D.B. Montefiore, Mr S.G. Hough and Mr H.V.M. Clark. Wilfrid Blunt had been nominated as the first President of the Society but had been disinclined to devote any time to its activities and in 1921 Mr Hough became President.

Blunt's last years were not happy. Racked with pain, he thought himself often to be on the point of death. 'When will it really be?' he wrote after a night of torture in 1921, and a month later, 'The only wonder to me has been how each morning I have been condemned to begin another.' His only consolations in 'this death in life' were the devotion of Miss Lawrence and Dorothy Carleton, and his expeditions in his perambulator, a remarkable affair consisting of a wooden platform built on pram wheels upon which he was pulled round the estate. His relationship with Judith never completely recovered from the bitterness between them in the past although after several approaches by Judith, a reconciliation of sorts did take place shortly before his death. On September 10th, 1922, Wilfrid Blunt died at the age of eighty-two.

He was buried in the woods behind Newbuildings. The ceremony was described by Sydney Cockerell.

> By his directions it took place as soon as possible and without coffin or religious or other ceremony – but the proceedings were very beautiful and dignified and just what he intended. The grave was immense, with steps down into it. The floor was covered with greenery over which we scattered his favourite everlasting flowers. Judith knelt for a little while beside the body, which was sewn in his favourite Eastern travelling carpet, and over and about which Miss Carleton, Miss Lawrence and Anne strewed fragrant pot pourri from Newbuildings roses . . . Whatever his shortcomings, he was a very wonderful being and quite unlike anyone else.

In his will Blunt left his lands at Worth and the Lordship of the Manor of Worth to Lady Mary Strickland. Dorothy Carleton was left Springfield Park and the Newbuildings estate. She spent the rest of her life at Newbuildings and on her death, over thirty years later, she bequeathed it to Lady Anne Lytton with succession to Lord Lytton's heir.

Skowronek quickly established himself at Crabbet. In 1922 he had two offspring of inestimable influence on Arab breeding throughout the world, the stallion Naseem (out of Nasra) and the mare Rifala (out of

Rissla). For the first few years that Skowronek was at Crabbet, about a third of the mares were put to him each season. Rasim, and Nadir who had been repurchased from Ruxton in 1919, were the other stallions mainly used at the time. Skowronek proved a remarkably successful outcross for the Crabbet mares. His most beautiful sons were probably the full brothers Naseem and Naziri but he sired many other excellent horses such as Raffles (out of Rifala), Raseyn (out of Rayya) and Raswan (out of Rim). The influence of Skowronek is examined in greater detail in Chapter 13. His beauty and the very high standard of his foals have made him renowned as a stallion and his exceptional prepotency ensured that these qualities were passed down through his descendants. He was also instrumental in reestablishing grey as a colour in the Stud.

As soon as Naseem was old enough, a high proportion of the mares at Crabbet were put to him and many fewer to Skowronek. Rasim had never been used at the Stud by the Blunts as Lady Anne thought his action faulty, though she considered him a very beautiful horse. But Lady Wentworth admired his type so much that when she took over the Stud she put a number of mares to him immediately. She described him as having 'a most lovely head, neck and front. Excellent legs, body and tail carriage' and 'particularly good feet'. Rasim won many championships and was the sire of Razina (out of Riyala), Sainfoin (out of Safarjal) and Raseem (out of Rim).

Another stallion at Crabbet in the early Twenties was Rafeef, by Nasik out of Riyala. He had 'magnificent style. Neck arched, tail in the air'. 'Everyone wanted this horse,' wrote Lady Wentworth. She eventually sold him for exportation to Argentina. Rafeef sired mostly colts, nearly all of which went abroad, but he did have two fine and influential daughters, Nezma (out of Nasra) and Risslina (out of Rissla).

Nureddin II had been bought by Mr S.G. Hough in 1918. In 1921 he was repurchased by Lady Wentworth for whom he sired, among others, Shareer (out of Selima), Faris (out of Fejr) and the important mare Neraida (out of Nasifa). Lady Wentworth described Nureddin as 'a tall showy chestnut with blaze and both hind stockings. Very strong hocks. Powerful all over. A grand type for getting brood mares'. Nureddin and Skowronek were very different in many respects but their qualities have blended well together in later generations when used in moderation. Too much Nureddin blood has tended to produce a certain coarseness and an increase in size. On the other hand inbreeding to Skowronek can lead to the opposite type.

When a stud has become as successful as Crabbet, it inevitably arouses jealousy and can lead to insinuations being made against some

above Lady Wentworth and Skowronek at the Richmond Show in 1924
left Lady Wentworth with, from left: Risala, Ajjam, Kibla, Riyala and Rim

above top Rafeef (Nasik–Riyala) outside the tennis court. 'Everyone wanted this horse'
below Nezma (Rafeef–Nasra) with Cecil Covey
above right Rasim (Feysul–Risala) and *below* Raseem (Rasim–Rim)

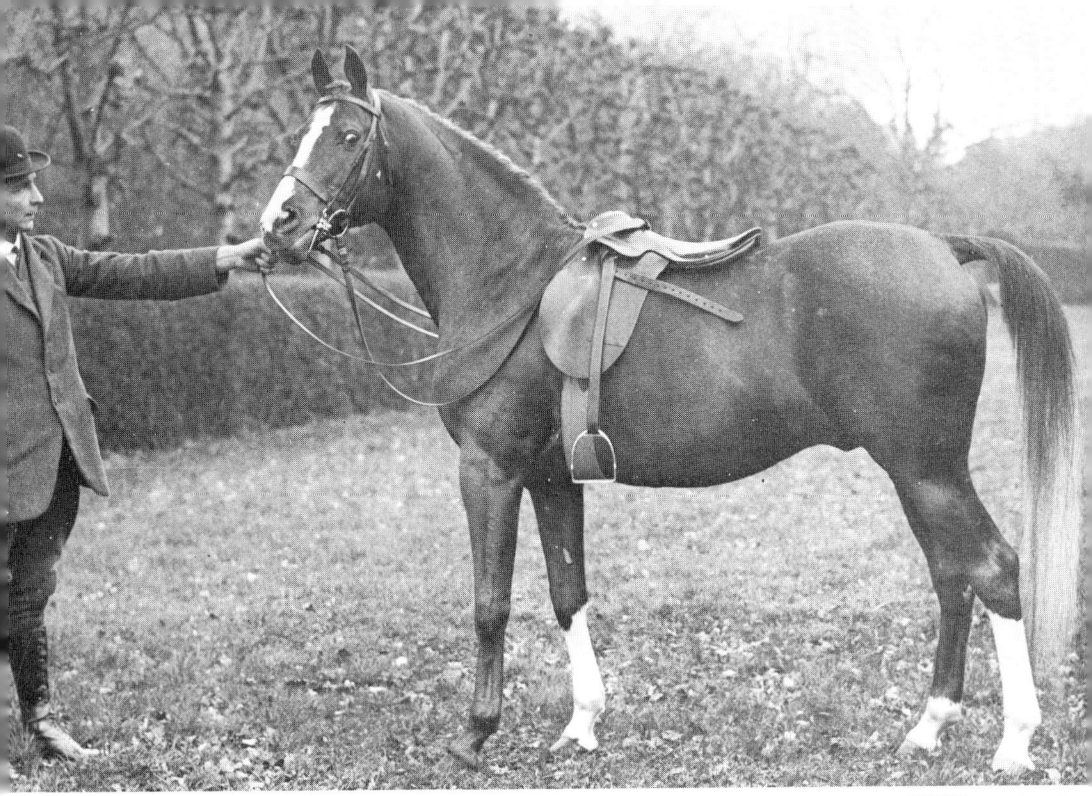

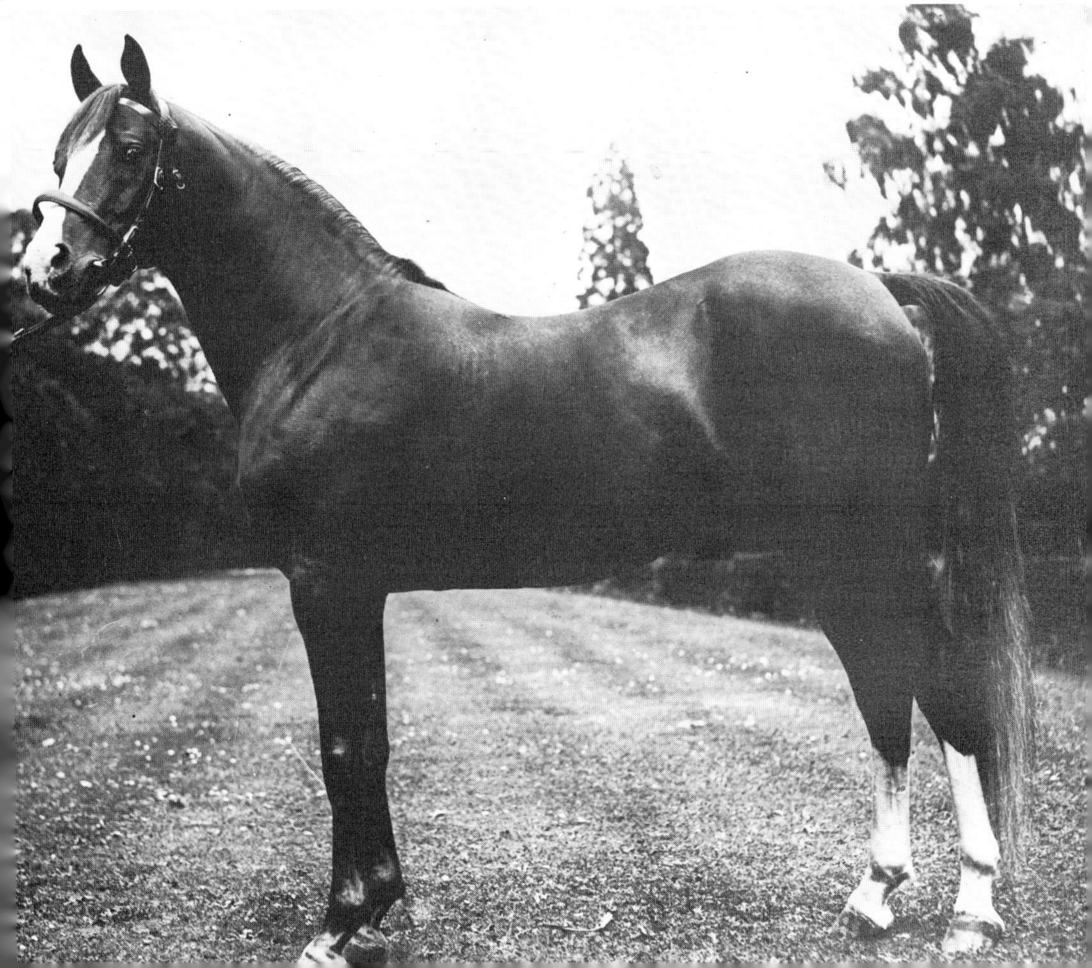

of the horses. Rumours, once started, have been as difficult to despatch at Crabbet as they have been elsewhere.

There are always breeders with a preference for Arabians that are larger or smaller than what may at the time be considered the norm. Lady Wentworth particularly admired larger ones and once said that she could not have 'too much of a good thing'. But she nevertheless bought the smaller ones too, such as Skowronek and Dargee, and kept horses of all sizes at Crabbet. Quality and type were the features that she prized above all others. In Wilfrid Blunt's opinion the smaller sires were the best, but that never prevented him from using and admiring their larger stallions such as Rijm and Nureddin II. Lady Anne Blunt also appreciated Rijm's 'splendid' qualities, and it may well be that the coarseness that occasionally appears in horses of this line comes from Rijm's sire, Mahruss (1893), the Ali Pasha Sherif horse that the Blunts imported.

The number of breeders of Arabians in England was steadily increasing and Lady Wentworth did not have to rely as exclusively as her parents had done on overseas buyers.

Mr S.G. Hough had started breeding pure Arabians with Nureddin II, by whom he had in 1920 Nuri Pasha (out of Ruth Kesia) and Nuri Sherif (out of Sheeba). When Lady Wentworth took over Crabbet he was among the first to buy from her, acquiring Amida (by Ibn Yashmak out of Ajramieh) and the seventeen-year-old Simrieh, the daughter of Seyal and Selma. After his death in the hunting field in 1923, the stud was taken over by his son Cecil who later became President of the Arab Horse Society on four occasions.

The oldest stud to have remained in the same ownership since its foundation is today that of Mr H.V.M. Clark, in Sussex. In 1910 he bought the Crabbet stallion Mansur. In 1917 and 1918 he acquired from Blunt the mares Feluka and Nessima (by Rijm out of Narghileh). For a time he also had Daoud at Courthouse. But the best known of all his Crabbet-bred horses was the mare Belka. Belka's sire was Rijm and her dam Bereyda, a daughter of Ahmar and Bozra. She was foaled in 1912 and bought by Mr Clark as a two-year-old. As well as achieving fame in the endurance tests which the Arab Horse Society organised in the early Twenties, Belka was a fine brood mare and left many notable descendants at the Courthouse Stud, among them Belkis II, Betina, Benjamin, Boaz and perhaps the most beautiful of them all, the stallion Bahram.

In 1923 Lady Wentworth presented Safarjal (by Berk out of Somra) to Mrs Clark. Safarjal was then in foal to Rasim. The bay colt that was born was named Sainfoin who together with Champurrado (who was bred by Lady Yule) had a tremendous influence on the Clarks' stud. Lady Wentworth had a high opinion of Mr Clark's judgement of Arabian type and regretted that two of his imported horses, Fedaan and Nimr, could not be registered in the G.S.B. because she would have liked to use them as stallions.

Despite its venerable age, Courthouse is not in fact the oldest stud in England today. This distinction belongs to the Harwood Stud. It was founded in 1896 when Colonel Lyon bought Howa (by Azrek) at the Crabbet sale. Howa was the great-granddaughter of the journey mare Hagar and it is through Howa and the Harwood Stud that one of the few surviving lines from Hagar is carried. After Colonel Lyon's death, his daughter May added other mares of Crabbet breeding. She later moved some of her horses to Rostrevor in Ireland and for many years ran two studs. She was an unmistakable figure and held forthright views which she aired in a penetrating voice. Like Mr Clark, she was a great admirer of Lady Anne Blunt. On her death, her property was inherited by Mr and Mrs R.H. Calvert and their daughter, who have continued to breed from Crabbet bloodlines.

Probably the most prominent breeder from Crabbet blood in Lady Wentworth's time was, however, Lady Yule. On July 11th, 1925, Lady Yule and her daughter Gladys paid their first visit to Crabbet. Though her main interest at the time was in breeding Anglo-Arabs, she was impressed by the parade of Arabians that Lady Wentworth gave her and bought the three-year-old Razina. As a yearling Razina had been sold to Mrs Carroll in Ireland and had been repurchased after she had had a colt named Radi. She was in foal to a Thoroughbred when she returned to Crabbet and in view of Lady Yule's preference for Anglo-Arabs, seemed an ideal choice. But in fact Lady Yule never put Razina to a Thoroughbred and only to Arab stallions.

Lady Wentworth was at first annoyed when Lady Yule started to breed pure Arabians. By 1932 Razina had had four foals, among them Nurschida, by Mr Hough's Nuri Sherif. That year Mr Kent, who was well known in pony breeding circles, came to Crabbet and said he wished to buy two mares. He chose Astrella (by Rasim out of Amida) and Naxina (by Skowronek out of Nessima) and departed professing himself well pleased. Within a week the mares were at Lady Yule's

above Astrella (Raseem–Amida) with Branch
centre Razina (Rasim–Riyala)
below Riffal (Naufal–Razina)

stud at Hanstead. Lady Wentworth would have been less than human had she resented the same methods by which she had acquired Skowronek, and agreed with Lady Yule that the Hanstead mares should come to Crabbet for covering. In 1933 Razina was put to Naseem. The foal born proved to be her finest son, Raktha. Razina returned to Crabbet in succeeding years and in 1936 had Riffal (by Naufal) and in 1939 Shamnar (by Naziri). For her foundation mare Lady Yule could scarcely have chosen better.

Until almost the end of the Second World War, Lady Yule continued to send her mares to Crabbet and the interchange of horses that thereby arose between the two studs was of tremendous value to each. One of Lady Yule's best colts was Grey Owl (by Raseem out of Naxina). Naxina also produced Naseel, by the Crabbet-bred Raftan. Naseel went to Mrs S.A. Nicholson in Ireland and there became a famous sire, particularly for the superb quality of the foals he got from pony mares. His part-bred daughter Pretty Polly founded a dynasty of highly successful show winners.

Lady Yule was wealthy and spared nothing to get the best, paying high prices for her mares and for the use of stallions. She sent her mares to Crabbet in an enormous and luxurious horse-box under the charge of Bishop, the stud groom. They would arrive in the morning, be covered immediately and then left in loose boxes while the grooms adjourned to a public house in Crawley for lunch. In the afternoon the mares would be covered again and then taken back to Hanstead.

As in the Blunts' days, a constant stream of English and overseas visitors came to Crabbet. One day it was a certain wealthy Duke, '6 foot 6 and very slow witted. Wasn't sure what he wanted but he wanted it for nothing'. On October 8th, 1926, Prince Faisal ibn Saoud 'arrived at 10.40 with the Jeddah Consul and saw all the horses. He picked out Blaze (Sultan Rasim) and Nureddin, Nasra, Nashisha and Ajjam. I don't think he is a real judge of horses according to Arab ideas as certainly Nureddin has not got the best head. The Amir is a young man of the true Nejd type with lovely eyes and teeth and a charming very shy manner. He was dressed in a beautiful head-dress and brown Nejd cloak but his *kaftan* was made of an indian shawl.' In July 1935 the Amir Saoud paid a visit to Crabbet with his interpreter and 'three flashing bodyguard Arabs and two Scotland Yard men'. Lady Wentworth pretended not to know any Arabic 'so heard all he said which was unstinted praise of the horses, which made a grand show'.

At the end of January, 1926, Carl Schmidt (as he then was: he later changed his name to Raswan) made his first appearance at Crabbet. After 'five hours of solid conversation' the Kellogg negotiations were under way. This was to be the first of Lady Wentworth's major sales overseas.

The essentials did not take long to settle. Within a week Kellogg had cabled Schmidt authorising him to accept Lady Wentworth's offer of twelve horses for a total price of £17,430. He also asked for an option (which was not taken up) on Nasra's daughter by Nadir called Nasira for ten thousand guineas. Among the mares were Farasin, Ferdisia, Ferda, Rossana and Rifla. To begin with there was only one stallion, Raseyn, then a three-year-old, and one colt, the yearling Rimal. But when the final details had been agreed, Lady Wentworth added two more as gifts – Nasik for Kellogg and Raswan for Schmidt himself, who had particularly wanted a son of Skowronek. She also sent the Welsh Mountain Pony stallion Silverlight for Mrs Kellogg.

The horses were not to be shipped until the end of March and in the intervening weeks, Schmidt was often at Crabbet. He appears at first to have impressed Lady Wentworth by his judgement. 'Mr Schmidt,' she wrote, 'with a glance from the other side of the street would buy you a better Arabian horse than any remount officer after a half hour examination with a couple of vets.' She did, however, think that his

Arabic was not all that he pretended it to be, while others at Crabbet felt that his knowledge of Arabians was less than might have been expected from a man spending very large sums on their purchase.

In the middle of February 'Carl Schmidt came down. We had another very long talk of the fairy tale variety. He paid a cheque for £1,150 on account which is not a fairy tale'. There was talk of Kellogg buying Skowronek but nothing came of it as Kellogg decided that he would like to see what he had got for his money before buying any more horses. At another point a proposal was made, apparently by Schmidt, that Kellogg endow a horse-breeding enterprise that would combine the advantages of his money with the Crabbet blood. Lady Wentworth was cautious, as 'the life and death of the Arabian horse in the world' would depend on her decision. The plan, as outlined by Schmidt, would entail virtually the whole of the Stud being moved to America and she was uncertain if she could entrust her horses to Kellogg, of whom she actually knew very little. Did he have, for instance, the 'fanatical spirit of the Bedouin Arab who would kill his mare and himself sooner than sell his mare or mismate her'? The most essential thing in breeding Arabians was 'the eye for type', a faculty that was born in people and not acquired like merchandise. She had no doubt that Kellogg had the money for the scheme but did he have the knowledge of breeding and the 'eye'?

The prospects for the endowment received a setback when soon after his return to America, Schmidt's relations with Kellogg began to deteriorate rapidly. One of several reasons for this was Schmidt's tendency to exceed his authority as Kellogg's agent. An instance of this was his offer on Kellogg's behalf of a gold cup to be awarded to the winner at the Richmond Show that summer. This annoyed Kellogg and embarrassed Lady Wentworth. When she won the cup with Raseem, she offered to return the prize money to Kellogg as evidence of her dissociation from Schmidt.

Meanwhile Kellogg had invited Lady Wentworth to go to California and to advise him on breeding policy. But she was reluctant to leave Crabbet and besides, she still remembered her disastrous trip to America with Neville Lytton in 1914. Her son Anthony* went to see Kellogg in her place. The principal matters discussed appear to have been whether Lady Wentworth would sell or loan Skowronek to Kellogg and whether Lady Wentworth would visit California. Lady Wentworth declined on

*The Hon. Anthony Lytton changed his name to Lytton-Milbanke in February, 1925. The Milbanke was dropped when he became the Earl of Lytton in 1951.

left King Fuad of Egypt admiring Naufal and
right Prince Faisal ibn Saoud at Crabbet

both accounts. She had still not met Kellogg; the sacrifice to Crabbet would be too great if she sent Skowronek; and as for going there, she felt that since conditions were not dissimilar to those in Egypt, she could advise him just as well by letter.

By 1930 the Depression was making itself felt at Crabbet. At the end of the year the overdrafts on the Stud and estate accounts were over £11,000 and something had to be done.

The Duke of Veragua had recently been to visit and had much admired Skowronek's stock. He now bought five of his daughters for his stud in Spain: Jalila, Shelifa, Reyna, Namira and Nasieda. Of more importance financially were the sales in 1930 and 1932 to Roger A. Selby of Portsmouth, Ohio. Selby had already bought from Crabbet in 1928, when he had acquired, among others, the influential mares Kareyma (by Naseem out of Julnar), Indaia (by Raseem out of Nisreen) and Rifala. His main purchase in 1930 was Mirage, an imported grey stallion of the Seglawi Jedran Dalia strain. Lady Wentworth described him as 'a very showy good horse. Excellent legs, splendid quarters and fine front. Very good in saddle but too bouncing for English taste as he gets English riders off.' But this was not the reason Mirage was sold. Weatherbys had by now closed their Stud Book to new imports and although Lady Wentworth tried to persuade them to accept Mirage, she was unsuccessful and therefore had no option but to sell him.

In 1932 Selby bought Raffles and in 1933 Nureddin II, then aged twenty-two. Raffles proved an extraordinarily popular stallion in America and like others of Selby's imports from Crabbet, has had a tremendous influence on Arabian breeding in that country. Despite the fact that he was himself inbred, his descendants have also been inbred and a definite 'Raffles type' has emerged. Raffles was the only experiment in close inbreeding to Skowronek that Lady Wentworth attempted – he was by Skowronek out of Rifala, a daughter of Skowronek. Another instance of inbreeding tried by Lady Wentworth was when she put a son of Rijm, Nureddin II, to a Rijm daughter, Fejr, to produce Faris. In this case she wanted a double cross to Rijm for the racing ability that he transmitted to his progeny.

More than once Lady Wentworth received an offer for the whole of the Crabbet Stud. One such occasion was in the autumn of 1931 when an American, Mr Drexel Castleton, cabled her with a proposal to buy all her stock for a very large figure. This Lady Wentworth accepted. But while waiting for a reply she began to have her doubts. There then

top left Reyna (Skowronek–Rissla) and *right* Jalila (Skowronek–Rasima)
below Mirage, purchased in 1923, ridden by Lady Wentworth

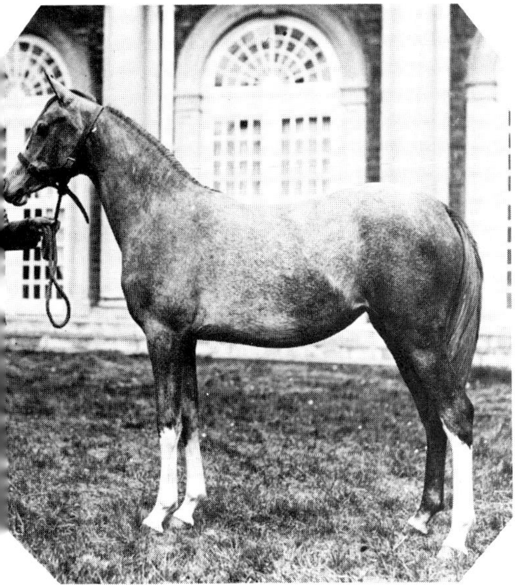
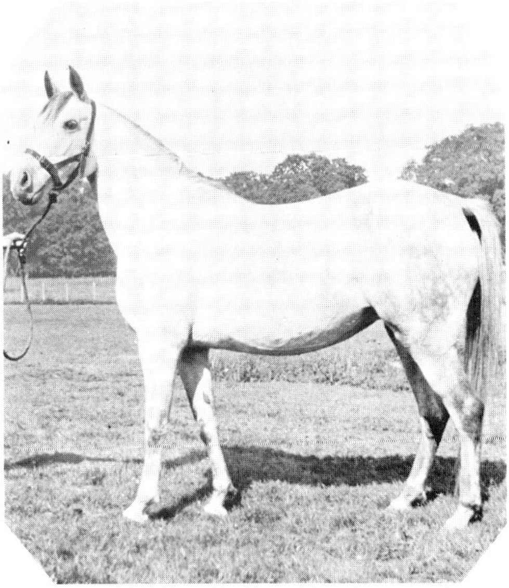
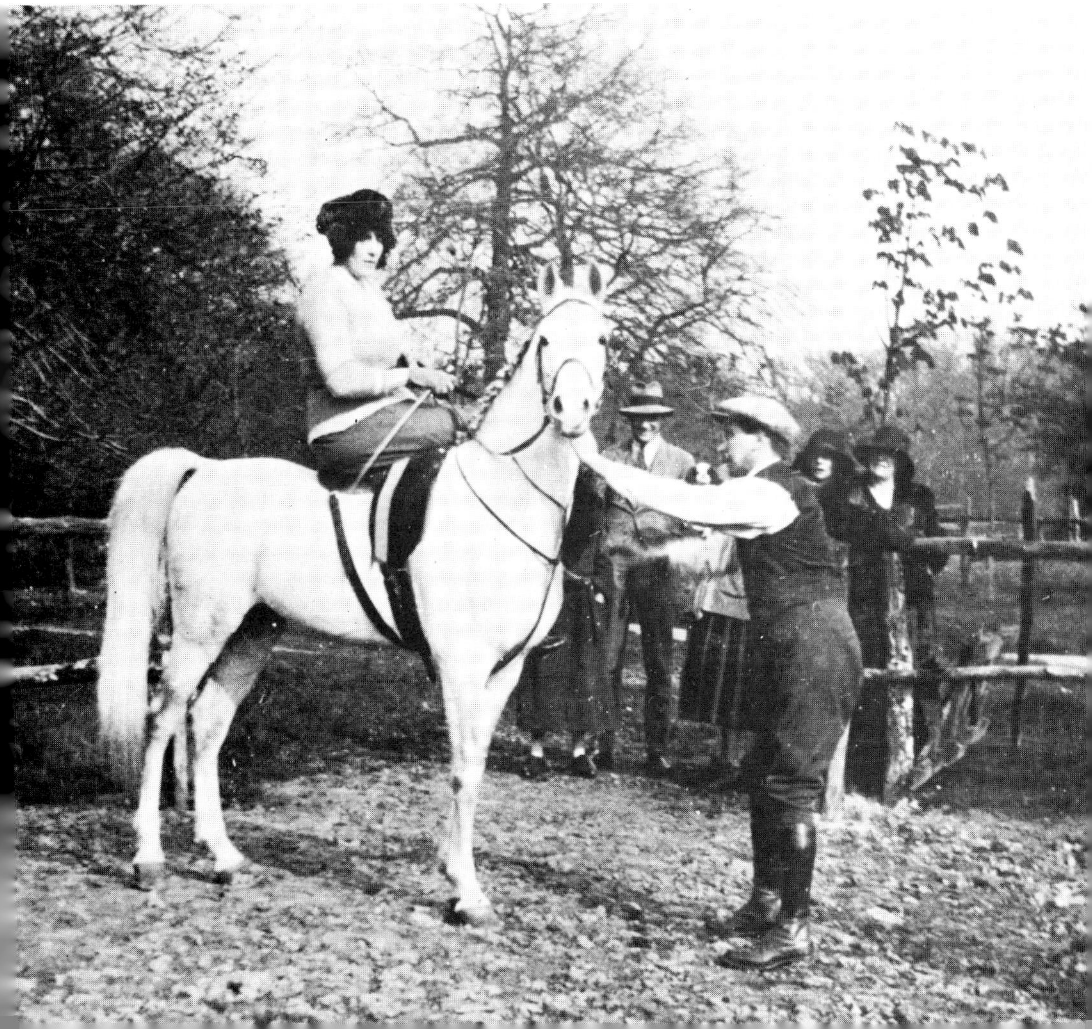

followed a promise of payment by Castleton but no money. The next she heard was that Castleton was spending a huge sum on building stables, so she promptly increased her price. Castleton agreed to this and went so far as to name the ship that was to take the horses to America. After a long delay she received an enquiry from him about the cost of keep and grooms' salaries for three months. But by this time Lady Wentworth had become disenchanted with Castleton and his procrastination and when a sailing date was proposed for the following April, she quickly withdrew from the negotiations.

Sales to English breeders helped but were by no means sufficient to keep Crabbet going. One of the older studs founded between the wars was that of the Hon. Mrs R.E.L. Vaughan-Williams, whose best mare was the chestnut Alfarouse (by Berk out of Mareesa). Alfarouse was memorable not only as one of the very few representatives of the Jilfa strain but also for her beautiful, elegant head and rare quality. In her old age she could be found grazing peacefully on her owner's lawn with nothing to prevent her from wandering wherever she pleased in the garden. In Yorkshire Mr W. Hay had bought Skowronek's son Rangoon (out of Rish) and Silver Fire's good daughter Somara (by Nureddin II). Miss Ianthe Bell had had Nisreen (by Nureddin II out of Nasra) from Crabbet and bred two very good daughters from her by Irex, Indian Flower and Indian Pride. In Gloucestershire, Mrs E.M. Murray was breeding excellent stock from Rissla's daughter Risslina, among them Risira, who together with Lord Moyne's Saladin II was among Naziri's few produce. There were other breeders too but their total demands could not prevent overstocks building up once again at Crabbet.

By 1936 the situation was more serious than ever before and Geoffrey Covey was becoming extremely worried. It may be mentioned here that Lady Wentworth relied implicitly upon the skills and loyalty of her staff and in return was never let down. She was immensely proud of the long service that so many gave her and never failed to pay them tribute whenever an opportunity arose. As manager, Geoffrey Covey had outstanding ability and held Lady Wentworth's complete trust. He had been in charge of the commercial side of the Stud for many years and besides being unafraid to speak his mind when he felt it necessary, had a ready appreciation of the financial dangers if the Stud became overstocked.

The sale to the Russians in 1936 is described later by Cecil Covey.

Lady Wentworth commented that they were the hardest people to deal with that she had ever met. After a month's strenuous bargaining she agreed to sell them six stallions and nineteen mares for breeding and no one could blame her at being depressed to see so many of her best horses leave. Among the mares were Nasifa, Neraida, Rissalma, Rixalina, Ruanda, Ruellia and Star of the Hills; and among the stallions Raseem, Naseem and Shareer. She might have been comforted had she been able to foresee the immense influence that many of these animals were to have on Arabian breeding not only in Russia and Poland but throughout the world.

CHAPTER 11

The End of an Era

In 1937 Cecil Covey was appointed manager at Crabbet upon the retirement of his father. His own recollections of the horses and events of the era are so ample that it is only necessary here to give the framework in which they lie.

In the decade before the Second World War, the principal stallions at Crabbet were Naseem, Raseem, Rissam, Ferhan, Faris and Shareer. Lady Wentworth considered Naseem to have ideal type, 'with perfect head and tiny muzzle'. Naziri, his full brother, was much less fertile than Naseem and when he died from colic in 1939, the post mortem revealed that he had three kidneys. In Lady Wentworth's estimation, Naziri was an even better horse than Naseem but 'I do not show him because he is so uproariously lively and the risk of boxing him is too great'.

Raseem, who was out of Rim, was Rasim's best son. He was a golden chestnut with 'a lovely head and neck. Brilliant shiny coat. Good legs and good all round. Rare quality'. Rissam was also a son of Rim, by Naseem. He was a dark chestnut of a 'wonderfully deep plum, almost purple' shade, with a lighter reddish mane. He had extraordinary style and very high tail carriage. But unfortunately, as Lady Wentworth noted, 'he never reproduced his own perfect head except in a few rare cases'.

Ferhan and Faris were both sons of Fejr, Feluka's daughter by Rijm. Ferhan (by Raswan) was a tall horse with 'a wonderful mane enormously long and silky and long full silky tail. Extra fine thin skin. Very beautiful all round.' Faris (by Nureddin II) was 'a grand type on the big scale. His head too straight for perfection but his sire qualities are outstanding. All his stock have fine frames and much style'.

Shareer was also by Nureddin II, out of Selima, and another large horse. Lady Wentworth could find no fault in him. 'Neck long, front fine, legs excellent. Quarters splendid, tail high set and carried high.'

Among the mares in the pre-war period, Rissla, Silver Fire (by Naseem out of Somra), Nisreen and Sharima (by Shareer out of Nashisha) were outstanding and left daughters in the Stud of equal merit.

During the war these horses and their descendants were to produce some of the finest Arabians ever foaled at Crabbet. Despite bombs and blackouts and the occupation of Crabbet by Canadian troops, Lady Wentworth continued to breed, albeit on a reduced scale. Her Welsh Mountain Ponies were disposed of and young Arab stock that showed no promise was quickly sold or given away. The Stud was more fortunate now than it had been during the First World War, when the Blunts had been continually worried about fodder restrictions, as special dispensations from wartime regulations were allowed for all breeding stock entered in the G.S.B., on the grounds of national importance.

Probably the two most important stallions at Crabbet during the war were Indian Gold and Raktha. Indian Gold (by Ferhan out of Nisreen) had been foaled in 1934. Similar in looks to his sire, he had an exceptionally fine head with enormous eyes and tiny muzzle and was a superb mover. He was Nisreen's best son and one of the most prepotent sires in the great 'N' family. Although he will be mainly remembered for his daughters, his son Sun Royal (out of Sharima) caused a sensation as a yearling when he won the Male Championship at the Arab Horse Society Show in 1947. (Sun Royal was exported to the United States in 1953.)

Indian Gold's wartime daughters were Rissiletta and Silver Gilt (1943), Silfina (1944) and Serafina (1945). Rissiletta, who was Rissla's last foal, was a beautiful mare but unlucky at stud. Her outstanding filly by Oran, Riffles, was made champion at the Windsor Show in 1948 as a yearling but tragically picked up an illness at the show from which she never recovered. Silver Gilt, one of the loveliest of Silver Fire's offspring, produced stock of the highest quality, of which the best was the unforgettable Silver Vanity (by Oran), who was considered by many to be one of the most beautiful stallions ever bred at Crabbet. He had all the qualities associated with the Silver Fire line, not least being his superlative head.

Silfina and Serafina were full sisters out of Sharfina, one of Sharima's most successful daughters. Silfina was the dam of Electric Silver (by Raktha) and Sindh (by Silver Vanity), both of whom went to Australia where they have founded important lines. Serafina's first foal was Serafix (by Raktha). Serafix was exported in 1954 to the stud of Mr John M. Rogers at Walnut Creek, California and at one time held the record as a sire of Champions in the United States.

Raktha had been foaled at the Hanstead Stud in 1934. In 1939 he was acquired by Lady Wentworth. His most famous sons in England were General Grant (out of Lady Yule's Samsie) and Indian Magic (out of Indian Crown) but Raktha will also be remembered for his many successful daughters such as Silverlet (out of Silver Gilt), who went to South Africa, Bint Razeena whom Raktha sired after being sold to South Africa, and Grey Royal (out of Sharima).

Indian Magic was particularly valued by Lady Wentworth for the double cross to Rasim in his breeding. Oran (by Riffal out of Astrella) also had a double cross to Rasim, besides five crosses to the Queen of Sheba line, by which Lady Wentworth set great store.

The interchange of horses between Crabbet and Hanstead continued into the war years. Ghezala, a Hanstead mare by Faris out of Rasana, came to Crabbet and Niseyra (by Rissam out of Neraida) went to Hanstead. Lady Wentworth then had Raktha and Lady Yule got the stallions Rissam and Rissalix (by Faris out of Rissla). The latter was one of the very few horses that Lady Wentworth regretted having sold. She was offered him back by Lady Yule during the war but could not take him as by then there were already too many colts and stallions at Crabbet. Rissalix was the sire of Blue Domino and Count Dorsaz.

Lady Wentworth believed that the main cause of the break between Crabbet and Hanstead was her refusal to sell Lady Yule a certain colt. This was Indian Grey, by Raktha out of Indian Crown, and therefore a full brother to Indian Magic and with the same crosses to Rasim. Lady Wentworth considered Indian Grey to be quite outstanding and would not part with him for any price that Lady Yule offered. (Indian Grey was put down suffering from acute colic in 1944, the same year that Indian Magic was foaled.) This did not help relations between the studs and in 1943 Lady Yule reciprocated the gesture by refusing Lady Wentworth's offer for Oran. A year later, however, she did sell Oran, to Mr C. McConnell, who then sold him to the British Bloodstock Agency from whom Lady Wentworth purchased him. So far as Lady Yule was concerned, Oran's arrival at Crabbet was the final straw and thereafter all horse dealings between the studs came to an end. In fact the mating that produced General Grant was among the last to take place between their horses.

In 1946 a new era began for the Arab Horse Society with their first post-war show at Roehampton. The spacious ground with its back drop of trees, the pleasant garden party atmosphere and the sight of England's finest Arabian horses, made the Roehampton shows an unfor-

above Faris
(Nureddin II–Fejr)
centre Rissalix
(Faris–Rissla)
below Blue Domino
(Rissalix–Niseyra) at
Roehampton

above Silver Fire
(Naseem–Somra)
centre Silver Gilt
(Indian Gold–Silver Fire)
with her foal Sunset
(by Bright Shadow) at
Frogshole Farm
below Silver Vanity
(Oran–Silver Gilt)

gettable experience. The sun always seemed to shine, the horses' coats gleamed with that iridescent sheen peculiar to the breed, and the ring was run like clock-work under the stewardship of Major Faudel-Phillips, popularly known as 'Fuddle'.

For many years the classes at Roehampton were dominated by the three studs of Crabbet, Hanstead and Courthouse, competing against each other with such horses as Grey Royal, Rissiletta, Indian Magic, Dargee, Silver Vanity, Blue Domino, Count Dorsaz, Shamnar, Bahram, Benjamin and Selma II. For sheer numbers of horses exhibited, Hanstead was the principal rival to Crabbet in these years and between them they often took the first four or five positions in each class. Expertly shown by Miss Lynn Lewis, the Courthouse horses also took their share of honours in the show ring. Although Mr Clark has at times introduced imported horses into his stud, his stock today is of almost pure Crabbet blood. He has strong views on breeding and considers the best Arabs to be not over 15 hands. Over the years he has evolved a 'Clark type' of its own which is especially notable for the excellence of head and the typically large eye.

The principal stallions at Crabbet after the war, apart from Indian Gold, were Oran and his sons Grand Royal and Silver Vanity, Dargee, Bright Shadow and Indian Magic.

Although Lady Wentworth was very proud of Indian Magic, she used him carefully at stud, as she did Shareer, Faris, Grand Royal and other large horses. He got some very good foals, but it may be that his real value will lie in later generations. Several of his sons have proved excellent sires. But whatever the future may show, Indian Magic was undoubtedly one of the most imposing stallions of all times and with his superb style and presence, stood out like a beacon every time he appeared in the show ring.

One of Crabbet's best show winners was Dargee. Dargee was bred by Mr Ruxton, by Manasseh (by Joseph out of Aatika) out of Myola (by Algol out of Rythma), and was bought by Lady Wentworth in 1946. He was a small horse with an especially good head and front and brilliant action. Lady Wentworth considered Dargee to be an exceptional horse, 'a freak', she once remarked, whose action she believed to be a throwback to his great-grandsire, Berk. She was uncertain whether his type would be passed on to his descendants and did not live long enough to see how his offspring bred. In fact Dargee sired several good horses, including Rissalma II (out of Rissiletta), Sirella (out of Shalina) and the Abel Smiths' Darjeel (out of Rajjela, by Grand Royal out of Nuhajjela). Born in 1962, Darjeel created a record by winning the Male Championship at the Arab Horse Society Show on three consecutive occasions.

Another stallion purchased by Lady Wentworth was Bright Shadow, bred by Mrs Mounsey-Heysham, by Radi out of Pale Shadow, a Rissalix mare. He left some good daughters, notably Silver Sheen out of Silver Grey, but like Dargee and many others he was not used a great deal at stud. The main reason for this was that Lady Wentworth always kept a large number of stallions in proportion to mares so that she had the widest possible choice of blood lines. As a result a stallion might have only one or two foals each year unless he was throwing really outstanding stock.

Oran, for instance, invariably had a large number of mares and rightly so, for a list of his offspring reads like a roll of champions. His sons include Silver Vanity, Royal Diamond and Grand Royal and his daughters Crown Royal, Silver Shadow, Nerinora and Umatella. It is interesting that Oran was the last stallion to be used at Crabbet of pure Blunt breeding, all the others at that time containing Skowronek's blood in their pedigrees, or, in the case of Dargee, the blood of Dwarka and others. Oran and Skowronek are particular examples of Lady Wentworth's genius as a breeder for recognising potential in horses that she had not herself bred.

Over the last twenty years of her life, Lady Wentworth was much occupied with writing. In 1938 *Thoroughbred Racing Stock and Its Ancestors* was published and seven years later appeared her most important work, *The Authentic Arabian Horse and His Descendants.* The text for the latter had been completed, and the type set and paper bought by its publishers before war broke out. This was most fortunate since with wartime paper restrictions and the post-war recession in the United Kingdom, it may be doubted whether the publishers would otherwise have been able to issue such a massive and expensive volume. When it did appear in 1945 (with the publication date meticulously altered in manuscript from 1943 in every copy), *The Authentic Arabian* was an instant success and by the end of the year had been sold out. Two years later, on the occasion of Princess Elizabeth's marriage to Prince Philip, Lady Wentworth was approached by the Committee of the Royal Windsor Horse Show. They had enquired what Princess Elizabeth would like as a wedding present and had been told that she wanted

centre Dargee (Manasseh–Myola)
top left Darjeel (Dargee–Rajjela) and *right* Royal Crystal (Dargee–Grey Royal)
below left Dancing Sunlight (Dargee–Shades of Night) and *right* Rissalma II (Dargee–Rissiletta)

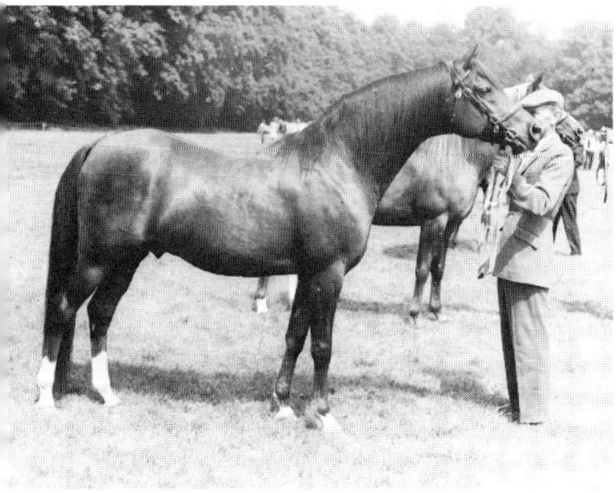

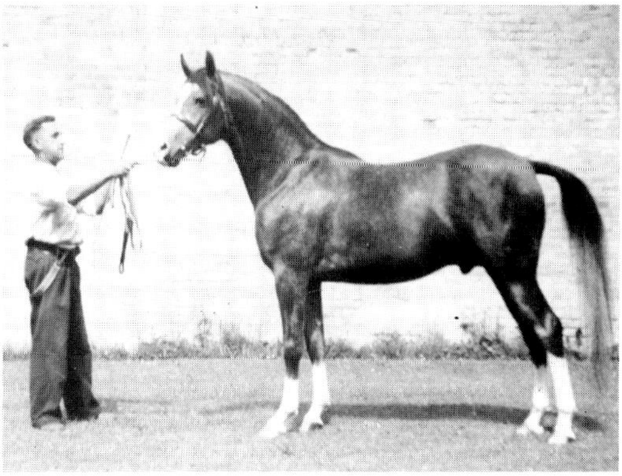

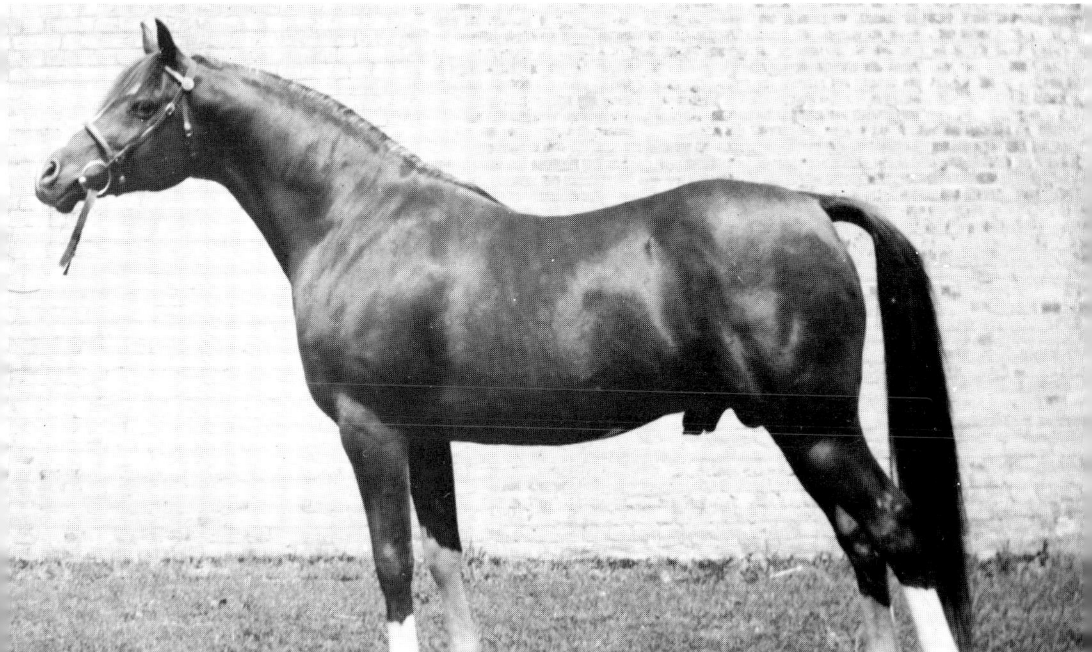

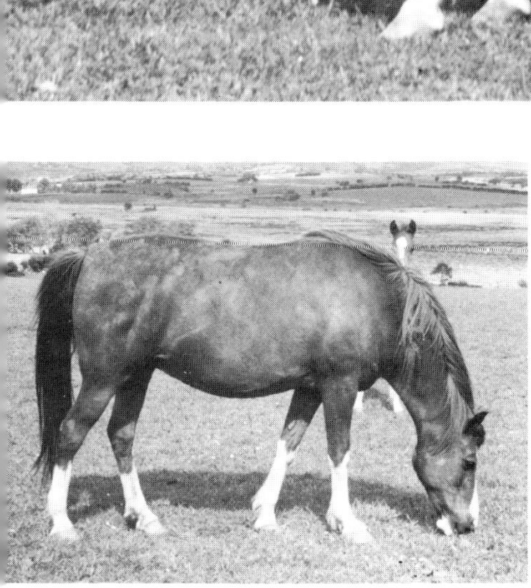

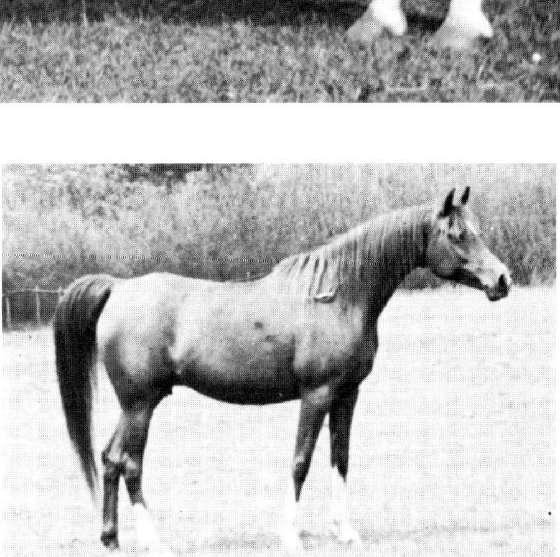

a copy of *The Authentic Arabian*. 'They are in a fix,' wrote Lady Wentworth, 'because they can't get one as it has sold out . . . I have got one to spare so they bought it and I added *Thoroughbred Racing Stock* to make the set complete.'

Further books followed: *Horses of Britain* (1944), *Arab Horse Nonsense* (1950), *Horses in the Making* (1951), *The Swift Runner* (1957) and posthumously, the *World's Best Horse* (1958). In addition to her own books she contributed to others (notably to Vesey-Fitzgerald's *Book of the Horse*, published in 1946) and wrote many articles for magazines. She was quick to challenge anyone whose views on Arabians differed from her own and greatly enlivened the correspondence pages of the press with trenchant comments upon the opinions of others.

She was particularly proud of her volumes of poetry. At heart she had much of her father's love for the freedom of mind and expression that the medium allowed and once remarked to her secretary, Mrs Barbara Scott, 'I would gladly follow Pegasus more closely, but I am always brought back to the horse on earth.' Her first book of poems, *Love in a Mist* (for which Neville Lytton did the woodcuts) had appeared in 1913. In 1930 *Flame of Life* was published. Her last two collections were *Drift of the Storm* and *Passing Hours* (1951 and 1952). In introducing them, Lord Dunsany wrote – with some licence – that 'the only poets with whom I can compare Lady Wentworth are the great ones – the immortals'.

There were no large sales overseas from Crabbet after the war. In 1951 Mr Botha of South Africa tried to buy a large number but although he acquired Raktha he was unable to buy as many as he wished. For during the war Lady Wentworth had inherited a considerable fortune from her aunt, Mary Lovelace (Ralph Lovelace's widow), and now no longer needed to sell.

Despite the frequency with which Crabbet horses appeared in the show ring, many of the best were in fact never seen in public – for instance Naziri, Indian Gold and Silver Gilt. Apart from the fact that she considered them too valuable to risk, Lady Wentworth also shared her parents' opinion, that the real value of the horses lay in the stock they produced. Nevertheless it must be said that Lady Wentworth was never averse to either the prestige or the publicity that stemmed from her successes in the show ring.

For those who had never had the opportunity to see all the best horses, the annual parades at Crabbet after the war were a welcome

THE END OF AN ERA

innovation. The horses were usually shown in families and the foals were allowed to run loose so that their action could be fully appreciated as their mothers were trotted across the lawn. To be able to watch, amid perfect surroundings on a summer's day, between 40 and 50 of Crabbet's best horses being superbly presented, was a unique experience for those who had the fortune to attend.

For the last few years of her life Lady Wentworth suffered from cataracts and in 1956 she engaged Mrs Scott as her secretary. Mrs Scott remembers Lady Wentworth with affection and admiration. Lady Wentworth used to talk of her life as a young girl at Crabbet, of her parents and in particular of her mother's courage. She spoke too of her fear of reporters and how she distrusted the press. She still recalled the despair she had felt on being launched into society as a young girl without any preparation at all, straight from the rural life at Crabbet into the whirl of London. She had had no idea how to behave and ever since had been intensely shy. She had no objection to meeting people on her home ground but hated the idea of being away and for the last thirty or so years of her life rarely spent a night away from Crabbet.

She had some engaging eccentricities, of which her style of dress was only one. Mrs Scott remembers an occasion when Lady Wentworth was invited out to luncheon. Nothing suitable could be found in her wardrobe so some material was bought from which Peggy Leppard, her Irish maid, ran up a dress. The next problem was shoes. For years Lady Wentworth had worn nothing but plimsolls, of which she possessed a great number and in particular a carmine pair with yellow laces which she kept for special occasions. But a more suitable pair of shoes was bought and seemed comfortable enough. At the last minute Lady Wentworth declared that they pinched and insisted upon the favourite carmine plimsolls. An aged hat was found in a cupboard, a priceless brooch and necklace in one drawer, some cheap glass beads in another and thus attired, Lady Wentworth set out for the day.

As she grew into old age, Lady Wentworth mellowed but her fiery reaction to adverse criticism of Arabians in general and of Crabbet stock in particular remained, and for many her pungent letters to the press were to be the only knowledge they had of her. Crabbet Park, its inmates and horses had become her whole life. Fit and active until the last few months of her life, she fell ill in the summer of 1957 and was moved to a hospital at Crawley. There she died on August 8th, 1957. She was buried in the grounds of the Franciscan Friary in Crawley, the church that contains her father's sculpture of his brother, Francis Blunt.

Her obituary notice in *The Times* spoke of her 'independence of mind, her eccentricities and her artistic pursuits'. But to the local press she was 'The Mistress of Crabbet':

> The death of Baroness Wentworth has snapped a link with an era that has, unhappily, vanished for ever... And so another chapter of this celebrated family's history is closed.

In her will, Lady Wentworth had left the Stud to Geoffrey Covey but as he had predeceased her by a few days it passed to his son Cecil.

There were then over 70 horses in the Stud and Cecil Covey was faced immediately with the problems of paying the very considerable death duties and of finding new accommodation for the horses.

Crabbet House, the stables and the park had all been left to Lady Wentworth's younger daughter, Lady Winifrid Tryon, who sold the estate to a timber merchant who later resold it in small units. Today the London to Brighton motorway cuts through the centre of the park but the land on the east remains much as it was before. The house has now been sympathetically converted into office accomodation and the tennis-court outwardly restored to its pristine splendour. To the west, urban development has taken place though with a fine sense of history, the authorities have given many of the new streets names linked with Crabbet – Lytton Drive, Wentworth Drive, The Covey, Stace Way, Short Gallop. Frogshole (where Wilfrid and Alice used to go fishing) has also been built over and is now called Maidenbower.

Cecil Covey had fortunately inherited other land from Lady Wentworth. It was only by selling it that he was able to pay the death duties and keep the Stud going. It soon became apparent that he would be unable to run the Stud at its previous size because of the cost and the loss of stabling. He therefore decided to sell enough animals to make it viable.

It was unlucky for Cecil Covey and for Arab horse breeding in England that shortly after Lady Wentworth's death, Miss Yule herself died* and most of the Hanstead horses also had to be sold. Not only had the country been thereby deprived within the same year of two of its greatest breeders but with so many horses offered for sale at the

---

*Lady Yule had died in 1950.

same time, supply was in danger of outstripping demand. It should be remembered that the Hanstead horses were wholly or very largely of Crabbet blood.

It was perhaps inevitable that many of these Arabians should go to the United States. Within weeks of Lady Wentworth's death, negotiations had begun which were to culminate in the sale that autumn of the largest single consignment of Arabians ever made from England, to Mrs Bazy Tankersley's Al Marah Stud. In all Mrs Tankersley bought 32 horses from Crabbet and Hanstead. Among those from Crabbet were Royal Diamond, Silver Shadow, Silwa, Silver Grand and Radeyra. Five years later Mrs Tankersley bought the stallion Silver Vanity in partnership with Mr Charles Prange.

From Hanstead Mrs Tankersley acquired Thorayya, Zulima, Blue Millet, Grey Stella, Kabara, Reenexa and Salinas. Miss Wolf, who had been left options by Miss Yule on some of the horses, kept Blue Domino, who continued to be a very popular sire until his death in 1966. She also kept Count Dorsaz but for one season only as she then leased, and later sold, him to Mrs Tankersley.

It is too early to say which of these horses will prove the most influential in America. Of the stallions, Royal Diamond has left some good daughters and Silver Vanity has undoubtedly made an impression, but it may well be that Count Dorsaz will prove the most important of them all. The Rissalix cross with Indraff and mares of 'old' Crabbet lines would appear to be producing some very fine animals.

The family tradition of breeding Arabians did not die with Lady Wentworth but has been carried on by her daughter, Lady Anne Lytton. After her mares Ferda and Rossana went to Kellogg in 1926, Lady Anne bred little for many years. During the Second World War she moved to Ashley Combe in Somerset, the family home of her brother Lord Lytton, and helped to run the estate while he was abroad. In 1951 Lady Anne was given as a birthday present by her mother the filly Mifaria, by Oran out of Rithyana, and later a filly foal Alyssa, by Raktha out of Somara. In 1955 Lady Anne moved to Newbuildings and there established the Blunt Stud. Mifaria was by then starting to prove herself a wonderful foundation mare. Not only did she produce champion sons, notably Manto (by Blue Domino) and El Meluk (by Mikeno) but also several first-class daughters. Her granddaughter Sahirah of the Storm (by Champurrado out of Mifaria's Indian Magic daughter Mellawieh) was a particularly fine mare. Mifaria lived until the age of 30 and of her direct descendants in the female line, there are now five fillies and mares at Newbuildings.

A number of new British breeders as well as some of the older studs profited from the Crabbet and Hanstead sales. One of the most successful breeders to have founded her stud with mares of Crabbet blood lines is Miss Margaret Greely. Many of the best colts bred at her Well House Stud in Sussex have gone abroad and contributed much to the success of Crabbet stock overseas. After the auction at Hanstead, Miss Greely acquired from Miss Wolf a daughter of Count Dorsaz called Princess Zia who proved a most valuable brood mare.

In 1952 Mr and Mrs H. Linney had bought the stallion Mikeno (by Rissalix out of Namilla) from the Hanstead Stud. Mikeno is a highly successful sire and has produced some notable stock from mares of Crabbet blood. The Linneys also breed Anglo-Arabs with which they have gained many prizes in the show ring.

Among new breeders who bought at the Hanstead auction were Major and Mrs T.W.I. Hedley. Later they also bought the Hanstead mare Umatella (by Oran out of Namilla) and the two stallions General Grant and Count Rapello (by Count Dorsaz out of Rafeena), and began to breed on a large scale in the Lake District.

One of the principal buyers from Cecil Covey was the late Mrs E.M. Thomas whose Metcombe Stud exerted considerable influence over Arabian breeding in England. Before Lady Wentworth's death she had

above Mikeno (Rissalix–Namilla) and
right Indian King (Oran–Indian Pride)

THE END OF AN ERA

acquired two Dargee fillies from Crabbet, Rissalma II and Incoronetta (out of Indian Crown). From Rissalma II she bred Astur (by Indian Magic), who had a very successful show career, and his full brother Indriss, who is proving a fine sire. Mrs Thomas enlarged her stud by purchasing several more fillies from Cecil Covey but was compelled by ill-health to cut back.

When Mrs Thomas died in 1974, her stock was sold to a number of British breeders. Mr W.W. Brogden in Cumbria had already had a number of mares from Metcombe, and in Worcestershire Mr and Mrs Munday had the stallion Risslan (by Oran out of Rissalma II) as well as some mares of Mrs Thomas's breeding. In Devon Mrs A.M. Roberts breeds stock of a high standard from Crabbet bloodlines.

Mr and Mrs Ronald Kydd had bought Indian King from Miss Bell in 1955 and they increased their stud after Lady Wentworth's death by buying the Heavenly Twins, Dancing Shadow and Dancing Sunlight (by Dargee out of Shades of Night), who produced several good show winners for them by Indian King.

One of the largest studs at present to have been founded with mares of predominantly Crabbet blood is the Tollard Park Stud in Wiltshire, which belongs to Mr M.A. Pitt-Rivers. One of his first purchases was the pure Crabbet mare Indian Snowflake (by Ludo out of Indian ved a wonderful foundation mare. Indian Snowy Mr and Mrs D.D. Wright, owners of the suc- in Norfolk from which have come a large number of show winners in the last twenty years.

It is impossible to mention all the studs that have incorporated Crabbet stock since Lady Wentworth's death. Perhaps the most important factor behind the distribution of the blood in Britain in recent years was Cecil Covey's decision to stand his stallions at public stud. This had not been possible in Lady Wentworth's time as she had been unable to accommodate many visiting mares owing to the numbers of her own horses. She had limited the available nominations to mares of Crabbet breeding and those belonging to friends like Miss Bell and Sir Henry and Lady May Abel Smith. Cecil Covey, however, was anxious that as many breeders as possible should have access to the Crabbet stallions and each year his stud was fully booked with visiting mares. Oran, Indian Magic, Dargee and Bright Shadow were his older stallions and, while he remained in England, Silver Vanity was the most prominent among the younger ones. There is no doubt that the availability of these horses was a great advantage to British breeders and particularly the smaller stud owners.

During the 1960s the demand from overseas for Crabbet stock continued. Shalwan (by Silver Vanity out of Shalina) went to Mr R. North in South Africa; Oran van Crabbet (by Oran out of Serafina) to Mr Dow in the United States, and Mahif (by Indian Magic out of Myolanda) to the Queensland Agricultural College in Australia. Possibly the most significant sale overseas was that of Sindh to Mrs A.D.D. Maclean in Australia. Sindh is by Silver Vanity out of Silfina and has proved himself to be a very important sire.

In England the Silver Gilt line has been much to the fore in the show ring with her daughter Silver Grey (by Royal Diamond) and her granddaughter Silver Sheen (by Bright Shadow out of Silver Grey) who between them won the Female Championship at the Arab Horse Society Show on no fewer than six occasions. Sirella was unbeaten in the mare classes and has bred some first-class foals. Her son Hanif (by Silver Vanity), who was kept by Cecil Covey, is the sire of Haroun, the winner of many championships for Mr Pitt-Rivers.

Other notable stallions bred by Cecil Covey include Orion (by Oran out of Dancing Diamond), who was bought by Major and Mrs Hedley and has got some outstanding fillies, and Indian Magic's son Indian Flame II (out of Nerinora), who has sired stock of the highest class for Mr and Mrs Calvert.

In 1971 work began on the construction of the London to Brighton

above left Sirella (Dargee–Shalina)
and *right* Hanif (Silver Vanity–Sirella).
centre Dancing Diamond
(Royal Diamond–Dancing Star)
below Haroun (Hanif–Indian Snowflake)

motorway, part of which was to run through Crabbet Park, and Cecil Covey realised that it would be impossible for him to carry on. He wanted English breeders to have the first chance of purchasing his horses since on all previous occasions it had been overseas breeders who had benefited from Crabbet disposals. The news of the disbandment spread like wildfire and within four days virtually every animal had been sold.

One of the principal buyers from Cecil Covey was Mr G. Plaister, who bought Hanif, Sunset (by Bright Shadow out of Silver Gilt) and two fillies. Bright Shadow went to the Duchess of Rutland with Dancing Diamond and Sirella, while Silver Grey joined her daughter Silver Sheen at the stud of Mrs I. Bowring. Mrs D. Gilbert bought the young mare Aurora (by Oran out of Shadowlight). Dalika (by Dargee out of Silver Gilt) went to Miss Pointer who already had Indian Star (by Indian Magic out of Nerinora), which she had bought from Cecil Covey as a two-year-old. Silver Gilt, now retired from stud, was given by Grace Covey to Mrs D.M. Campbell who had earlier bought her last daughter, Golden Gilt, by Bright Shadow. The only horse that Cecil Covey kept was Indian Magic, then aged twenty-seven.

It would be unrealistic not to mention that during the last thirty or so years of the existence of the Crabbet Arabian Stud, considerable numbers of Arabians of Egyptian, Polish, Russian and Spanish bloodlines have been imported into many countries besides Britain. As will be seen later, several of these horses have, to a greater or lesser degree, Crabbet blood in them and it will be of substantial interest to study in succeeding generations the results that will come from the blending of these various bloodlines.

Crabbet horses are not of course the sole possessors of the unique qualities of the Arabian. The admixture of their blood with that of other lines has been, and may well continue to be, advantageous to the breed as a whole. But it cannot be stressed too much how great a debt is owed throughout the world to animals of pure Crabbet origins. No private stud of comparable size, merit and importance has remained in existence for as long as Crabbet and none has had a greater influence throughout the world on Arabian horse breeding. It is to be hoped that this precious blood will be carefully preserved and that the work begun by Wilfrid and Lady Anne Blunt, and carried on by Lady Wentworth, will continue to benefit the breed as it has done for the last one hundred years.

CHAPTER 12

Some Memories of Crabbet

By Cecil Covey

Editor's note. Cecil Covey started work as a groom at the Crabbet Arabian Stud in 1926. He was 19, and had spent some years in the Merchant Navy and working on a farm in Sussex. He was to be at Crabbet during its most brilliant phase; was to manage it through the war, when Canadian troops requisitioned the house and stables, and it was he who had to take the decision to close it down. Now aged 71, he lives with his wife Grace in a bungalow overlooking Frogshole. He still takes a keen interest in Arab horse affairs and is much in demand as a judge. He has recently been appointed a Governor of the Arab Horse Society.
Cecil Covey died on March 9th, 1985 and his wife, Grace, four months later.

Cecil and Grace Covey with the farm buildings at Frogshole in the background

When I began at Crabbet my father was Lady Wentworth's general manager as well as the tennis professional. He later became her chief adviser with great influence on the Stud's financial affairs. He died in July 1957, when he was 75. Lady Wentworth died two weeks later. There were times when she had been close to selling up for lack of funds. My father had been with her throughout the negotiations with the Russians and it was he who had persuaded her to sell so many horses, as the Stud had been very near bankruptcy through being overstocked.

In 1926 there were about a dozen grooms employed to look after between 70 to 100 head of Arabian stock. There seemed to be horses everywhere and all available boxes and stalls were in use. Upwards of 20 stallions and 40 broodmares was our usual number, plus young stock, though this of course varied according to sales.

There were also Welsh Ponies – at least two stallions, King Cole and Springlight, and about 20 mares and young stock. The mares were covered in the spring and left to foal out. Except for the stallions and colts, all the ponies stayed out in winter. Some were shown and some were driven but the rest were seldom handled except for the few occasions when they had to have their feet pared or receive other attention. For this they were herded into one of the yards and it was quite a rodeo catching them. The herd grew in the Thirties but when war broke out it was drastically reduced.

There was also Old Billy, a cart-horse who lived in the brood mare yard and did all the carrying of manure and fodder to and from the stables.

Arabian mares and young stock were mostly driven in loose to their boxes at night in the Twenties and Thirties. All three and four-year-olds of both sexes were backed to saddle unless sold very young. The round indoor ring next to Windfalls Cottage was used for their initial training.

In a very large field of at least 50 acres called the Cricket Park, there was an old pavilion still in good repair and Lady Wentworth decided to use this for housing mares at night. We gutted it and put up stalls inside so that it held about eight brood mares. This was so successful that another large shed was erected and fitted out in the same manner. Only dry mares and late foalers were put out here but it left more boxes free in the brood mare yard.

Headcollars were never left on the mares at any time and seldom on youngsters. This was for several reasons; they look much better without a headcollar; secondly, they are liable to get hung up or to lose them; thirdly, after a time and especially in wet weather a bare patch is likely to form where the headcollar rubs; and finally it is good training for mares and young stock to get used to standing while a headcollar is put on out in the field.

All the farm work such as rolling and harrowing was done by teams of cart-horses. A few acres were kept ploughed up to provide green meat for the stallions – tares, sainfoin and quick-growing grasses. The coachman Rapson used to fetch a daily ration for the stallions with the pony and trap. In the autumn he would also take a load of grooms equipped with scythes in the trap up to the forest to cut the bracken that we used for bedding and yards. Peat-moss was also used in those days for bedding until we started to grow our own corn when of course straw was used exclusively.

All the stud hands were expected to help out on the farm during the summer. We had a lot of haying to do as we were entirely self-supporting and at that time it was all gathered and stacked by hand. The stacks could keep for as long as ten years so that in good summers we were able to lay in enough to tide us over the bad. Horses must have good hay and any that has had much rain on it before gathering has to be thrown away. We had several neighbouring farmers who were glad to clear any we found unsuitable for the Stud.

Stacks were cut out by hand with a large knife into bale-shaped trusses tied with string, and I have never fed better hay than that out of a well-made stack. We also cut our own chaff since a large ration was always mixed with the feeds. During the war, much of the land was ploughed up and put into corn.

The stud hands had to help here as well since the corn was all cut with a binder and stooked. Until we bought our own threshing drum we hired a traction-engine and all the rest of the paraphernalia for threshing. I found the tennis court, which was commandeered by the troops during the war, very useful for storing all the oats I had to keep. After the war we grew wheat, linseed, barley, sugar beet and roots for a flock of sheep. Here again the grooms were useful to help with the hoeing, all of which was done by hand. We also kept cattle to graze the land after the horses. In fact we were self-sufficient in everything after 1940.

There was a great bond of comradeship among the grooms at Crabbet. Most of the stallions were ridden out and the string of riders reminded one of a morning on Epsom Downs. The grooms were always willing to come out in the evenings haymaking or harvesting. They were paid overtime for any work out of hours on the farm, but not for extra work in the Stud or at weekends. The only time off in those early days was about six hours on Sunday, as no exercising or grooming was done that day and Lady Wentworth seldom allowed visitors to the Stud on a Sunday.

Medicine in the Twenties and early Thirties was very crude with no injections of any kind. The local vets were few and far between and some had little experience of tending breeding stock, especially horses. Our local vet came by horse and trap so we had to deal with emergencies ourselves. The usual cure for cuts and wounds was bathing and applying iodine. I remember one emergency where a mare had cut her heel very deeply and we couldn't stop the bleeding at all. But 'Old Pat', one of the grooms, recalled an ancient remedy, slapping on a handful of cobwebs from the stable roof, and believe it or not it did the trick.

The cure for stomach upsets and anything of that nature was by administering a ball. To give a ball successfully requires great skill and experience. The horse's mouth has to be opened and kept open by getting hold of the tongue and holding it outside and to one side of the mouth. The ball then has to be placed as far as possible into the gullet so that it can't be regurgitated, taking care of course that one's arm isn't chewed in the process.

To combat worms, the greatest menace of breeding studs, we periodically starved the horses for twenty-four hours and then dosed them with raw linseed oil and oil of turps. This was a difficult and messy job, requiring one or two men to hold the horse's head up while another administered the drench in the hope that it went down the patient's throat and not over us.

Feeding was strictly rationed and no animal, young or old, was ever over-fed. In fact by today's standards, I should say they were kept slightly under-fed. Brood mares were never 'steamed up' before foaling. The usual ration per day was three pounds of crushed oats and three pounds of broad bran with a large helping of chaff. This varied according to the age and sex of the animal and if a mare, whether it was dry or pregnant. In winter the mares were turned out in the morning without any feed but had a good bucket of mash to come back to at night.

Twice a week they were given a hot meal of well-simmered linseed mixed with barley and the usual feed. The nightly mash was always mixed in bulk in a large bin at least two hours before being fed to the mares and young stock. The stallions had less mash as their rations were split into three meals a day. Regular feeding is of great importance to the well-being of horses, especially for stallions if they are in their boxes most of the day. And mares in winter know to the minute when it's time to be fetched in.

We always sat up with mares that were due to foal. Apart from keeping an eye on them, we had also in those days to cut the umbilical cord as a precaution, so I understood, against any possibility of a rupture. This practice was done away with later, I think quite rightly.

Sitting up was a cold and tiring business since in the early days we had no sitting-up room but had to make do with an empty box and plenty of straw for warmth. If any complications arose we had to deal with them ourselves as it would have been impossible to get a vet out in time. In fact complications were very few, for the mares, being treated in a natural way, foaled as nature intended. They were left to get on with it and were never helped or interfered with until they were well in labour. I think that sometimes harm can be done by well-meaning owners rushing in to help far too soon. Mares usually take some time to decide when they will foal and nine times out of ten they get on with it quite well enough without any help.

Lady Wentworth liked to get her mares in foal as early in the year as possible, a practice then unusual in Arabian studs. Foaling would start late in January and go on until mid-June. Mares with foals at foot would get double rations of food. Dry mares stayed out at night from early in April until the second week in November and those with foals would stay out from about mid-May onwards, the foals only coming in when it was time for weaning. This was changed after the war as we found it better for the foals if we brought in the mares as well a week or two before weaning so that we could give the foals a bit more handling and get them used to putting their heads in the manger. Mares due to foal late in May or June were left to foal out in the field and I cannot remember ever having any trouble with them. In fact I noticed that foals were much quicker on their feet when foaled out and that they found the milk without any difficulty.

My first show was the Royal Richmond in 1926. All the horses were walked to Three Bridges station and put on the train for Richmond, which took most of the day. They were then walked through the streets from the station to the show ground at the Deer Park, next to Kew Gardens. We were there about two days and three nights. Several leads had to be found, not only for showing but for looking after the horses, since not too many grooms could be spared for so long. The porters and station-masters were always very helpful, both in making all the arrangements and during the loading and unloading of the horses. The boxes were very strong and well-padded and the animals mostly travelled loose with plenty of straw. There were often so many horses that the train amounted virtually to a Crabbet Special and until the railways went electric the boxes could be hitched to the back of passenger trains if there were not enough to make a separate train. Horses could be sent at any time, day or night, to any part of the British Isles, so long as the station had a loading platform. The staff at Three Bridges were exceptionally experienced in all this as we sent so many horses abroad. Lady Wentworth always sent them several brace of pheasants at Christmas as a thank-you for their help during the year.

About 1929 Lady Wentworth acquired Frogshole Farm, some 200 acres of grass with 100 acres of woodland. This came in most useful to relieve the paddocks at Crabbet during the summer. Since there were no boxes at Frogshole, we would take the mares down as soon as possible in the spring and leave them there until the autumn. It was about

The Richmond Show, 1928. From left: Reyna (with Cecil Covey), Nasra (with Fred Rice), Rissla (with Nugent), Riyala (with Leppard) and Rythma (with Walder)

a mile and a half from Crabbet. Of course foaling mares had to stay at Crabbet until the foals were old enough to be left out.

All the fields at Frogshole had shaws round most sides. A shaw is a strip of small trees and bushes varying in width between six and ten yards and they proved very handy for the mares and foals as shelter from both heat and bad weather. With all this cover round the fields we had a large rabbit population which had to be kept down by shooting and ferreting. I suppose a hundred a week were killed in the autumn and winter months and very good eating they were too.

It was the practice at Crabbet for one groom to look after four stallions. They were exercised by being either ridden or walked for about one and a half hours each day after which they were groomed thoroughly, half an hour to each horse. The stallions were never turned out as we had no paddocks available until we built some at Caxtons later on. Lady Wentworth was very strict about exercising, grooming and feeding. All mangers were inspected regularly and the hay was always put in a rack to save waste. Some stallions were rugged at night during the winter. All boxes had to be mucked out before breakfast and kept clean by picking up droppings during the day. Stallions being walked had surcingles and cruppers. They were kept well under control at all times and were trained to stand all-square so that they were prepared when either shown or paraded.

There were invariably many visitors, mostly from abroad, but none were allowed during the winter unless they were definite buyers. It was a strict rule that visitors were never allowed to take photographs. Nor were they ever shown horses in their boxes as Lady Wentworth always had them paraded, either singly or in groups according to the circumstances. No mare with a newly-born foal was ever shown to visitors, since mares often fall into a state of shock either just after foaling or after a day or so. Also they do not take kindly to strangers peering at them when they have newly-born foals.

Great importance was attached to the horses' feet and the mares' were regularly pared and kept in order. The stallions were usually given a new pair of shoes every other month; the month in between the shoes were removed and reset. We were lucky to have a very good blacksmith's within walking distance of the Stud. It was owned by two brothers called Steel whose nephew learned the trade and took over from them when they died.

We always had male grooms at Crabbet, not because we didn't like female ones but because in those days male grooms were much easier to find. I am quite sure that the grooms played a great part in the success of Crabbet. The one whose character and horsemanship most impressed me was Pat Cahill, or Old Pat as he was always called. He was in charge of the mares and also broke the youngsters and it was from him that I learned how to ride. He used to live in the Irish Hut, which still stands at Crabbet and is the office of the Equitation Centre. Old Pat died there in 1929.

There was another Irish groom at that time named Nugent. He looked after stallions and was a good rider although he rode jockey fashion, having been with Thoroughbreds before coming to Crabbet. His horses were kept in the stables next to the house and he lived in a flat above them. Naseem was one of his charges and he rode him every day. There was an amusing sequel to our different styles of riding. Nugent had to go away for a few days and I took over Naseem. He instantly took a dislike to my way of riding, which was longer than Nugent's, and gave me a most uncomfortable time until he got used to it. However, some time later when I was away, Nugent took over my horse Blaze and when I got back I heard that Blaze had tried to unseat Nugent because he rode so short!

Another groom who is well-known today in the Arabian horse world is Fred Rice. He spent all his life at the Stud and was still there when I had to give it up in 1972. He was also with the stallions and became our chief 'show' man. Burg Stace too served at Crabbet all his life. He looked after stallions or colts and helped foaling the mares. Another groom was Fred Branch. He started in the early Thirties and took over as stud groom during the war since most of my time was taken up with the farming. He left in 1954. There were many others besides and it is impossible to mention them all, but the Stud could never have been what it was without them.

Lady Wentworth took photography very seriously as it was her only way to present her horses to prospective buyers abroad. During my time more than half the horses that went abroad were sold entirely by photograph. Buyers used to write to Lady Wentworth enquiring what she had for sale and she would reply with photographs of those she could offer.

She was always very careful about the background. The early ones were taken in front of the tennis court but later they were taken in front of the garden wall, which had been specially painted for the purpose. The horses selected by Lady Wentworth, usually between eight and twelve in number, were got ready. Lady Wentworth had two Brownie cameras loaded, and then each horse was brought out in turn and made to stand in a marked area. When they were standing to satisfaction, an order was given and a white pony that had previously been hidden in the shrubbery was trotted out and back again. This seldom failed to attract the horse's attention and make it prick its ears and look alert.

I should say something about the photographs taken of Crabbet horses during the early years of the Stud. In the nineteenth century photography was in its infancy. Horses were not in the condition that they are today and when they were photographed it was usually done just where they stood and without any preparation. We should count ourselves very lucky to have so many photographs of these extremely interesting foundation horses.

Nearly all our sales were for export and of course they always went by sea. Since all other breeds of horses went by sea as well, the attendants who looked after them were very knowledgeable and good at their job. I don't remember that we had any mishaps on board ship.

In the case of the larger batches of horses sold abroad, the prospective buyer or his agent would come to inspect them and to bargain. The longest bargaining I can remember was with the Russians. They first appeared one afternoon early in 1936 and asked if they could see round the Stud. Not a word was said that they intended to buy anything. They were shown around, saw the horses and disappeared. However, after several weeks – I can't recall how long but I know I had forgotten all about them – they reappeared and announced that they wanted to buy a large number of Arabians of both sexes. This suited Lady Wentworth as the Stud was very overstocked.

There were five Russians in the party; the head man, well built and with a very strong character, a vet who was quite short and three others. They spoke very little English but all had dictionaries which they consulted continuously. By the time they left they had a good knowledge of the language.

After seeing most of the horses again and picking out those they were interested in, they retired to the house to negotiate with Lady Wentworth. These bargaining sessions went on for several hours each day over a number of weeks, with the Russians in one room and Lady Wentworth and my father in another, with someone else acting as messenger. Whenever a session was in progress, I had to be ready in the stable to show them any horse again or to let them compare one animal with another. When they had settled upon a horse, their vet and one other man would shut themselves in the box with it and I imagine test its eyes, heart, lungs and so on. They never let us see what they were doing and would spend a fair bit of time in the box with each horse.

The little vet was the most pleasant of the five and showed me an instrument he had for looking into horses' eyes. I had never seen anything like it before as we had always used the old bowler hat method, and he told me not to say a word to the others about having shown it to me.

Eventually the sale was completed and as a pleasant ending, the Russians very kindly asked me and my father to dinner with them at the Savoy Hotel in London, in the course of which we all toasted the success of the transaction in vodka.

There was, however, a tragic sequel. A colt that Lady Wentworth did not wish to sell at any price was hidden away down at Frogshole. He was an extremely fine yearling colt with very good type and action, called Indian Glory, by Raseem out of Incoronata, by Skowronek. If the Russians had seen him they would certainly never have rested until they had bought him. But he had been at Frogshole for only a few days when there was a violent thunderstorm and he was struck by lightning and killed on the spot. It was a terrible blow as Lady Wentworth had intended to keep him for breeding. She made a note in her stud book which I quote; 'Indian Glory. Struck by lightning and killed May 17th, 1936. The most perfect colt I have ever bred, with spectacular action.' I agree entirely and have never forgotten how lovely he was.

In September 1940, I drove Lady Wentworth to Lady Yule's Hanstead Stud. We had seen the horses in the morning and were having lunch with Lady Yule when, quite out of the blue, a message came through on the telephone that Crabbet was being taken over by the Canadian Army and that they were moving in then and there.

We hurried straight back to find that it was indeed true. There were Canadian soldiers in the stables and the house and two of the drives were guarded by sentries with fixed bayonets. Even the woods were full of soldiers. They apparently expected Lady Wentworth not only to move out of the house but also to give up most of the boxes. She was not the person to give in easily however, and after much argument she was allowed to stay in the house and we divided the boxes between us so that, for instance, the Canadians did their dentistry in one box while we kept our brood mares on either side.

The officers and NCO's were billeted in the house and they got on very well with Lady Wentworth, especially when they discovered how good she was at billiards. It was as well that she did stay in the house to keep an eye on things. There are three bullet holes in the weather vane above the Coronation Stables as a memento of the Canadians' high spirits. They also took over the tennis court for a sports centre but left the squash court to Lady Wentworth. I know the Canadians came to admire Lady Wentworth very much and we were in touch with them for a long time after the war. They left Crabbet just before D-Day, in 1944.

Early in the war Lady Wentworth bought a Thoroughbred stud near Petworth called Burton Park and its stock of mares and young horses. The stud consisted of about sixty acres of paddocks and a yard of between 30 and 40 boxes. It was very useful as a way of spreading the risk to our stock of death or injury from enemy action. The fact that there were 32 bombs dropped on Frogshole alone, apart from many incendiaries, was proof enough of the danger. Lady Wentworth sold a good number of the Thoroughbreds at Newmarket to make room for the Arabians. The grooms at Burton Park were not too pleased with this change and took some time to accept the Arabians. From my point of view, they were never as easy to manage as the men at Crabbet and I was continually having trouble with them. Lady Wentworth had always had an interest in Thoroughbred breeding. In 1930 she had bought a Thoroughbred mare called Forecastle and later bred a few at Crabbet. After the purchase of Burton Park she went in for breeding Thoroughbreds in a much bigger way and we bought and sold regularly at Newmarket.

The Arabs were greatly reduced during the war by cutting down breeding and selling off or giving away unwanted colts. Two trainers at Newmarket were presented with colts for riding out on the gallops.

Lady Wentworth was a very practical person and liked to see things for herself. She went round the whole Stud at least once a week to inspect the horses and talk to the grooms. She would look at all the feeding stuffs, the boxes and the mangers to see that they were clean. It was an inspection that gave no one offence. Compliments as well as criticism were handed out and we all looked forward to it. She was never sentimental about the horses and would have them put down, old or young, when there was no alternative. She had no favourites either and was never against a stallion being given a good hiding, provided it was really necessary. She was totally against swearing and never allowed smoking anywhere near the stables. She would always let you know what was on her mind and left you in no doubt when she was displeased. Her memory was astounding and I never knew her to be at a loss on a pedigree, be it one of her horses or somebody else's. I have been round many studs with her, including large Thoroughbred ones where we saw a great many horses, and on the way home she would discuss each and every individual she had seen.

One of her great loves at Crabbet was for the trees and particularly for the very fine oaks in the park. During all my time with her, there was a strict rule that no tree anywhere on the estate (except for elders, which she hated) could be felled or cut back unless it had died or become dangerous. This was very trying at times, for whenever we had to remove branches that weren't dead or dangerous – when they got in the way of the farm wagons, for instance – we had to be very careful to do it without her seeing us and then had to conceal the evidence afterwards.

Lady Wentworth had a ready wit and was an extremely interesting person to listen to on any subject. She was very athletic and had a fine eye, excelling at real tennis (which is a hard game for a woman) and playing squash almost until her death. She was very good at billiards and snooker and a more than useful shot, getting great pleasure from potting rabbits on the lawn from her bedroom window with a four-ten. One subject she was very touchy about was her age and she never liked to hear any mention of it. She was a punctual person and if she arranged to meet someone, be he a lord or a groom, she'd be there on time and expected others to do the same.

Timekeeping at the Stud was always strict, especially in the early morning. Our day went as follows: start at 7 a.m., breakfast from 8 to 8:45, midday meal from 1 to 2 p.m. and finish at 5. The only difference was that on Saturdays we stopped an hour early and on Sundays we had a break from 10 a.m. until feeding time at 4 p.m. After the war a rota system was introduced whereby grooms had every other weekend off.

At the end of 1937 I was appointed general manager in place of my father. I used to report to Lady Wentworth at nine o'clock every morning except Sundays. I would give her news of the Stud affairs and receive my orders for the day, such as matings of mares and moving them from one field to another, or, if there were visitors expected, arranging which horses were to be shown, how many at a time and so on. Visiting was always by appointment only. Lady Wentworth was very strict about this, especially after the war, when so many people wanted to come. She had to be informed as soon as a mare foaled and would come and look at it at the first opportunity. She always said the best time to judge a foal was when it was about ten days old. She picked the stallions for mating herself and usually waited until a mare had foaled before choosing the stallion. She had a telephone beside her bed in case anything serious happened in the night.

She used to keep the choicest stallions in the boxes adjoining the house. She loved to be able to pop out at any moment and feast her eyes on the likes of Naseem or Skowronek.

After the war Lady Wentworth rejoined the Arab Horse Society. She now went in for much more showing as the number of events for Arabs increased. To begin with, we were handicapped by a shortage of labour as several of the younger men who had been called up had not yet returned to the Stud and also because Lady Wentworth was expanding her breeding programme to meet an expected demand for Arabians.

We were also now farming on a fairly large scale. I had at least 200 acres under crops and even had to plough up part of Burton Park, so my time was rather stretched between farming, the Stud and Burton Park. With the amount of labour needed for harvesting the corn, which we still stooked in the field before stacking, it became a tug of war as to how many men could be spared for showing. The time factor was important not only in taking the horses to a show but also in preparing them for it.

The growing number of visitors to the Stud also took up a lot of time, and the idea occurred to us in the early Fifties of having one large parade each year so as to get all the visitors over at one time. A day would be fixed for the spring or early summer when there were most foals to be seen. A programme was drawn up with the order of showing and a loudspeaker was installed so that I could give information on each animal as it appeared. We held these parades on the lawns in front of the Coronation boxes and I'm sure the visitors enjoyed them.

above Silver Shadow (Oran–Silver Fire) standing against the garden wall
centre Bright Shadow (Radi–Pale Shadow)

and *below*
A post-war parade at Crabbet: Indian Magic is being held by Fred Rice. Standing next to **Lady** Wentworth is Fred **Branch**

If there were still people wanting to look round the Stud, another parade would be held in the autumn. As time went on the number of visitors grew enormously and at the end there were as many as two to three hundred, with many distinguished guests from abroad. The parades lasted almost until Lady Wentworth's death by which time, however, we had called a temporary halt because of the organisation required.

The war changed many things and running the Stud was never the same again. Labour was the chief problem and we even tried taking on boys. Some were a help and some just a hindrance but in any case they could never be asked to look after the stallions.

Riding had to be cut down a great deal and it was no longer possible to break in all the young stock to saddle. Most of the colts were backed but rarely the fillies, unless for some special reason. I must say though, that in the past we had always found it a great help when maiden mares came to be covered if they had already been backed to saddle.

Most of the stallions were moved to the paddocks at Caxtons where they could be turned out for the day instead of being led out for exercise. I found this change benefited them greatly. They became much less fractious by being out all day and being able to see the other stallions. Of course they were still brushed over daily but they were not groomed so much. They were also exercised by lungeing and walking but not every day, and quite some time and labour was thus saved.

Lady Wentworth remained active to her death although for some years she did use an electrically-operated chair to get round the estate. This was her only means of transport as she never learned to drive a car. Her sight also began to fail and I had to take on much of her correspondence. A number of sales were in negotiation at the time of her death.

In her will, the Stud was left to my father but as he had predeceased her it automatically came to me. I was overcome by the responsibility and the ensuing publicity. For several days I was beset by journalists and television people.

It was difficult to believe at first that I was now the owner of the Crabbet Arabian Stud. There were then about 75 Arabians and 15 or so Thoroughbred mares and fillies. The labour and food bills and all the other overheads involved were enormous and I soon learned that I would have to pay death duties at a rate of 80 per cent on everything, including the horses.

It was clearly a case of reducing the Stud to a manageable size as quickly as possible. Luckily there were several buyers already negotiating when Lady Wentworth died and others soon appeared in the hope of getting some of the renowned Crabbet stock. But there was little demand for Arabians in England. I was able to dispose of all the Thoroughbreds at the first auction at Newmarket. They were more expensive to keep than the Arabs but fetched more money.

I also had to plan where to keep the breeding stock I was retaining since I had to vacate the whole of the Crabbet stables. The stallions and colts were easy; I had been left Caxtons where there was enough room. The only place for the mares and fillies was Frogshole (which I had also inherited) where there was plenty of grazing but no buildings. So during the summer of 1958 I put up twenty loose boxes and foaling boxes, a feed room and a sitting-up room and these were ready for the mares by the winter.

The distance, about a mile and a half, between Caxtons and Frogshole was an added difficulty. It only mattered during the covering season when we had to walk the stallions to Frogshole but it did mean a lot of exercise for Fred Rice and Bright Shadow (who was our trying horse) as they had to go nearly every day while the other stallions went only when required. Another anxiety lay in walking the horses along the main road. I am quite sure it would be impossible to do that now.

The most important of my overseas sales was to Mrs Tankersley's Al Marah Stud. Her three representatives arrived unannounced at breakfast time on October 7th, 1957. They said they were interested in buying Arabians and in due course inspected all the horses that were for sale. The negotiations proceeded along very similar lines to those with the Russians in 1936, though they didn't take nearly so long. Mrs Tankersley used to telephone regularly every evening from America to discuss the prices of the animals she wanted. The horses were sent on a special train from Three Bridges to Glasgow to be shipped to America.

During a large sale of this nature one has to sell some against one's better judgement. The mare I most regretted selling was Silver Shadow, a grey mare by Oran out of Silver Fire and in foal to Silver Drift. She was really beautiful but she also proved a great loss to Mrs Tankersley. She had an accident soon after arriving at Al Marah and died in February the following year. I have often felt what a tragic waste it was. She was only twelve at the time.

The Stud was reduced by about half in the first year through sales to America, Canada, Australia, South Africa, Chile, Siam, Israel, Nassau, Pakistan and the Continent. I had in mind to cut it down to between 25 and 30 animals. Selling Arabians was not all that easy in the Fifties and Sixties. There had been a rush to buy when Lady Wentworth died, of which I had taken advantage, but this soon died down and I had always to guard against becoming overstocked, our continual worry in the past. I felt it would be a good policy to have only a few first-class horses for sale. Although buyers might come along and have to wait if there was nothing suitable, it was better than having too many horses for too few buyers. From the beginning I had to make the Stud pay its way since otherwise I could not afford to keep it. We had never previously been able to take in many visiting mares owing to the shortage of room but I immediately opened the Stud to as many outside mares as I could manage without impairing my own breeding programme. It brought in a steady revenue and also, I feel, helped considerably to popularize the Arabian in this country.

For twelve years the Stud ran smoothly with between twenty and thirty animals and the visiting mares until early in 1970, when I learned that the Government planned to build a motorway linking South London with Gatwick Airport and the coast. After a harrowing year of indecision the final route was announced. It was to run straight through the middle of Crabbet Park and apart from trimming several acres off my property at Caxtons, would involve the demolition of both of the grooms' cottages there.

My first instinct was to carry on as before, despite the upheaval and inconvenience it would cause. But when all the implications had been assessed I saw it would be impossible to continue a breeding stud in the middle of a virtual earthquake lasting at least a couple of years. With all the lorries and earth-moving equipment on the roads I would still have to get the stallions down to Frogshole. A more important factor was that I would be left with very little room at Caxtons for the stallions by the time I had used a few more acres to rebuild the grooms' cottages. So after much heart-searching, I reluctantly decided to sell the entire Stud. The only consolation was that this time all the horses went to breeders in this country.

Thinking back over the years at Crabbet and of all the horses it has been my privilege to know, there come to mind some outstanding individuals.

Naseem, for instance; a very strong and masculine type of horse, very good head and neck strong in the back, but very wilful and requiring firm handling. His full brother Naziri was also a character though much lighter in build and finer altogether than Naseem. He too was grey but so light in colour that when he died he had become almost pure white. Both Naseem and Naziri were tremendously powerful horses to ride. It was like driving a high-powered car. Naziri would walk quite as far on only his hind legs as he did on all four. He was extremely strong in the back and I have been riding him when he would just fetch his two fore legs off the ground and proceed, still in a horizontal position, for some distance without once touching the ground with his forefeet.

Raktha, by Naseem, was very different in temperament from his sire. He was a quiet and easy horse and very good to take to a show. In my opinion he was one of the very few perfect types of Arabian stallion. Raseem was another fine stallion with a wonderful back and loins and that lovely rich dark chestnut which comes from his dam Rim. Both Rim and Riyala were excellent brood mares and had splendid heads. Nasra was another top-class mare. She was the dam of Naseem and Naziri and had a fine shoulder and perhaps more length of neck than Rim and Riyala.

Another stallion I remember was Mirage, a very quiet horse to handle but as soon as you mounted him he became a different animal, full of fire and verve. When we were visited by King Fuad of Egypt, I was detailed to meet his convoy of cars at the gate of Crabbet Park and to escort them down the drive mounted on Mirage. We must have put on a spectacular display as Mirage hated combustion engines and gave

right Naziri (Skowronek–Nasra), full brother to Naseem and *above* Blaze

me a most awkward ride. When ridden he carried his head and tail high and had a very short gait which took a while to get used to. But once mastered he was exhilarating.

My favourite was the chestnut Sultan Rasim, or 'Blaze' as he was always called. He took after his sire Rasim, having a fine head and being very strong in the back and loins. When he arrived in about 1926, Old Pat rode him but Blaze, who was a hugely strong horse and quite indefatigable, used to rear a lot and once fell over backwards nearly squashing Old Pat who was by then getting rather old for that sort of caper. So I took on Blaze, with some trepidation, I might add. I usually tried to take the steam out of him first in the covered ring. But he still reared when I came out and would go up so high that I had to hang on to the branches of the mulberry trees that lined the path from the ring. There is very little one can do with a rearing horse except sit there and hope he doesn't go too high and lose his balance. In time, however, Blaze gave up his rearing and became a wonderful ride. I had at the time a fox terrier called George who came with me when I went riding and he became so keen that he would dance in front of Blaze's forelegs when going at the gallop. Blaze was eventually sold to Russia in 1936. I was truly sorry to see him go, for having looked after him for so long I had really lost my heart to him.

Nureddin II was a dark chestnut horse by Rijm. He stood 15.3 hands and was a very impressive horse, full of presence. He had superb conformation with a long and very well-placed neck, a good sloping shoulder and good bone and hocks. His one fault was his head, which was straight and rather thick through but as he was such a fine looking animal and carried himself so well he used to get away with it. Lady Wentworth used him extensively for improving the height and the length of neck and shoulders in the Stud and together with Skowronek, who was inclined to get a low shoulder, the two lines blended very well.

Skowronek was at the Stud for a few years during my time but I had more to do with his son Naseem.

Naufal was an exquisite type with very fine bone and a beautifully modelled head with prominent eyes and lovely little ears. He moved in the most delicate manner and had a fine trotting action. He was the darkest bay that I ever saw, being almost black.

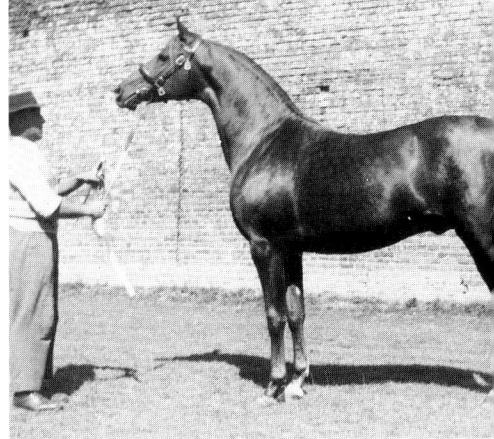

above Raktha
(Naseem–Razina)
centre General Grant
(Raktha–Samsie)
below Indian Magic
(Raktha–Indian Crown)

opposite Oran
(Riffal–Astrella)
below left Royal Diamond
(Oran–Grey Royal)
and right Grand Royal
(Oran–Sharima)

Indian Gold was dark chestnut. He had a beautiful head and long arched neck with a very good sloping shoulder. His back was long but in no way weak. He was, however, a very excitable horse and would roar all the way from the box when he was taken to cover mares, which frightened anyone not used to his ways.

There was also Oran, a chestnut of a very rich, almost deep red, colour. He proved a most successful sire and remained at the Stud until his death in 1968. He was a very strong horse, with good bone and loins and a lot of presence. I have noticed a great likeness to him in succeeding generations both through his colts and his fillies.

Bright Shadow was another chestnut. He was a well-balanced and compact horse with a very nice head. His temperament was out of this world. I have never had an easier horse to handle and he passed it all on to his stock. Lady Wentworth didn't use him much as a sire but I used him extensively and he has produced some fine stock.

Dargee was bought by Lady Wentworth after seeing him at Richmond in 1946. He was then a yearling and what a wonderful purchase he was! He also proved that Lady Wentworth didn't go entirely for the big ones as Dargee was only $14.2\frac{1}{2}$ hands. His record as a show horse and sire needs no mention here. It was a tragic loss for me when he died in 1963 of a twisted gut at the age of seventeen.

The 'Silver' line were all of outstanding quality and I knew them all from Somra onwards. Silver Fire was a particularly lovely mare who produced some excellent stock. Silver Gilt was also memorable as she lived to be 32, a record for a Crabbet mare in my time. All the Silver line had great presence though perhaps some lacked the best of hocks.

Rissla was another beautiful mare, with a lovely head and refined body, short back. She stood out on her own owing to her great quality and wonderful action. She was also quite a character and was the only mare I can remember being difficult to catch out in the field during the summer. She was never any bother in the winter when she knew there was a nice manger full of hot mash waiting. This little habit of Rissla's was passed on to several of her fillies. Traits like this are often passed on to the next generation, more so from mares than stallions.

The only horse I kept when I sold the Stud was Indian Magic, for whom I had always had a particular fondness. He was then twenty-seven and as Fred Rice had looked after him all his life I left him with Fred until the following autumn when we had to have him put down. And so it was that the Crabbet Arabian Stud came to an end.

CHAPTER 13

A Century's Work
The Families Summarised

That air of distinction which characterises the 'Crabbet type' cannot easily be explained. Lady Anne Blunt called it 'that indefinable thing "style"', and Blunt spoke of the 'almost electric thrill' he experienced when he saw a really first-class horse. It was this intangible quality, which every breeder recognises but none can describe, that the Blunts looked for and which remains the hallmark of the Crabbet type.

Style by itself does not make a horse. Both the Blunts and Lady Wentworth had extremely high standards of conformation and all three agreed that with knowledge of the blood, the only proper guide in the choice of breeding stock was close conformity to type. In Wilfrid Blunt's opinion it was a mistake to breed for any particular quality, such as speed. 'The natural Kehilan gallops easily and trots with the freest shoulder and hock action. Knee action, however, is not a characteristic of the breed nor should it be sought for. To breed for any special quality is to risk a loss of the general equilibrium.' Thus have arisen the fine free-moving action, the graceful arch of the throat and high tail-carriage that distinguish true Crabbet horses. The Blunts also attached great imhortance to good feet and as has been observed before, never regarded their horses as mere showpieces. For all their beauty, they were expected to work as hard as all other horses in that period and consequently their soundness was always fully tested.

Perhaps the main objective reason for the Blunts' success lay in their strict culling of stock. In a memorandum on breeding policy written in 1904, Blunt stated their views in detail.

> Lastly, to maintain the stud in its highest perfection, all individuals should be weeded out of it each year which fail to come up to a certain standard of physical form. It will be found at Crabbet, as is found in every Arabian tribe, that, while all are of the same original blood, certain strains only produce colts worthy of being used as

sires, for it must be remembered that as in nature there is a competition between the stallions for command in the herd, so in artificial breeding stallions must compete for preference at the breeder's hand. Thus the produce of certain imported mares, however good individually these were, will become eliminated from the stud and it will be idle out of sentiment to retain them. It is better such strains should be lost when after three generations they have failed to produce a sire of the first class.

At that time, he continued, three lines had come almost to monopolise the Stud at Crabbet but since this was the exact reproduction of the condition of things in the desert, it need not be regretted.

Blunt's comments are extremely significant. If one feature of Crabbet is more prominent than any other, it is the way in which year after year its finest stallions and colts were sold abroad and yet its mares continued to produce sons of the highest order. This was partly because the mares did indeed possess exceptional individual qualities but, more importantly, because they carried in their bloodlines that essential sire-bearing potential that the Blunts sought. It is impossible to say how and whence this potential originates but in the case of Crabbet it existed most noticeably in the foundation mares Rodania and Dajania. It is likely that the Arabs themselves knew of this in Rodania, for to them she was a 'celebrated' mare, but Dajania was bought when she was only a yearling. It is certain that in time the Blunts and Lady Wentworth learned to recognise which of their mares were capable of producing first-class colts and it is largely upon this facility that their achievements as breeders rest.

All three were fine judges and had a natural 'eye' for a horse. Lady Anne was more analytical in her approach than the other two. She would study every detail of a horse and its pedigree and make her decisions according to the evidence of the facts. Blunt and Lady Wentworth, on the other hand, had something which perhaps Lady Anne lacked; the rare gift of being able to discern the breeding potential of young stock. Blunt was always too occupied with other matters and had probably too little application ever to have achieved the highest rank as a breeder. But Lady Wentworth not only had the advantage of having lived with superb Arabians for most of her life; she also inherited a good measure of both her mother's persistence and her father's intuitive flair.

A case may readily be made for attributing the success of the Crabbet Arabian Stud to the horses themselves, whether to the original desert-bred importations, or to the Ali Pasha Sherif horses or to the later purchases such as Skowronek and Oran. But this ignores the perspicacity of the people who bought the animals in the first place. And acquisition is only one thing. But to continue to breed horses of the highest possible calibre for nearly a century and over the same period to sell many of the best ones abroad, requires either immoderately good fortune or a talent amounting to genius.

It is interesting to see how the families were assessed in 1897 when Blunt summarised the position after twenty years of breeding at Crabbet.

> Of the mares imported from Arabia and still represented at Crabbet all are strictly speaking of equal rank in point of blood, but the strains which have hitherto proved themselves the best are 1. Rodanias' 2. Dajania's through Nefisa 3. and 4. Meshura's and Basilisks' 5. Queen of Sheba's. Sherifa's descent has not yet produced a first class colt and Jerboa's is represented principally through Jeroboam's daughter Rosemary.
>
> Ferida's stock though excellent should not give sires to the stud, Ferida's pedigree having been insufficiently ascertained.* Hagar's stock also should not give sires, there being a doubt of her origin.
>
> All the Ali Pasha Sherif mares are worthy in point of blood to give stallions to the stud, but we have not sufficient experience yet to say which of the strains they represent is the best. [In fact only one female line, Sobha's, survived at Crabbet.]
>
> Of the stallions used at Crabbet by far our best has been Mesaoud. After him Azrek. Pharaoh's blood, what we have of it, is excellent and should be carefully preserved, especially the strains through Bozra and Rosemary. Kars' blood seems less good, his best strain being through Rose Diamond. Merzuk's is represented only in Ridaa where it should be carefully preserved.

We have since seen how various horses became important in Lady Wentworth's era. It is now appropriate to gather together all these

---

*Blunt's reasons for this assertion are not clear. Neither Lady Anne Blunt nor Lady Wentworth are known to have had any doubts about Ferida's authenticity; and Blunt himself selected Ferida's daughter Feluka at the Partition and bred from her Fejr (by Rijm) and Ferda (by Rustem).

threads and to trace the progress of the principal lines from the Crabbet foundation stock.

The following pages are intended only to give a guide to the families that have arisen around the world from Crabbet horses. For further details on British breeding, readers can do no better than to refer to that indispensable work, P.J. Gazder: *Arab Horse Families, an Introduction & Guide to the Stud Book*. Horses that are influential overseas are discussed at greater length under their relevant country.

The foundation horses have been divided into stallions and mares. Many of their descendants are mentioned under both dam and sire lines. For the purposes of consistency, stallion sections contain breeding details only of stallions, and mares' details only of mares. Where a stallion is important for his female lines (for instance Azrek), or a mare for her male lines (for instance Queen of Sheba), references to the appropriate family are given.

The principal British lines containing non-Crabbet blood that are mentioned here and in the overseas sections and tables, are those from Mootrub, Kesia, El Emir, Dwarka and Maidan. Their chief representatives are respectively Shahzada, Imamzada, Algol and Nuri Sherif.

STALLIONS

AZREK

Imported 1888. After his sale to South Africa in 1891, Lady Anne Blunt wrote: 'It is impossible not to feel a pang of regret at the departure of a horse such as Azrek whose stock are so satisfactory ... There should be a good many worthy sires to represent him, but they are still young.' In fact most of Azrek's colts were sold abroad and his only two sons to breed at Crabbet were Ahmar (out of Queen of Sheba) and Nejran (out of Nefisa). Ahmar was 'a bright bay with four white feet and narrow blaze, very beautiful head, small muzzle, fine shoulder and magnificent action both before and behind, tail set high and splendidly carried.' In 1901 he was sold to Belgium leaving no sons at Crabbet but important female lines through Selma and Siwa (see SOBHA), and Bukra and Bereyda (see BASILISK). Ahmar should be remembered as the grandsire of Berk (by Seyal out of Bukra).

Nejran too left only a female line, through his daughter Rish, the dam of Rangoon (by Skowronek).

Another female line from Azrek is the important one through his daughter Asfura (see QUEEN OF SHEBA).

Other lines from him run from his son Ben Azrek (out of Shemse) through Sheeba to Nuri Sherif and through Ruth Kesia to Nuri Pasha and Shahzada. Nuri Pasha has had widespread influence as a stallion in America.

Important lines overseas are, in Australia, through Azrek's son Rafyk (out of Rose of Sharon) and Ahmar's daughter Namusa (see table M3). In America Azrek's female line is represented through his daughter Rose Diamond, dam of Lal-i-Abdar (Abu Zeyd).

FEYSUL

Imported 1904, the last of the Ali Pasha stallions to come to England. His most important sons were Ibn Yashmak (out of Yashmak), exported to Egypt in 1920, and Rasim (out of Risala), exported to Baron Bicker in Poland in 1924.

Ibn Yashmak is strongest on the female side through his daughters Amida, and Amida's daughter Astrella (see QUEEN OF SHEBA), and Razieh who was exported to Egypt in 1920 and there renamed Bint Rissala (see table M11).

Rasim on the other hand has left flourishing male lines through Sainfoin (out of Safarjal) and Raseem (out of Rim), and very important female lines through Lady Yule's foundation mare Razina (see RODANIA) and through Nashisha (see DAJANIA).

HADBAN

Imported 1884. Hadban was sold to Australia in 1885, an unfortunate decision in view of the astonishing records of his only two daughters, Nefisa and Rose of Sharon (see DAJANIA and RODANIA respectively).

KARS

Imported 1878 and sold to Australia in 1885. Kars was the first stallion to be used by the Blunts and was somewhat disappointing at stud. His main lines are through his daughters Dahna in Australia (see table M1), and Rose of Jericho, the dam of Rose Diamond and therefore granddam of the American stallion Abu Zeyd (by Mesaoud).

MAHRUSS (1893)

Imported 1897. Though only at Crabbet for three years, Mahruss (1893) has exerted a profound influence on breeding in England and overseas through his son Rijm, out of Rodania's daughter Rose of Sharon. Rijm was the sire of the full brothers Nasik, in 1908, and Nureddin II in 1911, out of the Dajania line mare Narghileh.

Nasik was a bay with 'superlative style. A real peacock. Fiery rolling eyes of immense size and a metallic golden coat of amazing brilliance. A highly strung excitable temperament full of fire. Lovely head'. Nasik sired mostly colts, of which the majority were exported though one, Miraze (out of Bereyda) did start useful lines in Britain through his sons Rix (out of Rim) and Fayal (out of Fejr). The finest of Nasik's sons was Rafeef (out of Riyala) who had two very influential daughters in Nezma (see DAJANIA) and Risslina (see RODANIA). Risslina's American grandson Abu Farwa was sired by Rabiyas who also traces to Nasik. Another line from Rabiyas exists in South Africa (see table s24).

Nasik was included in the Kellogg consignment on account of his age – he was then eighteen. He lived to the age of thirty and sired a total of 32 foals in America and left many lines there, of which perhaps the most famous is through his son Farana to Farawi, Bint Sahara and Fadjur.

Rijm's other son was Nureddin II. His male line is carried principally through Faris (out of Fejr), Shareer (out of Selima) and Mr Hough's Nuri Sherif (out of Sheeba).

Faris left a number of sons of which the most influential have been Rifari (out of Risslina) and in particular Rissalix (out of Rissla), who was the sire of the stallions Count Dorsaz (out of Shamnar) and Blue Domino (out of Niseyra).

Shareer's main influence is through his daughters Sharima (see DAJANIA) and Rissalma (see RODANIA).

Lady Wentworth also valued Nureddin II as a sire of brood mares, though she used him carefully. His best daughters were Nisreen, dam of Indian Gold, Indian Crown and Indian Pride; and Neraida, dam of Niseyra who was the mother of Blue Domino, Champurrado (by Irex) and the lovely mare Tehoura. In Russia and Poland also the Nureddin daughters Ramayana, Ryama and Ruellia have left significant lines (see tables M14, M15).

MERZUK
Imported in 1891. This horse had only one season at Crabbet before being sold to South Africa. He left no colts but is extremely important for his daughter Ridaa, out of Rose of Sharon (see RODANIA).

MESAOUD
Imported 1891. Of the seven stallions brought to England from Egypt,

above Rijm
(Mahruss (1893)
Rose of Sharon
centre Nureddin II
(Rijm–Narghileh)
below Shareer
(Nureddin II–Selima)

Mesaoud is by far the most important. Strong male lines from him can be found throughout the world. His principal sons in order of birth were Seyal (out of Sobha), Daoud (out of Bint Nura), Nejef (out of Nefisa), Astraled (out of Queen of Sheba), Nadir (out of Nefisa) and Lal-i-Abdar (out of Rose Diamond).

Seyal is significant as the sire of Berk, whose brilliant action may, however, be due to the influence of his maternal grandsire Ahmar (see AZREK).

Daoud was a very fine sire of mares, among them Nasra (see DAJANIA), and Somra (see SOBHA).

Nadir's sire lines in England are mainly through Rishan (out of Rish) and Joseph (out of Maisuna) and thus to Manasseh (out of Aatika) and Dargee (out of Myola). Lal-i-Abdar is justly famed in both England and America as a sire of fine horses, of which the most important in England has been the stallion Sher-i-Khurshid (out of Mazna).

Mesaoud's most famous son is undoubtedly Astraled. Foaled in 1900, Astraled is very important for his male line through Sotamm (out of Selma) to Naufal (out of Narghileh) to Riffal (out of Razina) to Oran (out of Astrella) and Silver Vanity (out of Silver Gilt). Riffal went to Australia in 1947 (see table S11) as did others of Astraled's descendants, notably Shafreyn, Sindh and Grand Royal (see tables S11, S14). In Egypt, Astraled's granddaughter Bint Rustem and his grandson Kasmeyn (by Sotamm out of Kasima, out of Kasida) have been influential, the latter being the grandsire of the preeminent stallion Nazeer.

In 1909 Astraled was sold to the American, Lothrop Ames, in whose hands Blunt remarked sanguinely, 'all horse fanciers will see Astraled and spread our Crabbet fame'. Renown did indeed come when Astraled was crossed with Rose of Sharon's granddaughter Gulnare to produce in 1924 the important American stallion Gulastra.

On the female side both Mesaoud and Astraled have left their mark, the former with Narghileh (see DAJANIA) and Risala (see RODANIA); and Astraled with Rim and Riyala (see RODANIA) and Selima (see SOBHA).

MIRAGE

Purchased in 1923. Mirage was sold in 1930 to Mr Selby in Ohio for reasons already stated. He has left no lines in Britain which is this country's loss as his influence in American breeding has been considerable.

above Sotamm (Astraled–Selma)
centre Naufal (Sotamm–Narghileh) and
below left Sindh (Silver Vanity–Silfina)
right Shafreyn (Royal Diamond–Sharfina)

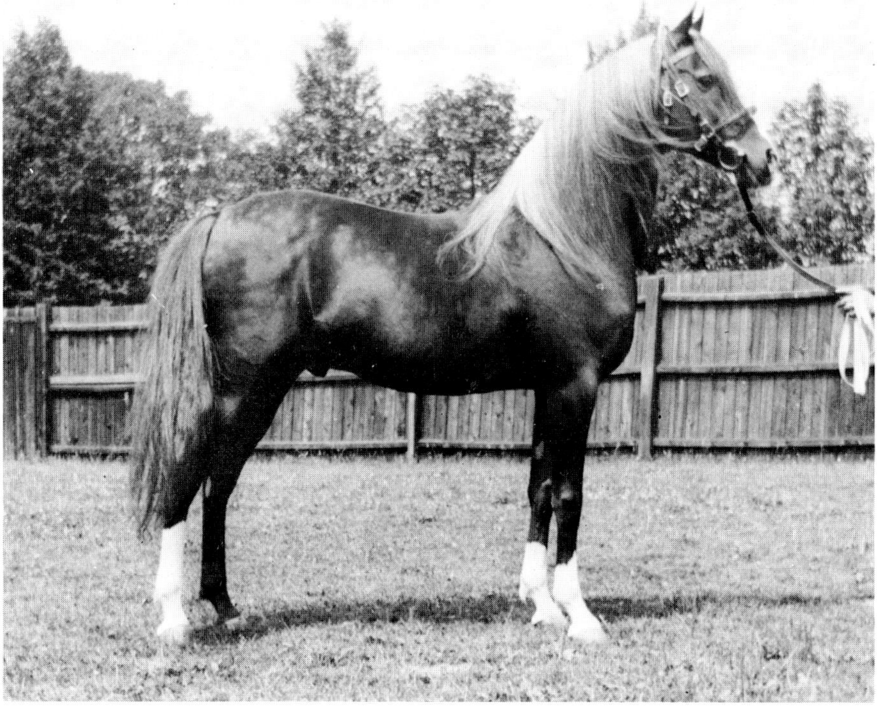

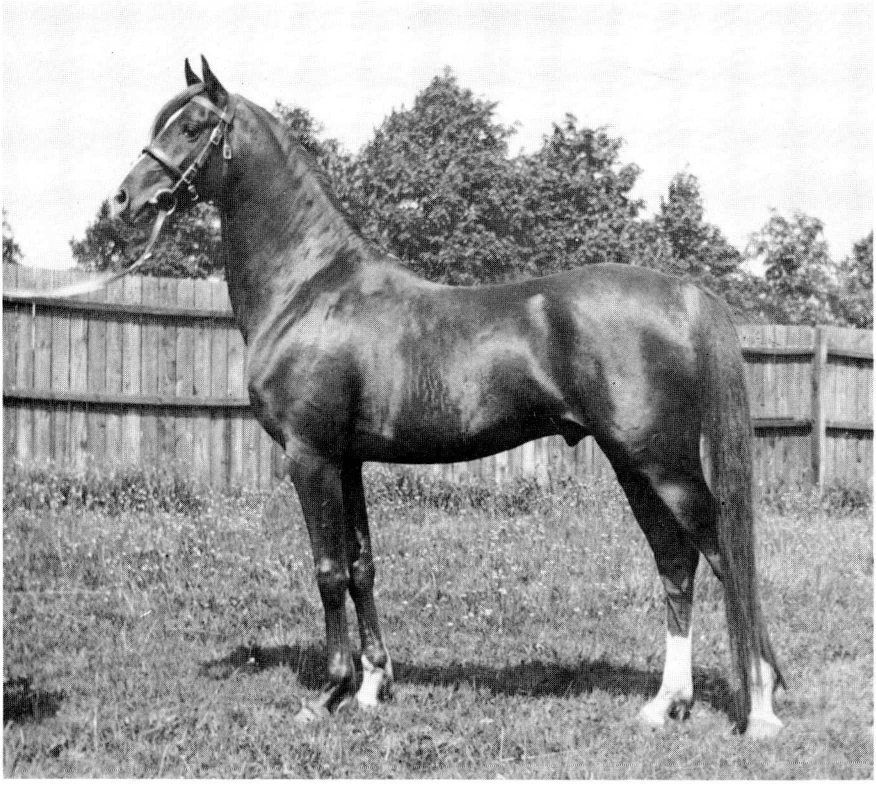

PHARAOH

Imported 1879. Pharaoh was at Crabbet for only three years during which he sired a very good colt out of Jerboa called Jeroboam who was the sire of Rosemary (see RODANIA). Jeroboam died at sea in 1887. Pharaoh has also left an important line through his daughter Bozra (see BASILISK) and a less important one through his grandson Ben Azrek (by Azrek out of Shemseh, out of Sherifa).

SHAHWAN

Imported 1892. He too was at Crabbet for only three years. His only line extant is through his daughter Yashmak out of Yemama who was foaled at Sheykh Obeyd. Yashmak, when crossed with Feysul, produced Ibn Yashmak (see FEYSUL).

SKOWRONEK

Purchased in 1920. The decision to buy Skowronek, and the manner in which she used him at stud, are among Lady Wentworth's greatest achievements as a breeder. The nick between Skowronek and the mare lines of Dajania and Rodania has, taken all in all, been of paramount influence in Arabian breeding throughout the world.

From the Rodania line came Raswan (out of Rim) and Rangoon (out of Rish). Raswan's principal son was Ferhan (out of Fejr) who, when crossed with Nureddin II's daughter Nisreen, produced the very important stallion Indian Gold: 'a wonderfully beautiful horse with exceptionally long neck. Fine striding action covering a lot of ground. Lovely carriage and style. Beautiful head and very long mane. Deep chestnut. Shoulder very long and sloping and girth deep. A first class sire type'. Indian Gold is most influential through his daughters Silver Gilt, Silfina and Serafina. Raswan has also left a very strong female line in Russia and Poland through his daughter Star of the Hills (see table M18).

From the Dajania line came the two full brothers Naseem and Naziri (out of Nasra). Naseem's importance throughout the world has been colossal. Before being sold to Russia in 1936 he had sired the stallions Indian Light (see table S5), Raftan (out of Riyala), Rissam (out of Rim), Irex (out of Rissla) and Raktha (out of Razina). Raftan's male line continues through Naseel (out of Naxina), Rissam's through Nizzam (out of Nezma) and Irex's through Champurrado (out of Niseyra). In 1951 Raktha was sold to South Africa where he got first-class produce (see table S22) but by then he had already sired the stallions Electric

above Ferhan (Raswan–Fejr)
below Indian Gold (Ferhan–Nisreen)

Silver (see table s8), and Silver Drift and Serafix (both out of Serafina), between them of great importance in Australian and American breeding. Before being exported Raktha also sired two prominent stallions in post-war Britain, Indian Magic (out of Indian Crown) and General Grant (out of Samsie).

Naseem's daughters include Sulka, who was exported to Holland, and the famous mare Silver Fire, founder of the 'Silver' line (see SOBHA). Naseem's career was far from finished when he left England. His extraordinary influence in post-war Russia and Poland, and hence throughout the world, is discussed in the section for those countries.

With descendants such as the above, Skowronek scarcely needs further renown. But he has it through his inbred son Raffles (out of Rifala, by Skowronek out of Rissla) whose progeny have been sufficiently numerous and important in America to have a book devoted to them. Apart from Rifala, other Skowronek mares to have left families are Rose of the Sea, Naxina and in Australia Nasirieh (see table M4).

The only imported stallion in Appendix I to have left a line is RATAPLAN. Bought for the Newmarket race, Rataplan was imported in 1884 and perished *en route* for Egypt three years later. His line survives in Hagar's family through his daughter Harra (out of Harik) and in Australia through his granddaughter El Lahr (see table M2).

MARES

BASILISK
Imported 1878. Blunt considered the Basilisk line to be one of the best of the early importations but by Lady Wentworth's time it had died out in the direct female line at Crabbet.

Basilisk had three fillies before being sold in 1884, of which only one was kept. This was Bozra (by Pharaoh), who produced a total of fourteen foals. Eight died young (two from accidents) and her three colts were sold. Of the three surviving fillies, the line through Bushra was lost as a result of sales and deaths. Her next daughter Bukra (by Ahmar) was the dam of the stallion Berk. Bukra also had Balis (by Seyal) and Battla (by Razaz). Battla was sold to the United States in 1918 and was repurchased by Lady Wentworth in 1924 when in foal to Rizvan (by Ibn Yashmak out of Rijma). The resulting produce was named Bahreyn who returned to America in the Kellogg sale of 1926 and there established a line through her son Ronek.

above left Irex (Naseem–Rissla) and *right* Rissam (Naseem–Rim)
below Naseem (Skowronek–Nasra) with Pat Nugent

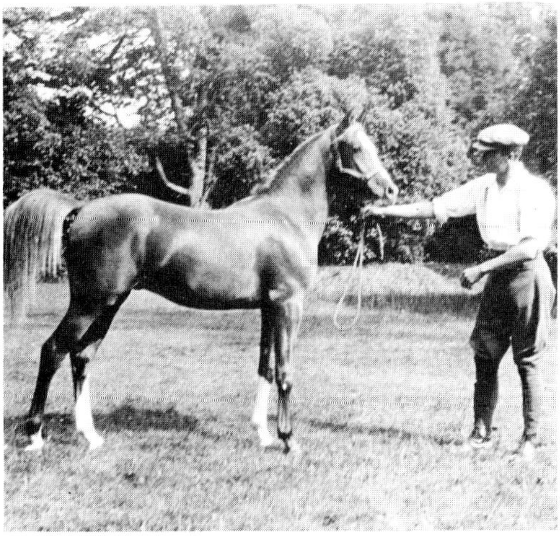

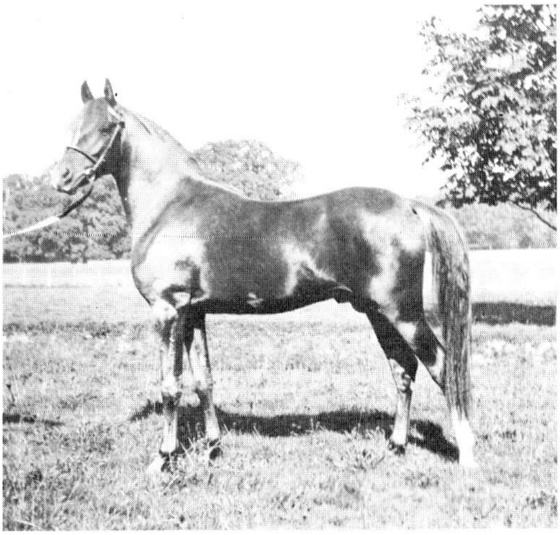

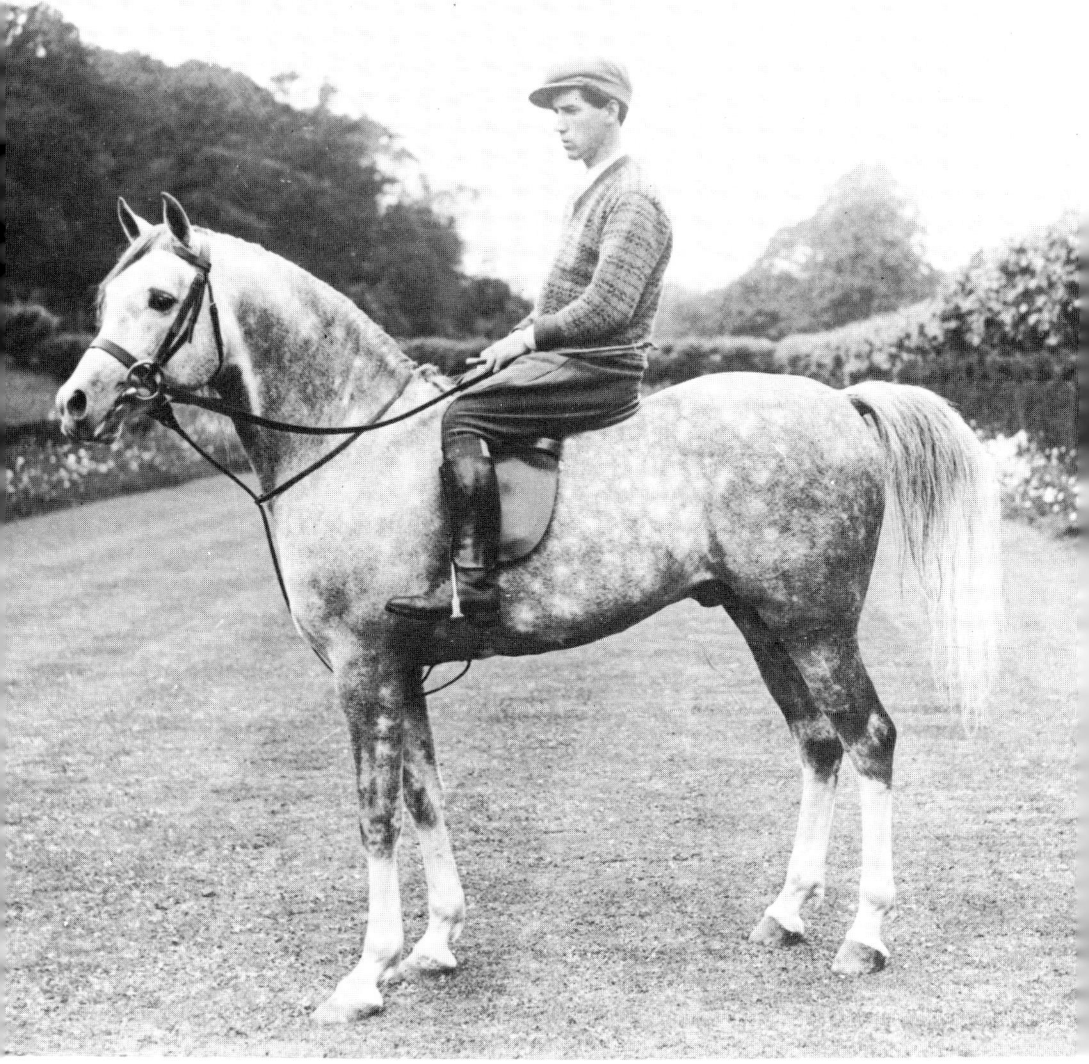

Bozra's last live filly was Bereyda (a full sister to Bukra), who was the dam of the fine mare Belka (by Rijm) through whom the Basilisk female line has been continued.*

BINT HELWA

Imported 1897. Bint Helwa's line died out quite quickly at Crabbet. It is prominent in America through her daughter Ghazala (by Ibn Sherara) who was the dam of Gulnare and granddam of Gulastra. Bint Helwa is also the dam of Harb and therefore the granddam of Rodan, the sire of Gulnare. This line was reintroduced into England in the Thirties with the mares Gara and Gayza but not into Crabbet. Another line from Bint Helwa in America is through her daughter Hamasa (by Mesaoud) and Hamasa's daughter Hazna (by Razaz, by Astraled out of Rose of Hind). A small line also exists in Australia through Bint Helwa's grandson Harir (see table s4).

BINT NURA

Imported 1897. Bint Nura is important for her sons MAHRUSS (1893) and Daoud (see MESAOUD).

DAFINA

Imported 1927. Dafina has a small family from her daughter Dafinetta (by Naziri), and another in Russia from her daughter Ryama (by Nureddin II: see table M14).

DAJANIA

Imported 1878 and progenitor of the 'N' line. The families of Dajania and Rodania are of paramount importance and it is possible only to mention the most influential of their descendants. Dajania's contribution is perhaps the more remarkable since it is attributable to precisely one mare, Nefisa (by Hadban).

Foaled in 1885, Nefisa was an outstanding brood mare, having in all 21 foals, the last at the age of 27. The most notable of her colts was Nadir (by MESAOUD, q.v.) and it is through her daughters Narghileh (also by Mesaoud) and Nasra (by Daoud) that her importance lies.

The ability of mares of the 'N' line to produce stallions of the highest quality for generation upon generation is truly astonishing and several notable horses such as Serafix, Champurrado and Indian Magic have close crosses to this line on both sides of their pedigrees. From Narghileh came Nureddin II and Nasik—see MAHRUSS (1893)—while Nasra

* For the importance of the Basilisk line in America, see footnote on p. 245

would have achieved fame merely by being the dam of Naseem and Naziri (see SKOWRONEK).

On the female side Narghileh is mainly important for the line through Nessima (by Rijm) to Naxina (by Skowronek) who had four very good daughters – Raxina (by Raktha), Samsie and Nariffa (both by Riffal) and Naxindra (by Indian Gold). Raxina had three fillies in Ireland, all by Naseel: Nizreen went to America in 1961 but both Nafisa and Nazli were retained and now have descendants in Britain. Samsie was the dam of, in particular, General Grant (the sire of General Gold and a string of show-winning fillies) and Samson who left sons in Britain and grandsons in America. Naxindra has left a large family, mainly through Magnindra (by Magnet) and Naxiffa (by Hanif). She was also the dam of the stallion Masjid (by Bright Shadow).

Nasra's main daughters are Nezma (by Rafeef), Nasira (by Nadir), Nasifa (by Skowronek), Nisreen (by Nureddin II) and Nashisha (by Rasim).

Nezma was the dam of the stallion Nizzam (by Rissam) who produced stock of high quality first in Holland and then in the United States. Her daughter Nazziria (by Naziri) was the dam of Yavroum (by Raktha) whose daughter Surprise of Harwood has left many descendants.

Nasifa was the dam of Neraida (by Nureddin II) who produced Niseyra (by Rissam) who was the dam of the important stallions Blue Domino and Champurrado. Niseyra's daughter Tehoura (by Radi) went to Holland where she had Nishida (by Nizzam) who was exported to England and there produced numerous foals by Ludo, including the important mare Ludmilla.

Nisreen was the dam of the fine stallion Indian Gold and of the mares Nasirieh (see table M4), Indian Crown (by Raseem), Indian Pride and Indian Flower (full sisters by Irex). Indian Crown is best known as the dam of Indian Magic but her daughter Incoronetta (by Dargee) produced a good family which includes Silvanetta, African Queen and Azara. Indian Pride's principal son was Indian King (by Oran) but her daughter Indian Starlight (by Indian Magic) was also important: among her issue (nearly all of whom were by Ludo), Indian Snowflake and Indian Golddust may be singled out for mention. Indian Flower was the dam of Indian Diamond (by Oran) who was exported to the United States in 1957 but her line has been continued in Britain through another daughter, Indian Rhapsody by Greatheart.

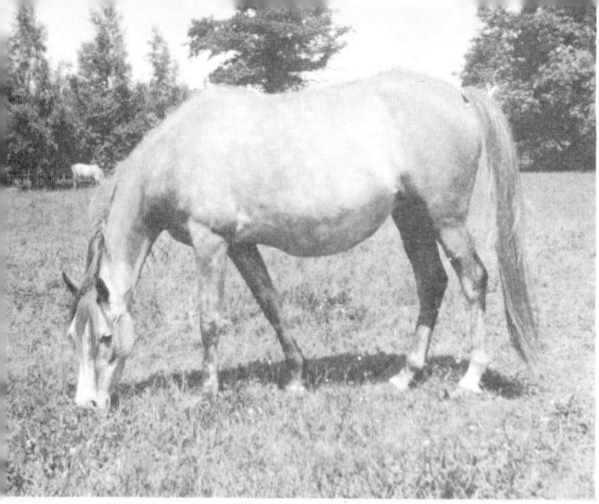
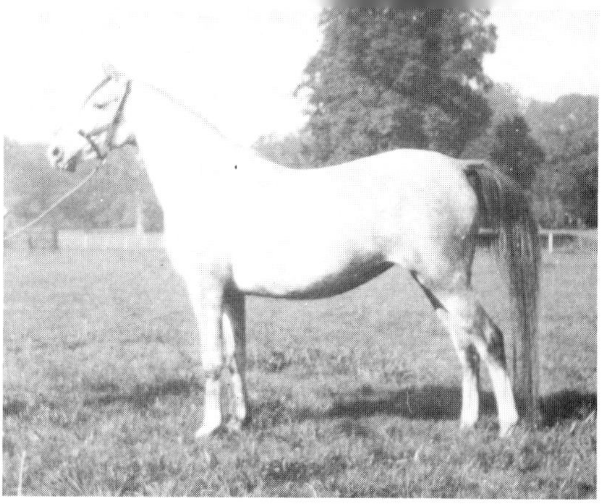
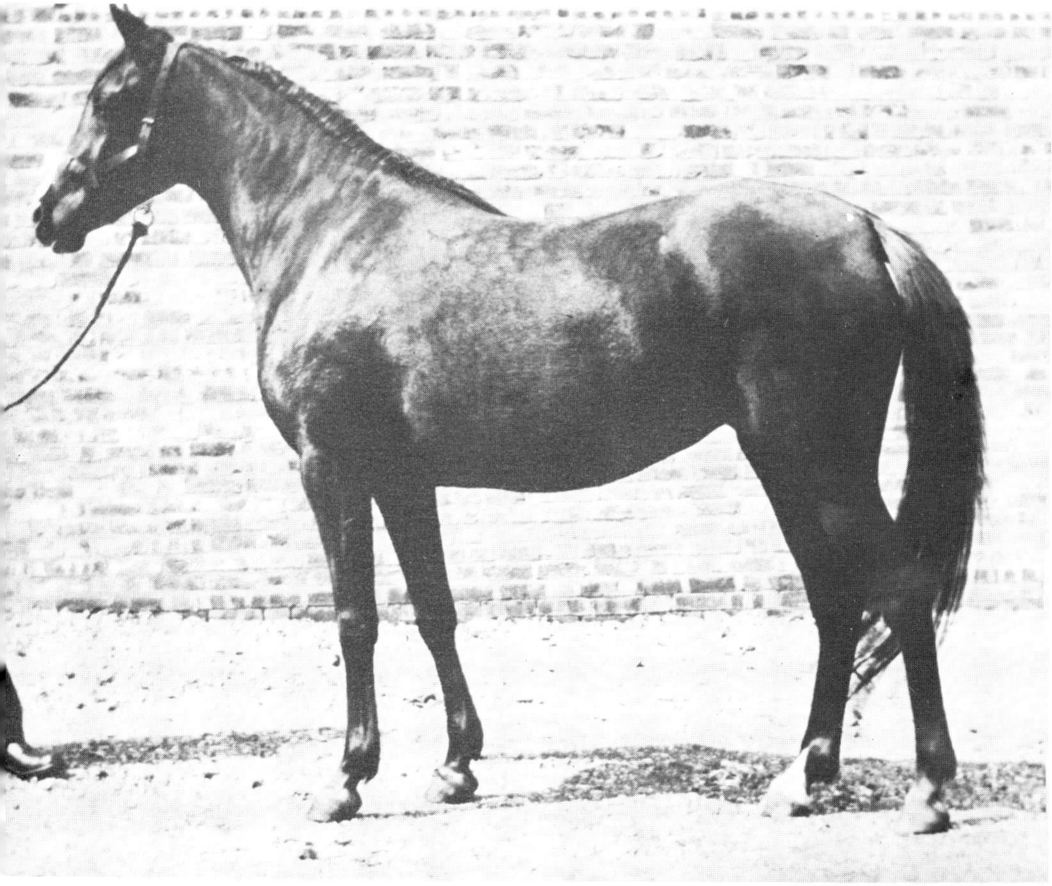
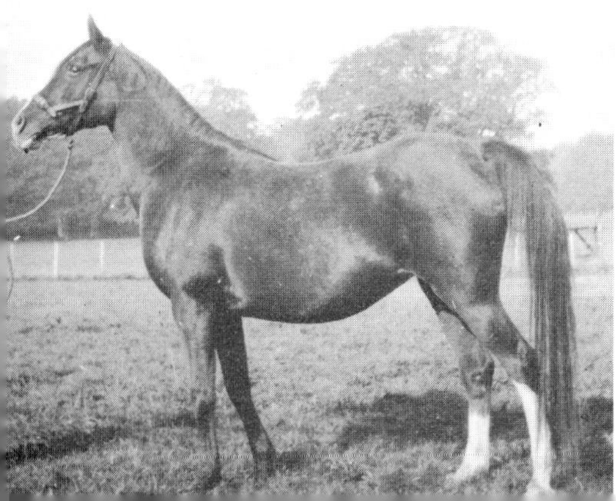
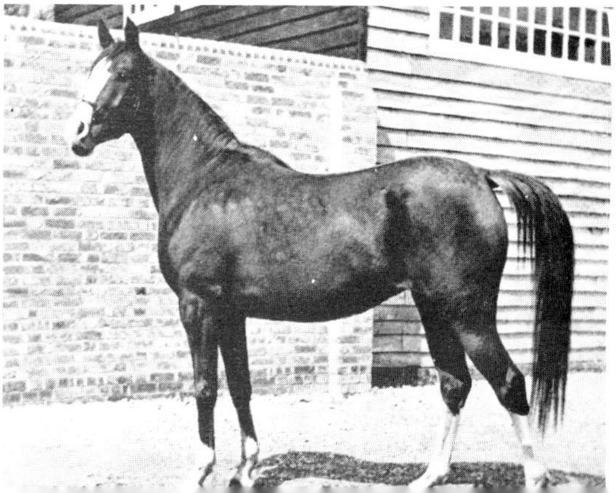

Opposite
top left Nasifa (Skowronek–Nasra)
top right Neraida (Nureddin II–Nasifa)
centre Niseyra (Rissam–Neraida)
below left Nisreen (Nureddin II–Nasra) and
right Indian Crown (Raseem–Nisreen)

above top left Sharima (Shareer–Nashisha)
and *right* Grey Royal (Raktha–Sharima)
centre Sharfina (Rytham–Sharima)
right Serafilla (Raktha–Sharfina)

Nashisha was the dam of Sharima (by Shareer) whose influential line has been continued principally through her daughter Sharfina (by Rytham), dam of Shafreyn (see table S14). Another daughter, Grey Royal (by Raktha) was the dam of Serafire and Royal Diamond, both of whom were exported to the United States, and of Royal Crystal, who went to South Africa.

Sharfina's family is immense. Her daughter Silfina (by Indian Gold) was the dam of Sindh (see table S14), Silindra (by Raktha) and Silent Wings (by Oran). The latter's daughter Yemama (by Indian Magic) produced the important stallion Ludomino (by Ludo) and several good fillies including Golden Ludo, dam of Golden Silver.

In 1945, Sharfina had Serafina, also by Indian Gold, who was the dam of Serafix and Silver Drift (full brothers by Raktha), both of which were sent to America (see table S28) and had a colossal influence there.

The lovely Shades of Night (by Rissam) was another important daughter of Sharfina being the dam in particular of the twin fillies by Dargee, Dancing Sunlight and Dancing Shadow, the latter of whose daughter Tarantella (by Indian King) founded a good family. Shalina, full sister to Shades of Night, produced Sirella (by Dargee) who has also left a large family and was the dam of Hanif (by Silver Vanity).

The influence of the male and female lines of the 'N' family is amply demonstrated by the tables for each country. In America, where the tables are constructed on different lines, particular mention should be made of Indaia (by Raseem out of Nisreen) and her son Indraff (by Raffles), Incoronata (by Skowronek out of Nisreen), Serafina and her son Serafix, Silfina, Serafire and of course Narghileh's son Nasik.

Narghileh is also notable in another context, as the dam of Narda (II) —by Rejeb. Narda's son Crabbet (by Rijm) and to a lesser degree her daughter Noam (by Rijm) achieved considerable celebrity as a result of their performance in the early American endurance tests.

FERIDA

Imported 1891. Ferida had two colts, both of whom were sold abroad. Of her seven fillies only one, Feluka (by Mesaoud) remained at Crabbet.

Feluka's first five foals were all colts and were sold. She then had three fillies of which Fejr (by Rijm) and Ferda (by Rustem) are the most important.

Fejr was purchased by Mr H.V.M. Clark as a young mare but returned in 1922 and in 1924 produced Faris—see MAHRUSS (1893). In 1925 Fejr had Ferhan (by Raswan). Through these two stallions the blood of Ferida remained at Crabbet although after the death of Fejr in 1931 it was no longer represented on the female side.

Feluka's other daughter, Ferda, was exported to the United States in the Kellogg sale of 1926 with her daughter Farasin (by Rasim). Between them they have founded a large family to which Ferda's son Ferseyn (by Raseyn, by Skowronek out of Rayya) has contributed significantly. Ferda also left a daughter in Britain, Fantana (by Nasik) who in 1933 had Dil Fireb (by Joseph) whose descendants are numerous.

FULANA

Imported 1897. The only descendants of Fulana appear to be in Australia where her son Faraoun (by Mesaoud) has influenced the lines of Namusa and Dahna (see tables M3 and M1).

JELLABIEH

Imported 1898. The only line from Jellabieh appears to be through her daughter Jask (by Berk) who was exported to Brazil in 1921.

JERBOA

Imported 1878. For her son Jeroboam, see PHARAOH. Jerboa also had a daughter by Pharaoh called Jerud who, when mated with Miss Dillon's stallion Maidan, produced the colt Jamrood who appears in the pedigree of Nuri Sherif and in Hagar's line from Zem Zem.

JOHARA

Imported 1897. Johara has left a small line through her daughter Jalmuda (by Mesaoud) to Jawi-Jawi.

KASIDA

Imported 1898. Kasida's greatest influence is through her grandson Kasmeyn (by Sotamm, see MESAOUD), who was sold to Egypt in 1920 and is important in bloodlines there.

MAKBULA

Imported 1898. Makbula was the dam of KASIDA (q.v.).

MESHURA

Imported 1881. On the male side Meshura's influence lies through her daughter Maisuna (by Mesaoud) to Maisuna's son Joseph (by Nadir, see MESAOUD). Meshura's granddaughter Mazna (by Astraled) was the dam of the stallion Sher-i-Khurshid (by Lal-i-Abdar).

QUEEN OF SHEBA

Imported 1879. The Queen of Sheba line is very important. But it has been an unlucky family and there are few representatives now left in the female line.

Of her four filly foals, one was born dead, two died as yearlings and only Asfura (by Azrek), who was described as having 'splendid action', survived. Two of Asfura's fillies were kept, Abla and Ajramieh (both by Mesaoud). Lady Anne Blunt wrote of Abla that she 'has action like a deer, singularly tame, perfect hack'. Abla became Wilfrid Blunt's favourite riding mare after Shieha died and was one of the few horses to remain at Newbuildings after the lawsuit.

Ajramieh's best daughter was Amida (by Ibn Yashmak) and it is through Amida's daughter Astrella (by Raseem) that the female line of Queen of Sheba is chiefly represented today, although another line does come from Amida's daughter Almas (by Nuri Pasha) through her granddaughter Arabian Dawn who was sired by the non-Crabbet stallion Jair.

On the male side, however, Queen of Sheba's sons Ahmar and Astraled have left strong lines (see AZREK and MESAOUD respectively). It is interesting to note that Astraled's great-great-grandson Oran was out of Astrella, Queen of Sheba's great-great-granddaughter.

RODANIA

Imported 1881 and progenitor of the 'R' line. The invasion of Arabian horse breeding by the Rodania family has been even more widespread than that by Dajania's line. No less than 45% of the mares in AHSB Volume XII (1970–73) trace in tail female to Rodania, as opposed to 10% for Dajania and 9% for Sobha. The bias in the United States is less pronounced but still striking: 11%* of the 1985 stud-book entries go back to Rodania, 3% to Dajania and 2% to Sobha. Only the Davenport mare, Urfah Or.Ar., has a higher rating, with 13%. Nor has the influence of

* Information compiled by Cadranell, Schulz, Dirks and Dirks for members of the A.H.H.A. and reproduced by kind permission. Interestingly, the line from Basilisk which is nearly extinct in tail female in Britain, had become by 1985 the third most prolific in the United States (9.5%).

THE FAMILIES SUMMARISED

Rodania been confined to those English-speaking countries whose breeders traditionally bought direct from Britain. Strong colonies have at various times been established in Spain, Egypt, Russia and Poland where they have been successfully bred with indigenous mares and stallions to produce descendants who have in their turn been exported to found yet more outposts of the Rodania gene. The ability of this family (as indeed of all of the world's great dam-lines) to transmit for a century and more certain unique and desirable characteristics is surely a cause of wonderment to breeders and laymen alike.

Insofar as overseas countries are concerned, the various bifurcations from Rodania are described in detail in the text and table between pages 265 and 358. Additionally, a new table has been compiled to chart the diaspora from Rodania and this lies between pages 359 and 371.

Rodania had three main daughters: Rose of Jericho (by Kars), Rosemary (by Jeroboam) and Rose of Sharon (by Hadban).

Rose of Jericho was sold to Sir J.P. Boucaut in Australia in 1891. Her daughter Rose Diamond (by Azrek) was sold to Savile in 1903. Rose Diamond was the dam of Lal-i-Abdar, and left a line at Crabbet through her daughter Rose of Hind.

Rosemary's two main daughters were Riada and Rabla (both by Mesaoud). Riada's daughter Rayya (by Rustem) produced Raseyn, of considerable influence in the United States. From Rabla the lines of her daughters Rish (by Nejran) and Rangha (by Berk) are important, the former through her daughter Rishna (by Nureddin II) and the latter mainly through her son Algol (by Aldebaran).

Rodania's principal line is through Rose of Sharon. Lady Wentworth made an interesting comment on her colour: 'Rose of Sharon. Golden chestnut with white mane and tail. The colour constantly reappears in her descendants and after crossing with brown develops maroon almost black chestnut with flaxen or golden manes and tails. With golden bay cross instead of brown it sometimes reappears as a vivid iridescent buttercup gold of dazzling brilliancy with lighter gold mane.'

In 1892 Rose of Sharon produced Ridaa (by Merzuk). Ridaa had three important daughters: Risala (by Mesaoud) and Riyala and Rim (both by Astraled).

Risala, whom Blunt described as the finest mare at Crabbet 'without question', was foaled in 1900 Her main son was Rasim (by FEYSUL, q.v.). Of her daughters, Rafina founded a good line in Australia (see table M5); Rythma (by Berk) had Myola (by Algol) who was the dam of Dargee, while

Rijma has left prolific lines through Riz to Rizada (by Shahzada). Risala's most important daughter, though, was undoubtedly Rissla (by Berk) who combined the beauty, quality and style which are so striking in her family with the brilliant action of her sire. These characteristics have been transmitted very noticeably to her descendants.

Rissla's stock are numerous. Rifala (by Skowronek) and her son Raffles were exported to the United States (see SKOWRONEK). Reyna (by Skowronek) was originally important in Spanish lines. Rissalma (by Shareer) was sold to Russia with her daughter Florencia (by Faris). There she produced the extremely important stallion Priboj and Florencia had a mare called Parfumeria (by Piolun) who was the dam of the influential stallion Knippel (by Korej). Rixalina (by Raseem) was also sold to Russia where she produced Korej (by Kann). Risslina (by Rafeef) had a foal by Naseem called Rissletta who was sold to the United States where she produced the brilliant American sire Abu Farwa (by Rabiyas). It is through Risslina that Rissla's line is most strongly represented in Britain today.

Rissla's male lines through her sons Rissalix and Irex are of great importance both in Britain and overseas through their several sons, notably Count Dorsaz, Blue Domino, Mikeno, Greatheart and Champurrado.

Rose of Sharon's second daughter was Riyala. Foaled in 1905, Riyala's female line is represented by her daughters Ranya (by Nasik) and Razina

Risala (Mesaoud–Ridaa) in the field called Short Gallop

above Rissla (Berk–Risala) and *below* Risslina (Rafeef–Rissla)

(by Rasim), Lady Yule's foundation mare; and by Razina's daughter Nurschida (by Nuri Sherif). Razina also had two highly important sons in Raktha (see SKOWRONEK) and Riffal (see MESAOUD). In Russia, Riyala's line has been perpetuated by her daughter Ruellia.

Rim, who was full sister to Ramla, the American endurance test winner, as well as to Riyala, is strongest through her sons Rissam, Raseem and Raswan. In America she is represented through her daughter Rifla (by

Rasim) and Rifla's son Rifda. In Russia she has a powerful line through Raswan's daughter Star of the Hills and in Australia she has lines through Rissam's daughters Carlina and Rizala.

The chief progenitor of this astonishing line, Rose of Sharon, has left her mark not only through her daughters. For she was also the dam of Rijm—see MAHRUSS (1893).

At the age of 20, when in foal to Harb, she was sold to Spencer Borden in the United States. There she produced the colt Rodan, the sire of Gulnare; and Rosa Rugosa (by Imamzada), the dam of Sidi.

SHERIFA

Imported 1878. All of Sherifa's five daughters were sold leaving no issue at Crabbet. One of her granddaughters Shieha (by Azrek out of Shiraz, by Kars) did return to the Stud but bred only colts. Shieha was sent back as her owner complained that she was a bad ride. Lady Anne Blunt tried her and found her only 'raw and nervous' when first mounted. She had a very fast walk and trot and it was thought that she had probably outdistanced the cobs at her previous owner's estate. Lady Anne found her willing, though 'she pulled a bit, like Sherifa and has same peculiar amble'. Shieha became Blunt's favourite riding mare. She collapsed and died out hunting in 1908, aged twenty.

Sherifa's most important line extant today is through her grandson Ben Azrek (by Azrek out of Shemseh, by Pharaoh).

SOBHA

Imported 1891 and the only Ali Pasha Sherif mare to leave descendants at Crabbet by the 1930s. Lady Anne described Sobha as 'delightful as a companion and to ride'.

Sobha had five living foals. Two were born in Egypt, Antar, who was sold there in 1899, and SAFRA (see below) . Of the remaining three, one was a son by Mesaoud called Seyal (the sire of Berk). The other two were the fillies Selma and Siwa (full sisters by Ahmar) from whom lines have spread all over the world.

Selma's main daughter was Selima (by Astraled), the dam of the stallion Shareer and the fine mare Star of the Hills. Selma, who was foaled dark brown and remained a very dark grey for some years, has also left a strong male line through her son Sotamm (see MESAOUD).

In many ways, however, it is Siwa, Sobha's other daughter, who is the more important of the two since she was the dam of Somra (by Daoud).

above Selma
(Ahmar–Sobha)
centre Somra (Daoud–Siwa)
with Pat Cahill
below left Silver Grey
(Royal Diamond–
Silver Gilt) and
right Selima
(Astraled–Selma)
with her daughter
Star of the Hills
(by Raswan)

Somra had three important daughters: Safarjal (by Berk), Seriya (by Skowronek) and Silver Fire (by Naseem). Apart from being the dam of Sainfoin (by Rasim), Safarjal also had Sukr (by Atesh imported horse) and Somra II (by Fedaan imported horse) who both founded families at the Courthouse Stud of Mr H.V. Musgrave Clark.

Seriya was the dam of the bay Shabryeh (by Algol) who, when put to Rissalix, had Shabrette. The bay colour died out in the Crabbet Stud but Shabrette's daughter Farette (by Rifari) has left one of the few families of almost entirely Crabbet blood-lines in which bays regularly appear.

Silver Fire can be said to have founded a dynasty in her own right. The striking characteristics of the 'Silver' line are their quality and extreme beauty, particularly of the head. Silver Fire's principal daughters were Somara (by Nureddin II), Silver Shadow (by Oran) and Silver Gilt (by Indian Gold).

Somara was the dam of Senga and Silver Crystal, both by Rangoon. Senga's large family includes Shtaura, the dam of Ahmoun, and Scindia, the dam of Scindian Magic. Silver Crystal was sold to the United States in 1951 but before that she produced Silver Bell (by Raktha) who in due course had Platinum Bell and Grey Crystal.

Silver Shadow was also sold to America (in 1957) but left two fillies at Crabbet, Shadow Light and Wentworth Golden Shadow, full sisters by Indian Gold. Shadow Light's main daughters are Magic Pearl (by Indian Magic) and Aurora (by Oran) while Wentworth Golden Shadow has left a large line, chiefly through Maracanda (by Mikeno) and Silver Mantle (by Manto).

The crowning glory, however, of Silver Fire's female descent is Silver Gilt, dam of the outstanding Silver Vanity (see MESAOUD) and several choice mares. Silver Vanity was exported to America at the relatively tender age of twelve but he had meantime sired some first-class horses: Sindh who went to Australia in 1961 (see table S14), the prominent stallion Hanif and the mares Indira and Silver Ripple who have numerous descendants of quality. Another line from Silver Vanity was introduced to Britain by the importation from the United States at the beginning of the 70s of his daughter, Vain Love.

Of Silver Gilt's daughters, four went abroad: Silver Grand and Silver Diamond to the United States, Silverlet to South Africa and Royal Radiance to Australia. In Britain, her line is represented by several notable mares. Silver Grey (by Royal Diamond) left a number of sons and daughters among which Silver Sheen (by Bright Shadow) stands out, not least for her remarkable record in the show-ring. Her progeny includes the stallion Silver Blue and Silver Mantilla. Silver Gilt also had Dalika (by Dargee) who was the dam of Enchantment (by Indian Magic) and some good sons by Indian Star one of which, Diamond Star, was the sire of Aboud. Silver Gilt's last two daughters, Sunset and Golden Gilt, foaled in 1965 and 1968 respectively, have also established more than useful families.

The Crabbet foundation mares BADIA, KHATILA and SAFRA left no stock at Crabbet.

The following mares that were sold by the Blunts have left lines outside the Stud.

DAHMA
Imported 1881. This line survives in Australia, through Dahma's daughter Dahna (by Kars) and Dahna's granddaughter El Lahr (see tables M1 and M2).

HAGAR
Imported 1878. After being sold to Miss Dillon, Hagar produced seven foals before her death in 1898, the second of which was Zem Zem (by El Emir). A small line continues from Zem Zem to this day, as does another from the Crabbet-bred Howa (by Azrek), the great-granddaughter of Hagar. Hagar was also the great-great-grandmother of Nuri Sherif.

JEDRANIA
Imported 1881 and sold to Miss Dillon in 1886. In 1893 she produced the colt Jezail (by Imam) who was the sire of Hauran (out of Hagar, above). This horse was left in Miss Dillon's will to Spencer Borden, went to America in 1910 and there sired Bathsheba who appears in many pedigrees through her only foal Bazrah (by Rodan).

JILFA
Imported 1888. Jilfa has left a small line through Jamusa (by Azrek), whose granddaughter was Alfarouse (by Berk out of Mareesa, by Mareb).

WILD THYME
Imported 1878. Wild Thyme had a daughter by Kars called Raschida, who

was purchased by Miss Dillon. Raschida had several offspring, of which two, Mahal and Nessa, were imported by Spencer Borden into America where their lines appear to have continued. Raschida also has a line through Nuri Sherif.

above Silent Wings
(Oran-Silfina)
centre Indian Sylphette
(Indian King-Blue Sylphide)
Photo B. Finke
below Hanif
(Silver Vanity-Sirella)
Photo P. Sweet

above Nerinora (Oran-Nerin)
centre Rikitea
(Rissalix-Nurschida)
below Ludo
(Blue Domino-Rithyana)

above Golden Treasure
(Blue Domino-Gleaming
Gold)
Photo B. Finke
centre King Cotton Gold
(Fari II-Dreaming Gold)
Photo P. Sweet
below Somerled, aged 21.
Bred in Australia
by Baz (Rakib-Barada II)
out of Silver Radiance
(Electric Silver-Royal
Radiance).
Photo R. Flynn

top left Aliha
(Indian Silver-AK Atallah)
Photo C. Massey
top right Carmargue
(White Lightning-Velvet Shadow)
Photo Gari Dill-Marlow
left Seheran (Silver Flame-Shottifa)
Champion long distance racehorse.
One of the last foals bred by
Lady Anne Lytton who had always
wanted to breed a race winner.
Photo J.M. Ratcliff

Appendix I

Horses imported by the Blunts from whom no descendants remained in the Crabbet Arabian Stud in 1897

ABEYAN
A bay stallion foaled about 1869, an Abeyan Sherrak of the Maoyaja tribe of Sebaa Anazeh. Imported 1884. Sold in 1885 to the Earl of Antrim.

ABU KHASHEB
A Dahman Nejib. A grey stallion bred by Ali Pasha Sherif in Cairo in 1894. Sire: Mahruss. Dam: Bint Bint Nura. Purchased from Ali Pasha Sherif December 1896. Imported in 1898. Sold 1901 for Government of India.

ASHGAR
A dark chestnut stallion foaled in 1883, a Seglawi Obeyran, strain from the Shammar of Mesopotamia. Bred by Othman el Ibrahim el Akeyli of Deyr on the Euphrates. Dam: a Seglawieh Obeyrieh of the Saekh tribe of Shammar. Sire: an Abeyan Sherrak. Imported 1888. Sold in Sept. 1890 for exportation to Gibraltar.

BURNING BUSH
Foaled about 1869, a Kehilet el Krush. Sire: a Kehilan Abu Janub of the Mizrab. A dark chestnut mare with 3 white feet and star. Purchased by Mr Skene April 1878 at Hama. Imported 1878. Given to Miss Dillon 1884.

CANORA
A chestnut mare foaled in 1874, said to be a Kehileh Ajuz of the Nowak strain. Purchased 1879 at Baghdad, from Anton Latinik a Christian of Baghdad who stated that she was brought to him from the desert by a shepherd who was supposed to have stolen her. Imported 1881. Sold July 1882 to Sir Donald Currie.

DAHMA
Foaled in 1876, a Dahmeh Omm Amr of Ibn Hemsi of the Gomussa tribe of Sebaa Anazeh. Sire a bay Abeyan Sherrak (related to Queen of Sheba) also of Gomussa tribe. A dark bay mare with four white feet, near hind leg a stocking $\frac{1}{2}$ way up to hock off hind foot a very small mark of white, star a little to off side on forehead snip going up from lip in a narrow line to level of eyes. Purchased April 11th 1881 in the desert of Oueyman ibn Said of the Gomussa tribe of Sebaa Anazeh. Imported 1881. Sold 1888 to Mr Stephens M.P.

DAMASK ROSE
Foaled in 1873, said to be a Seglawieh El Abd of the Roala. A chestnut mare

with two white hind feet and blaze ending pink. Purchased April 1878 at Damascus from the Greek Patriarch Georgius who bred her out of a mare he obtained from the Roala. Imported 1878. Sold 1882 to Lord Hardinge.

DARLEY
Foaled in 1876, a Kehilan Ajuz of the Ras el Fedawi strain or a Kehilan el Fedawi of the Fedaan Anazeh. Purchased in December 1877 at Aleppo of Mr Skene who had procured him as a foal some months before of Seyd Ahmed Sheykh of the Hannadi tribe settled near Aleppo. Imported 1878. Sold in the July sale 1882.

FRANCOLIN
Foaled in 1875, a Saadeh Tokan. A grey mare, became flea bitten. Purchased at Deyr January 1878 from Abd el Huseyn. Imported 1879. Sold at the July sale 1882 to Mr Dangar who sent her to his stud in Australia, with Purple Stock.

HAGAR
Foaled in 1872, a Kehilet Ajuz of the Sebaa Anazeh. 15 hands, girth $71\frac{5}{8}$, below knee $7\frac{1}{4}$ inches. A bay mare with black points no white, fairly good head profile better than front view, large prominent eyes long well placed nostril, rather ewe necked (when thin) fine and long shoulder racing like appearance, legs good and remarkably sound, hocks rather small but not defective in any way and having stood hard work under heavy weights, fine mover especially galloping, tail well placed. Purchased in Aleppo Jan 4th 1878 from an Arab of the Moali who had recently bought her from the Roala who had taken her in war from the Sebaa Anazeh. Imported 1878. Sold in September 1886 to the Hon. Miss Dillon.

JEDRANIA
Foaled in 1875, a Seglawieh Jedranieh of Ibn Sbeyni of the Mehed tribe of Fedaan Anazeh. Sire a bay Kehilan Nowak of the Moayaja tribe of Sebaa Anazeh. Dam a grey Seglawieh Jedranieh of Ibn Sbeyni of the Mehed tribe. A bay mare with black points no white except small star on forehead. Purchased in Aleppo April 24th 1881 from Ali Agha, a Kurd. Sold to Miss Dillon in July 1886. Jedrania was given by Miss Dillon in 1898 to H. C. Stephens.

JILFA
Foaled in 1884, a Jilfeh Stamm el Bulad. A bay mare. Star no other white. Bred by Khashman el Kasab of the Moahib tribe of the Sebaa Anazeh. Purchased in the summer of 1887 from her breeder. Imported 1888. Given in August 1896 to Hon. Terence Bourke for exportation to Tunis.

PROXIMO
Foaled about 1875, a Kehilan of the strain belonging to Ibn Khoreyssan or

a Kehilan el Akhras (the dumb) of Ibn Khoreyssan of the Jemaat of Beteyen ibn Mirshid of the Gomussa tribe. Sire a Managhy ibn Sbeyel. A bright bay stallion with 3 white feet and blaze ending in a pink muzzle. Purchased at Bombay in February 1884 from Abd ul Rahman ibn Minni who obtained him from Aid ed Temini by whom he was brought from Arabia in the spring of 1880-1. Imported in 1884. There were but 2 foals by him in three years, both remarkably fine but both died. Given to Count Joseph Potocki in 1887.

PURPLE STOCK
A bay mare foaled in 1874, said to be a Kehilet Ajuz bred by Thami Ibn Jebail of the Ajajera tribe of Fedaan Anazeh. Purchased in Aleppo, 1878 by Mr Skene. Imported 1878. Sold July 1882 to Mr Dangar.

RATAPLAN
Foaled about 1873, a Dahman Om Amr of Ibn Hemsi of the Gomussa tribe. A dark bay or brown stallion with black points, two near feet white up to fetlock joints, and star on forehead. Purchased in Bombay in February 1884 from Abd ul Rahman ibn Minni. Rataplan's dam a Dahmeh Om Amr of that strain belonging to Ibn Hemsi. It has not been possible to obtain information as to his sire without reference to the family of the Hemsi, but their Dahman strain has too great a reputation in the desert as *mazbut* to allow of any doubt as to the care that would be taken in the choice of sires. Imported 1884. Rataplan was shipped for Egypt and perished at sea in the autumn of 1887 with Jeroboam in a steamer of only 500 tons or so.

TAMARISK
Foaled about 1867, a Saadeh Tokan of the Obeyd tribe. A chestnut mare with 3 white feet, off fore foot chestnut, star and blaze down the muzzle. Purchased Jan 20 at Deyr. Imported 1878. Sold July 1884 to Mons. Tanfi for the Hungarian Stud of Babolna.

WILD THYME
Foaled in 1876, said to be a Kehilet Ajuz of the Ras el Fedawi strain. A bay mare with no white except star. Purchased in the spring of 1878, for Mr Blunt, by Mr Skene, from Hamid el Abbas Sheykh of Beni Jamil branch of the Baggara tribe, left bank of the Euphrates. Imported 1878. Sold to Mr G. Watson July 1882. Repurchased 1884. In 1887 was given to Mr C. E. Tebbutt.

ZEFIFIA
Foaled in 1873, a Kebeysheh Zefifieh, of the strain described as El Olahyeh (the tall). A grey mare with black mane and tail, flea bitten, black skin. Bred by Ibn Erdzi of the Ibn Haddal Amarat (Anazeh) tribe. Purchased April 4th 1881. Imported 1881. Sold in 1888 to a Mr Harrison. [A well known mare. In Lady Wentworth's opinion, the Blunts were wrong to sell her.]

Appendix II

SHEYKH OBEYD

First attempt: horses from which no descendants were kept

ABU ZEYD

Stated to be an Abeyan Sherrak. A dark bay stallion foaled about 1883. Brought from the Arabian desert to Syria and from there to Egypt by Karkur, a Smyrna man, a dealer in Cairo. Purchased Dec. 1893. Sent to Tunis Dec. 1895 to Hon. Terence Bourke.

ATWA

A Kehileh Nowakieh of the Debbe Nowak strain of the Gomussa tribe. A bay mare foaled 1884. Bred by the late Nazir Agha, her dam Daifa given to Nazir Agha by Prince Ahmed Pasha. Purchased from Mohammed Kuddr Ibn Kuddr Agha March 25 1892. Exchanged Dec. 7 1898 for Feysul, a ch. horse. [See FEYSUL under Foundation Stock.]

MAHRUSSA

A grey mare foaled about 1882. Bred by Kazim Agha (chief Eunuch to the late Khedive Towfik Pasha), dam a bay mare purchased from the Roala tribe. Purchased from Boghos Bey Achikian Dec. 30th 1894. Died Dec. 29, 1895, foaling.

NEJIMA

Stated to be a Seglawieh. A bay mare foaled 1890. Purchased from Khuddr Jemal el Din, March 30, 1894. Sold May 1896.

SAADA

A Kehilet Ajuz stated to be of Ibn Aafas's strain. A chestnut mare foaled about 1883. Said to have been bred by Ibn Aafuz of the Beni Husseyn tribe of Dafir and taken in war by the Fedaan tribe, from whom she was taken by the Roala tribe. Purchased from Ahmed Ibn Jamil, Feb. 3rd, 1891. Given away April 15, 1897.

SAFURA

Stated to be an Abeyeh Sharrakieh. A chestnut mare foaled 1887. Bred by Mohammed es Safuri, a Turi Sheykh residing at Tell el Yahudieh. Purchased from Mohammed es Safuri Jan. 23, 1892. Sold January 1896 to Sheykh Salame Abu Shedid.

SHIEHA

Stated to be a Kehilet Ajuz. A grey mare foaled 1883. Bred by Abd el

Wahab Bey el Afifi of Zowanin, who purchased her dam from Mohammed Agha Haj Hamed of the Abu Hamed family of Nasrieh. Purchased from Abd el Azim el Afifi, nephew of Abd el Wahab Bey, March 18, 1892. [Fate unknown. Given to Mutlak as a riding horse.]

TARFA

Stated to be a Hamdanieh Simrieh. A bay mare foaled 1889. Bred by the Beni Sokhr tribe and purchased from Mutalleb Ibn Abd el Kerim of that tribe by Ahmed Ibn Jamil (the Akeyle) who brought her to Egypt. Purchased from Ahmed Ibn Jamil, Dec. 14, 1891. Died August 1894.

TIHAWIEH

A Kehilet Ajuz. A chestnut mare foaled 1891-2. Bred by Ghadir Aamr el Tihawi in the Sherkieh province. Purchased from him Feb. 19, 1894. Given away 1896.

TOEYSSA

A Toeysseh Algami (stated to be). A bay mare foaled 1887. Stated to have been bred by Sha-er Ibn ed Dukhi of the Weled Ali tribe. Purchased from Khalid Ibn Ghanim Jan. 11, 1894. Given away 1897.

PART TWO

The Influence of Crabbet Blood Overseas

by Colin Pearson
with Betty Finke

Introduction

The purpose of the following sections is to examine in detail the influence of Crabbet blood overseas. The word 'Crabbet' is used here as a portmanteau and has been taken to include all animals whose pedigrees trace, wholly or substantially, to horses bred or owned by the Blunts and Lady Wentworth.

The text provides a brief history of the principal importations of Crabbet blood into each country where these have not been covered in previous chapters, together with such explanations and amplifications as are necessary.

The tables have been designed to show how families have become established and not to pay court to individuals of current, and perhaps ephemeral, fame. In this way the reader can, with a minimum of trouble, relate the horses of today both to preceding generations and to other contemporary branches of the same family. An exception to this is the United States of America where the number of relevant horses is too great to permit extended tables similar to those for other countries.

Two particular problems of presentation have arisen of which the reader should be aware.

Non-Crabbet horses. It has not been possible to indicate these, nor the percentage by which such animals are not of Crabbet blood. The major British lines with non-Crabbet blood of which representatives will be found on the tables have been given in Chapter 13. Horses bred outside Britain and not of Crabbet ancestry are obviously more numerous and more difficult to summarise. In the tables for Australia and South Africa, horses of non-Crabbet and non-British breeding are relatively few but in those for Egypt, and Russia and Poland, they are more common. It can only be said that every effort has been made in the text to differentiate clearly between horses of Crabbet ancestry and those of indigenous or non-Crabbet imported bloodlines.

Name changes. Many horses registered under one name in their country of birth have been given different names when exported. This applies especially in Egypt, and Russia and Poland. Thus Azmi (1951: also known as Nahr el Nil) is registered in Russia as Nil; Raafat (1958) is Aswan; Tilal (1957) is Talal; Kamel (1952) is Hadban Enzahi; Namet (1969) is Namiet and his dam Naturshitsa (1963) is registered in Poland as Naturszczica. Also Nabor (1950) is Naborr in America. No attempt has been made to give all variant names.

The tables are divided into stallion and mare lines. Important male produce by females and female produce by males are either given as notes on the tables or explained in the text.

Dates on tables are dates of birth.

Stallions are printed in **bold** type on the tables.

Each indentation to the right on the tables represents one generation.

In the United States of America, numerals against horses are the registration numbers in its stud-book.

Finally, the horses that appear in the tables are only those with lines extant today. The apparent cessation of, for instance, a stallion line is caused usually by the horse in question having left daughters, but no sons to have bred on. The same applies, *mutatis mutandis,* for mares' tables.

Publisher's Note: Colin Pearson having died in November 1987, the work of revising his text has been kindly undertaken by Rosemary Archer (Australia and South Africa) and Betty Finke (Europe). Only minimal changes have been made to the sections on Argentina and the United States of America and none to that on Egypt. Additional material has been introduced by Mrs Archer on New Zealand and Canada and by Betty Finke on Europe.

The areas where material revision has taken place are Australia, South Africa, Russia and Poland. This work has not involved any significant corrections but a number of changes have been made to reflect current opinion concerning some of the later horses mentioned by Mr Pearson and to bring to readers' attention certain animals that have become prominent since the first publication of this book.

ARGENTINA

The influence of Crabbet blood has been as marked in South America in general and Argentina in particular, as it has been elsewhere. Of the horses listed as sires in the 1970 Argentina Stud Book, well over half are direct male descendants of horses from Crabbet.

It must be stated, however, that some of the horses bred in South

America and described as pure-bred in their own countries have yet to be accepted as such in other parts of the world.

Señor Ayerza's El Aduar Stud was for many years the most important in South America. His* principal purchases of Crabbet stock were in 1913 with the mare Nadima (Daoud/Nefisa) and the stallion Rukham (Berk/Rabla).

Nadima, who was full sister to the remarkable mare Nasra, had two daughters, Tual (by Rukham) in 1915 and a full sister, Helib, the following year. Both bred on well and by the 1930s Nadima's line was well established. The family was then depleted by exports to Brazil but the branch from Tual re-established itself and by 1970 had developed a strong line of brood mares.

It is, however, the Berk son Rukham who has contributed most to the breed in Argentina. He had four sons, Heil, Nebal, Setuhan and Zedak of which the line from Nebal (see table s3) has prospered to such an extent that the Berk male line has become the largest in Argentina. This is of particular interest for Berk had relatively few get and although his daughters have become famous throughout the world, his male lines have been of much less consequence. His son Ribal had many produce in the United States and while important, was in no way able to influence the entire population of Arabians in that country as Nebal has done in Argentina.

Ajman was another Crabbet stallion to be imported into South America, in 1912. By Feysul out of Ajramieh, his produce appear in many pedigrees in Brazil, Uruguay and Argentina. More recently, Silver Sun (Sun Royal/Silver Shadow) has made an impression (see table s1) as also has the North American-bred stallion Al Marah Ibn Rapture who is a double grandson of Raffles, being by the Raffles son Rapture out of Rafla (Raffles/Indaia). Indaia herself was a granddaughter of Nasra and therefore related to Nadima. A Silver Sun daughter called Sun Diamond (out of Twinkling Diamond) was imported to Britain in 1973.

*In fact these were purchased not by Hernán Ayerza, the owner of El Aduar, but by his brother Alfonso.

LIST OF TABLES
s = *Stallions*

s1 Silver Sun
s2 Skowronek's line
s3 Rukham

S1 SILVER SUN

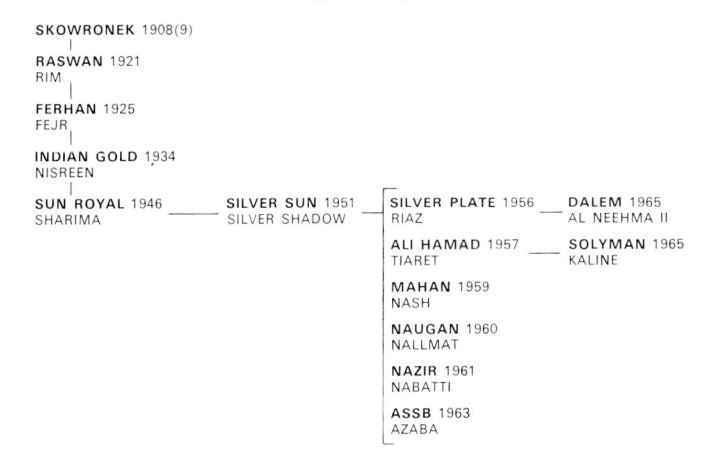

SKOWRONEK 1908(9)
|
RASWAN 1921
RIM
|
FERHAN 1925
FEJR
|
INDIAN GOLD 1934
NISREEN
|
SUN ROYAL 1946 — SILVER SUN 1951 — ⎡ SILVER PLATE 1956 — DALEM 1965
SHARIMA   SILVER SHADOW   ⎢ RIAZ   AL NEEHMA II
                                    ⎢
                                    ⎢ ALI HAMAD 1957 — SOLYMAN 1965
                                    ⎢ TIARET   KALINE
                                    ⎢
                                    ⎢ MAHAN 1959
                                    ⎢ NASH
                                    ⎢
                                    ⎢ NAUGAN 1960
                                    ⎢ NALLMAT
                                    ⎢
                                    ⎢ NAZIR 1961
                                    ⎢ NABATTI
                                    ⎢
                                    ⎣ ASSB 1963
                                      AZABA

S2 SKOWRONEK'S LINE

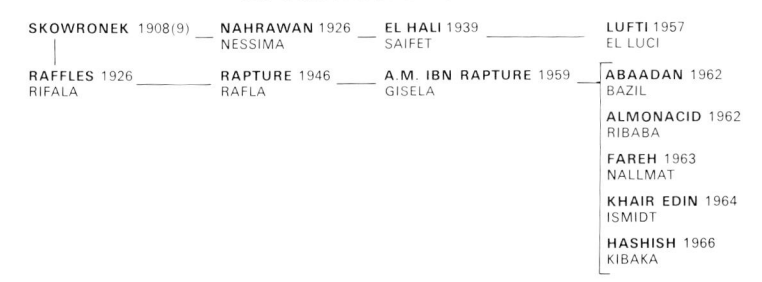

SKOWRONEK 1908(9) — NAHRAWAN 1926 — EL HALI 1939 ———————— ⎡ LUFTI 1957
| NESSIMA   SAIFET   ⎢ EL LUCI
RAFFLES 1926 — RAPTURE 1946 — A.M. IBN RAPTURE 1959 ——————⎢ ABAADAN 1962
RIFALA   RAFLA   GISELA   ⎢ BAZIL
                                                           ⎢
                                                           ⎢ ALMONACID 1962
                                                           ⎢ RIBABA
                                                           ⎢
                                                           ⎢ FAREH 1963
                                                           ⎢ NALLMAT
                                                           ⎢
                                                           ⎢ KHAIR EDIN 1964
                                                           ⎢ ISMIDT
                                                           ⎢
                                                           ⎣ HASHISH 1966
                                                             KIBAKA

S3 RUKHAM

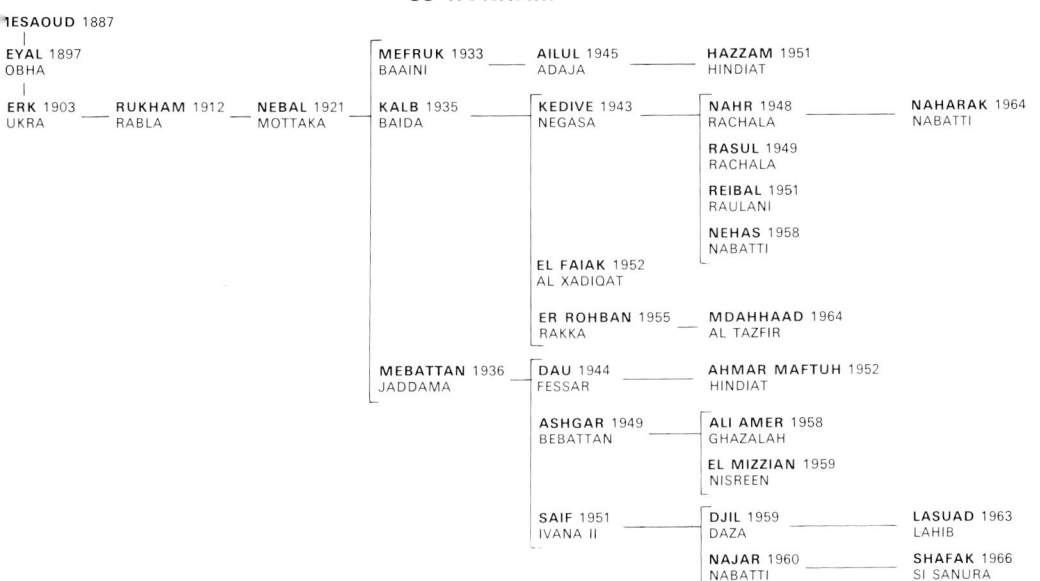

MESAOUD 1887
|
EYAL 1897
OBHA
|
ERK 1903 — RUKHAM 1912 — NEBAL 1921 — ⎡ MEFRUK 1933 — AILUL 1945 ————— HAZZAM 1951
UKRA   RABLA   MOTTAKA   ⎢ BAAINI   ADAJA   HINDIAT
                                      ⎢
                                      ⎢ KALB 1935 — ⎡ KEDIVE 1943 — ⎡ NAHR 1948 ————— NAHARAK 1964
                                      ⎢ BAIDA   ⎢ NEGASA   ⎢ RACHALA   NABATTI
                                      ⎢   ⎢   ⎢
                                      ⎢   ⎢   ⎢ RASUL 1949
                                      ⎢   ⎢   ⎢ RACHALA
                                      ⎢   ⎢   ⎢
                                      ⎢   ⎢   ⎢ REIBAL 1951
                                      ⎢   ⎢   ⎢ RAULANI
                                      ⎢   ⎢   ⎢
                                      ⎢   ⎢   ⎣ NEHAS 1958
                                      ⎢   ⎢   NABATTI
                                      ⎢   ⎢
                                      ⎢   ⎢ EL FAIAK 1952
                                      ⎢   ⎢ AL XADIQAT
                                      ⎢   ⎢
                                      ⎢   ⎣ ER ROHBAN 1955 — MDAHHAAD 1964
                                      ⎢   RAKKA   AL TAZFIR
                                      ⎢
                                      ⎣ MEBATTAN 1936 — ⎡ DAU 1944 — AHMAR MAFTUH 1952
                                        JADDAMA   ⎢ FESSAR   HINDIAT
                                                        ⎢
                                                        ⎢ ASHGAR 1949 — ⎡ ALI AMER 1958
                                                        ⎢ BEBATTAN   ⎢ GHAZALAH
                                                        ⎢   ⎢
                                                        ⎢   ⎣ EL MIZZIAN 1959
                                                        ⎢   NISREEN
                                                        ⎢
                                                        ⎣ SAIF 1951 — ⎡ DJIL 1959 ————— LASUAD 1963
                                                          IVANA II   ⎢ DAZA   LAHIB
                                                                      ⎢
                                                                      ⎣ NAJAR 1960 ———— SHAFAK 1966
                                                                        NABATTI   SI SANURA

267

AUSTRALIA AND NEW ZEALAND

The first Australian purchases from the Crabbet Arabian Stud were Francolin and Purple Stock, bought by Mr Dangar at the 1882 sale. In 1885 Mr D. Mackay of New South Wales bought Kars, the first stallion to have been used at Crabbet, and Hadban. It was said that Kars obtained a fine reputation in Australia as a sire of buggy horses.

The most important of the early acquisitions from Crabbet were those of Sir James Penn Boucaut for his pure Arabian stud at Quambi Springs in South Australia. In 1891 he bought the yearling colt Rafyk and the mares Dahna (Kars/Dahma) and Rose of Jericho (Kars/Rodania). Rafyk was the first foal out of Rose of Sharon and was sired by Azrek.

In 1901 Boucaut made further purchases from Crabbet; the mares Namusa (Ahmar/Narghileh) and El Lahr (Imamzada/Dinarzade) and the Mesaoud son Faraoun, one of the few offspring of the Ali Pasha Sherif mare Fulana.

There was at this time in Australia neither a printed studbook nor a register in which details of matings could be recorded so while we may safely assume that many of these early imports were used to breed pure Arabs as well as crosses, we unfortunately know nothing about their descendants. Although Kars and Hadban had no purebred sons in Australia of which we are presently aware, they are nevertheless represented both through Kars' two daughters, Dahna and Rose of Jericho, and through Rafyk, his dam Rose of Sharon being by Hadban.

El Lahr, though purchased by Boucaut from the Blunts, was not in fact bred by them but came to Crabbet as a foal with her dam. Her background is unusual: her sire, Imamzada, combined the relatively rare blood of four non-Crabbet desert-bred horses – El Emir, Ishtar, Kesia and Kesia II. Her dam, Dinarzade, was by Rataplan out of Dahna. Rataplan was the only stallion imported by the Blunts to have left no lines at Crabbet but some outside the stud, of which this is his largest. Dahma, the dam of Dahna, also left no lines at Crabbet or indeed anywhere else except Australia.

above Rossfennick
(Indian Magic–Rosinella)
centre Silver Moonlight
Indian Magic–Silver Fire)
below Rakib
(Nax–Rythama)

Dinarzade was sold by the Blunts to a Mr Martin as a riding horse for his wife. Mrs Martin, however, found her 'too much' and after a sale to Spencer Borden fell through, the mare was purchased by Miss Dillon. She also took against Dinarzade and in 1899 exchanged her, by this time with El Lahr at foot, for Jerboa's daughter Jerud. Dinarzade was then sold to Russia, leaving the Blunts with her problem filly. Lady Anne's feelings about El Lahr were unequivocal. 'I should much prefer not to have had it as it will have to be got rid of whatever good qualities it may possess for these could not make up for its being half of a strain one cannot vouch for. Moreover, if sold from this stud it will be counted as of our breeding no matter what precautions be taken to contradict statements to that effect.' Lady Anne's concern has not deterred Australian breeders. For El Lahr's large family, see table M2.

Shortly before his death in 1908, Boucaut sold his entire stud except for two mares. He was then aged 77 and unable to cope any longer with the management. 'I miss dear old Rafyk very much,' he wrote to Blunt, 'he was more kindly in his nature and much more sensible than many Christians.' Boucaut had not been wholly successful in upgrading local stock with his Arabian blood. 'You may more satisfactorily preach to a horse-box than a farmer,' he wrote – although some of Rafyk's get were making people think, 'or rather I should say, beginning to think'. Rafyk's influence on the pure Arabian stock in Australia has been considerable, as may be seen throughout the earlier tables. But it has been somewhat overshadowed by the importance of the Boucaut mares Dahna and Namusa (see tables M1 and M3).

Among the buyers at the Quambi sale were the Hon. Samuel Winter-Cooke of Murndal, Victoria and Mr G. Leonard Brown of Gurlargambone, N.S.W. In 1911 Cooke imported from Crabbet the Rijm son Fakreddin out of Feluka and two years later Brown bought Berk's son Harir (see table S4). Later his sister-in-law, Mrs W.D. Brown, imported into Australia the stallion Rief (Sotamm/Ridaa) who sired the important stallion Raisuli, out of Ayesha.

During the 1920s, a small group of breeders began registering the Arabians they had bred in the Arab Horse Society Stud Book. Most of them were at this period using sons of the non-Crabbet stallion Shahzada who was by Mootrub out of Ruth Kesia and who was imported into Australia in 1925 by Mr A.E. Grace together with the desert-bred Nejdmieh and Miriam (Nadir/Ranya, table M7), who had been bred by Colonel J. Hamilton Leigh. Shahzada had had an excellent record in

above Nuralina
(Hazzam–Nasira)
centre Rafina
(Rustem–Risala)
below Nasirieh
(Skowronek–Nisreen)

Endurance Tests in England, winning one of 250 miles, one of 300 miles and coming second in a third, also of 300 miles, and went on to win numerous championships in Australia and to become a popular sire. As is evident from the tables, the bloodlines from these horses have combined well with those of the previous imports from Crabbet.

Jos Jelbart of Stony Park East had also bought several mares from Winter-Cooke's stud and his collection included representatives of all the earlier breeders. In 1949 his entire stud was purchased by the New South Wales Department of Agriculture and to it they later added the Hanstead stallion Sala (Grey Owl/Hama, table S13) and, in 1955, Razaz (Champurrado/Rahab) of Crabbet descent and bred by Mr H.V. Musgrave Clark at Courthouse.

The greatest influence, however, on Australian Crabbet bloodlines has been the stud of Mrs A.D.D. Maclean, the breeder who has been described as 'the Lady Wentworth of Australia'. She visited Crabbet in 1924 and there bought Rafina (Rustem/Risala, table M5) and her colt foal Raseel (by Nureddin II, table S12) to found her famous stud at Fenwick in Victoria. She sought out remnants of earlier studs, purchasing three mares at the Winter-Cooke sale and ten from Mr A.J. McDonald's Tehama stud, all of which traced to Boucaut mares. Amongst these was Barada II (Raisuli/Gadara) who turned out to be one of the most influential mares of Australia. Her large family (see table M3) is of particular interest in that it combines most of the early Crabbet blood-lines.

Over the next thirty-six years, Mrs Maclean continued to import horses from England and thus built her stud into the largest concentration of Crabbet blood in Australia. Among the stallions she bought may be mentioned Indian Light (table S5), Fayrial (Fayal/Raxina), Electric Silver (table S8), Silver Moonlight (table S6: sold at the age of twenty by his then owners, the Queensland Agricultural College, to the United States where he died soon after his arrival) and Rossfennick (table S6). She also bought from Hanstead, including the influential Riffal (table S11) who at the height, it is said, of just over 16 hands, was the tallest of the imported stallions. In fact Mrs Maclean tended to prefer taller Arabians because at that time they were considered more useful for cross-breeding in order to produce bigger horses for working with cattle.

Other Hanstead-bred horses imported by Mrs Maclean were two Rissam daughters, Carlina out of Shamnar and Rizala out of Ghezala. Rakib (table S9), originally brought over by Edward Hirst in 1938, was also purchased by Mrs Maclean as was his son Baz, out of Barada II.

right Indian Light
(Naseem–Nisreen)
centre Ralvon Pilgrim
(Rikham–Trix Silver)
below left Greylight
(Bright Shadow–
Royal Radiance) and
right Electric Silver
(Raktha–Silfina)

Another outstanding stallion from Crabbet that Mrs Maclean acquired was Shafreyn (table s14). In 1966 one of his sons Shalawi (out of Helawi, by Rakib out of Carlina) won the first Tom Quilty 100 Mile Endurance Ride in what was claimed to be the world's record time of 11 hours and 24 minutes, with his rider completing the course bare-back. Shalawi's pedigree has crosses to both Rijm and Astraled, both of whom feature prominently in the pedigrees of the early American Endurance Test winners.

In 1961 Mrs Maclean made one of her last, and as it transpired, most significant purchases from Crabbet: the magnificent stallion Sindh (table s14). This Silver Vanity son sired over 200 foals altogether in Australia and has had tremendous influence on Arab horse breeding in that country.

Besides Rafina, Mrs Maclean bought three other distinguished mares from Crabbet that deserve to be mentioned: Nasirieh in 1935 (table M4), Nuralina in 1936 (table M6) and Rosinella in 1956 (table M5). Of these, Rosinella was the most prolific as well as being the dam of the important stallion Rossfennick which she was carrying at the time of her importation.

Since Mrs Maclean's death in 1978, the stud has been greatly reduced and is now carried on by her granddaughter Vicky. Greylight (table s10), the last surviving Crabbet-bred stallion, died as recently as 1992 at the fine age of thirty-three.

During the last three decades, additional Crabbet blood has been introduced into Australia both from Crabbet itself and from other studs in Britain. Some also arrived from the United States though not all the latter horses were of pure Crabbet breeding.

From Crabbet, the stallions Silwan (table s10) and Spindrift (table s8) together with the mare Silver Magic (Indian Magic/Silver Fire) went to Mrs M. Leicht. When her stud was sold, all the horses were purchased by the Queensland Agricultural College where they were later joined by the Crabbet stallions Grand Royal (table s14) and Mahif (Indian Magic/Myolanda), the latter being bred by Cecil Covey, and by the mare Bright Light (Bright Shadow/ Shadow Light).

Mrs Elwyn Bligh and her daughter also imported several good horses of predominantly Crabbet blood-lines. Count Manilla (table s12) from Hanstead and Crystal Fire (Dargee/Rosinella), bred by Mrs S. Bomford, were popular show horses and sires in the 60s. The mare Scherzade (Irex/Shamal) went out from Margaret Greely's stud in foal to Blue

Domino and the resulting colt, Royal Domino, has had a marked influence as a sire.

Another of the Blighs' imports, the stallion Abiram (Noran/Rythoura), bred by Dr Pieter Houtappel at his stud in Holland and of pure Crabbet descent, was particularly well-known as a sire of top-class saddle horses. Reference must also be made to the superlative grey stallion Gai General (Gay Count/Gai Moonbeam). Bred in the United States by Gainey Arabians in 1973, his pedigree is over 80% Crabbet and traces in almost every line to the horses exported from Crabbet to America in the 1920s and 30s. Of especial interest is the fact that on the bottom line (Gajala, by *Raffles out of Rageyma who was by *Mirage out of *Kareyma), it goes back to the Keheileh Jellabieh mare Makbula. This horse, bred by Ali Pasha Sherif and imported to Britain by the Blunts, has left only one other line apart from those in America and that through Kasmeyn who was sold by Lady Wentworth to Egypt in 1920 (see pages 298 to 300). Gai General has been a noted show-winner in Australia.

At one time the Bremervale Stud of Mr and Mrs G. Toft had Arabians of largely Crabbet blood-lines. Stallions exported by them include Bremervale Destiny who went to Mrs Bazy Tankersley's Al-Marah Stud in the United States, and Bremervale Emperor who was purchased by Mrs P.A.M. Murray and thus brought back to Britain some of the 'old' Crabbet lines. More recently Bremervale, like other large studs, has started to go elsewhere for its stallions though not a few of these have material elements of Crabbet blood in their pedigrees.

Mr and Mrs R. Males still retain a high concentration of Crabbet in their Ralvon Stud and their horses have a fine record in performance events as well as in the show-ring. The best known of their stallions was the International Champion Ralvon Pilgrim (Rikham/Trix Silver) who was taken to England in 1977 and became Supreme Champion at the first International Show to be held at Ascot. A most successful sire in Australia, Pilgrim died in 1992 at the age of twenty-three.

Stallions such as Banderol (Sindh/Balsora) and his son Bandom (out of Domtif), are amongst many which have lately played their part in perpetuating the qualities associated with Crabbet-bred Arabs. Others include the striking bay Akhu (Remembrance/Kai) and the grey Somerled (Baz/Silver Radiance) who shows strongly the characteristics of the Silver Fire family.

The most recent stallion produce lists demonstrate the high percentage of Crabbet blood which still exists in Australia. Horses of largely Crabbet breeding have not only held their own in the show-ring but their progeny are in great demand for performance work. This is especially the case in endurance riding where horses of Crabbet descent are much respected both for their soundness and temperament.

Another sign of the continuing appeal of Crabbet horses can be seen in the flourishing Crabbet Groups which have been formed round the country in recent years. By circulating regular newsletters and organising shows specifically for horses of Crabbet blood, they do much to promote a cause which at one time looked like losing ground to more fashionable blood-lines. A review of this nature cannot conclude without drawing attention to the fact that Australia, like America, now has its own Crabbet magazine.

NEW ZEALAND

By comparison with Australia, Arab horse breeding in New Zealand is still in its infancy, having only begun in earnest twenty-five years ago. Most of its foundation stock came from Australia and its rapidly expanding Arab horse population therefore contains much Crabbet blood.

Alan Sisam of the Qaimeha Stud imported three stallions from Fenwick: Shereef (Riffal/Senabra), Grey Swirl (Electric Silver/Grey Coronet) and Crescendo (Greylight/Carla). But the most important stallion of the earlier days was Silver Sparkle, foaled in 1947, by Oran out of Silver Fire. He was purchased by a Mr Booth, a timber merchant who lived in the North Island. It is related that he wrote to Lady Wentworth asking the price of the best colt she had available: the following year Silver Sparkle arrived in New Zealand. Although the stallion was primarily for his personal enjoyment, Mr Booth felt obliged to stand him at public stud, which he did *via* an advertisement announcing 'No Common Mares Entertained'.

In 1961 Lester Marshall of Holly Farm, South Island started to look for pure-bred Arabians. He bought Sadik (Rakib/Dahana), a Fenwick-bred mare, and began searching for a stallion. Five years later, he saw two Anglo-Arabs by Silver Sparkle which so impressed him that he decided at once to purchase their sire. He also acquired Ghanimeh (Grey Owl/Risira) who had been bred by Mrs E.M. Murray in England, together with her two daughters Adah and Zillah.

Silver Sparkle proved a highly successful sire at Holly Farm. His daughters include Silver Lady, out of Sadik, who has been a remarkable brood mare with twenty-one foals to her name, several of which have taken top honours in the show-ring: she herself was Royal Show Champion Mare in 1977. Silver Sparkle was also much admired for his excellent temperament, a characteristic that he bequeathed to his progeny. In 1969 he was sold to the United States with Silver Moonlight, his half-brother, but sadly died there soon after his arrival.

More Crabbet blood has recently been introduced to New Zealand through sons of Ralvon Pilgrim and, from America, through the importation of the stallion Gai Cadet from Gainey Arabians. Among other new arrivals may be mentioned Indian Firedance (Dancing King/Indian Gem) who was purchased as a colt from the wellknown Victorian breeder Mrs C. Luckock who had bought his dam from Mr and Mrs D.D. Wright when carrying Indian Firedance.

As in Australia, the demand for horses of Crabbet blood-lines for all spheres of ridden work is on the increase, with flourishing riding clubs encouraging continually more people to take up mounted activities.

LIST OF TABLES

Stallions
- S4 Harir
- S5 Indian Light: Rikham
- S6 Silver Moonlight: Rossfennick
- S7 Yourouk: Risheem: Razaz
- S8 Electric Silver: Spindrift
- S9 Rakib
- S10 Crystal Fire: Silwan: Greylight
- S11 Rief: Riffal
- S12 Raseel: Count Manilla: Royal Domino
- S13 Sala
- S14 Sindh: Shafreyn: Grand Royal

Mares
- M1 Dahna
- M2 El Lahr
- M3 Namusa
- M4 Nasirieh
- M5 Rafina: Rosinella
- M6 Nuralina
- M7 Miriam

S4 HARIR

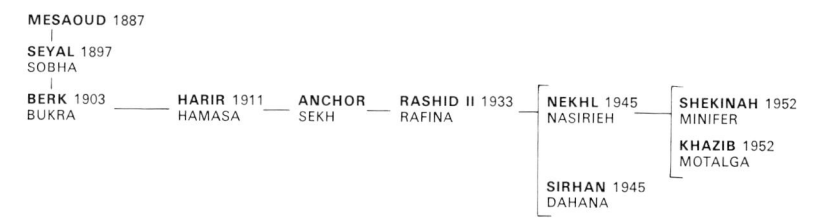

```
MESAOUD 1887
  |
SEYAL 1897
SOBHA
  |
BERK 1903 ──── HARIR 1911 ──── ANCHOR ──── RASHID II 1933 ──┬── NEKHL 1945 ──┬── SHEKINAH 1952
BUKRA            HAMASA          SEKH         RAFINA         │   NASIRIEH    │   MINIFER
                                                             │               │
                                                             │               └── KHAZIB 1952
                                                             │                   MOTALGA
                                                             │
                                                             └── SIRHAN 1945
                                                                 DAHANA
```

S5 INDIAN LIGHT · RIKHAM

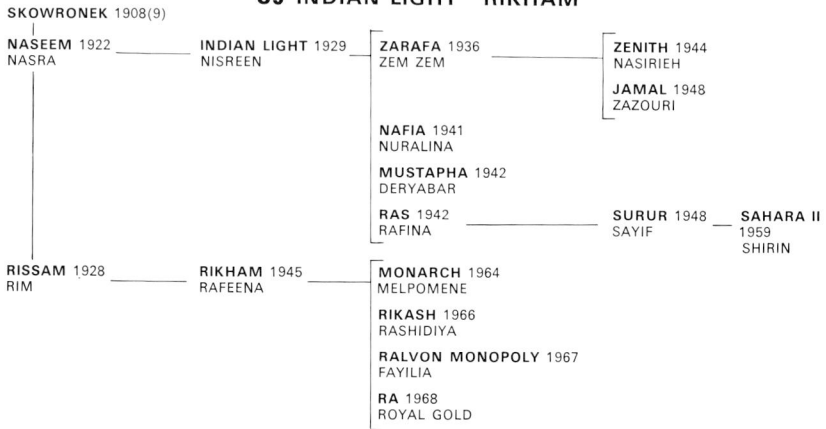

```
SKOWRONEK 1908(9)
  |
NASEEM 1922 ──── INDIAN LIGHT 1929 ──┬── ZARAFA 1936 ──┬── ZENITH 1944
NASRA             NISREEN             │   ZEM ZEM      │   NASIRIEH
  |                                   │                │
  |                                   │                └── JAMAL 1948
  |                                   │                    ZAZOURI
  |                                   │
  |                                   ├── NAFIA 1941
  |                                   │   NURALINA
  |                                   │
  |                                   ├── MUSTAPHA 1942
  |                                   │   DERYABAR
  |                                   │
  |                                   └── RAS 1942 ──── SURUR 1948 ──── SAHARA II
  |                                       RAFINA        SAYIF            1959
  |                                                                      SHIRIN
  |
RISSAM 1928 ──── RIKHAM 1945 ──┬── MONARCH 1964
RIM               RAFEENA       │   MELPOMENE
                                │
                                ├── RIKASH 1966
                                │   RASHIDIYA
                                │
                                ├── RALVON MONOPOLY 1967
                                │   FAYILIA
                                │
                                └── RA 1968
                                    ROYAL GOLD
```

S6 SILVER MOONLIGHT · ROSSFENNICK

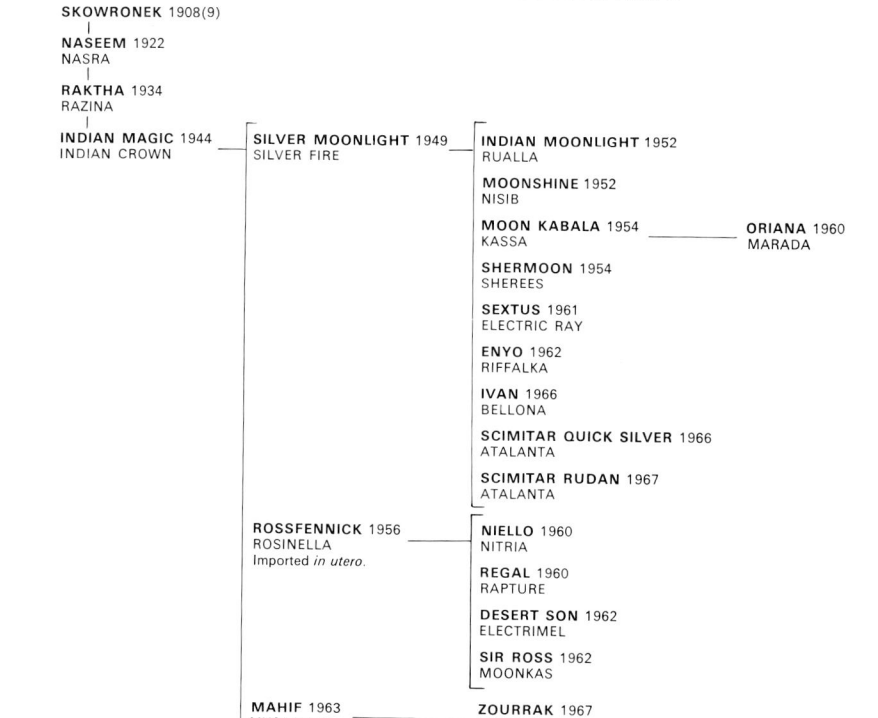

```
SKOWRONEK 1908(9)
  |
NASEEM 1922
NASRA
  |
RAKTHA 1934
RAZINA
  |
INDIAN MAGIC 1944 ──┬── SILVER MOONLIGHT 1949 ──┬── INDIAN MOONLIGHT 1952
INDIAN CROWN        │    SILVER FIRE            │    RUALLA
                    │                           │
                    │                           ├── MOONSHINE 1952
                    │                           │    NISIB
                    │                           │
                    │                           ├── MOON KABALA 1954 ──── ORIANA 1960
                    │                           │    KASSA                 MARADA
                    │                           │
                    │                           ├── SHERMOON 1954
                    │                           │    SHEREES
                    │                           │
                    │                           ├── SEXTUS 1961
                    │                           │    ELECTRIC RAY
                    │                           │
                    │                           ├── ENYO 1962
                    │                           │    RIFFALKA
                    │                           │
                    │                           ├── IVAN 1966
                    │                           │    BELLONA
                    │                           │
                    │                           ├── SCIMITAR QUICK SILVER 1966
                    │                           │    ATALANTA
                    │                           │
                    │                           └── SCIMITAR RUDAN 1967
                    │                                ATALANTA
                    │
                    ├── ROSSFENNICK 1956 ──┬── NIELLO 1960
                    │    ROSINELLA          │    NITRIA
                    │    Imported in utero. │
                    │                       ├── REGAL 1960
                    │                       │    RAPTURE
                    │                       │
                    │                       ├── DESERT SON 1962
                    │                       │    ELECTRIMEL
                    │                       │
                    │                       └── SIR ROSS 1962
                    │                            MOONKAS
                    │
                    ├── MAHIF 1963 ──── ZOURRAK 1967
                    │    MYOLANDA        MOONAMET
                    │
                    └── MUTLAK 1963
                         MIFARIA
```

S7 YOUROUK · RISHEEM · RAZAZ

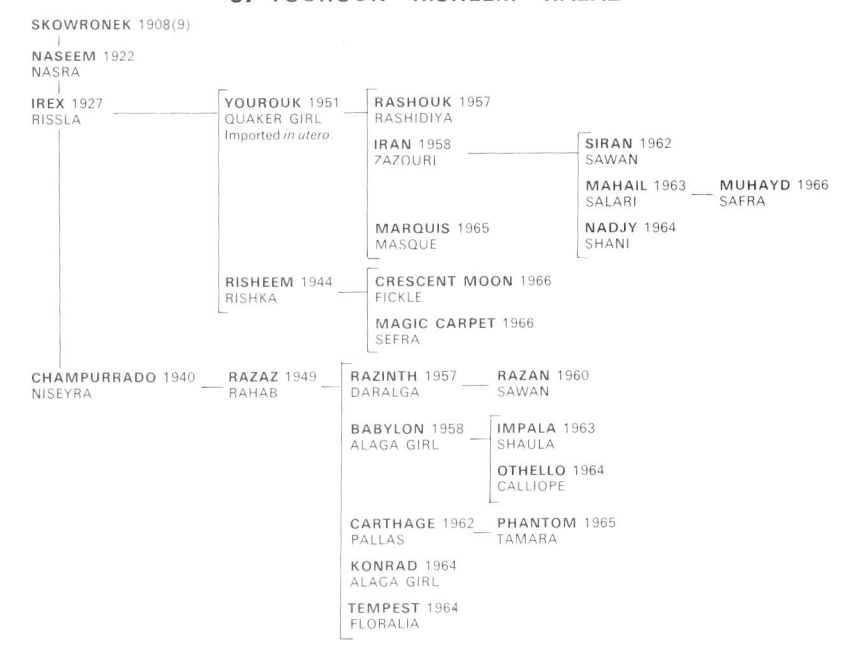

SKOWRONEK 1908(9)
NASEEM 1922
NASRA
IREX 1927
RISSLA
YOUROUK 1951
QUAKER GIRL
Imported in utero.
RASHOUK 1957
RASHIDIYA
IRAN 1958
ZAZOURI
SIRAN 1962
SAWAN
MAHAIL 1963
SALARI
MUHAYD 1966
SAFRA
MARQUIS 1965
MASQUE
NADJY 1964
SHANI
RISHEEM 1944
RISHKA
CRESCENT MOON 1966
FICKLE
MAGIC CARPET 1966
SEFRA
CHAMPURRADO 1940
NISEYRA
RAZAZ 1949
RAHAB
RAZINTH 1957
DARALGA
RAZAN 1960
SAWAN
BABYLON 1958
ALAGA GIRL
IMPALA 1963
SHAULA
OTHELLO 1964
CALLIOPE
CARTHAGE 1962
PALLAS
PHANTOM 1965
TAMARA
KONRAD 1964
ALAGA GIRL
TEMPEST 1964
FLORALIA

S8 ELECTRIC SILVER · SPINDRIFT

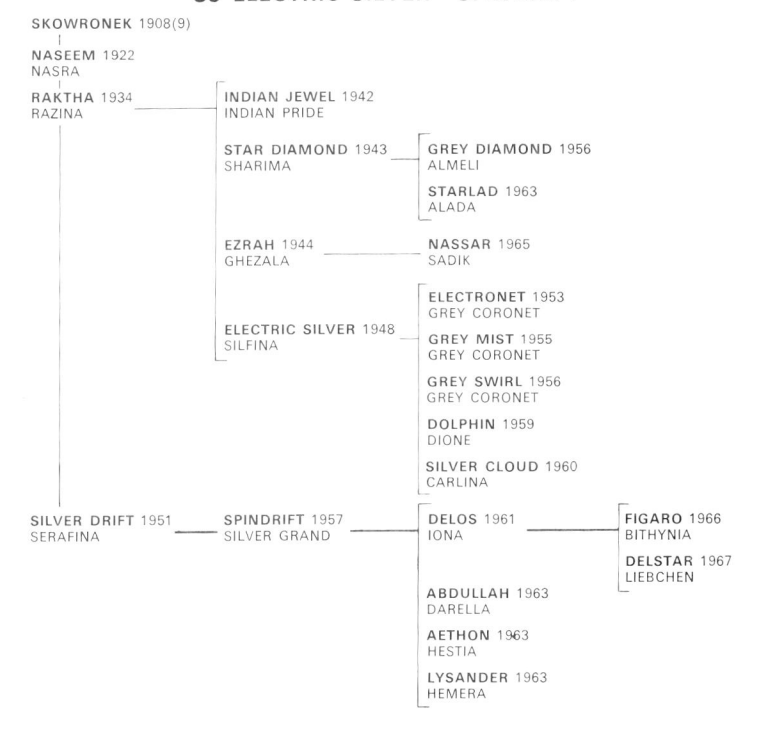

SKOWRONEK 1908(9)
NASEEM 1922
NASRA
RAKTHA 1934
RAZINA
INDIAN JEWEL 1942
INDIAN PRIDE
STAR DIAMOND 1943
SHARIMA
GREY DIAMOND 1956
ALMELI
STARLAD 1963
ALADA
EZRAH 1944
GHEZALA
NASSAR 1965
SADIK
ELECTRIC SILVER 1948
SILFINA
ELECTRONET 1953
GREY CORONET
GREY MIST 1955
GREY CORONET
GREY SWIRL 1956
GREY CORONET
DOLPHIN 1959
DIONE
SILVER CLOUD 1960
CARLINA
SILVER DRIFT 1951
SERAFINA
SPINDRIFT 1957
SILVER GRAND
DELOS 1961
IONA
FIGARO 1966
BITHYNIA
DELSTAR 1967
LIEBCHEN
ABDULLAH 1963
DARELLA
AETHON 1963
HESTIA
LYSANDER 1963
HEMERA

S9 RAKIB

SKOWRONEK 1908(9)
|
NAX 1925 ────────── RAKIB 1934 ─┬─ RAMI 1946
NESSIMA   RYTHAMA   │ RISSANI
                                │
                                ├─ MALIK 1946
                                │ MEYMOONEH
                                │
                                ├─ NEFUDH 1946
                                │ NASIRIEH
                                │
                                ├─ YARAL 1946
                                │ YUSSEF
                                │
                                ├─ HOUSSAIN 1947
                                │ SABIYAH
                                │
                                ├─ MEKILI 1947
                                │ MELIHA
                                │
                                ├─ NAR 1947 ────── NASSABA 1960
                                │ NASIFA   NURMANA
                                │
                                ├─ SABAH 1948
                                │ DAHANA
                                │
                                ├─ SHEHAB 1949
                                │ DAHANA
                                │
                                ├─ ANOUK 1949 ──── SANTARABIA THE CALIPH 1961
                                │ ARABETTE   RASHIDIYA
                                │
                                ├─ BAHRI 1949
                                │ BARADA II
                                │
                                └─ BAZ 1950
                                   BARADA II

S10 CRYSTAL FIRE · SILWAN · GREYLIGHT

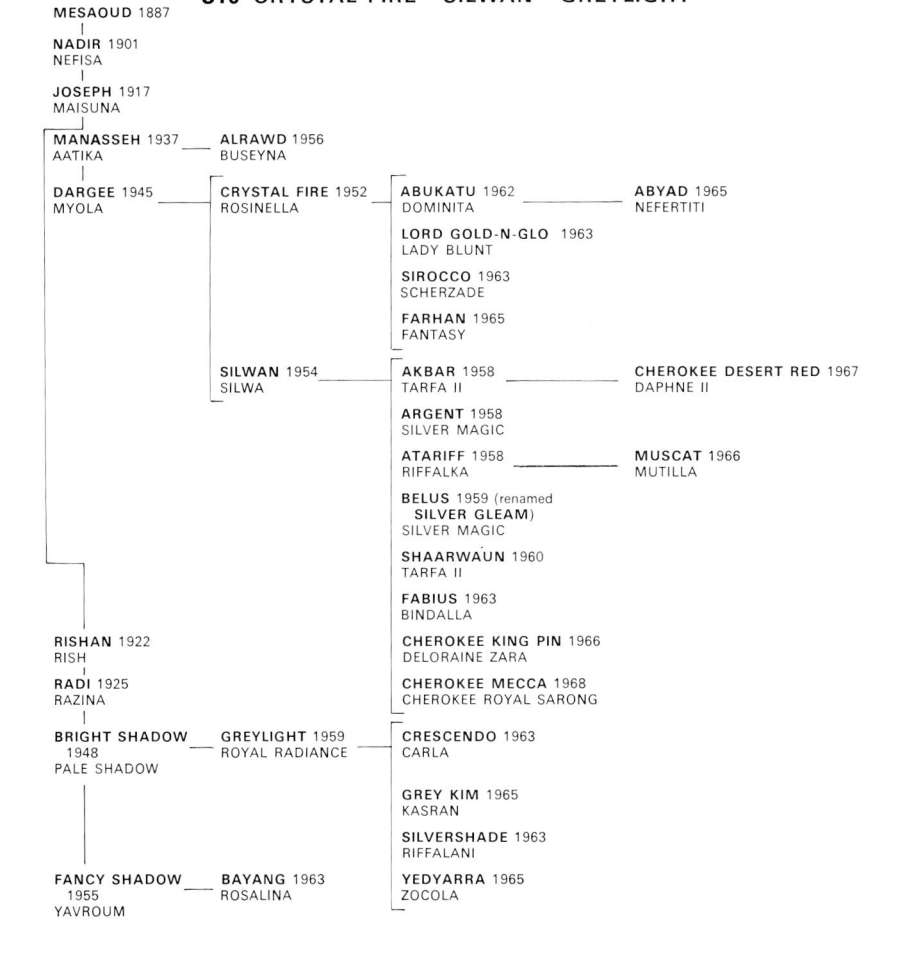

MESAOUD 1887
|
NADIR 1901
NEFISA
|
JOSEPH 1917
MAISUNA
|
MANASSEH 1937 ──── ALRAWD 1956
AATIKA   BUSEYNA
|
DARGEE 1945 ──┬── CRYSTAL FIRE 1952 ─┬─ ABUKATU 1962 ────── ABYAD 1965
MYOLA   │   ROSINELLA   │ DOMINITA   NEFERTITI
              │   │
              │   ├─ LORD GOLD-N-GLO 1963
              │   │ LADY BLUNT
              │   │
              │   ├─ SIROCCO 1963
              │   │ SCHERZADE
              │   │
              │   └─ FARHAN 1965
              │   FANTASY
              │
              └── SILWAN 1954 ─┬─ AKBAR 1958 ────── CHEROKEE DESERT RED 1967
                  SILWA   │ TARFA II   DAPHNE II
                               │
                               ├─ ARGENT 1958
                               │ SILVER MAGIC
                               │
                               ├─ ATARIFF 1958 ───── MUSCAT 1966
                               │ RIFFALKA   MUTILLA
                               │
                               ├─ BELUS 1959 (renamed
                               │   SILVER GLEAM)
                               │ SILVER MAGIC
                               │
                               ├─ SHAARWAUN 1960
                               │ TARFA II
                               │
                               ├─ FABIUS 1963
                               │ BINDALLA
                               │
                               ├─ CHEROKEE KING PIN 1966
                               │ DELORAINE ZARA
                               │
                               └─ CHEROKEE MECCA 1968
                                  CHEROKEE ROYAL SARONG

RISHAN 1922
RISH
|
RADI 1925
RAZINA
|
BRIGHT SHADOW ──── GREYLIGHT 1959 ─┬─ CRESCENDO 1963
1948   ROYAL RADIANCE │ CARLA
PALE SHADOW   │
                                   ├─ GREY KIM 1965
                                   │ KASRAN
                                   │
                                   ├─ SILVERSHADE 1963
                                   │ RIFFALANI
                                   │
FANCY SHADOW ──── BAYANG 1963 ─────┴─ YEDYARRA 1965
1955   ROSALINA   ZOCOLA
YAVROUM

280

S11 RIEF · RIFFAL

MESAOUD 1887

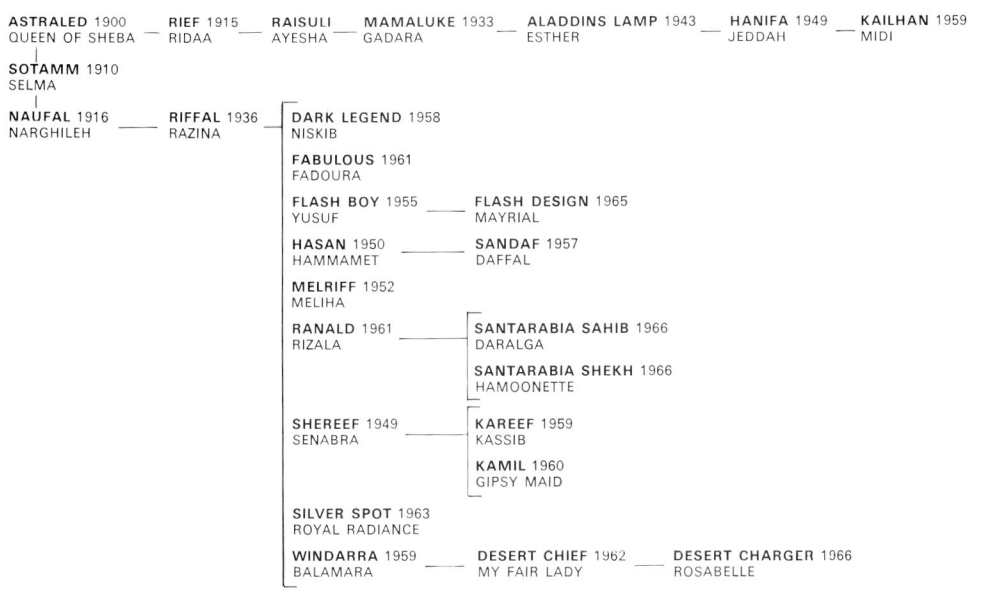

ASTRALED 1900 — RIEF 1915 — RAISULI — MAMALUKE 1933 — ALADDINS LAMP 1943 — HANIFA 1949 — KAILHAN 1959
QUEEN OF SHEBA — RIDAA — AYESHA — GADARA — ESTHER — JEDDAH — MIDI

SOTAMM 1910
SELMA

NAUFAL 1916 — RIFFAL 1936 — DARK LEGEND 1958
NARGHILEH — RAZINA — NISKIB

FABULOUS 1961
FADOURA

FLASH BOY 1955 — FLASH DESIGN 1965
YUSUF — MAYRIAL

HASAN 1950 — SANDAF 1957
HAMMAMET — DAFFAL

MELRIFF 1952
MELIHA

RANALD 1961 — SANTARABIA SAHIB 1966
RIZALA — DARALGA

SANTARABIA SHEKH 1966
HAMOONETTE

SHEREEF 1949 — KAREEF 1959
SENABRA — KASSIB

KAMIL 1960
GIPSY MAID

SILVER SPOT 1963
ROYAL RADIANCE

WINDARRA 1959 — DESERT CHIEF 1962 — DESERT CHARGER 1966
BALAMARA — MY FAIR LADY — ROSABELLE

S12 RASEEL · COUNT MANILLA · ROYAL DOMINO

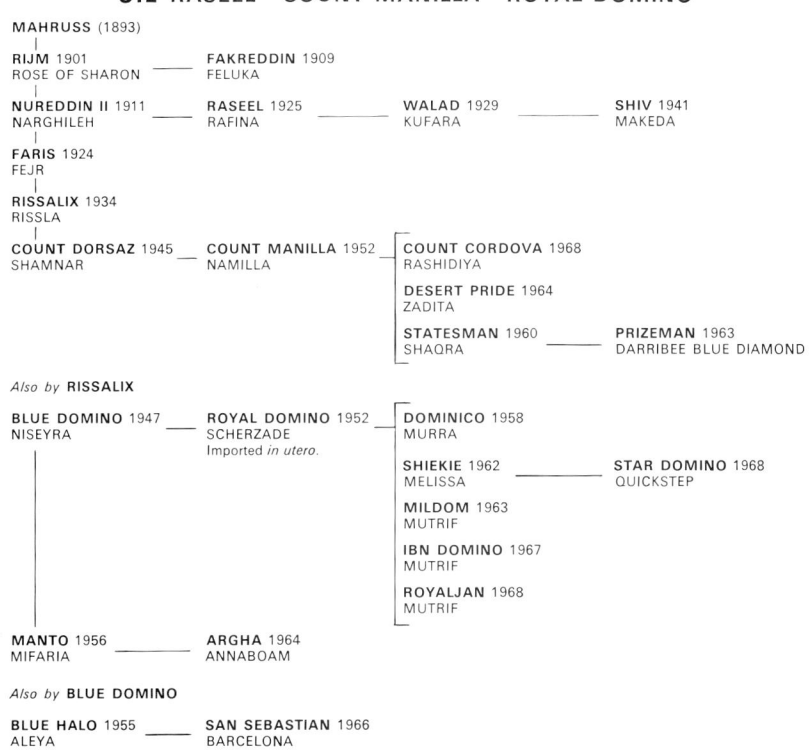

MAHRUSS (1893)

RIJM 1901 — FAKREDDIN 1909
ROSE OF SHARON — FELUKA

NUREDDIN II 1911 — RASEEL 1925 — WALAD 1929 — SHIV 1941
NARGHILEH — RAFINA — KUFARA — MAKEDA

FARIS 1924
FEJR

RISSALIX 1934
RISSLA

COUNT DORSAZ 1945 — COUNT MANILLA 1952 — COUNT CORDOVA 1968
SHAMNAR — NAMILLA — RASHIDIYA

DESERT PRIDE 1964
ZADITA

STATESMAN 1960 — PRIZEMAN 1963
SHAQRA — DARRIBEE BLUE DIAMOND

Also by RISSALIX

BLUE DOMINO 1947 — ROYAL DOMINO 1952 — DOMINICO 1958
NISEYRA — SCHERZADE — MURRA
Imported in utero.

SHIEKIE 1962 — STAR DOMINO 1968
MELISSA — QUICKSTEP

MILDOM 1963
MUTRIF

IBN DOMINO 1967
MUTRIF

ROYALJAN 1968
MUTRIF

MANTO 1956 — ARGHA 1964
MIFARIA — ANNABOAM

Also by BLUE DOMINO

BLUE HALO 1955 — SAN SEBASTIAN 1966
ALEYA — BARCELONA

S13 SALA

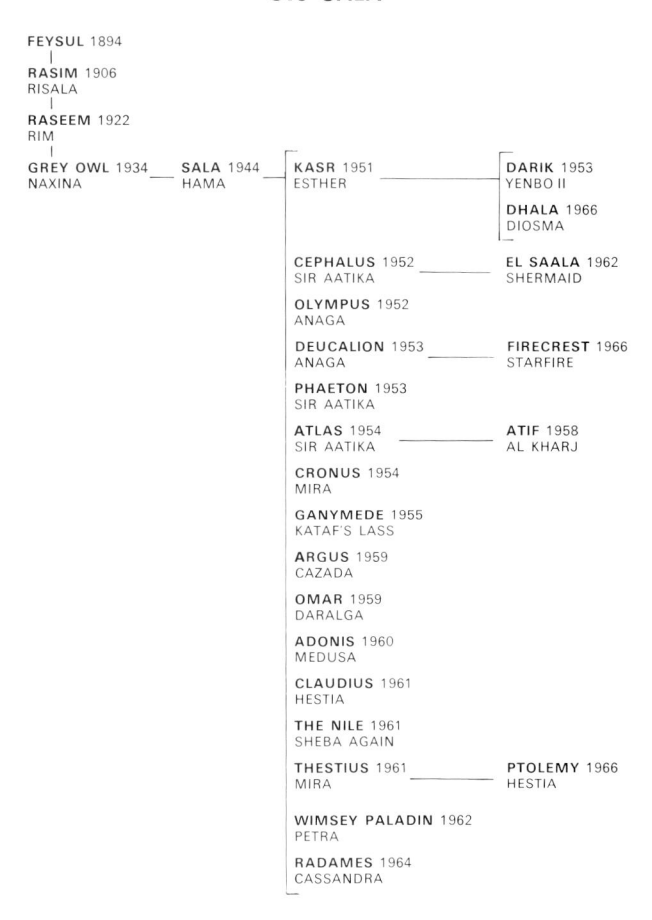

```
FEYSUL 1894
  |
RASIM 1906
RISALA
  |
RASEEM 1922
RIM
  |
GREY OWL 1934 ── SALA 1944 ── KASR 1951 ─────────── DARIK 1953
NAXINA              HAMA        ESTHER               YENBO II
                                                     DHALA 1966
                                                     DIOSMA

                                CEPHALUS 1952 ────── EL SAALA 1962
                                SIR AATIKA           SHERMAID

                                OLYMPUS 1952
                                ANAGA

                                DEUCALION 1953 ───── FIRECREST 1966
                                ANAGA                STARFIRE

                                PHAETON 1953
                                SIR AATIKA

                                ATLAS 1954 ────────── ATIF 1958
                                SIR AATIKA           AL KHARJ

                                CRONUS 1954
                                MIRA

                                GANYMEDE 1955
                                KATAF'S LASS

                                ARGUS 1959
                                CAZADA

                                OMAR 1959
                                DARALGA

                                ADONIS 1960
                                MEDUSA

                                CLAUDIUS 1961
                                HESTIA

                                THE NILE 1961
                                SHEBA AGAIN

                                THESTIUS 1961 ─────── PTOLEMY 1966
                                MIRA                 HESTIA

                                WIMSEY PALADIN 1962
                                PETRA

                                RADAMES 1964
                                CASSANDRA
```

S14 SINDH · SHAFREYN · GRAND ROYAL

MESAOUD 1887

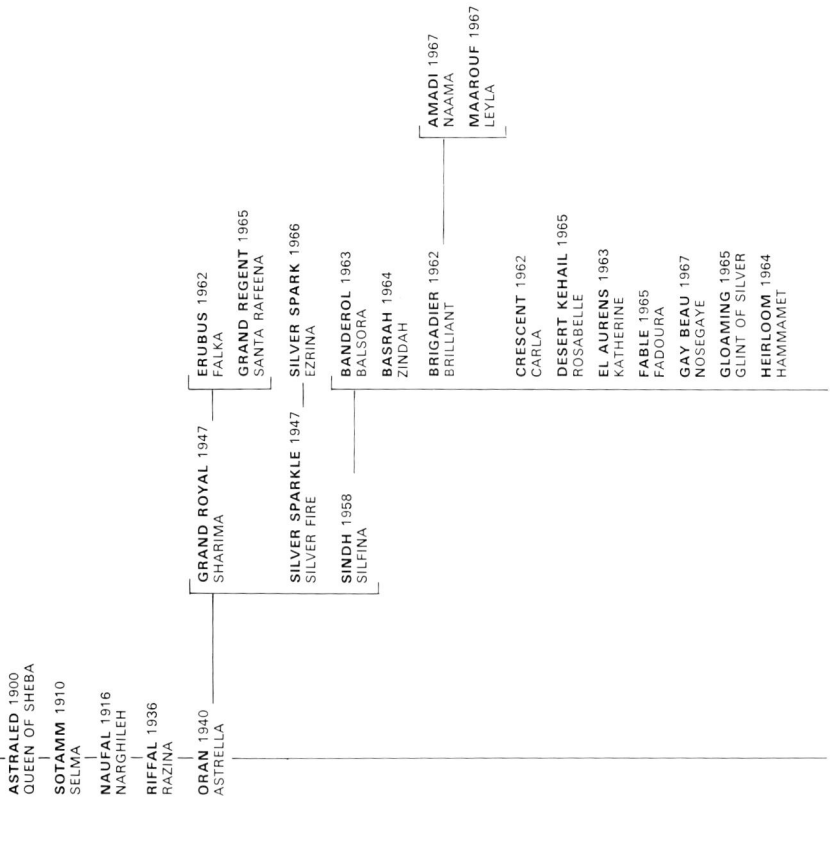

ASTRALED 1900
QUEEN OF SHEBA

SOTAMM 1910
SELMA

NAUFAL 1916
NARGHILEH

RIFFAL 1936
RAZINA

ORAN 1940
ASTRELLA

GRAND ROYAL 1947
SHARIMA
- ERUBUS 1962
  FALKA
- GRAND REGENT 1965
  SANTA RAFEENA

SILVER SPARKLE 1947
SILVER FIRE
- SILVER SPARK 1966
  EZRINA

SINDH 1958
SILFINA
- BANDEROL 1963
  BALSORA
- BASRAH 1964
  ZINDAH
- BRIGADIER 1962
  BRILLIANT
  - AMADI 1967
    NAAMA
  - MAAROUF 1967
    LEYLA
- CRESCENT 1962
  CARLA
- DESERT KEHAIL 1965
  ROSABELLE
- EL AURENS 1963
  KATHERINE
- FABLE 1965
  FADOURA
- GAY BEAU 1967
  NOSEGAYE
- GLOAMING 1965
  GLINT OF SILVER
- HEIRLOOM 1964
  HAMMAMET

Sindh was not by Oran but by Oran's son, Silver Vanity out of Silver Gilt foaled in 1950.

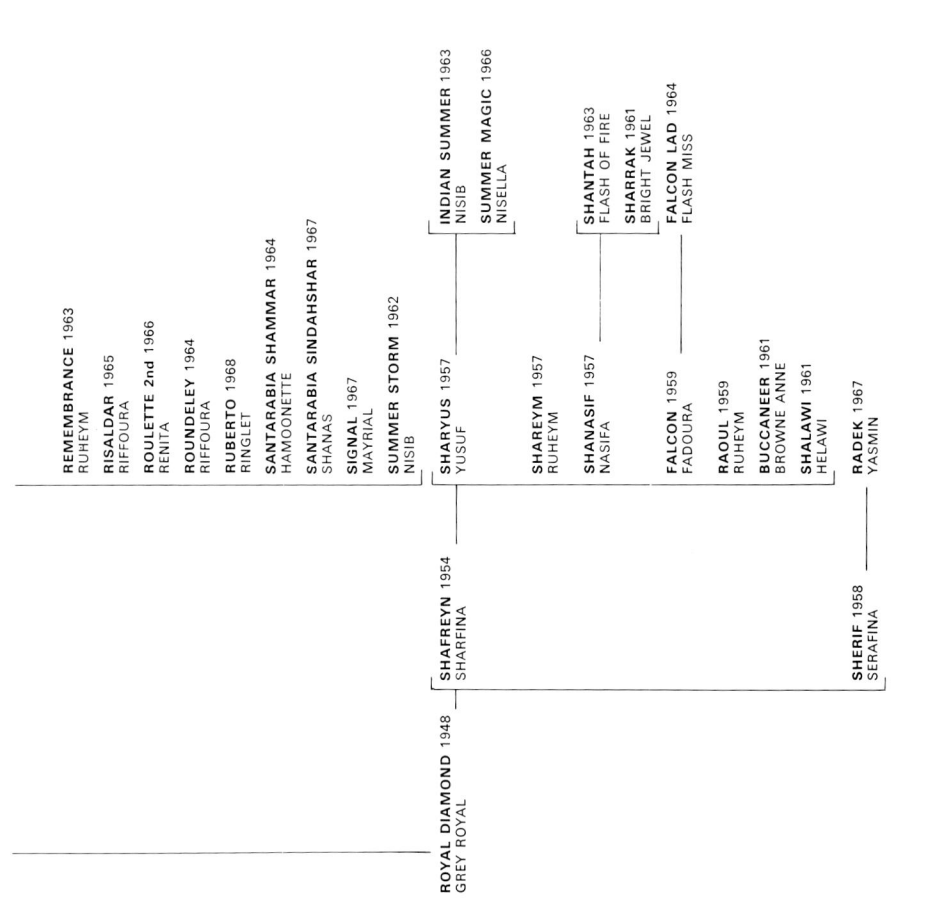

ROYAL DIAMOND 1948
GREY ROYAL
├── SHAFREYN 1954
│   SHARFINA
│   ├── REMEMBRANCE 1963
│   │   RUHEYM
│   ├── RISALDAR 1965
│   │   RIFFOURA
│   ├── ROULETTE 2nd 1966
│   │   RENITA
│   ├── ROUNDELEY 1964
│   │   RIFFOURA
│   ├── RUBERTO 1968
│   │   RINGLET
│   ├── SANTARABIA SHAMMAR 1964
│   │   HAMOONETTE
│   ├── SANTARABIA SINDAHSHAR 1967
│   │   SHANAS
│   ├── SIGNAL 1967
│   │   MAYRIAL
│   ├── SUMMER STORM 1962
│   │   NISIB
│   ├── SHARYUS 1957
│   │   YUSUF
│   │   ├── INDIAN SUMMER 1963
│   │   │   NISIB
│   │   └── SUMMER MAGIC 1966
│   │   NISELLA
│   ├── SHAREYM 1957
│   │   RUHEYM
│   ├── SHANASIF 1957
│   │   NASIFA
│   │   ├── SHANTAH 1963
│   │   │   FLASH OF FIRE
│   │   └── SHARRAK 1961
│   │   BRIGHT JEWEL
│   ├── FALCON 1959
│   │   FADOURA
│   │   └── FALCON LAD 1964
│   │   FLASH MISS
│   ├── RAOUL 1959
│   │   RUHEYM
│   ├── BUCCANEER 1961
│   │   BROWNE ANNE
│   └── SHALAWI 1961
│   HELAWI
└── SHERIF 1958
    SERAFINA
    └── RADEK 1967
        YASMIN

M1 DAHNA

```
DAHMA 1876
  │
DAHNA 1883 ─── SHERIFA ─── LABADAH ─── KHADIJAD ─── ALCOUZA ─── ALFILA 1936 ─── ZAHLE 1941
  KARS          RAFYK       MAHBOUB      FARAOUN      KHAMASIN    INDIAN LIGHT    ZARAFA
                          (imported from              │
                            India)                    │
                                                    DERYABAR          DAHNA 1934
                                                    KHAMASIN          RASEEL
```

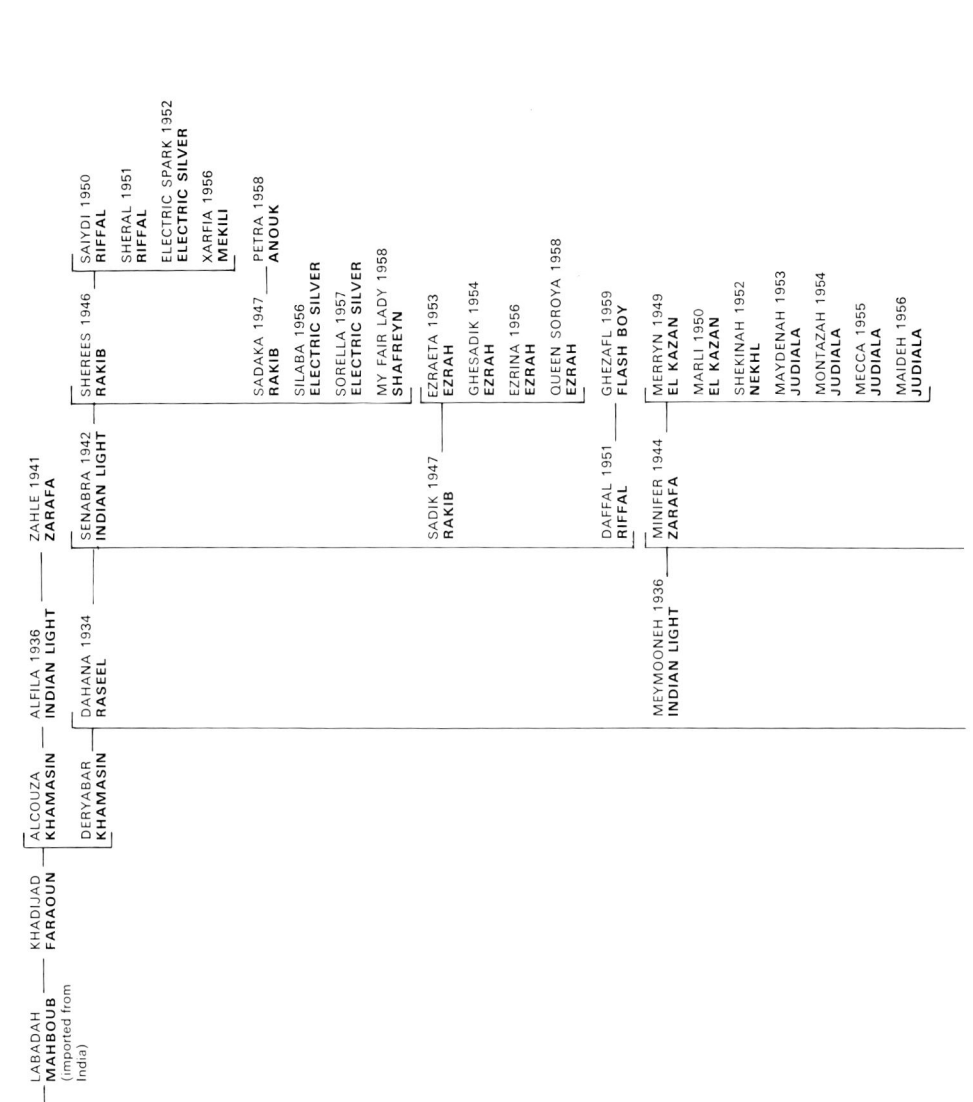

Descendants (right side):

- SENABRA 1942 INDIAN LIGHT
  - SHEREES 1946 RAKIB
    - SAIYDI 1950 RIFFAL
    - SHERAL 1951 RIFFAL
    - ELECTRIC SPARK 1952 ELECTRIC SILVER
    - XARFIA 1956 MEKILI
    - PETRA 1958 ANOUK
  - SADAKA 1947 RAKIB
  - SILABA 1956 ELECTRIC SILVER
  - SORELLA 1957 ELECTRIC SILVER
  - MY FAIR LADY 1958 SHAFREYN
  - SADIK 1947 RAKIB
    - EZRAETA 1953 EZRAH
    - GHESADIK 1954 EZRAH
    - EZRINA 1956 EZRAH
    - QUEEN SOROYA 1958 EZRAH
  - DAFFAL 1951 RIFFAL
    - GHEZAFL 1959 FLASH BOY
  - MINIFER 1944 ZARAFA
    - MERRYN 1949 EL KAZAN
    - MARLI 1950 EL KAZAN
    - SHEKINAH 1952 NEKHL
    - MAYDENAH 1953 JUDIALA
    - MONTAZAH 1954 JUDIALA
    - MECCA 1955 JUDIALA
    - MAIDEH 1956 JUDIALA
- MEYMOONEH 1936 INDIAN LIGHT

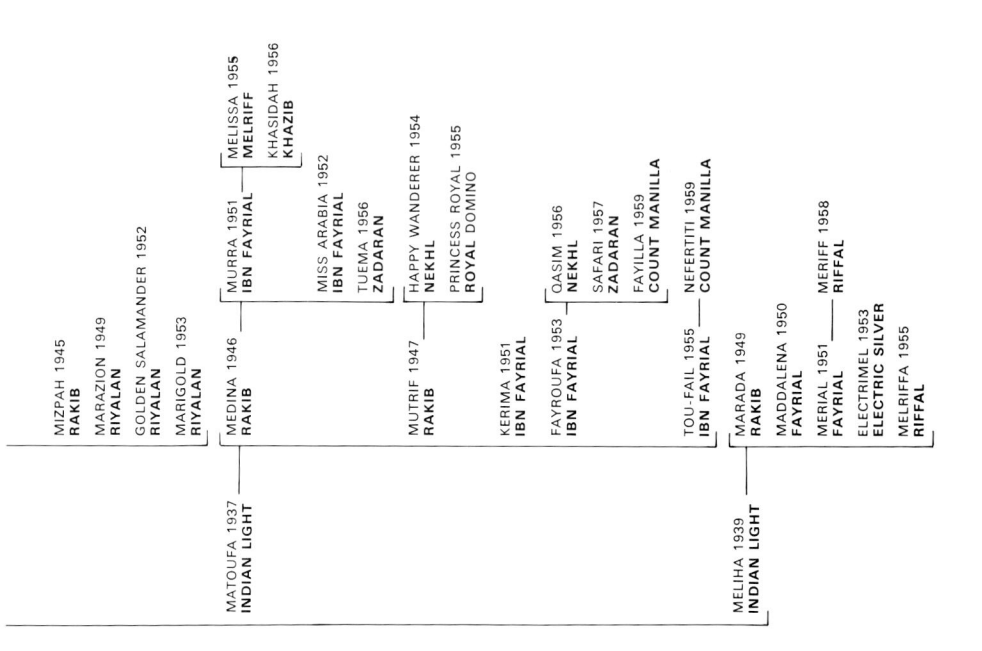

MATOUFA 1937
INDIAN LIGHT
├─ MIZPAH 1945
│ **RAKIB**
├─ MARAZION 1949
│ **RIYALAN**
├─ GOLDEN SALAMANDER 1952
│ **RIYALAN**
├─ MARIGOLD 1953
│ **RIYALAN**
├─ MEDINA 1946
│ **RAKIB**
│ ├─ MURRA 1951
│ │ **IBN FAYRIAL**
│ │ ├─ MELISSA 1955
│ │ │ **MELRIFF**
│ │ └─ KHASIDAH 1956
│ │   **KHAZIB**
│ ├─ MISS ARABIA 1952
│ │ **IBN FAYRIAL**
│ ├─ TUEMA 1956
│ │ **ZADARAN**
│ ├─ HAPPY WANDERER 1954
│ │ **NEKHL**
│ └─ PRINCESS ROYAL 1955
│   **ROYAL DOMINO**
├─ MUTRIF 1947
│ **RAKIB**
├─ KERIMA 1951
│ **IBN FAYRIAL**
└─ FAYROUFA 1953
   IBN FAYRIAL
   ├─ QASIM 1956
   │ **NEKHL**
   ├─ SAFARI 1957
   │ **ZADARAN**
   ├─ FAYILLA 1959
   │ **COUNT MANILLA**
   └─ TOU-FAIL 1955 ── NEFERTITI 1959
      IBN FAYRIAL   **COUNT MANILLA**

MELIHA 1939
INDIAN LIGHT
├─ MARADA 1949
│ **RAKIB**
├─ MADDALENA 1950
│ **FAYRIAL**
├─ MERIAL 1951 ── MERIFF 1958
│ **FAYRIAL**   **RIFFAL**
├─ ELECTRIMEL 1953
│ **ELECTRIC SILVER**
└─ MELRIFFA 1955
   RIFFAL

M2 EL LAHR

```
EL LAHR 1899 ─┬─ AL CASWA
IMAMZADA     │   RAFYK
             │
DINARZADE 1887
RATAPLAN
   │
DAHNA 1883
KARS
DAHMA 1876
```

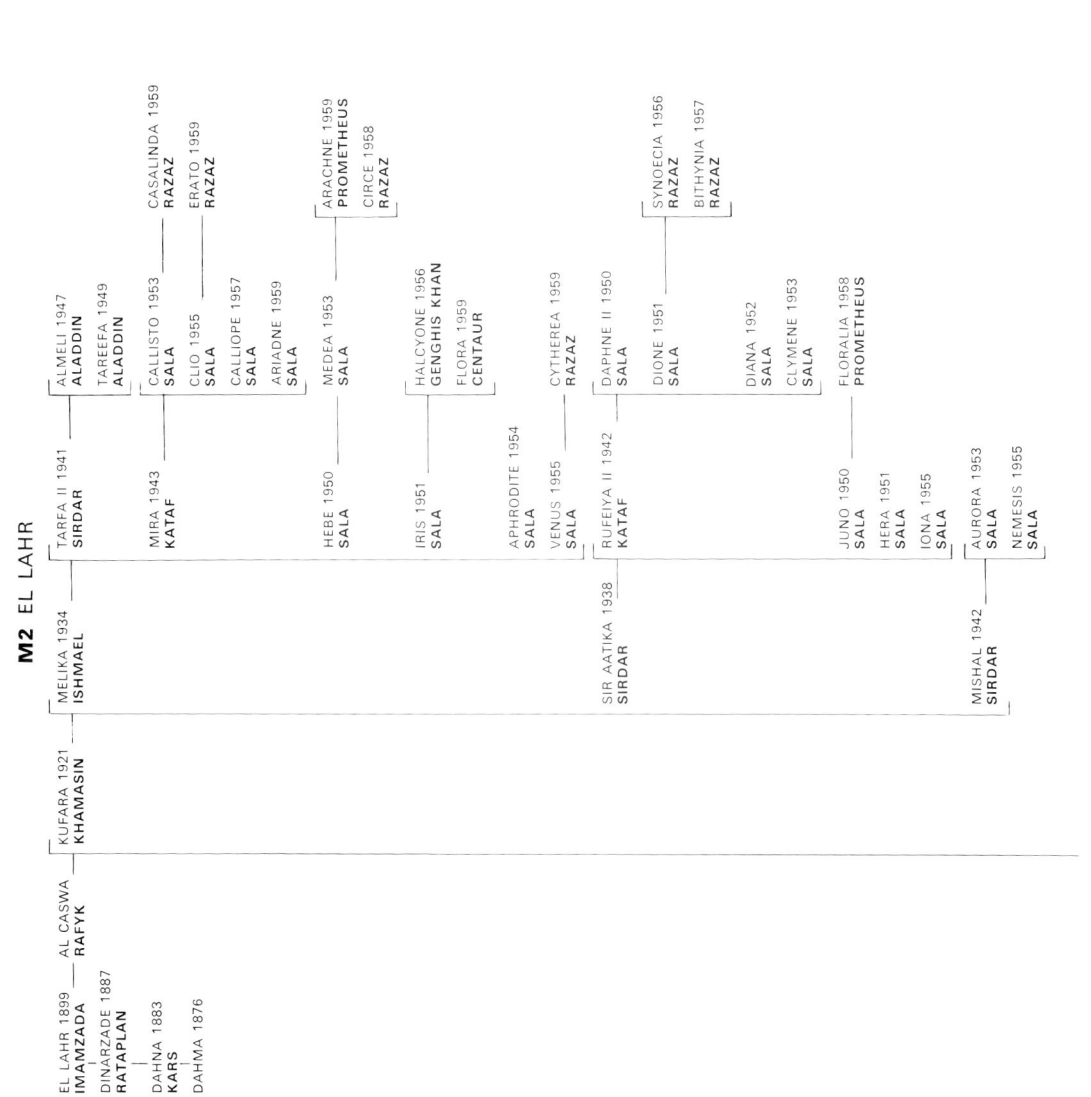

```
KUFARA 1921 ─┬─ MELIKA 1934 ─┬─ TARFA II 1941 ─┬─ ALMELI 1947
KHAMASIN     │   ISHMAEL     │   SIRDAR        │   ALADDIN
             │               │                 │
             │               │                 └─ TAREEFA 1949
             │               │                     ALADDIN
             │               │
             │               │                 ┌─ CALLISTO 1953 ─┬─ CASALINDA 1959
             │               ├─ MIRA 1943 ─────┤   SALA           │   RAZAZ
             │               │   KATAF         │                  └─ ERATO 1959
             │               │                 │                      RAZAZ
             │               │                 ├─ CLIO 1955
             │               │                 │   SALA
             │               │                 ├─ CALLIOPE 1957
             │               │                 │   SALA
             │               │                 └─ ARIADNE 1959
             │               │                     SALA
             │               │
             │               ├─ HEBE 1950 ───── MEDEA 1953 ─┬─ ARACHNE 1959
             │               │   SALA           SALA        │   PROMETHEUS
             │               │                              └─ CIRCE 1958
             │               │                                  RAZAZ
             │               │
             │               ├─ IRIS 1951 ─┬─ HALCYONE 1956
             │               │   SALA      │   GENGHIS KHAN
             │               │             └─ FLORA 1959
             │               │                 CENTAUR
             │               │
             │               ├─ APHRODITE 1954
             │               │   SALA
             │               │
             │               ├─ VENUS 1955 ─── CYTHEREA 1959
             │                   SALA          RAZAZ
             │
             ├─ SIR AATIKA 1938 ─┬─ RUFEIYA II 1942 ─┬─ DAPHNE II 1950
             │   SIRDAR          │   KATAF           │   SALA
             │                   │                   │
             │                   │                   └─ DIONE 1951 ─┬─ SYNOECIA 1956
             │                   │                       SALA        │   RAZAZ
             │                   │                                   └─ BITHYNIA 1957
             │                   │                                       RAZAZ
             │                   │
             │                   ├─ JUNO 1950
             │                   │   SALA
             │                   ├─ DIANA 1952
             │                   │   SALA
             │                   ├─ HERA 1951      CLYMENE 1953
             │                   │   SALA          SALA
             │                   └─ IONA 1955  ─── FLORALIA 1958
             │                       SALA          PROMETHEUS
             │
             └─ MISHAL 1942 ─┬─ AURORA 1953
                 SIRDAR      │   SALA
                             └─ NEMESIS 1955
                                 SALA
```

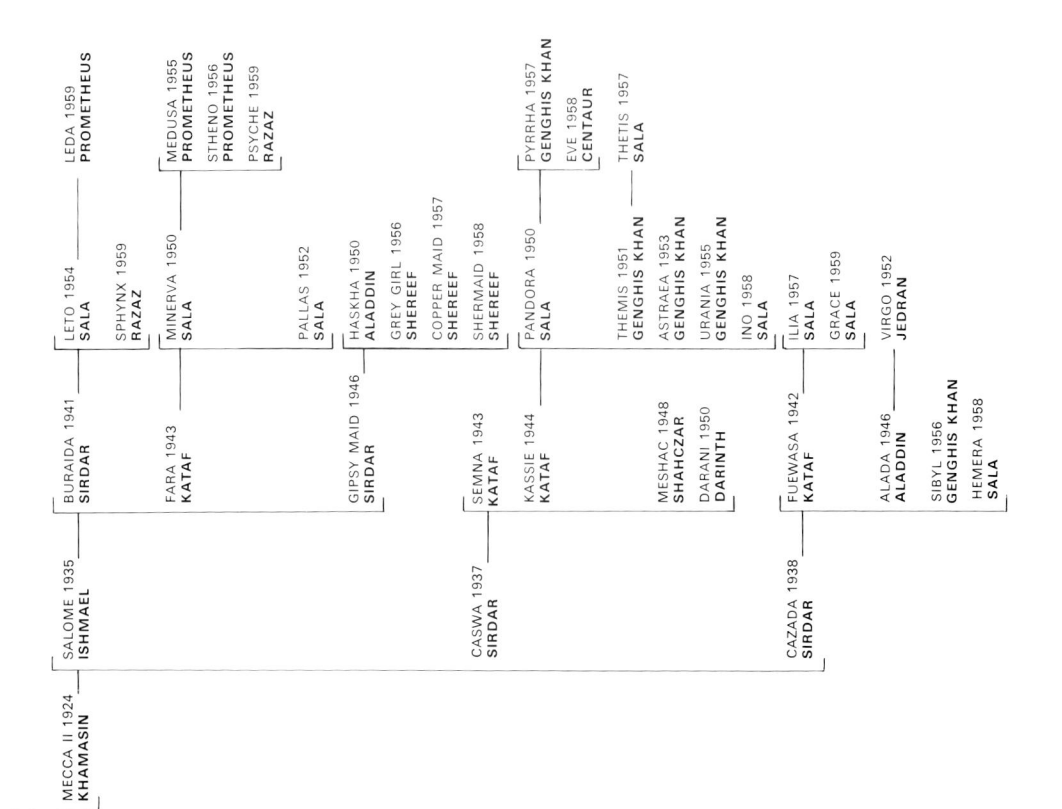

- MECCA II 1924 **KHAMASIN**
  - SALOME 1935 **ISHMAEL**
    - BURAIDA 1941 **SIRDAR**
      - LETO 1954 **SALA**
        - LEDA 1959 **PROMETHEUS**
      - SPHYNX 1959 **RAZAZ**
    - FARA 1943 **KATAF**
      - MINERVA 1950 **SALA**
        - MEDUSA 1955 **PROMETHEUS**
        - STHENO 1956 **PROMETHEUS**
        - PSYCHE 1959 **RAZAZ**
      - PALLAS 1952 **SALA**
    - GIPSY MAID 1946 **SIRDAR**
      - HASKHA 1950 **ALADDIN**
      - GREY GIRL 1956 **SHEREEF**
      - COPPER MAID 1957 **SHEREEF**
      - SHERMAID 1958 **SHEREEF**
  - CASWA 1937 **SIRDAR**
    - SEMNA 1943 **KATAF**
    - KASSIE 1944 **KATAF**
      - PANDORA 1950 **SALA**
        - PYRRHA 1957 **GENGHIS KHAN**
        - EVE 1958 **CENTAUR**
      - THEMIS 1951 **GENGHIS KHAN**
        - THETIS 1957 **SALA**
      - ASTRAEA 1953 **GENGHIS KHAN**
      - URANIA 1955 **GENGHIS KHAN**
      - INO 1958 **SALA**
    - MESHAC 1948 **SHAHCZAR**
    - DARANI 1950 **DARINTH**
  - CAZADA 1938 **SIRDAR**
    - FUEWASA 1942 **KATAF**
      - ILIA 1957 **SALA**
      - GRACE 1959 **SALA**
    - ALADA 1946 **ALADDIN**
      - VIRGO 1952 **JEDRAN**
    - SIBYL 1956 **GENGHIS KHAN**
    - HEMERA 1958 **SALA**

M3 NAMUSA

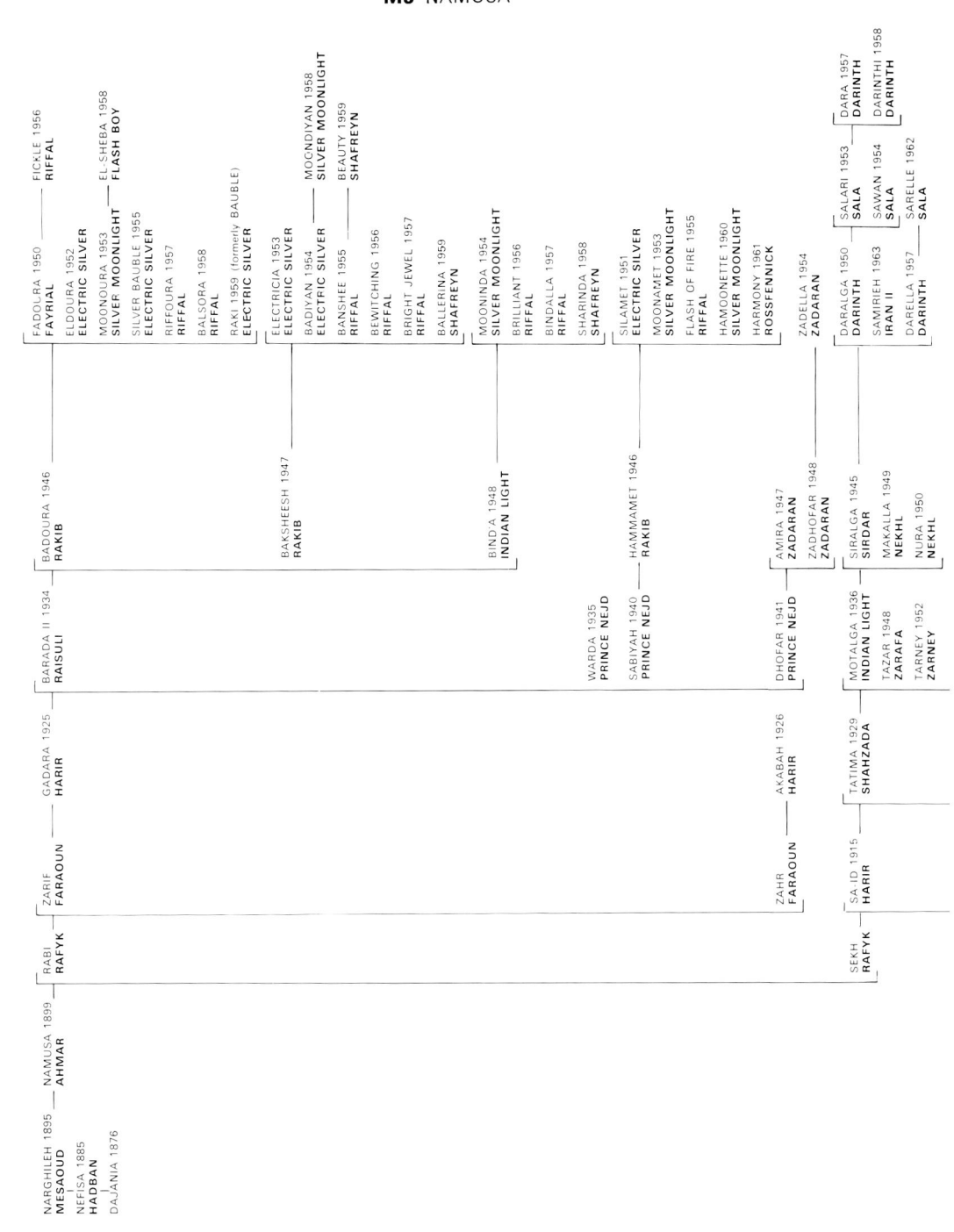

NARGHILEH 1895 — NAMUSA 1899 — RABI — ZARIF — GADARA 1925 — BARADA II 1934 — BADOURA 1946
MESAOUD   AHMAR   RAFYK   FARAOUN HARIR   RAISULI   RAKIB

NEFISA 1885
HADBAN

DAJANIA 1876

FADOURA 1950 ——————————————— FICKLE 1956
FAYRIAL   RIFFAL

ELDOURA 1952
ELECTRIC SILVER

MOONOURA 1953 ——————————————— EL-SHEBA 1958
SILVER MOONLIGHT   FLASH BOY

SILVER BAUBLE 1955
ELECTRIC SILVER

RIFFOURA 1957
RIFFAL

BALSORA 1958
RIFFAL

RAKI 1959 (formerly BAUBLE)
ELECTRIC SILVER

BAKSHEESH 1947 — ELECTRICIA 1953
RAKIB   ELECTRIC SILVER

BADIYAN 1954 ——————————————— MOONDIYAN 1958
ELECTRIC SILVER   SILVER MOONLIGHT

BANSHEE 1955 ——————————————— BEAUTY 1959
RIFFAL   SHAFREYN

BEWITCHING 1956
RIFFAL

BRIGHT JEWEL 1957
RIFFAL

BALLERINA 1959
SHAFREYN

BINDA 1948 — MOONINDA 1954
INDIAN LIGHT SILVER MOONLIGHT

BRILLIANT 1956
RIFFAL

BINDALLA 1957
RIFFAL

SHARINDA 1958
SHAFREYN

WARDA 1935
PRINCE NEJD

SABIYAH 1940 — HAMMAMET 1946 — SILAMET 1951
PRINCE NEJD   RAKIB   ELECTRIC SILVER

MOONAMET 1953
SILVER MOONLIGHT

FLASH OF FIRE 1955
RIFFAL

HAMOONETTE 1960
SILVER MOONLIGHT

HARMONY 1961
ROSSFENNICK

ZAHR — AKABAH 1926 — DHOFAR 1941 — AMIRA 1947
FARAOUN HARIR   PRINCE NEJD   ZADARAN

ZADHOFAR 1948
ZADARAN

ZADELLA 1954
ZADARAN

SEKH — SA'ID 1915 — TATIMA 1929 — MOTALGA 1936 — SIRALGA 1945 — DARALGA 1950 — DARA 1957
RAFYK   HARIR   SHAHZADA   INDIAN LIGHT   SIRDAR   DARINTH   DARINTH

SALARI 1953
SALA

SAWAN 1954
SALA

DARINTHI 1958
DARINTH

SARELLE 1962
SALA

TAZAR 1948 — MAKALLA 1949
ZARAFA   NEKHL

TARNEY 1952 — NURA 1950
ZARNEY   NEKHL

SAMIRIEH 1963
IRAN II

DARELLA 1957
DARINTH

289

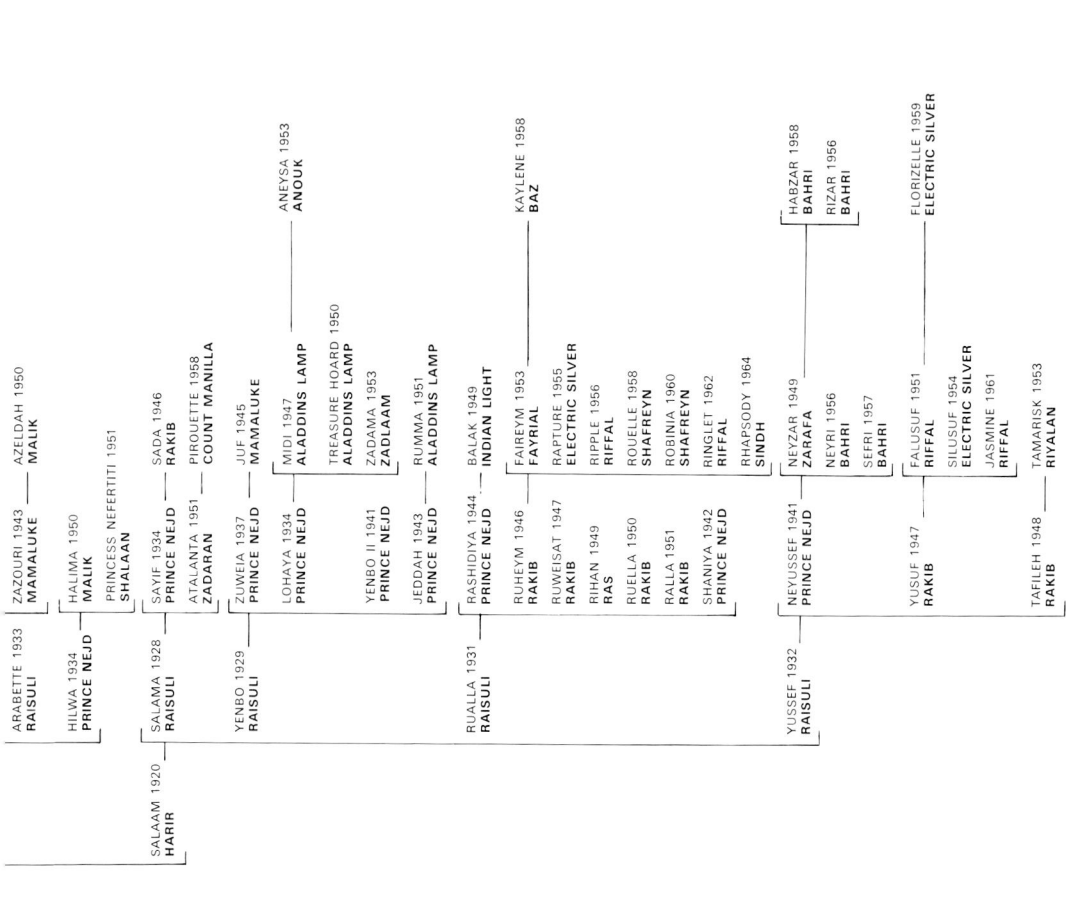

			ARABETTE 1933 **RAISULI**	ZAZOURI 1943 **MAMALUKE**	AZELDAH 1950 **MALIK**	
			HILWA 1934 **PRINCE NEJD**	HALIMA 1950 **MALIK**		
				PRINCESS NEFERTITI 1951 **SHALAAN**		
			SALAMA 1928 **RAISULI**	SAYIF 1934 **PRINCE NEJD**	SADA 1946 **RAKIB**	
				ATALANTA 1951 **ZADARAN**	PIROUETTE 1958 **COUNT MANILLA**	
			YENBO 1929 **RAISULI**	ZUWEIA 1937 **PRINCE NEJD**	JUF 1945 **MAMALUKE**	
				LOHAYA 1934 **PRINCE NEJD**	MIDI 1947 **ALADDINS LAMP**	ANEYSA 1953 **ANOUK**
					TREASURE HOARD 1950 **ALADDINS LAMP**	
				YENBO II 1941 **PRINCE NEJD**	ZADAMA 1953 **ZADLAAM**	
				JEDDAH 1943 **PRINCE NEJD**	RUMMA 1951 **ALADDINS LAMP**	
			RUALLA 1931 **RAISULI**	RASHIDIYA 1944 **PRINCE NEJD**	BALAK 1949 **INDIAN LIGHT**	
				RUHEYM 1946 **RAKIB**	FAIREYM 1953 **FAYRIAL**	KAYLENE 1958 **BAZ**
				RUWEISAT 1947 **RAKIB**	RAPTURE 1955 **ELECTRIC SILVER**	
				RIHAN 1949 **RAS**	RIPPLE 1956 **RIFFAL**	
				RUELLA 1950 **RAKIB**	ROUELLE 1958 **SHAFREYN**	
				RALLA 1951 **RAKIB**	ROBINIA 1960 **SHAFREYN**	
				SHANIYA 1942 **PRINCE NEJD**	RINGLET 1962 **RIFFAL**	
					RHAPSODY 1964 **SINDH**	
SALAAM 1920 **HARIR**		YUSSEF 1932 **RAISULI**	NEYUSSEF 1941 **PRINCE NEJD**	NEYZAR 1949 **ZARAFA**	HABZAR 1958 **BAHRI**	
					RIZAR 1956 **BAHRI**	
				NEYRI 1956 **BAHRI**		
				SEFRI 1957 **BAHRI**		
			YUSUF 1947 **RAKIB**	FALUSUF 1951 **RIFFAL**	FLORIZELLE 1959 **ELECTRIC SILVER**	
				SILUSUF 1954 **ELECTRIC SILVER**		
				JASMINE 1961 **RIFFAL**		
			TAFILEH 1948 **RAKIB**	TAMARISK 1953 **RIYALAN**		

M4 NASIRIEH

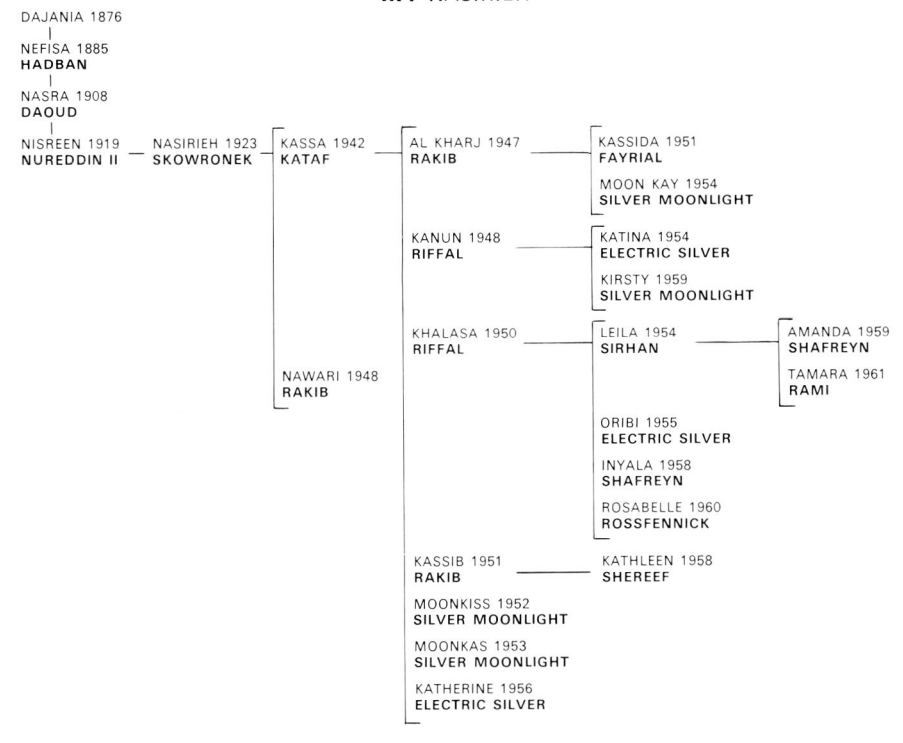

```
DAJANIA 1876
  |
NEFISA 1885
HADBAN
  |
NASRA 1908
DAOUD
  |
NISREEN 1919 ─── NASIRIEH 1923 ┬─ KASSA 1942 ┬─ AL KHARJ 1947 ┬─ KASSIDA 1951
NUREDDIN II      SKOWRONEK     │  KATAF      │  RAKIB         │  FAYRIAL
                               │             │                │
                               │             │                └─ MOON KAY 1954
                               │             │                   SILVER MOONLIGHT
                               │             │
                               │             ├─ KANUN 1948 ┬─ KATINA 1954
                               │             │  RIFFAL     │  ELECTRIC SILVER
                               │             │             │
                               │             │             └─ KIRSTY 1959
                               │             │                SILVER MOONLIGHT
                               │             │
                               │             └─ KHALASA 1950 ┬─ LEILA 1954 ┬─ AMANDA 1959
                               │                RIFFAL       │  SIRHAN     │  SHAFREYN
                               │                             │             │
                               │                             │             └─ TAMARA 1961
                               │                             │                RAMI
                               │                             │
                               │                             ├─ ORIBI 1955
                               │                             │  ELECTRIC SILVER
                               │                             │
                               │                             ├─ INYALA 1958
                               │                             │  SHAFREYN
                               │                             │
                               │                             └─ ROSABELLE 1960
                               │                                ROSSFENNICK
                               │
                               ├─ NAWARI 1948
                               │  RAKIB
                               │
                               ├─ KASSIB 1951 ─── KATHLEEN 1958
                               │  RAKIB           SHEREEF
                               │
                               ├─ MOONKISS 1952
                               │  SILVER MOONLIGHT
                               │
                               ├─ MOONKAS 1953
                               │  SILVER MOONLIGHT
                               │
                               └─ KATHERINE 1956
                                  ELECTRIC SILVER
```

M5 RAFINA · ROSINELLA

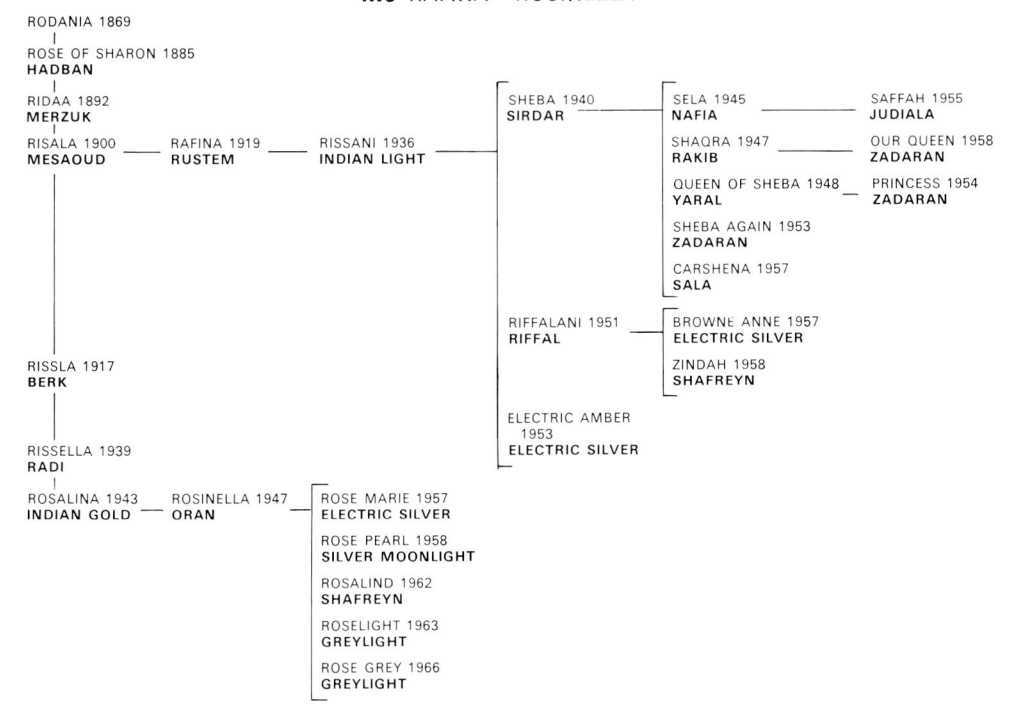

```
RODANIA 1869
  |
ROSE OF SHARON 1885
HADBAN
  |
RIDAA 1892
MERZUK
  |
RISALA 1900 ─── RAFINA 1919 ─── RISSANI 1936 ┬─ SHEBA 1940 ┬─ SELA 1945 ─── SAFFAH 1955
MESAOUD         RUSTEM          INDIAN LIGHT │  SIRDAR     │  NAFIA          JUDIALA
                                             │             │
                                             │             ├─ SHAQRA 1947 ─── OUR QUEEN 1958
                                             │             │  RAKIB            ZADARAN
                                             │             │
                                             │             ├─ QUEEN OF SHEBA 1948 ─── PRINCESS 1954
                                             │             │  YARAL                    ZADARAN
                                             │             │
                                             │             ├─ SHEBA AGAIN 1953
                                             │             │  ZADARAN
                                             │             │
                                             │             └─ CARSHENA 1957
                                             │                SALA
                                             │
                                             ├─ RIFFALANI 1951 ┬─ BROWNE ANNE 1957
                                             │  RIFFAL         │  ELECTRIC SILVER
                                             │                 │
                                             │                 └─ ZINDAH 1958
                                             │                    SHAFREYN
                                             │
                                             └─ ELECTRIC AMBER 1953
                                                ELECTRIC SILVER

RISSLA 1917
BERK
  |
RISSELLA 1939
RADI
  |
ROSALINA 1943 ─── ROSINELLA 1947 ┬─ ROSE MARIE 1957
INDIAN GOLD       ORAN           │  ELECTRIC SILVER
                                 │
                                 ├─ ROSE PEARL 1958
                                 │  SILVER MOONLIGHT
                                 │
                                 ├─ ROSALIND 1962
                                 │  SHAFREYN
                                 │
                                 ├─ ROSELIGHT 1963
                                 │  GREYLIGHT
                                 │
                                 └─ ROSE GREY 1966
                                    GREYLIGHT
```

M6 NURALINA

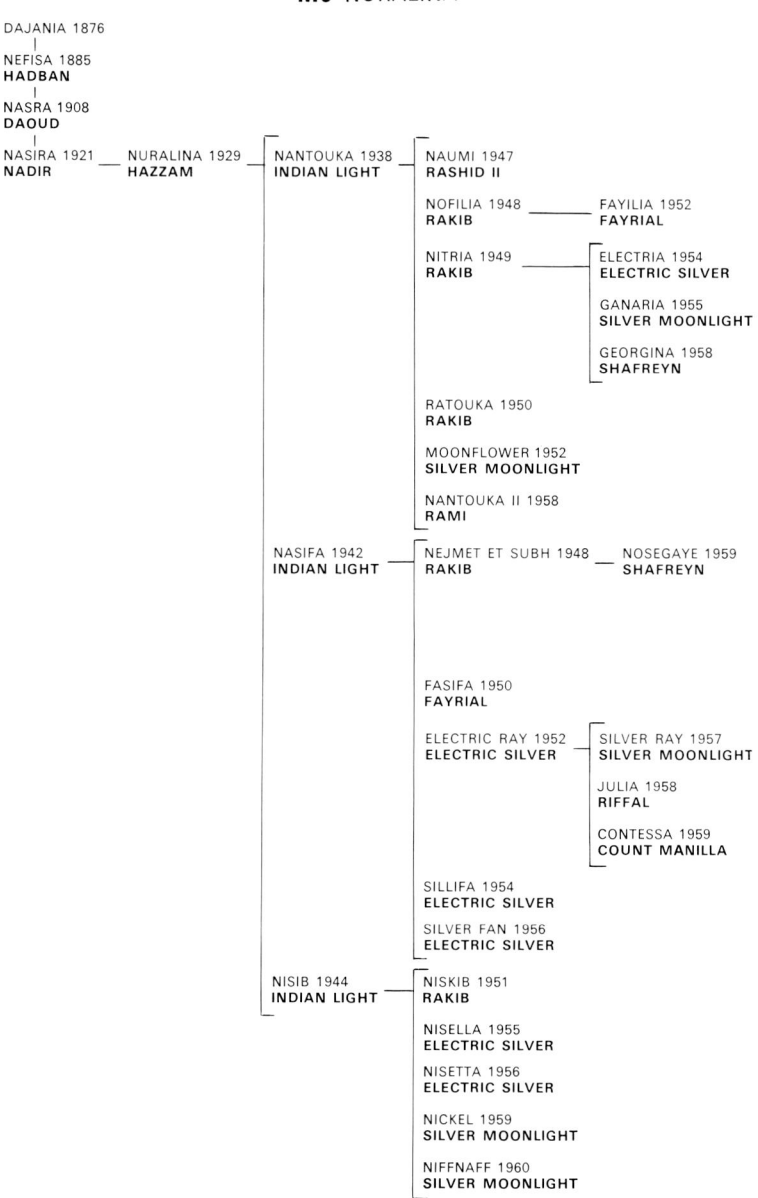

```
DAJANIA 1876
  |
NEFISA 1885
HADBAN
  |
NASRA 1908
DAOUD
  |
NASIRA 1921 ── NURALINA 1929 ─┬─ NANTOUKA 1938 ─┬─ NAUMI 1947
NADIR           HAZZAM         │  INDIAN LIGHT   │  RASHID II
                               │                 │
                               │                 ├─ NOFILIA 1948 ──── FAYILIA 1952
                               │                 │  RAKIB              FAYRIAL
                               │                 │
                               │                 ├─ NITRIA 1949 ──┬─ ELECTRIA 1954
                               │                 │  RAKIB          │  ELECTRIC SILVER
                               │                 │                 │
                               │                 │                 ├─ GANARIA 1955
                               │                 │                 │  SILVER MOONLIGHT
                               │                 │                 │
                               │                 │                 └─ GEORGINA 1958
                               │                 │                    SHAFREYN
                               │                 │
                               │                 ├─ RATOUKA 1950
                               │                 │  RAKIB
                               │                 │
                               │                 ├─ MOONFLOWER 1952
                               │                 │  SILVER MOONLIGHT
                               │                 │
                               │                 └─ NANTOUKA II 1958
                               │                    RAMI
                               │
                               ├─ NASIFA 1942 ──┬─ NEJMET ET SUBH 1948 ── NOSEGAYE 1959
                               │  INDIAN LIGHT  │  RAKIB                   SHAFREYN
                               │                │
                               │                ├─ FASIFA 1950
                               │                │  FAYRIAL
                               │                │
                               │                ├─ ELECTRIC RAY 1952 ─┬─ SILVER RAY 1957
                               │                │  ELECTRIC SILVER    │  SILVER MOONLIGHT
                               │                │                     │
                               │                │                     ├─ JULIA 1958
                               │                │                     │  RIFFAL
                               │                │                     │
                               │                │                     └─ CONTESSA 1959
                               │                │                        COUNT MANILLA
                               │                │
                               │                ├─ SILLIFA 1954
                               │                │  ELECTRIC SILVER
                               │                │
                               │                └─ SILVER FAN 1956
                               │                   ELECTRIC SILVER
                               │
                               └─ NISIB 1944 ──┬─ NISKIB 1951
                                  INDIAN LIGHT │  RAKIB
                                               │
                                               ├─ NISELLA 1955
                                               │  ELECTRIC SILVER
                                               │
                                               ├─ NISETTA 1956
                                               │  ELECTRIC SILVER
                                               │
                                               ├─ NICKEL 1959
                                               │  SILVER MOONLIGHT
                                               │
                                               └─ NIFFNAFF 1960
                                                  SILVER MOONLIGHT
```

For Nejmet et Subh read Nejmet es Subh.

M7 MIRIAM

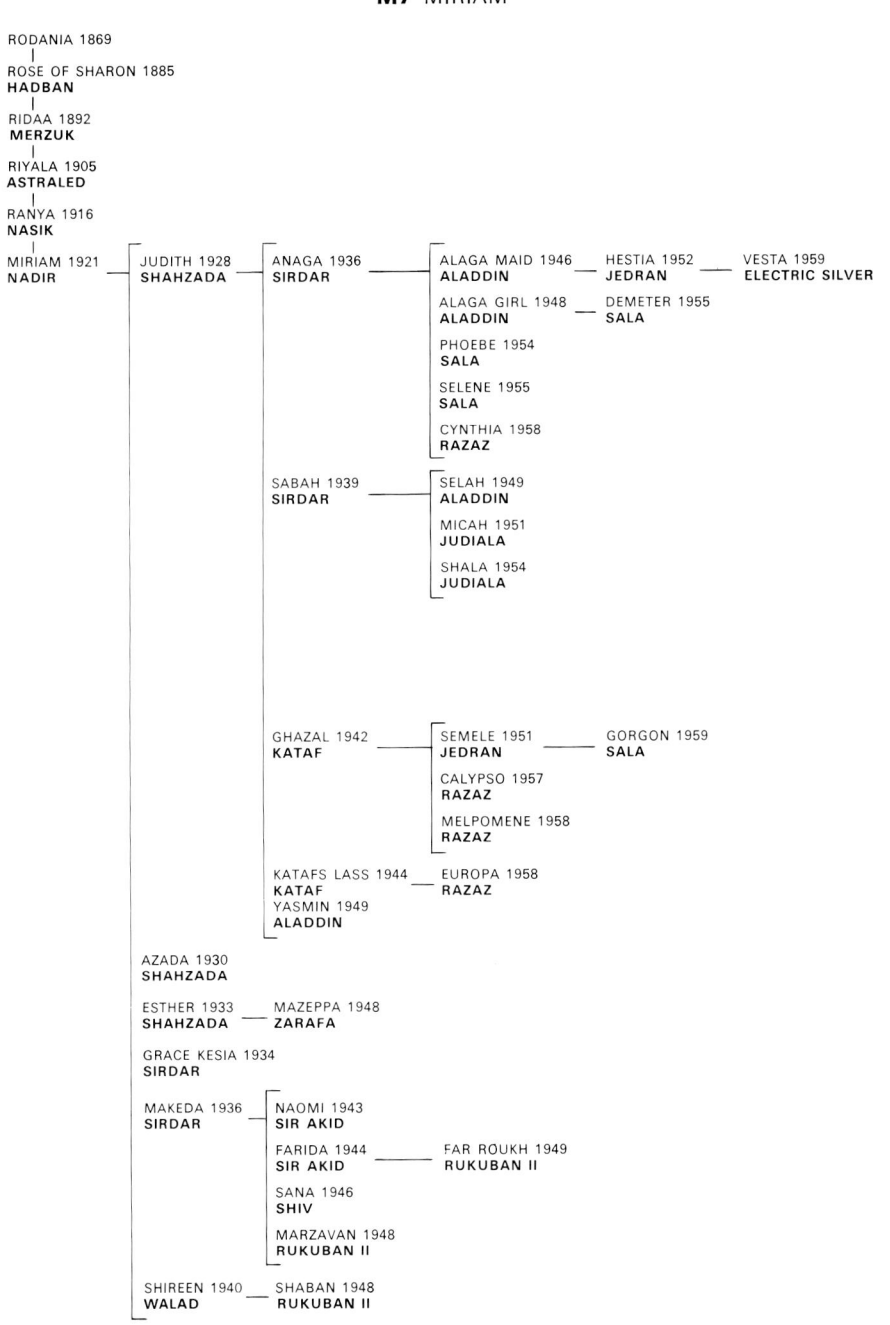

RODANIA 1869
|
ROSE OF SHARON 1885
HADBAN
|
RIDAA 1892
MERZUK
|
RIYALA 1905
ASTRALED
|
RANYA 1916
NASIK
|
MIRIAM 1921
NADIR
— JUDITH 1928
SHAHZADA
— ANAGA 1936
SIRDAR
— ALAGA MAID 1946
ALADDIN
— HESTIA 1952
JEDRAN
— VESTA 1959
ELECTRIC SILVER

ALAGA GIRL 1948
ALADDIN
— DEMETER 1955
SALA

PHOEBE 1954
SALA

SELENE 1955
SALA

CYNTHIA 1958
RAZAZ

SABAH 1939
SIRDAR
— SELAH 1949
ALADDIN

MICAH 1951
JUDIALA

SHALA 1954
JUDIALA

GHAZAL 1942
KATAF
— SEMELE 1951
JEDRAN
— GORGON 1959
SALA

CALYPSO 1957
RAZAZ

MELPOMENE 1958
RAZAZ

KATAFS LASS 1944
KATAF
— EUROPA 1958
RAZAZ

YASMIN 1949
ALADDIN

AZADA 1930
SHAHZADA

ESTHER 1933
SHAHZADA
— MAZEPPA 1948
ZARAFA

GRACE KESIA 1934
SIRDAR

MAKEDA 1936
SIRDAR
— NAOMI 1943
SIR AKID

FARIDA 1944
SIR AKID
— FAR ROUKH 1949
RUKUBAN II

SANA 1946
SHIV

MARZAVAN 1948
RUKUBAN II

SHIREEN 1940
WALAD
— SHABAN 1948
RUKUBAN II

293

EGYPT

The Blunts' Stud at Sheykh Obeyd was founded in 1889 and nine years later was purged by Lady Anne of all doubtful animals. Details of the horses discarded and of those comprising the New Venture are given in Appendix 2 and in Chapter Six.

Before discussing the relationships between Blunt horses and the present 'New Egyptian', it may be useful for readers unfamiliar with the highways and byways of Egyptian horse-breeding to present in tabular form the connections between the principal studs involved.

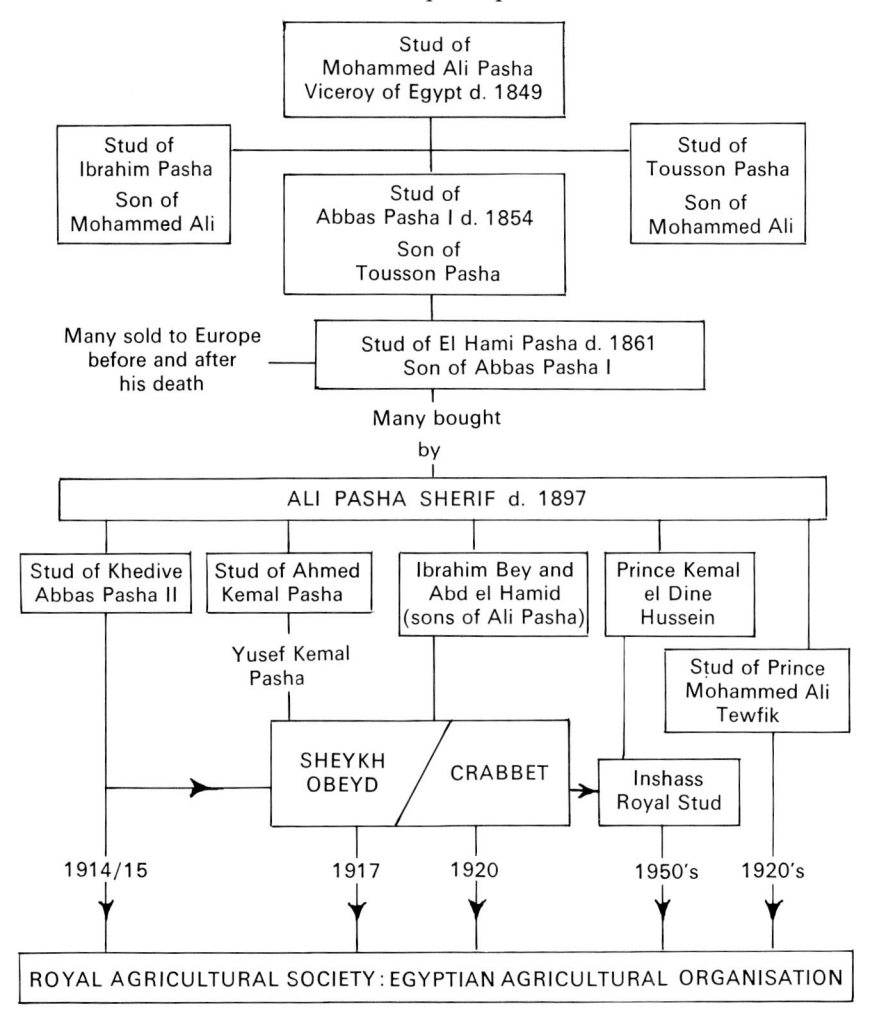

```
                          Stud of
                     Mohammed Ali Pasha
                    Viceroy of Egypt d. 1849
    ┌─────────────────────┬─────────────────────┐
   Stud of              Stud of              Stud of
  Ibrahim Pasha       Abbas Pasha I d. 1854  Tousson Pasha
    Son of              Son of                 Son of
  Mohammed Ali        Tousson Pasha          Mohammed Ali
                          │
                          │
Many sold to Europe   Stud of El Hami Pasha d. 1861
before and after  ──  Son of Abbas Pasha I
his death
                     Many bought
                         by
  ┌──────────────────────────────────────────────────────┐
  │           ALI PASHA SHERIF d. 1897                   │
  └──────────────────────────────────────────────────────┘
    │            │              │                │
  Stud of     Stud of       Ibrahim Bey and   Prince Kemal
  Khedive     Ahmed         Abd el Hamid      el Dine
  Abbas       Kemal Pasha   (sons of Ali      Hussein
  Pasha II                   Pasha)
                │                              │
            Yusef Kemal                    Stud of Prince
            Pasha                          Mohammed Ali
                                           Tewfik
            SHEYKH   /  CRABBET           Inshass
            OBEYD    /                    Royal Stud

   1914/15      1917        1920          1950's    1920's
     │           │            │              │        │
     ▼           ▼            ▼              ▼        ▼
  ┌──────────────────────────────────────────────────────────┐
  │ ROYAL AGRICULTURAL SOCIETY: EGYPTIAN AGRICULTURAL ORGANISATION │
  └──────────────────────────────────────────────────────────┘
```

Sixteen mares and forty-one stallions are listed as root stock in the stud book of the Royal Agricultural Society of Egypt (renamed the Egyptian Agricultural Organisation in 1952). Of these nearly one half were bred either at Sheykh Obeyd or at Crabbet. Six female lines only have persisted from this original stock, of which four come from Blunt foundations. The six families exist within four strains; Seglawi Jedran, Kehilan Rodan, Dahman Shahwan and Hadban Enzahi.

SEGLAWI JEDRAN

The continuation of this strain is attributable solely to two mares: Ghadia and Bint Roga.

Ghadia (renamed Radia by the R.A.S.) was foaled at Sheykh Obeyd on March 3rd 1904, by Feysul out of Ghazala. The latter was a daughter of Bint Helwa and therefore the great-great-granddaughter of the original Abbas Pasha mare Ghazieh. Ghadia (Radia) was presented by Lady Anne Blunt to the R.A.S. in 1917 with her half sister Jemla (by Jamil 1896). Jemla (renamed Jamila) failed to establish a continuing family in Egypt though her granddaughter Bint Serra (by Sotamm out of Serra, by Sahab) was exported to Henry Babson's stud in the United States where she has left a strong line through Fay El Dine and FaSerr and her several daughters.

Radia's main influence has been through her daughter Bint Radia (see table M8), the dam of Zamzam and Samira. Samira was the dam of Zaafarana who in turn had the famous stallion Talal and Talal's full sister (Ansata) Bint Zaafarana. For Radia's very important male line through Bint Radia to Hamdan and Shahloul, see table S16.

The second source of the Seglawi strain endures from the mysterious mare Bint Roga. The normal attribution of Bint Roga is that she was owned by Lady Anne Blunt and that she traces in tail female to Bint Horra. This deserves comment since there is no Bint Roga in the Sheykh Obeyd records, only Bint Roda and Roda; and for Bint Roga to trace to Bint Horra (born in 1889) would require four generations within the space of fourteen years – Bint Roga's granddaughter Dalal was born in 1903. Such fecundity is unlikely in the conditions of the time. An alternative explanation may be found in Lady Anne Blunt's papers.

'Dec. 2, 1907. Saw Prince Yusef's mares:
gr. Segl Jedranieh bint Roja abuha Jamila abt 16 yrs [1].
gr. Segl Jed. (Shieha) bint es Shakra bint bint Roja abuha *Abeyan* Hanaydis from the Sebaa (Mutlak says *mazbut* strain) abt. 5 or 6.

Bay Segl Jedranieh bint ez Zerka bint Roja, abuha Rabdan. 2 in spring [2].

'Dec. 17, 1907. To H.H. (Mohammed Ali) . . . It was a brilliant show. I do not know that I covet anything of it very much, though I should not *mind* having the chestnut Seglawieh (bint Roga). There was *first* a fine flea bitten mare [1]. Prince Moh. Ali *said* that 'they call her Roja' in case she shld be only the *dam* of Roja. I think she is the old mare Moharrem Pasha advised me to buy, and that the Prince has taken her *since* my visit to the Ahmed Pasha stud. For there was no other mare of that stamp connected with Roja. Then the handsome 3 y.o./or 4 Dalal . . .'

The horse marked [1], the grey Seglawieh Jedranieh and a fine fleabitten mare, was purchased by Lady Anne Blunt in April 1909 from Prince Yusef (the son and inheritor of Prince Ahmed Pasha) and is recorded in the Sheykh Obeyd Stud Book as Bint Roda. (See Chapter 6.) Lady Anne gives her date of birth here as 1896. Elsewhere she has said 1895. Raswan has 1894.

The horse marked [2], the bay Seglawieh Jedranieh bint ez Zerka bint Roja, was purchased by Lady Anne in January 1908 and is entered as Roda in the Sheykh Obeyd Stud Book. (See Chapter 6.)

Although the evidence is by no means conclusive, it seems likely that Lady Anne Blunt's Bint Roda is the same animal as the R.A.S.'s Bint Roga. This removes the problem of fitting four generations into fourteen years and matches the R.A.S.'s records with those of Lady Anne. It must be said, however, that it would still mean having two generations within eight or nine years. Were this hypothesis correct Bint Roga would trace to Jamil (Prince Ahmed Pasha's Jamil) and Roda (an Ali Pasha mare) and not to Bint Horra. But owing to the lack of proof, it has been preferred to list Bint Roga without attribution to either Bint Horra or Roda.

Nevertheless, the influence of the Bint Roga line has been considerable (see table M10).

Taken all in all, the Seglawi Jedran strain has been responsible for some of the most renowned horses bred in Egypt in recent years; Mabrouka and her son Morafic, Moniet el Nefous and her sons Tuhotmos and Fakher el Din, Lubna and her son Sultan; Samira, and Zaafarana and her daughters.

KEHILAN RODAN

The Rodania family is as vigorous in Egypt as elsewhere. The strain has developed from two mares exported by Lady Wentworth in 1920; Razieh (renamed Bint Rissala), by Ibn Yashmak out of Risala; and Risama (renamed Bint Riyala), by Nadir out of Riyala.

Bint Rissala (see table M11) has been successful in both male and female lines. Her daughter Kateefa was the granddam of two outstandingly beautiful stallions, Kaysoon and Farag. Kaysoon (by Nazeer) was exported to West Germany in 1963 where he has been widely used while Farag (by Morafic) has offspring in Hungary as well as in Germany. Another Morafic son in Hungary is Ghalion, out of Lubna.

Yashmak, another daughter of Bint Rissala, has also produced well. Of her three daughters, Rahma produced Hanadi who went to Babolna. Hanadi's sire was Alaa el Din whose own pedigree is so strongly infused with Blunt blood (see table s15) that Hanadi is almost 50 per cent Blunt stock. A second Yashmak daughter, Om el Saad, is of particular note as a brood mare and is perhaps most famous for her lovely daughter Bint Om el Saad (by Nazeer) whose daughter Sonbolah, renamed Serenity Sonbolah in the United States, has achieved world renown. Sonbolah's sire Sameh is a son of El Moez (see table s16), who also contains a substantial portion of Blunt blood.

Bint Rissala's third daughter, Yaquota, also founded a notable family. For some reason this is listed in the Egyptian stud books under the Ubayan strain.

The other Kehilan Rodan import into Egypt is Risama (Bint Riyala). Her line has spread through her granddaughter Malaka, an outstanding brood mare. Malaka had three fine daughters by Nazeer (Samia, Mamlouka and Nazeera) and a fourth, Salomi, by El Sareei. As may be seen from table M12 the produce of these mares has spread throughout the world. Malaka should also be mentioned as the dam of Nil who went to Russia in 1958 and there sired the important stallion Naslednik out of Naseem's daughter Nitochka.

DAHMAN SHAHWAN

This strain developed in Egypt from two lines; Lady Anne Blunt's Bint el Bahreyn and Ali Pasha Sherif's mare, El Dahma.

Bint el Bahreyn was bought by Lady Anne from Abbas Pasha II in 1907. Three years later she gave birth to the filly Dalal (not to be confused with Dalal 1903), sired by Jamil 1896 (the Blunts' Jamil). In

1917 Dalal produced Durra (by Saadun, a desert-bred horse acquired by Lady Anne in 1911). It is probable that Durra was one of the horses bought by the Greek, Mr Casdugli, from the executors of Lady Anne's will. In 1924 the R.A.S. acquired Durra from Casdugli and bred from her two mares of note, Bint Durra (by Eid) and Zareefa (by Kasmeyn).

Bint Durra was the dam of Bint Bint Durra who went to Henry Babson's stud. She also deserves mention on account of the supposedly unknown origins of her sire Eid. Raswan has recorded that Eid was bought as a racehorse by Casdugli from a trader in Qasim. It is in fact probable that Eid is the same horse as the Eid who was bred by Lady Anne Blunt at Sheykh Obeyd in 1917, by Jamil 1896 out of Aida (for whom see the entry in Chapter 6); and that he was one of the horses purchased by Casdugli when Lady Anne died. The link between this and Raswan's version may lie in the fact that Aida's dam came from Abdallah el Bassam, of the Bassam family of Oneyzeh in Qasim.

Durra's more important daughter, however, was Zareefa, by the Blunt horse Kasmeyn. Zareefa is doubly meritorious for as well as founding a strong female line (see table M9) she was also the dam of the famous stallion El Sareei, who was the sire of the equally prominent Tuhotmos. El Sareei has other Blunt blood through his granddam Bint Radia. It is unfortunate that Zareefa's family was not larger since many of her descendants have been exported from their mother stud.

Of Zareefa's daughters, Badia was the dam of the stallion Gassir; Bint Zareefa (1936) is significant with a great-great-granddaughter (Bint Azza I) at Babolna; Maisa contributed two daughters to America in Bint Maisa el Saghira and Bint Maisa, while the youngest, Elwya, produced in 1959 a colt by Mashhour named Seef who has been widely used as a stallion in Egypt.

The second strain of the Dahman Shahwan family is from the Ali Pasha Sherif mare El Dahma, from whom one line is given on table M13. Little is known of this mare other than her strain making it possible only to surmise at the links which she undoubtedly had with other Ali Pasha Sherif Dahman Shahwan stock. The connection between the Dahman strains of Ali Pasha Sherif and those in the Blunt animals is discussed under the Egyptian foundation stallion **Gamil el Ahmar**.

HADBAN ENZAHI

The perpetuation of this strain is due to descendants from the mare Venus, brought to Egypt by Hassan Aga in 1893. The line progresses through the two branches of her great-granddaughters, Bint Rustem and Samiha.

Bint Rustem was by the Crabbet stallion Rustem whom Lady Wentworth sold to Egypt in 1920. Bint Rustem's female line runs to Yosreia, the dam of Aswan. On the male side Bint Rustem was the dam of the important stallion Mashhour (by Shahloul).

Samiha's pedigree traces to Bint Roga. In 1924 she was mated to Kasmeyn to give birth the following year to Bint Samiha, the dam of one of the most influential Egyptian stallions of the last half century, Nazeer (by Mansour). Nazeer has two crosses to Bint Roga.

Bint Samiha is also important through her daughter Samha who in 1942 produced Kamla, by Sheikh el Arab. Kamla in turn had the very important stallion Hadban Enzahi, by Bint Samiha's son Nazeer. Hadban Enzahi therefore has three crosses to Kasmeyn. As the senior sire at the Marbach State Stud in Germany he has assumed world-wide importance.

The main stallion lines that have survived in Egypt are those of Gamil el Ahmar, Saklawi I, El Dere and Zobeyni, although the latter appears only through the middle of present day pedigrees.

The line of Gamil el Ahmar through his son the grey Dahman and Dahman's son Rabdan is an extremely important one. The relationships between Dahman and Rabdan, and horses owned by the Blunts and the Princes are important though obscure. The dam of Dahman was Farida el Debbani, a daughter of Gayza, an original Abbas Pasha I mare of the Dahman Shahwan strain. Now two of the known branches of this strain, namely Khalil el Hajry and Faras Nakadan, both of whom also come from Abbas Pasha stock, feature significantly in several Blunt stallions such as Feysul, Jamil 1896, Mahruss 1893 and Shahwan, and in the pedigrees of many Blunt mares. Whilst positive linkage is unproven, it is highly probable that a greater or lesser degree of consanguinity exists between Dahman and many Blunt horses. This would also apply on the female side. In analysing the foundation stock in the early twentieth century, one is struck by the relatively small number of Arabians involved. This is in contrast to the extravagant numbers given for the mid-19th century and after allowing for the ravages of the horse plague, it would indicate the probability of these few remaining animals having been bred together in order to have existed.

The influence of Blunt horses on the Gamil el Ahmar line multiplies surprisingly the further one gets from the lines progenitor, in much the same way as it does in the Saklawi I family. On the Gamil el Ahmar table (S16) it comes with Radia's daughter Bint Radia, dam of Hamdan and Shahloul, and with Bint Zareefa (1926), the dam of El Moez. In the case of Shahloul it becomes even more pronounced at the next generation. Zareefa, the dam of El Sareei (and thus the granddam of Tuhotmos) was 100 per cent Blunt blood and Bint Rustem, dam of Mashhour, was by the Blunt stallion Rustem.

Saklawi I was a Seglawi Jedran stallion born, it is believed, in 1886 and imported to Egypt by Ali Pasha Sherif. Again, the further one goes the higher becomes the proportion of named animals in the pedigree that were owned or bred by the Blunts. Thus Alaa El Din, Morafic and Shaarawi all relate to around 45 per cent or more Blunt stock. Note should also be taken of the dam of Saklawi II, namely El Dahma. This matriarchal mare is recorded as being owned at one time by Ali Pasha Sherif and being a Dahmeh Shahwanieh highlights once again the probable ties with other horses of this prized strain.

El Dere was brought into the R.A.S. in 1934 from the royal stables of King Fuad. Little is known of his parentage but his strain is given as Seglawi Sheifi. It is believed he was a complete outcross for breeding purposes although of course a pure-bred Arab. His line is continued through Sid Abouhom, whose dam Layla was a granddaughter of the Blunt horse Kasmeyn.

The final stallion line to be considered is that of Zobeyni, a horse which features often in the pedigrees of Crabbet horses. Zobeyni was purchased from Arabia by Abbas Pasha I and mated by him to the original mare Ghazieh to produce first the mare Horra and later the famous stallion Wazir. Horra was the granddam of the Blunt mares Bint Helwa and Johara. Wazir was the sire of Shahwan and Merzuk and the grandsire of Mahruss (1893), while Harkan, another son of Zobeyni, was the grandsire of Mesaoud. Thus the Zobeyni male line at Crabbet is twin-branched through Harkan to Mesaoud and Wazir to Mahruss (1893). In Egypt the Mesaoud Crabbet line is most influential through Astraled's sons Rustem and Sotamm. A truncated line is included for reference. Particular notice should be taken of Kasmeyn, Sotamm's son out of Kasima (Narkise/Kasida). Kasmeyn is thus of pure Blunt breeding and, as we have already seen, of great importance in Egyptian bloodlines. The progeny of Mekdam also appear fairly frequently in the breeding of Inshass horses, as for instance in the stallion Anter.

The incorporation in recent years into the E.A.O. of stock from the

Inshass stud has not substantially affected the original source content of the pedigrees of horses bred. It is common for today's Egyptian Arabian horse to be termed the 'New Egyptian'. This is no more than an exercise in semantics. The Arabian in Egypt is Arabian by virtue of the purity of its blood which was saved from extinction by its dedicated breeders. The horses they loved trace to a tiny source of pedigrees, inextricably interwoven and all closely related to each other and to the Crabbet horses of yesterday and today.

LIST OF TABLES

Stallions

- S15 Saklawi I
- S16 Gamil el Ahmar
- S17 El Dere
- S18 Zobeyni

Mares

- M8 Ghadia (Radia)
- M9 Bint el Bahreyn
- M10 Bint Roga
- M11 Razieh (Bint Rissala)
- M12 Risama (Bint Riyala)
- M13 El Dahma

S15 SAKLAWI I

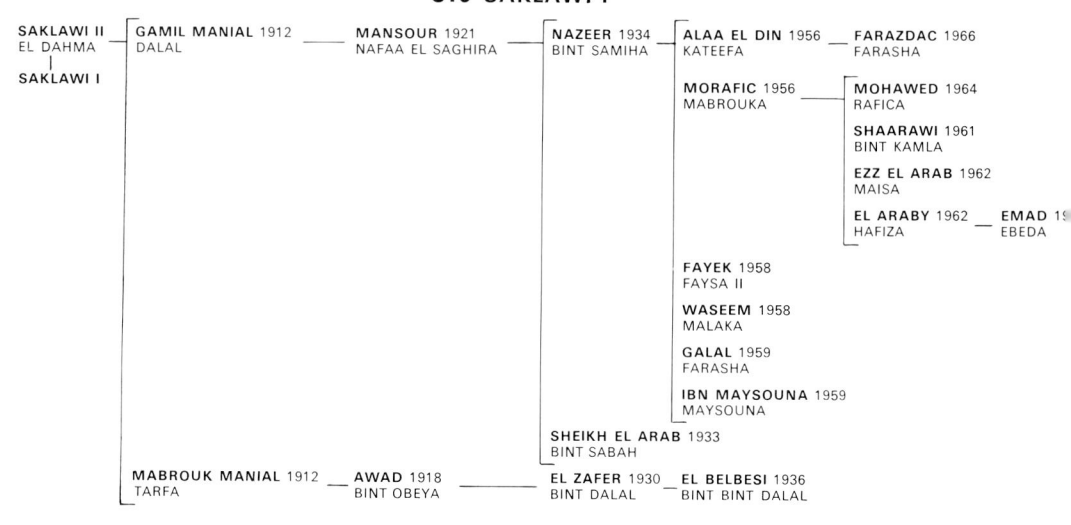

- SAKLAWI II
  EL DAHMA
- SAKLAWI I
  - GAMIL MANIAL 1912
    DALAL
    - MANSOUR 1921
      NAFAA EL SAGHIRA
      - NAZEER 1934
        BINT SAMIHA
        - ALAA EL DIN 1956
          KATEEFA
          - FARAZDAC 1966
            FARASHA
        - MORAFIC 1956
          MABROUKA
          - MOHAWED 1964
            RAFICA
          - SHAARAWI 1961
            BINT KAMLA
          - EZZ EL ARAB 1962
            MAISA
          - EL ARABY 1962
            HAFIZA
            - EMAD 19
              EBEDA
        - FAYEK 1958
          FAYSA II
        - WASEEM 1958
          MALAKA
        - GALAL 1959
          FARASHA
        - IBN MAYSOUNA 1959
          MAYSOUNA
      - SHEIKH EL ARAB 1933
        BINT SABAH
  - MABROUK MANIAL 1912
    TARFA
    - AWAD 1918
      BINT OBEYA
      - EL ZAFER 1930
        BINT DALAL
        - EL BELBESI 1936
          BINT BINT DALAL

S16 GAMIL EL AHMAR

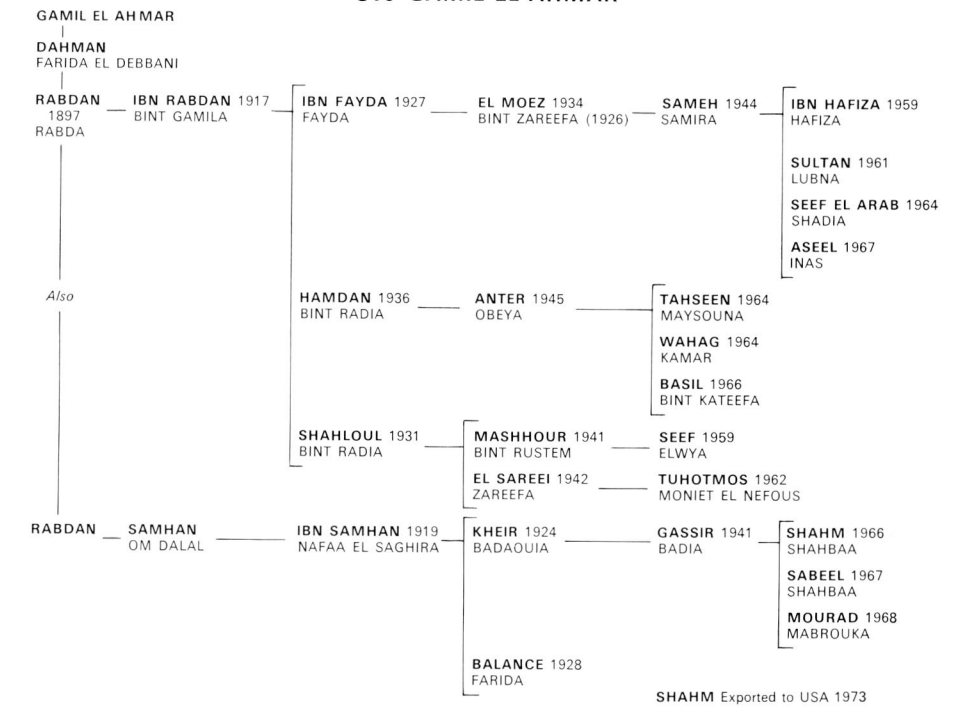

- GAMIL EL AHMAR
  - DAHMAN
    FARIDA EL DEBBANI
    - RABDAN 1897
      RABDA
      - IBN RABDAN 1917
        BINT GAMILA
        - IBN FAYDA 1927
          FAYDA
          - EL MOEZ 1934
            BINT ZAREEFA (1926)
            - SAMEH 1944
              SAMIRA
              - IBN HAFIZA 1959
                HAFIZA
              - SULTAN 1961
                LUBNA
              - SEEF EL ARAB 1964
                SHADIA
              - ASEEL 1967
                INAS
        - HAMDAN 1936
          BINT RADIA
          - ANTER 1945
            OBEYA
            - TAHSEEN 1964
              MAYSOUNA
            - WAHAG 1964
              KAMAR
            - BASIL 1966
              BINT KATEEFA
        - SHAHLOUL 1931
          BINT RADIA
          - MASHHOUR 1941
            BINT RUSTEM
            - SEEF 1959
              ELWYA
          - EL SAREEI 1942
            ZAREEFA
            - TUHOTMOS 1962
              MONIET EL NEFOUS
    Also
    - RABDAN
      - SAMHAN
        OM DALAL
        - IBN SAMHAN 1919
          NAFAA EL SAGHIRA
          - KHEIR 1924
            BADAOUIA
            - GASSIR 1941
              BADIA
              - SHAHM 1966
                SHAHBAA
              - SABEEL 1967
                SHAHBAA
              - MOURAD 1968
                MABROUKA
          - BALANCE 1928
            FARIDA

SHAHM Exported to USA 1973

S17 EL DERE

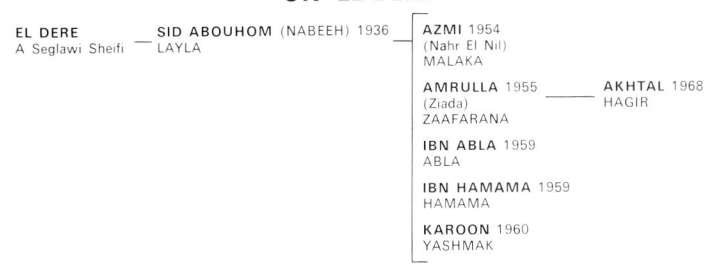

```
EL DERE ──── SID ABOUHOM (NABEEH) 1936 ──┬── AZMI 1954
A Seglawi Sheifi    LAYLA                │    (Nahr El Nil)
                                         │    MALAKA
                                         │
                                         ├── AMRULLA 1955 ──── AKHTAL 1968
                                         │    (Ziada)              HAGIR
                                         │    ZAAFARANA
                                         │
                                         ├── IBN ABLA 1959
                                         │    ABLA
                                         │
                                         ├── IBN HAMAMA 1959
                                         │    HAMAMA
                                         │
                                         └── KAROON 1960
                                              YASHMAK
```

S18 ZOBEYNI

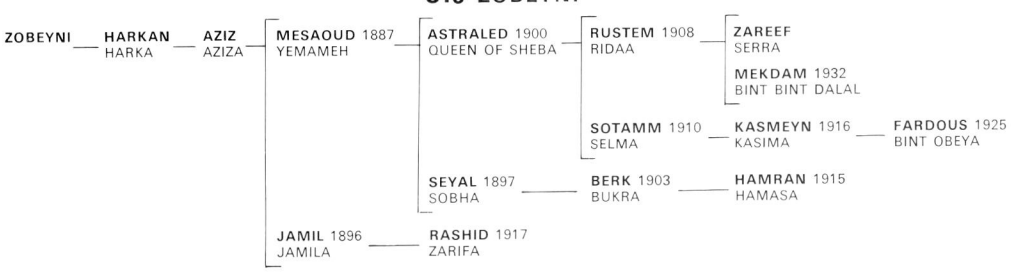

```
ZOBEYNI ── HARKAN ── AZIZ ── MESAOUD 1887 ──┬── ASTRALED 1900 ──┬── RUSTEM 1908 ──┬── ZAREEF
           HARKA     AZIZA    YEMAMEH       │    QUEEN OF SHEBA │    RIDAA         │    SERRA
                                            │                   │                  │
                                            │                   │                  └── MEKDAM 1932
                                            │                   │                       BINT BINT DALAL
                                            │                   │
                                            │                   └── SOTAMM 1910 ──── KASMEYN 1916 ──── FARDOUS 1925
                                            │                        SELMA              KASIMA              BINT OBEYA
                                            │
                                            ├── SEYAL 1897 ──── BERK 1903 ──── HAMRAN 1915
                                            │    SOBHA           BUKRA            HAMASA
                                            │
                                            └── JAMIL 1896 ──── RASHID 1917
                                                 JAMILA           ZARIFA
```

M8 GHADIA (RADIA)

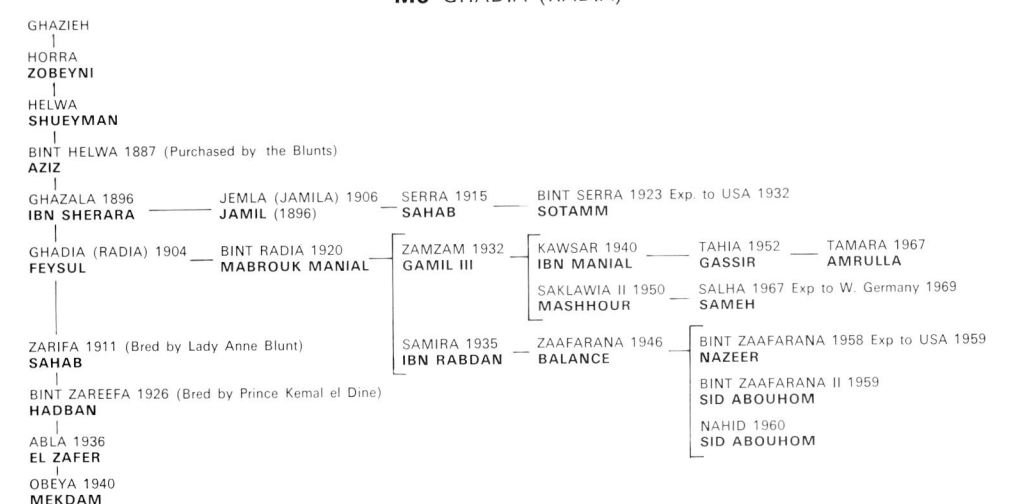

GHAZIEH
 |
HORRA
ZOBEYNI
 |
HELWA
SHUEYMAN
 |
BINT HELWA 1887 (Purchased by the Blunts)
AZIZ
 |
GHAZALA 1896 ──── JEMLA (JAMILA) 1906 ──── SERRA 1915 ──── BINT SERRA 1923 Exp. to USA 1932
IBN SHERARA   **JAMIL (1896)**   **SAHAB**   **SOTAMM**
 |
GHADIA (RADIA) 1904 ──── BINT RADIA 1920 ──── ZAMZAM 1932 ──┬── KAWSAR 1940 ──── TAHIA 1952 ──── TAMARA 1967
FEYSUL   **MABROUK MANIAL**   **GAMIL III**   │   **IBN MANIAL**   **GASSIR**   **AMRULLA**
                                                                         │
                                                                         └── SAKLAWIA II 1950 ──── SALHA 1967 Exp to W. Germany 1969
                                                                              MASHHOUR   **SAMEH**
 |
ZARIFA 1911 (Bred by Lady Anne Blunt)   SAMIRA 1935 ──── ZAAFARANA 1946 ──┬── BINT ZAAFARANA 1958 Exp to USA 1959
SAHAB   **IBN RABDAN**   **BALANCE**   │   **NAZEER**
 | │
BINT ZAREEFA 1926 (Bred by Prince Kemal el Dine)   ├── BINT ZAAFARANA II 1959
HADBAN   │   **SID ABOUHOM**
 | │
ABLA 1936   └── NAHID 1960
EL ZAFER   **SID ABOUHOM**
 |
OBEYA 1940
MEKDAM

BINT ZAREEFA was dam of **EL MOEZ** 1934 exported to South Africa.
OBEYA was dam of **ANTER** 1946 stud horse in EAO Stud.
SERRA was dam of **IBN SERRA** 1931 stud horse in Inshass Stud.
ZAAFARANA was dam of **TALAL** 1957 exported to USA 1967.
ZARIFA was dam of **RASHID** 1917 stud horse in Inshass Stud.

M9 BINT EL BAHREYN

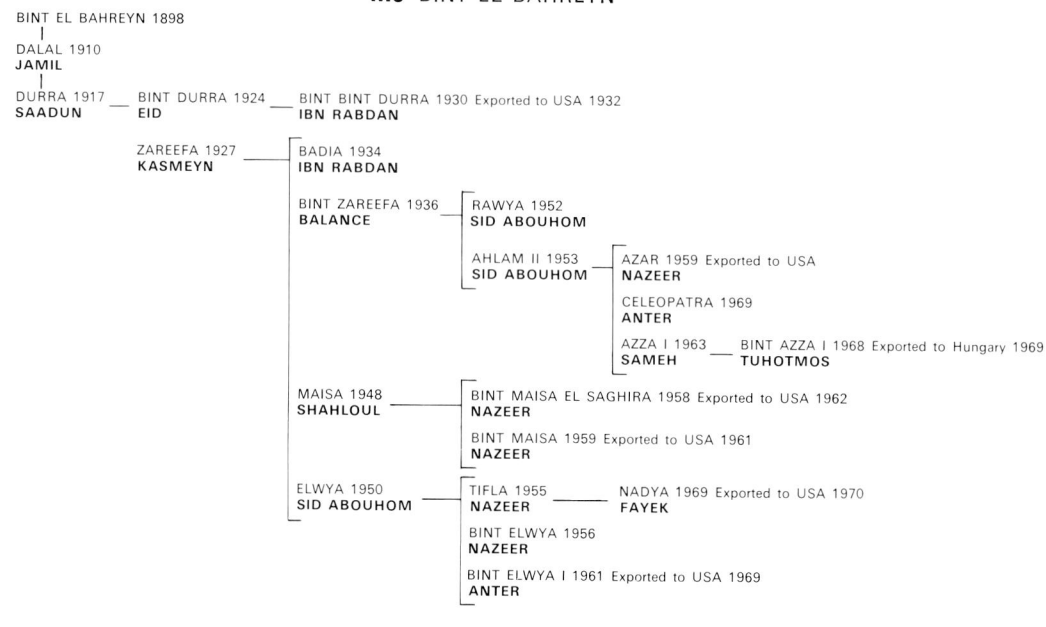

```
BINT EL BAHREYN 1898
 |
DALAL 1910
JAMIL
 |
DURRA 1917 ── BINT DURRA 1924 ── BINT BINT DURRA 1930 Exported to USA 1932
SAADUN        EID                 IBN RABDAN
              │
              ├─ ZAREEFA 1927 ──┬─ BADIA 1934
              │  KASMEYN        │  IBN RABDAN
              │                 │
              │                 ├─ BINT ZAREEFA 1936 ──┬─ RAWYA 1952
              │                 │  BALANCE             │  SID ABOUHOM
              │                 │                      │
              │                 │                      ├─ AHLAM II 1953 ──┬─ AZAR 1959 Exported to USA
              │                 │                      │  SID ABOUHOM     │  NAZEER
              │                 │                      │                  │
              │                 │                      │                  ├─ CELEOPATRA 1969
              │                 │                      │                  │  ANTER
              │                 │                      │                  │
              │                 │                      │                  └─ AZZA I 1963 ── BINT AZZA I 1968 Exported to Hungary 1969
              │                 │                      │                     SAMEH          TUHOTMOS
              │                 │
              │                 ├─ MAISA 1948 ──┬─ BINT MAISA EL SAGHIRA 1958 Exported to USA 1962
              │                 │  SHAHLOUL     │  NAZEER
              │                 │               │
              │                 │               └─ BINT MAISA 1959 Exported to USA 1961
              │                 │                  NAZEER
              │                 │
              │                 └─ ELWYA 1950 ──┬─ TIFLA 1955 ── NADYA 1969 Exported to USA 1970
              │                    SID ABOUHOM  │  NAZEER        FAYEK
              │                                 │
              │                                 ├─ BINT ELWYA 1956
              │                                 │  NAZEER
              │                                 │
              │                                 └─ BINT ELWYA I 1961 Exported to USA 1969
              │                                    ANTER
```

M10 BINT ROGA

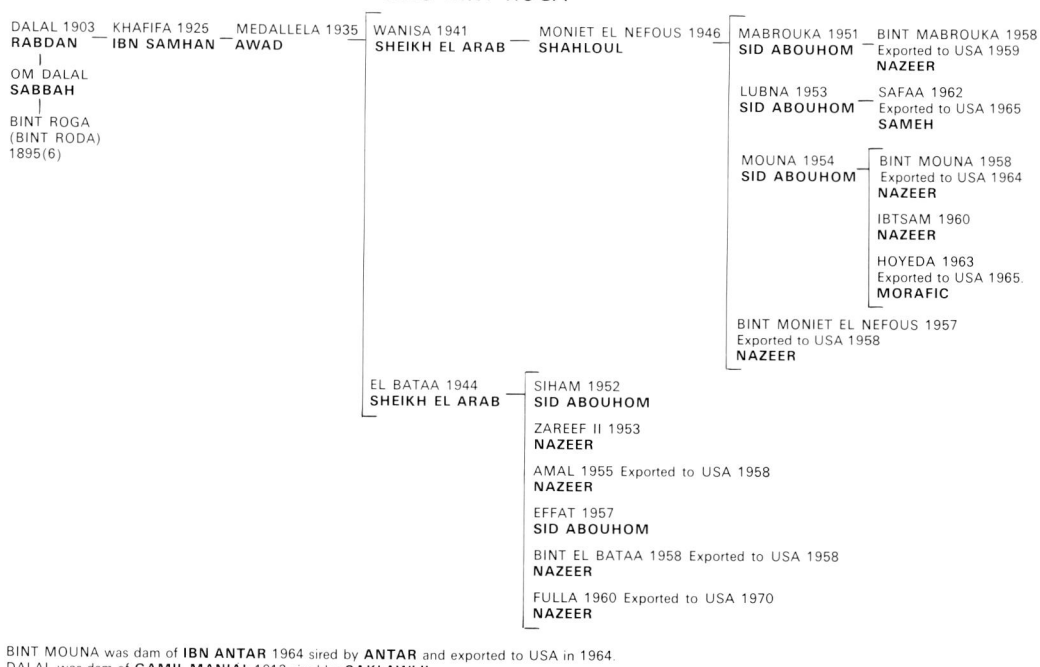

```
DALAL 1903 ── KHAFIFA 1925 ── MEDALLELA 1935 ── WANISA 1941 ── MONIET EL NEFOUS 1946 ──┬─ MABROUKA 1951 ── BINT MABROUKA 1958
RABDAN        IBN SAMHAN      AWAD              SHEIKH EL ARAB  SHAHLOUL                │  SID ABOUHOM      Exported to USA 1959
 │                                                                                      │                  NAZEER
OM DALAL                                                                                │
SABBAH                                                                                  ├─ LUBNA 1953 ── SAFAA 1962
 │                                                                                      │  SID ABOUHOM   Exported to USA 1965
BINT ROGA                                                                               │                SAMEH
(BINT RODA)                                                                             │
1895(6)                                                                                 ├─ MOUNA 1954 ──┬─ BINT MOUNA 1958
                                                                                        │  SID ABOUHOM  │  Exported to USA 1964
                                                                                        │               │  NAZEER
                                                                                        │               │
                                                                                        │               ├─ IBTSAM 1960
                                                                                        │               │  NAZEER
                                                                                        │               │
                                                                                        │               └─ HOYEDA 1963
                                                                                        │                  Exported to USA 1965.
                                                                                        │                  MORAFIC
                                                                                        │
                                                                                        └─ BINT MONIET EL NEFOUS 1957
                                                                                           Exported to USA 1958
                                                                                           NAZEER

                                                EL BATAA 1944 ──┬─ SIHAM 1952
                                                SHEIKH EL ARAB  │  SID ABOUHOM
                                                                │
                                                                ├─ ZAREEF II 1953
                                                                │  NAZEER
                                                                │
                                                                ├─ AMAL 1955 Exported to USA 1958
                                                                │  NAZEER
                                                                │
                                                                ├─ EFFAT 1957
                                                                │  SID ABOUHOM
                                                                │
                                                                ├─ BINT EL BATAA 1958 Exported to USA 1958
                                                                │  NAZEER
                                                                │
                                                                └─ FULLA 1960 Exported to USA 1970
                                                                   NAZEER
```

BINT MOUNA was dam of **IBN ANTAR** 1964 sired by **ANTAR** and exported to USA in 1964.
DALAL was dam of **GAMIL MANIAL** 1912 sired by **SAKLAWI II**.
LUBNA was dam of **SULTAN** 1961 sired by **SAMEH** and exported to USA.
MABROUKA was dam of **MORAFIC** 1956 sired by **NAZEER** and exported to USA 1965.
MONIET EL NEFOUS was dam of **TUHOTMOS** 1962 sired by **EL SAREEI** and exported to USA.
MONIET EL NEFOUS was dam of **IBN MONIET EL NEFOUS** 1964 sired by **MORAFIC** and exported to USA.
MONIET EL NEFOUS was dam of **SOUFIAN** 1968 sired by **ALAA EL DIN** and exported to USA 1968.
MONIET EL NEFOUS was dam of **FAKHER EL DIN** 1960 sired by **NAZEER** and exported to USA 1967.

M11 RAZIEH (BINT RISSALA)

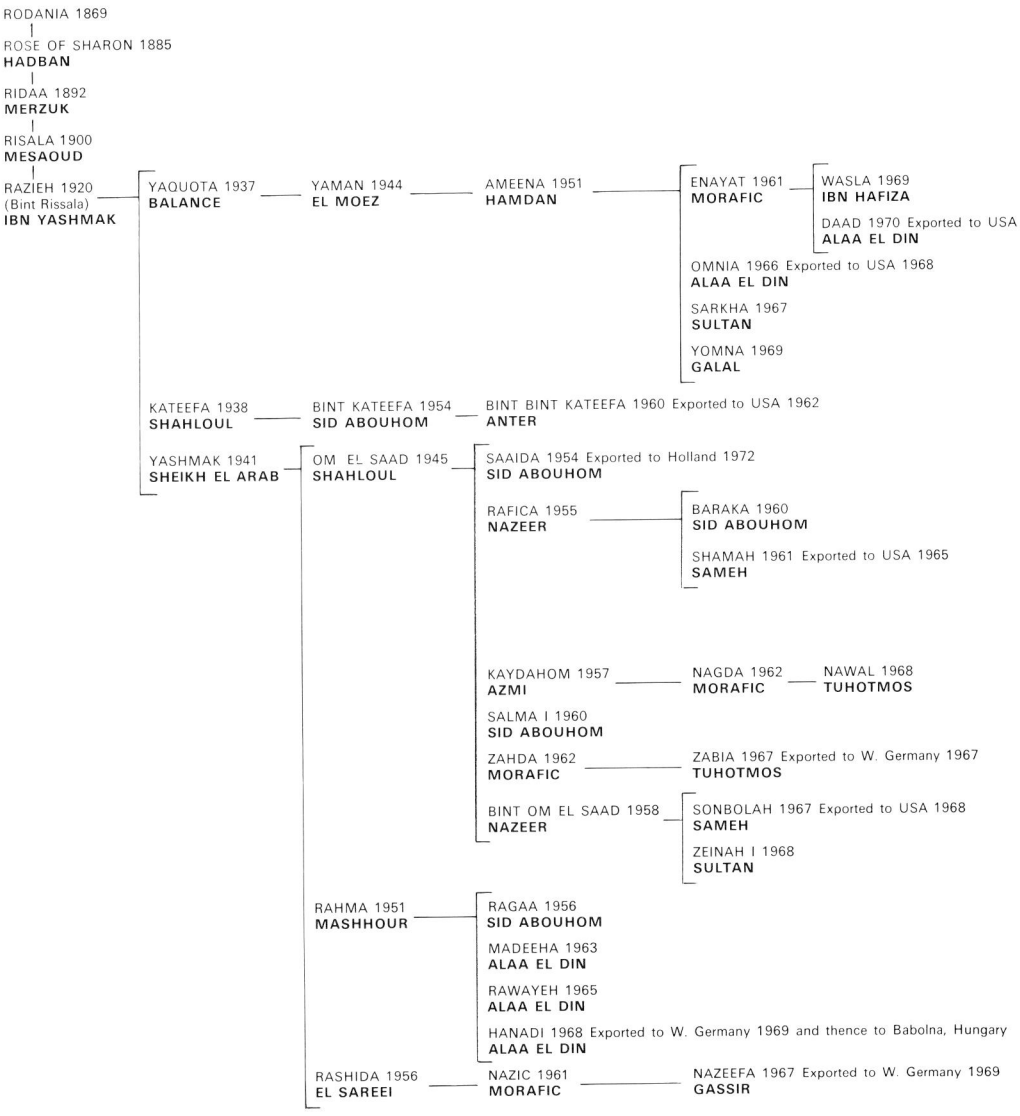

RODANIA 1869
|
ROSE OF SHARON 1885
HADBAN
|
RIDAA 1892
MERZUK
|
RISALA 1900
MESAOUD
|
RAZIEH 1920 ── YAQUOTA 1937 ── YAMAN 1944 ── AMEENA 1951 ── ENAYAT 1961 ── WASLA 1969
(Bint Rissala)   **BALANCE**   **EL MOEZ**   **HAMDAN**   **MORAFIC**   **IBN HAFIZA**
IBN YASHMAK
                                                                                   DAAD 1970 Exported to USA
                                                                                   ALAA EL DIN

                                                                 OMNIA 1966 Exported to USA 1968
                                                                 ALAA EL DIN

                                                                 SARKHA 1967
                                                                 SULTAN

                                                                 YOMNA 1969
                                                                 GALAL

            KATEEFA 1938 ── BINT KATEEFA 1954 ── BINT BINT KATEEFA 1960 Exported to USA 1962
            SHAHLOUL   **SID ABOUHOM**   **ANTER**

            YASHMAK 1941 ── OM EL SAAD 1945 ── SAAIDA 1954 Exported to Holland 1972
            SHEIKH EL ARAB **SHAHLOUL**   **SID ABOUHOM**

                                              RAFICA 1955 ── BARAKA 1960
                                              NAZEER   **SID ABOUHOM**

                                                             SHAMAH 1961 Exported to USA 1965
                                                             SAMEH

                                              KAYDAHOM 1957 ── NAGDA 1962 ── NAWAL 1968
                                              AZMI   **MORAFIC**   **TUHOTMOS**

                                              SALMA I 1960
                                              SID ABOUHOM

                                              ZAHDA 1962 ── ZABIA 1967 Exported to W. Germany 1967
                                              MORAFIC   **TUHOTMOS**

                                              BINT OM EL SAAD 1958 ── SONBOLAH 1967 Exported to USA 1968
                                              NAZEER   **SAMEH**

                                                                       ZEINAH I 1968
                                                                       SULTAN

            RAHMA 1951 ── RAGAA 1956
            MASHHOUR   **SID ABOUHOM**

                           MADEEHA 1963
                           ALAA EL DIN

                           RAWAYEH 1965
                           ALAA EL DIN

                           HANADI 1968 Exported to W. Germany 1969 and thence to Babolna, Hungary
                           ALAA EL DIN

            RASHIDA 1956 ── NAZIC 1961 ── NAZEEFA 1967 Exported to W. Germany 1969
            EL SAREEI   **MORAFIC**   **GASSIR**

BINT KATEEFA was dam of **KAYSOON** 1958 sired by **NAZEER** and exported to W. Germany 1963.
BINT KATEEFA was dam of **FARAG** 1962 sired by **MORAFIC** exported to Hungary 1969 and thence to W. Germany.
BINT OM EL SAAD was dam of **SANAD** 1962 sired by **AMRULLA** exported and to USA.
ENAYAT was dam of **SAKR** 1968 sired by **SULTAN** and exported to USA 1968.
KAYDAHOM was dam of **THABIT** 1964 sired by **ALAA EL DIN** and exported to USA 1966.
RAFICA was dam of **REFKY** 1963 sired by **MORAFIC** and exported to USA 1965.
YASHMAK was dam of **RASHAD** 1955 sired by **NAZEER** and exported to USA 1958.
YASHMAK was dam of **NISR** 1957 sired by **EL SAREEI** and exported to Yemen.

M12 RISAMA (BINT RIYALA)

RODANIA 1869
|
ROSE OF SHARON 1885
HADBAN
|
RIDAA 1892
MERZUK
|
RIYALA 1905
ASTRALED
|
RISAMA 1920 — BINT BINT RIYALA 1924 — MALAKA 1941 — SAMIA 1952 — BINT SAMIA 1957 — *NOHA sold to USA 1970.
(Bint Riyala) **GAMIL MANIAL** **KHEIR** **NAZEER** **EL SAREEI**
NADIR

                 Note: MALAKA was dam of **AZMI** (Nahr El Nil) 1954   *NOHA 1958 — SET ABOUHOM 1962 — NESMA 1969
                 sired by **SID ABOUHOM** and exported to Russia 1958.   **MASHHOUR**   **ALAA EL DIN**   **GASSIR**

                                                                    HEKMAT 1961 Exported to USA 1965
                                                                   ANTER

                                                                   SAGDA 1966 Exported to USA 1968
                                                                  ANTER

                                MAMLOUKA 1953 — BINT MAMLOUKA 1959
                                NAZEER   **MASHHOUR**

                                                           SET EL WADI 1962
                                                           EL SAREEI

                                                           FIFI 1963 — SENDIBAD 1968
                                                          ANTER   **SULTAN**

                                                                          FARHA 1970
                                                                          GALAL

                                                          FAWKIA 1965 Exported to USA 1966
                                                          SAMEH

                                                          MOMTAZA 1967 Exported to Hungary 1969 thence to W. Germany
                                                          SAMEH

                              NAZEERA 1954 — BINT NAZEERA 1858
                              NAZEER   **GASSIR**

                                                HAMDIA 1959 Exported to USA 1963
                                                ANTER

                                              AMANI 1962 — MAWAHEB 1969
                                              EL SAREEI   **IBN HAFIZA**

                                              ROMANA II 1963 Exported to USA 1966
                                              SAMEH

                                              OMAYMA 1964
                                              SAMEH

                                              KAWMIA 1965
                                              ANTER

                                              BINT NAZEERA 1968 Exported to Hungary 1969 thence to W
                                              ANTER   Germany

                                              HEBAH 1970
                                              IBN HAFIZA

                              SALOMI 1957 Exported to USA 1961
                              EL SAREEI

M13 EL DAHMA

EL DAHMA
|
OBEYA 1894
KOHEILAN EL MOSSEN
|
BINT OBEYA 1912 — SABAH 1920 — BINT SABAH 1925 — LAYLA 1929 — NUZHA 1935
EL HALABI   **MABROUK MANIAL**   **KASMEYN**   **IBN RABDAN**   **MANSOUR**
                                                                            Sold to Trouncer

                                                      KOMEIRA 1937 — KAMAR 1953 — HAGIR 1957 — ZARAFA 1961
                                                      NABRAS   **NAZEER**   **EL SAREEI**   **SAMEH**

                                                      TURRA 1946   KAHRAMANA 1966
                                                      BALANCE   Exported to USA 1968
                                                                             ANTER

                                                                               TAMRIA 1967
                                                                               Exported to Hungary 1967
                                                                               TUHOTMOS

                                    BINT BINT SABAH 1930   HAKIMA 1970
                                    Sold to Henry Babson USA 1932   **FAYEK**
                                    BAIYAD

                                  BUKRA 1942 — BINT BUKRA 1957 — NAGWA 1961 — NADEEMAH 1966
                                    SHAHLOUL   **NAZEER**   **SAMEH**   **AMRULLA**

                                                      HUSNIA 1959
                                                      Sold to USA 1965
                                                      NAZEER

                   EL YATIMA 1931 — ZAHRA 1938 — AMARA 1945
                   IBN RABDAN   **HAMRAN II**   **KHEIR**

EUROPE

RUSSIA

The influence of Crabbet blood in this country derives principally from Lady Wentworth's sale to the Russian Government in 1936.

These were not the first purchases made from Crabbet. In 1882 Pharaoh was sold to Count Joseph Potocki who three years later resold him to the Imperial Russian Stud. Some time later the Blunts made enquiries with a view to his repurchase but were informed by Potocki that if the opportunity ever arose he would buy Pharaoh for his own use.

In 1899 de Sdanovitch bought five horses at the Blunts' summer auction – Dijleh, Dinarzade, Fezara, Jeyneyna and Naaman – and afterwards the Ali Pasha mare Sobha, then aged twenty. In 1900 Count Stroganoff bought Makbula and in 1903 the great Mesaoud was sold to the Kleniewski Stud. Unfortunately none of these horses, nor any of their descendants, are known to have survived the First World War and the Revolution.

The Russian sale of 1936 comprised six stallions and nineteen mares for breeding purposes. A list of the consignment is now given.

STALLIONS

FERHAN	1925	Raswan	Fejr
JERUAN	1920	Nureddin II	Rose of Persia
NASEEM	1922	Skowronek	Nasra
RASEEM	1922	Rasim	Rim
RYTHAM	1929	Shareer	Rythma
SHAREER	1923	Nureddin II	Selima

MARES

BISARIEH	1928	Naseem	Battla
FLORENCIA	1936	Faris	Rissalma
GREY CRABBET	1935	Raseem	Silver Fire

NAHARINA	1927	Nureddin II	Nasira
NAJERA	1930	Rahal	Nasirieh
NASHISHA	1920	Rasim	Nasra
NASIFA	1924	Skowronek	Nasra
NERAIDA	1928	Nureddin II	Nasifa
NISSAMA	1936	*Rissam	Neraida
RASHIFA	1931	Shareer	Rishafa
RIMULA	1928	Nureddin II	Rimini
RISSALMA	1932	Shareer	Rissla
RIXALINA	1929	Raseem	Rissla
ROSE OF AFRICA	1929	Nureddin II	Jalila
RUANDA	1926	Najib	Rythma
RUELLIA	1926	Nureddin II	Riyala
RYAMA	1931	Nureddin II	Dafina
SILKA	1929	Nureddin II	Somra
STAR OF THE HILLS	1927	Raswan	Selima

*Incorrectly transliterated in the Russian Arab Stud Book as Raseem.

The selection process applied by the Russians at the Tersk Stud has always been very strict. Their overall breeding programme consists of achieving a balanced admixture between certain proven families and has led to the total rejection of any unwanted lines. Of the 1936 batch from Crabbet only one stallion, Naseem, and five mares, Rissalma, Ruanda, Ruellia, Ryama and Star of the Hills, have established lines that are extant today. Of the others, Ferhan, Rytham and Rixalina are found in indirect lines. This treatment is applied impartially to all imported horses and its results demonstrate the importance of Crabbet blood, which even now emerges rarely as less than 25 per cent and often as much as 75 per cent.

The most influential of the Crabbet horses have been Naseem, Rissalma, and Star of the Hills.

Naseem (table s19) was used at Tersk for seventeen years, many of them as senior sire. Nineteen of his daughters were incorporated into the stud, a large number bearing in mind the selection process. The most important are probably Nitochka (out of Taraszcza and a full sister of Negatiw), Nagrada (out of Rixalina) and Naturalistka (out of Rissalma).

Naseem's sons used at Tersk were Nomer (out of Oaza), Negatiw, and Normativ (out of Mulatka).

Nomer sired two mares that were retained, Nera and Napraslina. Nera was the daughter of Rezeda II, by Rytham out of Ruellia, and in 1957 produced Nerpa (by Rissalma's son Priboj), through whom the Ruellia line continues to this day. Napraslina (out of Plotka) is probably better known than her half-sister. A lovely grey, she was exported to England in 1965 and her blood is carried by her daughters Nepriadwa (by Pomeranets) in Russia, Nasmeshka (by Semen) in England and Naadirah (by Aswan) in Australia. At Tersk, Nepriadwa's son Naftalin (by the Priboj son Topol), foaled in 1977, became one of the most significant sires in the 80s and his offspring have excelled at the racetrack.

Though Normativ was used for six years at stud, his blood has not survived to the present day. It is to his paternal half-brother Negatiw that the credit for the succession of Naseem's line must be given.

Negatiw stood for eleven years at Tersk and during that period sired 105 Arabian foals. This very high figure is surprising since he was standing at the same time as Priboj and Rixalina's son Korej were senior sires.
Negatiw had only two daughters of note at Tersk, Karmen and Linka, and it is through his six sons that his reputation has been ensured. These were Nabor(out of Lagodna), Nimrod (out of Mulatka), Pinsk (out of Privilegia), Patron (out of Provincia and not be confused with the elegant Patron by Aswan out of Podruga) and the full brothers Suvenir and Salon (out of Sonata).

Salon has been widely used with a large group of daughters retained as broodmares on a scale rivalling that of his grandsire Naseem. Four of his sons have been used at Tersk: the full brothers Muscat and Moment (out of the Priboj daughter Malpia) and the full brothers Posol and Parus (out of Palba, a granddaughter of Priboj). Of these, Muscat and Moment were by far the more influential. Both were exported to the United States (Moment detouring *via* Bulgaria), where their influence has been even greater than at Tersk. Another Salon son Namiet (1969) was exported to Poland in 1973 and used at stud at Janow Podlaski until 1976 when he was transferred to Michalow stud and from there *via* Holland to the United States. Namiet's dam Naturshitsa traces to both Naseem and Rissalma. Salon's last son to be used in Russia was Nespokoini (1972, out of the Naseem granddaughter Novinka) who was used as a sire for the small Arabian herd at Stavropol Stud in the Eighties.

Salon was sold to Germany in 1971, where his value was not appreciated. Towards the end of his life he was sold again, this time to the United States. His American-bred inbred son Ponomarev is emerging as one of the most successful sires of show mares in Europe in this decade.

Negatiw himself was sold to Poland in 1962 at the age of seventeen, where he was possibly even more influential than in Russia: his impact there is discussed under the section on that country.

Naseem's only contemporary rival at Tersk was the French stallion Kann. Most of Kann's produce were of purely French bloodlines, but when mated with Rixalina he sired a noteworthy stallion, the chestnut Korej. In 1954, Korej was crossed with Nagrada, Rixalina's daughter by Naseem, to produce the predominantly Crabbet stallion Kankan who stood at Tersk throughout the Sixties.

The dominance of Naseem in Russian bloodlines must not be allowed to overshadow the importance of other Crabbet-bred horses. Particular mention should be made of Rodania's descendants Rixalina, Rissalma, and Ruanda, and of the family established by Star of the Hills.

Rixalina is significant as the dam of Nagrada and of the stallion Korej, mentioned above. Korej's son Mak established a line through his son Kumir, whose dam Kapella was descended from Rissalma and Rixalina. Though Kumir died prematurely, the continuation of his line is ensured through his sons Mukomol (1979), Pakistan (1980), and Vatican (1983).

Mukomol, out of the Salon granddaughter Malinka, was a chief sire at Tersk during the Eighties: his progeny includes the winner of the 1992 Russian Derby, Naum. Pakistan, descended from Star of the Hills in his dam line, was used at Tersk during the late Eighties, where he sired the international show winner Bespechni. He was sold to Abu Dhabi in 1992 for a very high sum. Vatican, a major winner of races in Russia and Poland, was leased to Holland and has emerged as a highly successful sire in the Nineties.

Rissalma has perpetuated the Rodania line through two daughters, Naturalistka (by Naseem) and Praga (by Patent). Naturalistka's daughter Pienoczka was sold to Poland and established a branch of the family there through her Nabor daughter Planeta. In Russia, Rissalma's influence lies mainly through her son Priboj (by Piolun) who stood at Tersk from 1948 to 1958 and is credited with the massive total of 203 progeny, of whom 48 were retained for stud purposes. Four of his sons were used at stud, of whom Krepish (out of Knopka) left nothing. Pietuszok (out of Taktika, tracing to Star of the Hills in the female line) was an important broodmare sire in Poland and was later sold to America; Pomeranets (out of Mammona) was an excellent sire of broodmares at Tersk in the Fifties and Sixties. Priboj's male line was continued at Tersk by Pietuszok's full

above Rixalina (Raseem – Rissla)
below Rissalma (Shareer – Rissla)

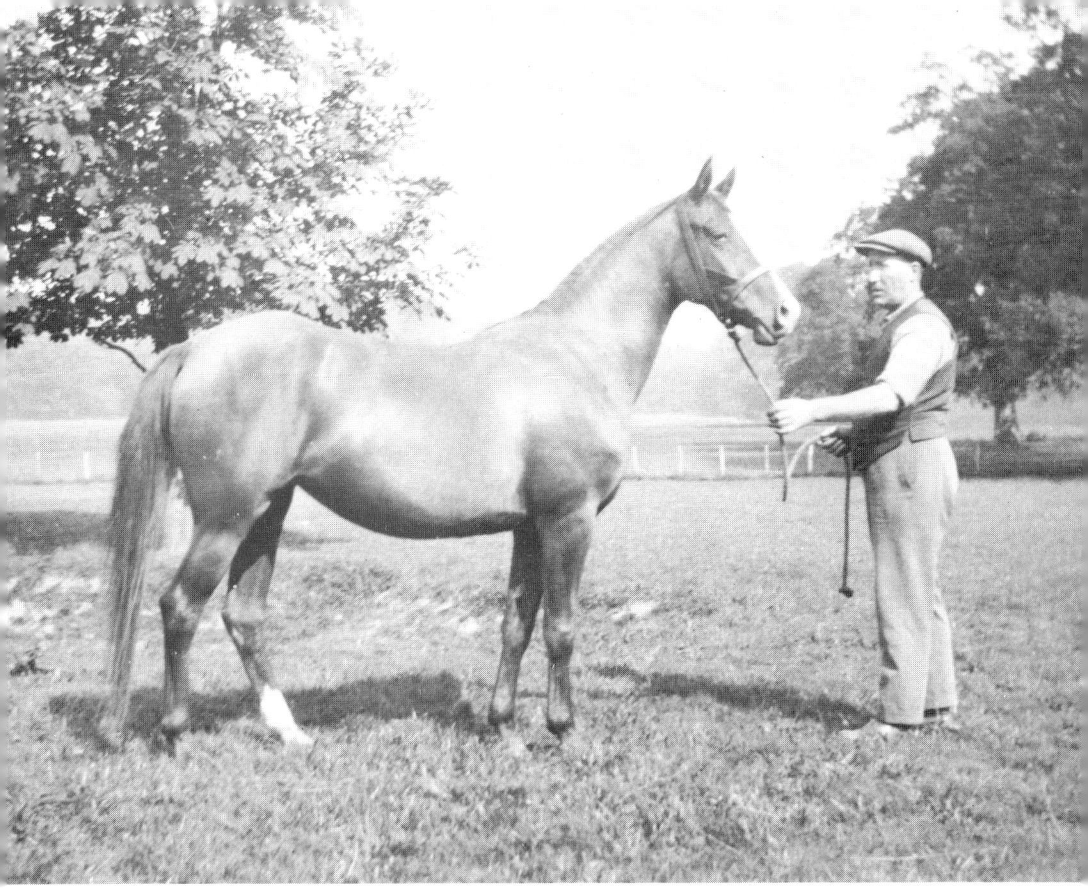

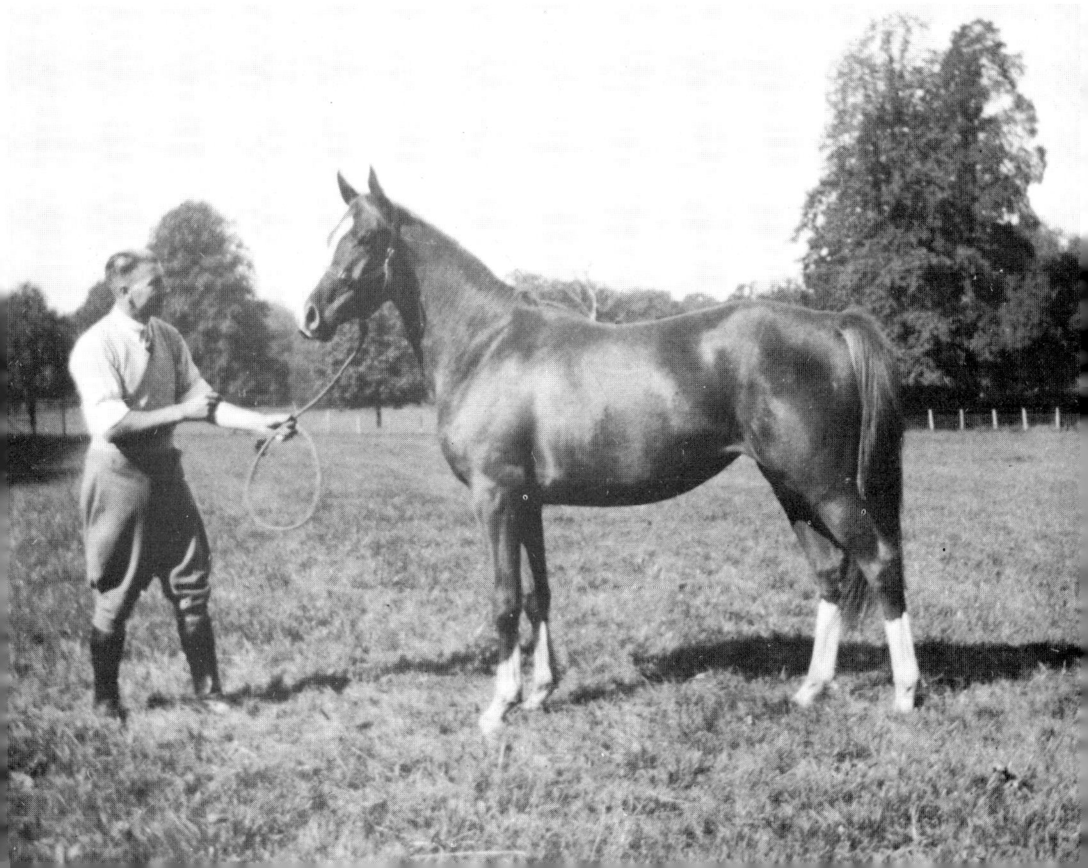

brother Topol, who sired several fine producing daughters and the stallion Naftalin (see above).

Four Priboj daughters were sold to Poland by the Russians; in 1956 Piewica and Potencia, both of whom also trace to Star of the Hills, and in 1958 Porfira and Prowierka. Piewica established a most successful line in Poland whose best known descendants include the glamorous multi-champion mare Pilarka, who also traces to Star of the Hills, Kazmeen, and Bint Riyala through her Russian-bred sire Palas. More on this branch may be found in the Polish section.

Ruanda, out of the Berk daughter Rythma (full sister to Rissla, the dam of Rissalma), founded a family at Tersk through her daughter Raduga (by Rytham). Raduga had two offspring entered as broodmares, Kreatura (by Kann) and Otrada (by Ofir). Kreatura's line has flourished through her Priboj daughter Plaksa and Plaksa's daughters Perikola (by Knippel), Prisma (by Arax) and Passia (by Salon). The stock of all these mares has been retained at Tersk.

Another line from Rodania at Tersk is through the stallion Knippel (by Korej out of Parfumeria, by Piolun out of Florencia) who is line bred to Rissla and with two crosses to her also. Knippel had eleven daughters kept as broodmares at Tersk and held the 7000 metre speed record in Russia. He also sired two record-breaking fillies, Perikola, holder of the 1400 and 1600 metre records, and Monogramma (out of Monopolia), holder of the 1500 metre two-year-old record. The line of Rissla occurs in the pedigrees of many race and record winners throughout the world. This is particularly so in Russia where the progeny of the Rissla grandson Priboj hold almost half the total of the Russian Arabian speed records. Priboj is, moreover, the sire of the dams of several more speed record holders. It may be argued that athletic ability has been achieved at the expense of Arabian characteristics but this is not supported by the evidence in Russia. Between 1954 and 1975 Priboj and his son Pomeranets sired the winners of 16 out of 37 show awards listed for the period. During this time their produce won 23 out of a total of 44 speed records.

One of these records was held by Priboj's son Sport (out of Soljanka), whose son Neron (out of Nitochka by Naseem) was exported to West Germany where he became well known for winning show-jumping contests against warmblood horses. Neron's son Susdal (out of Salomea by Sport), who is inbred to Sport, in 1987 established the world record time for 2200 metres in Holland. It may also be mentioned in passing that Pomeranets' partbred son Hockey II sired the Olympic competitor Almox

above Star of the Hills (Raswan – Selima)
below Ruellia (Nureddin II – Riyala)

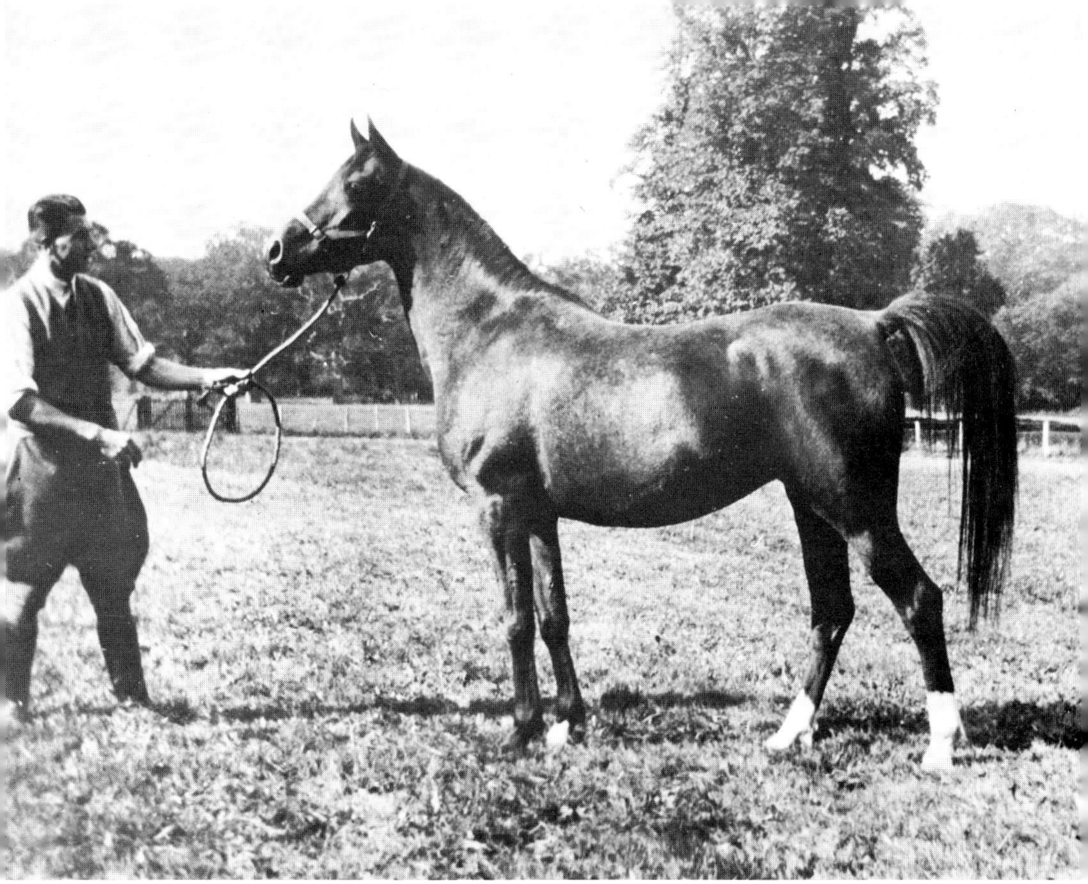

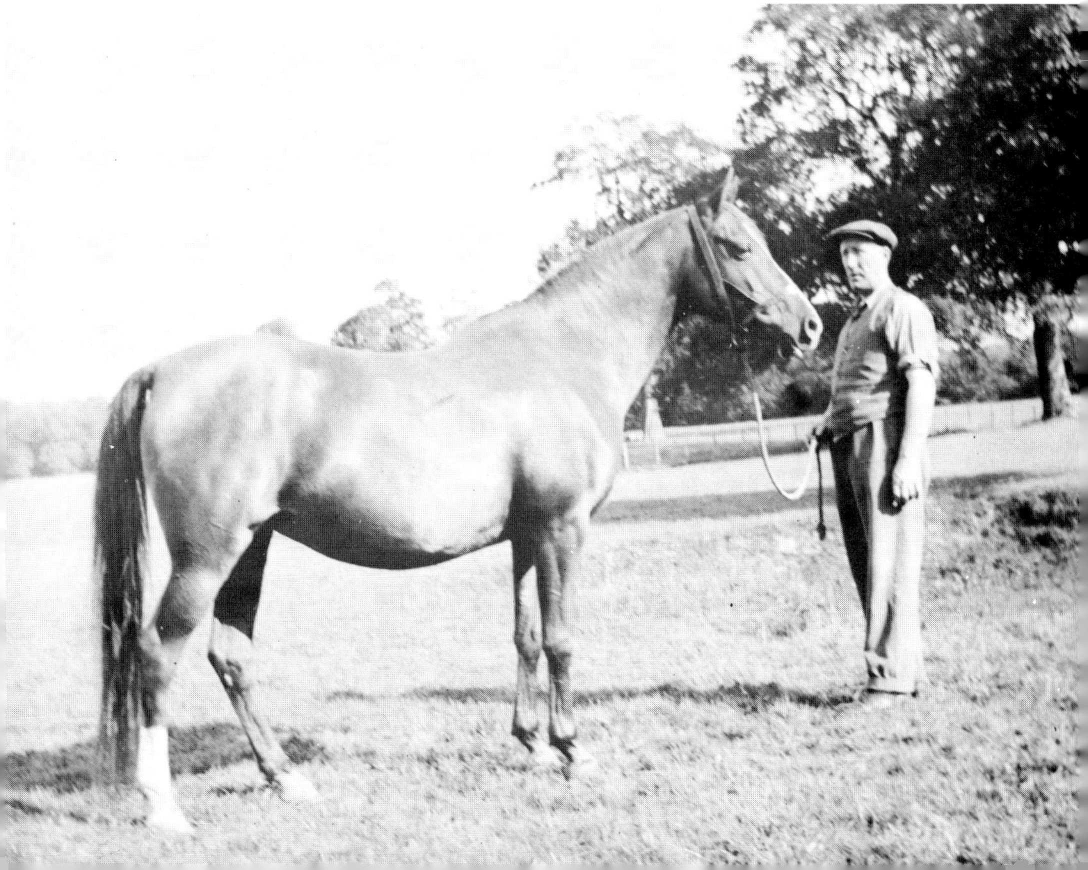

Prints J, who in the early Nineties became one of the most sought-after sires in the breeding of show jumpers in Europe.

The remaining Crabbet import to be discussed is Star of the Hills, the great-granddaughter of the Abbas Pasha mare Sobha. The line became established with Star of the Hills' granddaughter Taktika (by Taki Pan) and Taktika's daughters Platina (by Priboj), Ptashka (by Priboj) and Trapecia (by Pomeranets); and with her great-grandsons (also by Priboj), Pietuszok and Topol. Platina's line becomes multi-branched with her daughters Panel, Ptichka, Panama and Panorama. With the exception of Panama, who was exported to Holland in 1971, all these horses have founded families at Tersk.

The line from Ptashka is especially strong, with seven daughters kept as broodmares. Trapecia had two daughters at Tersk while another one, Tiwiriada, went to Poland and a son, Tamerlan, went to Holland and later to the United States. One particularly notable fact about the line of Star of the Hills is its ability to produce top class stallions and sires: besides Topol, these include Palas (Aswan/Panel) in Poland, Plakat (Aswan/Pchelka) in Holland, Potomak (Muscat/Panomara), Pakistan (Kumir/Panagia), Balaton (Menes/Panagia) and Aspirant (Naslednik/Panagia) at Tersk; Peleng (Nabeg/Palmira) at Tersk and in Holland, Paks 7 (Aswan/Pandora) in Italy, Pesniar (Nabeg/Pesnia) at Tersk and in the USA, Pesennik (Kumir/Pesnia) in Poland, and Top (Pesniar/Trapecia) in Germany.

Two other stallions with Crabbet blood are worthy of remark: Nil and Aswan. These horses were presented to Russia by President Nasser in 1958 and 1964 respectively. The pedigree of Nil (by Sid Abouhom out of Malaka) traces directly in tail female line to the Crabbet mare Riyala and to other Blunt horses through his paternal grandmother Layla. Unfortunately Nil died leaving only sixteen descendants. His son Naslednik (out of Nitochka and therefore a grandson of Naseem) was used widely as his successor at stud. Four of his six daughters were also retained as broodmares, of which the most influential were Panel (out of Platina) and Naina (out of Nomenklatura). Panel produced Palas (by Aswan), exported to Poland and the most succesful sire there in the Eighties, and Naina produced – both by Aswan – Nevada, one of the most influential broodmares in Germany, and the international show winner and sire Nrav (Narav Ibn Aswan).

Aswan was by Nazeer out of Yosreia. Nazeer's dam Bint Samiha was by the Crabbet-bred Kasmeyn. Yosreia traces through her sire to both

Kasmeyn and Bint Roga, and through her dam, Hind, to Rustem. Aswan was used extensively at Tersk. Of his sons, the full brothers Mashuk and Maskat (out of Malutka by Salon) have been retained as his successors. His offspring, both male and female, may be found throughout the world, especially in the United States of America.

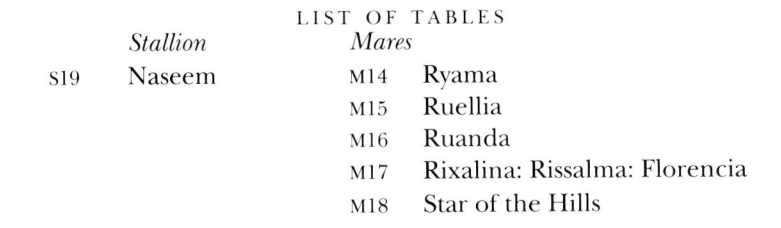

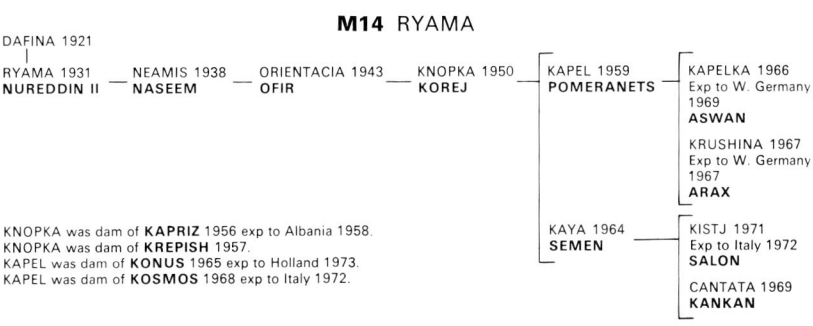

LIST OF TABLES

	Stallion	Mares	
S19	Naseem	M14	Ryama
		M15	Ruellia
		M16	Ruanda
		M17	Rixalina: Rissalma: Florencia
		M18	Star of the Hills

M14 RYAMA

DAFINA 1921
|
RYAMA 1931 — NEAMIS 1938 — ORIENTACIA 1943 — KNOPKA 1950 — KAPEL 1959 — KAPELKA 1966
NUREDDIN II   NASEEM   OFIR   KOREJ   POMERANETS   Exp to W. Germany 1969
                                                                              ASWAN

                                                                              KRUSHINA 1967
                                                                              Exp to W. Germany 1967
                                                                              ARAX

KNOPKA was dam of **KAPRIZ** 1956 exp to Albania 1958.
KNOPKA was dam of **KREPISH** 1957.   KAYA 1964 — KISTJ 1971
KAPEL was dam of **KONUS** 1965 exp to Holland 1973.   SEMEN   Exp to Italy 1972
KAPEL was dam of **KOSMOS** 1968 exp to Italy 1972.   SALON

                                                                          CANTATA 1969
                                                                          KANKAN

M15 RUELLIA

RODANIA 1869
|
ROSE OF SHARON 1885
HADBAN
|
RIDAA 1892
MERZUK
|
RIYALA 1905
ASTRALED
|
RUELLIA 1926 — REZEDA II 1939 — NERA 1948 — NERPA 1957 — NASTAVNITSA 1962 — NAZRA 1967
NUREDDIN II   RYTHAM   NOMER   PRIBOJ   ARAX   SPORT

                                                                              SOLOMKA 1971
                                                                              Exp to France 1973
                                                                              SALON

NERA was dam of **NAKAL** 1968 Exp to Italy 1972.   NARGIS 1970
                                                                              Exp to Holland 1972
                                                                              KANKAN

                                             NEVZGODA 1964 Exp to UK 1965
                                             ARAX

                                             NINI 1968 Exp to W. Germany 1970
                                             ASWAN

                                             NEPOSLUSHNAJA 1971 Exp to France 1973
                                             SEMEN

                                             NINEVIA 1973 Exp to W. Germany 1975
                                             NABEG

M16 RUANDA

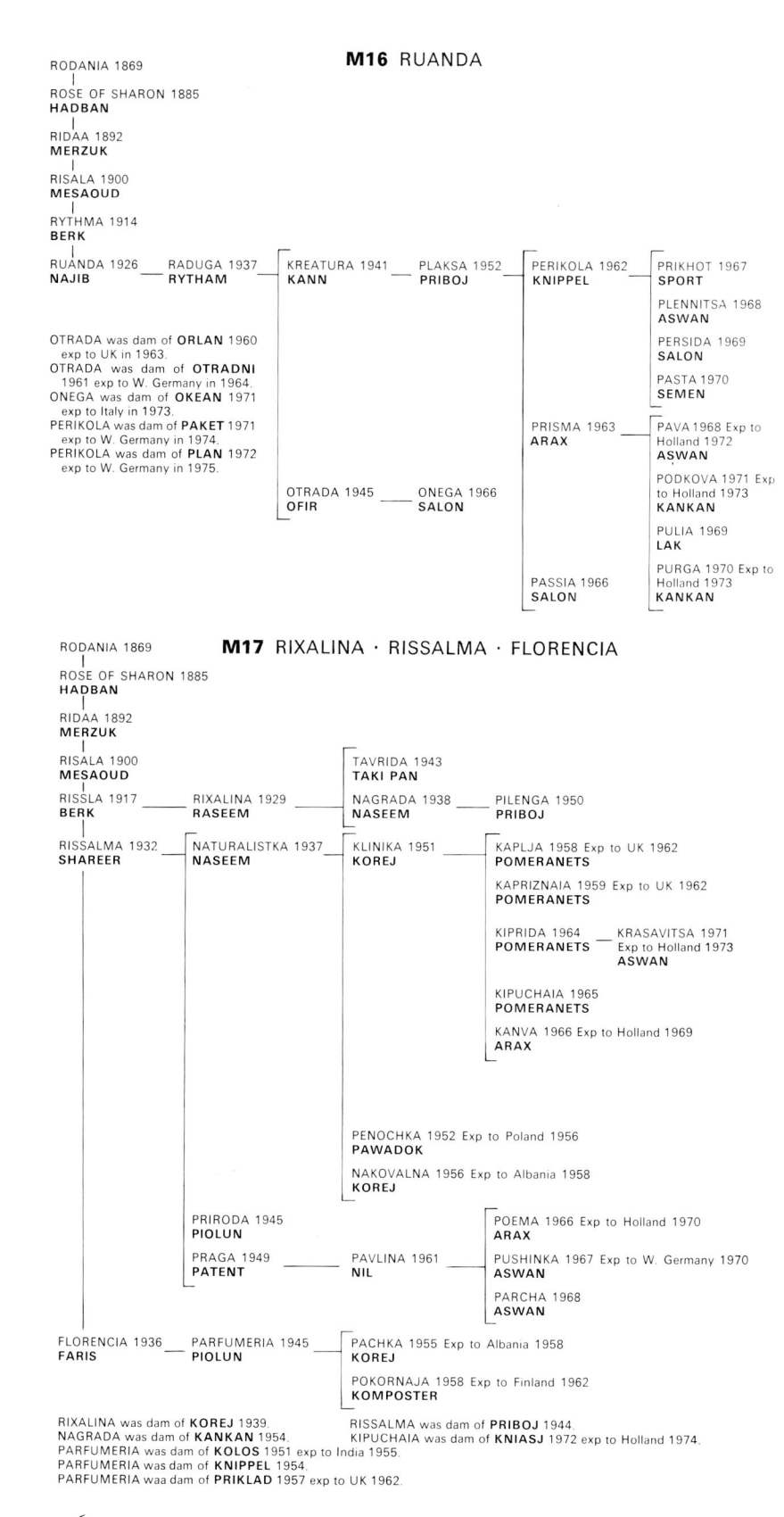

RODANIA 1869
|
ROSE OF SHARON 1885
HADBAN
|
RIDAA 1892
MERZUK
|
RISALA 1900
MESAOUD
|
RYTHMA 1914
BERK
|
RUANDA 1926 ─── RADUGA 1937 ─── KREATURA 1941 ─── PLAKSA 1952 ─── PERIKOLA 1962 ─── PRIKHOT 1967
NAJIB **RYTHAM** **KANN** **PRIBOJ** **KNIPPEL** **SPORT**

PLENNITSA 1968
ASWAN

PERSIDA 1969
SALON

PASTA 1970
SEMEN

OTRADA was dam of **ORLAN** 1960 exp to UK in 1963.
OTRADA was dam of **OTRADNI** 1961 exp to W. Germany in 1964.
ONEGA was dam of **OKEAN** 1971 exp to Italy in 1973.
PERIKOLA was dam of **PAKET** 1971 exp to W. Germany in 1974.
PERIKOLA was dam of **PLAN** 1972 exp to W. Germany in 1975.

PRISMA 1963 ─── PAVA 1968 Exp to
ARAX Holland 1972
ASWAN

PODKOVA 1971 Exp to Holland 1973
KANKAN

OTRADA 1945 ─── ONEGA 1966
OFIR **SALON**

PULIA 1969
LAK

PURGA 1970 Exp to Holland 1973
PASSIA 1966 **KANKAN**
SALON

M17 RIXALINA · RISSALMA · FLORENCIA

RODANIA 1869
|
ROSE OF SHARON 1885
HADBAN
|
RIDAA 1892
MERZUK
|
RISALA 1900
MESAOUD
|
RISSLA 1917 ─── RIXALINA 1929
BERK **RASEEM**

TAVRIDA 1943
TAKI PAN

NAGRADA 1938 ─── PILENGA 1950
NASEEM **PRIBOJ**

RISSALMA 1932 ─── NATURALISTKA 1937 ─── KLINIKA 1951 ─── KAPLJA 1958 Exp to UK 1962
SHAREER **NASEEM** **KOREJ** **POMERANETS**

KAPRIZNAIA 1959 Exp to UK 1962
POMERANETS

KIPRIDA 1964 ─── KRASAVITSA 1971
POMERANETS Exp to Holland 1973
ASWAN

KIPUCHAIA 1965
POMERANETS

KANVA 1966 Exp to Holland 1969
ARAX

PENOCHKA 1952 Exp to Poland 1956
PAWADOK

NAKOVALNA 1956 Exp to Albania 1958
KOREJ

PRIRODA 1945
PIOLUN

POEMA 1966 Exp to Holland 1970
ARAX

PRAGA 1949 ─── PAVLINA 1961 ─── PUSHINKA 1967 Exp to W. Germany 1970
PATENT **NIL** **ASWAN**

PARCHA 1968
ASWAN

FLORENCIA 1936 ─── PARFUMERIA 1945 ─── PACHKA 1955 Exp to Albania 1958
FARIS **PIOLUN** **KOREJ**

POKORNAJA 1958 Exp to Finland 1962
KOMPOSTER

RIXALINA was dam of **KOREJ** 1939.   RISSALMA was dam of **PRIBOJ** 1944.
NAGRADA was dam of **KANKAN** 1954.   KIPUCHAIA was dam of **KNIASJ** 1972 exp to Holland 1974.
PARFUMERIA was dam of **KOLOS** 1951 exp to India 1955.
PARFUMERIA was dam of **KNIPPEL** 1954.
PARFUMERIA waa dam of **PRIKLAD** 1957 exp to UK 1962.

M18 STAR OF THE HILLS

SOBHA 1879
|
SELMA 1894
|
AHMAR
|
SELIMA 1908
|
ASTRALED
|
STAR OF THE HILLS 1927 — KRONA 1939 — TAKTIKA 1943 — PLATINA 1950 — PANEL 1960 — PCHELKA 1964
RASWAN   KANN   TAKI PAN   PRIBOJ   NIL   KNIPPEL

                                PRIVICHIKA 1945   POVEST 1966
                                PLOMBIR   Exp to W. Germany 1969
                                                                             SALON

                                                                             POPRINGUNIA 1969
                                                                             POMERANETS

                                                                             PAUZA 1971
                                                                             ASWAN

KRONA was dam of **OPTIK** 1944.
TAKTIKA was dam of **PIETUSZOK** 1954 exp to Poland 1956 and thence to Canada in 1973.
TAKTIKA was dam of **TOPOL** 1958.
TRAPECIA was dam of **TALANT** 1965.
TRAPECIA was dam of **TAMERLAN** 1967 exp to Holland 1972.
PANEL was dam of **PROCENT** 1970 exp to Holland 1974.
PANEL was dam of **PALAS** 1968 exp to Poland 1974.
PANAMA was dam of **POKLON** 1971 exp to Holland 1971.
PCHELKA was dam of **PAMIR** 1969 exp to Czechoslovakia 1973.
PCHELKA was dam of **PLAKAT** 1970 exp to Holland 1973.
PCHELKA was dam of **PASYNOK II** 1972 exp to W. Germany 1975.
PLATINA was dam of **PEGAS** 1967.
PLATINA was dam of **PIRS** 1968 exp to Holland 1972.

                                                PTICHKA 1962
                                                KNIPPEL

                                                PANAMA 1964   PANIKA 1969
                                                Exp to Holland 1971   Exp to W. Germany 1971
                                                ARAX   KANKAN

                                                                      PALITRA 1970
                                                                      Exp to W. Germany 1972
                                                                      SALON

                                                PANORAMA 1966   PASTUCHKA 1971
                                                ASWAN   Exp to Italy 1972
                                                                      SEMEN

                                                                      PESENKA 1972
                                                                      SALON

                                                PLIASKA 1970
                                                Exp to France 1972
                                                SEMEN

                                PTASHKA 1953   PUSTINIA 1965   PEIZAGE 1970
                                PRIBOJ   SALON   Exp to Italy 1972
                                                                      KANKAN

                                                PANTERA 1966
                                                ASWAN

                                                PALMIRA 1967   PRISTAN 1972
                                                SALON   ASWAN

                                                PALLADA 1968
                                                SALON

                                                PESNIA 1969
                                                ASWAN

                                                PARKETNAIA 1971
                                                ASWAN

                                TRAPECIA 1961   TIVERIADA 1966
                                POMERANETS   Exp to Poland 1968
                                                ASWAN

                                                TIEN 1968   TESEMKA 1972
                                POTENCIA 1952   ARAX   SPORT
                                Exp to Poland 1956
                                PRIBOJ   TOSKA 1969
                                                ARAX

S19 NASEEM

SKOWRONEK 1908(9)
NASEEM 1922
NASRA

NOMER 1943
OAZA

NEGATIW 1945
Exp to Poland 1962
TARASZCZSA

NABOR 1950
Exp to Poland 1957
and thence to USA in
1963
LAGODNA

KING 1956
KOMPOSITIA

NIMROD 1952
MULATKA

PINSK 1956
PRIVILEGIA

PATRON 1957
PROVINCIA

SUVENIR 1957
SONATA

SALON 1959
Exp to W. Germany 1971
SONATA

KORALL 1966
Exp to W. Germany 1972
KAPELLA

NIKEL 1947
KONFEDERACJA

NAMET II 1947
TARASZCZA

NORMATIV 1947
MULATKA

NEAPOL II 1948
PAPROC

NIMB 1948
MAMMONA

MUSLIN 1968
Exp to Holland 1972
MAGNOLIA

POMPEY 1967
Exp to Holland 1970
PANEL

POSOL 1967
PALBA

PILOT 1971
Exp to W. Germany
PILINKA 1975

PROMETEY 1967
Exp to Holland 1972
PTICHKA

PODSNEJNIK 1968
Exp to W. Germany 1971
PANKARTA

PROGRESS 1968 Exp to W Germany 1971
PROGRESSIA

NAMET 1969 Exp to Poland 1973
NATURSHITSA

PARNAS 1969 Exp to Italy 1971
PIKA

MOMENT 1969 Exp to Bulgaria 1972
MALPIA

MUSSON 1971 Exp to Italy 1974
MONOGRAMMA

NAL 1970 Exp to W. Germany 1972
NAGRADA

MUSCAT 1971
MALPIA

PARUS 1971 Exp to Italy 1974
PALBA

NEBOSKLON 1972
NERPA

NESPOKOINI 1972
NOVINKA

NONIUS 1972
NIAGARA

PERSTEN 1972 Exp to Holland 1974
PARCHA

POLAND

For geopolitical reasons, it is difficult to separate the start of Crabbet influence in Poland from that in Russia since a good deal of the later Crabbet blood came to Poland through Russian imports. However, there are several distinct Crabbet lines that are particular to Poland.

The first purchase from Crabbet was Pharaoh, sold in 1882 to Count Joseph Potocki, who three years later resold him to the Imperial Russian Stud. He did, however, have a number of foals for Potocki and from them indirect lines of descent continue even to this day. In 1896 Countess Branicka bought Anbar and Rishan for her stud in Russian Poland but these horses perished the following year when the stables were fired by a vengeful English groom who had been discharged for theft. The imports from Crabbet to leave the greatest mark on Polish breeding were the horses imported by Baron Bicker in the late 1920s to his wife's stud at Ujazd. These were one stallion and four mares:

RASIM	1906	Feysul	Risala
FASILA	1923	Rasim	Fejr
SARDHANA	1924	Nureddin II	Selima
RAMAYANA	1924	Nureddin II	Riyala
NITLA	1926	Nureddin II	Nashisha

Like many Polish horses, the Crabbet imports fell victim to World War II but with the exception of Nitla, their blood has survived to the present day. Ramayana's line continues *via* a detour through Tersk. In 1937 she was bred to Rasim III (by Rasim) to produce the mare Maddy, with 75 per cent Crabbet blood. In 1942 Maddy gave birth to Madila, by the Polish stallion Lowelas. During the War Madila fell first into German and then Russian hands and thereafter established another branch of the Rodania line at Tersk.

Rasim was unable to establish a sire line in Poland but is found frequently today in indirect lines. His only son to breed on was Rasim III (out of Karima), who besides Maddy, sired the stallion Rasim Pierwszy (out of Fasila, and thus inbred to Rasim) and the mare El-Zabibe, a full sister to Rasim III. Rasim Pierwszy sired Rasima (out of Sardhana), who established a flourishing family in Poland with equally active branches in Holland and Denmark.

Rasim Pierwszy and El-Zabibe are jointly responsible for perpetuating Rasim's bloodline in Poland. Bred together in 1941, they produced the bay mare Elza, who was linebred to Rasim. Elza produced a famous trio of full sisters by Witraz: Celina, Ellora, and Elzunia.

Celina was exported to England, where she was a major show ring sensation, leaving one breeding son, Chazar, in Poland. Ellora was the most important of the three for Poland: she produced the chief sires El Azrak (by Faher), sire of the even more popular Banat; El Paso (by Czort), Ellorus (by Krezus) and El Paso's full brother Elfur, who left nothing in Poland but was used as a chief sire at Tersk for some years and left some good broodmares. Ellora's daughter Eliza (by Pietuszok) produced the sire Elef (by Almifar) and the Janow broodmare Elita (by Celebes). Ellora also established a female line through her daughter Elewacja (by Celebes). Elzunia was exported to Holland but left one very influential daughter in Poland, Etna (by Faher), who must rank among Janow Podlaski's best producing mares. Her foals include the chief sires Etap (by Celebes) and Eternit (by Bandos), and the multiple champion mare Etruria (by Palas). One interesting aspect of Rasim's influence in Poland remains visible to the present day. It is not unusual for a pair of modestly marked bay Polish horses to suddenly produce a chestnut foal with more white markings than usual – an examination of the pedigree of such a foal will invariably reveal the presence of Rasim.

The influence of Fasila is impossible to separate from Rasim's since she was his daughter and her only offspring to breed on in Poland was Rasim Pierwszy. However, she also had two sons by the Polish stallion Fetysz, Sulejman (1934) and Adonah (1936), who were exported to the United States and to Germany respectively and left existing lines there.

Sardhana's importance is also difficult to quantify, as again, her one continuing line comes through a Rasim Pierwszy daughter, Rasima. This mare, who was descended from three of Baron Bicker's imports from Crabbet, produced three foals by Witraz: the mares Cesima and Rokiczana, whose lines still exist in Poland, and the stallion Rustan, who was sold to Germany and has offspring there. Cesima proved of particular importance through her daughter Zlota Iwa (by Arax) who produced Zamiec (by Czardasz), Zbroja (by Kord) and Zazula (by Negatiw). Zamiec and Zazula rank among Poland's top producing mares, while Zbroja was sold to Germany and later to Denmark and founded a very successful dam line there. Rasima's daughter by Wielki Szlem, Rega, was sold to Holland.

It is interesting to note that Sardhana, when she was sold to Poland, was in foal to Skowronek. In 1929 she foaled a filly named Uadyah, the only Skowronek foal to be born in Poland. Uadyah was not, however, used for purebred breeding.

While the Bicker imports were Poland's only direct source of Crabbet blood, more has come in from Russia. There is a branch of Rissalma's dam line through her granddaughter Pienoczka: a tail female descendant of this family, Pohaniec (Comet/Planeta) was exported to Sweden, from where his son Probat returned to Poland to become a much-used chief sire in the Eighties.

More Rissalma blood was introduced through the four daughters of Rissalma's son Priboj – Potencja, Porfira, Prowierka, and Piewica – and one Priboj son, Pietuszok. Piewica in particular has founded a highly successful dam line whose representatives include the stallions Pepton (Bandos/Pemba), Penitent (Partner/Penza), Piechur (Banat/Pierzeja) and the Derby winner Pierrot (Czort/Pierzga), whose son Santhos is one of the leading sires of race-winners in Europe. Pietuszok, who was also descended from Star of the Hills in tail female, was a first-class broodmare sire whose daughters include Algonkina (dam of Algomej and granddam of Aloes), Andorra, Banda, Orla, Wilma, and Beatrice. The family of Orla is another line noted for its racing ability.

A further line from Crabbet came to Poland through the Russian-bred Naseem son Negatiw and his son Nabor. Negatiw arrived in Poland in 1962 at the age of 17, after a successful career as chief sire at Tersk. He sired many valuable broodmares in his new country as well as several stallions such as Bandos (out of Bandola) who succeeded him as chief sire until his sale to the United States in 1982. Other Negatiw sons born in Poland include Buszmen, Cebion, and Etiw now in the United States, Baj at the French National Stud at Pompadour, Gon in Holland, and Diem in Germany.

Nabor preceded his sire to Poland by five years, having been used only sparingly at Tersk, where none of his blood remains. Six years later he was sold to the United States where he was to become one of its most important stallions. Most of his foals followed him across the Atlantic, leaving in fact very little of his blood in Poland. Most of what there now is comes from his daughters Estebna and Eskapada (out of Estokada). His male line was reintroduced to Poland in the early Nineties through two imported stallions, Gadir (Saudi/Garda) from Germany and Grandorr (Nabor/Gwadiana) from America.

The last introduction of Crabbet blood to Poland was the stallion Burkan, bred in England in 1964 by Lord Moyne and leased to Poland in exchange for Banat in 1975. Burkan was by Saladin II out of Biruta, a Polish mare imported into England. Saladin II was by Naziri out of Starilla, who was by Raseem out of Star of the Hills. Saladin II was therefore very closely related to many Russian Arabians. Burkan left no sons in Poland, but several good daughters that have been used in Polish breeding with excellent results.

SPAIN

More than one famous Crabbet horse has disappeared without trace after being exported. In the case of Spain it was Rijm, who was imported in 1915 but left no descendants in that country.

Further Crabbet blood was introduced by Cristobál Colón, 15th Duke of Veragua and a direct linear descendant of Christopher Columbus. He founded a stud farm at Valjuanete in 1926 and imported a substantial number of foundation animals from England. These were as follows:

Imported

1926	**AJLUN**	1923	Rasim	Mejamieh
	RAZADA	1925	Shahzada	Ranya
	RANYA	1916	Nasik	Riyala
1928	SHALIMAR	1921	Yakoot	Jawi-Jawi
1930	JALILA	1922	Skowronek	Rasima
	REYNA	1925	Skowronek	Rissla
	NAMIRA	1928	Skowronek	Nessima
	SHELIFA	1922	Skowronek	Selima
	NASIEDA	1927	Skowronek	Nasra
1934	INSILLA	1930	Naseem	Nisreen
	RITLA	1926	Jeruan	Rissla

The 1930 and 1934 imports were from Crabbet Park directly. Of the 1926 imports, Ranya was of pure Crabbet breeding. Her son Razada was by

Shahzada, the produce of the desertbred stallion Mootrub and Ruth Kesia, a mare combining early Blunt and other desert lines. Ajlun was by a Crabbet stallion out of a desertbred mare. Shalimar's sire Yakoot was by the desertbred Zoowar out of Husn-u-Gul, a mainly Crabbet mare; her dam Jawi-Jawi was by Rijm out of Jiwa and of pure Crabbet breeding.

Of these imports, only the stallions Razada and Ajlun and the mares Reyna, Jalila, and Shalimar have left verifiable lines, and only Reyna founded a dam line that still exists in Spain. Shalimar's dam line is still in existence, though it has died out in Spain; her fourth generation tail female descendant Flora was exported in 1971 to Holland, where her line continues. Nevertheless, the Veragua horses as a whole, comprising both English and old Spanish bloodlines, have played a highly important part in the development of the Arabian breed in Spain.

Razada was undoubtedly the most influential of the English horses, though it is almost impossible to separate him from the Crabbet mares Reyna and Jalila who produced his most important foals. Bred to Reyna, he sired the stallions Ifni and Kashmir. Ifni, through whom the sire line continues, sired Almozabor (out of Duquesa) who was given to King Abdullah of Jordan where, under the name Ushaahe, he had some influence. Kashmir remained in Spain and sired a total of 88 foals. His blood is found today mainly through his daughter Kayan (out of Sara) and Kayan's daughters Batista (by Sherif, a grandson of Ajlun) and Arilla (by Malvito, tracing to Razada and Jalila). Batista's daughter Prometida was exported to Germany where she was a successful broodmare. Another daughter Rumbosa produced Gual Ghazir (by Galeon), a popular sire in Germany, and his full sister Gual Boukra who was exported to Australia along with another mare of this family, Polaca (Hacho/Batista). Arilla produced Pintor (by Jaguay), a successful sire in the Netherlands, and Finta (by Tabal) who founded a flourishing family also in the Netherlands.

Razada's most influential son was Nana Sahib, foaled in 1934 out of the Crabbet mare Jalila. He sired 41 daughters and 30 sons, six of which were used extensively: Fabuloso (out of Beni Amer), Habano (out of Saboya), Habon (out of Yalina), Kako (out of Carola), Karabe (out of Rizosa) and Nana Sahib II (out of Alhambra II). But it is for his daughters that he is chiefly noted, especially the following four: Famula (out of Sara), Egina (out of Saboya), Kantista (out of Morayma) and Habladuria (out of Sara). Famula and Egina produced, respectively, the two very influential stallions Maquillo and Malvito, both sired by Gandhy.

Malvito sired the important Spanish sires Zurich (out of Extranjera) and Corinto (out of Undina II) and several good mares, including Arilla (above), Comedia II, Egipcia, Agata III and Aldebaran II. The latter was exported to the USA in foal to Zurich and there produced the important American sire Barich de Washoe. Maquillo sired the stallions Sacudir (out of Jabonera by Nana Sahib), Saludo (out of Jacobita), Uzacur (out of Veranda), and Bambu (out of Ocalina, a granddaughter of Kashmir), besides many others. His daughters include Baldosa (out of Habladuria), the dam of the great Spanish sire Garbo, and Motasen II (out of Morayma II by Karabe).

Nana Sahib's daughter Kantista was of all-English breeding, as her dam Morayma was by Razada out of Reyna. Kantista's crowning achievement was the noted sire Alhabac (by Cairel), whose offspring are found in both Spain and France. Alhabac's daughter Ispahan (out of Chavali) produced the stallion AN Malik (by Galero), a popular sire in America. The latter carries an additional line to Razada through Chavali, whose grandsire Tetuan was out of Razada's daughter Teutonica. Nana Sahib was also the sire of Habladuria, dam of Baldosa, already mentioned under her sire Maquillo as the dam of Garbo.

The lines of Razada, Jalila, and Reyna came together in the mare Jalila III, foaled in 1946 by Jalila's son Nana Sahib out of Reyna. Jalila III was instrumental in carrying on the Rodania dam line in Spain through her daughters Teja (by Damasco III) and Sagaz (by Habienta), and Sagaz's daughter Ebanista. A mare of this family, Niharra (Jaguay/Jabalina II), was exported to Germany and became an important foundation mare for the renowned Om El Arab Stud.

Ajlun, the Rasim son imported with Razada, was sold on to Portugal but he did establish one line in Spanish breeding through his daughter Rebeca (out of Gomara). She was the dam of the stallion Sherif (by Ilustre), who can be found in several Spanish lines today. The mare Rumbosa (see above) was inbred to Sherif.

It is fairly certain that lines to the other Veragua imports exist today, but it is impossible to trace them. The Veragua Stud suffered greatly during the Spanish Civil War of 1936 to 1939, in which the Duke was killed and his horses scattered. His heirs were able to gather the remaining horses after the war and to continue the breeding programme but among them were twenty young fillies that had not been registered. They were identified by their brands as being purebred Arabians from the Duke's stud, but it was impossible to say what their breeding was. The closest one can come is to say that some must have been by Razada and some by the Duke's Spanish stallion Sirio III, as those were the sires he was then using. In the days before the advent of blood-typing, it is anyone's guess who was by whom and who their dams were. The fillies that went into breeding eventually were registered under names beginning with "Vera"; and six of these – Veracruz, Veralina, Verana, Veranda, Verapaz, and Veraz – established families. Given the nature of the Duke's breeding programme, it is virtually certain that they had Crabbet blood to some extent; it is possible that some of them were mostly or even entirely English.

Verana, foaled in 1934, produced Imelina, the dam of the sire Zangano and the granddam of the celebrated Estopa, besides being the great-granddam in tail female of Chavali. Veracruz, also foaled in 1934, produced Galatife who had Zalema, the dam of the sires Galero and Jaguay, and Teorica, the dam of the sires Jacio and Kadi. Veranda produced two important stallions, Habiente and Uzacur (by Maquillo). The exact amount of Crabbet blood in these horses is impossible to determine but one can be certain that it is there. It would be very difficult today, if not impossible, to find a Spanish Arabian that does not descend in some way from the Veragua imports.

A more recent import to Spain with Crabbet breeding was the English stallion Cranleigh Karim, imported in 1973. He was by the Polish stallion Grojec out of Tatiama, a mare of all-Crabbet breeding except for one line to Shahzada. His daughter Radiada produced the stallion Sol d'Oa, who was successful at international shows in the early Eighties but whether his blood establishes itself permanently remains to be seen.

THE NETHERLANDS

From its very beginning, Arab breeding in the Netherlands rested on a Crabbet foundation. The first pure Arab to be registered in the Dutch Arabian Stud Book in 1935 was the stallion Houbaran (Aldebaran/Arusa), foaled in 1923. Houbaran was three-quarter Crabbet, both parents descending in tail female from the Blunt's celebrated Queen of Sheba. The line, the oldest in the Netherlands, is still in existence today and is found in the pedigrees of many winning Dutch Arab horses.

The only importations directly from Crabbet Park were those made by

Dr H.C.E.M. Houtappel during 1937 and the following years. Dr Houtappel imported three stallions from Crabbet Park:

NISSAM	1943	Rissam	Nezma
NORAN	1956	Oran	Nerina
RYTHAL	1933	Shareer	Rythma

In addition, he imported a number of both pure and predominantly Crabbet horses from the Hanstead Stud, including the stallion The Chief 1943 (Riffal/Astrella), a full brother to Oran, and the mares Sulka 1934 (Naseem/Nurschida) and Tehoura 1946 (Radi/Niseyra), who in Holland foaled Bashida by General Grant. All these horses except Sulka were of pure Crabbet breeding. Sulka had one line to the desertbred Maidan through her dam's sire Nuri Sherif, though tracing to Crabbet imports in all other lines.

Rythal, the first Crabbet import, did not excel in Dutch breeding. Of his 15 foals, only three were used for breeding. One, the pure Crabbet mare Hadassa (out of Bashida), left no foals in Holland but became a foundation mare for the Fairfield Stud in England. Rythal's most successful foal in Holland was the pure Crabbet Rythoura (out of Tehoura), who produced the three sires Nisry (by Nizzam) and Abiram and Achar, both by Noran: all are found in modern pedigrees.

Nizzam fared better. His daughter Fatma (out of Sulka) produced four daughters by Noran that were used for breeding: Adaja, Norama, Abida, and Attalaia. Norama and Abida were exported to England, while Adaja (by the Houbaran son Saoud) founded an important dam line in Holland. Samantha (out of Ziada, a pure Crabbet mare) is found in current pedigrees through her daughter Chadiga (by Achim by Noran), and Nishida (out of Bashida) established a dam line in England. Of Nizzam's sons, Aatik (out of Farida) and Nisry (out of Rythoura) were used for breeding, and Nizar (out of Sulka) was sold to Germany where he founded a sire line. At an advanced age, Nizzam was sold to the United States where his influence exceeded that in Holland.

Noran was the most important of Dr Houtappel's Crabbet imports. With 32 purebred foals in the Dutch Stud Book, he was one of the most used stallions of his time. His sons used for breeding were Abiram (out of Rythoura), Achim (out of Tehoura), Adar (out of Bashida), Witel (out of Elzunia), Fahred (out of Elzunia), Achar (out of Rythoura) and Esmir (out of Fatma). Another good daughter in Holland was Mielka (out of Fatma) who has had considerable influence through her daughters

top left Amal
(Abdullah-Naomi by Darjeel)
World Champion
Photo B. Finke
top right Bint Sylvan Lass
(El Zahra [E.A.O] – Sylvan Lass)
Multi-Champion in Germany.
Photo B. Finke
centre Mangani
(Nuri Schalan-Metelica)
1987 Nations Cup Champion
Photo B. Finke
right Warandes Plakat
(Plakat-Barwna by Iridos)
Photo B. Finke

Callista (by Saoud) and Dabrana (by Little Star). Noran also sired the Anglo-Arab Rex the Robber, one of the most successful show-jumpers of all time.

Of the Hanstead imports, The Chief only sired six foals and of these, only a son Hamad (out of Tehoura) and a daughter Chieka (out of Sulka) have been much used.

The two mares Sulka and Tehoura had considerable influence, as can already be seen from the horses listed previously. Tehoura produced the mares Bashida (imported *in utero*, by General Grant) and Rythoura (by Rythal), as well as the pure Crabbet stallion Achim (by Noran). Achim left several daughters that bred on in Holland before going to England with the entire Rodania Stud. There he was greatly appreciated and became British National Champion at the age of 23 before emigrating again, this time to the United States.

Bashida produced seven foals, five of which bred on: Hadassa, Nishida, Adar, and Mielka, as well as Rachida, by the Polish stallion Rustan – who was a grandson of the Crabbet mare Sardhana (see page 320). Sulka's four foals all bred on, the most important being the mare Fatma and the stallion Nizar, both by Nizzam.

Aside from the Houtappel imports, one other stallion was imported directly from Crabbet Park. This was Silver Royal (Grand Royal/Silver Gilt). He sired only eight foals, including the licensed stallion Royal (out of Sibylla by Saoud) who represented Dutch Crabbet breeding at the 1985 Crabbet Convention.

A considerable number of English horses have since 1957 been imported to the Netherlands that were of pure or predominantly Crabbet breeding. Those listed in Volume I of the Dutch Stud Book and which also bred on are, in alphabetical order, as follows:

ADAGIO	1969	Bright Shadow	Tarantella
AUNT CARA	1968	Kedowa	Raffinda
BERAK	1968	General Grant	Bona Blue
BLUE DIAMOND	1964	Blue Domino	Ambria
BRIGHT WINGS	1965	Bright Shadow	Silent Wings
CHANTAL	1969	Fancy Shadow	Mafika
CYANELLA	1966	Oran	Bona Blue
DARDANELLA	1968	Ringing Gold	Crystal Magic
DHARMENDRA	1973	Darzee	Ranee
DJINN	1965	General Dorsaz	Sugar Plum Fairy
EDH-DAHAB	1928	Sher-i-Khurshid	Fantana

NETHERLANDS

FIRE PRINCESS	1964	Indian King	Cinders
GAMAR	1964	Iran	Merrymount Emma
GHIBLI	1966	Ludo	Yasmina
GOLDBEY	1966	Ludo	Abeya
HALIDE	1963	Count Roland	Halfa
HAMU	1962	Indian Fakir	Harima
INDIAN FIRE	1969	Indian Flame II	Yanni
INDIAN TAMARISK	1968	Indian King	Dancing Shadow
LAELIA	1965	Bright Shadow	Vanda
LUREX	1968	Ludrex	Yemama
MAGIC GOLD	1966	Indian Magic	Magnindra
MANTILLA	1965	My Man	Cinders
MY FAIR LADY II	1965	My Man	Blue Moon
MY PET	1958	Sole Hope	Yavroum
NAXINDOS	1968	Iridos	Naxindra
QUICK MAN	1967	My Man	My Pet *in utero*
RASHMARI	1967	Indian Star	Rashayna
RETSINA	1959	Iridos	Ragassa
RISSAZ	1965	Indriss	Kazra
ROBERT E. LEE	1953	General Grant	Ragassa
SALEEMIE	1968	Sumatra	Golden Charm
SERINDA	1969	Seradin	Cinders
SHAKRA	1959	Indian Magic	Rissada
SITHARA	1962	Sahran	Pitti Sing
SKY MINUET	1975	Indriss	Masqueen
SONATA	1967	Indian King	Dancing Sunlight
SUSQUEHANNA	1955	General Grant	Ragassa
SWEET SINCERITY	1973	Crystal King	Royal Serenity
TAMARAK	1970	Berak	Tahiti
TAZEE	1932	Joseph	Rasana
TERRISA	1965	General Grant	Indian Fair
ZELDA	1964	Russlan of Pelere	Raffinda
ZIADA	1944	Fayal	Raxina

Some of these horses were actually imported to Belgium but registered in the Dutch Stud Book, and it is therefore not easy to keep them apart. Two of the Belgian imports were Adagio and Ghibli, who between them produced the champion mares Selina and Primula.

Bright Wings sired the mare Odessa, out of Serinda, who became famous as the dam of the U.S. Champion and sire of champions, Padron. Chantal was the dam of the multi-champions Hassan and Khouros, sired by Plakat, a tail female descendant of Star of the Hills. Rissaz is among the stallions with the most foals listed in Volume I of the Dutch Stud Book; he especially excelled as a broodmare sire. His son Hoekhorst Shiraz sired the World Champion Mare Orinda. Zelda produced the *in utero* import Naomi, by Darjeel, who is the dam of the World Champion and successful sire Amal.

Two mares with a considerable amount of Crabbet blood who also deserve mention are Baranta 1971 (Manto/Baraka) and Barwna 1972 (Iridos/Baraka). Both were prolific and successful broodmares. Barwna in particular is famous for her many foals by Plakat, all of which are major show-winners. The best known are the stallions Warandes Plakat, Warandes Pasha and Tamarek, and the mare Saskia RJ.

It goes without saying that more Crabbet blood arrived in Holland through the numerous imports made from Russia. Holland was in fact the first country to import significant numbers of Russian Arabs and to make them popular the world over. The resulting Crabbet/Russian cross has become something of a Dutch trademark and includes many celebrated horses such as Padron, Amal, and Warandes Plakat.

GERMANY

There have never been any direct Crabbet exports to Germany, nor has Crabbet blood ever achieved the popularity and influence in Germany that it has had elsewhere. Nevertheless it can be found and has a loyal, if small, following.

One of the foundation sires of the breed in post-war Western Germany was Nizar, bred in 1953 by Dr Houtappel in Holland by Nizzam out of Sulka. Nizar was pure Crabbet with the exception of one line far back in his pedigree to the desertbred Maidan. He was discovered in a circus by Carl-Heinz Dömken, who bought him and made him the foundation sire for his new stud.

Nizar sired a total of nineteen foals, fifteen colts and only four fillies – a lot by the standard of those days. Moreover ten of his sons became licensed stallions and all four daughters went into breeding. Nizar lived to the age of thirty, which seems to be typical for his line; in 1993, four of his sons were still alive and well at the ages of twenty-nine, twenty-seven, and twenty-six respectively.

Nizar's most significant sons were Nazir (out of Sachara) and Nuri Schalan (out of Wega). Nazir sired some of Germany's most successful broodmares which include Nazira, Meneptah, Wahana, Brawura, and Padua, all of whom are dams of national and international champions. Brawura's son Ibn Mohafez ranks among Germany's most prolific and successful sires. Nazir also sired Marwan, a celebrated performance stallion who was one of Germany's leading endurance horses in his younger days and also excelled at hunting and jumping.

Nuri Schalan was another notable sire of broodmares; his daughters, often out of Russian mares, have been highly successful both in the showring and as producers. Many of their foals have been exported to the United States. The most famous is Mangani (out of Metelica), an international winner who also produced a National Champion Stallion, Mangan (by Plakat). Resalah (out of Rajana) is another international winner, whose produce include the successful endurance stallion Re Schalan (by Madkour).

Nizar's only four daughters Nishi (out of Joschi), Nizara (out of Wega), Ninive (out of Joschi) and Salome (out of Sarah) have all been active breeders.

Another import from Dr Houtappel's stud in Holland was the stallion Witel, who was by Noran out of the Polish mare Elzunia. Witel sired a number of good broodmares, most notably Semiramis (out of Surijah).

English imports were then few and far between until in 1966, a private breeder imported from the United States the three-quarter Crabbet mare A.M. Midnight Sun (Al-Marah Shahriar/Shades of Night): her son Count Rubin, by Count Bazy, imported *in utero*, became a licensed stallion and has left stock that is breeding on. Another American import of Crabbet bloodlines worth mentioning is Sylvan Lass (A.M. Sylvan Sheikh/Gallasaa), whose daughter Bint Sylvan Lass (by El Zahra, an Egyptian stallion) was one of the most prolific show winners in Germany during the Eighties.

Two mares were also privately imported from Sweden, the pure Crabbet Rozita (Samba/Rizara) and the Crabbet/Old English Rosalind (Nimran/Rosjanka). Both have left breeding stock, in particular Rozita's son, the licensed stallion Raskal (by Gharib).

The first major importation of horses directly from England was made in the early 1970s by Hans Vorderbrüggen, who brought over the stallions Rodanieh Rafaqa (Grojec/Lilac Time), Prince Azfar (Fari II/Princess

Amara), and Ibn Naxor (Naxor/Maid of Medina), and eight mares:

CONSTANZE	1972	Harwood Asif	Consuella *in utero*
CONSUELLA	1962	Magnet	Misery
GOLDA	1971	Harwood Asif	Magda
HALO'S IRIS	1972	Seradin	Halo's Miracle *in utero*
HALO'S MIRACLE	1966	Blue Halo	Rare Magic
IONE	1972	Fancy Shadow	Misery
SOPHRONIA	1974	Donax	Krysia
VANESSA	1965	Magic Fire	Rexbaya

Of the stallions, Prince Azfar was not used in purebred breeding. Rodanieh Rafaqa, renamed Gromet in Germany, became a moderately prolific sire and Ibn Naxor sired a number of good broodmares. The Vorderbrüggen stud was dispersed ten years after its founding but the horses remained in Germany and have bred on.

Since then, a number of horses of Crabbet breeding have been imported from Britain or Holland by various private breeders. They include the stallions Rustem Pasha (Indian King/Bint Roxana), Lurex (Ludrex/Yemama), Indian Fire (Indian Flame II/Yanni), Agamemnon (Ahmoun/Kamisha), Rexan (Magic Myth/Ivory Star), and Safrano (Aboud/Dancing Rose). A pure Crabbet stallion, Pedro (Ghibli/Delilah) was imported from Belgium. He has done very well under saddle and was German Reserve National Champion Stallion in 1982.

Imported mares include Seductive Magic (Scindian Magic/Countess Amarilla), Sahrilla (Sahar/Sad'ha Raheng), Teleri (Sahar/Fleur Rouge), Luisa (Magnet/Zaphara), Anchusa (Taqah/Zaphara), Haryad (Haroun/Baiyad), and Shiriba (Crystal King/Hadassa), all of which have bred on.

During the last few years, Russian Arabs have become very popular in Germany and many have been and are being imported, adding another strong Crabbet component to German breeding.

DENMARK

The Danish Arab Horse Society was formed in 1967. Many of the early Danish imports were from Britain, though not a few of these were of Polish and Russian rather than Crabbet breeding.

DENMARK

One of the earliest imports of Crabbet breeding to Denmark was the mare Indian Trinket (Crystal Fire/Sapphire), who was imported in 1964 by Baroness Bille-Brahe-Selby, one of the first Danish Arab breeders. Indian Trinket was in foal to the Crabbet stallion Bright Shadow. The resulting colt, Ibn El Hamra (a full brother to Crystal Clear), became a breeding stallion and was still siring foals during the early 1980s.

Since then there have been several imports of horses of predominantly Crabbet breeding from England. Volume III of the Danish Arab Stud Book lists the following such imports that were still actively breeding between 1983 and 1987:

STALLIONS

CONDOR	1970	Shirar	Zena
DUSHARA	1964	Zeus II	Dura
IBN EL HAMRA	1965	Bright Shadow	Indian Trinket *in utero*
SILVER SOLOMON	1974	Marwin	Silmana
STAR CRYSYAL	1976	Crystal King	Countess Ireena

MARES

COUNTESS MARITZA	1966	Count Roland	Rosmarita
ECURB ROYAL HABIBA	1968	Sharrik	Shemali Magic
KERRIA	1977	Kami	Rishmuna
MAZANINA	1973	Kemal	Manzanilla
OPAL	1973	Silver Rain	Turquoise
SILVER DOVE	1965	Ludo	Yemama
SILVER SHOWER	1975	Royal Gold	Silver Rainbow
SILVER SPARKLER	1975	Silver Rain	Faery Snow

Another predominantly Crabbet mare used for breeding in Denmark was Velisa of Yeomans, foaled in 1968 by Marengo out of Doniazad. She was later sold to Germany along with two of her daughters by Polish stallions which are breeding on there.

SWEDEN

Sweden is generally associated with straight Polish rather than Crabbet Arabians. But here too, as in so many cases, the earliest imports were from

England and several of them have left traces.

Two breeders in Sweden with Crabbet connections are Mrs Asta Ohlsson of Hammarshus Stud and Countess Penelope Lewenhaupt of Claestorps Arabian Stud. Mrs Ohlsson owned the Crabbet-bred gelding Silvershaft (Oran/Silver Gilt) and later imported her foundation breeding stock from Britain: the pure Crabbet stallion Samba 1963 (Bright Shadow/Simra) and the predominantly Crabbet mares Noureena 1961 (Greatheart/Nouronnihar) and Puteh 1961 (Magnet/Rafika). They were later joined by the mares Grey Elf 1954 (Grey Owl/Elvira), Orena 1971 (Oran/Reema) and Rizara 1966 (Rayyan/Disa). A daughter of Samba and Rozita, Rizara, was later exported to Germany and has offspring there, including a licensed stallion.

Countess Lewenhaupt, who was born in Britain and is a niece of Mrs E.M. Murray, took several predominantly Crabbet Arabs with her when she moved to Sweden, among them the stallion Kariba 1956 (Rifari/Moraea) and the mare Farissla 1960 (Count Orlando/Farette), both of whom have bred on.

The pure Crabbet mares Ambretta 1960 (Oran/Ambria), Rhapsody in Blue 1966 (General Grant/Blue Rhapsody), Blue Horizon 1966 (Blue Domino/Aleya) and Silver Silhouette 1962 (Silver Drift/Aletta), imported by smaller breeders, have also left offspring in Sweden. The descendants of Blue Horizon and especially of Silver Silhouette have been successful at international shows in recent years.

FRANCE

Mention must finally be made of France and in particular of the purchase in 1987 of seven mares and two stallions by Emile Buttigieg and Pierre Courtial:

STALLIONS
RAMOTH	1982	Shammar	Rosa-Maria
SALTRAM	1982	Samhan	Sceptre

MARES
CAVITA	1984	Shammar	Calpurnia

ROCKDOVE	1979	Samhan	Rosemary
ROSA-MARIA	1977	Samhan	Rosemary
SAREK	1983	Bend Or	Signorinetta
SIGNORINETTA	1978	Samhan	Salome IV
SPILLETTA	1988	Kantaka	Sceptre
SUMERIA	1987	Ramoth	Signorinetta

This transaction was remarkable on two counts: that it was the first substantial single sale of Arab horses from Britain to France, and second that it comprised the major part of the breeding stock that was either at the Courthouse Stud when Bill Musgrave Clark died in 1981 or had been bred subsequently by his son, Derek. Mr Clark had not of course used Crabbet blood exclusively during his long and selective career as a breeder (see also page 176) but his principal foundation mares, Belka, Rangha and Safarjal, were Crabbet through and through and it will be of no little interest to see how this enterprise fares.

It should also be mentioned that in the 1980s, the entire Hawkhurst Stud of Derek and Rosemary Bretherton, composed of pure and mainly Crabbet horses, was relocated to France. It too remains to be seen what becomes of their breeding programme there and what impact it has on French Arab breeding.

Jamani Rashani (Jamani Shabani – Bint Razena)
See page 339

SOUTH AFRICA

The early history of Crabbet horses in South Africa was distressingly similar to that in Russia. In both cases, some of the best Crabbet blood was purchased and lost. In Russia it was Mesaoud and Pharaoh, in South Africa Azrek and Merzuk. The first volume of the Arab Horse Stud book of South Africa gives only seven horses as having been bought from the Blunts during the initial period, 1891 to 1914, but it is apparent from the returns published in the General Stud Book that many more than these were exported but never registered in South Africa.

Of course some, if not all, of these horses were purchased with a view to upgrading local stock as opposed to pure-bred breeding and it is for this reason that their lines have been lost. But horses of the calibre of Azrek and Merzuk are not easily come by and had their pure blood been preserved in the country, it would today have been of inestimable value.

The turning-point for Arab breeding in South Africa may be said to have occurred in 1938 when Mr Claude Orpen of Cape Province imported the stallion Jiddan. He had been bred in 1930 by the Hon. George Savile, by Sher-i-Khurshid out of Baida, a mare whose dam line was that of Hagar, the Blunts' journey mare during their desert travels. By his style and ability as a riding horse, Jiddan attracted much attention in the Eastern Cape and the success of his progeny with locally bred mares led to a revival of interest in the breed and a number of subsequent importations.

One of the first people involved was Mr G.C. Kock who, shortly after the Second World War, imported the stallions Indian Gem (Raktha/Indian Crown), Indian Red (Raktha/Nezma) and Shahim (Rangoon/Somara) amongst others, and the mares Ghezala (Faris/Rasana) and Nazziria (Naziri/Nezma) with her daughter Nazrina by Star Royal. Mr Kock's stud was dispersed in 1951 and these three mares were bought by Mr P.J. van der Merwe who also brought in from the United States horses of predominantly Crabbet bloodlines including, in 1954, Rabiyas, the sire of Abu Farwa. Mr van der Merwe used Rabiyas extensively (see table S24) and his Vlinkfontein Stud provided many new breeders with their foundation stock.

top Grantchester (General Grant–Rafeena)
above Shalwan (Silver Vanity–Shalina)
right Raktha Scha (Raktha–Shadilla)

Another of these early breeders was Mr E.M. Hind who in 1948 bought the young stallion Indian Flyer (Faris/Indian Flower) and the mare Shirama (Raktha/Sharfina), together with her foal Shireen by Whirlstorm.

Probably the most influential horse in South Africa of pure Crabbet bloodlines has been Raktha, by Naseem out of Razina. Though actually foaled at Hanstead, he was acquired by Lady Wentworth and in 1951 sold by her at the age of sixteen to Mr A. J. Botha. With him went the mare Silviana, by Oran out of Silver Fire.

Raktha (see table s22), his sons Quantock II and Indian Red, and his grandsons Chief Kasalo and Grantchester – all imported from England – together with Timarie Major Grant – imported *in utero* – have had a widespread effect on Arabian pedigrees in South Africa. Raktha's importance has been further emphasised by his imported daughters Silverlet and Serafilla and his granddaughters Silsilla, Endora, Lanisa and Rinessa, the last three all being by General Grant, Raktha's son out of Samsie. Lanisa (out of Shamnar) and Rinessa (out of Rikitea) were both bred at Hanstead and imported by Mr W.P. du Toit, the owner of the Quimran Stud which flourished during the 1950s and 1960s.

Silverlet (out of Silver Gilt) and Silsilla (Rithan/Somara) were imported to South Africa by Mrs E.B. Arnold in 1951, though the latter was sold on soon afterwards. Mrs Arnold also owned two sons of Dargee; Dancing Wings (out of Shades of Night), bought from Crabbet in 1952, and Royal Crystal (out of Grey Royal) which had been originally imported by Mr Botha in 1957.

Mr and Mrs J.D.D. Kettlewell imported Fayalina (Fayal/Naama) and her daughter Irexia by Irex. In 1956 the latter had a daughter called Jerico Sherifa by Chief Kasalo (General Grant/Rikitea) who turned into a

left Dancing Wings (Dargee–Shades of Night) and *right* Zena (Blue Domino–Queen Zenobia) marvellous foundation mare for their stud. In 1970 they introduced a new line to Raktha by bringing over from England Barabaz whose sire, Stargard, was a son of Raktha.

One of the most important Arab studs in South Africa has been Jamani, started in 1955 by Mr and Mrs J.B. Grobbelaar with the Hanstead-bred mare Correze, by Count Dorsaz out of Namilla. Three years later they imported Grantchester (General Grant/Rafeena) and the combination of this stallion with Correze and their other foundation mares – which included two more from Hanstead, namely Garance (Grey Owl/Rikitea) and Zena (Blue Domino/Queen Zenobia) – proved a happy one in every way. Not only did the horses themselves achieve outstanding results in the show-ring but they also went on to produce stock of consistently high quality that have in their turn been used to found numerous other studs.

It can be seen that a large proportion of these imports from Britain were bred at Hanstead and it is arguable that South Africa has been the country most influenced by horses bred by Lady Yule and her daughter. A further instance is Mrs T.E.M. Murray's Timarie Stud which was started in 1952 with the importation of Kumara (Grey Owl/Hama) and Kasala (Sala/Queen Zenobia) and produced first-rate stock for over twenty years. Another breeder whose stud was founded with mares from both Crabbet and Hanstead was Mrs M.P. Trollip who bought Silsilla from Mrs Arnold and also owned Chief Kasalo for a number of years. A stallion she bred called Chez Nous Shah Rukh, by Al Burak out of Silsilla,had a great influence on the Vidiko Stud of Mr V.V. Voorendyk.

One of the last stallions to be exported directly from Crabbet was Shalwan (Silver Vanity/Shalina), who was bought by Mr North from Cecil Covey in 1962. Shalwan was National Champion in 1966 and fourteen years later, when owned by Mrs Arnold, became South African Supreme Champion.

More recently, Mrs E. Chapman imported Falouk 1969 (El Meluk/Farette), a stallion that has since become highly successful for a new owner, Mrs D. Richardson and in 1982 Professor and Mrs P.A. Boyazoglu imported Ibn Chantarella(Orion/Chantarella) to use on his Jamani Prince Zayani daughters.

LIST OF TABLES

Stallions

S20	Rissalix's line	S23	Riffal's line
S21	Manasseh's line	S24	Rabiyas
S22	Raktha		

S20 RISSALIX'S LINE

```
MAHRUSS (1893)
│
RIJM 1901
ROSE OF SHARON
│
NUREDDIN II 1911
NARGHILEH
│
FARIS 1924
FEJR
│
RISSALIX 1934
RISSLA
      ├── COUNT DORSAZ 1945 ──┬── ROBDON DESERT DUST 1955
      │   SHAMNAR             │   YASIMET
      │                       ├── REIBARA MANSOUR 1955 ── RYNET SULDOURE-SHA 1962
      │                       │   ENDORA                  SULEENA
      ├── BLUE DOMINO 1947 ───┼── THERON 1955 ─────────── ESTERVILLE HASEEM 1960
      │   NISYRA              │   TERESITA                CHEZ NOUS CHEZAZ
      │                       ├── ROBDON RED DEMON 1955
      │                       │   DAWN SHADOW
      │                       └── AZRAK 1964
      │                           SILENT WINGS
      ├── MIKENO 1949
      │   NAMILLA
      │
      └── EL MELUK 1959 ────────── FALOUK 1969
          MIFARIA                  FARETTE
```

S21 MANASSEH'S LINE

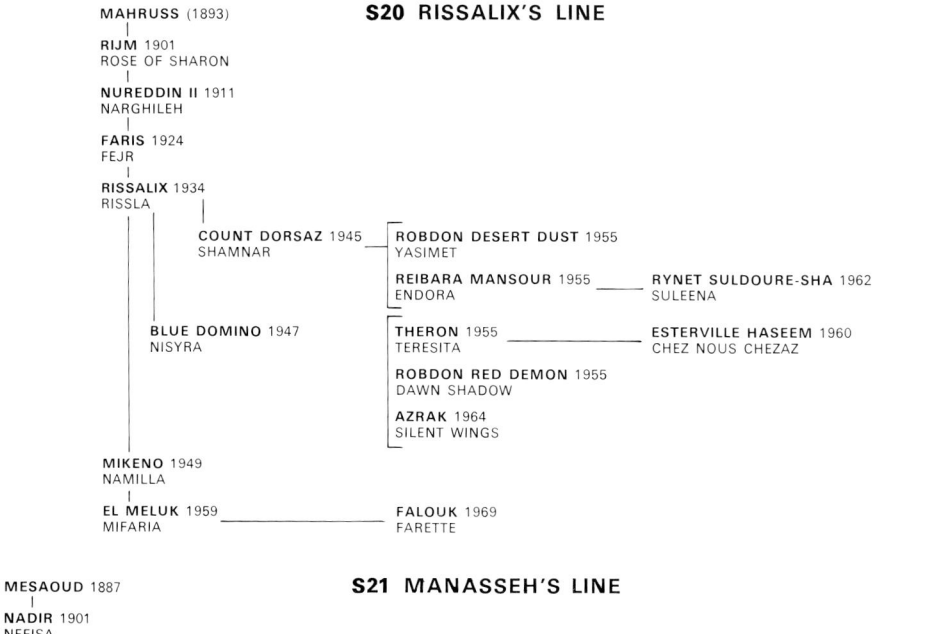

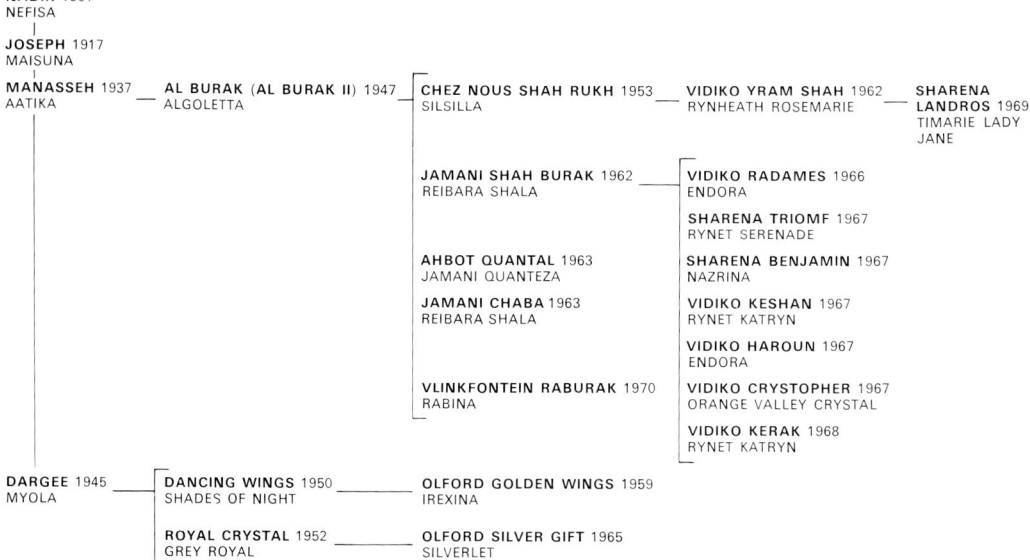

```
MESAOUD 1887
│
NADIR 1901
NEFISA
│
JOSEPH 1917
MAISUNA
│
MANASSEH 1937 ── AL BURAK (AL BURAK II) 1947 ─┬── CHEZ NOUS SHAH RUKH 1953 ── VIDIKO YRAM SHAH 1962 ── SHARENA
AATIKA           ALGOLETTA                    │   SILSILLA                     RYNHEATH ROSEMARIE       LANDROS 1969
                                              │                                                         TIMARIE LADY
                                              │                                                         JANE
                                              ├── JAMANI SHAH BURAK 1962 ──┬── VIDIKO RADAMES 1966
                                              │   REIBARA SHALA            │   ENDORA
                                              │                            ├── SHARENA TRIOMF 1967
                                              │                            │   RYNET SERENADE
                                              │                            ├── SHARENA BENJAMIN 1967
                                              │                            │   NAZRINA
                                              ├── AHBOT QUANTAL 1963       ├── VIDIKO KESHAN 1967
                                              │   JAMANI QUANTEZA          │   RYNET KATRYN
                                              ├── JAMANI CHABA 1963        ├── VIDIKO HAROUN 1967
                                              │   REIBARA SHALA            │   ENDORA
                                              │                            ├── VIDIKO CRYSTOPHER 1967
                                              └── VLINKFONTEIN RABURAK 1970│   ORANGE VALLEY CRYSTAL
                                                  RABINA                   └── VIDIKO KERAK 1968
                                                                               RYNET KATRYN

DARGEE 1945 ─┬── DANCING WINGS 1950 ──── OLFORD GOLDEN WINGS 1959
MYOLA        │   SHADES OF NIGHT          IREXINA
             │
             └── ROYAL CRYSTAL 1952 ───── OLFORD SILVER GIFT 1965
                 GREY ROYAL               SILVERLET
```

S20: Blue Domino was the sire of Theron, Robdon Red Demon and Azrak.
S21: Chez Nous Shah Rukh was the sire of Vidiko Yram Shah and the horses listed beneath him.

S22 RAKTHA

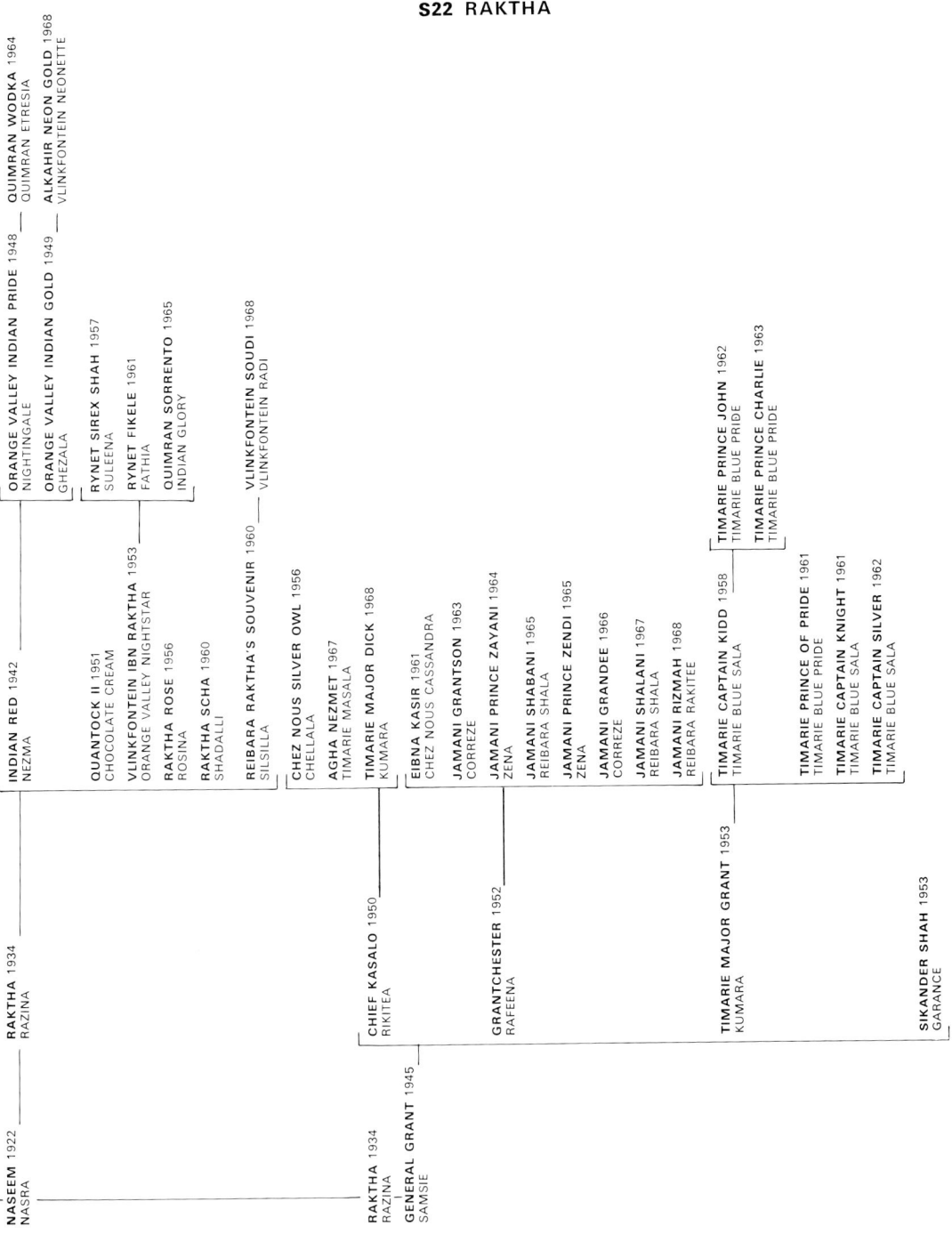

```
NASEEM 1922 ── RAKTHA 1934 ── INDIAN RED 1942 ──┬── ORANGE VALLEY INDIAN PRIDE 1948 ──┬── QUIMRAN WODKA 1964
NASRA          RAZINA           NEZMA           │   NIGHTINGALE                       │   QUIMRAN ETRESIA
                                                │                                     └── ORANGE VALLEY INDIAN GOLD 1949
                                                │                                         GHEZALA                       ── ALKAHIR NEON GOLD 1968
                                                │                                                                          VLINKFONTEIN NEONETTE
                                                ├── RYNET SIREX SHAH 1957
                                                │   SULEENA
                                                ├── RYNET FIKELE 1961
                                                │   FATHIA                    ── QUIMRAN SORRENTO 1965
                                                │                                INDIAN GLORY
                                                │
                                                ├── QUANTOCK II 1951
                                                │   CHOCOLATE CREAM
                                                ├── VLINKFONTEIN IBN RAKTHA 1953
                                                │   ORANGE VALLEY NIGHTSTAR
                                                ├── RAKTHA ROSE 1956
                                                │   ROSINA
                                                ├── RAKTHA SCHA 1960
                                                │   SHADALLI
                                                ├── REIBARA RAKTHA'S SOUVENIR 1960  ── VLINKFONTEIN SOUDI 1968
                                                │   SILSILLA                           VLINKFONTEIN RADI
                                                ├── CHEZ NOUS SILVER OWL 1956
                                                │   CHELLALA
                                                ├── AGHA NEZMET 1967
                                                │   TIMARIE MASALA
                                                └── TIMARIE MAJOR DICK 1968
                                                    KUMARA

RAKTHA 1934 ── GENERAL GRANT 1945 ── CHIEF KASALO 1950 ── GRANTCHESTER 1952 ──┬── EIBNA KASIR 1961
RAZINA         SAMSIE                RIKITEA              RAFEENA              │   CHEZ NOUS CASSANDRA
                                                                               ├── JAMANI GRANTSON 1963
                                                                               │   CORREZE
                                                                               ├── JAMANI PRINCE ZAYANI 1964
                                                                               │   ZENA
                                                                               ├── JAMANI SHABANI 1965
                                                                               │   REIBARA SHALA
                                                                               ├── JAMANI PRINCE ZENDI 1965
                                                                               │   ZENA
                                                                               ├── JAMANI GRANDEE 1966
                                                                               │   CORREZE
                                                                               ├── JAMANI SHALANI 1967
                                                                               │   REIBARA SHALA
                                                                               └── JAMANI RIZMAH 1968
                                                                                   REIBARA RAKITEE

                                     TIMARIE MAJOR GRANT 1953 ──┬── TIMARIE CAPTAIN KIDD 1958 ──┬── TIMARIE PRINCE JOHN 1962
                                     KUMARA                     │   TIMARIE BLUE SALA          │   TIMARIE BLUE PRIDE
                                                                │                              └── TIMARIE PRINCE CHARLIE 1963
                                                                │                                  TIMARIE BLUE PRIDE
                                                                ├── TIMARIE PRINCE OF PRIDE 1961
                                                                │   TIMARIE BLUE PRIDE
                                                                ├── TIMARIE CAPTAIN KNIGHT 1961
                                                                │   TIMARIE BLUE SALA
                                                                └── TIMARIE CAPTAIN SILVER 1962
                                                                    TIMARIE BLUE SALA

                                     SIKANDER SHAH 1953
                                     GARANCE
```

Quantock II was the sire of Rynet Sirex Shah and the horses listed beneath him.

341

S23 RIFFAL'S LINE

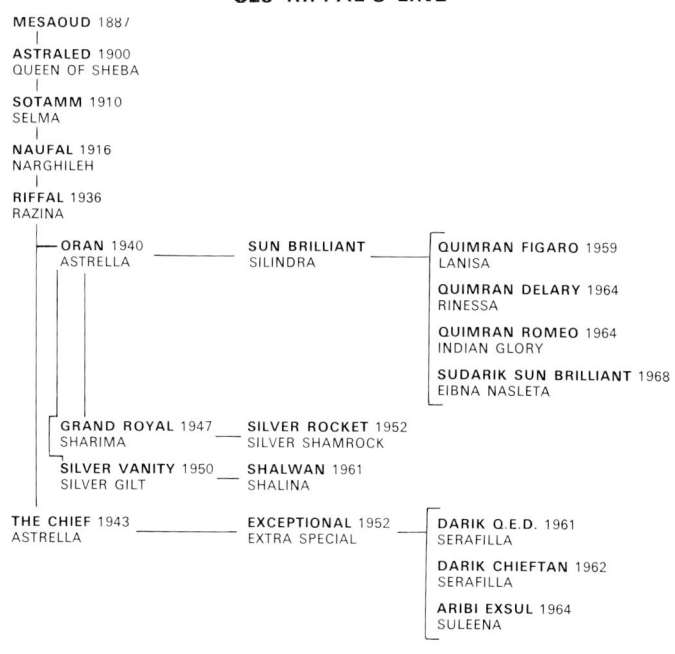

MESAOUD 1887
|
ASTRALED 1900
QUEEN OF SHEBA
|
SOTAMM 1910
SELMA
|
NAUFAL 1916
NARGHILEH
|
RIFFAL 1936
RAZINA
├── ORAN 1940 ──── SUN BRILLIANT ──── QUIMRAN FIGARO 1959
│   ASTRELLA   SILINDRA   LANISA
│   QUIMRAN DELARY 1964
│   RINESSA
│   QUIMRAN ROMEO 1964
│   INDIAN GLORY
│   SUDARIK SUN BRILLIANT 1968
│   EIBNA NASLETA
├── GRAND ROYAL 1947 ── SILVER ROCKET 1952
│   SHARIMA   SILVER SHAMROCK
├── SILVER VANITY 1950 ── SHALWAN 1961
│   SILVER GILT   SHALINA
THE CHIEF 1943 ──── EXCEPTIONAL 1952 ──── DARIK Q.E.D. 1961
ASTRELLA   EXTRA SPECIAL   SERAFILLA
                                          DARIK CHIEFTAN 1962
                                          SERAFILLA
                                          ARIBI EXSUL 1964
                                          SULEENA

S24 RABIYAS

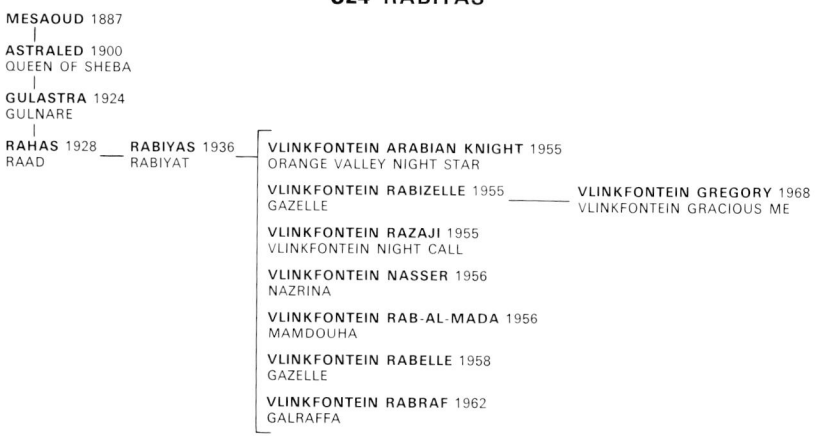

MESAOUD 1887
|
ASTRALED 1900
QUEEN OF SHEBA
|
GULASTRA 1924
GULNARE
|
RAHAS 1928 ── RABIYAS 1936 ── VLINKFONTEIN ARABIAN KNIGHT 1955
RAAD   RABIYAT   ORANGE VALLEY NIGHT STAR
                              VLINKFONTEIN RABIZELLE 1955 ──── VLINKFONTEIN GREGORY 1968
                              GAZELLE   VLINKFONTEIN GRACIOUS ME
                              VLINKFONTEIN RAZAJI 1955
                              VLINKFONTEIN NIGHT CALL
                              VLINKFONTEIN NASSER 1956
                              NAZRINA
                              VLINKFONTEIN RAB-AL-MADA 1956
                              MAMDOUHA
                              VLINKFONTEIN RABELLE 1958
                              GAZELLE
                              VLINKFONTEIN RABRAF 1962
                              GALRAFFA

THE UNITED STATES OF AMERICA AND CANADA

With 90 per cent of the world's population of Arab horses and a long history of numerous purchases both from Crabbet and from Crabbet-based studs, the United States gives obvious problems of presentation because of the sheer volume of relevant horses. The tables have therefore been constructed so as to illustrate the relationships between exported animals and not, as is the case elsewhere, the influence of their produce in America.

The first importation from the Crabbet Stud took place in 1893 when William H. Forbes purchased the colt Bedr 239 (Azrek/Bozra) and the mare Jamila 240 (Roala/Jerboa). Two years later Mr J.A.P. Ramsdell bought Shahwan 241, the white son of Wazir bred by Ali Pasha Sherif. In 1900 Mr Eustis bought three horses from the Blunts (one *in utero*) but it was only through the purchases by Spencer Borden between 1906 and 1911, and by Homer Davenport in 1910 that Crabbet lines became firmly established in America.

A full account of Spencer Borden's dealings with Lady Anne Blunt has been given already and it need only be noted here that his most important purchases from Crabbet were Rose of Sharon 246, Rodan 258, and Ghazala 211.

In 1910 Homer Davenport bought Berid 80 and Jahil 81 from Crabbet and Lal-i-Abdar (Mesaoud/Rose Diamond) from Captain the Hon. George Savile. Jahil is of interest as being a son of Berk but although he had a number of produce, he failed to found a continuing line. Lal-i-Abdar (renamed Abu Zeyd 82) has on the other hand had considerable influence. In due course he was purchased by W.R. Brown for his Maynesboro Stud where he was used as a senior sire. In all Abu Zeyd left 46 sons and daughters bred and registered in America. His male line continues in that country through his sons Gharis 623 and Bazleyd 648, the latter being a successful sire in General Dickinson's Travelers Rest Stud between 1931 and 1936. The most notable of Abu Zeyd's many daughters was the beautiful Bazikh 618, a full sister to Bazleyd and dam of several good mares. Another fine daughter was Ghazil 635 (out of the pure Crabbet Hamida 509), bred by Brown and bought by General Dickinson. Other daughters of Abu Zeyd whose names appear in modern pedigrees are Domow 267 and Larkspur 199.

Brown had founded the Maynesboro Stud in 1912 and by 1929 had seven stallions and some thirty mares and colts. He had acquired his foundation stock from a variety of sources, principally Wilfrid Blunt, Prince Mohammed Ali and fellow American breeders such as Spencer Borden and Lothrop Ames.

Ames bought four horses from Newbuildings in 1909: Shibine 160, Narda (II) 164, Crabbet 309 and Astraled 238. Narda was carrying a foal by Rijm when imported (in 1910) that was subsequently named Noam 167. In 1919 Noam had a daughter, Nusara 371 (by Abu Zeyd) whose descendants feature in predigrees today. As had been observed earlier, Ames's importations had, directly and indirectly, a remarkable record in the American endurance tests. For Noam, Crabbet and Astraled's daughter Ramla 347 all performed well over long distances. It should be mentioned here that Ramla's sire is Astraled and not Rijm as was erroneously stated in the 1917 Crabbet catalogue. Raswan's grounds for reviving doubts upon this score in *The Raswan Index* appear tendentious, to say the least.

Astraled passed through the hands of the United States Army Remount Department before he was acquired by Brown, together with Rodan, who had been imported *in utero* by Spencer Borden. In 1923 he was mated to Gulnare 278 (Rodan/Ghazala) to produce the famous sire Gulastra 521. The breeding of Gulnare is interesting since Rodan's grandsire was Mesaoud whose female source traces to the common root also shared by Ghazala and Bint Helwa (the dam of Rodan's sire, Harb), thus intensifying the strain of Seglawi Jedran. Rodan's dam was the Rodania daughter Rose of Sharon.

The horses purchased by Brown from Wilfrid Blunt in 1918 were:

343	Berk (Seyal/Bukra)	350	Rajafan – gelding (Feysul/Rijma)
356	Nafia (Ibn Yashmak/Nessima)	344	Baraza (Razaz/Bereyda)
345	Battla (Razaz/Bukra)	348	Ramim (Berk/Rim)
347	Ramla (Astraled/Ridaa)	346	Rijma (Rijm/Risala)
349	Rishrash (Nasik/Riyala)	351	Rokhsa (Nasik/Rokhama)
352	Kasima (Narkise/Kasida)	353	Kerbela (Ibn Yashmak/Kantara)

355 Numera (Sotamm/Nueyra)   354 Nueyra (Daoud/Nefisa)
357 Hazna (Razaz/Hamasa)   358 Simawa (Rustem/Sarama)
359 Felestin (Ibn Yashmak/Fejr)

Ramla, Rishrash, Kerbela, and Nueyra had no produce. The lines from Kasima and Numera died out after one generation. Hazna 357 is founder of two strong lines through her daughters Ghazayat 584 and Nafud 820.

One of Brown's most significant purchases was that of Berk, then fifteen years old. With him he also bought Berk's daughter Ramim who in 1923 bred Rehal 504, a chestnut colt who has left a strong line through his sons and grandsons. Berk sadly sired only one crop of foals in America. It consisted of three fillies, Tahdik 396 (out of Nessa), Roshana 401 (out of Rokhsa) and Nardina 459 (out of Narda II), and the colt Ribal 397 (out of Rijma). Ribal was used extensively by Brown and later in the studs of John A. George and Robert T. Wilson, and contributed much to the breed with over 67 registered produce. It is most unfortunate that Berk's get were so few as his three American daughters have all founded creditable families while the fame of his daughters and their produce in England, particularly that of Rissla, is verging on legendary.

In 1923 Brown bought the Crabbet-bred mares Hamida 509 and Hama 510 on the death of their owner, Mr S.G. Hough. Nine years later he made further importations, from Prince Mohammed Ali's Manial Stud: the stallions Zarife 885, Nasr 889 and Silver Yew 801; and the mares Roda 886, Hamama 887, Aziza 888 and Hamida 890. The relationship between Blunt horses and those in the studs of the Princes and of the Royal Agricultural Organisation is discussed in the section on Egypt.

The next major importation of Crabbet horses into America was by Mr Kellogg in 1926, the first of two major purchases for his stud that did so much to publicise Arab horse breeding in the 1930s.

The first consignment included the following stallions:

613 Ferdin (Nurreddin II/Ferda)   604 Nasik (Rijm/Narghileh)
     in utero   607 Raswan (Skowronek/Rim)
597 Raseyn (Skowronek/Rayya)   599 Rimal (Hazzam/Rim)
612 Razam (Hazzam/Rasima)   gelded
     in utero

above Rissletta
(Naseem–Risslina)
centre Ferda
(Rustem–Feluka)
below left Incoronata
(Skowronek–Nisreen)
with Holman and
right Crabbet Sura
(Skowronek–Sardhana)

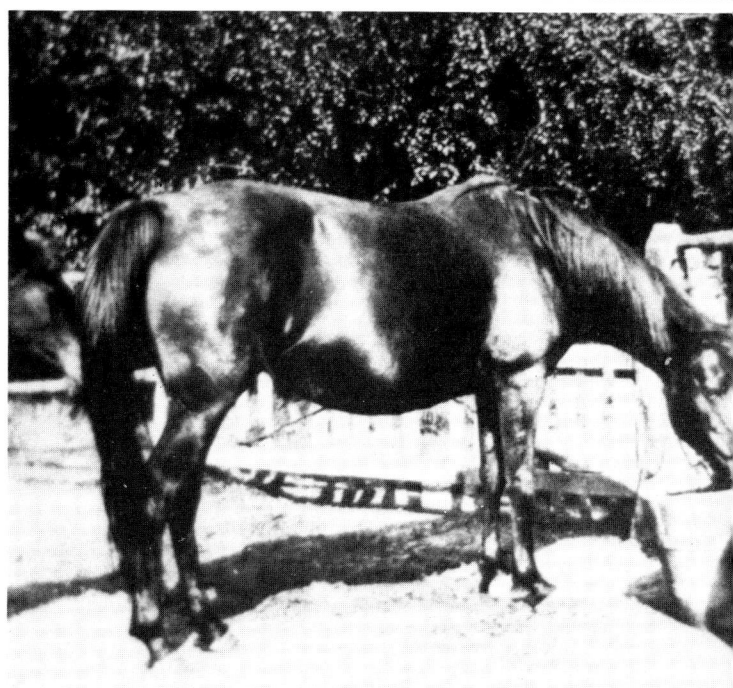

above Nasik
(Rijm–Narghileh)
centre Anne Lytton with
Rifala
(Skowronek–Rissla)
and Raffles
(Skowronek–Rifala)
below Raffles in
America in 1934

Several of these horses have influenced succeeding generations. The most important has probably been Raseyn, with 135 sons and daughters to his credit. The most prominent of his sons are Ferseyn 1381, Sureyn 1886, Ronek 807, Moneyn 1044 and Ralet 759. Nasik has also made an impression. He was an elder brother of Nureddin II, a horse later imported into America by Roger Selby. (For the benefit of the curious, Nureddin I was a half brother, by Daoud, and was exported from Crabbet to India as a three-year-old in 1906.)

Among the females bought by Kellogg in 1926 were:

603	Bahreyn (Rizvan/Battla)	608	Bint (Shareer/Farasin)
615	Farasin (Rasim/Ferda)	596	Ferda (Rustem/Feluka)
595	Ferdisia (Rafeef/Ferda)	600	Raida (Skowronek/Rabla)
602	Rasafa (Rafeef/Rasima)	606	Rasima (Daoud/Rose of Hind)
605	Rifda (Nureddin II/Rifla)	601	Rifla (Rasim/Rim)
598	Rossana (Skowronek/Rose of Hind)		

A few years after this, W.R. Brown's Maynesboro Stud was dispersed and a large group of his horses were acquired by Kellogg to add to those of Crabbet blood he already possessed. His Maynesboro purchases included: Bakmal 961 (Rahas/Bazrah), Bazikh 618 (Abu Zeyd/Bazrah), Ghazayat 584 (Rehal/Hazna), Nusara 371 (Abu Zeyd/Noam), Raab 627 (Abu Zeyd/Raad), Raad 474 (Sidi/Rijma), Rabiyat 577 (Rehal/Rokhsa), Rayik 582 (Rehal/Roshana) and Roshana 401 (Berk/Rokhsa). They combined so successfully with Kellogg's earlier purchases that several years later the whole stud was substantially of Crabbet descent. The horses that Kellogg had acquired from other sources, mainly of Davenport lines, were in most cases not retained in the stud.

In 1936 Kellogg added to his stud three superlative mares bred by Lady Wentworth:

1200 Incoronata (Skowronek/Nisreen)
1201 Rissletta (Naseem/Risslina)
1199 Sura, renamed Crabbet Sura (Skowronek/Sardhana).

Rissletta produced a son in 1940 called Abu Farwa who has since influenced American breeding to a very large extent. An extension of Abu Farwa's pedigree is interesting as it illustrates how Crabbet lines have combined with others to produce one of the most significant horses of his generation.

THE UNITED STATES OF AMERICA

ABU FARWA'S PEDIGREE

ABU FARWA 1960
born 1940

- Rabiyas 1236
  - Rahas 651
    - Gulastra 521
      - Astraled 238
      - Gulnare 278
    - Raad 474
      - Sidi 223
      - Rijma 346
  - Rabiyat 577
    - Rehal 504
      - Sidi 223
      - Ramim 348
    - Rokhsa 351
      - Nasik 604
      - Rokhama
- Rissletta 1201
  - Naseem
    - Skowronek
      - Ibrahim
      - Yaskoulka
    - Nasra
      - Daoud
      - Nefisa
  - Risslina
    - Rafeef
      - Nasik 604
      - Riyala
    - Rissla
      - Berk 343
      - Risala

The influence of the Rodania female line in America, as exemplified in Abu Farwa's pedigree, is in many ways comparable to its importance in Russian breeding.

Crabbet Sura has not bred extensively in the female line but she has had considerable effect through her son Sureyn.

The other most important pre-war importations direct from Crabbet were those of Roger A. Selby of Ohio, who bought from Lady Wentworth in 1928, 1930, 1932 and 1933. The horses are as follows.

STALLIONS

808 Mirzam (Rafeef/Marhaba)
953 Menzil (Nureddin II/Marhaba)
950 Rahal (Nureddin II/Rim)
974 Nureddin II (Rijm/Narghileh)

790 Mirage - original horse
952 Raffles (Skowronek/Rifala)
951 Selmian (Naseem/Selima)

MARES

813 Indaia (Raseem/Nisreen)
815 Rifala (Skowronek/Rissla)
819 Jerama (Jeruan/Kiyama)
855 Namilla (Nureddin II/Nejmia)
814 Raselma (Raseem/Selmnab)
812 Selmnab (Nawab/Simrieh)
973 Rimini (Skowronek/Rim)

811 Kareyma (Naseem/Julnar)
810 Hilwe (Najib/Hafra)
809 Kiyama (Rafeef/Julnar)
856 Rasmina (Shareer/Jalila)
857 Rose of France (Raswan/Jalila)
954 Rishafieh (Jeruan/Rishafa)

The Selby imports made a notable and far-reaching contribution to the development of Arab breeding. The combined effects of Mirage, Raffles, Indaia and Rifala are out of all proportion to the scale of Selby's enterprise. Raffles, of course, has especially distinguished himself. Through a legion of his own offspring and his grandsons and granddaughters, Raffles dominated the show scene to an extent that was challenged closely only by the Kellogg stallion Raseyn. The importance of Raffles and his sons Aaraf 2748, Garaff 5021, Geym 2363, Handeyraff 3940, Indraff 1575, Rapture 3783 and Rifraff 4350 has been immense in America.

Raffles' dam, Rifala 815, was a worthy representative of that grand producer Rissla. Rifala was four years old when she had Raffles and in America she went on to produce the stallions Image 1008 (by Mirage), Rifage 1286 (also by Mirage) and Phantom 2186 (by Image), and a daughter called Ragala 1091 (by Mirage). The stallions have been widely used and it is interesting to note in their breeding the way in which Mirage was constantly used as an outcross.

In 1932 Henry B. Babson brought into America seven horses bred in Egypt. There were two stallions (one of which died shortly after arrival) and five mares, and between them they have made a substantial impact on American breeding. The mares are of interest here as four of them contain Blunt blood:

Bint Bint Durra (Ibn Rabdan/Bint Durra), Bint Bint Sabbah (Baiyad/Bint Sabbah), Bint Saada (Ibn Samhan/Saada) and Bint Serra I (Sotamm/Serra). The lines of these animals are discussed in the section on Egypt. One of Mr Babson's later purchases (in 1958) was the stallion Nimrod 13005 (Champurrado/Nautch Girl) from the Courthouse Stud in Sussex. Nimrod was the sire in America of the well-known stallion Bay Rod, out of Sheeba. Mr Babson also imported to the United States the Polish-bred Sulejman whose dam was the Crabbet mare Fasila (Rasim/Fejr); Sulejman is considered by some to have been among the best stallions to go to America from Poland.

Importations continued in the late Thirties and the early post-war years from various sources including Poland. By 1949 over 5,000 Arabian horses had been registered in North America of which almost one half were recorded between 1944 and 1948. As an illustration of the dominance of Crabbet blood during those years, it may be mentioned that 40 per cent of all foals registered were by stallions of 100 per cent Crabbet blood and that 70 per cent were by horses of over 50 per cent Crabbet ancestry. The situation continued more or less unchanged up to Lady Wentworth's death by which time the total number or Arabians listed had increased to over 14,000.

The only importation of Crabbet blood after 1957 on a scale to rival those of earlier years was that by Mrs Bazy Tankersley whose Al-Marah Stud has been in existence for over fifty years. The encouragement and help she has given to smaller breeders has done much to further the development of Crabbet lines in the States. Some of these horses, notably Count Dorsaz 14388, have made a substantial impression on American breeding, as also have other post-war importations of Crabbet stock such as Nizzam 16070, Serafix 8955, Silver Crystal 7183, Serafire 7426 and Silver Drift 23494. Serafix has been particularly influential and by the end of 1968 had the record number of 46 Champions among his offspring. Another important stallion has been the Raseyn grandson Ferzon who was owned by the Gainey Foundation. Daniel C. Gainey began the Foundation in the 1950s with purchases of horses of mainly Crabbet blood-lines from Albert Harris and Roger Selby and his subsequent breeding programme has been a source of inspiration to many.

Other recent horses in America with a high percentage of Crabbet blood include Gai Parada; Al-Marah Canadius who has sired National Champions in halter and performance as well as having a fine career in the show-ring; Padron who has sired thirty-three National Winners and, above all, Khemosabi. This horse who is by Amerigo out of Jurneeka and so a grandson of Ferseyn, has had more registered foals than any other stallion, living or dead and is the leading living sire with no less than 268 Champions and 57 National Champions amongst his progeny.

A great strength of Arab horse breeding in the United States is the existence of many small independent studs whose owners are content to pursue their personal visions. Horses of largely Crabbet blood-lines are still being bred at numerous studs – Gai General (see page 275) is a case in point – and imports from England continue to be made. This robust individuality in the face of the current fashion for horses of Egyptian and other blood-lines is fostered by the availability of journals such as the *CMK Heritage Catalogue* and *The Crabbet Influence in Arabians Today* which offer their readers a depth of generally impartial research which cannot but be beneficial to the whole breed in the long term.

CANADA

The first Crabbet horse to reach Canada was the mare Narda (Rejeb/Narghileh) who in 1910 had been sold to Lothrop Ames in the United States where she had been named Narda II. She was later purchased by Mr Simmons Brown of Quebec who registered her in the Canadian Thoroughbred Studbook since there was at that time no Arabian studbook in which to enter her. She was followed by Rokhsa (Nasik/Rokhama) who had been sold in 1918 to W.R. Brown for whom she had produced the famous mare Rabiyat, and by two horses bred in the United States: the stallion Nazil (Rodan/Nusara) and the mare Rayif (Rodan/Raad). Rayif had three foals by Nazil but none appears to have bred on. Though he was only half Crabbet, mention must also be made of the stallion Aldebaran, sire of Algol, who was exported from England to Canada in 1929 and there named Aldebar. His dam was Amida, of Queen of Sheba's line, and his sire the desert-bred Dwarka.

Dwarka also features in the pedigree of Victory Day II who is probably the best-known of these early imports. Bred by Mr T.C. Armitage in 1944, Victory Day was by the Hanstead stallion Riffal out of Shabryeh, whose paternal grandsire was Dwarka. Victory Day had considerable influence in Canada: he was unbeaten in his classes in British Columbia, won

top Xanthium by Count Rafla by Count Dorsaz out of Expectation, a granddaughter of *Raffles, competing in the Tevis 100 miles Ride in the U.S.A
left Khemosabi (Amerigo by Ferseyn out of Jurneeka) *Photo Rees*
right AM Canadian Beau (Ranix – Al-Marah Caliope by Indraff) *Photo Louise Serpa*

numerous championships, in-hand and under saddle, and left a son, Mrs V. Breakwell's Royal Victory, who sired over 300 foals and through his progeny did much to promote the value of Arabian blood both in the show-ring and in performance.

In 1949, Mrs M. Trethewey purchased from the United States the Crabbet mare Rishafieh (Jeruan/Rishafa) who had been among the horses sold by Lady Wentworth to Roger A. Selby of Ohio. With her came her colt foal Ferishal who later developed into a brilliant show-jumper and dressage horse whose style and personality made him a prominent public figure in the 1960s.

In Ontario, Mrs M.A. Smith imported Iorana (Radi/Namilla) from Lady Yule in 1945. She was in foal to Rissalix at the time and the resulting colt, Ranix, went on to become Grand Champion at the Royal Winter Fair in 1955. He was eventually bought by Mrs Bazy Tankersley for the Al-Marah Stud in the United States and there proved himself an important sire. Among many good offspring was the outstanding bay, Canadian Beau.

The last sale to be made directly from Crabbet took place shortly after Lady Wentworth's death when Mr S.G. Bennett, also of Ontario, purchased several mares and fillies from Cecil Covey. These included Indian Peril (Dargee/Indian Pearl), who won at the Richmond Show just before being exported and who was then made Female Champion in Toronto soon after her arrival in Canada. But the most distinguished of Mr Bennett's imported horses was the splendid mare Serafina (Indian Gold/Sharfina). She lived to the age of thirty-one and produced seventeen foals, the last at the age of twenty-seven. Amongst these was Bright Gold, by Bright Shadow, which she had been carrying when sold, and Seralixa (by Ranix), who has turned out to be a fine brood mare.

As in the United States, there are many small studs in Canada which still concentrate on breeding from stock that is basically Crabbet in origin and several horses of Crabbet bloodlines have been imported from Britain in recent years.

LIST OF TABLES

Stallions

| S25 | Mahruss (1893) | S27 | Feysul |
| S26 | Mesaoud | S28 | Skowronek |

above Abu Zeyd
(Mesaoud–Rose Diamond)
centre Serafix
(Raktha–Serafina)
below left Silver Drift
(Raktha–Serafina) and
right Nizzam
(Rissam–Nezma)

S25 MAHRUSS (1893)

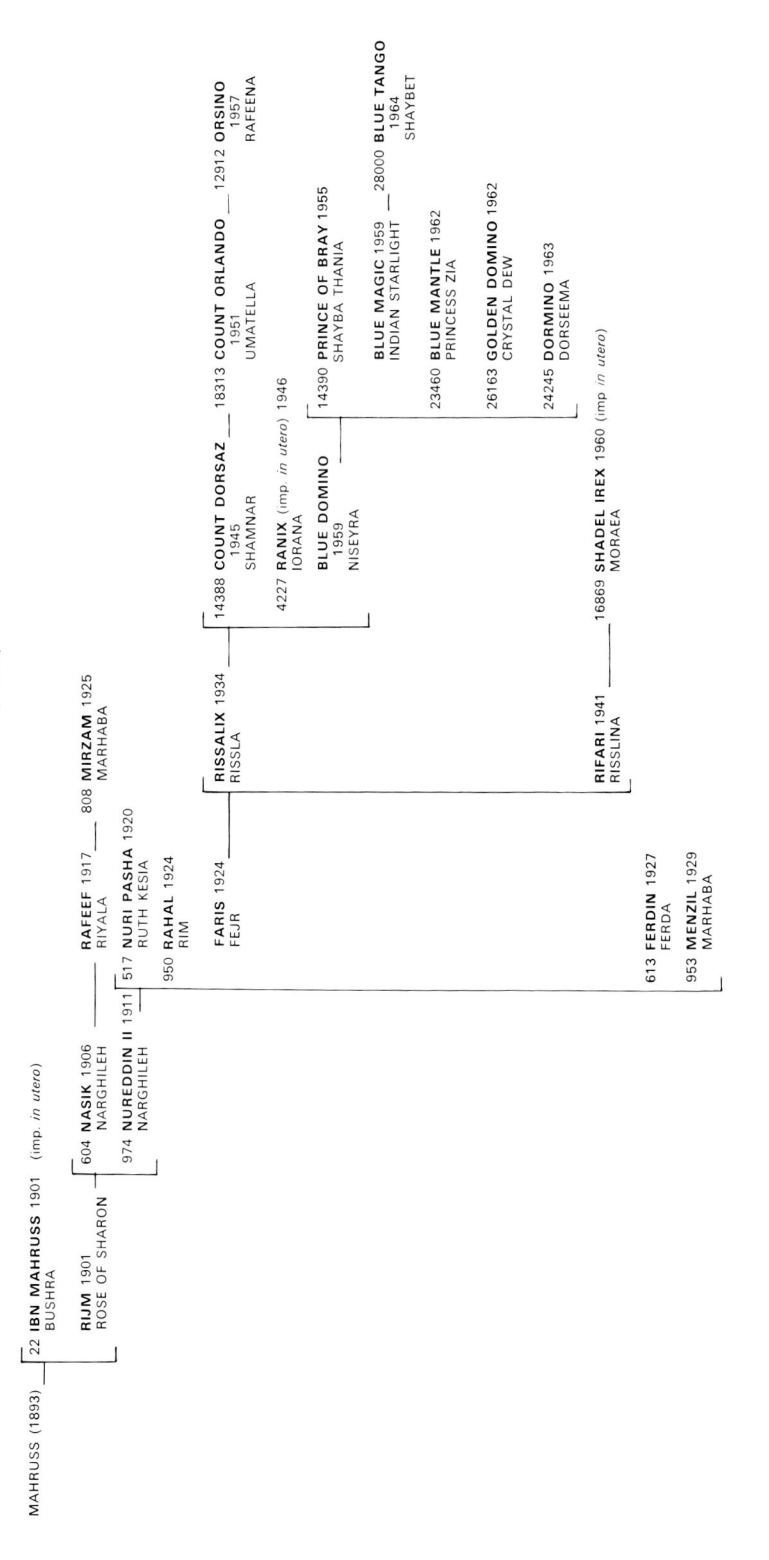

MAHRUSS (1893)
- 22 **IBN MAHRUSS** 1901 (imp. in utero)
  BUSHRA
- **RIJM** 1901
  ROSE OF SHARON
  - 604 **NASIK** 1906
    NARGHILEH
  - 974 **NUREDDIN II** 1911
    NARGHILEH
    - **RAFEEF** 1917 ── 808 **MIRZAM** 1925
      RIYALA   MARHABA
    - 517 **NURI PASHA** 1920
      RUTH KESIA
    - 950 **RAHAL** 1924
      RIM
      - **FARIS** 1924
        FEJR
        - **RISSALIX** 1934 ── 14388 **COUNT DORSAZ** ── 18313 **COUNT ORLANDO** ── 12912 **ORSINO**
          RISSLA   1945   1951   1957
                                    SHAMNAR   UMATELLA   RAFEENA
          - 4227 **RANIX** (imp. in utero) 1946
            IORANA
          - **BLUE DOMINO** 1959 ── 14390 **PRINCE OF BRAY** 1955 ── 28000 **BLUE TANGO**
            NISEYRA   SHAYBA THANIA   1964
                                                                        SHAYBET
            - **BLUE MAGIC** 1959
              INDIAN STARLIGHT
            - 23460 **BLUE MANTLE** 1962
              PRINCESS ZIA
            - 26163 **GOLDEN DOMINO** 1962
              CRYSTAL DEW
            - 24245 **DORMINO** 1963
              DORSEEMA
      - **RIFARI** 1941 ── 16869 **SHADEL IREX** 1960 (imp in utero)
        RISSLINA   MORAEA
- 613 **FERDIN** 1927
  FERDA
- 953 **MENZIL** 1929
  MARHABA

356

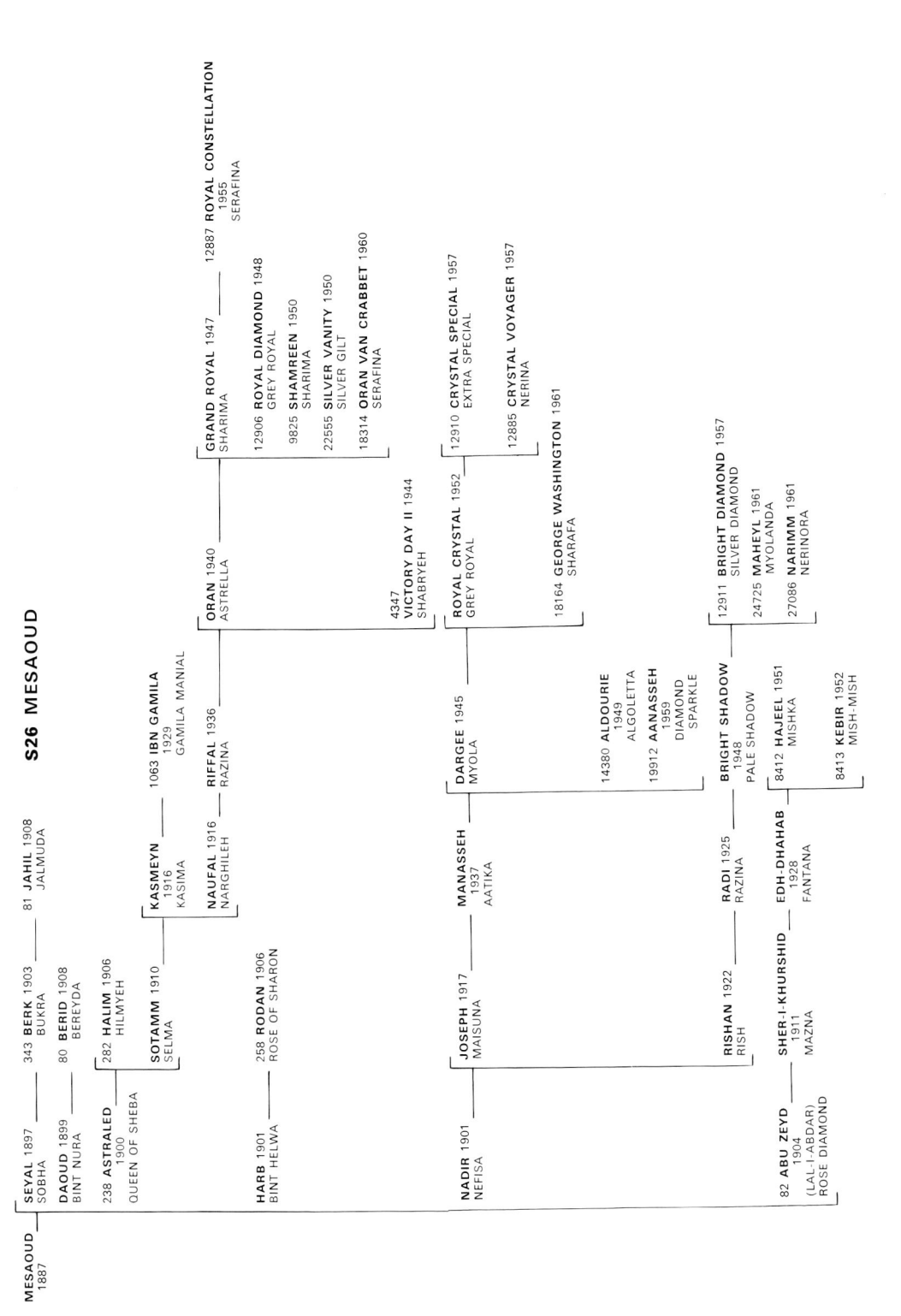

S26 MESAOUD

```
MESAOUD
1887
├── SEYAL 1897 ─── 343 BERK 1903 ─── 81 JAHIL 1908
│   SOBHA          BUKRA              JALMUDA
│
├── DAOUD 1899 ─── 80 BERID 1908
│   BINT NURA       BEREYDA
│
├── 238 ASTRALED ─── 282 HALIM 1906
│   1900              HILMYEH
│   QUEEN OF SHEBA
│              │
│              └── SOTAMM 1910 ─── KASMEYN 1916 ─── 1063 IBN GAMILA 1929
│                  SELMA            KASIMA            GAMILA MANIAL
│                                         │
│                                         └── NAUFAL 1916 ─── RIFFAL 1936 ─── ORAN 1940 ─── GRAND ROYAL 1947 ─── 12887 ROYAL CONSTELLATION 1955
│                                             NARGHILEH        RAZINA          ASTRELLA      SHARIMA                SERAFINA
│                                                                                   │
│                                                                                   ├── 12906 ROYAL DIAMOND 1948
│                                                                                   │         GREY ROYAL
│                                                                                   ├── 9825 SHAMREEN 1950
│                                                                                   │        SHARIMA
│                                                                                   ├── 22555 SILVER VANITY 1950
│                                                                                   │         SILVER GILT
│                                                                                   └── 18314 ORAN VAN CRABBET 1960
│                                                                                             SERAFINA
│
│                                                              4347
│                                                              VICTORY DAY II 1944 ─── ROYAL CRYSTAL 1952 ─── 12910 CRYSTAL SPECIAL 1957
│                                                              SHABRYEH                GREY ROYAL              EXTRA SPECIAL
│                                                                                           │
│                                                                                           └── 12885 CRYSTAL VOYAGER 1957
│                                                                                                     NERINA
│
│                                                                                  18164 GEORGE WASHINGTON 1961
│                                                                                        SHARAFA
│
├── HARB 1901 ─── 258 RODAN 1906
│   BINT HELWA    ROSE OF SHARON
│
│                           DARGEE 1945 ─── BRIGHT SHADOW ─── 12911 BRIGHT DIAMOND 1957
│                           MYOLA            1948                    SILVER DIAMOND
│                                            PALE SHADOW
│                                                       ├── 24725 MAHEYL 1961
│                                                       │         MYOLANDA
│                                                       └── 27086 NARIMM 1961
│                                                                 NERINORA
│
│                           14380 ALDOURIE 1949
│                                 ALGOLETTA
│                           19912 AANASSEH 1959
│                                 DIAMOND SPARKLE
│
├── NADIR 1901 ─── MANASSEH 1937 ─── JOSEPH 1917
│   NEFISA          AATIKA             MAISUNA
│                                        │
│                                        ├── RISHAN 1922 ─── RADI 1925 ─── HAJEEL 1951 ─── 8413 KEBIR 1952
│                                        │   RISH            RAZINA         MISHKA           MISH-MISH
│                                        │                                  8412
│                                        └── SHER-I-KHURSHID ─── EDH-DHAHAB
│                                            1911                 1928
│                                            MAZNA                FANTANA
│
└── 82 ABU ZEYD
    1904
    (LAL-I-ABDAR)
    ROSE DIAMOND
```

357

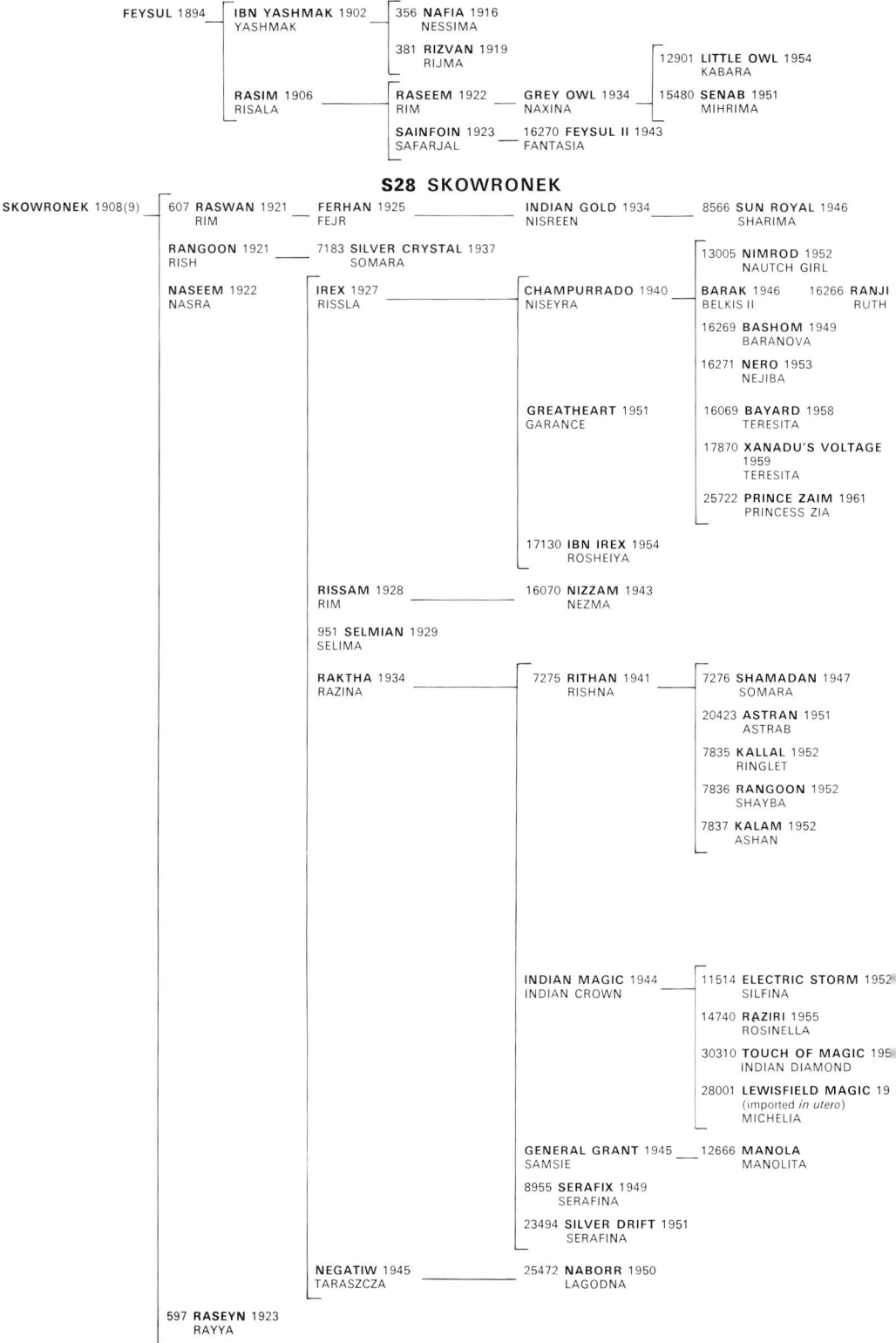

S27 FEYSUL

- FEYSUL 1894
  - IBN YASHMAK 1902 / YASHMAK
    - 356 NAFIA 1916 / NESSIMA
    - 381 RIZVAN 1919 / RIJMA
  - RASIM 1906 / RISALA
    - RASEEM 1922 / RIM
      - GREY OWL 1934 / NAXINA
        - 12901 LITTLE OWL 1954 / KABARA
        - 15480 SENAB 1951 / MIHRIMA
    - SAINFOIN 1923 / SAFARJAL
      - 16270 FEYSUL II 1943 / FANTASIA

S28 SKOWRONEK

- SKOWRONEK 1908(9)
  - 607 RASWAN 1921 / RIM
  - RANGOON 1921 / RISH
  - NASEEM 1922 / NASRA
    - FERHAN 1925 / FEJR
      - INDIAN GOLD 1934 / NISREEN
        - 8566 SUN ROYAL 1946 / SHARIMA
    - 7183 SILVER CRYSTAL 1937 / SOMARA
    - IREX 1927 / RISSLA
      - CHAMPURRADO 1940 / NISEYRA
        - 13005 NIMROD 1952 / NAUTCH GIRL
        - BARAK 1946 / BELKIS II   16266 RANJI / RUTH
        - 16269 BASHOM 1949 / BARANOVA
        - 16271 NERO 1953 / NEJIBA
      - GREATHEART 1951 / GARANCE
        - 16069 BAYARD 1958 / TERESITA
        - 17870 XANADU'S VOLTAGE 1959 / TERESITA
        - 25722 PRINCE ZAIM 1961 / PRINCESS ZIA
      - 17130 IBN IREX 1954 / ROSHEIYA
    - RISSAM 1928 / RIM
      - 16070 NIZZAM 1943 / NEZMA
    - 951 SELMIAN 1929 / SELIMA
    - RAKTHA 1934 / RAZINA
      - 7275 RITHAN 1941 / RISHNA
        - 7276 SHAMADAN 1947 / SOMARA
        - 20423 ASTRAN 1951 / ASTRAB
        - 7835 KALLAL 1952 / RINGLET
        - 7836 RANGOON 1952 / SHAYBA
        - 7837 KALAM 1952 / ASHAN
      - INDIAN MAGIC 1944 / INDIAN CROWN
        - 11514 ELECTRIC STORM 1952 / SILFINA
        - 14740 RAZIRI 1955 / ROSINELLA
        - 30310 TOUCH OF MAGIC 195 / INDIAN DIAMOND
        - 28001 LEWISFIELD MAGIC 19 (imported *in utero*) / MICHELIA
      - GENERAL GRANT 1945 / SAMSIE
        - 12666 MANOLA / MANOLITA
      - 8955 SERAFIX 1949 / SERAFINA
      - 23494 SILVER DRIFT 1951 / SERAFINA
    - NEGATIW 1945 / TARASZCZA
      - 25472 NABORR 1950 / LAGODNA
  - 597 RASEYN 1923 / RAYYA
  - 952 RAFFLES 1926 / RIFALA

Greatheart was the sire of Bayard and the horses listed beneath him.

RODANIA Or.Ar.

This table has three main purposes: to assemble in one place the breeding details of many of the horses that have been discussed in previous chapters; to put on record horses of Crabbet ancestry that have been important in America but which, for reasons of space, were not touched upon – or only very slightly – in that section; and, in a wider context, to illustrate how the descent from one desert-bred mare, dam of only five known live foals, has come to influence the entire world of Arab horse breeding.

Readers looking for unarguable criteria for the selection of the listed horses will be disappointed. Good sense must prevail unassisted when faced with a data base that in the case of the Rodania line runs to several thousand horses in tail female alone. Generally speaking, lines have been continued until either the Rodania element ceases to be material or the breeding record of an animal does not warrant its inclusion. The exception is America where descents have not been extended beyond the 1930s and 40s simply because the number of relevant horses becomes too great. Those listed should, however, be enough to give readers a platform from which they can reach modern pedigrees without difficulty. Cross-references (for example 'See M2') are to the tables in the overseas section dealing with Australia, Egypt and Russia.

RODANIA Or.Ar.

An asterisk before a horse's name, i.e. *Rossana, indicates an import to the United States of America. A dagger after a horse's name, i.e. Bazrah†, indicates that its breeding is given elsewhere on this table. Breeders' names are given following the sire or dam.

Rodania was a chestnut Kehailet Ajuz, an 'old and celebrated' mare. She was foaled in 1869 and bred by Ibn Roala of the Roala tribe. She was captured in 1880 by the Gomussa from whom she was purchased the following year by Wilfrid and Lady Anne Blunt. She was imported to Crabbet in 1881 and died in 1889.

RODANIA Or.Ar.
  ROSE OF JERICHO B. 1883 (**Kars Or.Ar.**) Crabbet. Australia 1891
    ROSE DIAMOND B. 1890 (**Azrek Or.Ar**) Crabbet
      ROSE OF HIND B. 1902 (**Rejeb**†) Crabbet
        RAZAZ B. 1907 (**Astraled**) Crabbet. Egypt 1920
          HAZNA B. 1914 (Hamasa) Crabbet. USA 1918
          BARAZA B. 1915 (Bereyda) Crabbet. USA 1918
            BABYAT B. 1922 (**Sidi**†) W.R. Brown
          BATTLA Gr. 1915 (Bukra) Crabbet. USA 1918. UK 1924
        RASIMA Ch. 1917 (**Daoud**) Crabbet. USA 1926
          JALILA Gr. 1922 (**Skowronek**) Crabbet. Spain 1930
            NANA SAHIB Gr. 1934 (**Razada**†) Veragua
            ROSE OF FRANCE Gr. 1926 (**Raswan**†) Crabbet. USA 1930
              BRIDE ROSE Gr. 1938 (**Ronek**†) J.M. Dickinson
          RASAFA Ch. 1926 (**Rafeef**†) Crabbet. USA 1926
            ANTAFA Ch. 1930 (**Antez**) W.K. Kellogg
        ROSSANA Gr. 1921 (**Skowronek**) Crabbet. USA 1926
          FERDANA Gr. 1931 (*****Ferdin**) W.K. Kellogg
          ROSSDIN Gr. 1933 (*****Ferdin**) W.K. Kellogg
          TAMMA B. 1937 (**Rifnas**†) W.K. Kellogg
          FARASA Gr. 1939 (**Farana**†) W.K. Kellogg
  LAL-I-ABDAR Ch. 1904 (**Mesaoud**) Hon. G. Savile. USA 1910 as Abu Zeyd
    NUSARA Ch. 1919 (*Noam) W.R. Brown
    BAZIKH Ch. 1927 (Bazrah†) W.R. Brown
    BAZLEYD Ch. 1928 (Bazrah†) W.R. Brown

RODANIA Or.Ar .
   ROSE OF SHARON Ch. 1885 (**Hadban Or.Ar.**) Crabbet . USA 1905
      RAFYK B. 1890 (**Azrek Or.Ar.**) Crabbet. Aust. 1891. See M1, M2 and M3
         AYESHA 1907 (Namusa) Sir J.P. Boucaut
      RIDAA Ch. 1892 (**Merzuk**) Crabbet
         RISALA Ch. 1900 (**Mesaoud**) Crabbet
            RASIM Ch. 1906 (**Feysul**) Crabbet. Poland 1924
               RIFLA Ch. 1920 (Rim†) Crabbet. USA 1926
               FARASIN B. 1920 (Ferda†) Crabbet. USA 1926
                  FARANA B. 1929 (**Nasik**†) W.K. Kellogg
                  FARNASA B. 1935 (**Nasik**†)W.K. Kellogg
               NASHISHA B. 1920 (Nasra) Crabbet. USSR 1936
                  SHARIMA Ch. 1932 (**Shareer**) Crabbet
               RASEEM Ch. 1922 (Rim†) Crabbet. USSR 1936
                  INDAIA B. 1927 (Nisreen)Crabbet. USA 1928
                  RIXALINA Ch. 1929 (Rissla†) Crabbet. USSR 1936. See M17
                  GREY OWL Gr. 1934 (Naxina) Lady Yule. See S13
                  INDIAN CROWN Ch. 1935 (Nisreen) Crabbet
            AJLUN B. 1923 (Mejamieh Or.Ar.) Brig. F.F. Lance. Spain 1926
            SAINFOIN B. 1923 (Safarjal) Mrs H.V. Musgrave Clark
            FASILA Ch. 1923 (Fejr) Crabbet. Poland 1927
               SULEJMAN Gr. 1934 (**Fetysz**) Baron Bicker. USA 1938
               RASIM PIERWSZY B. 1937 (**Rasim III**†) Baron Bicker
                  RASIMA B. 1943 (Sardhana) Baron Bicker
            RASIM III B. 1931 (Karima) Baron Bicker
               EI-ZABIBE Gr. 1938 (Karima) Baron Bicker
                  ELZA B. 1942 (**Rasim Pierwszy**†) Baron Bicker
         RIJMA Ch. 1911 (**Rijm**†) Crabbet. USA 1918
            RIZ B. **1916** (**Razaz**†) Crabbet
               REGISTAN Gr. 1927 (**Skowronek**) Crabbet. Egypt
            RIZVAN Ch. 1919 (**Ibn Yashmak**) W.R. Brown. USA i.u.
               BAHREYN B. 1924 (*Battla) Crabbet. UK i.u. USA 1926
               NADIRAT Ch. 1927 (Nusara†) W.R. Brown
            RIBAL Ch. 1920 (*Berk) W.R. Brown
               GHADAF Ch. 1929 (Gulnare†) W.R. Brown
               GHANIGAT Gr. 1930 (Guemura) W.R. Brown
               BINT SEDJUR Gr. 1935 (Sedjur) R. Wilson
               CARAVAN Ch. 1938 (Fasal) R. Wilson

RODANIA Or.Ar.
  ROSE OF SHARON
    RIDAA
      RISALA
        RIJMA (cont.)
          RAAD Ch. 1922 (**Sidi**†) W.R. Brown
            RAHAS Ch. 1928 (**Gulastra**†) W.R. Brown
        RYTHMA B. 1914 (**Berk**) Crabbet
          RUANDA B. 1926 (**Najib**) Crabbet. USSR 1936. See M16
          RADUGA B. 1937 (**Rytham**†) Tersk. See M16
          RYTHAM Ch. 1929 (**Shareer**) Crabbet. USSR 1936
            SHARFINA Ch. 1937 (**Sharima**†) Crabbet
            RADUGA B. 1937 (**Ruanda**†) Tersk. See M16
            REZEDA II Ch. 1939 (**Ruellia**†) Tersk. See M15
          RYTHAMA B. 1930 (**Shareer**) Crabbet
            RAKIB Gr. 1934 (**Nax**) Mrs G. Bromley. Aust. 1938. See S9
          ALGOLETTA Ch. 1935 (**Algol**†) G. Ruxton
          MYOLA B. 1937 (**Algol**†) G. Ruxton
            DARGEE Ch. 1945 (**Manasseh**) G. Ruxton
            MYOLETTA Ch. 1946 (**Manasseh**) G. Ruxton
            MYOLANDA Ch. 1948 (**Manasseh**) G. Ruxton
        RISSLA Ch. 1917 (**Berk**) Crabbet
          RIFALA Gr. 1922 (**Skowronek**) Crabbet. USA 1928
            RAFFLES Wh. 1926 (**Skowronek**) Crabbet. USA 1932
              INDRAFF Gr. 1938 (**Indaia**†) R. Selby
              RAFLA Ch. 1941 (**Indaia**†) R. Selby
              GEYM Gr. 1942 (**Rageyma**) R. Selby
              RALLAF Ch. 1942 (**Chrallah**) R. Selby
              AARAF Gr. 1943 (**Aarah**) Mrs B. Tormohlen
              RAPTURE B. 1946 (**Rafla**†) R. Selby
              ROSE-MARIE Gr. 1947 (**Rodetta**) M. Shuey
              AZRAFF Gr. 1949 (**Azja IV**) W. Ross
              CASSANDRA Gr. 1946 (**Rodetta**) M. Shuey
              GARAFF B. 1948 (**Woengran**) R. Selby
              RAFFERTY Gr. 1953 (**Masrufa**) Alice Payne
            IMAGE Ch. 1933 (*****Mirage Or.Ar.**) R. Selby
            RAGALA Gr. 1934 (*****Mirage Or.Ar.**) R. Selby
            RIFAGE Gr. 1936 (*****Mirage Or.Ar.**) R. Selby
            PHANTOM Gr. 1941 (**Image**†) R. Selby

RODANIA Or.Ar.
  ROSE OF SHARON
    RIDAA
      RISALA
        RISSLA
          REYNA Gr. 1925 (**Skowronek**) Crabbet. Spain 1930
            MORAYMA Ch. 1933 (**Razada**†) Veragua
              KANTISTA Gr. 1947 (**Nana Sahib**†) Yeguada Militar
                ALHABAC Gr. 1956 (**Cairel**) Belalcázar
            KASHMIR Gr. 1934 (**Razada**†) Veragua
            IFNI Gr. 1937 (**Razada**†) Veragua
            JALILA III Ch. 1946 (**Nana Sahib**†) Yeguada Militar
              SAGAZ Ch. 1954 (**Habiente**) Yeguada Militar
                DAKAR Gr. 1962 (**Congo**) Yeguada Militar
                EBANISTA Gr. 1963 (**Congo**) Yeguada Militar
          RISSLINA Ch. 1926 (**Rafeef**†) Crabbet
            RISSLETTA Ch. 1930 (**Naseem**) Crabbet. USA 1936
              ABU FARWA Ch. 1940 (**Rabiyas**†) W.K. Kellogg
              JOANNA Ch. 1943 (**Rabiyas**†) W.K. Kellogg
            RISIRA Gr. 1939 (**Naziri**) Mrs E.M. Murray
              RISSEEFA Ch. 1943 (**Faris**†) Mrs E.M. Murray
                SILVER RIPPLE Gr. 1960 (**Silver Vanity**) Mrs R. Archer
              RISSALIRA Gr. 1947 (**Rissalix**†) Mrs E.M. Murray. USA 1957
                RISANIRA Br. 1952 (**Manasseh**) Mrs E.M. Murray
              NERINA Ch. 1950 (**Rissalix**†) Mrs E.M. Murray
              GLEAMING GOLD Ch. 1952 (**Indian Gold**) Mrs E.M. Murray
              CRYSTAL DEW Ch. 1957 (**Rifari**†) Mrs E.M. Murray
              DREAMING GOLD Ch. 1963 (**Blue Domino**†) Mrs E.M.
                                                          Murray
                GOLDEN TREASURE Ch. 1966 (**BIue Domino**†) Mrs E.M.
                                                       Murray
                AUTUMN GOLD Ch. 1969 (**Fari II**†) Mrs P.A.M. Murray
            RIFARI Ch. 1941 (**Faris**†) Mrs E.M. Murray
        IREX Ch. 1927 (**Naseem**) Crabbet
          INDIAN PRIDE Ch. 1938 (Nisreen) Crabbet
            INDIAN STARLIGHT Ch. 1951 (**Indian Magic**†) Ianthe Bell
          ZEHRAA Ch. 1951 (Nurmana) Lady May Abel Smith
          GREATHEART Ch. 1951 (**Garance**†) Miss M. Greely
          IRIDOS Gr. 1951 (**Rafeena**†) Miss G. Yule

RODANIA Or.Ar.
  ROSE OF SHARON
    RIDAA
      RISALA
        RISSLA
          RIXALINA Ch. 1929 (**Raseem**†) Crabbet. USSR 1936. See M17
            NAGRADA Gr. 1938 (**Naseem**) Tersk
            KOREJ Ch. 1939 (**Kann**) Tersk
              KANKAN Gr. 1954 (Nagrada†) Tersk
              KNIPPEL Ch. 1954 (Parfumeria†) Tersk
              MAK Ch. 1956 (Madila†) Tersk
                KUMIR Ch. 1973 (Kapella†) Tersk
          RISSALMA Ch. 1932 (**Shareer**) Crabbet. USSR 1936. See M17
            FLORENCIA Ch. 1936 (**Faris**†) Crabbet. USSR 1936. See M17
              PARFUMERIA Ch. 1945 (**Piolun**) Tersk
                KNIPPEL Ch. 1945 (**Korej**†) Tersk
            NATURALISTKA Ch. 1937 (**Naseem**) Tersk
              KLINIKA Ch. 1951 (**Korej**†) Tersk
              PENOCHKA Gr. 1952 (**Pawadok**) Tersk. Poland 1956
            PRIBOJ Ch. 1944 (**Piolun**) Tersk
              POTENCJA B. 1952 (Taktika) Tersk. Poland 1956
              PLAKSA Ch. 1952 (Kreatura) Tersk
              POMERANETS Ch. 1952 (Mammona) Tersk
              PORFIRA Ch. 1953 (Operetka) Tersk. Poland 1958
              PIEWICA B. 1953 (Wlodarka) Tersk. Poland 1956.
              PIETUSZOK B. 1954 (Taktika) Tersk. Poland 1958.
                                                             Canada 1973
              MONOPOLIA B. 1956 (Mammona) Tersk
              KAPELLA Ch. 1957 (Kanitel) Tersk
              TOPOL B. 1958 (Taktika) Tersk
          RISSALIX Ch. 1934 (**Faris**†) Crabbet
          RISSELLA Ch. 1939 (**Radi**†) Crabbet
            ROSALINA Ch. 1943 (**Indian Gold**) Crabbet
              ROSINELLA Ch. 1947 (**Oran**†) Crabbet. Aust. 1956. See M5
                CRYSTAL FIRE Ch. 1952 (**Dargee**†) Mrs Bomford. Aust.
                                                       61. See S10
              MAGNET Ch. 1951 (**Dargee**†) Miss M. Lyon
            RISSILETTA Ch. 1943 (**Indian Gold**) Crabbet. USA 1956
              RISSALMA Ch. 1954 (**Dargee**†) Crabbet
                INDRISS Ch. 1962 (**Indian Magic**†) Mrs E.M. Thomas

RODANIA Or.Ar.
  ROSE OF SHARON
    RIDAA
      RISALA
        RAFINA Ch. 1919 (**Rustem**[†]), Crabbet. Australia 1925. See M5
        RAZIEH Ch. 1920 (**Ibn Yashmak**) Cr. Egypt 1920 as Bint Rissala. M11
      RIYALA Ch. 1905 (**Astraled**) Crabbet
        RANYA B. 1916 (**Nasik**[†]) Crabbet. Spain 1926
          RAZADA Gr. 1925 (**Shahzada**) C. Hough. Spain 1926
            KASHMIR Gr. 1934 (Reyna[†]) Veragua
              KAYAN Gr. 1947 (Sara) Yeguada Militar
                BATISTA Ch. 1960 (**Sherif**) Yeguada Militar
                ARILLA Gr. 1961 (**Malvito**[†]) Osuna
            NANA SAHIB Gr. 1934 (Jalila[†]) Veragua
            FABULOSO Ch, 1942 (Beni Amer) Yeguada Militar
            EGINA B. 1941 (Saboya) Yeguada Militar
              MALVITO B. 1949 (**Gandhy**) Yeguada Militar
            FAMULA Gr. 1942 (Sara) Yeguada Militar
              MAQUILLO Ch. 1949 (**Gandhy**) Yeguada Militar
            HABLADURIA Ch. 1944 (Sara) Yeguada Militar
              BALDOSA Ch. 1960 (**Maquillo**[†]) Yeguada Militar
            KANTISTA Gr. 1947 (Morayma[†]) Yeguada Militar
          IFNI Gr. 1937 (Reyna[†]) Veragua
            ALMOZABOR Gr. 1942 (Duquesa) Valdés. Jordan 1949 as
                                            Ushaahe
        MIRIAM Ch. 1921 (**Nadir**) J. Hamilton Leigh. Aust. 1926. See M7
        RANYA II B. 1922 (**Redif**[†]) J. Hamilton Leigh
          ROXANA Gr. 1932 (**Ruskov**) Miss M. Russell
            ROSH Gr. 1939 (**Joseph**) Miss M. Russell
            ROXELANA Gr. 1937 (**Joseph**) Miss M. Russell
              BLUE RHAPSODY Ch. 1954 (**Blue Domino**[†]) Gibson
              BINT ROXANA Gr. 1957 (**Greatheart**[†]) Miss M.J. Stevens
          RUFEIYA B. 1938 (**Aluf**) Miss M. Russell
            ROSHEIYA B. 1943 (**Rosh**[†]) Miss M.J. Stevens
              ROSHNARA Ch. 1949 (**Hassan II**) Miss M.J. Stevens
          RAFEENA Gr. 1940 (**Aluf**) Miss M. Russell
            IRIDOS Gr. 1951 (**Irex**[†]) Miss G. Yule
            COUNT RAPELLO Ch. 1954 (**Count Dorsaz**[†]) Miss G. Yule

RODANIA Or.Ar.
  ROSE OF SHARON
    RIDAA
      RIYALA
        RAFEEF Ch. 1917 (**Nasik**†) Crabbet. Argentina 1926
        NEZMA B. 1926 (Nasra) Crabbet
        RISSLINA Ch. 1926 (Rissla†) Crabbet
        RISAMA B. 1920 (**Nadir**) Crabbet. Egypt 1920 as Bint Riyala. See M12
          BINT BINT RIYALA Gr. 1924 (**Gamil Manial**) R.A.S. Egypt
        RAZINA Ch. 1922 (**Rasim**†) Crabbet
          RADI B. 1925 (**Rishan**†) Mrs E. Carroll
            TEHOURA Ch. 1946 (Niseyra†) Miss G. Yule
          BRIGHT SHADOW Ch. 1948 (Pale Shadow†) Mounsey-Heysham
          NURSCHIDA Ch. 1930 (**Nuri Sherif**) Lady Yule
            SULKA Ch. 1934 (**Naseem**) Lady Yule
              QUEEN ZENOBIA B. 1942 (**Radi**†) Lady Yule
            NAMILLA Ch. 1937 (**Algol**†) Lady Yule
              UMATELLA Ch. 1945 (**Oran**†) Lady Yule
                COUNT ORLANDO Ch. 1951 (**Count Dorsaz**†)
                                            Miss G. Yule. USA 1960
                  DOMATELLA Ch. 1960 (**Blue Domino**†) Mrs T.W.I.
                                            Hedley
            MIKENO Ch. 1949 (**Rissalix**†) Miss G. Yule
            CORREZE Ch. 1950 (**Count Dorsaz**†) Miss G. Yule.
                                  South Africa 1955
            COUNT MANILLA Ch. 1952 (**Count Dorsaz**†)Miss G. Yule.
                                  Aust. 57. See S12
          MANZANA B. 1938 (**Naufal**) Lady Yule
            MORAEA B. 1950 (**Irex**†) Mrs E.M. Murray. USA 1959
          RIKITEA Ch. 1942 (**Rissalix**†) Lady Yule
            GARANCE Gr. 1946 (**Grey Owl**†) Miss G. Yule
              PERLE D'OR Gr. 1956 (**Count Dorsaz**†) Miss M. Greely
            TERESITA Ch. 1951 (**General Grant**†) Miss G. Yule
              ESTHER II Ch. 1960 (**Greatheart**†) Miss M. Greely
            TAHEKI Ch. 1953 (**Grey Owl**†) Miss G. Yule. USA 1957
        RAKTHA Gr. 1934 (**Naseem**) Lady Yule. Sth. Africa 1951. See S22
        INDIAN MAGIC Gr. 1944 (Indian Crown†) Crabbet
        GENERAL GRANT Ch. 1945 (Samsie) Lady Yule
        ELECTRIC SILVER Gr. 1948 (Silfina) Crabbet. Australia 1950.
                                                    See S8
      RIFFAL B. 1936 (**Naufal**) Lady Yule. Aust. 47. See S11, S23
        ORAN Ch. 1940 (Astrella) Lady Yule

RODANIA Or.Ar.
  ROSE OF SHARON
    RIDAA
      RIYALA
        RAZINA (cont.)
          SHAMNAR Ch. 1939 (**Naziri**) Lady Yule
            PALE SHADOW Ch. 1944 (**Rissalix**†) Lady Yule
              BRIGHT GLEAM Ch. 1958 (**Aldourie**) Mrs Rowcliffe
            COUNT DORSAZ Ch. 1945 (**Rissalix**†) Lady Yule. USA 1958
            SALINAS Gr. 1947 (**Grey Owl**†) Miss Yule. USA 1957
              YATEEMAH Gr. 1954 (**Blue Domino**†) Miss Yule
                CINDERS Ch. **1959** (**Algolson**) Mrs J. Ratcliff
          RAMAYANA Ch. 1924 (**Nureddin II**†) Crabbet. Poland 1928
            MADDY Ch. 1937 (**Rasim III**†) Baron Bicker
              MADILA Ch. 1942 (**Lowelas**) USSR 1945
          RUELLIA Ch. 1926 (**Nureddin II**) Crabbet. USSR 1936. See M15
            RIYALAN Wh. 1930 (**Naseem**) Crabbet. Australia 1934
            REZEDA II Ch. 1939 (**Rytham**†) Tersk. See M15
      RUSTEM B. 1908 (**Astraled**) Crabbet. Egypt 1920
        FERDA B. 1913 (Feluka) Crabbet. USA 1926
        RAFINA Ch. 1919 (**Risala**†) Crabbet. Australia 1925. See M5
        BINT RUSTEM Br. 1922 (Bint Hadba el Saghira) R.A.S. Egypt
          HIND B. 1929 (**Ibn Rabdan**) R.A.S. Egypt
          MASHHOUR Br. 1941 (**Shahloul**) R.A.S. Egypt
        RASALA B. 1926 or 27 (Serra) Prince Kemal ed Dine
        KASBANA B. (**Registan**†) T.G.B. Trouncer
          MAHASIN Gr. 1942 (**Sheikh el Arab**) T.G.B. Trouncer
      RIM Ch. 1910 (**Astraled**) Crabbet
        RAMIM B. 1915 (**Berk**) Crabbet. USA 1918
          REHAL Ch. 1923 (**Sidi**†) W.R. Brown
            RABIYAT B. 1926 (*Rokhsa†) W.R. Brown
            RAMGHAZA B. 1933 (**Ghazi**) P. Houston
        RIFLA Ch. 1920 (**Rasim**†) Crabbet. USA 1926
          RIFDA Ch. 1926 (**Nureddin II**†) Crabbet. USA 1926
          RIFNAS Ch. 1932 (**Nasik**†) W.K. Kellogg
            AULANI Ch. 1940 (Follyat) H.H. Reese
        RASWAN Gr. 1921 (**Skowronek**) Crabbet. USA 1926
        STAR OF THE HILLS B. 1927 (Selima) Crabbet. USSR 1936.
                                                        See M18
          STARILLA B. 1935 (**Raseem**†) Crabbet

RODANIA Or.Ar.
  ROSE OF SHARON
    RIDAA
      RIM (cont.)
        RASEEM Ch. 1922 (**Rasim**†) Crabbet. USSR 1936
          INDAIA B. 1927 (Nisreen) Crabbet. USA 1928
            INDRAFF Gr. 1938 (*****Raffles**†) R. Selby
            RAFLA Ch. 1941 (*****Raffles**†) R. Selby
          RIMINI Gr. 1923 (**Skowronek**) Crabbet. USA 1933
            NAHARIN Gr. 1941 (**Gulastra**†) J.M. Dickinson
        RAHAL Ch. 1924 (**Nureddin II**†) Crabbet. USA 1932
        RISSAM Ch . 1928 (**Naseem**) Crabbet
          NISEYRA Ch. 1935 (Neraida) Crabbet
          NIZZAM B. 1943 (Nezma) Crabbet. Netherlands 1948. USA 1960
            RIKHAM Gr. 1945 (Rafeena†) Mrs Armstrong Jones. Australia 1948.
                                                        See S5
            RALVON PILGRIM Ch. 1969 (Trix Silver) Mrs V. Males
          SHADES OF NIGHT Ch. 1946 (Sharfina†) Crabbet. USA 1957
      RIEF B. 1915 (**Sotamm**) Crabbet. Australia 1918. See S11
        RAISULI (Ayesha†) G.L. Brown
          BARADA II B. 1934 (Gadara) A.J. McDonald
    RIJM Ch. 1901 (**Mahruss 1893**) Crabbet
      NASIK B. 1908 (Narghileh) Crabbet. USA 1926
        RAFEEF Ch. 1917 (Riyala†) Crabbet. Argentina 1926
      NUREDDIN II Ch. 1911 (Narghileh) Crabbet
        FARIS Ch. 1924 (Fejr) Crabbet
          RISSALIX Ch. 1934 (Rissla†) Crabbet
            COUNT DORSAZ Ch. 1945 (Shamnar†) Lady Yule. USA 1958
              COUNT ORLANDO Ch. 1951 (Umatella†) G. Yule. USA 1960
              COUNT MANILLA Ch. 1952 (Namilla†) Yule. Aust. 1957. S12
              COUNT RAPELLO Ch. 1954 (Rafeena†) Miss G. Yule
              COUNT ROLAND Ch. 1957 (Rithyana†) Miss M. Greely
                ROXAN Gr. 1964 (Bint Roxana†) Miss M.J. Stevens
            BLUE DOMINO Ch. 1947 (Niseyra†) Miss G. Yule
              LUDO Ch. 1953 (Rithyana†) B. Dixon
                LUDOMINO Gr. 1964 (Yemama) D.D. Wright
              MANTO Ch. 1956 (Mifaria†) Lady Anne Lytton
              FARI II B, 1965 (Farette†) Mrs R. Brown
            MIKENO Ch. 1949 (Namilla†) Miss G. Yule
              EL MELUK Ch. 1959 (Mifaria†) Lady Anne Lytton
              RINGING GOLD Ch. 1961 (Gleaming Gold†)
                                                    Mrs E.M. Murray
            KAZRA Ch. 1961 (Razehra) Lady May Abel Smith

RODANIA Or.Ar.
  ROSE OF SHARON
    RIJM
      NUREDDIN II
        FARIS (cont.)
          RIFARI Ch. 1941 (Risslina†) Mrs E.M. Murray
            FARETTE B. 1954 (Shabrette) Mrs E.M. Murray
    RODAN Ch. 1906 (**Harb**) S. Borden. USA i.u.
      GULNARE Gr. 1914 (*Ghazala) S. Borden
        GULASTRA Ch. 1924 (*Astraled) W.R. Brown
          RAHAS Ch. 1928 (Raad†) W.R. Brown
            RABIYAS Ch. 1936 (Rabiyat†) W.R. Brown
              ABU FARWA Ch. 1940 (Rissletta†) W.K. Kellogg
                GA'ZI Ch. 1949 (Ghazna) L. Mekeel
                ANTEZEYN SROWRONEK Ch. 1949 (Sharifa) E. Boyer
                ABU BAHA Ch. 1948 (Surrab) H.H. Reese
                ABU GAMWA Gr. 1953 (Gamyla) Cal-Poly
                SCHARIFA Ch. 1948 (Schilastra) L. Mekeel
                FARLANE Ch. 1957 (Alleyna) H.H. Reese
                SHAMA Ch. 1947 (Shamrah) L. Hinckley
                TAMARLANE Ch. 1945 (Ritama) J. & M. Flowers
                ABLA Ch. 1949 (Valla) F. Jorgensen
      BAZRAH B. 1919 (Bathsheba) W.R. Brown
      RAAF B. 1925 (*Rokhsa†) W.R. Brown
      GHAZI Gr. 1925 (Guemura) W.R. Brown
      FATH Ch. 1926 (*Kola) W.R. Brown
    ROSA RUGOSA Ch. 1907 (*Imamzada) S. Borden
      SIDI Ch. 1917 (**Khaled**) W.R. Brown
        BABYAT B. 1922 (*Baraza†) W.R. Brown
        RAAD Ch. 1922 (*Rijma†) W.R. Brown
        REHAL Ch. 1923 (Ramim†) W.R. Brown
          RABIYAT B. 1926 (*Rokhsa†) W.R. Brown
          RIBAGH Ch. 1933 (Raaf†) W.R. Brown
          RABKHAL Ch. 1937 (Rabk†) Hearst Corp.
ROSEMARY B. 1886 (**Jeroboam**) Crabbet. Sold 1888, repurchased 1890
  REJEB Ch. 1897 (**Mesaoud**) Crabbet. Japan 1901
    ROSE OF HIND B. 1902 (Rose Diamond†) Crabbet
    NARDA Ch. 1902 (Narghileh) Crabbet. USA 1910 as Narda II

RODANIA Or.Ar.
  ROSEMARY (cont.)
    RABLA B. 1899 (**Mesaoud**) Crabbet
      RISH B. 1903 (**Nejran**) Crabbet
        RANGOON Gr. 1921 (**Skowronek**) Crabbet
        RISHAN B. 1922 (**Nadir**) Crabbet
          RADI B. 1925 (Razina†) Mrs E.M. Carroll
            BRIGIIT SHADOW Ch. 1948 (Pale Shadow†)
                                Mrs P. Mounsey-Heysham
        RISHNA Ch. 1923 (**Nureddin II**†) Crabbet
        RISHKA B. 1928 (**Naufal**) Crabbet
          RISHYANA Ch. 1939 (**Rissam**†) Crabbet. South Africa 1945
            RITHYANA Ch. 1943 (**Raktha**†) Crabbet
              MIFARIA Ch. 1947 (**Oran**†) C. McConnell
                MELLAWIEH Ch. 1951 (**Indian Magic**†) Lady A. Lytton.
                                  USA 1961
                  MANTO Ch. 1956 (**Blue Domino**†) Lady Anne Lytton
                  EL MELUK Ch. 1959 (**Mikeno**†) Lady Anne Lytton
              LILAC DOMINO Ch. 1952 (**Blue Domino**†) B. Dixon
              LUDO Ch. 1953 (**Blue Domino**†) B. Dixon
              PRINCESS TROUBADOUR Ch. 1955 (**Blue Domino**†)
                                  B. Dixon
            GHAZALI Ch. 1961 (**Count Rapello**†) Mrs T.W.I Hedley
          RAFIKA Gr. 1943 (**Ruskov**) Dr E. Maconochie
        MARISHNA Ch. 1950 (**Manasseh**) Mrs N. Elms
      RISHAFA Ch. 1924 (**Nureddin II**†) Crabbet
        RISHAFIEH Ch. 1930 (**Jeruan**) Crabbet. USA 1932
          RAFFIEH Ch. 1938 (*****Raffles**†) R. Selby
    ROKHAMA Ch. 1906 (**Astraled**) Crabbet
      ROKHSA B. 1915 (**Nasik**†) Crabbet. USA 1918
        RABIYAT B. 1926 (Rehal†) W.R. Brown
          RABK Ch. 1931 (**Gulastra**†) W.R. Brown
            RABKHAL Ch. 1937 (**Rehal**†) Hearst Corp.
          RABIYAS Ch. 1936 (**Rahas**†) W . R . Brown
          TAWALI B. 1938 (**Raseyn**†) W.K. Kellogg
        ROSHANA B. 1920 (**Berk**) W.R. Brown
          ROSEYNA Gr. 1939 (**Raseyn**†) W.K. Kellogg
      RAAF B. 1925 (**Rodan**†) W.R. Brown
        RIBAGH Ch. 1933 (**Rehal***) W.R. Brown
        FEJR B . 1942 (**Bazikin**) R . Wing

371

RODANIA Or.Ar.
  ROSEMARY
    RABLA (cont.)
      RANGHA Ch. 1911 (**Berk**) Crabbet
        KAROOSHA B. 1921 (**Dwarka Or.Ar.**) The Prince of Wales
          ALGOL Ch. 1928 (**Aldebaran**) The Prince of Wales
          RAHAB B. 1931 (**Sainfoin**†) H.V. Musgrave Clark
            RAZAZ Ch. 1949 (**Champurrado**) H.V.M. Clark. Australia 1955. See S7
          RHEOBOAM Ch. 1936 (**Sainfoin** †) H.V. Musgrave Clark
      RUKHAM B. 1912 (**Berk**) Crabbet. Argentina 1913
      RAIDA Gr. 1922 (**Skowronek**) Crabbet. USA 1926
        RAIDAANA Gr. 1931 (**Jadaan**) W.K. Kellogg
    ROSETTA Ch. 1903 (**Mesaoud**) Crabbet. USA 1906
    RIADA Br. 1904 (**Mesaoud**) Crabbet
      RAYYA Br. 1915 (**Rustem**†) Crabbet
        RASEYN Gr. 1923 (**Skowronek**) Crabbet. USA 1926
          RALET B. 1930 (Sherlet) W K. Kellogg
          RONEK Gr. 1931 (*Bahreyn†) W.K. Kellogg
            ALYF Gr. 1938 (Fath†) J.M. Dickinson
          MONEYN Gr. 1934 (Monica) W.K. Kellogg
          MONEYNA Gr. 1937 (Monica) W.K. Kellogg
          FERSEYN Gr. 1937 (*Ferda†) W.K. Kellogg
            FERNEYN Gr. 1944 (Moneyna $) H. Ellis
              FERZON Gr. 1952 (Fersara $) F.B. McCoy
            FERSARA Gr. 1947 (Bint Sahara) F.B. McCoy
            SAKI Gr. 1950 (Ferdia) Mary Brown
            AMERIGO Gr. 1962 (*Szarza) F. Mari
          SUREYN Gr. 1940 (*Crabbet Sura) W.K. Kellog
    REDIF B. 1906 (**Daoud**) Crabbet.
  ROALA B. 1884 (**Kars Or.Ar.**) Crabbet. Sold and died 1888
   JAMILA Ch. 1887 (Jerboa) Crabbet. USA 1893
     JOKTAN Ch. 1891 (**Ashgar Or. Ar.**) Crabbet. Sold 1893
     ABDALLAH Gr. 1897 (*Bedr) J.M. Forbes. Gelded
   DEBORA B. 1888 (Dahma Or. Ar.) Crabbet. Sold 1895
    QUEEN OF RAIN B. 1888 (Queen of Sheba Or. Ar.) Crabbet. Died 1888
  REHOBOAM B. 1887 (**Jeroboam**) Crabbet. Sold 1888

GENERAL INDEX

Abassieh Stud 48
Abbas Pasha I 16, 49, 72, 78, 83, 97, 101, 108, 109, 112, 146, 294, 295, 299, 300
Abbas Pasha II, The Khedive, 83, 87, 110, 112, 122, 146, 294, 296
    Ismail 85
    Tewfik 260
Abd el Azim el Afifi 261
Abd el Jadir 95
Abd el Kadr 66
Abd el Wahab 110, 261
Abdullah, King of Jordan 323
Abdur Rahman Minni 56, 57, 259
Abel Smith, Col. Sir H. and Lady May 192, 200
Abu Fayal, wells of 49, 106
Ahmed ibn Jamil 260, 261
Ahmed Kemal Pasha, Prince 84, 86, 110, 112, 113, 260, 294, 296
    Yusuf Kemal (son) 110, 113, 294, 296
Ahmed Shafee 111
Alderney cattle 55
Aleppo 18, 19, 33, 34, 35, 37, 40, 41, 49, 50, 51, 57, 96, 99, 102, 103, 105, 107, 258, 259
Alexandretta 19, 20, 33, 50
Aleysh, Abdur Rahman 26
Algeria 70
Ali Agha 50, 258
Ali el Abdallah el Bassam 109, 111, 112, 113, 298
Ali ibn Amr 97
Ali Pasha Sherif 47–9, 66, 70, 77–9, 80, 81, 82–3, 86, 87, 88–92, 93, 95, 96, 97, 98, 100, 101, 106, 108, 109, 110, 111, 112, 113, 114, 120, 146, 162, 176, 227, 229, 268, 294, 296, 297, 298, 300, 307, 343
    Abd el Hamid (son) 91, 111, 294
    Ibrahim Bey (son) 91, 99, 294
    Othman Bey (son) 110, 113
Ali Pasha, Governor of Deyr 50, 102–3
Al Marah Stud *see* Tankersley, Mrs B.
Ames, Lothrop 144, 145, 232, 344
Anazeh, tribes of 19, 33, 42, 44, 94, 95, 99, 101, 102, 103, 104, 107, 108, 111, 147, 257, 258, 259, 260
    see also Gomussa *and* Ruala
Andrews, Dr 68
Anglo-Arabs 177, 198
Antoniny 54, 170
Antrim, Earl of 257
A Pilgrimage to Nejd 44
Arabi Pasha 73, 75, 76, 151
Arab Horse Society, The 118, 167, 170, 171, 176, 188, 192, 200, 203, 215
Arabian Horse Club of America, The 108, 153, 158
Arabian Horse Historians Association 244
Arabian Horse, Its Country and People 69
Arab's Farewell to His Steed, The 14
Arab's Ride to Cairo, The 14
Armenia 99
Armitage, T.C. 352
Arnold, Mrs E.B. 338
Ashley Combe 197
Authentic Arabian Horse, The 44, 66, 68, 192–3
Automobile Club, The 124
Ayerza, Señor 148, 266
Ayub Bey 98

Babbage, C. 26
Babolna Stud 259, 297, 298
Babson, Henry 295, 298, 350, 351
Baghdad 18, 35, 45, 257
Bedouin Tribes of the Euphrates 44
Bedr Mohammed 113
Beeding Farm 126, 157
Behtim 112
Beirut 19, 94
Bell, Sir H. 138
Bell, Ianthe 184, 200
Beni Khaled, tribe of 44
Bennett, S.G. 354
Bernhardt, Sarah 70
Beteyen ibn Mirshid 37, 43, 104, 105, 259
Bicker, Baron 229, 319, 321
Bickley, J. 143
Bille-Brahe-Selby, Baroness 333
Bishop, J. 179
Blackwater Farm 151, 152
Bligh, Mrs E. 274–5
Blunt, Alice, Mrs W.F.Wheatley 23, 30, 152
    Anne Isabella King, Lady 15th Baroness Wentworth 24, 25–33, 37–9, 40, 42, 44–5, 47–9, 53–4, 57–8, 64, 65, 66–8, 69, 70–1, 76–82, 83–5, 86, 87, 88–92, 93, 114, 116–7, 118, 120, 122, 124–36, 137–41, 143, 145–6, 147, 148–9, 150–5, 156–7, 158–9, 160, 163–4, 165, 167, 172, 177, 202, 225, 226, 243, 246, 268, 270, 294, 295, 343
    Francis Scawen, Blunt's father 23, 30
    Francis Scawen, Blunt's brother 23, 24, 30, 196
    Judith Anne Dorothea, *see* Wentworth, 16th Baroness
    Wilfrid Scawen 17, 19, 23–5, 26, 28, 29–33, 34, 37, 38, 40–1, 42, 44, 46–7, 49, 53–8, 61–70, 73–6, 77, 78, 79, 82–3, 86, 87, 88–9, 91, 92, 93, 94, 95, 96, 99, 104, 107, 114, 116–22, 124–36, 137–8, 140–1, 143, 144–5, 146–52, 153, 156–64, 165–6, 168, 171, 176, 196, 202, 225–7, 232, 236, 243, 244, 246, 259, 270, 344
    Wilfrid and Lady Anne
        Marriage 23
        In Algeria 32
        In Arabia 17, 32, 44–5, 49, 73, 76
        In Egypt 32, 47–8, 66, 73–92, 116
        In Syria 34–8, 49–50
        Attitudes to horses and breeding 39, 46, 51, 54–5, 56, 63–4, 65, 87, 94, 107, 143, 147, 153, 154, 165–6, 176, 225–7
        Stud-books of 39, 84, 93, 94, 95, 212, 295
    Wilfrid Scawen (son) 29
    See also Crabbet Arabian Stud, Sheykh Obeyd *and* Newbuildings
Boghos Bey, Achikian 260
Bombay 56, 97, 259
Bomb Proof, The 56
Bomford, Mrs S. 274
Booth, Mr 276
Borden, Spencer 111, 115, 139–41, 158, 248, 252, 270, 343, 344
Botha, A.J. 194, 338
Boucaut, Sir J.P. 59, 65, 245, 268–9
Bourke, Hon. T. 258, 260

GENERAL INDEX

Boxer Rebellion, the 118
Bowring, Mrs I. 202
Boyazoglu, Prof. and Mrs P. 339
Brackton 154
Brahms, J. 28
Branch, Dr A.E. 162, 167
Branicka, Countess 319
Branicki, Count 13
Breakwell, Mrs V. 354
Bretherton, D. and R. 335
British Bloodstock Agency, The 188
British Empire League, The 123
British Expeditionary Force, The 148
Brogden, W.W. 199
Brown, G.L. 270
Brown, W.R. 145, 158, 160, 164, 170, 343, 344–5, 348
Browne, Capt. R. 160
Browne, Gen. 131
Brudermann, Col. von 13, 18, 19
Burton Park Stud 213, 215
Bush–Brown, H.K. 153, 159
Buttigieg, E. 335
Byron, Anne Isabella Milbanke, Lady 24, 25
Byron, Lord George 23, 25, 126

Caffin, A.C. 71, 150, 157, 164
Cahill, Pat 206, 210, 221
Cairo 32, 72, 73, 75, 76, 77, 79, 81, 89, 100, 108, 109, 111, 116, 131, 260
Calvert, R.H. 177, 200
Cambridge Review, The 69
Campbell, Mrs D.M. 202
Carleton, Guy 131, 133, 138
Carleton, Miss M.T. (Dorothy) 133, 137, 138, 143, 149, 171
Carruthers, D. 16, 17
Carroll, Mrs E.M. 177
Casdugli, Mr 157, 298
Castleton, Drexel 182–3
Caxtons 72, 131, 136, 144, 146, 147, 150, 152, 157, 158, 160, 217, 218, 219
Chandler, E. 121, 150, 151
Chandler, Mary 23
Chaplin, H. 20
Chapman, Mrs E. 339
Chesney, Col. F.R. 32
Cheyne Gardens 121
Chipping Norton 115
Chrestowka Stud 70
Churchill, Lord Randolph 147
    Rt. Hon. Winston 147
Clark, H.V.Musgrave 98, 170, 176–7, 191, 243, 250, 272, 335, 351
    Mrs H.V.M. 177
Clery, Léon 100
CMK Heritage Catalogue 352
Cockerell, Sir S. 129, 162, 171
Constantinople 16, 18, 20, 24, 30, 32, 34, 41, 50, 69, 70, 77
Cooke, Hon. S. Winter 270
Courthouse Stud *see* Clark, H.V.Musgrave
Covey, Geoffrey 143, 148, 166, 184, 186, 196, 204, 217
    Cecil 184, 186, 196, 198, 199, 200, 202, 203–224
    Grace 202, 203
Cowie, Isabella 29, 38, 76, 77, 79, 116
Crabbet Arabian Stud, The 13, 25, 32, 34, 37, 38, 40, 42, 43, 47, 49, 51, 59, 64, 66, 81, 86, 87, 93, 94, 101, 105, 115, 118, 122, 126, 132–6, 149, 156–64, 165–70, 173, 179, 182, 184, 185, 186–92, 194, 196–7, 200, 202, 203–24, 224–8, 261, 294, 295, 307, 336, 343, 345
    "The Plan" 34–5, 38, 41, 42
    Auctions 53–5, 58, 60, 102, 104, 117, 118, 122, 132, 144, 147
    Colours of horses 70–1, 118, 146, 159, 168, 172
    Endurance tests 145, 239, 247, 274, 344

Finances of 53, 71, 116, 120–1, 131, 132, 138, 153, 156, 161, 163, 164, 167, 182, 184, 194, 196, 204
Lawsuit over 156–64, 166, 244
Partition of 126–36, 140, 141, 150, 157, 159
Racing 40, 47, 51, 55–8, 81, 236, 312
Showing 47, 71, 114, 120, 144, 170, 179, 181, 186, 187, 191, 194, 207–8, 224
Crabbet Influence in Arabians Today 352
Crabbet Park 23, 25, 30, 37, 51, 53, 59, 61–3, 69, 71, 72, 99, 117, 118, 124– 6, 138, 143, 144, 148, 149–52, 160, 164, 196, 202
Crookhorn Farm 116, 138, 150, 164
Cromer, Evelyn Baring, 1st Earl of 76, 117, 122
Currie, Sir D. 225

Da Croz, F. 29
Damascus 19, 32, 37, 42, 43, 44, 49, 66, 94, 103, 127
Dambly, M. 18, 19
Damoiseau, L 18
Dangar, A.A. and W.J. 20, 54, 258, 259, 268
Daumas, Gen. E. 66
Davenport, Homer 146–7, 343, 348
Dawson, Mat 57
Dean, Col. 131
De Portes, M. 18
Derkoul Stud, The 104, 108
De Wiart, C. 91
Deyr 96, 98, 103, 257
Dickinson, Gen J.M. 343
Digby, Jane 42, 43
Dillon, Hon. Miss Etheldred 51, 59, 115, 138, 243, 251, 252, 257, 258, 270
Dömken, C–H. 330
Dorgan 144
Doughty, C.M. 16, 17, 65
Dow, R.H. 200
Drummonds Bank 132
Dunsany, Lord 194
Du Toit, W.P. 338
Dzieduszycki, Count 13

Edward VII, King 47, 76, 122
Edward VIII, King 141
Egyptian Agricultural Organisation 294, 295, 301
Egyptian Gazette, The 155
Egyptian Horse Breeding Commission, The 113
Egypt, Royal Agricultural Society of 98, 153, 294, 295, 296, 298, 300
El Hami Pasha 78, 294
Elizabeth II, Queen 192
El Khamsa 17
El Kheyshi 80, 83, 131, 137
Elms, Mrs Nina 108
Eustis, Mr 118, 343
Evening Globe, The 124
Exmoor ponies 118
Ezbet en Nakhle 117

Fairhurst, Lord 55
Faisal I. King of Iraq 108
Faris Assaat 95
Faudel-Phillips, Maj. H.F. 191
Fechtig. Baron von 13
Fernycroft 117, 118, 121
Field, The 20, 53, 121
"First Attempt" *see* Sheykh Obeyd
Fitzgerald, Mr 47
Flemotomo, Paul 79, 80, 81, 83
Forbes, W.H. 314
Forest Cottage 124, 129, 133, 143, 152
Francis, S. 39, 40, 47, 57
Frogshole Farm 147, 151, 152, 203, 208, 209, 212, 213, 218, 219
Fuad, King of Egypt 220, 300
Fulton, Col. 153
Future of Islam, The 73

Gainey, Daniel 275, 277, 351
Gazder, Dr P.J. 228
General Stud Book, The 59, 84, 94, 95, 108, 146, 166, 170, 177, 182, 187
George V, King 161
George, J.A. 345
Ghadir Aamr el Tihawi 261
Gilbert, Mrs D. 202
Gladstone, Rt.Hon. W.E. 47
Glyns Bank 127
Gomussa, tribe of 37, 49, 98, 103, 104, 105, 106, 257, 259, 260
Goodwood Cup, The 58
Gorst, Sir E. 87
Grace 114, 124
Grace, A.E. 270
Grant, A. 162
Greely, Miss M. 198, 274
Gregory, R. 95
Greville, H.Brook 109
Grobbelaar, Mrs C. 339
Guarmani, C.C. 16, 17, 18, 19

Haig, Earl of 159
Haïl 19, 44, 45, 77
Hama 19
Hamilton Leigh, Col. J. 100, 142
Hannadi, tribe of 34, 96, 258
Hanstead Stud see Yule, Lady
Hardinge, Lord 258
Harris, A. 351
Harrison, Mr 259
Hassan Aga 298
Hay, W. 184
Hayden, C. 158, 160, 170
Hedley, Maj. T.W.I. 199, 200
Henderson, P. 41, 50
Herbert, Maj. von 18, 19
Hillside 146
Hind, E.M. 338
Hirst, E. 272
Hogarth, D.G. 16, 17, 19, 35
Holman, Fred 66, 145, 149, 152, 157, 158, 160
Homs 19
Horsham Times, The 117
Hough, S.G. 160, 171, 173, 176, 177, 345
  Cecil (son) 176
Houtappel, Dr P. 275, 326, 328, 330
Hunt, Vere D. 15
Hussars, 11th, The 121
Huxley, Prof. T. 68, 69

Ibn Aafas 113
Ibn ed Derri 76, 94, 95, 101, 102, 103, 104,
  Abtan 106
  Berghi 102
  Mashlab 94
  Neddi 94, 95, 102, 104
Ibn Khalifeh, Sheykh of Bahreyn 97, 98, 100, 101, 106, 110, 112, 113
Ibn Nakadan 101
Ibn Ulema 107
Ibrahim 51
Ibrahim Bey see Ali Pasha Sherif
Ibrahim Pasha see Mohammed Ali, Viceroy
Inshass Royal Stud 294, 301

Janow Podlaski Stud 320
Jebel Shammar 18, 19
Jockey Club, The 55, 57, 58

Karkur 253
Kasim 113, 298
Kazim Agha 260
Kellogg, W.K. 168, 180-2, 230, 236, 243, 345, 348
  Mrs W.K. 180

Kemal el Dine, Prince 153, 162, 294
Kent, Mr 177
Kettlewell, J.D.D. 338
Khabra el Mashluk 37
Khalid ibn Ghanim 261
Khalil 51
Khedive, The, see Abbas Pasha II
Khuddr, Mohammed 83, 96, 260
Kirkwood, Dr 85
Kliniewski Stud 102, 307
Knebworth 116
Kock, C.G. 336
Kubba Palace 112, 153
Kuwait, Emir of 112
Kydd, Ronald 199

Lansdowne, Henry, 5th Marquis of 121
Laprimaudaye, Captain 43, 71
Latham, P. 143
Lawrence, Miss E. 127, 128, 129, 149, 171
Leicht, Mrs M. 274
Leppard, Peggy 195
Les Chevaux du Sahara 66
Lewenhaupt, Countess P. 334
Lewis, Miss L. 191
Linney, H. 198
Loates 57
Loch, Sir H. 101
Lovelace, William, 1st Earl of 26, 71
  Ralph, 13th Baron Wentworth, 2nd Earl of 26, 32, 33, 38, 39, 40, 41, 42, 71, 132, 134, 136, 137, 154
  Ada, wife of 1st Earl of 26
  Mary, wife of 2nd Earl of 136, 167, 194
Luckock, Mrs C. 277
Lydekker, R. 68
Lyon, Col. F.L.H. 177
May 177
Lytton, Robert, 1st Earl of 65, 116

  Neville, 3rd Earl of 28, 116, 117, 121, 124, 128, 131, 133, 143, 148, 181, 194
  Anthony, 4th Earl of 124, 157, 171, 181, 197
  Edith, wife of 1st Earl 116
  Lady Anne 124, 149, 150, 156, 159, 161, 167, 168, 171, 182-3
  Hon. Emily, Lady Lutyens 127
  Hon. Mrs Neville see Wentworth, 16th Baroness
  Hon. Winifrid, Lady Tryon 124, 156, 159, 161, 167, 196

Mackay, D. 97, 100, 268
Maclean, Mrs A.D.D. 200, 272, 274
  Vicky 274
Mahmud Aga 99
Mahmud Bey 81, 87, 106, 108, 109, 113
Males, Mr and Mrs R. 275
Mannington, Yousiffe 56
Marbach Stud 299
Married Women's Property Act, 1882, 137
Marshall, L. 276
Martin, Mrs 270
Martino, S. de 108
Mason, F.E. 112
Mataria 110, 113
Matinah 77
Maynesboro Stud see Brown, W.R.
McConnell, C. 188
Meshur Agid 49
Meynell, Dr C. 24
Milbankes, Stud of the 33
Mizrab, Mijuel 43
  Afet el 106
Mohammed Ahmed el Minshawi 112
Mohammed Ali Tewfik, Prince 143, 146, 153, 162, 294, 296, 344, 345

GENERAL INDEX

Mohammed Ali, Viceroy of Egypt 15, 16, 75, 77, 78, 154
  Tousson Pasha (son) 294
  Ibrahim Pasha (son) 75, 294
Mohammed er Robaa 49
Mohammed es Safuri 260
Mohammed Sadyk Pasha 70, 83, 106
Moharrem Pasha 113, 296
Molony, Mr 29
Montefiore, Rev. D.B. 118, 167, 171
Montefyk, Sheikhs of 70, 100, 113
Mounsey-Heysham, Mrs I.M. 192
Mount Street 71
Moyne, Lord 322
Munday, T.J.C. 199
Murray, Mrs E.M. 184, 276
Murray, Mrs P.A.M. 275
Murray, Mrs T.E.M. 339
Muscat 18
Muteyr, tribe of 44, 92
Mutlak el Bataal 88, 89, 91, 92, 117, 121, 140, 146, 152, 254, 295
Mutlak, Mahmud 109
My Diaries 77

Napier, Col. E. 15
Napier, Lord, of Magdala 65
Napier, Philip 152, 154, 156, 157, 161
Napoleon III, Emperor 17
Nasser, G., President 314
Nazir Agha 260
Nejd 16, 17, 18, 20, 43, 44, 50, 107, 108, 140
Newbuildings Place 23, 29, 30, 64, 71, 114, 116, 118, 121, 124, 126, 129, 131, 133, 136, 137, 138, 141, 149, 151, 157, 158, 161, 162, 164, 167, 171, 198
  stud at 134, 138, 141, 143, 145, 146, 147, 148, 150, 165–6, 344
"New Venture, The" *see* Sheykh Obeyd
New York World, The 146
Nicholson, Mrs S.A. 179
Nineteenth Century 47, 69
Noel, B.V. 112
Nolan, Capt. L.–E. 15
North, G. 200
Norton, Mrs C. 14
Nugent, Pat 210

Obeyd, tribe of 98
Ockham 71, 137
Old House, the 137, 152
Oneyzeh 113, 298
Orpen, Claude 336
Osborn, Prof. H.F. 144
Oscott 24
Oteybeh, tribe of 56, 83, 97
Othman Bey *see* Ali Pasha Sherif
Othman el Abd 98
Ottoman Horse Show, The 120
Ouston 148, 156

Palgrave, W.G. 16, 17, 19, 44
Pall Mall Gazette, The 60–4
Palmyra 37, 49, 104
Paris 38, 39, 47, 65, 89, 117, 127
  International Horse Show 101, 120
Pearce, Mrs 99
Philby, H. St. J. 17
Pink House, the 83, 117, 137, 138
Pitt-Rivers, M.A. 199, 200
Plaister, G. 202
Pointer, Miss P.J. 202
Portland, Duke of, The 58, 161
Potocki, Count Joseph 54, 104, 108, 170, 259, 307, 309
  Count Roman 170

Prange, C. 197
Public Trustee, The 151, 156, 157, 158, 160, 161, 162, 163, 167
Pückler-Muscau, Prince 18

Queensland Agricultural College 197, 274
Quilty, Tom, Endurance Ride 274

Ramsdell, J.A.P. 71, 106, 343
Rasham (hawk) 50
Rashid, Mohammed ibn, Emir of Nejd 44, 45, 49, 70, 113
Raswan, C. 180–1
Raswan Index, The 296, 298, 344
Reuter 76
Rhodes, Cecil 66, 94
Riad 44, 107
Ribblesdale, Lord 161, 166
Rice, Fred 210, 218, 224
Ridgeway, Prof. W. 69
Roberts, Mrs A.M. 199
Roosevelt, Theodore 146, 147
Rostrevor 177
Ruala, tribe of 19, 101, 104, 106, 108, 111, 258, 260
Ruskin, J. 28
Rustem Pasha, H.E. 96
Rutland, Frances, Duchess of 202
Ruxton, G.H. 100, 141, 172, 191
Rzewuski, Count 18

Sabit Pasha 88, 89, 91, 111
Sabunji, L. 26
Sadlier, G.F. 16
St Valentine's Day 46
Saleh Bey Sherif 97
Salisbury. Robert, 3rd Marquis of 76
Sandeman, A. 170
Sanguszko, Princes of 13, 18, 56, 70
Saoud
  Abdul Aziz ibn, King 108, 179
  Faisal ibn, Prince 179
  Feysul ibn Turki 97, 101
  Saoud ibn, Emir of Riad 107
Savile, Capt. the Hon. George 142, 147, 245, 336, 343
Scherbatoff, Prince 117
Schleswig-Holstein, Princess Louise of 124
Schmidt, C. *see* Raswan, C.
Schumann, Clara 28
Scott, Mrs B. 194, 195
Sdanovitch, Col. A. de 104, 108, 117, 307
Selby, Roger A. 182, 232, 348, 350
Seven Golden Odes, The 68
Seyd Ahmed 96
Seyyid Mohammed Fathi 97
Shalaan, Beneyeh ibn 106
  Sotamm ibn 106
Shammar, tribes of 44, 96, 102, 257
Shelley, P.B. 25
Shepheards Hotel 47
Sheykh Obeyd 75, 76, 77, 79, 83, 86–7. 92, 121, 131, 157
  "First Attempt" 87, 92, 93, 260–1, 294
  "New Venture" 87, 109–13, 260–1, 294
  Stud at 79–92, 95, 96, 97, 98, 99, 100, 101, 117, 126, 131, 140, 141, 146, 152–3, 157, 165, 168, 235, 259, 295, 298
Shoubra 15, 154
Simmons Brown, Mr 352
Sisam, A. 276
Sitwell 81
Skene, J.H. 33, 34–42, 50, 95, 96, 104, 105, 107, 257, 258, 259
  Mrs 40, 41
Smith, F. 121, 133, 137
Smith, Mrs M.A. 354

Smuts, J.C. 161
Speaker, The 69
Springfield House 23, 126, 171
South Down, The 99
Stace, Burg 210
Stealing of the Mare, The 68
Stephens, H.C., M.P. 257, 258
Storrs, Sir R. 128
Streatham Hurdle Plate 40
Strickland, Lady Mary 171
Stroganoff, Count 117, 120, 307
Suarès, M. 112
Suffolks 118
Suleyman Bey 108
Sultan el Duish, Sheykh 112
Sultan of Turkey, The, Abdul Hamid II 70, 75, 120
Sussex and Surrey Courier, The 54
Syria 16, 18, 32, 33, 35, 43, 75, 105

Taïs ibn Sharban 106
Tanfi, M. 259
Tankersley, Mrs B. 197, 218, 275, 351
Tattersall, Mr 54
Tattersalls 108, 132, 156
Tebbutt, C.E. 259
Thomas, Mrs E.M. 198, 199
Thompson, Mr 66, 94
Thoroughbred horse, the 14–15, 33, 37, 40, 54–5, 58, 63, 69, 71, 83, 99, 122, 145, 210, 213, 218
Thoroughbred Horse, The Origin and Influence of 69
Three Bridges 39, 40, 60, 85, 122, 124, 136, 149, 152, 207, 218
Three Voices, The 68
Times, The 68, 76, 117, 196
Timur Bey 113
Toft, G. 275
Tousson Pasha *see* Mohammed Ali, Viceroy
Toy Dogs and Their Ancestors 68
Travelers Rest Stud 314
Travels in Arabia Deserta 65
Trawlers Farm 114, 118
Trethewey, Mrs M. 354
Trollip, Mrs M.P. 339
Tryon, Admiral G. 57
Tweedie, Maj.-Gen. W. 69

Ujazd Stud 319
Upton, Maj. R.D. 19–20, 34, 37, 54, 170, 270
R.H.E. 54

Valensin, J. 109, 110, 111, 112
Van der Merwe, P.J. 336

Vaughan-Williams, Hon. Mrs R. 184
Veragua, Duke of 182, 322, 324–5
Vesey-Fitzgerald, B. 194
Victoria, Queen 116, 117
Vivian, General 34
Vorderbrüggen, H. 331
Vyse, Col. A. 15

Wales, Prince of *see* Edward VII *and* Edward VIII
Wallin, Dr G.A. 16, 19
Watson, G. 259
Watts, G.F. 24
Weatherbys 56, 100, 146, 170, 182
Webb, Sam 66, 72, 85, 86, 92, 97, 114, 120
Webb-Ware, W. 170
Weil 18
Welsh Mountain Ponies 180, 187, 204
Wentworth, Byron, 12th Baron 26
Ralph, 13th Baron *see* Lovelace, 2nd Earl of
Mary, 14th Baroness 153, 154
Anne Isabella, 15th Baroness *see* Blunt, Lady Anne
Judith Anne Dorothea, 16th Baroness 13, 20, 24, 25, 29–30, 65–8, 71, 77, 78, 79, 80, 82, 92, 93, 116–7, 121, 124–6, 127, 129, 132, 133, 137, 138, 141, 143, 144, 145, 146, 147, 148–52, 156–64, 165, 166–70, 173–6, 177, 179–85, 186–96, 197, 199, 200, 202, 204, 207, 208, 209, 210, 211, 212, 213, 214–5, 217, 219, 222, 24, 225, 226, 227, 236, 259, 297, 299, 307, 348
Books by 68, 193 *see also Authentic Arabian, The*
Westminster, 1st Duke of 95, 168
Wheatley, W.F. (Nep) 30, 38, 43
Wilson, Sir Charles Rivers 85
Wilson, R.T. 345
Winans, W. 108, 170
Wolf, Miss P. 197, 198
Woolborough Farm 151, 152, 157
Worleys 147, 166
Worth, Manor and Forest of 23, 124, 147, 149, 171
Wright, D.D. 193, 277
Württemburg 18, 56
Wyndham, Rt. Hon. George 71, 124
Mary, Lady Leconfield 24

Yule, Lady 177–8, 188, 196, 212, 247
Gladys (daughter) 177, 196
Yusuf Effendi 49
Yusef Kemal Pasha *see* Ahmed Kemal Pasha

Zeyd Saad el Muteyri 76, 80, 94
Zeytun 75, 109, 117

INDEX OF HORSES

Text references are in roman type, tables in italics (except for the table for Rodania, entries for which are indicated by an asterisk*) and illustrations in **bold**. Horses with identical names are differentiated between Sheykh Obeyd (Sh.Ob.) and Crabbet (Cr.), or by country (Aust. for Australia, Eg. for Egypt etc.).

Aanasseh *357*
*Aaraf *350, 362*
Aatik *326*
Aatika *357*, 191, 232
Abaadan *267*
*Abdallah *371*
Abdullah *279*
Abeyan *257*
Abida *326*
Abiram 275, *326*
Abla (UK) 138, 244
Abla (Eg.) *303, 304*
Abla (USA) *369*
Aboud 251, *332*
*Abu Farwa 230, 246, *336, 340, 348, 349*
*Abu Gamwa *369*
Abukatu *280*
Abu Khasheb 88, 89, 100, 120, *257*
Abu Zeyd (Sh.Ob.) *260*
*Abu Zeyd (UK) *357*, 142, 147, 229, *343, 344, 348, 360*, **355** see also Lal-i-Abdar
Abyad *280*
Achar *326*
Achim *326*, *328*
Adagio *328*
Adah *276*
Adaja (Aust.) *267*
Adaja (Neth.) *326*
Adar *326*, *328*
Adonah *320*
Adonis *282*
Aethon *279*
Agamemnon *332*
Agata III *324*
Agha Nezmet *341*
Ahbot Quantal *340*
Ahlam II *304*
Ahmar 289, 65, 66, 71, 118, 126, 134, 176, 228, 229, 232, 236, 244, 248, 268, **125**
Ahmar Maftuh *267*
Ahmoun 250, *332*
Aida 109, *298*
Ailul *267*
Ajjam 179, **169**, **172**
*Ajlun *322, 323, 324, 361*
Ajman *266*
Ajramieh 134, 138, 176, 244, 266

Akabah *289*
Akbar *280*
Akhtal *303*
Akhu *275*
Alaa el Din *302, 304, 305, 306, 297, 300*
Alada *279, 287*
Aladdin *287, 293*
Aladdins Lamp *281, 289*
Alaga Girl *279, 293*
Alaga Maid *293*
Al Burak (II) *340*, 339
Al Caswa *287*
Alcouza *285*
Aldebaran 244, *325, 352*
Aldebaran II *324*
Aldourie *357*
Alfarouse 184, 251
*Algol *141, 191, 228, 244, 245, 246, 352, 371*
*Algoletta *340, 357, 362*
Algomej *321*
Algonkina *321*
*Alhabac *324, 363*
Ali Amer *267*
Alif 54
Aliha **256**
Ali Hamad *267*
Alkahir Neon Gold *341*
Al Kharj *282, 291*
Al-Marah Canadius *351*
Al Marah Ibn Rapture *267*, 266
Almas 244
Almeli *279, 287*
Almonacid *267*
Almox Prints J *314*
*Almozabor *323, 365*
Al Neehma II *267*
Aloes *321*
Alrawd *280*
Al Tazfir *267*
Al Xadiqat *267*
*Alyf *371*
Alyssa 197
Amadi *283*
Amal (Eg.) *304*
Amal (Neth.) *330*, **327**
Amanda *291*
Amani *306*
Ambretta *334*
AM Canadian Beau *354*, **353**

Ameena *305*
*Amerigo *352, 371*
Amida 176, 177, 229, 244, *352*
Amir 82
Amira *289*
A.M. Midnight Sun *331*
Amrulla *303, 304, 305, 306*
Anaga *282, 293*
Anbar *319*
Anchor *278*
Anchusa *332*
Andorra *321*
Aneysa *289*
AN Malik *324*
Annaboam *281*
Anouk *280, 285, 289*
*Antafa *360*
Antar (Eg.) *304*
Antar (Sh.Ob.) 87, 109, 248
Antar (Ibn Moniet el Nefous) 112
Anter *302, 304, 305, 306*, *301*.
Antezeyn Skowronek *369*
Antika 140
Aphrodite *287*
Arabette *280, 289*
Arabian Dawn 244
Arachne *287*
Arax *315, 316*, *312, 320*
Argent *280*
Argha *281*
Argus *282*
Ariadne *287*
*Arilla *323, 324, 365*
Arusa *325*
Aseel *302*
Asfura 65, 134, 228, 244
Ashan *358*
Ashgar (Cr.) 76, 94, 257
Ashgar (Arg.) *267*
Asil 57, 58
Aspirant *314*
Assb *267*
Astrab *358*
Astraea *287*
Astraled *303, 357*, 122, 129, 134, 138, 140, 142, 143, 145, 149, 232, 238, 242, 244, 245, 248, 274, 300, 314, 344, 349
Astran *358*
Astrella *357*, 177, 178, 229, 232,

INDEX OF HORSES

244, 326
Astur 199
Aswan *315, 316, 317*, 264, 299, 309, 314, 315
Atalanta *278, 289*
Atesh 250
Atlas *282*
Attalaia 326
Atwa 260
*Aulani 367
Aunt Cara 328
Aurora (Cr.) 202, 250
Aurora (Aust.) *287*
*Autumn Gold 363
*Ayesha 270, 361
Azaba 267
Azada *293*
Azar *304*
Azara 239
Azeldah *289*
Aziz *303*, 48, 78, 82, 87, 95, 96, 98, 100, 101, 109, 110, 111
Aziza (Sh.Ob.) 109, 112
Aziza (USA) 345
Aziza (Eg.) *303*
Azmi *303, 305*, 264 see also Nil
*Azraff 362
Azrek 59, 65, 76, 94, 104, 118, 120, 126, 141, 142, 146, 177, 227, 228
229, 232, 235, 244, 248, 251, 268, 336, 343, **104**
Azz 110, 113
Azza I *304*

Baaini 267
*Babyat 360, 369
Babylon *279*
Babylonia 94
Badouia *302*
Badia (Cr.) 88, 89, 91, 92, 95, 100, 251
Badia (Eg.) *302, 304*, 298
Badiyan *289*
Badoura *289*
*Bahreyn 236, 348, 361
Bahri *280, 289*
Baida 267
Baiyad (Bayyad) *306*, 351
Baj 321
Bakmal 348
Baksheesh *289*
Balak *289*
Balamara *281*
Balance *302, 304, 305, 306*
Balaton 314
*Baldosa 324, 365
Balis 134, 236
Ballerina *289*
Balsora *283, 289*, 275
Bambu 324
Banat 320, 321, 322
Banda 321
Banderol *283*, 275

Bandola 321
Bandom 275
Bandos 320, 321
Banshee *289*
Barabaz 339
*Barada II *280, 289*, 272, 368
Barak *358*
Baraka *305*
Barakat 118
Baranova *358*
Baranta 330
*Baraza *344, 360*
Barcelona *281*
Barich de Washoe 324
Barwna 330
Bashida 326, 328
Bashom *358*
Basil *302*
Basilisk 48, 49, 94, 95, 105, 120, 168, 227, 228, 236, 238, 244, **104**
Basrah 283
Bathsheba 251
*Batista 323, 365
*Battla 157, 236, 307, 344, 348, 360
Bauble see Raki
Bayard *358*
Bay Rod 351
Baz *280, 289*, 272, 275
*Bazikh 343, 348, 360
*Bazleyd 343, 360
*Bazrah 251, 369
Beatrice 321
Beauty *289*
Bebattan 267
Bedr 343
Belka 176, 238, 334
Belkis 134
Bellona *278*
Belus see Silver Gleam
Ben Azrek 229, 235, 248
Benjamin 176, 191
Berak 328
Bereyda *357*, 134, 176, 228, 230, 238, 344
Berid *357*, 147, 343
Berk *303, 357*, 126, 134, 141, 144, 158, 177, 184, 191, 228, 232, 236, 243, 245, 246, 248, 250, 251, 266, 270, 343, 344, 348, 349, **125**
Bespechni 310
Betina 176
Bewitching *289*
Binda *289*
Bindalla *280, 289*
Bint 348
Bint Azz 88, 91, 110
Bint Azza I *304*, 298
Bint Bint-Azz see Azz
Bint Bint Dalal *302, 303*
Bint Bint Fereyha see Fulana
Bint Bint Helwa see Ghazala

Bint Bint Horra see Ghazieh (Sh.Ob.)
Bint Bint Jamila el Kebira 91, 110
Bint Bint Jellabieh Feysul see Jellabieh
Bint Bint Jellabiet Feysul 97, 98
Bint Bint Kateefa *305*
*Bint Bint Riyala *306*, 366
Bint Bint Sabbah *306*, 351
Bint Bukra *306*
Bint Dalal *302*
Bint Durra *304*, 298, 351
Bint el Bahreyn (line of) *304*
Bint el Bahreyn 110, 297
Bint el Bataa *304*
Bint Elwya *304*
Bint Elwya I *304*
Bint es Shakra Bint Roja 295
Bint es Zerka Bint Roja 296
Bint Fereyha 88, 89, 91, 97, 110, 111
Bint Gamila *302*
Bint Helwa *357*, 88, 89, 92, 95, 111, 114–5, 131, 134, 138, 141, 238, 295, 300, 344, **115**
Bint Helwa es Shakra see Johara
Bint Horra 110, 111, 295, 296
Bint Jamila 109, 110, 111, 112
Bint Jellabiet–Feysul 97, 98
Bint Kamla *302*
Bint Kateefa *302, 305*
Bint Mabrouka *304*
Bint Maisa *304*, 298
Bint Makbula see Manokta
Bint Makbula es Shakra see Kasida
Bint Mamlouka *306*
Bint Moniet el Nefous *304*
Bint Mouna *304*
Bint Mumtaza see Badia (Cr.)
Bint Nazeera (1958) *306*
Bint Nazeera (1968) *306*
(Bint) Noma 110
Bint Nura (Eg.) 96, 111
Bint Nura (Cr.) *357*, 91, 92, 95, 100, 113, 114, 120, 122, 134, 140, 232, 238, 257
Bint Obeya *302, 303, 306*
Bint Om el Saad *305*, 297
Bint Radia *302, 303*, 295, 298, 300
Bint Razeena 188
*Bint Rissala *305*, 229, 297, 365
*Bint Riyala *306*, 297, 312
Bint Roda (Bint Roga) *304*, 110, 112, 295–6, 299, 315
*Bint Roxana 332, 365
*Bint Rustem *302*, 232, 299, 300, 367
Bint Saada 351
Bint Sab(b)ah *302, 306*, 351
Bint Sahara 230
Bint Samia *306*

INDEX OF HORSES

Bint Samiha *302*, 299, 314
*Bint Sedjur *361*
Bint Serra (I) *304*, 295, 351
Bint Sylvan Lass 331, **327**
Bint Zaafarana *304*, 295
Bint Zaafarana II *304*
Bint Zareefa (1926) *302*, *304*, 300
Bint Zareefa (1936) *304*, 298
Biruta 322
Bisarieh 307
Bithynia 279, 287
Blaze 179, 210, 221, **220**
Blot 40
Blue Diamond 328
*Blue Domino *356*, 188, 191, 197, 230, 239, 246, 274, 368, **190**
Blue Horizon 334
Blue Magic *356*
Blue Mantle *356*
*Blue Rhapsody 334, 365
Blue Tango *356*
Boaz 176
Borack 99
Bozra 120, 134, 168, 176, 227, 235, 236, 238, 343, **119**
Brawura 331
Bremervale Destiny 275
Bremervale Emperor 275
*Bride Rose 360
Brigadier *283*
Bright Diamond *357*
*Bright Gleam 367
Bright Gold 354
Bright Jewel *283*, *289*
Bright Light 274
*Bright Shadow *357*, 192, 200, 202, 218, 224, 239, 250, 274, 333, 334, 354, 366, 370, **216**
Bright Wings 328, 330
Brilliant *283*, *289*
Browne Anne *283*, *291*
Buccaneer *283*
Bukra *303*, *357*, 126, 134, 228, 236, 238, 344, **125**
Buraida 287
Burkan 322
Burning Bush 39, 40, 257
Buseyna 280
Bushra *356*, 236
Bustard 95
Buszmen 321

Calliope 279, 287
Callista 326
Callisto 287
Calypso *293*
Canora 45, 48, 54, 257
Cantata *315*
*Caravan 361
Carlina 279, 248, 272, 274,
Carmargue **256**
Carshena *291*
Carthage 279

Casalinda 287
*Cassandra 362
Caswa 287
Cavita 334
Cazada 282, 287
Cebion 321
Celeopatra 282
Celina 320
Centaur 287
Cephalus 282
Cesima 320
Chadiga 326
Champurrado 279, *358*, 177, 197, 230, 235, 239, 246, 272, 351
Chantal 328, 330
Chavali 325
Chazar 320
Chellala *341*
Cherokee Desert Red 280
Cherokee King Pin 280
Cherokee Mecca 280
Cherokee Royal Sarong 280
Chez Nous Cassandra *341*
Chez Nous Chezaz 340
Chez Nous Shah Rukh 340, 339
Chez Nous Silver Owl *341*
Chief Kasalo *341*, 338
Chieka 328
Chocolate Cream *341*
Cinders 367
Circe 287
Claudius 282
Clio 287
Clymene 287
Comedia II 324
Condor 333
Constanze 332
Consuella 332
Contessa 292
Copper Maid 287
Corinto 324
*Correze *341*, 339, 366
Count Bazy 331
Count Cordova *281*
*Count Dorsaz *356*, 188, 191, 197, 198, 230, 246, 339, 351, 367, 368
Countess Maritza 333
*Count Manilla *281*, *285*, *289*, 292, 274, 366, 368
*Count Orlando *356*, 334, 366, 368
*Count Rapello 198, 365, 368
*Count Roland 368
Count Rubin 331
Crabbet 145, 239, 344
Crabbet Sura 348, 349, **317**
Cranleigh Karim 325
Crescendo 280, 276
Crescent Moon 279
Cronus 282
Crystal Clear 333
*Crystal Dew *356*, 363
*Crystal Fire 280, 274, 333, 364

Crystal Special *357*
Crystal Voyager *357*
Cyanella 328
Cynthia *293*
Cytherea 287
Czort 320, 321

Daad 305
Dabrana 328
Daffal *281*, *285*
Dafina (line of) *315*
Dafina 93, 108, 238, 308
Dafinetta 238
Dahana 278, 280, 285, 276
Dahma (line of) *285*, 287
Dahma 49, 50, 65, 251, 257, 268, **51**
Dahman *302*, 299
Dahman el Azrak 110
Dahna 65, 229, 243, 251, 268, 270
Daifa 260
Dajania (lines of) *289*, *291*, *292*
Dajania 20, 35, 39, 47, 48, 53, 54, 96, 226, 227, 229, 230, 232, 235, 238–9, 244, **104**
*Dakar 363
Dalal (1903) *302*, *304*, 296, 297
Dalal (1910) *304*, 154, 297, 298
Dalem 267
Dalika 202, 251
Damask Rose 40, 54, 257–8
Dancing Diamond 200, 202, **201**
Dancing King 277
Dancing Shadow 199, 242
Dancing Sunlight 199, 242, **193**
Dancing Wings 340, 338, **310**
Daoud *357*, 59, 122, 129, 134, 140, 176, 232, 238, 248, 260, 344, 348, 349, **130**
Daphne II 280, 287
Dara *283*
Daralga 279, 281, 282, 289
Darani 287
Dardanella 328
Darella 279, 289
*Dargee *357*, 176, 191, 192, 199, 200, 202, 224, 232, 242, 246, 251, 338, 354, 362, **193**
Darik 282
Darik Chieftain 342
Darik Q.E.D. 342
Darinth 287, 289
Darinthi 289
Darjeel 192, 330, **193**
Dark Legend 281
Darley 34, 35, 38, 40, 54, 258
Darley Arabian, The 33, 34, 35
Darribee Blue Diamond *281*
Dau 267
Dawn Shadow 340
Daza 267
Debora 371
Deloraine Zara 280
Delos 279

INDEX OF HORSES

Delstar 279
Demeter 293
Dervish 108
Deryabar 278, 285
Desert Charger 281
Desert Chief 281
Desert Kehail 283
Desert Son 278
Deucalion 282
Dhala 282
Dharmendra 328
Dhofar 289
Diamond Sparkle 357
Diamond Star 251
Diana 287
Dictator 56, 57
Diem 321
Dijleh 307
Dil Fireb 168, 243
Dinarzade 268, 307
Dione 279, 287
Diosma 282
Djil 267
Dohayya 111
Doheymeh Nejib 48, 78
Dolphin 279
*Domatella 366
Dominico 281
Dominita 280
Domow 344
Domtif 275
Doniazad 333
Dormino 356
Dorseema 356
*Dreaming Gold 363
Dungannon 99
Durra 304, 157, 298
Dushara 333
Dwarka 142, 192, 228, 352

*Ebanista 324, 363
Ebeda 302
Ecurb Royal Harida 333
Edh–Dhahab 357, 328
Effat 304
*Egina 323, 365
Egipcia 324
Eibna Kasir 341
Eibna Nasletta 342
Eid 304, 298
El Araby 302
El Aurens 283
El Azrak 320
El Bataa 304
El Dahma (line of) 306
El Dahma 302, 297, 298, 300
El Dere (line of) 303
El Dere 300
Eldoura 289
Electria 292
Electric Amber 291
Electric Ray 278, 292
*Electric Silver 279, 285, 289, 291, 292, 187, 235, 272, 276, **265**

Electric Spark 285
Electric Storm 358
Electrimel 278, 285
Electronet 279
Elef 320
El Emir 53, 115, 228, 251, 268
Elewacja 320
El Faiak 267
Elfur 320
El Halabi 306
El Hali 267
Elita 320
Eliza 320
El Kazan 285
El Lahr 287, 236, 251, 268, 270
Ellora 320
Ellorus 320
El Luci 267
*El Meluk 187, 339, 368, 370
El Mizzian 267
El Moez 302, 304, 305, 297, 298, 300
El Paso 320
El Saala 282
El Sareei 302, 304, 305, 306, 297, 298, 300
El Sheba 289
El Tafuk 84
Elwya 302, 304, 298
El Yatima 306
*Elza 320, 361
*El-Zabibe 319, 361
El Zafer 302, 304
Elzunia 320, 326, 331
Emad 302
Enayat 305
Enchantment 251
Endora 340, 338
Enyo 278
Epopeja 108
Erato 287
Er Rohban 267
Erubus 283
Eskapada 321
Esmir 326
Estebna 321
Esterville Haseem 357
*Esther II 366
Esther 281, 282, 293,
Estopa 325
Etap 320
Eternit 320
Etiw 321
Etna 320
Etruria 320
Europa 293
Eve 287
Exceptional 342
Extra Special 342, 357
Ezraeta 285
Ezrah 279, 285
Ezrina 283, 285
Ezz el Arab 302

Fabius 280
Fable 283
*Fabuloso 323, 365
Fabulous 281
Fadek 304
Fadjur 230
Fadoura 281, 283, 289
Faher 320
Faireym 289
Fakher el Din 304, 296
Fakreddin 281, 270
Falcon 283
Falcon Lad 283
Falka 283
Falouk 340, 339
Falusuf 289
*Famula 323, 365
Fantana 357, 168, 243
Fantasia 358
Fantasy 280
Fara 287
*Farana 230, 361
Faraoun 285, 289, 243, 268
*Farasa 360
Farasha 302
*Farasin 168, 180, 243, 348, 361
Faras Nakadan 299
Farawi 230
Farazdac 302
Fardous 303
Fareh 267
*Farette 340, 250, 334, 339, 369
Farha 306
Farhan 280
*Fari II 331, 368
Farida (Aust.) 293
Farida (Eg.) 302
Farida el Debbani 302, 299
Faris (1879) 54
*Faris (1924) 316, 356, 173, 182, 186, 188, 239, 243, 246, 307, **190**
Farissla 334
*Farlane 369
*Farnasa 361
Farrash 168
Far Roukh 293
FaSerr 295
Fasifa 292
Fasiha 91, 111
*Fasila 319, 320, 351, 361
*Fath 369
Fathia 341
Fatma 326, 328
Fawkia 306
Fayal 230, 272, 338
Fayalina 338
Fayda 302
Fayek 302, 306
Fayilia 278, 292
Fayrial 285, 289, 291, 292, 272
Fayoufa 285
Faysa II 302
Fedaan 177, 250

INDEX OF HORSES

*Fejr *356, 358,* 142, 173, 182, 186, 227, 230, 235, 239, 242, 243, 307, 345
Fejran 168
Felestin 345
Feluka *281,* 138, 142, 168, 176, 186, 227, 242–3, 270, 348
*Ferda *356,* 168, 180, 197, 227, 239, 243, 348, 367, **346**
*Ferdana *360*
Ferdin *356,* 345
Ferdisia 168, 180, 348
Fereyha 110
Ferhan *358,* 186, 187, 235, 243, 307, **234**
Ferida 96, 104, 134, 138, 227, 239, 242
Ferishal 354
*Ferneyn *371*
*Fersara *371*
*Ferseyn 243, 348, 352, 371
*Ferzon 351, 371
Fessar 267
Feysul (lines of) *282, 358*
Feysul *304,* 97, 98, 126, 134, 148, 229, 235, 245, 260, 266, 295, 299, 344, **105**
Feysul II *358*
Fezara 307
Fickle *279, 289*
Fifi *306*
Figaro *279*
Finta 323
Firecrest *282*
Firefly 168
Fire Princess 328
Flash Boy *281, 285, 289*
Flash Design *281*
Flash Miss *283*
Flash of Fire *283, 289*
Flora (Aust.) *287*
Flora (Sp.) 323
Floralia *279, 287*
*Florencia *316,* 246, 307, 312, 364
Florizelle *289*
Forecastle 213
Francolin 54, 105, 258, 268
Fuewasa *287*
Fulana 38, 89, 92, 97, 114, 243, 268
Fulla *304*

Gadara *281, 289,* 272
Gadir 322
Gai Cadet 277
Gai General 275, 352
Gai Moonbeam 275
Gai Parada 351
Gajala 275
Galal *302, 305, 306*
Galatife 325
Galero 325

Galraffa *342*
Gamar 329
Gamil III *304*
Gamil el Ahmar (line of) *302*
Gamil el Ahmar 298, 299, 300
Gamil Manial 357
Gamila Manial 357
Ganaria 292
Gandhy 323
Ganymede *282*
Gara 238
*Garaff 350, 362
*Garance *341, 358,* 339, 366
Garbo 324
Gassir *302, 304, 305, 306,* 298
Gay Beau *283*
Gay Count 275
Gayza (UK) 238
Gayza (Eg.) 299
Gazelle *342*
*Ga'zi 369
General Gold 239
*General Grant *358,* 188, 198, 236, 239, 326, 338, 366, **223**
Genghis Khan *287*
George Washington 357
Georgina 292
*Geym 350, 362
*Ghadaf 361
Ghadia *see* Radia
Ghalion 297
*Ghanigat 361
Ghanimeh 276
Gharis 343
Ghazal *293*
Ghazala *304,* 88, 92, 111, 141, 238, 295, 343, 344
Ghazalah 267
*Ghazali 370
Ghazayat 345, 348
Ghazieh (Sh.Ob.) 111
Ghazieh (Eg., line of) *304*
Ghazieh (Eg.) 108, 295, 300
Ghazil 344
Ghesadik *285*
Ghezaff *285*
Ghezala *279, 341,* 181, 272, 336
Ghibli 329, 332
Gipsy Maid *281, 287*
Gisela 267
*Gleaming Gold 363
Glint of Silver *283*
Gloaming *283*
Godolphin Arabian, The 48
Golda 332
Goldbey 329
Golden Domino *356*
Golden Gilt 202, 251
Golden Ludo 242
Golden Salamander *285*
Golden Silver 242
Golden Treasure **255**
Gon 321
Gorgon *293*

Grace *287*
Grace Kesia *293*
Grandorr 322
Grand Regent *283*
Grand Royal *283, 357,* 191, 192, 232, 274, 328, **222**
Grantchester *341,* 338, **309**
*Greatheart *358,* 239, 246, 334, 363
Grey Coronet *279, 276*
Grey Crabbet 307
Grey Crystal 250
Grey Diamond *279*
Grey Girl *287*
Grey Kim *280*
Greylight *280, 291, 274, 276,* **273**
*Grey Owl *358,* 179, 272, 276, 334, 339, 361
Grey Royal *340, 357,* 188, 191, 242, 338, **241**
Grey Stella 197
Grey Swirl *279, 276*
Grojec 325, 331
Gromet *see* Rodanieh Rafaqa
Gual Boukra 323
GualGhazir 323
*Gulastra 140, 145, 232, 238, 344, 349, 369
*Gulnare 232, 238, 248, 344, 349, 369

Habano 323
Habiente 324, 325
*Habladuria 323, 324, 365
Habon 323
Habzar *289*
Hadassa 326, 328, 332
Hadban (Cr.) 56, 59, 97–8, 141, 229, 238, 245, 268, 336, **104**
Hadban (Eg.) *304*
Hadban Enzahi 264, 299
Hadramaut 57, 58
Hafiza *302*
Hafra 350
Hagar 35, 37, 39, 53, 56, 93, 177, 227, 236, 243, 251, 258, 336, **51**
Hagir *303, 306*
Hajeel 357
Hakima *306*
Halcyone *287*
Halfa 56, 57, 58
Halide 329
Halim 357
Halima *289*
Halo's Iris 332
Halo's Miracle 332
Hama (1921) 345
Hama (1940) *282, 272,* 339
Hamad 328
Hamama (USA) 345
Hamama (Eg.) *303*
Hamasa *278, 303,* 138, 238, 345

Hamdan 302, 305, 295, 300
Hamdia 306
Hamida (USA) 345
Hamida (UK) 344, 345
Hammamet 281, 283, 289
Hamoonette 281, 283, 289
Hamran 303
Hamran II 306
Hamu 329
Hanadi 305, 297
Handeyraff 350
Hanif 200, 202, 239, 242, 250, **201**, **253**
Hanifa 281
Happy Wanderer 285
Harb 357, 131, 140, 238, 344
Harik 236
Harir 278, 289, 238, 270
Harka 303
Harkan 303, 300
Harmony 289
Haroun 200, 332, **201**
Harra 236
Haryad 332
Hasan 281
Hashish 267
Hashka 287
Hassan 330
Hauran 251
*Hazna 238, 345, 348, 360
Hazzam (Cr.) 291, 164, 345
Hazzam (Arg.) 267
Heavenly Twins, The see Dancing Shadow and Dancing Sunlight
Hebah 306
Hebe 287
Heil 266
Heirloom 283
Hekmat 306
Helawi 283
Helib 266
Helwa 95, 98
Hemera 279, 287
Hera 287
Hermit 58
Hestia 279, 282, 293
Hilmyeh 357
Hilwa 289
Hilwe 350
*Hind 315, 367
Hindiat 267
Hockey II 314
Hoekhorst Shiraz 330
Horra (Hora) 48, 79, 82, 110, 300
Houbaran 325
Housain 280
Howa 177, 251
Hoyeda 304
Husnia 306
Husn-u-Gul 323

Ibn Abla 303

Ibn Antar 304
Ibn Bint Nura see Abu Khasheb
Ibn Chantarella 339
Ibn Domino 281
Ibn El Hamra 333
Ibn Fayda 302
Ibn Fayrial 285
Ibn Gamila 357
Ibn Hafiza 302, 305, 306
Ibn Hamama 303
Ibn Irex 358
Ibn Mahruss (1893) see Mahruss (1893)
Ibn Mahruss (1901) 356.72
Ibn Manial 304
Ibn Maysouna 302
Ibn Mesaoud 83, 94
Ibn Mohafez 331
Ibn Moniet el Nefous 304
Ibn Nadir 78, 79, 87, 91, 113
Ibn Naxor 332
Ibn Nura 88, 91, 92, 97, 98, 110, 111, **90**
Ibn Rabdan 302, 304, 306, 351
Ibn Samhan 302, 304, 351
Ibn Serra 304
Ibn Sherara 304, 88, 91, 111, 113, 141, 238
Ibn Yashmak 305, 358, 98, 126, 138, 144, 158, 162, 176, 229, 235, 244, 297, 344
Ibn Yemama 94, 126
Ibn Zarifa 80
Ibrahim 108, 349
Ibtsam 304
*Ifni 323, 363, 365
*Image 350, 362
Imam 251
Imamzada 287, 115, 228, 248, 268
Imelina 325
Impala 279
Inas 302
Incoronata 212, 242, 348, **346**
Incoronetta 199, 239
*Indaia 182, 242, 266, 350, 361, 368
*Indian Crown 278, 358, 188, 199, 230, 236, 239, 336, 361, **240**
Indian Diamond 358, 239
Indian Fire 329, 332
Indian Firedance 277
Indian Flame II 200
Indian Flower 184, 239, 336
Indian Flyer 338
Indian Gem 277, 336
Indian Glory (Cr.) 212
Indian Glory (SA) 341, 342
Indian Gold 358, 187, 191, 194, 224, 230, 235, 239, 242, 250, 354, **234**
Indian Golddust 239
Indian Grey 188

Indian Jewel 279
Indian King 199, 239, 242, 332, **199**
Indian Light 278, 285, 289, 291, 235, 272, **273**
*Indian Magic 278, 358, 188, 191, 197, 199, 200, 202, 224, 236, 238, 239, 242, 250, 366, **216**, **223**
Indian Moonlight 278
Indian Pearl 354
Indian Peril 354
*Indian Pride 279, 184, 230, 363
Indian Red 341, 336, 338
Indian Rhapsody 239
Indian Snowflake 199, 239
Indian Star 202, 251
*Indian Starlight 356, 199, 239, 363
Indian Summer 283
Indian Sylphette **253**
Indian Tamarisk 329
Indian Trinket 333
Indira 250
*Indraff 197, 242, 350, 362, 368
*Indriss 199, 364
Ino 287
Insilla 322
Inyala 291
Iona 279, 287
Ione 332
Iorana 356, 354
Iran 279
*Irex 358, 184, 230, 235, 274, 336, 337, 338, 363, **237**
Irexia 338
Irexina 340
*Iridos 330, 363, 365
Iris 287
Ishmael 287
Ishtar 268
Ismidt 267
Ivan 278
Ivana II 267

Jacio 325
Jaddama 267
Jaguay 323, 324, 325
Jahil 357, 147, 343
Jair 244
*Jalila 182, 308, 322-3, 350, 360
*Jalila III 324, 363
Jalmuda 357, 243
Jamal 278
Jamani Chaba 340
Jamani Grandee 341
Jamani Grantson 341
Jamani Prince Zayani 341
Jamani Prince Zendi 341
Jamani Quanteza 340
Jamani Rashani **335**
Jamani Rizmah 341
Jamani Shabani 341
Jamani Shah Burak 340

INDEX OF HORSES

Jamani Shalani *341*
Jamil (Eg.) 110, *296*
Jamil (Sh.Ob.) *303, 304,* 111, 141, 153, 295, 297, 298, 299
Jamila (Eg.) 110
Jamila (Sh.Ob. 1901) 112
Jamila (Sh.Ob. 1906) *303, 304,* 153, 295
*Jamila (Cr.) *343,* 371
Jamrood 243
Jamusa 251
Jask 243
Jasmine *see* Dajania
Jauza 112, 154
Jawi-Jawi 243, *322*
Jeddah *281, 289*
Jedran *287, 289*
Jedrania 50, 53, 251, 258
Jellabieh 92, 98, 243
Jellabiet-Feysul 97
Jemima 54
Jerama 350
Jerboa 39, 40, 53, 54, 55, 98, 104, 227, 235, 243, *343*
Jerico Sherifa 338
Jeroboam 59, 71, 227, 235, 243, 245, 259
Jeruan 307, 350, 354
Jerud 53, 243, 270
Jeyneyna 307
Jezail 251
Jiddan 336
Jilfa 76, 93, 94, 184, 251, 258
Jiwa *323*
*Joanna *363*
Johara 92, 98, 99, 114, 243
*Joktan *371*
Joseph *357,* 141, 191, 232, 243, 244
Josepha 168
Judiala *285, 291, 293*
Judith *293*
Juf *289*
Julia *292*
Julnar 182, 350
Juno *287*
Jurneeka 352

Kabara *358,* 197
Kadi *325*
Kaftan 168, **169**
Kahramana *306*
Kai 275
Kailhan *281*
Kako *323*
Kalam *358*
Kalb *267*
Kaline *267*
Kallal *358*
Kamil *281*
Kamla *299*
*Kankan *315, 316, 317,* 310, *364*
Kann *316, 317,* 246, 310, 312

Kantara 138, *344*
*Kantista *323, 324, 363, 365*
Kanun *291*
Kanva *316*
Kapel *315*
Kapelka *315*
*Kapella *318,* 310, *364*
Kaplja *316*
Kapriz *315*
Kapriznaia *316*
Karabe *323*
Kareef *281*
Kareyma 182, 275, 350
Kariba *334*
Karima *319*
Karmen *309*
Karoon *303*
*Karoosha *371*
Kars *285,* 37, 39, 40, 46, 47, 48, 53, 56, 65, 93, 99-100, 104, 227, 229, 245, 251, 268, **27, 46**
Karun 160
Kasala *339*
*Kasbana *367*
*Kashmir *323, 324, 363, 365*
Kasida 92, 100, 232, 243, 300, *344*
Kasima *303, 357,* 232, 300, *344*
Kasmeyn *303, 304, 306, 357,* 232, 243, 275, 298, 299, 300, 315
Kasr *282*
Kasran *280*
Kassa *278, 291*
Kassib *281, 291*
Kassida *291*
Kassie *287*
Kataf *287, 291, 293*
Kataf's Lass *282, 293*
Kateefa *302, 305,* 297
Katherine *283, 291*
Kathleen *291*
Katina *291*
Kaukab 113
Kawmia *306*
Kawsar *304*
Kaya *315*
*Kayan *323, 365*
Kaydahom *305*
Kaylene *289*
Kaysoon *305,* 297
*Kazra *368*
Kebir *357*
Kedive *267*
Kerbela *344*
Kerima *285*
Kerria *333*
Kesia 20, 228, 268
Kesia II 268
Khadijad *285*
Khafifa *304*
Khair Edin *267*
Khalasa *291*
Khamasin *285, 287*
Khasidah *285*
Khatila 79, 82, 100, 251

Khazib *278, 285*
Kheir *302, 306*
Khemosabi 352, **353**
Khouros 330
Kibaka *267*
Kibla 138, **172**
King *318*
King Cole 204
King Cotton Gold **255**
Kiprida *316*
Kipuchaia *316*
Kirsty *291*
Kismet 56, 57, 58
Kistj *315*
Kiyama 350
*Klinika *316, 364*
Kniasj *316*
*Knippel *316, 317,* 246, 312, *364*
Knopka *315,* 310
Koheilan el Mossen *306*
Kolos *316*
Komeira *306*
Komposita *318*
Komposter *316*
Konfederacja *318*
Konrad *279*
Konus *315*
Korall *318*
*Korej *315, 316,* 246, 309, 310, *364*
Kosmos *315*
Krasavitsa *316*
Kreatura *316,* 312
Krepish *315,* 310
Krona *317*
Krush 112, 146
Krushina *315*
Kufara *281, 287*
Kumara *341, 339*
*Kumir 310, *364*

Labadah *285*
Lady Blunt *280*
Lady Hester *see* Dajania
Laelia *329*
Lagodna *318, 358,* 309
Lahib *267*
*Lal-i-Abdar 142, 147, 232, 244, 245, *343,* 360 *see also* Abu Zeyd
Lanisa *342,* 338
Larkspur *344*
Lasuad *267*
Layla *303, 306,* 300, 314
Leda *287*
Leila *291*
Leto *287*
Lewisfield Magic *358*
Leyla *283*
Liebchen *279*
*Lilac Domino *370*
Lilac Time *331*
Linka *309*
Litle Owl *358*

Little Star 328
Lohaya 289
Lord Gold-n-Glo 280
Lowelas 319
Lubna 302, 304, 296
Ludmilla 239
*Ludo 199, 239, 242, 368, 370, **254**
*Ludomino 242, 368
Lufti 267
Luisa 332
Lurex 329, 332
Lyra 108
Lysander 279

Maarouf 283
Mabrouka 302, 304, 296
Mabrouk Manial 302, 304, 306
Mabruk 160
Mabruka 120, 138, 142
Maddalena 285
*Maddy 319, 367
Madeeha 305
*Madila 319, 367
Madkour 331
Magic Carpet 279
Magic Gold 329
Magic Pearl 250
*Magnet 239, 332, 334, 364
Magnindra 239
Magnolia 318
Mahail 279
Mahal 252
Mahan 267
*Mahasin 367
Mahboub 285
Maheyl 357
Mahif 278, 200, 274
Mahruss 72, 100, 257
Mahruss (1893, lines of) 281, 340
Mahruss (1893) 72, 87, 92, 100, 142, 176, 229–30, 238, 243, 248, 299, 300, **104**
Mahrussa 91, 260
Maidan 53, 228, 243, 326
Maideh 285
Maisa 302, 304
Maisuna 357, 141, 232, 244
*Mak 310, 364
Makbula (Eg.) 100
Makbula (Cr.) 88, 89, 92, 100, 112, 120, 243, 275, 307
Makeda 281, 289
Malaka 302, 303, 306, 297, 314
Malik 280, 289
Malinka 310
Malpia 318, 309
Malutka 315
*Malvito 323, 324, 365
Mamaluke 281, 289
Mamdouha 342
Mamlouka 306, 297
Mammona 318, 310
Manasseh 357, 191, 232

Mangan 331
Mangani 331, **327**
Manokta 91, 92, 112
Manola 358
Manolita 358
Mansour 302, 306, 299
Mansur 176
Mantilla 329
*Manto 197, 250, 330, 368, 370
*Manzana 366
*Maquillo 323, 325, 365
Maracanda 250
Marada 278, 285
Marazion 285
Mareb 251
Mareesa 184, 251
Marengo 333
Marhaba 356, 350
Marigold 285
Marquis 279
Marwan 331
Marzavan 293
*Mashhour 302, 304, 305, 306, 298, 299, 300, 367
Mashuk 315
Masjid 239
Maskat 315
Masque 279
Matoufa 285
Mawaheb 306
Maydenah 285
Mayrial 281, 283
Maysouna 302
Mazanina 333
Mazeppa 293
Mazna 357, 142, 232, 244
Mdahhaad 267
Mebattan 267
Mecca 285
Mecca II 287
Medallela 304
Medea 287
Medina 285
Medusa 282, 287
Mefruk 267
Mejamieh 322
Mekdam 303, 304, 300
Mekili 280, 285
Meliha 280, 281, 285
Melika 287
Melissa 281, 285
Mellawieh 197, 370
Melpomene 278, 293
Melriff 281, 285
Melriffa 285
Meneptah 331
Menzil 356, 350
Merial 285
Meriff 285
Meroe 39
Merryn 285
Merzuk 59, 66, 79, 81, 82, 101, 141, 227, 230, 245, 300, 336
Mesa'd 91

Mesaoud (lines of) 267, 278, 280, 281, 283, 340, 342, 357
Mesaoud 289, 303, 48, 59, 66, 70, 72, 79, 80, 81, 82, 83, 101–2, 114, 115, 117, 118, 120, 122, 131, 134, 138, 141, 142, 145, 149, 162, 168, 227, 229, 230–1, 238, 239, 242, 243, 244, 245, 247, 248, 250, 268, 300, 307, 336, 343, 344, **104**
Meshac 287
Meshura (Cr.) 50, 51, 102–3, 106, 120, 141, 227, 244, **67**
Meshura (Eg.) 112
Meymooneh 280, 285
Mezna 112, 113
Micah 293
Michelia 358
Midi 281, 289
Mielka 326, 328
*Mifaria 278, 197, 370
Mihrima 358
*Mikeno 197, 198, 246, **198**
Mildom 281
Minerva 287
Minifer 278, 285
Mira 282, 287
Mirage 93, 108, 182, 220, 232, 275, 350, **183**
Miraze 230
*Miriam 293, 270, 365
Mirzam 356, 350
Mishal 287
Mishka 357
Mish–Mish 357
Mizpah 285
Mohawed 302
Moment 318, 309
Momtaza 306
Monarch 278
*Moneyn 348, 371
*Moneyna 371
Moniet el Nefous 302, 304, 296
Monogramma 318, 312
*Monopolia 312, 364
Montaza 82
Montazah 285
Moonamet 278, 289
Moondiyan 289
Moonflower 292
Moon Kabala 278
Moonkas 278, 291
Moon Kay 291
Moonkiss 291
Moonoura 289
Moonshine 278
Mootrub 228, 270
*Moraea 356, 366
Morafic 302, 304, 305, 296, 300
*Morayma 323, 363
Morayma II 324
Motalga 278, 289
Motasen II 324
Mottaka 267

INDEX OF HORSES

Mouna *304*
Mourad *302*
Muhayd *279*
Mukomol *310*
Mulatka *318*, 309
Mumtaza 95
Murra *281, 285*
Muscat (Rus.) *318*, 309
Muscat (Aust.) *280*
Muslin *318*
Musson *318*
Mustapha *278*
Mutlak *278*
Mutilla *280*
Mutrif *281, 285*
My Fair Lady *281, 285*
My Fair Lady II 329
Myola *357*, 191, 232, 246
*Myolanda *278, 357,* 200, 274, 362
*Myoletta *362*
My Pet *329*

Naadirah 309
Naama *283*
Naaman 59, 307
Nabatti *267*
Nabeg *315*
Nabor(r) *318, 358*, 309, 311, 321–2
Nabras *306*
Nadeemah *306*
Nadima *266*
Nadir (Cr.) *293, 306, 357*, 141, 144, 168, 172, 180, 232, 239, 244, 356
Nadir (Eg.) 113
*Nadirat *361*
Nadjy *279*
Nadya *304*
Nafaa el Saghira *302*
Nafia (Cr.) *358*, 215, 344
Nafia (Aust.) *278, 291*
Nafisa 239
Naftalin 309, 312
Nafud *345*
Nagda *289*
*Nagrada *316, 318*, 308, 310, 364
Nagwa *306*
Naharak *267*
*Naharin *368*
Naharina 308
Nahid *304*
Nahr *267*
Nahrawan *267*
Naina 314
Najar *267*
Najera 308
Najib *316*, 308, 350
Nakal *315*
Nakovalina *316*
Nal *318*
Namet *318*, 309
Namet II *318*

Namilla (1929) 350
*Namilla (1937) *281*, 198, 339, 354, 366
Namira 182, 322
Namusa *289*, 229, 243, 268, 270
*Nana Sahib 323, 324, 360, 365
Nana Sahib II 323
Nantouka *292*
Nantouka II *292*
Naomi (Aust.) *293*
Naomi (Neth.) 330
Napraslina 309
Nar *280*
*Narda (II) 138, 145, 239, 344, 345, 352, 369
Nardina 345
Narenk 59
Narghileh *356, 357*, 59, 134, 138, 154, 162, 168, 176, 229, 232, 238, 239, 268, 345, 350, 352, **135**
Nargis *315*
Nariffa 239
Narimm *357*
Narkise 59, 300, 345
Naseel 179, 235, 239
Naseem *315, 316, 318, 358,* 171, 172, 179, 182, 185, 186, 210, 215, 219, 220, 222, 23, 5, 236, 239, 246, 250, 297, 307, 308–9, 312, 314, 326, 349, 350, **237**
Nash *267*
*Nashisha 179, 186, 229, 239, 308, 361
Nasieda 322
Nasifa (Cr.) 173, 185, 239, 308, **240**
Nasifa (Aust.)*280, 283, 292*
*Nasik *356*, 142, 153, 157, 160, 162, 167, 168, 173, 180, 229, 230, 238, 242, 247, 344, 345, 349, **347**
Nasira 180, 239
Nasirieh *278, 280, 291*, 236, 239, 274, **271**
Naslednik 297, 314
Nasmeshka 309
Nasr (USA) 345
Nasr (Eg.) 100, 112
Nasra *358*, 59, 164, 171, 173, 179, 184, 220, 232, 235, 238, 239, 266, 349, **130**
Nassaba *280*
Nassar *279*
Nastavnitsa *315*
*Naturalistka *316*, 308, 310, 364
Naturshitsa *318*, 309
Naufal *357*, 162, 179, 222, 232, **232**
Naugan *267*
Naum 310
Naumi *292*
Nautch Girl *358*, 351

Nawab 350
Nawari *291*
Naxiffa 239
Naxina *358*, 177, 235, 239
Naxindos 329
Naxindra 239
Nazeefa *305*
Nazeer *302, 304, 305,* 232, 297, 299, 314
Nazeera *306*, 297
Nazic *305*
Nazil 352
Nazir (Arg.) *267*
Nazir (Ger.) 331
Nazira 331
Naziri 172, 179, 184, 186, 194, 219, 220, 235, 239, 322, 336, **221**
Nazli 239
Nazra *315*
Nazrat 82
Nazrina *340, 342*, 336
Nazziria 239, 336
Neamis *315*
Neapol II *318*
Nebal *267*, 266
Nebosklon *318*
Nejdmieh 270
Nefertiti *280, 285*
Nefisa *357*, 59, 98, 120, 134, 141, 227, 228, 229, 232, 238, 266, 344, 349, **60**
Nefudh *280*
Negasa *267*
Negatiw *318, 358*, 308, 309, 310, 320, 321
Nehas *267*
Nejef 232
Nejiba (1892) 120, 168, **169**
Nejiba (1939) *358*
Nejima 260
Nejmet es Subh *292*
Nejmia 350
Nejran 118, 228, 245
Nekhl *278, 285, 289*
Nemesis 287
Nemrud 59
Neposlushnaja *315*
Nepriadwa 309
Nera *315*, 309
Neraida 173, 185, 188, 230, 239, 308, **240**
*Nerina *357*, 326, 363
Nerinora *357*, 192, 200, 202, **255**
Nero *358*
Neron 312
Nerpa *315, 318*, 309
Nesma *306*
Nespokoini *318*, 309
Nessa 252, 345
Nessima *267, 280, 358*, 176, 177, 239, 344
Nevada 314
Nevzgoda *315*

INDEX OF HORSES

Neyri 289
Neyussef 289
*Nezma 341, 358, 173, 230, 235, 239, 326, **174**
Niagara 318
Nickel 292
Niello 278
Niffnaff 292
Nightingale 341
Niharra 324
Nikel 318
Nil 316, 317, 297, 314 see also Azmi
Nimb 318
Nimr 177
Nimrod (UK) 358, 351
Nimrod (Rus.) 318, 309
Ninevia 315
Nini 315
Ninive 331
Nisella 283, 292
Nisetta 292
*Niseyra 279, 356, 358, 188, 230, 235, 239, 326, **240**
Nishi 331
Nishida 239, 326, 328
Nisib 278, 281, 292
Niskib 281, 292
Nisr 305
Nisreen (Arg.) 267
Nisreen (Cr.) 278, 358, 182, 184, 186, 187, 230, 235, 239, 348, 350, **240**
Nisry 326
Nissam 326
Nissama 308
Nitla 319
Nitochka 297, 308, 312, 314
Nitria 278, 292
Nizar 328, 330
Nizara 331
Nizreen 239
*Nizzam 358, 235, 239, 326, 328, 330, 351
Noam 145, 239, 344, 348
Nofilia 292
Noha 306
Noma 110
Nomenklatura 314
Nomer 315, 318, 308
Nonius 318
Norah 48
Norama 326
Noran 275, 326
Normativ 318, 309
Nosegaye 283, 292
Noureena 334
Novinka 318, 309
Nrav 314
Nueyra 345
Nuhajjela 192
Numera 345
Nura (Dahmeh Nejiba) 96
Nura (Managhieh) 84

Nura (Aust.) 289
Nuralina 278, 292, 274, **271**
Nureddin I 348
*Nureddin II 315, 356, 154, 158, 160, 173, 176, 179, 182, 184, 186, 222, 229, 230, 235, 238, 245, 345, 348, 350, 368, **231**
Nuri Pasha 356, 176, 229, 244
Nuri Schalan 331
Nuri Sherif 176, 177, 228, 229, 230, 243, 247, 251, 252, 326
*Nurschida 177, 247, 326, 366
*Nusara 344, 348, 352, 360
Nuzha 306

Oaza 318, 308
Obeya 302, 304, 306
Odessa 330
Ofir 315, 316, 312
Okean 316
Old Billy 204
Olford Golden Wings 340
Olford Silver Gift 340
Olympus 282
Omar 282
Omayma 306
Om Dalal 302, 304
Om el Saad 305, 297
Omnia 305
Onega 316
Opal 333
Optik 317
*Oran 291, 357, 187, 191, 192, 197, 199, 200, 202, 218, 224, 227, 232, 244, 250, 276, 326, 334, 338, 366, **222**
Orange Valley Crystal 340
Orange Valley Indian Gold 341
Orange Valley Indian Pride 341
Orange Valley Night Star 341, 342
Oran Van Crabbet 357, 200
Orena 334
Oriana 278
Oribi 291
Orientacia 315
Orinda 330
Orion 200
Orla 321
Orlan 316
Orsino 356
Othello 279
Otrada 316, 312
Otradni 316
Our Queen 291

Pachka 316
Padron 330, 351
Padua 331
Paket 316
Pakistan 310, 314
Paks 7 314
Palas 318, 312, 314

Palba 318, 309
*Pale Shadow 357, 192, 367
Palitra 317
Pallada 317
Pallas 279, 287
Palmira 317
Pamir 317
Panama 317, 314
Pandora 287
Panel 317, 318, 314
Panika 317
Pankarta 318
Panorama 317, 314
Pantera 317
Paproc 318
Parcha 316, 318
*Parfumeria 316, 246, 312, 364
Parketnaia 317
Parnas 318
Parus 318, 309
Passia 316, 312
Pasta 316
Pastuchka 317
Pasynok II 317
Patent 316, 310
Patron (1957) 318, 309
Patron (1966) 309
Pauza 317
Pava 316
Pavlina 316
Pawadok 316
Pchelka 317
Pedro 332
Pegas 317
Peizage 317
Peleng 314
Penitent 321
*Penochka 316, 310, 321, 364
Pepton 321
Perikola 316, 312
*Perle d'Or 366
Persida 316
Persten 318
Pesenka 317
Pesennik 314
Pesnia 317
Pesniar 314
Petra 282, 285
Phaeton 282
*Phantom (USA) 350, 362
Phantom (Aust.) 279
Pharaoh 28, 42, 47, 51, 54, 93, 102, 103, 104, 105, 107, 120, 141, 227, 235, 236, 243, 248, 307, 319, **52**
Phoebe 293
Piechur 321
Pierrot 321
*Pietuszok 317, 310, 314, 320, 321, 364
*Piewica 312, 364
Pika 318
Pilarka 312
Pilenga 316

INDEX OF HORSES

Pilinka *318*
Pilot *318*
Pinsk *318*, 309
Pintor 323
Piolun *316*, 246, 310, 312
Pirouette 289
Pirs *317*
Plakat *317*, 314, 330, 331,
*Plaksa *316*, 312, 364
Plan *316*
Planeta 310, 321
Platina *317*, 314
Platinum Bell 250
Plennitsa *316*
Pliaska *317*
Plombir *317*
Plotka 309
Podkova *316*
Podruga 309
Podsnejnik *318*
Poema *316*
Pohaniec 321
Poklon *317*
Pokornaja *316*
Polaca 323
*Pomeranets *315*, *316*, *317*, 309, 310, 364
Pompey *318*
Ponomarev 310
Popringunia *317*
Porfira 312, 321, 364
Posol *318*, 309
*Potencia *317*, 312, 321, 364
Potomak 314
Povest *317*
Praga *316*, 310
Pretty Polly 179
*Priboj *315*, *316*, *317*, 246, 309, 310–11, 314, 321, 364
Prikhot *316*
Priklad *316*
Primula 329
Prince Azfar 331, 332
Prince Nejd 289
Prince of Bray *356*
Princess 291
Princess Nefertiti 289
Princess Royal 285
*Princess Troubadour 370
Princess Zia *356*, *358*, 198
Prince Zaim *358*
Prisma *316*, 312
Pristan *317*
Privichika *317*
Privilegia *318*, 309
Prizeman 281
Probat 321
Procent *317*
Progress *318*
Progressia *318*
Prometida 323
Prometey *318*
Prometheus *316*
Provincia *318*, 309

Prowierka 312, 321
Proximo 56, 57, 58, 59, 258–9
Psyche 287
Ptashka *317*, 314
Ptichka *317*, *318*, 314
Ptolemy 282
Pulia *316*
Purga *316*
Purple Emperor 54
Purple Iris 54
Purple Stock 40, 54, 259, 268
Pushinka *316*
Pustinia *317*
Puteh 334
Pyrrha 287

Qasim 285
Quaker Girl 279
Quantock II *341*, 338
*Queen of Rain 371
Queen of Sheba (Cr.) *303*, 357, 37–9, 41, 42, 43, 46, 49, 53, 54, 65, 104–5, 122, 126, 188, 227, 228, 229, 232, 244, 325, **104**
Queen of Sheba (Aust.) 291
Queen Soraya 285
*Queen Zenobia 339, 366
Quick Man 329
Quickstep 281
Quimran Delary 342
Quimran Etresia *341*
Quimran Figaro 342
Quimran Romeo 342
Quimran Wodka *341*

Ra 278
Raab 348
*Raad 348, 349, 352, 369
*Raaf 369, 370
Raafat see Aswan
Rabda 302
Rabdan (Cr.) 84
Rabdan (Eg.) *302*, *304*, 113, 299
Rabi 289
Rabina 340
*Rabiyas *342*, 230, 246, 336, 340, 349, 369, 370
*Rabiyat *341*, 348, 352, 367, 369, 370
*Rabk 370
*Rabkhal 369, 370
*Rabla 267, 134, 142, 245, 348, 370
Rachala 267
Rachida 328
Radames 282
Radek 283
Radeyra 197
*Radi *357*, 177, 192, 239, 326, 354, 366, 370
Radia *304*, 92, 153, 295, 300
Radiada 325
*Raduga *316*, 312, 362

*Rafeef *356*, 168, 173, 230, 239, 246, 348, 349, 350, 366, 368, **174**
*Rafeena *341*, *356*, 198, 365, **271**
*Rafferty 362
*Raffieh 370
*Raffles *358*, 172, 183, 236, 239, 242, 246, 266, 275, 350, 362, **347**
Rafica *302*, 305
*Rafika 370
*Rafina 278, 281, 291, 246, 272, 365
*Rafla 267, 266, 362, 368
Raftan 179, 235
*Rafyk 285, 287, 289, 59, 65, 229, 268
Ragaa 305
*Ragala 350, 362
Rageyma 275
*Rahab 279, 272, 371
*Rahal *356*, 350, 368
*Rahas 348, 349, 362, 369
Rahma 305
*Raida 348, 371
*Raidaana 371
*Raisuli 281, 289, 270, 272, 368
Rajafan 344
Rajjela 192
Raki 289
*Rakib 280, 285, 289, 291, 292, 272, 276, 362, **269**
Rakima 114, 138, 147
Rakka 267
*Raktha *341*, *358*, 179, 187, 188, 194, 197, 220, 235, 236, 239, 247, 250, 336, 338, 339, 366, **223**
Raktha Rose *341*
Raktha Scha 337, **337**
*Ralet 348, 371
Ralla 289
*Rallaf 362
Ralvon Monopoly 278
*Ralvon Pilgrim 275, 277, 368, **273**
*Ramayana 230, 319, 367
*Ramghaza 367
Rami 291, 292
*Ramim 344, 345, 349, 367
Ramla 145, 157, 247, 344
Ramoth 334
Ranald 281
*Rangha 144, 245, 334, 371
*Rangoon *358*, 184, 228, 235, 250, 336, 370
Ranix *356*, 354
Ranji *358*
*Ranya 142, 247, 322, 365
*Ranya II 365
Raoul 283
*Rapture (USA) 267, 266, 350, 362
Rapture (Aust.) 278, 289

INDEX OF HORSES

Ras *278, 289*
*Rasafa 348, *360*
*Rasala 367
Rasana 188
Raschida 53, 251–2
Raseel *281, 285*, 272
*Raseem *316, 358*, 172, 179, 181, 182, 185, 186, 212, 220, 229, 239, 242, 244, 247, 307, 308, 322, 350, 361, 368, **175**
Raselma 350
*Raseyn *358*, 142, 172, 180, 243, 345, 348, 350, **371**
Rashad *305*
Rashid *303, 304*
Rashid II *278*, 292
Rashida *305*
Rashidiya *278, 279, 280, 281,* 289
Rashifa 308
Rashmari 329
Rashouk 279
*Rasim *358*, 148, 157, 158, 162, 163, 164, 168, 172, 177, 186, 188, 221, 229, 239, 243, 245, 247, 319–20, 348, 361, **175**
*Rasim III 319, 361
*Rasima (1917) 348, 360
*Rasima (1943) 320, 321, 361
*Rasim Pierwszy 319–20, 361
Raskal 331
Rasmina 350
Rasul 267
*Raswan *317, 358*, 172, 180, 235, 243, 247, 345, 350, 367
Rataplan 56, 57, 71, 93, 236, 259, 268
Ratouka 292
Raulani 267
Rawya *304*
Raxina 239
Rayif 352
Rayik 348
*Rayya *358*, 142, 172, 243, 245, 345, *371*,
*Razada 322, 324, 325, 365
Razam 345
Razan 279
*Razaz (1907) 157, 164, 238, 344, 360
*Razaz (1949) *279, 287, 293*, 272, *371*
*Razieh see Bint Rissala
*Razina *279, 281, 341, 357, 358*, 172, 177, 179, 229, 232, 235, 247, 366, **178**
Razinth 279
Raziri *358*
Rebeca 324
*Redif *371*
Refky *305*
Rega 321
Regal *278*
Regib 122
*Registan 361

*Rehal 345, 348, 367, 369
*Rehoboam *371*
Reibal 267
Reibara Mansour *340*
Reibara Rakitee *341*
Reibara Raktha's Souvenir *341*
Reibara Shala *340, 341*
*Rejeb 118, 138, 239, 352, 369
Remembrance *283*, 275
Renita *283*
Resalah 331
Re Schalan 331
Retsina 329
Rexan 332
Rex The Robber 328
*Reyna 182, 246, 322–3, 324, 363, **183**
*Rezeda II *315*, 309, 362, 367
Rhapsody *289*
Rhapsody in Blue 334
*Rheoboam *371*
*Riada 142, 245, *371*
Riaz (Cr.) 122
Riaz (Arg.) 267
Ribaba 267
*Ribagh 369, 370
Ribal 345, 361
*Ridaa *281, 303*, 59, 131, 134, 138, 140, 145, 149, 160, 162, 227, 230, 232, 245, 270, 344, 361, **119, 135**
*Rief *281*, 160, 270, 368
Rifaat 131, 138
*Rifage 350, 362
*Rifala *358*, 172, 182, 236, 246, 350, 362, **347**
*Rifari *356*, 230, 250, 334, 363, 369
*Rifda 247, 348, 367
*Riffal *281, 285, 289, 291, 292, 357*, 179, 188, 232, 239, 247, 272, 276, 352, 366, **178**
Riffalani *280, 291*
Riffalka *278, 280*
Riffles 187
Riffoura *283*, 289
*Rifla 180, 247, 348, 361, 367
*Rifnas 367
Rifraff 350
Rihan 289
*Rijm *356*, 59, 100, 129, 131, 134, 138, 140, 141, 142, 145, 146, 147, 154, 160, 162, 168, 176, 182, 186, 222, 227, 229, 230, 238, 239, 242, 250, 274, 322, 344, 345, 350, 368, **231**
*Rijma *358*, 236, 246, 344, 345, 348, 349, 361
Rikash 278
*Rikham *278*, 275, 368
*Rikitea *341*, 338, 366, **254**
*Rim *278, 356, 358*, 59, 164, 172, 186, 220, 229, 230, 235, 247–8, 344, 345, 350, 367, **139, 172**
Rimal 180, 345
*Rimini 308, 350, 368
Rimula 308
Rinessa *342*, 338
*Ringing Gold 368
Ripple 289
*Risala *358*, 59, 141, 148, 157, 162, 229, 232, 245–6, 344, 350, 361, **119, 172, 246**
Risaldar *283*
*Risama see Bint Riyala
*Risanira 363
*Rish *357, 358*, 184, 228, 232, 245, 370
*Rishafa 308, 350, 354, 370
*Rishafieh 350, 354, 370
Rishan (1894) 319
*Rishan (1922) *357*, 232, 370
Risheem 279
*Rishka *279*, 370
*Rishna *358*, 245, 370
Rishrash 344
*Rishyana 370
*Risira 184, 276, 363
*Rissalix *356*, 188, 192, 197, 198, 230, 246, 250, 354, 364, 368, **190**
*Rissalma (1932) *316*, 185, 230, 246, 308, 309, 310, 321, 364, **311**
*Rissalma II (1954) 191, 199, 364, **192**
*Rissam *278*, 186, 188, 235, 239, 247, 326, 368, **237**
Rissani *280, 291*
Rissaz 329, 330
*Risseefa 363
*Rissella 364
*Rissiletta 187, 191, 364
*Rissla *279, 356, 358*, 144, 172, 173, 184, 186, 187, 188, 224, 230, 235, 246, 312, 345, 349, 350, 362, **247**
Risslan 199
*Rissletta 246, 348, 363, **346**
*Risslina *356*, 173, 184, 230, 246, 348, 349, 363, 366, **245**
Rithan *358*
*Rithyana 197, 370
Ritla 322
Rix 329
*Rixalina *316*, 185, 246, 308, 310, 361, 364, **311**
*Riyala *356*, 59, 140, 141, 142, 158, 163, 172, 220, 230, 235, 245, 247, 344, 365, **139**
*Riyalan *285, 289*, 367
*Riz 246, 361
Rizada 246
Rizala *281*, 248, 272
Rizar *289*
Rizara 331, 334
*Rizvan *358*, 236, 348, 361

INDEX OF HORSES

Roala 343, 371
Robdon Desert Dust *340*
Robdon Red Demon *340*
Robert E. Lee 329
Robinia 289
Rockdove 334
Roda (USA) 345
Roda (Eg.) 110, 296
Roda (Sh.Ob.) 112, 296
*Rodan (USA) *357*, 140, 238, 248, 343, 344, 352, 369
Rodan (Cr.) 147
*Rodania (lines of) *291*, *293*, *305*, *306*, *315*, *316*, 360–71
*Rodania 16, 49, 50, 65, 71, 105–6, 226, 227, 229, 230, 232, 235, 238, 244–8, 297, 349, 360, **51**
Rodanieh Rafaqa 331, 332
*Rokhama 142, 344, 349, 352, 370
*Rokhsa 344, 349, 352, 370
Rokiczana 320
Romana II *306*
*Ronek 236, 348, 371
Rosabelle *281*, *283*, *291*
*Rosalina *280*, 364
Rosalind (Aust.) *291*
Rosalind (Ger.) 331
Rosa-Maria 334
*Rosa Rugosa 248, 369
*Rose Diamond *357*, 138, 142, 227, 229, 232, 245, 360
Rose Grey *291*
Roselight *291*
*Rose-Marie 362
*Rosemary 59, 71, 114, 118, 134, 227, 235, 245, 369 **135**
Rose of Africa 308
Rose of Dawn 71
*Rose of France 350, 360
*Rose of Hind 138, 168, 238, 245, 348, 360, 369
*Rose of Jericho 65, 71, 142, 229, 245, 268, 360, **67**
Rose of Persia 307
*Rose of Sharon *356*, *357*, 59, 98, 100, 138, 140, 229, 232, 245, 248, 268, 340, 343, 344, 361, **61, 119**
Rose of the Sea 236
Rose Pearl *291*
*Rosetta 140, 371
Rosewater 71
*Roseyna 370
*Rosh 365
*Roshana 345, 348, 370
*Rosheiya 358, 365
*Roshnara 365
Rosina *341*
*Rosinella *278*, *280*, *291*, *358*, 274, 364
Rosjanka 331
*Rossana 168, 180, 197, 348, 360

*Rossdin 360
Rosfennick *278*, *289*, *291*, 272, 274, **269**
Rouelle *289*
Roulette 2nd *283*
Roundeley *283*
*Roxan 368
*Roxana 365
*Roxelana 365
Royal 328
Royal Constellation *357*
Royal Crystal *340*, *357*, 242, 338, **193**
Royal Diamond *357*, 192, 197, 200, 242, 250, **222**
Royal Domino *281*, *285*, 275
Royal Gold *278*
Royaljan *281*
Royal Radiance *280*, *281*, 250
Royal Victory 354
Rozita 331
Rualla *278*, *289*
*Ruanda *316*, 185, 308, 312, 362
Ruberto *283*
Ruella *289*
*Ruellia *315*, 185, 230, 247, 308, 309, 367, **313**
*Rufeiya 365
Rufeiya II 287
Ruheym *283*, *289*
*Rukham 267, 266, 371
Rukuban II *293*
Rumbosa 323, 324
Rumeliya 140
Rumma *289*
Rustan 320, 328
*Rustem *291*, *303*, 142, 149, 158, 162, 168, 227, 239, 242, 245, 272, 299, 300, 367
Rustem Pasha 332
Ruth II *358*
Ruth Kesia *356*, 176, 229, 270
Ruweisat *289*
Ryama *315*, 238, 308
Rymnik 108
Rynet Fikele *341*
Rynet Katryn *340*
Rynet Serenade *340*
Rynet Sirex Shah *341*
Rynet Suldoure-Sha *340*
Rynheath Rosemarie *340*
Rythal 326
*Rytham *315*, *316*, 242, 307, 309, 312, 362
*Rythama *280*, 362
*Rythma 141, 144, 191, 246, 307, 312, 326, 362
Rythoura 275, 326

Saada (Sh.Ob.) 83, 260
Saada (Eg.) 351
Saade 113
Saadun *304*, 113, 154, 298
Saaida *305*

Sabah (Sh.Ob.) 113
Sabah (Eg.) *306*
Sabah (Aust.) *280*, *293*
Sabbah *304*, 112
Sabeel *302*
Sabiyah *280*, *289*
Saboya 323
Sacudir 324
Sada *289*
Sadaka *285*
Sadik *279*, *285*, 276
Safaa *304*
Safari *285*
Safarjal *358*, 144, 172, 177, 229, 250, 334
Saffah *291*
Safra (Cr.) 106, 248, 251
Safra (Aust.) *279*
Safrano 332
Safura 260
*Sagaz 324, 363
Sagda *306*
Saha 70
Sahab *304*, 113, 295
Sahara II *278*
Sahrilla 332
Sa-id *289*
Saif 267
Saifet 267
*Sainfoin *358*, 172, 177, 229, 250, 361
Saiydi *285*
*Saki 371
Saklawi I (line of) *302*
Saklawi I 299, 300
Saklawi II *304*, 300
Saklawia II *304*
Sakr *305*
Sala *282*, *287*, *289*, *291*, *293*, 272, 339
Salaam *289*
Saladin II 322
Salari *279*, *289*
Saleemie 329
Salha *304*
*Salinas 197, 367
Salma I *305*
Salome (Aust.) 287
Salome (Ger.) 331
Salomea 312
Salomi *306*, 297
Salon *315*, *316*, *317*, *318*, 309–10, 312, 315
Saltram 334
Saludo 324
Samantha 326
Samba 334
Sameh *302*, *304*, *305*, *306*, 297
Samha (Seg. Jed.) 113
Samha (Hadban Enzahi) 299
Samhan *302*
Samia *305*, 297
Samiha 299
Samira *302*, *304*, 295, 296

Samirieh 289
Samsie 358, 188, 236, 239
Samson 239
Sana 293
Sanad 305
Sandaf 281
San Sebastian 281
Santarabia Sahib 281
Santarabia Shammar 283
Santarabia Shekh 281
Santarabia Sindashar 283
Santarabia the Caliph 280
Santa Rafeena 283
Santhos 321
Saoud 40, 51, 54
Sara 323
Sarama 344
Sardhana 319, 320, 328, 348
Sarek 334
Sarelle 289
Sarkha 305
Saskia R.J. 330
Sayif 278, 289
*Scharifa 369
Scherzade 280, 281, 274
Scimitar Quicksilver 278
Scimitar Rudan 278
Scindia 250
Scindian Magic 250, 332
Seductive Magic 332
Seef 302, 298
Seef el Arab 302
Sefina 118
Sefra 279
Sefri 289
Seheran 256
Sekh 278, 289,
Sela 291
Selah 293
Selene 293
Selima 358, 173, 186, 230, 232, 248, 250, 308, 350, **249**
Selina 329
Selma (Eg.) 108
Selma (Cr.) 303, 357, 149, 176, 228, 232, 248, 350, **249**
Selma II 191
Selmian 358, 350
Selmnab 350
Semele 293
Semen 315, 316, 317, 309
Semiramis 331
Semna 287
Senab 358
Senabra 281, 285, 276
Sendibad 306
Senga 250
Serafilla 342, 239, 338, **241**
Serafina 279, 283, 357, 358, 187, 200, 235, 236, 239, 242, 354
Serafire 242, 322, 351
Serafix 358, 187, 236, 238, 242, 322, 351, **355**
Seralixa 354

Serinda 329, 330
Seriya 250
Serra 303, 304, 295, 322
Set Abouhom 306
Set el Wadi 306
Setuhan 266
Sextus 278
Seyal 303, 357, 70, 118, 120, 126, 129, 134, 176, 232, 236, 248, 344
Shaarawi 302, 300
Shaarwaun 280
Shaban 293
Shabrette 250
Shabryeh 357, 250, 352
Shadel Irex 356
*Shades of Night 340, 199, 242, 338, 368
Shadia 302
Shadilla 341
Shadow Light 202, 250, 274
Shafak 267
Shafreyn 283, 285, 289, 291, 292, 232, 242, 274, **233**
Shah 66
Shahbaa 302
Shahczar 287
Shahim 336
Shahloul 302, 304, 305, 306, 295, 299, 300
Shahm 302
Shahwan 70, 71, 83, 84, 85, 98, 106, 146, 235, 299, 300, 343, **86**
Shahzada 289, 293, 228, 229, 246, 270–1, 322, 325
Shakra 329
Shala 293
Shalaan 289
Shalawi 283, 274
Shalimar 322–3
Shalina 342, 191, 200, 242, 339
Shalwan 342, 200, 339, **337**
*Shama 369
Shamadan 358
Shamah 305
Shamal 274
Shammar 334
*Shamnar 356, 179, 191, 230, 272, 338, 367
Shamreen 357
Shanas 283
Shanasif 283
Shani 279
Shaniya 289
Shantah 283
Shaqra 281, 291
Sharafa 357
Shareer 316, 173, 185, 186, 230, 239, 242, 246, 248, 250, 307, 326, 348, 350, **231**
Sharena Benjamin 340
Sharena Landros 340
Sharena Triomf 340

Shareym 283
*Sharfina 283, 242, 354, 362, **241**
*Sharima 279, 283, 357, 358, 186, 187, 188, 230, 242, **241**
Sharinda 289
Sharrak 283
Sharyus 283
Shaula 279
Shayba 358
Shayba Thania 356
Shaybet 356
Sheba 291
Sheba Again 282, 291
Sheeba 176, 229, 230
Shehab 280
Shehrezad 57
Sheikh el Arab 302, 304, 305, 299
Shekinah 278, 285
Shelifa 182, 322
Shemse(h) 235, 248
Sheral 285
Shereef 281, 287, 291, 276
Sherees 278, 285
Sherif (Sh.Ob.) 87, 113
Sherif (Aust.) 283
Sherif (Sp.) 323, 324
Sherifa (Cr.) 40, 42, 49, 51, 66, 107, 227, 235, 248, **31, 51, 62, 74**
Sherifa (Aust.) 285
Sher-i-Khurshid 357, 142, 232, 244, 336
Shermaid 281, 287
Shermoon 278
Shibine 145, 344
Shieha (Cr.) 39, 138, 244, 248
Shieha (Sh.Ob.) 117, 260
Shiekie 281
Shirama 338
Shiraz 248
Shireen 293, 338
Shiriba 332
Shirin 278
Shiv 281, 293
Shobha 145
Shtaura 250
Shueyman Sebaa 48, 106, 110
Sibyl 287
Sibylla 328
Sid Abouhom 303, 304, 305, 300, 314
*Sidi 248, 349, 369
Signal 283
Signorinetta 334
Siham 304
Sikander Shah 341
Silaba 285
Silamet 289
Silent Wings 340, 242, **253**
Silfina 279, 283, 358, 187, 200, 235, 242
Silindra 342, 242
Silka 308
Sillifa 292

INDEX OF HORSES

Silsilla *340, 341*, 338, 339
Silusuf *289*
Silvanetta 239
Silver Bauble *289*
Silver Bell 250
Silver Blue 251
Silver Cloud *279*
Silver Crystal *358*, 250, 351
Silver Diamond *357*, 250
Silver Dove 333
Silver Drift *279, 358*, 218, 236, 242, 334, 351, **355**
Silver Fan *292*
Silver Fire *278, 283*, 184, 186, 218, 224, 236, 250, 276, 338, **189**
Silver Gilt *357*, 187, 188, 194, 202, 224, 232, 235, 236, 250, 251, 328, 334, 338, **189**
Silver Gleam *280*
Silver Grand *279*, 197, 250
Silver Grey 192, 200, 202, 250, **249**
Silver Lady 276
Silverlet *340*, 188, 250, 338
Silverlight 180
Silver Magic *280*, 274
Silver Mantilla 251
Silver Mantle 250
Silver Moonlight *278, 289, 291, 292*, 250, 272, 277, **269**
Silver Plate 267
Silver Radiance 275
Silver Ray *292*
*Silver Ripple 250, 363
Silver Rocket *342*
Silver Royal 328
Silver Shadow *267*, 197, 218, 250 **216**
Silvershaft 334
Silver Shamrock *342*
Silver Sheen 192, 200, 202, 250
Silver Shower 333
Silver Silhouette 334
Silver Solomon 333
Silver Spark *283*
Silver Sparkle *283*, 276, 277
Silver Sparkler 333
Silver Spot *281*
Silver Sun *267*, 266
Silver Vanity *357*, 187, 191, 192, 197, 200, 232, 242, 250, 274, 339, **189**
Silver Yew 345
Silviana 338
Silwa *280*, **197**
Silwan *280*, 274
Simawa 345
Simrieh 176, 350
Sindh *283, 289*, 187, 200, 232, 242, 250, 274, **233**
Sir Aatika *282*, 287
Sir Akid *293*
Siralga *289*

Siran *279*
Sirdar *287, 289, 290, 293*
Sirella 191, 200, 202, 242, **201**
Sirhan *278, 291*
Sirio III 325
Sirocco *280*
Sir Ross *278*
Si Sanura *267*
Sithara 329
Siwa 118, 134, 228, 248
Skowronek (lines of) *267, 278, 279, 280, 318, 341, 356*
Skowronek *291*, 93, 108–9, 167, 168, 170, 171, 172, 173, 176, 177, 179, 180, 181, 182, 184, 192, 212, 215, 222, 227, 228, 235–6, 239, 246, 321, 322, 348, 349, 350, **173**
Sky Minuet 329
Sobha (line of) *317*
Sobha *303, 357*, 70, 81, 86, 106, 108, 109, 113, 117, 118, 227, 228, 232, 236, 244, 248–51, 307, **119**
Sol d'Oa 325
Soljanka 312
Solomka *315*
Solyman *267*
Somara *358*, 184, 197, 250, 338
Somerled 275, **255**
Somra 177, 182, 224, 232, 250
Somra II 250
Sonata (Rus.) *318*, 309
Sonata (Neth.) 329
Sonbolah *305*, 297
Sophronia 332
Sorella 285
Sotamm (Cr.) *303, 304, 357*, 149, 157, 160, 162, 167, 232, 248, 295, 300, 344, 351, **233**
Sotamm (Eg.) 111
Soufian *304*
Sphynx 287
Spilletta 334
Spindrift *279*, 274
Sport *315, 316*, 312
Springlight 204
Star Crystal 333
Star Diamond *279*
Star Domino *281*
Star Royal 336
Starfire *282*
Stargard 339
*Starilla *315*, 322, 367
Starlad *279*
*Star of the Hills *317*, 185, 235, 248, 308, 310, 314, 315, 322, 330, 367, **313**
Statesman *281*
Stheno 287
St. Simon 58
Sudarik Sun Brilliant *342*
Sueyd 111
Sukr 250

Suleena *340, 341, 342*
*Sulejman 320, 351, 361
*Sulka 326, 328, 330, 366
Sultan *302, 304, 305, 306*, 296
Sumeria 334
Summer Magic *283*
Summer Storm *283,*
Sun Brilliant *342*
Sun Diamond 266
Sun Royal *358*, 187
Sunset 202, 251
Sura *see* Crabbet Sura
*Sureyn 348, 349, 371
Surprise of Harwood 239
Surur *278*
Susdal 312
Susquehanna 329
Suvenir *318*, 309
Sweet Sincerity 329
Sylvan Lass 331
Synoecia 287

Tabal 323
Tafileh *289*
Tahdik 345
*Taheki 366
Tahia *304*
Tahseen *302*
Taki Pan *316*, 314, 317
Taktika *317*, 310, 314
Talal *304*, 295
Talant *317*
Tamara (Eg.) *304*
Tamara (Aust.) *279, 291*
Tamarak 329
Tamarek 330
Tamarisk (Cr.) 40, 259
Tamarisk (Aust.) *289*
Tamarisk (Neth.) 330
*Tamarlane 369
Tamerlan *317*, 314
*Tamma 360
Tamria *306*
Tarantella 242
Taraszcza *318, 358*, 308
Tareefa 287
Tarfa (Sh.Ob.) 261
Tarfa (Eg.) *302*
Tarney *289*
Tatiama 325
Tatima *289*
Tavrida *316*
*Tawali 370
Tazar *289*
Tazee 329
*Tehoura 230, 239, 326, 328, 366
Teja 324
Tclcri 332
Tempest *279*
Teorica 325
*Teresita *340, 358*, 366
Terrisa 329
Tesemka 317
Tetuan 324

INDEX OF HORSES

Teutonica 324
Thabit 305
The Chief 326, 328
Themis 287
The Nile 282
Theron 357
Thestius 282
Thetis 287
Thorayya 197
Tiaret 267
Tien 317
Tifla 304
Tihawieh 261
Timarie Blue Pride 341
Timarie Blue Sala 341
Timarie Captian Kidd 341
Timarie Captain Knight 341
Timarie Captain Silver 341
Timarie Lady Jane 340
Timarie Major Dick 341
Timarie Major Grant 341, 338
Timarie Masala 341
Timarie Prince Charlie 341
Timarie Prince John 341
Timarie Prince of Pride 341
Tiwiriada 317, 314
Toeyssa 261
Top 314
*Topol 317, 309, 312, 314, 364
Toska 317
Touch of Magic 358
Tou-Fail 285
Trapecia 317, 314
Treasure Hoard 289
Trix Silver 275
Tual 266
Tuema 285
Tuhotmos 302, 304, 305, 306, 296, 298, 300
Turkeycock 32, **31**
Turra 306
Twinkling Diamond 266

Uadyah 321
*Umatella 356, 192, 198, 366
Urania 287
Urfah 244
Ushaahe see Almozabor
Uzacur 324, 325

Vain Love 250
Vanessa 332
Vatican 310
Velisa of Yeomans 333
Venus (Eg.) 298
Venus (Aust.) 287
"Vera-" mares 325
Vesta 293
Victory Day II 357, 352–3
Vidiko Chrystopher 340

Vidiko Haroun 340
Vidiko Kerak 340
Vidiko Keshan 340
Vidiko Radames 340
Vidiko Yram Shah 340
Virgo 287
Vlinkfontein Arabian Knight 342
Vlinkfontein Gracious Me 342
Vlinkfontein Gregory 342
Vlinkfontein Ibn Raktha 341
Vlinkfontein Nasser 342
Vlinkfontein Neonette 341
Vlinkfontein Night Call 342
Vlinkfontein Rabelle 342
Vlinkfontein Rab-el-Mada 342
Vlinkfontein Rabizelle 342
Vlinkfontein Rabraf 342
Vlinkfontein Raburak 340
Vlinkfontein Radi 341
Vlinkfontein Razaji 342
Vlinkfontein Soudi 341

Wahag 302
Wahana 331
Walad 281, 293
Wanisa 304
Warandes Pasha 330
Warandes Plakat 330, **327**
Warda 289
Waseem 302
Wasla 305
Wazir 48, 79, 100, 101, 106, 108, 300, 343
Wega 331
Wentworth Golden Shadow 250
Whirlstorm 338
White Krush, The 112
Wild Thyme 39, 51, 54, 251–2
Wilma 321
Wimsey Paladin 282
Windarra 281
Witel 326, 331
Witraz 320

Xanadu's Voltage 358
Xanthium **353**
Xarfia 285

Yakoot 323
Yaman 305
Yaquota 305, 297
Yaral 280, 291
Yaskoulka 108, 349
Yashmak (Sh.Ob.) 358, 98, 110, 229, 235
Yashmak (Eg.) 303, 305, 297
Yasimet 340
Yasmin 283, 293
*Yateemah 367
Yavroum 239
Yedyarra 280

Yemama (1885) 92, 93, 98, 113, 128, 235, **128**
Yemama (1959) 242
Yemameh 303, 101
Yenbo 289
Yenbo II 282, 289
Yomna 305
Yosreia 299, 314
Yourouk 279
Yussef 280, 289
Yusuf 281, 283, 289

Zaafarana 303, 304, 295, 296
Zabia 305
Zadama 289
Zadaran 285, 289, 291
Zadella 289
Zadhofar 289
Zadita 281
Zadlaam 289
Zahda 305
Zahle 285
Zahr 289
Zahra 306
Zalema 325
Zamiec 320
Zamzam 304, 295
Zangano 325
Zarafa (Eg.) 306
Zarafa (Aust.) 278, 285, 289, 293
Zareef 303
Zareef II 304
Zareefa 302, 304, 298, 300
Zarif 289
Zarifa 303, 304
Zarife 345
Zarney 289
Zazouri 278, 279, 289
Zazula 320
Zbroja 320
Zedak 266
Zefifia 49, 50, 259, **51**
*Zehraa 363
Zeinah I 305
Zelda 329, 330
Zem Zem (UK) 243, 251
Zem Zem (Aust.) 278
Zena 341, 339, **338**
Zenith 278
Ziada 326, 329
Zillah 276
Zindah 283, 291
Zlota Iwa 320
Zobeyni (line of) 303
Zobeyni 96, 108, 299, 300
Zocola 280
Zoowar 323
Zourrak 278
Zulima 197
Zurich 324
Zuweia 289

TENNIS PARK

B
C
C
D
E
F
G
H

ICE
HOUSE
WOOD